Landmark Decisions of the U.S. Supreme Court

Landmark Decisions of the U.S. Supreme Court

Edited by

JAMES DALEY

DOVER PUBLICATIONS, INC.
Mineola, New York

Bibliographical Note

Landmark Decisions of the U.S. Supreme Court is a new work, first published by Dover Publications, Inc., in 2006.

Library of Congress Cataloging-in-Publication Data

Landmark decisions of the U. S. Supreme Court / edited by James Daley.
    p. cm.
  ISBN 0-486-45141-0 (pbk.)
    1. Constitutional law—United States—Cases. I. Daley, James, 1979– II. United States. Supreme Court.

KF4549.L369 2007
342.73—dc22

2006050212

Manufactured in the United States of America
Dover Publications, Inc., 31 East 2nd Street, Mineola, N.Y. 11501

Introductory Note

THE HISTORY and influence of the United States Supreme Court is as broad as it is intricate. It could be argued that every decision made by the Court is a landmark, as each one affects, in some way, the laws and lives of the people of the United States of America for years after its conclusion. Thus, it was with an aim towards creating a broad and representative collection of the most influential cases heard by the Supreme Court that these ten decisions were chosen for this anthology. In the interest of space, only the majority and dissenting opinions are included, while concurring opinions have been omitted. Furthermore, each decision is preceded by a brief history and explanation, intended to provide the reader with a basic knowledge of the case, with which to better understand their meaning and significance in history.

James Daley, Editor

Contents

Marbury v. Madison
1803

Following Thomas Jefferson's defeat of John Adams in the presidential election of 1800, Adams went about appointing sixteen new circuit judges and forty-two new justices of the peace for the District of Columbia. However, when Adams failed to deliver four of the justices of the peace (including William Marbury) before his last day in office, Jefferson's new secretary of state, James Madison, refused to give these four men their commissions. Marbury, in turn, called upon the Supreme Court to exercise a power Congress had bestowed upon it in the Judiciary Act of 1789 by issuing a writ of mandamus ordering Madison to deliver the four appointees to their commissions.

It was the decision of the court that, because the jurisdiction bestowed upon it in the Judiciary Act was not enumerated in the Constitution, the Judiciary Act was null and void, and therefore the court did not have the authority to issue the requested writ of mandamus. The great significance of this case, however, comes from the fact that in order to reach this decision, the court found that it had the power and authority to review acts of Congress for their conformity to the Constitution.

U.S. SUPREME COURT

MARBURY v. MADISON, 5 U.S. 137 (1803)

5 U.S. 137 (Cranch)

WILLIAM MARBURY
V.
JAMES MADISON, SECRETARY OF STATE
OF THE UNITED STATES.

February Term, 1803

AT THE December term 1801, William Marbury, Dennis Ramsay, Robert Townsend Hooe, and William Harper, by their counsel [5 U.S. 137, 138] severally moved the court for a rule to James Madison, secretary of state of the United States, to show cause why a mandamus should not issue commanding him to cause to be delivered to them respectively their several commissions as justices of the peace in the district of Columbia.

This motion was supported by affidavits of the following facts: that notice of this motion had been given to Mr. Madison; that Mr. Adams, the late president of the United States, nominated the applicants to the senate for their advice and consent to be appointed justices of the peace of the district of Columbia; that the senate advised and consented to the appointments; that commissions in due form were signed by the said president appointing them justices, &c. and that the seal of the United States was in due form affixed to the said commissions by the secretary of state; that the applicants have requested Mr. Madison to deliver them their said commissions, who has not complied with that request; and that their said commissions are withheld from them; that the applicants have made application to Mr. Madison as secretary of state of the United States at his office, for information whether the commissions were signed and sealed as aforesaid; that explicit and satisfactory information has not been given in answer to that inquiry, either by the secretary of state, or any officer in the department of state; that application has been made to the secretary of the senate for a certificate of the nomination of the applicants, and of the advice and consent of the senate, who has declined giving such a certificate; whereupon a rule was made to show cause on the fourth day of this term. This rule having been duly served—[5 U.S. 137, 139] Mr. Jacob Wagner and Mr. Daniel Brent, who had been summoned to attend the court, and were required to give evidence, objected to be sworn, alleging that they were clerks in the department of state, and not bound to disclose any facts relating to the business or transactions of the office.

The court ordered the witnesses to be sworn, and their answers taken in writing; but informed them that when the questions were asked they might state their objections to answering each particular question, if they had any.

Mr. Lincoln, who had been the acting secretary of state, when the circumstances stated in the affidavits occurred, was called upon to give testimony. He objected to answering. The questions were put in writing.

The court said there was nothing confidential required to be disclosed. If there had been, he was not obliged to answer it, and if he thought any thing was communicated to him confidentially he was not bound to disclose, nor was he obliged to state any thing which would criminate himself.

The questions argued by the counsel for the relators were, 1. Whether the supreme court can award the writ of mandamus in any case. 2. Whether it will lie to a secretary of state, in any case whatever. 3. Whether in the present case the court may award a mandamus to James Madison, secretary of state.

[5 U.S. 137, 153]

Mr. Chief Justice MARSHALL delivered the opinion of the court.

At the last term, on the affidavits then read and filed with the clerk, a rule was granted in this case, requiring the secretary of state to show cause why a mandamus [5 U.S. 137, 154] should not issue, directing him to deliver to William Marbury his commission as a justice of the peace for the county of Washington, in the district of Columbia.

No cause has been shown, and the present motion is for a mandamus. The peculiar delicacy of this case, the novelty of some of its circumstances, and the real difficulty attending the points which occur in it, require a complete exposition of the principles on which the opinion to be given by the court is founded.

These principles have been, on the side of the applicant, very ably argued at the bar. In rendering the opinion of the court, there will be some departure in form, though not in substance, from the points stated in that argument.

In the order in which the court has viewed this subject, the following questions have been considered and decided.

1. Has the applicant a right to the commission he demands?

2. If he has a right, and that right has been violated, do the laws of his country afford him a remedy?

3. If they do afford him a remedy, is it a mandamus issuing from this court?

The first object of inquiry is,

1. Has the applicant a right to the commission he demands?

His right originates in an act of congress passed in February 1801, concerning the district of Columbia.

After dividing the district into two counties, the eleventh section of this law enacts, "that there shall be appointed in and for each of the said counties, such number of discreet persons to be justices of the peace as the president of the United States shall, from time to time, think expedient, to continue in office for five years." [5 U.S. 137, 155] It appears from the affidavits, that in compliance with this law, a commission for William Marbury as a justice of peace for the county of Washington was signed by John Adams, then president of the United States; after which the seal of the United States was affixed to it; but the commission has never reached the person for whom it was made out.

In order to determine whether he is entitled to this commission, it becomes necessary to inquire whether he has been appointed to the office. For if he has been appointed, the law continues him in office for five years, and he is entitled to the possession of those evidences of office, which, being completed, became his property.

The second section of the second article of the constitution declares, "the president shall nominate, and, by and with the advice and consent of the senate, shall appoint ambassadors, other public ministers and consuls, and all other officers of the United States, whose appointments are not otherwise provided for."

The third section declares, that "he shall commission all the officers of the United States."

An act of congress directs the secretary of state to keep the seal of the United States, "to make out and record, and affix the said seal to all civil commissions to officers of the United States to be appointed by the president, by and with the consent of the senate, or by the president alone; provided that the said seal shall not be affixed to any commission before the same shall have been signed by the president of the United States."

These are the clauses of the constitution and laws of the United States, which affect this part of the case. They seem to contemplate three distinct operations:

1. The nomination. This is the sole act of the president, and is completely voluntary.

2. The appointment. This is also the act of the president, and is also a voluntary act, though it can only be performed by and with the advice and consent of the senate. [5 U.S. 137, 156]

3. The commission. To grant a commission to a person appointed, might perhaps be deemed a duty enjoined by the constitution. "He shall," says that instrument, "commission all the officers of the United States."

The acts of appointing to office, and commissioning the person appointed, can scarcely be considered as one and the same; since the power to perform them is given in two separate and distinct sections of the constitution. The distinction between the appointment and the commission will be rendered more apparent by adverting to that provision in the second section of the second article of the constitution, which authorises congress "to vest by law the appointment of such inferior officers as they think proper, in the president alone, in the courts of law, or in the heads of departments;" thus contemplating cases where the law may direct the president to commission an officer appointed by the courts or by the heads of departments. In such a case, to issue a commission would be apparently a duty distinct from the appointment, the performance of which perhaps, could not legally be refused.

Although that clause of the constitution which requires the president to commission all the officers of the United States, may never have been applied to officers appointed otherwise than by himself, yet it would be difficult to deny the legislative power to apply it to such cases. Of consequence the constitutional distinction between the appointment to an office and the commission of an officer who has been appointed, remains the same as if in practice the president had commissioned officers appointed by an authority other than his own.

It follows too, from the existence of this distinction, that, if an appointment was to be evidenced by any public act other than the commission, the performance of such public act would create the officer; and if he was not removable at the will of the president, would either give him a right to his commission, or enable him to perform the duties without it.

These observations are premised solely for the purpose of rendering more intelligible those which apply more directly to the particular case under consideration. [5 U.S. 137, 157] This is an appointment made by the president, by and with the advice and consent of the senate, and is evidenced by no act but the commission itself. In such a case therefore the commission and the appointment seem inseparable; it being almost impossible to show an appointment otherwise than by proving the existence of a commission: still the commission is not necessarily the appointment; though conclusive evidence of it.

But at what stage does it amount to this conclusive evidence?

The answer to this question seems an obvious one. The appointment being the sole act of the president, must be completely evidenced, when it is shown that he has done every thing to be performed by him.

Should the commission, instead of being evidence of an appointment, even be considered as constituting the appointment itself; still it would be made when the last act to be done by the president was performed, or, at furthest, when the commission was complete.

The last act to be done by the president, is the signature of the commission. He has then acted on the advice and consent of the senate to his own nomination. The time for deliberation has then passed. He has decided. His judgment, on the advice and consent of the senate concurring with his nomination, has been made, and the officer is appointed. This appointment is evidenced by an open, unequivocal act; and being the last act required from the person making it, necessarily excludes the idea of its being, so far as it respects the appointment, an inchoate and incomplete transaction.

Some point of time must be taken when the power of the executive over an officer, not removable at his will, must cease. That point of time must be when the constitutional power of appointment has been exercised. And this power has been exercised when the last act, required from the person possessing the power, has been performed. This last act is the signature of the commission. This idea seems to have prevailed with the legislature, when the act passed converting the department [5 U.S. 137, 158] of foreign affairs into the department of state. By that act it is enacted, that the secretary of state shall keep the seal of the United States, "and shall make out and record, and shall affix the said seal to all civil commissions to officers of the United States, to be appointed by the president:" "provided that the said seal shall not be affixed to any commission, before the same shall have been signed by the president of the United States; nor to any other instrument or act, without the special warrant of the president therefor."

The signature is a warrant for affixing the great seal to the commission; and the great seal is only to be affixed to an instrument which is complete. It attests, by an act supposed to be of public notoriety, the verity of the presidential signature.

It is never to be affixed till the commission is signed, because the signature, which gives force and effect to the commission, is conclusive evidence that the appointment is made.

The commission being signed, the subsequent duty of the secretary of state is prescribed by law, and not to be guided by the will of the president. He is to affix the seal of the United States to the commission, and is to record it.

This is not a proceeding which may be varied, if the judgment of the executive shall suggest one more eligible, but is a precise course accurately marked out by law, and is to be strictly pursued. It is the duty of the secretary of state to conform to the law, and in this he is an officer of the United States, bound to obey the laws. He acts, in this respect, as has been very properly stated at the bar, under the authority of law, and not by the instructions of the president. It is a ministerial act which the law enjoins on a particular officer for a particular purpose.

If it should be supposed, that the solemnity of affixing the seal, is necessary not only to the validity of the commission, but even to the completion of an appointment, still when the seal is affixed the appointment is made, and [5 U.S. 137, 159] the commission is valid. No other solemnity is required by law; no other act is to be performed on the part of government. All that the executive can do to invest the person with his office, is done; and unless the appointment be then made, the executive cannot make one without the co-operation of others.

After searching anxiously for the principles on which a contrary opinion may be supported, none have been found which appear of sufficient force to maintain the opposite doctrine.

Such as the imagination of the court could suggest, have been very deliberately examined, and after allowing them all the weight which it appears possible to give them, they do not shake the opinion which has been formed.

In considering this question, it has been conjectured that the commission may have been assimilated to a deed, to the validity of which, delivery is essential.

This idea is founded on the supposition that the commission is not merely evidence of an appointment, but is itself the actual appointment; a supposition by no means unquestionable. But for the purpose of examining this objection fairly, let it be conceded, that the principle, claimed for its support, is established.

The appointment being, under the constitution, to be made by the president personally, the delivery of the deed of appointment, if necessary to its completion, must be made by the president also. It is not necessary that the livery should be made personally to the grantee of the office: it never is so made. The law would seem to contemplate that it should be made to the secretary of state, since it directs the secretary to affix the seal to the commission after it shall have been signed by the president. If then the act of livery be necessary to give validity to the commission, it has been delivered when executed and given to the secretary for the purpose of being sealed, recorded, and transmitted to the party.

But in all cases of letters patent, certain solemnities are required by law, which solemnities are the evidences [5 U.S. 137, 160] of the validity of the instrument. A formal delivery to the person is not among them. In cases of commissions, the sign manual of the president, and the seal of the

United States, are those solemnities. This objection therefore does not touch the case.

It has also occurred as possible, and barely possible, that the transmission of the commission, and the acceptance thereof, might be deemed necessary to complete the right of the plaintiff.

The transmission of the commission is a practice directed by convenience, but not by law. It cannot therefore be necessary to constitute the appointment which must precede it, and which is the mere act of the president. If the executive required that every person appointed to an office, should himself take means to procure his commission, the appointment would not be the less valid on that account. The appointment is the sole act of the president; the transmission of the commission is the sole act of the officer to whom that duty is assigned, and may be accelerated or retarded by circumstances which can have no influence on the appointment. A commission is transmitted to a person already appointed; not to a person to be appointed or not, as the letter enclosing the commission should happen to get into the post-office and reach him in safety, or to miscarry.

It may have some tendency to elucidate this point, to inquire, whether the possession of the original commission be indispensably necessary to authorize a person, appointed to any office, to perform the duties of that office. If it was necessary, then a loss of the commission would lose the office. Not only negligence, but accident or fraud, fire or theft, might deprive an individual of his office. In such a case, I presume it could not be doubted, but that a copy from the record of the office of the secretary of state, would be, to every intent and purpose, equal to the original. The act of congress has expressly made it so. To give that copy validity, it would not be necessary to prove that the original had been transmitted and afterwards lost. The copy would be complete evidence that the original had existed, and that the appointment had been made, but not that the original had been transmitted. If indeed it should appear that [5 U.S. 137, 161] the original had been mislaid in the office of state, that circumstance would not affect the operation of the copy. When all the requisites have been performed which authorize a recording officer to record any instrument whatever, and the order for that purpose has been given, the instrument is in law considered as recorded, although the manual labour of inserting it in a book kept for that purpose may not have been performed.

In the case of commissions, the law orders the secretary of state to record them. When therefore they are signed and sealed, the order for their being recorded is given; and whether inserted in the book or not, they are in law recorded.

A copy of this record is declared equal to the original, and the fees to be paid by a person requiring a copy are ascertained by law. Can a keeper of a public record erase therefrom a commission which has been recorded? Or can he refuse a copy thereof to a person demanding it on the terms prescribed by law?

Such a copy would, equally with the original, authorize the justice of peace to proceed in the performance of his duty, because it would, equally with the original, attest his appointment.

If the transmission of a commission be not considered as necessary to give validity to an appointment; still less is its acceptance. The appointment is the sole act of the president; the acceptance is the sole act of the officer, and is, in plain common sense, posterior to the appointment. As he may resign, so may he refuse to accept: but neither the one nor the other is capable of rendering the appointment a nonentity.

That this is the understanding of the government, is apparent from the whole tenor of its conduct.

A commission bears date, and the salary of the officer commences from his appointment; not from the transmission or acceptance of his commission. When a person, appointed to any office, refuses to accept that office, the successor is nominated in the place of the person who [5 U.S. 137, 162] has declined to accept, and not in the place of the person who had been previously in office and had created the original vacancy.

It is therefore decidedly the opinion of the court, that when a commission has been signed by the president, the appointment is made; and that the commission is complete when the seal of the United States has been affixed to it by the secretary of state.

Where an officer is removable at the will of the executive, the circumstance which completes his appointment is of no concern; because the act is at any time revocable; and the commission may be arrested, if still in the office. But when the officer is not removable at the will of the executive, the appointment is not revocable and cannot be annulled. It has conferred legal rights which cannot be resumed.

The discretion of the executive is to be exercised until the appointment has been made. But having once made the appointment, his power over the office is terminated in all cases, where by law the officer is not removable by him. The right to the office is then in the person appointed, and he has the absolute, unconditional power of accepting or rejecting it.

Mr. Marbury, then, since his commission was signed by the president and sealed by the secretary of state, was appointed; and as the law creating the office gave the officer a right to hold for five years independent of the executive, the appointment was not revocable; but vested in the officer legal rights which are protected by the laws of his country.

To withhold the commission, therefore, is an act deemed by the court not warranted by law, but violative of a vested legal right.

This brings us to the second inquiry; which is,

2. If he has a right, and that right has been violated, do the laws of his country afford him a remedy? [5 U.S. 137, 163] The very essence of civil liberty certainly consists in the right of every individual to claim the protection of the laws, whenever he receives an injury. One of the first duties of government is to afford that protection. In Great Britain the king himself is sued in the respectful form of a petition, and he never fails to comply with the judgment of his court.

In the third volume of his Commentaries, page 23, Blackstone states two cases in which a remedy is afforded by mere operation of law.

> "In all other cases," he says, "it is a general and indisputable rule, that where there is a legal right, there is also a legal remedy by suit or action at law whenever that right is invaded."

And afterwards, page 109 of the same volume, he says, "I am next to consider such injuries as are cognizable by the courts of common law. And herein I shall for the present only remark, that all possible injuries whatsoever, that did not fall within the exclusive cognizance of either the ecclesiastical, military, or maritime tribunals, are, for that very reason, within the cognizance of the common law courts of justice; for it is a settled and invariable principle in the laws of England, that every right, when withheld, must have a remedy, and every injury its proper redress."

The government of the United States has been emphatically termed a government of laws, and not of men. It will certainly cease to deserve this high appellation, if the laws furnish no remedy for the violation of a vested legal right.

If this obloquy is to be cast on the jurisprudence of our country, it must arise from the peculiar character of the case.

It behoves us then to inquire whether there be in its composition any ingredient which shall exempt from legal investigation, or exclude the injured party from legal redress. In pursuing this inquiry the first question which presents itself, is, whether this can be arranged [5 U.S. 137, 164] with that class of cases which come under the description of damnum absque injuria—a loss without an injury.

This description of cases never has been considered, and it is believed never can be considered as comprehending offices of trust, of honour or of profit. The office of justice of peace in the district of Columbia is such an office; it is therefore worthy of the attention and guardianship of the laws. It has received that attention and guardianship. It has been created by special act of congress, and has been secured, so far as the laws can give security to the person appointed to fill it, for five years. It is not then on account of the worthlessness of the thing pursued, that the injured party can be alleged to be without remedy.

Is it in the nature of the transaction? Is the act of delivering or withholding a commission to be considered as a mere political act belonging to the executive department alone, for the performance of which entire confidence is placed by our constitution in the supreme executive; and for any misconduct respecting which, the injured individual has no remedy.

That there may be such cases is not to be questioned; but that every act of duty to be performed in any of the great departments of government constitutes such a case, is not to be admitted.

By the act concerning invalids, passed in June 1794, the secretary at war is ordered to place on the pension list all persons whose names are contained in a report previously made by him to congress. If he should refuse to do so, would the wounded veteran be without remedy? Is it to be contended that where the law in precise terms directs the performance of an act in which an individual is interested, the law is incapable of securing obedience to its mandate? Is it on account of the character of the person against whom the complaint is made? Is it to be contended that the heads of departments are not amenable to the laws of their country?

Whatever the practice on particular occasions may be, the theory of this principle will certainly never be maintained. [5 U.S. 137, 165] No act of the legislature confers so extraordinary a privilege, nor can it derive countenance from the doctrines of the common law. After stating that personal injury from the king to a subject is presumed to be impossible, Blackstone, Vol. III. p. 255, says, "but injuries to the rights of property can scarcely be committed by the crown without the intervention of its officers: for whom, the law, in matters of right, entertains no respect or delicacy; but furnishes various methods of detecting the errors and misconduct of those agents by whom the king has been deceived and induced to do a temporary injustice."

By the act passed in 1796, authorizing the sale of the lands above the mouth of Kentucky river, the purchaser, on paying his purchase money, becomes completely entitled to the property purchased; and on producing to the secretary of state the receipt of the treasurer upon a certificate required by the law, the president of the United States is authorized to grant him a patent. It is further enacted that all patents shall be countersigned by the secretary of state, and recorded in his office. If the secretary of state should choose to withhold this patent; or the patent being lost, should refuse a copy of it; can it be imagined that the law furnishes to the injured person no remedy?

It is not believed that any person whatever would attempt to maintain such a proposition.

It follows then that the question, whether the legality of an act of the head of a department be examinable in a court of justice or not, must always depend on the nature of that act.

If some acts be examinable, and others not, there must be some rule of law to guide the court in the exercise of its jurisdiction.

In some instances there may be difficulty in applying the rule to particular cases; but there cannot, it is believed, be much difficulty in laying down the rule.

By the constitution of the United States, the president is invested with certain important political powers, in the [5 U.S. 137, 166] exercise of which he is to use his own discretion, and is accountable only to his country in his political character, and to his own conscience. To aid him in the performance of these duties, he is authorized to appoint certain officers, who act by his authority and in conformity with his orders.

In such cases, their acts are his acts; and whatever opinion may be entertained of the manner in which executive discretion may be used, still there exists, and can exist, no power to control that discretion. The subjects are political. They respect the nation, not individual rights, and being entrusted to the executive, the decision of the executive is conclusive. The application of this remark will be perceived by adverting to the act of congress for establishing the department of foreign affairs. This officer, as his duties were prescribed by that act, is to conform precisely to the will of the president. He is the mere organ by whom that will is communicated. The acts of such an officer, as an officer, can never be examinable by the courts.

But when the legislature proceeds to impose on that officer other duties; when he is directed peremptorily to perform certain acts; when the rights of individuals are dependent on the performance of those acts; he is so far the officer of the law; is amenable to the laws for his conduct; and cannot at his discretion sport away the vested rights of others.

The conclusion from this reasoning is, that where the heads of departments are the political or confidential agents of the executive, merely to execute the will of the president, or rather to act in cases in which the executive possesses a constitutional or legal discretion, nothing can be more perfectly clear than that their acts are only politically examinable. But where a specific duty is assigned by law, and individual rights depend upon the performance of that duty, it seems equally clear that the individual who considers himself injured has a right to resort to the laws of his country for a remedy.

If this be the rule, let us inquire how it applies to the case under the consideration of the court. [5 U.S. 137, 167] The power of nominating to the senate, and the power of appointing the person nominated, are political powers, to be exercised by the president according to his own discretion. When he has made an appointment, he has exercised his whole power, and his discretion has been completely applied to the case. If, by law, the officer be removable at the will of the president, then a new appointment may be immediately made, and the rights of the officer are terminated. But as a fact which has existed cannot be made never to have existed, the appointment cannot be annihilated; and consequently if the officer is by law not removable at the will of the president, the rights he has acquired are protected by the law, and are not resumable by the president. They cannot be extinguished by executive authority, and he has the privilege of asserting them in like manner as if they had been derived from any other source.

The question whether a right has vested or not, is, in its nature, judicial, and must be tried by the judicial authority. If, for example, Mr. Marbury had taken the oaths of a magistrate, and proceeded to act as one; in consequence of which a suit had been instituted against him, in which his defence had depended on his being a magistrate; the validity of his appointment must have been determined by judicial authority.

So, if he conceives that by virtue of his appointment he has a legal right either to the commission which has been made out for him or to a copy of that commission, it is equally a question examinable in a court, and the decision of the court upon it must depend on the opinion entertained of his appointment.

That question has been discussed, and the opinion is, that the latest point of time which can be taken as that at which the appointment was complete, and evidenced, was when, after the signature of the president, the seal of the United States was affixed to the commission.

It is then the opinion of the court,

1. That by signing the commission of Mr. Marbury, the president of the United States appointed him a justice [5 U.S. 137, 168] of peace for the county of Washington in the district of Columbia; and that the seal of the United States, affixed thereto by the secretary of state, is conclusive testimony of the verity of the signature, and of the completion of the appointment; and that the appointment conferred on him a legal right to the office for the space of five years.

2. That, having this legal title to the office, he has a consequent right to the commission; a refusal to deliver which is a plain violation of that right, for which the laws of his country afford him a remedy.

It remains to be inquired whether,

3. He is entitled to the remedy for which he applies. This depends on,

1. The nature of the writ applied for. And,

2. The power of this court.

1. The nature of the writ.

Blackstone, in the third volume of his Commentaries, page 110, defines a mandamus to be, "a command issuing in the king's name from the court of king's bench, and directed to any person, corporation, or inferior court of judicature within the king's dominions, requiring them to do some particular thing therein specified which appertains to their office and duty, and which the court of king's bench has previously determined, or at least supposes, to be consonant to right and justice."

Lord Mansfield, in 3 Burrows, 1266, in the case of The King v. Baker et al. states with much precision and explicitness the cases in which this writ may be used.

> "Whenever," says that very able judge, "there is a right to execute an office, perform a service, or exercise a franchise (more especially if it be in a matter of public concern or attended with profit), and a person is kept out of possession, or dispossessed of such right, and [5 U.S. 137, 169] has no other specific legal remedy, this court ought to assist by mandamus, upon reasons of justice, as the writ expresses, and upon reasons of public policy, to preserve peace, order and good government." In the same case he says, "this writ ought to be used upon all occasions where the law has established no specific remedy, and where in justice and good government there ought to be one."

In addition to the authorities now particularly cited, many others were relied on at the bar, which show how far the practice has conformed to the general doctrines that have been just quoted.

This writ, if awarded, would be directed to an officer of government, and its mandate to him would be, to use the words of Blackstone, "to do a particular thing therein specified, which appertains to his office and duty, and which the court has previously determined or at least supposes to be consonant to right and justice." Or, in the words of Lord Mansfield, the applicant, in this case, has a right to execute an office of public concern, and is kept out of possession of that right.

These circumstances certainly concur in this case.

Still, to render the mandamus a proper remedy, the officer to whom it is to be directed, must be one to whom, on legal principles, such writ may be directed; and the person applying for it must be without any other specific and legal remedy.

1. With respect to the officer to whom it would be directed. The intimate political relation, subsisting between the president of the United States and the heads of departments, necessarily renders any legal investigation of the acts of one of those high officers peculiarly irksome, as well as delicate; and excites some hesitation with respect to the propriety of entering into such investigation. Impressions are often received without much reflection or examination; and it is not wonderful that in such a case as this, the assertion, by an individual, of his legal claims in a court of justice, to which claims it is the duty of that court to attend,

should at first view be considered [5 U.S. 137, 170] by some, as an attempt to intrude into the cabinet, and to intermeddle with the prerogatives of the executive.

It is scarcely necessary for the court to disclaim all pretensions to such a jurisdiction. An extravagance, so absurd and excessive, could not have been entertained for a moment. The province of the court is, solely, to decide on the rights of individuals, not to inquire how the executive, or executive officers, perform duties in which they have a discretion. Questions, in their nature political, or which are, by the constitution and laws, submitted to the executive, can never be made in this court.

But, if this be not such a question; if so far from being an intrusion into the secrets of the cabinet, it respects a paper, which, according to law, is upon record, and to a copy of which the law gives a right, on the payment of ten cents; if it be no intermeddling with a subject, over which the executive can be considered as having exercised any control; what is there in the exalted station of the officer, which shall bar a citizen from asserting, in a court of justice, his legal rights, or shall forbid a court to listen to the claim; or to issue a mandamus, directing the performance of a duty, not depending on executive discretion, but on particular acts of congress and the general principles of law?

If one of the heads of departments commits any illegal act, under colour of his office, by which an individual sustains an injury, it cannot be pretended that his office alone exempts him from being sued in the ordinary mode of proceeding, and being compelled to obey the judgment of the law. How then can his office exempt him from this particular mode of deciding on the legality of his conduct, if the case be such a case as would, were any other individual the party complained of, authorize the process?

It is not by the office of the person to whom the writ is directed, but the nature of the thing to be done, that the propriety or impropriety of issuing a mandamus is to be determined. Where the head of a department acts in a case in which executive discretion is to be exercised; in which he is the mere organ of executive will; it is [5 U.S. 137, 171] again repeated, that any application to a court to control, in any respect, his conduct, would be rejected without hesitation.

But where he is directed by law to do a certain act affecting the absolute rights of individuals, in the performance of which he is not placed under the particular direction of the president, and the performance of which the president cannot lawfully forbid, and therefore is never presumed to have forbidden; as for example, to record a commission, or a patent for land, which has received all the legal solemnities; or to give a copy of such record; in such cases, it is not perceived on what ground the courts of the country are further excused from the duty of giving judgment, that right to be done to an injured individual, than if the same services were to be performed by a person not the head of a department.

This opinion seems not now for the first time to be taken up in this country.

It must be well recollected that in 1792 an act passed, directing the secretary at war to place on the pension list such disabled officers and soldiers as should be reported to him by the circuit courts, which act, so far as the duty was imposed on the courts, was deemed unconstitutional; but some of the judges, thinking that the law might be executed by them in the character of commissioners, proceeded to act and to report in that character.

This law being deemed unconstitutional at the circuits, was repealed, and a different system was established; but the question whether those persons, who had been reported by the judges, as commissioners, were entitled, in consequence of that report, to be placed on the pension list, was a legal question, properly determinable in the courts, although the act of placing such persons on the list was to be performed by the head of a department.

That this question might be properly settled, congress passed an act in February 1793, making it the duty of the secretary of war, in conjunction with the attorney general, to take such measures as might be necessary to obtain an adjudication of the supreme court of the United [5 U.S. 137, 172] States on the validity of any such rights, claimed under the act aforesaid.

After the passage of this act, a mandamus was moved for, to be directed to the secretary at war, commanding him to place on the pension list a person stating himself to be on the report of the judges.

There is, therefore, much reason to believe, that this mode of trying the legal right of the complainant, was deemed by the head of a department, and by the highest law officer of the United States, the most proper which could be selected for the purpose.

When the subject was brought before the court the decision was, not, that a mandamus would not lie to the head of a department, directing him to perform an act, enjoined by law, in the performance of which an individual had a vested interest; but that a mandamus ought not to issue in that case—the decision necessarily to be made if the report of the commissioners did not confer on the applicant a legal right.

The judgment in that case is understood to have decided the merits of all claims of that description; and the persons, on the report of the commissioners, found it necessary to pursue the mode prescribed by the law subsequent to that which had been deemed unconstitutional, in order to place themselves on the pension list.

The doctrine, therefore, now advanced is by no means a novel one.

It is true that the mandamus, now moved for, is not for the performance of an act expressly enjoined by statute.

It is to deliver a commission; on which subjects the acts of congress are silent. This difference is not considered as affecting the case. It has already been stated that the applicant has, to that commission, a vested legal right, of which the executive cannot deprive him. He has been appointed to an office, from which he is not removable at the will of the executive; and being so [5 U.S. 137, 173] appointed, he has a right to the commission which the secretary has received from the president for his use. The act of congress does not indeed order the secretary of state to send it to him, but it is placed in his hands for the person entitled to it; and cannot be more lawfully withheld by him, than by another person.

It was at first doubted whether the action of detinue was not a specific legal remedy for the commission which has been withheld from Mr. Marbury; in which case a mandamus would be improper. But this doubt has yielded to the consideration that the judgment in detinue is for the thing itself, or its value. The value of a public office not to be sold, is incapable of being ascertained; and the applicant has a right to the office itself, or to nothing. He will obtain the office by obtaining the commission, or a copy of it from the record.

This, then, is a plain case of a mandamus, either to deliver the commission, or a copy of it from the record; and it only remains to be inquired,

Whether it can issue from this court.

The act to establish the judicial courts of the United States authorizes the supreme court "to issue writs of mandamus, in cases warranted by the principles and usages of law, to any courts appointed, or persons holding office, under the authority of the United States."

The secretary of state, being a person, holding an office under the authority of the United States, is precisely within the letter of the description; and if this court is not authorized to issue a writ of mandamus to such an officer, it must be because the law is unconstitutional, and therefore absolutely incapable of conferring the authority, and assigning the duties which its words purport to confer and assign.

The constitution vests the whole judicial power of the United States in one supreme court, and such inferior courts as congress shall, from time to time, ordain and establish. This power is expressly extended to all cases arising under the laws of the United States; and consequently, in some form, may be exercised over the present [5 U.S. 137, 174] case; because the right claimed is given by a law of the United States.

In the distribution of this power it is declared that "the supreme court shall have original jurisdiction in all cases affecting ambassadors, other public ministers and consuls, and those in which a state shall be a party. In all other cases, the supreme court shall have appellate jurisdiction."

It has been insisted at the bar, that as the original grant of jurisdiction to the supreme and inferior courts is general, and the clause, assigning original jurisdiction to the supreme court, contains no negative or restrictive words; the power remains to the legislature to assign original jurisdiction to that court in other cases than those specified in the article which has been recited; provided those cases belong to the judicial power of the United States.

If it had been intended to leave it in the discretion of the legislature to apportion the judicial power between the supreme and inferior courts according to the will of that body, it would certainly have been useless to have proceeded further than to have defined the judicial power, and the tribunals in which it should be vested. The subsequent part of the section is mere surplusage, is entirely without meaning, if such is to be the construction. If congress remains at liberty to give this court appellate jurisdiction, where the constitution has declared their jurisdiction shall be original; and original jurisdiction where the constitution has declared it shall be appellate; the distribution of jurisdiction made in the constitution, is form without substance.

Affirmative words are often, in their operation, negative of other objects than those affirmed; and in this case, a negative or exclusive sense must be given to them or they have no operation at all.

It cannot be presumed that any clause in the constitution is intended to be without effect; and therefore such construction is inadmissible, unless the words require it. [5 U.S. 137, 175] If the solicitude of the convention, respecting our peace with foreign powers, induced a provision that the supreme court should take original jurisdiction in cases which might be supposed to affect them; yet the clause would have proceeded no further than to provide for such cases, if no further restriction on the powers of congress had been intended. That they should have appellate jurisdiction in all other cases, with such exceptions as congress might make, is no restriction; unless the words be deemed exclusive of original jurisdiction.

When an instrument organizing fundamentally a judicial system, divides it into one supreme, and so many inferior courts as the legislature may ordain and establish; then enumerates its powers, and proceeds so far to distribute them, as to define the jurisdiction of the supreme court by declaring the cases in which it shall take original jurisdiction, and that in others it shall take appellate jurisdiction, the plain import of the words seems to be, that in one class of cases its jurisdiction is original, and not appellate; in the other it is appellate, and not original. If any other construction would render the clause inoperative, that is an additional reason for rejecting such other construction, and for adhering to the obvious meaning.

To enable this court then to issue a mandamus, it must be shown to be an exercise of appellate jurisdiction, or to be necessary to enable them to exercise appellate jurisdiction.

It has been stated at the bar that the appellate jurisdiction may be exercised in a variety of forms, and that if it be the will of the legislature that a mandamus should be used for that purpose, that will must be obeyed. This is true; yet the jurisdiction must be appellate, not original.

It is the essential criterion of appellate jurisdiction, that it revises and corrects the proceedings in a cause already instituted, and does not create that case. Although, therefore, a mandamus may be directed to courts, yet to issue such a writ to an officer for the delivery of a paper, is in effect the same as to sustain an original action for that paper, and therefore seems not to belong to [5 U.S. 137, 176] appellate, but to original jurisdiction. Neither is it necessary in such a case as this, to enable the court to exercise its appellate jurisdiction.

The authority, therefore, given to the supreme court, by the act establishing the judicial courts of the United States, to issue writs of mandamus to public officers, appears not to be warranted by the constitution; and it becomes necessary to inquire whether a jurisdiction, so conferred, can be exercised.

The question, whether an act, repugnant to the constitution, can become the law of the land, is a question deeply interesting to the United States; but, happily, not of an intricacy proportioned to its interest. It seems only necessary to recognise certain principles, supposed to have been long and well established, to decide it.

That the people have an original right to establish, for their future government, such principles as, in their opinion, shall most conduce to their own happiness, is the basis on which the whole American fabric has been erected. The exercise of this original right is a very great exertion; nor can it nor ought it to be frequently repeated. The principles, therefore, so established are deemed fundamental. And as the authority, from which they proceed, is supreme, and can seldom act, they are designed to be permanent.

This original and supreme will organizes the government, and assigns to different departments their respective powers. It may either stop here; or establish certain limits not to be transcended by those departments.

The government of the United States is of the latter description. The powers of the legislature are defined and limited; and that those limits may not be mistaken or forgotten, the constitution is written. To what purpose are powers limited, and to what purpose is that limitation committed to writing; if these limits may, at any time, be passed by those intended to be restrained? The distinction between a government with limited and unlimited powers is abolished, if those limits do not confine the persons on whom they are imposed, and if acts prohibited [5 U.S. 137, 177] and acts allowed are of equal obligation. It is a proposition too plain to be contested, that the constitution controls any legislative act repugnant to it; or, that the legislature may alter the constitution by an ordinary act.

Between these alternatives there is no middle ground. The constitution is either a superior, paramount law, unchangeable by ordinary means, or it is on a level with ordinary legislative acts, and like other acts, is alterable when the legislature shall please to alter it.

If the former part of the alternative be true, then a legislative act contrary to the constitution is not law: if the latter part be true, then written constitutions are absurd attempts, on the part of the people, to limit a power in its own nature illimitable.

Certainly all those who have framed written constitutions contemplate them as forming the fundamental and paramount law of the nation, and consequently the theory of every such government must be, that an act of the legislature repugnant to the constitution is void.

This theory is essentially attached to a written constitution, and is consequently to be considered by this court as one of the fundamental principles of our society. It is not therefore to be lost sight of in the further consideration of this subject.

If an act of the legislature, repugnant to the constitution, is void, does it, notwithstanding its invalidity, bind the courts and oblige them to give it effect? Or, in other words, though it be not law, does it constitute a rule as operative as if it was a law? This would be to overthrow in fact what was established in theory; and would seem, at first view, an absurdity too gross to be insisted on. It shall, however, receive a more attentive consideration.

It is emphatically the province and duty of the judicial department to say what the law is. Those who apply the rule to particular cases, must of necessity expound and interpret that rule. If two laws conflict with each other, the courts must decide on the operation of each. [5 U.S. 137, 178] So if a law be in opposition to the constitution: if both the law and the constitution apply to a particular case, so that the court must either decide that case conformably to the law, disregarding the constitution; or conformably to the constitution, disregarding the law: the court must determine which of these conflicting rules governs the case. This is of the very essence of judicial duty.

If then the courts are to regard the constitution; and the constitution is superior to any ordinary act of the legislature; the constitution, and not such ordinary act, must govern the case to which they both apply.

Those then who controvert the principle that the constitution is to be considered, in court, as a paramount law, are reduced to the necessity of maintaining that courts must close their eyes on the constitution, and see only the law.

This doctrine would subvert the very foundation of all written constitutions. It would declare that an act, which, according to the principles and theory of our government, is entirely void, is yet, in practice, completely obligatory. It would declare, that if the legislature shall do what is expressly forbidden, such act, notwithstanding the express prohibition, is in reality effectual. It would be giving to the legislature a practical and real omnipotence with the same breath which professes to restrict their powers within narrow limits. It is prescribing limits, and declaring that those limits may be passed at pleasure.

That it thus reduces to nothing what we have deemed the greatest improvement on political institutions—a written constitution, would of itself be sufficient, in America where written constitutions have been viewed with so much reverence, for rejecting the construction. But the peculiar expressions of the constitution of the United States furnish additional arguments in favour of its rejection.

The judicial power of the United States is extended to all cases arising under the constitution. [5 U.S. 137, 179] Could it be the intention of those who gave this power, to say that, in using it, the constitution should not be looked into? That a case arising under the constitution should be decided without examining the instrument under which it arises?

This is too extravagant to be maintained.

In some cases then, the constitution must be looked into by the judges. And if they can open it at all, what part of it are they forbidden to read, or to obey?

There are many other parts of the constitution which serve to illustrate this subject.

It is declared that "no tax or duty shall be laid on articles exported from any state." Suppose a duty on the export of cotton, of tobacco, or of flour; and a suit instituted to recover it. Ought judgment to be rendered in such a case? Ought the judges to close their eyes on the constitution, and only see the law?

The constitution declares that "no bill of attainder or ex post facto law shall be passed."

If, however, such a bill should be passed and a person should be prosecuted under it, must the court condemn to death those victims whom the constitution endeavours to preserve?

"No person," says the constitution, "shall be convicted of treason unless on the testimony of two witnesses to the same overt act, or on confession in open court."

Here the language of the constitution is addressed especially to the courts. It prescribes, directly for them, a rule of evidence not to be departed from. If the legislature should change that rule, and declare one witness, or a confession out of court, sufficient for conviction, must the constitutional principle yield to the legislative act?

From these and many other selections which might be made, it is apparent, that the framers of the constitution [5 U.S. 137, 180] contemplated that instrument as a rule for the government of courts, as well as of the legislature.

Why otherwise does it direct the judges to take an oath to support it? This oath certainly applies, in an especial manner, to their conduct in their official character. How immoral to impose it on them, if they were to be used as the instruments, and the knowing instruments, for violating what they swear to support!

The oath of office, too, imposed by the legislature, is completely demonstrative of the legislative opinion on this subject. It is in these words: "I do solemnly swear that I will administer justice without respect to persons, and do equal right to the poor and to the rich; and that I will faithfully and impartially discharge all the duties incumbent on me as according to the best of my abilities and understanding, agreeably to the constitution and laws of the United States."

Why does a judge swear to discharge his duties agreeably to the constitution of the United States, if that constitution forms no rule for his government? if it is closed upon him and cannot be inspected by him.

If such be the real state of things, this is worse than solemn mockery. To prescribe, or to take this oath, becomes equally a crime.

It is also not entirely unworthy of observation, that in declaring what shall be the supreme law of the land, the constitution itself is first mentioned; and not the laws of the United States generally, but those only which shall be made in pursuance of the constitution, have that rank.

Thus, the particular phraseology of the constitution of the United States confirms and strengthens the principle, supposed to be essential to all written constitutions, that a law repugnant to the constitution is void, and that courts, as well as other departments, are bound by that instrument.

The rule must be discharged.

Scott v. Sandford
1856

Dred Scott was an American slave whose master, army physician John Emerson, moved often to posts at various military bases. Throughout the course of his servitude, Scott was moved to Illinois, a free state, Minnesota, a free territory, and then back to Missouri, which at the time was still a slave state. After Dr. Emerson's death, Scott attempted to purchase his own and his wife's freedom from Emerson's widow. When she refused to accept this offer, Scott successfully sued for his freedom in a Missouri lower court, citing the commonly accepted precedent that slaves who are moved to a free state become free. This decision was quickly reversed, however, upon appeal to the Missouri Supreme Court, after which Scott unsuccessfully appealed to the Federal Circuit Court in St. Louis, before taking his case to the United States Supreme Court.

The Supreme Court ruled that only Missouri law applied in this case, and thus Scott was forced to return to slavery. In addition, the court ruled that no person of African descent could ever be a citizen, as they were "beings of an inferior order," and thus not included in the phrase "all men" in the Declaration of Independence or the Constitution. Furthermore, in coming to this decision, the court ruled that the Missouri Compromise—which prohibited slavery for all new states north of the 36° 30' line, excluding Missouri—was unconstitutional, as it violated the Fifth Amendment by depriving citizens of property without due process. This decision had the effect of strengthening legal precedent in favor of slaveholders until 1868, when the Fourteenth Amendment provided citizenship to all freed slaves. Dred Scott did not live to see the passing of this amendment, as he died of tuberculosis less than two years after this decision.

U.S. SUPREME COURT

DRED SCOTT v. SANDFORD, 60 U.S. 393 (1856)

60 U.S. 393 (How.)

DRED SCOTT, PLAINTIFF IN ERROR,
V.
JOHN F. A. SANDFORD.
December Term, 1856

[60 U.S. 393, 396] THIS case was brought up, by writ of error, from the Circuit Court of the United States for the district of Missouri.

It was an action of trespass vi et armis instituted in the Circuit Court by Scott against Sandford.

Prior to the institution of the present suit, an action was brought by Scott for his freedom in the Circuit Court of St. Louis county, (State court,) where there was a verdict and judgment in his favor. On a writ of error to the Supreme Court of the State, the judgment below was reversed, and the case remanded to the Circuit Court, where it was continued to await the decision of the case now in question.

The declaration of Scott contained three counts: one, that Sandford had assaulted the plaintiff; one, that he had assaulted Harriet Scott, his wife; and one, that he had assaulted Eliza Scott and Lizzie Scott, his children.

Sandford appeared, and filed the following plea:

DRED SCOTT
v.
JOHN F. A. SANDFORD.
Plea to the Jurisdiction of the Court.
APRIL TERM, 1854.

And the said John F. A. Sandford, in his own proper person, comes and says that this court ought not to have or take further cognizance of the action aforesaid, because he says that said cause of action, and each and every of them, (if any such have accrued to the said Dred Scott,) accrued to the said Dred Scott out of the jurisdiction of this court, and exclusively within the jurisdiction of the courts of the State of Missouri, for that, to wit: the said plaintiff, Dred Scott, is not a citizen of the State of Missouri, as alleged in his declaration, because [60 U.S. 393, 397] he is a negro of African descent; his ancestors were of pure African blood, and were brought into this country and sold as negro slaves, and this the said Sandford is ready to verify. Wherefore, he prays judgment whether this court can or will take further cognizance of the action aforesaid.

JOHN F. A. SANDFORD.

To this plea there was a demurrer in the usual form, which was argued in April, 1854, when the court gave judgment that the demurrer should be sustained.

In May, 1854, the defendant, in pursuance of an agreement between counsel, and with the leave of the court, pleaded in bar of the action:

1. Not guilty.

2. That the plaintiff was a negro slave, the lawful property of the defendant, and, as such, the defendant gently laid his hands upon him, and thereby had only restrained him, as the defendant had a right to do.

3. That with respect to the wife and daughters of the plaintiff, in the second and third counts of the declaration mentioned, the defendant had, as to them, only acted in the same manner, and in virtue of the same legal right.

In the first of these pleas, the plaintiff joined issue; and to the second and third, filed replications alleging that the defendant, of his own wrong and without the cause in his second and third pleas alleged, committed the trespasses, &c.

The counsel then filed the following agreed statement of facts, viz:

In the year 1834, the plaintiff was a negro slave belonging to Dr. Emerson, who was a surgeon in the army of the United States. In that year, 1834, said Dr. Emerson took the plaintiff from the State of Missouri to the military post at Rock Island, in the State of Illinois, and held him there as a slave until the month of April or May, 1836. At the time last mentioned, said Dr. Emerson removed the plaintiff from said military post at Rock Island to the military post at Fort Snelling, situate on the west bank of the Mississippi river, in the Territory known as Upper Louisiana, acquired by the United States of France, and situate north of the latitude of thirty-six degrees thirty minutes north, and north of the State of Missouri. Said Dr. Emerson held the plaintiff in slavery at said Fort Snelling, from said last-mentioned date until the year 1838.

In the year 1835, Harriet, who is named in the second count of the plaintiff's declaration, was the negro slave of Major Taliaferro, who belonged to the army of the United States. [60 U.S. 393, 398] In that year, 1835, said Major Taliaferro took said Harriet to said Fort Snelling, a military post, situated as hereinbefore stated, and kept her there as a slave until the year 1836, and then sold and delivered her as a slave at said Fort Snelling unto the said Dr. Emerson hereinbefore named. Said Dr. Emerson held said Harriet in slavery at said Fort Snelling until the year 1838.

In the year 1836, the plaintiff and said Harriet at said Fort Snelling, with the consent of said Dr. Emerson, who then claimed to be their master and owner, intermarried, and took each other for husband and wife. Eliza and Lizzie, named in the third count of the plaintiff's declaration, are the fruit of that marriage. Eliza is about fourteen years old, and was born on board the steamboat Gipsey, north of the north line of the State of Missouri, and upon the river Mississippi. Lizzie is about seven years old, and was born in the State of Missouri, at the military post called Jefferson Barracks.

In the year 1838, said Dr. Emerson removed the plaintiff and said Harriet and their said daughter Eliza, from said Fort Snelling to the State of Missouri, where they have ever since resided.

Before the commencement of this suit, said Dr. Emerson sold and conveyed the plaintiff, said Harriet, Eliza, and Lizzie, to the defendant, as slaves, and the defendant has ever since claimed to hold them and each of them as slaves.

At the times mentioned in the plaintiff's declaration, the defendant, claiming to be owner as aforesaid, laid his hands upon said plaintiff, Harriet, Eliza, and Lizzie, and imprisoned them, doing in this respect, however, no more than what he might lawfully do if they were of right his slaves at such times.

Further proof may be given on the trial for either party.

It is agreed that Dred Scott brought suit for his freedom in the Circuit Court of St. Louis county; that there was a verdict and judgment in his favor; that on a writ of error to the Supreme Court, the judgment below was reversed, and the same remanded to the Circuit Court, where it has been continued to await the decision of this case.

In May, 1854, the cause went before a jury, who found the following verdict, viz: "As to the first issue joined in this case, we of the jury find the defendant not guilty; and as to the issue secondly above joined, we of the jury find that before and at the time when, &c., in the first count mentioned, the said Dred Scott was a negro slave, the lawful property of the defendant; and as to the issue thirdly above joined, we, the jury, find that before and at the time when, &c., in the second and third counts mentioned, the said Harriet, wife of [60 U.S. 393, 399] said Dred Scott, and

Eliza and Lizzie, the daughters of the said Dred Scott, were negro slaves, the lawful property of the defendant."

Whereupon, the court gave judgment for the defendant.

After an ineffectual motion for a new trial, the plaintiff filed the following bill of exceptions.

On the trial of this cause by the jury, the plaintiff, to maintain the issues on his part, read to the jury the following agreed statement of facts, (see agreement above.) No further testimony was given to the jury by either party. Thereupon the plaintiff moved the court to give to the jury the following instruction, viz:

"That, upon the facts agreed to by the parties, they ought to find for the plaintiff. The court refused to give such instruction to the jury, and the plaintiff, to such refusal, then and there duly excepted."

The court then gave the following instruction to the jury, on motion of the defendant:

"The jury are instructed, that upon the facts in this case, the law is with the defendant." The plaintiff excepted to this instruction.

Upon these exceptions, the case came up to this court.

It was argued at December term, 1855, and ordered to be reargued at the present term.

It was now argued by Mr. Blair and Mr. G. F. Curtis for the plaintiff in error, and by Mr. Geyer and Mr. Johnson for the defendant in error.

The reporter regrets that want of room will not allow him to give the arguments of counsel; but he regrets it the less, because the subject is thoroughly examined in the opinion of the court, the opinions of the concurring judges, and the opinions of the judges who dissented from the judgment of the court.

Mr. Chief Justice TANEY delivered the opinion of the court.

This case has been twice argued. After the argument at the last term, differences of opinion were found to exist among the members of the court; and as the questions in controversy are of the highest importance, and the court was at that time much pressed by the ordinary business of the term, it was deemed advisable to continue the case, and direct a reargument on some of the points, in order that we might have an opportunity of giving to the whole subject a more deliberate [60 U.S. 393, 400] consideration. It has accordingly been again argued by counsel, and considered by the court; and I now proceed to deliver its opinion. There are two leading questions presented by the record: 1. Had the Circuit Court of the United States jurisdiction to hear and determine the case between these parties? And 2. If it had jurisdiction, is the judgment it has given erroneous or not? The plaintiff in error, who was also the plaintiff in the court below, was, with his wife and children, held as slaves by the defendant, in the State of Missouri; and he brought this action in the Circuit Court of the United States for that district, to assert the title of himself and his family to freedom. The declaration is in the form usually adopted in that State to try questions of this description, and contains the averment necessary to give the court jurisdiction; that he and the defendant are citizens of different States; that is, that he is a citizen of Missouri, and the defendant a citizen of New York. The defendant pleaded in abatement to the jurisdiction of the court, that the plaintiff was not a citizen of the State of Missouri, as alleged in his declaration, being a negro of African descent, whose ancestors were of pure African blood, and who were brought into this country and sold as slaves. To this plea the plaintiff demurred, and the defendant joined in demurrer. The court overruled the plea, and gave judgment that the defendant should answer over. And he thereupon put in sundry pleas in bar, upon which issues were joined; and at the trial the verdict and judgment were in his favor. Whereupon the plaintiff brought this writ of error. Before we speak of the pleas in bar, it will be proper to dispose of the questions which have arisen on the plea in abatement. That plea denies the right of the plaintiff to sue in a court of the United States, for the reasons therein stated. If the question raised by it is legally before us, and the court should be of opinion that the facts stated in it disqualify the plaintiff from becoming a citizen, in the sense in which that word is used in the Constitution of the United States, then the judgment of the Circuit Court is erroneous, and must be reversed. It is suggested, however, that this plea is not before us; and that as the judgment in the court below on this plea was in favor of the plaintiff, he does not seek to reverse it, or bring it before the court for revision by his writ of error; and also that the defendant waived this defence by pleading over, and thereby admitted the jurisdiction of the court. [60 U.S. 393, 401] But, in making this objection, we think the peculiar and limited jurisdiction of courts of the United States has not been adverted to. This peculiar and limited jurisdiction has made it necessary, in these courts, to adopt different rules and principles of pleading, so far as jurisdiction is concerned, from those which regulate courts of common law in England, and in the different States of the Union which have adopted the common-law rules.

In these last-mentioned courts, where their character and rank are analogous to that of a Circuit Court of the United States; in other words, where they are what the law terms courts of general jurisdiction; they are presumed to have jurisdiction, unless the contrary appears. No averment in the pleadings of the plaintiff is necessary, in order to give jurisdiction.

If the defendant objects to it, he must plead it specially, and unless the fact on which he relies is found to be true by a jury, or admitted to be true by the plaintiff, the jurisdiction cannot be disputed in an appellate court.

Now, it is not necessary to inquire whether in courts of that description a party who pleads over in bar, when a plea to the jurisdiction has been ruled against him, does or does not waive his plea; nor whether upon a judgment in his favor on the pleas in bar, and a writ of error brought by the plaintiff, the question upon the plea in abatement would be open for revision in the appellate court. Cases that may have been decided in such courts, or rules that may have been laid down by common-law pleaders, can have no influence in the decision in this court. Because, under the Constitution and laws of the United States, the rules which govern the pleadings in its courts, in questions of jurisdiction, stand on different principles and are regulated by different laws.

This difference arises, as we have said, from the peculiar character of the Government of the United States. For although it is sovereign and supreme in its appropriate sphere of action, yet it does not possess all the powers which usually belong to the sovereignty of a nation. Certain specified powers, enumerated in the Constitution, have been conferred upon it; and neither the legislative, executive, nor judicial departments of the Government can lawfully exercise any authority beyond the limits marked out by the Constitution. And in regulating the judicial department, the cases in which the courts of the United States shall have jurisdiction are particularly and specifically enumerated and defined; and they are not authorized to take cognizance of any case which does not come within the description therein specified. Hence, when a plaintiff sues in a court of the United States, it is necessary that he should [60 U.S. 393, 402] show, in his pleading, that the suit he brings is within the jurisdiction of the court, and that he is entitled to sue there. And if he omits to do this, and should, by any oversight of the Circuit Court, obtain a judgment in his favor, the judgment would be reversed in the appellate court for want of jurisdiction in the court below. The jurisdiction would not be presumed, as in the case of a common-law English or State court, unless the contrary appeared. But the record, when it comes before the appellate court, must show, affirmatively, that the inferior court had authority, under the Constitution, to hear and determine the case. And if the plaintiff claims a right to sue in a Circuit Court of the United States, under that provision of the Constitution which gives jurisdiction in controversies between citizens of different States, he must distinctly aver in his pleading that they are citizens of different States; and he cannot maintain his suit without showing that fact in the pleadings.

This point was decided in the case of Bingham v. Cabot, (in 3 Dall.,

382,) and ever since adhered to by the court. And in Jackson v. Ashton, (8 Pet., 148,) it was held that the objection to which it was open could not be waived by the opposite party, because consent of parties could not give jurisdiction.

It is needless to accumulate cases on this subject. Those already referred to, and the cases of Capron v. Van Noorden, (in 2 Cr., 126,) and Montalet v. Murray, (4 Cr., 46,) are sufficient to show the rule of which we have spoken. The case of Capron v. Van Noorden strikingly illustrates the difference between a common-law court and a court of the United States.

If, however, the fact of citizenship is averred in the declaration, and the defendant does not deny it, and put it in issue by plea in abatement, he cannot offer evidence at the trial to disprove it, and consequently cannot avail himself of the objection in the appellate court, unless the defect should be apparent in some other part of the record. For if there is no plea in abatement, and the want of jurisdiction does not appear in any other part of the transcript brought up by the writ of error, the undisputed averment of citizenship in the declaration must be taken in this court to be true. In this case, the citizenship is averred, but it is denied by the defendant in the manner required by the rules of pleading, and the fact upon which the denial is based is admitted by the demurrer. And, if the plea and demurrer, and judgment of the court below upon it, are before us upon this record, the question to be decided is, whether the facts stated in the plea are sufficient to show that the plaintiff is not entitled to sue as a citizen in a court of the United States. [60 U.S. 393, 403] We think they are before us. The plea in abatement and the judgment of the court upon it, are a part of the judicial proceedings in the Circuit Court, and are there recorded as such; and a writ of error always brings up to the superior court the whole record of the proceedings in the court below. And in the case of the United States v. Smith, (11 Wheat., 172,) this court said, that the case being brought up by writ of error, the whole record was under the consideration of this court. And this being the case in the present instance, the plea in abatement is necessarily under consideration; and it becomes, therefore, our duty to decide whether the facts stated in the plea are or are not sufficient to show that the plaintiff is not entitled to sue as a citizen in a court of the United States.

This is certainly a very serious question, and one that now for the first time has been brought for decision before this court. But it is brought here by those who have a right to bring it, and it is our duty to meet it and decide it.

The question is simply this: Can a negro, whose ancestors were imported into this country, and sold as slaves, become a member of the political community formed and brought into existence by the Constitution of the United States, and as such become entitled to all the rights, and privileges, and immunities, guarantied by that instrument to the citizen? One of which rights is the privilege of suing in a court of the United States in the cases specified in the Constitution.

It will be observed, that the plea applies to that class of persons only whose ancestors were negroes of the African race, and imported into this country, and sold and held as slaves. The only matter in issue before the court, therefore, is, whether the descendants of such slaves, when they shall be emancipated, or who are born of parents who had become free before their birth, are citizens of a State, in the sense in which the word citizen is used in the Constitution of the United States. And this being the only matter in dispute on the pleadings, the court must be understood as speaking in this opinion of that class only, that is, of those persons who are the descendants of Africans who were imported into this country, and sold as slaves.

The situation of this population was altogether unlike that of the Indian race. The latter, it is true, formed no part of the colonial communities, and never amalgamated with them in social connections or in government. But although they were uncivilized, they were yet a free and independent people, associated together in nations or tribes, and governed by their own laws. Many of these political communities were situated in territories to which the white race claimed the ultimate [60 U.S. 393, 404] right of dominion. But that claim was acknowledged to be subject to the right of the Indians to occupy it as long as they thought proper, and neither the English nor colonial Governments claimed or exercised any dominion over the tribe or nation by whom it was occupied, nor claimed the right to the possession of the territory, until the tribe or nation consented to cede it. These Indian Governments were regarded and treated as foreign Governments, as much so as if an ocean had separated the red man from the white; and their freedom has constantly been acknowledged, from the time of the first emigration to the English colonies to the present day, by the different Governments which succeeded each other. Treaties have been negotiated with them, and their alliance sought for in war; and the people who compose these Indian political communities have always been treated as foreigners not living under our Government. It is true that the course of events has brought the Indian tribes within the limits of the United States under subjection to the white race; and it has been found necessary, for their sake as well as our own, to regard them as in a state of pupilage, and to legislate to a certain extent over them and the territory they occupy. But they may, without doubt, like the subjects of any other foreign Government, be naturalized by the authority of Congress, and become citizens of a State, and of the United States; and if an individual should leave his nation or tribe, and take up his abode among the white population, he would be entitled to all the rights and privileges which would belong to an emigrant from any other foreign people.

We proceed to examine the case as presented by the pleadings.

The words "people of the United States" and "citizens" are synonymous terms, and mean the same thing. They both describe the political body who, according to our republican institutions, form the sovereignty, and who hold the power and conduct the Government through their representatives. They are what we familiarly call the "sovereign people," and every citizen is one of this people, and a constituent member of this sovereignty. The question before us is, whether the class of persons described in the plea in abatement compose a portion of this people, and are constituent members of this sovereignty? We think they are not, and that they are not included, and were not intended to be included, under the word "citizens" in the Constitution, and can therefore claim none of the rights and privileges which that instrument provides for and secures to citizens of the United States. On the contrary, they were at that time considered as a subordinate [60 U.S. 393, 405] and inferior class of beings, who had been subjugated by the dominant race, and, whether emancipated or not, yet remained subject to their authority, and had no rights or privileges but such as those who held the power and the Government might choose to grant them.

It is not the province of the court to decide upon the justice or injustice, the policy or impolicy, of these laws. The decision of that question belonged to the political or law-making power; to those who formed the sovereignty and framed the Constitution. The duty of the court is, to interpret the instrument they have framed, with the best lights we can obtain on the subject, and to administer it as we find it, according to its true intent and meaning when it was adopted.

In discussing this question, we must not confound the rights of citizenship which a State may confer within its own limits, and the rights of citizenship as a member of the Union. It does not by any means follow, because he has all the rights and privileges of a citizen of a State, that he must be a citizen of the United States. He may have all of the rights and privileges of the citizen of a State, and yet not be entitled to the rights and privileges of a citizen in any other State. For, previous to the adoption of the Constitution of the United States, every State had the undoubted right to confer on whomsoever it pleased the character of citizen, and to endow him with all its rights. But this character of course was confined to the boundaries of the State, and gave him no rights or privileges in other States beyond those secured to him by the laws of nations and the comity of States. Nor have the several States surrendered the power of conferring these rights and privileges by adopting the

Constitution of the United States. Each State may still confer them upon an alien, or any one it thinks proper, or upon any class or description of persons; yet he would not be a citizen in the sense in which that word is used in the Constitution of the United States, nor entitled to sue as such in one of its courts, nor to the privileges and immunities of a citizen in the other States. The rights which he would acquire would be restricted to the State which gave them. The Constitution has conferred on Congress the right to establish an uniform rule of naturalization, and this right is evidently exclusive, and has always been held by this court to be so. Consequently, no State, since the adoption of the Constitution, can by naturalizing an alien invest him with the rights and privileges secured to a citizen of a State under the Federal Government, although, so far as the State alone was concerned, he would undoubtedly be entitled to the rights of a citizen, and clothed with all the [60 U.S. 393, 406] rights and immunities which the Constitution and laws of the State attached to that character.

It is very clear, therefore, that no State can, by any act or law of its own, passed since the adoption of the Constitution, introduce a new member into the political community created by the Constitution of the United States. It cannot make him a member of this community by making him a member of its own. And for the same reason it cannot introduce any person, or description of persons, who were not intended to be embraced in this new political family, which the Constitution brought into existence, but were intended to be excluded from it.

The question then arises, whether the provisions of the Constitution, in relation to the personal rights and privileges to which the citizen of a State should be entitled, embraced the negro African race, at that time in this country, or who might afterwards be imported, who had then or should afterwards be made free in any State; and to put it in the power of a single State to make him a citizen of the United States, and endue him with the full rights of citizenship in every other State without their consent? Does the Constitution of the United States act upon him whenever he shall be made free under the laws of a State, and raised there to the rank of a citizen, and immediately clothe him with all the privileges of a citizen in every other State, and in its own courts?

The court thinks the affirmative of these propositions cannot be maintained. And if it cannot, the plaintiff in error could not be a citizen of the State of Missouri, within the meaning of the Constitution of the United States, and, consequently, was not entitled to sue in its courts.

It is true, every person, and every class and description of persons, who were at the time of the adoption of the Constitution recognised as citizens in the several States, became also citizens of this new political body; but none other; it was formed by them, and for them and their posterity, but for no one else. And the personal rights and privileges guarantied to citizens of this new sovereignty were intended to embrace those only who were then members of the several State communities, or who should afterwards by birthright or otherwise become members, according to the provisions of the Constitution and the principles on which it was founded. It was the union of those who were at that time members of distinct and separate political communities into one political family, whose power, for certain specified purposes, was to extend over the whole territory of the United States. And it gave to each citizen rights and privileges outside of his State [60 U.S. 393, 407] which he did not before possess, and placed him in every other State upon a perfect equality with its own citizens as to rights of person and rights of property; it made him a citizen of the United States.

It becomes necessary, therefore, to determine who were citizens of the several States when the Constitution was adopted. And in order to do this, we must recur to the Governments and institutions of the thirteen colonies, when they separated from Great Britain and formed new sovereignties, and took their places in the family of independent nations. We must inquire who, at that time, were recognised as the people or citizens of a State, whose rights and liberties had been outraged by the English Government; and who declared their independence, and assumed the powers of Government to defend their rights by force of arms.

In the opinion of the court, the legislation and histories of the times, and the language used in the Declaration of Independence, show, that neither the class of persons who had been imported as slaves, nor their descendants, whether they had become free or not, were then acknowledged as a part of the people, nor intended to be included in the general words used in that memorable instrument.

It is difficult at this day to realize the state of public opinion in relation to that unfortunate race, which prevailed in the civilized and enlightened portions of the world at the time of the Declaration of Independence, and when the Constitution of the United States was framed and adopted. But the public history of every European nation displays it in a manner too plain to be mistaken.

They had for more than a century before been regarded as beings of an inferior order, and altogether unfit to associate with the white race, either in social or political relations; and so far inferior, that they had no rights which the white man was bound to respect; and that the negro might justly and lawfully be reduced to slavery for his benefit. He was bought and sold, and treated as an ordinary article of merchandise and traffic, whenever a profit could be made by it. This opinion was at that time fixed and universal in the civilized portion of the white race. It was regarded as an axiom in morals as well as in politics, which no one thought of disputing, or supposed to be open to dispute; and men in every grade and position in society daily and habitually acted upon it in their private pursuits, as well as in matters of public concern, without doubting for a moment the correctness of this opinion.

And in no nation was this opinion more firmly fixed or more [60 U.S. 393, 408] uniformly acted upon than by the English Government and English people. They not only seized them on the coast of Africa, and sold them or held them in slavery for their own use; but they took them as ordinary articles of merchandise to every country where they could make a profit on them, and were far more extensively engaged in this commerce than any other nation in the world.

The opinion thus entertained and acted upon in England was naturally impressed upon the colonies they founded on this side of the Atlantic. And, accordingly, a negro of the African race was regarded by them as an article of property, and held, and bought and sold as such, in every one of the thirteen colonies which united in the Declaration of Independence, and afterwards formed the Constitution of the United States. The slaves were more or less numerous in the different colonies, as slave labor was found more or less profitable. But no one seems to have doubted the correctness of the prevailing opinion of the time.

The legislation of the different colonies furnishes positive and indisputable proof of this fact.

It would be tedious, in this opinion, to enumerate the various laws they passed upon this subject. It will be sufficient, as a sample of the legislation which then generally prevailed throughout the British colonies, to give the laws of two of them; one being still a large slaveholding State, and the other the first State in which slavery ceased to exist.

The province of Maryland, in 1717, (ch. 13, s. 5,) passed a law declaring "that if any free negro or mulatto intermarry with any white woman, or if any white man shall intermarry with any negro or mulatto woman, such negro or mulatto shall become a slave during life, excepting mulattoes born of white women, who, for such intermarriage, shall only become servants for seven years, to be disposed of as the justices of the county court, where such marriage so happens, shall think fit; to be applied by them towards the support of a public school within the said county. And any white man or white woman who shall intermarry as aforesaid, with any negro or mulatto, such white man or white woman shall become servants during the term of seven years, and shall be disposed of by the justices as aforesaid, and be applied to the uses aforesaid."

The other colonial law to which we refer was passed by Massachusetts in 1705, (chap. 6.) It is entitled "An act for the better preventing of a spurious and mixed issue," &c.; and it provides, that "if any negro or mulatto shall presume to smite or strike any person of the English or other

Christian nation, such negro or mulatto shall be severely whipped, at [60 U.S. 393, 409] the discretion of the justices before whom the offender shall be convicted."

And "that none of her Majesty's English or Scottish subjects, nor of any other Christian nation, within this province, shall contract matrimony with any negro or mulatto; nor shall any person, duly authorized to solemnize marriage, presume to join any such in marriage, on pain of forfeiting the sum of fifty pounds; one moiety thereof to her Majesty, for and towards the support of the Government within this province, and the other moiety to him or them that shall inform and sue for the same, in any of her Majesty's courts of record within the province, by bill, plaint, or information."

We give both of these laws in the words used by the respective legislative bodies, because the language in which they are framed, as well as the provisions contained in them, show, too plainly to be misunderstood, the degraded condition of this unhappy race. They were still in force when the Revolution began, and are a faithful index to the state of feeling towards the class of persons of whom they speak, and of the position they occupied throughout the thirteen colonies, in the eyes and thoughts of the men who framed the Declaration of Independence and established the State Constitutions and Governments. They show that a perpetual and impassable barrier was intended to be erected between the white race and the one which they had reduced to slavery, and governed as subjects with absolute and despotic power, and which they then looked upon as so far below them in the scale of created beings, that intermarriages between white persons and negroes or mulattoes were regarded as unnatural and immoral, and punished as crimes, not only in the parties, but in the person who joined them in marriage. And no distinction in this respect was made between the free negro or mulatto and the slave, but this stigma, of the deepest degradation, was fixed upon the whole race.

We refer to these historical facts for the purpose of showing the fixed opinions concerning that race, upon which the statesmen of that day spoke and acted. It is necessary to do this, in order to determine whether the general terms used in the Constitution of the United States, as to the rights of man and the rights of the people, was intended to include them, or to give to them or their posterity the benefit of any of its provisions.

The language of the Declaration of Independence is equally conclusive:

It begins by declaring that, "when in the course of human events it becomes necessary for one people to dissolve the political bands which have connected them with another, and to [60 U.S. 393, 410] assume among the powers of the earth the separate and equal station to which the laws of nature and nature's God entitle them, a decent respect for the opinions of mankind requires that they should declare the causes which impel them to the separation."

It then proceeds to say: "We hold these truths to be self-evident: that all men are created equal; that they are endowed by their Creator with certain unalienable rights; that among them is life, liberty, and the pursuit of happiness; that to secure these rights, Governments are instituted, deriving their just powers from the consent of the governed."

The general words above quoted would seem to embrace the whole human family, and if they were used in a similar instrument at this day would be so understood. But it is too clear for dispute, that the enslaved African race were not intended to be included, and formed no part of the people who framed and adopted this declaration; for if the language, as understood in that day, would embrace them, the conduct of the distinguished men who framed the Declaration of Independence would have been utterly and flagrantly inconsistent with the principles they asserted; and instead of the sympathy of mankind, to which they so confidently appealed, they would have deserved and received universal rebuke and reprobation.

Yet the men who framed this declaration were great men—high in literary acquirements—high in their sense of honor, and incapable of asserting principles inconsistent with those on which they were acting. They perfectly understood the meaning of the language they used, and how it would be understood by others; and they knew that it would not in any part of the civilized world be supposed to embrace the negro race, which, by common consent, had been excluded from civilized Governments and the family of nations, and doomed to slavery. They spoke and acted according to the then established doctrines and principles, and in the ordinary language of the day, and no one misunderstood them. The unhappy black race were separated from the white by indelible marks, and laws long before established, and were never thought of or spoken of except as property, and when the claims of the owner or the profit of the trader were supposed to need protection.

This state of public opinion had undergone no change when the Constitution was adopted, as is equally evident from its provisions and language.

The brief preamble sets forth by whom it was formed, for what purposes, and for whose benefit and protection. It declares [60 U.S. 393, 411] that it is formed by the people of the United States; that is to say, by those who were members of the different political communities in the several States; and its great object is declared to be to secure the blessings of liberty to themselves and their posterity. It speaks in general terms of the people of the United States, and of citizens of the several States, when it is providing for the exercise of the powers granted or the privileges secured to the citizen. It does not define what description of persons are intended to be included under these terms, or who shall be regarded as a citizen and one of the people. It uses them as terms so well understood, that no further description or definition was necessary.

But there are two clauses in the Constitution which point directly and specifically to the negro race as a separate class of persons, and show clearly that they were not regarded as a portion of the people or citizens of the Government then formed.

One of these clauses reserves to each of the thirteen States the right to import slaves until the year 1808, if it thinks proper. And the importation which it thus sanctions was unquestionably of persons of the race of which we are speaking, as the traffic in slaves in the United States had always been confined to them. And by the other provision the States pledge themselves to each other to maintain the right of property of the master, by delivering up to him any slave who may have escaped from his service, and be found within their respective territories. By the first above-mentioned clause, therefore, the right to purchase and hold this property is directly sanctioned and authorized for twenty years by the people who framed the Constitution. And by the second, they pledge themselves to maintain and uphold the right of the master in the manner specified, as long as the Government they then formed should endure. And these two provisions show, conclusively, that neither the description of persons therein referred to, nor their descendants, were embraced in any of the other provisions of the Constitution; for certainly these two clauses were not intended to confer on them or their posterity the blessings of liberty, or any of the personal rights so carefully provided for the citizen.

No one of that race had ever migrated to the United States voluntarily; all of them had been brought here as articles of merchandise. The number that had been emancipated at that time were but few in comparison with those held in slavery; and they were identified in the public mind with the race to which they belonged, and regarded as a part of the slave population rather than the free. It is obvious that they were not [60 U.S. 393, 412] even in the minds of the framers of the Constitution when they were conferring special rights and privileges upon the citizens of a State in every other part of the Union.

Indeed, when we look to the condition of this race in the several States at the time, it is impossible to believe that these rights and privileges were intended to be extended to them.

It is very true, that in that portion of the Union where the labor of the negro race was found to be unsuited to the climate and unprofitable to the master, but few slaves were held at the time of the Declaration of Independence; and when the Constitution was adopted, it had entirely worn out in one of them, and measures had been taken for its gradual abolition in several others. But this change had not been produced by any change of opinion in relation to this race; but because it was discovered, from experience, that slave labor was unsuited to the climate and productions of these States: for some of the States, where it had ceased or nearly ceased to exist, were actively engaged in the slave trade, procuring cargoes on the coast of Africa, and transporting them for sale to those parts of the Union where their labor was found to be profitable, and suited to the climate and productions. And this traffic was openly carried on, and fortunes accumulated by it, without reproach from the people of the States where they resided. And it can hardly be supposed that, in the States where it was then countenanced in its worst form—that is, in the seizure and transportation—the people could have regarded those who were emancipated as entitled to equal rights with themselves.

And we may here again refer, in support of this proposition, to the plain and unequivocal language of the laws of the several States, some passed after the Declaration of Independence and before the Constitution was adopted, and some since the Government went into operation.

We need not refer, on this point, particularly to the laws of the present slaveholding States. Their statute books are full of provisions in relation to this class, in the same spirit with the Maryland law which we have before quoted. They have continued to treat them as an inferior class, and to subject them to strict police regulations, drawing a broad line of distinction between the citizen and the slave races, and legislating in relation to them upon the same principle which prevailed at the time of the Declaration of Independence. As relates to these States, it is too plain for argument, that they have never been regarded as a part of the people or citizens of the State, nor supposed to possess any political rights which the dominant race might not withhold or grant at their pleasure. [60 U.S. 393, 413] And as long ago as 1822, the Court of Appeals of Kentucky decided that free negroes and mulattoes were not citizens within the meaning of the Constitution of the United States; and the correctness of this decision is recognized, and the same doctrine affirmed, in 1 Meigs's Tenn. Reports, 331.

And if we turn to the legislation of the States where slavery had worn out, or measures taken for its speedy abolition, we shall find the same opinions and principles equally fixed and equally acted upon.

Thus, Massachusetts, in 1786, passed a law similar to the colonial one of which we have spoken. The law of 1786, like the law of 1705, forbids the marriage of any white person with any negro, Indian, or mulatto, and inflicts a penalty of fifty pounds upon any one who shall join them in marriage; and declares all such marriage absolutely null and void, and degrades thus the unhappy issue of the marriage by fixing upon it the stain of bastardy. And this mark of degradation was renewed, and again impressed upon the race, in the careful and deliberate preparation of their revised code published in 1836. This code forbids any person from joining in marriage any white person with any Indian, negro, or mulatto, and subjects the party who shall offend in this respect, to imprisonment, not exceeding six months, in the common jail, or to hard labor, and to a fine of not less than fifty nor more than two hundred dollars; and, like the law of 1786, it declares the marriage to be absolutely null and void. It will be seen that the punishment is increased by the code upon the person who shall marry them, by adding imprisonment to a pecuniary penalty.

So, too, in Connecticut. We refer more particularly to the legislation of this State, because it was not only among the first to put an end to slavery within its own territory, but was the first to fix a mark of reprobation upon the African slave trade. The law last mentioned was passed in October, 1788, about nine months after the State had ratified and adopted the present Constitution of the United States; and by that law it prohibited its own citizens, under severe penalties, from engaging in the trade, and declared all policies of insurance on the vessel or cargo made in the State to be null and void. But, up to the time of the adoption of the Constitution, there is nothing in the legislation of the State indicating any change of opinion as to the relative rights and position of the white and black races in this country, or indicating that it meant to place the latter, when free, upon a level with its citizens. And certainly nothing which would have led the slaveholding States to suppose, that Connecticut designed to claim for them, under [60 U.S. 393, 414] the new Constitution, the equal rights and privileges and rank of citizens in every other State.

The first step taken by Connecticut upon this subject was as early as 1774, when it passed an act forbidding the further importation of slaves into the State. But the section containing the prohibition is introduced by the following preamble:

"And whereas the increase of slaves in this State is injurious to the poor, and inconvenient."

This recital would appear to have been carefully introduced, in order to prevent any misunderstanding of the motive which induced the Legislature to pass the law, and places it distinctly upon the interest and convenience of the white population—excluding the inference that it might have been intended in any degree for the benefit of the other.

And in the act of 1784, by which the issue of slaves, born after the time therein mentioned, were to be free at a certain age, the section is again introduced by a preamble assigning a similar motive for the act. It is in these words:

"Whereas sound policy requires that the abolition of slavery should be effected as soon as may be consistent with the rights of individuals, and the public safety and welfare'—showing that the right of property in the master was to be protected, and that the measure was one of policy, and to prevent the injury and inconvenience, to the whites, of a slave population in the State."

And still further pursuing its legislation, we find that in the same statute passed in 1774, which prohibited the further importation of slaves into the State, there is also a provision by which any negro, Indian, or mulatto servant, who was found wandering out of the town or place to which he belonged, without a written pass such as is therein described, was made liable to be seized by any one, and taken before the next authority to be examined and delivered up to his master—who was required to pay the charge which had accrued thereby. And a subsequent section of the same law provides, that if any free negro shall travel without such pass, and shall be stopped, seized, or taken up, he shall pay all charges arising thereby. And this law was in full operation when the Constitution of the United States was adopted, and was not repealed till 1797. So that up to that time free negroes and mulattoes were associated with servants and slaves in the police regulations established by the laws of the State.

And again, in 1833, Connecticut passed another law, which made it penal to set up or establish any school in that State for the instruction of persons of the African race not inhabitants of the State, or to instruct or teach in any such school or [60 U.S. 393, 415] institution, or board or harbor for that purpose, any such person, without the previous consent in writing of the civil authority of the town in which such school or institution might be.

And it appears by the case of Crandall v. The State, reported in 10 Conn. Rep., 340, that upon any information filed against Prudence Crandall for a violation of this law, one of the points raised in the defence was, that the law was a violation of the Constitution of the United States; and that the persons instructed, although of the African race, were citizens of other States, and therefore entitled to the rights and privileges of citizens in the State of Connecticut. But Chief Justice Dagget, before whom the case was tried, held, that persons of that description were not citizens of a State, within the meaning of the word citizen in the Constitution of the United States, and were not therefore entitled to the privileges and immunities of citizens in other States.

The case was carried up to the Supreme Court of Errors of the State, and the question fully argued there. But the case went off upon another point, and no opinion was expressed on this question.

We have made this particular examination into the legislative and judicial action of Connecticut, because, from the early hostility it displayed to the slave trade on the coast of Africa, we may expect to find the laws of that State as lenient and favorable to the subject race as those of any other State in the Union; and if we find that at the time the Constitution was adopted, they were not even there raised to the rank of citizens, but were still held and treated as property, and the laws relating to them passed with reference altogether to the interest and convenience of the white race, we shall hardly find them elevated to a higher rank anywhere else.

A brief notice of the laws of two other States, and we shall pass on to other considerations.

By the laws of New Hampshire, collected and finally passed in 1815, no one was permitted to be enrolled in the militia of the State, but free white citizens; and the same provision is found in a subsequent collection of the laws, made in 1855. Nothing could more strongly mark the entire repudiation of the African race. The alien is excluded, because, being born in a foreign country, he cannot be a member of the community until he is naturalized. But why are the African race, born in the State, not permitted to share in one of the highest duties of the citizen? The answer is obvious; he is not, by the institutions and laws of the State, numbered among its people. He forms no part of the sovereignty of the State, and is not therefore called on to uphold and defend it. [60 U.S. 393, 416] Again, in 1822, Rhode Island, in its revised code, passed a law forbidding persons who were authorized to join persons in marriage, from joining in marriage any white person with any negro, Indian, or mulatto, under the penalty of two hundred dollars, and declaring all such marriages absolutely null and void; and the same law was again re-enacted in its revised code of 1844. So that, down to the last-mentioned period, the strongest mark of inferiority and degradation was fastened upon the African race in that State.

It would be impossible to enumerate and compress in the space usually allotted to an opinion of a court, the various laws, marking the condition of this race, which were passed from time to time after the Revolution, and before and since the adoption of the Constitution of the United States. In addition to those already referred to, it is sufficient to say, that Chancellor Kent, whose accuracy and research no one will question, states in the sixth edition of his Commentaries, (published in 1848, 2 vol., 258, note b,) that in no part of the country except Maine, did the African race, in point of fact, participate equally with the whites in the exercise of civil and political rights.

The legislation of the States therefore shows, in a manner not to be mistaken, the inferior and subject condition of that race at the time the Constitution was adopted, and long afterwards, throughout the thirteen States by which that instrument was framed; and it is hardly consistent with the respect due to these States, to suppose that they regarded at that time, as fellow-citizens and members of the sovereignty, a class of beings whom they had thus stigmatized; whom, as we are bound, out of respect to the State sovereignties, to assume they had deemed it just and necessary thus to stigmatize, and upon whom they had impressed such deep and enduring marks of inferiority and degradation; or, that when they met in convention to form the Constitution, they looked upon them as a portion of their constituents, or designed to include them in the provisions so carefully inserted for the security and protection of the liberties and rights of their citizens. It cannot be supposed that they intended to secure to them rights, and privileges, and rank, in the new political body throughout the Union, which every one of them denied within the limits of its own dominion. More especially, it cannot be believed that the large slaveholding States regarded them as included in the word citizens, or would have consented to a Constitution which might compel them to receive them in that character from another State. For if they were so received, and entitled to the privileges and immunities of citizens, it would exempt them from the operation of the special laws and from the police [60 U.S. 393, 417] regulations which they considered to be necessary for their own safety. It would give to persons of the negro race, who were recognised as citizens in any one State of the Union, the right to enter every other State whenever they pleased, singly or in companies, without pass or passport, and without obstruction, to sojourn there as long as they pleased, to go where they pleased at every hour of the day or night without molestation, unless they committed some violation of law for which a white man would be punished; and it would give them the full liberty of speech in public and in private upon all subjects upon which its own citizens might speak; to hold public meetings upon political affairs, and to keep and carry arms wherever they went. And all of this would be done in the face of the subject race of the same color, both free and slaves, and inevitably producing discontent and insubordination among them, and endangering the peace and safety of the State.

It is impossible, it would seem, to believe that the great men of the slaveholding States, who took so large a share in framing the Constitution of the United States, and exercised so much influence in procuring its adoption, could have been so forgetful or regardless of their own safety and the safety of those who trusted and confided in them.

Besides, this want of foresight and care would have been utterly inconsistent with the caution displayed in providing for the admission of new members into this political family. For, when they gave to the citizens of each State the privileges and immunities of citizens in the several States, they at the same time took from the several States the power of naturalization, and confined that power exclusively to the Federal Government. No State was willing to permit another State to determine who should or should not be admitted as one of its citizens, and entitled to demand equal rights and privileges with their own people, within their own territories. The right of naturalization was therefore, with one accord, surrendered by the States, and confided to the Federal Government. And this power granted to Congress to establish an uniform rule of naturalization is, by the well-understood meaning of the word, confined to persons born in a foreign country, under a foreign Government. It is not a power to raise to the rank of a citizen any one born in the United States, who, from birth or parentage, by the laws of the country, belongs to an inferior and subordinate class. And when we find the States guarding themselves from the indiscreet or improper admission by other States of emigrants from other countries, by giving the power exclusively to Congress, we cannot fail to see that they could never have left with the States a much [60 U.S. 393, 418] more important power—that is, the power of transforming into citizens a numerous class of persons, who in that character would be much more dangerous to the peace and safety of a large portion of the Union, than the few foreigners one of the States might improperly naturalize. The Constitution upon its adoption obviously took from the States all power by any subsequent legislation to introduce as a citizen into the political family of the United States any one, no matter where he was born, or what might be his character or condition; and it gave to Congress the power to confer this character upon those only who were born outside of the dominions of the United States. And no law of a State, therefore, passed since the Constitution was adopted, can give any right of citizenship outside of its own territory.

A clause similar to the one in the Constitution, in relation to the rights and immunities of citizens of one State in the other States, was contained in the Articles of Confederation. But there is a difference of language, which is worthy of note. The provision in the Articles of Confederation was, "that the free inhabitants of each of the States, paupers, vagabonds, and fugitives from justice, excepted, should be entitled to all the privileges and immunities of free citizens in the several States."

It will be observed, that under this Confederation, each State had the right to decide for itself, and in its own tribunals, whom it would acknowledge as a free inhabitant of another State. The term free inhabitant, in the generality of its terms, would certainly include one of the African race who had been manumitted. But no example, we think, can be found of his admission to all the privileges of citizenship in any State of the Union after these Articles were formed, and while they continued in force. And, notwithstanding the generality of the words "free inhabitants," it is very clear that, according to their accepted meaning in that day, they did not include the African race, whether free or not: for the fifth section of the ninth article provides that Congress should have the power "to agree upon the number of land forces to be raised, and to make requisitions from each State for its quota in proportion to the number of white inhabitants in such State, which requisition should be binding."

Words could hardly have been used which more strongly mark the line of distinction between the citizen and the subject; the free and the subjugated races. The latter were not even counted when the inhabitants of a State were to be embodied in proportion to its numbers for the general defence. And it cannot for a moment be supposed, that a class of [60 U.S. 393, 419] persons thus separated and rejected from those who formed the sovereignty of the States, were yet intended to be included under the words "free inhabitants," in the preceding article, to whom privileges and immunities were so carefully secured in every State.

But although this clause of the Articles of Confederation is the same in principle with that inserted in the Constitution, yet the comprehensive word inhabitant, which might be construed to include an emancipated slave, is omitted; and the privilege is confined to citizens of the State. And this alteration in words would hardly have been made, unless a different meaning was intended to be conveyed, or a possible doubt removed. The just and fair inference is, that as this privilege was about to be placed under the protection of the General Government, and the words expounded by its tribunals, and all power in relation to it taken from the State and its courts, it was deemed prudent to describe with precision and caution the persons to whom this high privilege was given—and the word citizen was on that account substituted for the words free inhabitant. The word citizen excluded, and no doubt intended to exclude, foreigners who had not become citizens of some one of the States when the Constitution was adopted; and also every description of persons who were not fully recognised as citizens in the several States. This, upon any fair construction of the instruments to which we have referred, was evidently the object and purpose of this change of words.

To all this mass of proof we have still to add, that Congress has repeatedly legislated upon the same construction of the Constitution that we have given. Three laws, two of which were passed almost immediately after the Government went into operation, will be abundantly sufficient to show this. The two first are particularly worthy of notice, because many of the men who assisted in framing the Constitution, and took an active part in procuring its adoption, were then in the halls of legislation, and certainly understood what they meant when they used the words "people of the United States" and "citizen" in that well-considered instrument.

The first of these acts is the naturalization law, which was passed at the second session of the first Congress, March 26, 1790, and confines the right of becoming citizens "to aliens being free white persons."

Now, the Constitution does not limit the power of Congress in this respect to white persons. And they may, if they think proper, authorize the naturalization of any one, of any color, who was born under allegiance to another Government. But the language of the law above quoted, shows that citizenship [60 U.S. 393, 420] at that time was perfectly understood to be confined to the white race; and that they alone constituted the sovereignty in the Government.

Congress might, as we before said, have authorized the naturalization of Indians, because they were aliens and foreigners. But, in their then untutored and savage state, no one would have thought of admitting them as citizens in a civilized community. And, moreover, the atrocities they had but recently committed, when they were the allies of Great Britain in the Revolutionary war, were yet fresh in the recollection of the people of the United States, and they were even then guarding themselves against the threatened renewal of Indian hostilities. No one supposed then that any Indian would ask for, or was capable of enjoying, the privileges of an American citizen, and the word white was not used with any particular reference to them.

Neither was it used with any reference to the African race imported into or born in this country; because Congress had no power to naturalize them, and therefore there was no necessity for using particular words to exclude them.

It would seem to have been used merely because it followed out the line of division which the Constitution has drawn between the citizen race, who formed and held the Government, and the African race, which they held in subjection and slavery, and governed at their own pleasure.

Another of the early laws of which we have spoken, is the first militia law, which was passed in 1792, at the first session of the second Congress. The language of this law is equally plain and significant with the one just mentioned. It directs that every "free able-bodied white male citizen" shall be enrolled in the militia. The word white is evidently used to exclude the African race, and the word "citizen" to exclude unnaturalized foreigners; the latter forming no part of the sovereignty, owing it no allegiance, and therefore under no obligation to defend it. The African race, however, born in the country, did owe allegiance to the Government, whether they were slave or free; but it is repudiated, and rejected from the duties and obligations of citizenship in marked language.

The third act to which we have alluded is even still more decisive; it was passed as late as 1813, (2 Stat., 809,) and it provides: "That from and after the termination of the war in which the United States are now engaged with Great Britain, it shall not be lawful to employ, on board of any public or private vessels of the United States, any person or persons except citizens of the United States, or persons of color, natives of the United States. [60 U.S. 393, 421] Here the line of distinction is drawn in express words. Persons of color, in the judgment of Congress, were not included in the word citizens, and they are described as another and different class of persons, and authorized to be employed, if born in the United States.

And even as late as 1820, (chap. 104, sec. 8,) in the charter to the city of Washington, the corporation is authorized "to restrain and prohibit the nightly and other disorderly meetings of slaves, free negroes, and mulattoes," thus associating them together in its legislation; and after prescribing the punishment that may be inflicted on the slaves, proceeds in the following words: "And to punish such free negroes and mulattoes by penalties not exceeding twenty dollars for any one offence; and in case of the inability of any such free negro or mulatto to pay any such penalty and cost thereon, to cause him or her to be confined to labor for any time not exceeding six calendar months." And in a subsequent part of the same section, the act authorizes the corporation "to prescribe the terms and conditions upon which free negroes and mulattoes may reside in the city."

This law, like the laws of the States, shows that this class of persons were governed by special legislation directed expressly to them, and always connected with provisions for the government of slaves, and not with those for the government of free white citizens. And after such an uniform course of legislation as we have stated, by the colonies, by the States, and by Congress, running through a period of more than a century, it would seem that to call persons thus marked and stigmatized, "citizens" of the United States, "fellow-citizens," a constituent part of the sovereignty, would be an abuse of terms, and not calculated to exalt the character of an American citizen in the eyes of other nations.

The conduct of the Executive Department of the Government has been in perfect harmony upon this subject with this course of legislation. The question was brought officially before the late William Wirt, when he was the Attorney General of the United States, in 1821, and he decided that the words "citizens of the United States" were used in the acts of Congress in the same sense as in the Constitution; and that free persons of color were not citizens, within the meaning of the Constitution and laws; and this opinion has been confirmed by that of the late Attorney General, Caleb Cushing, in a recent case, and acted upon by the Secretary of State, who refused to grant passports to them as "citizens of the United States."

But it is said that a person may be a citizen, and entitled to [60 U.S. 393, 422] that character, although he does not possess all the rights which may belong to other citizens; as, for example, the right to vote, or to hold particular offices; and that yet, when he goes into another State, he is entitled to be recognised there as a citizen, although the State may measure his rights by the rights which it allows to persons of a like character or class resident in the State, and refuse to him the full rights of citizenship.

This argument overlooks the language of the provision in the Constitution of which we are speaking.

Undoubtedly, a person may be a citizen, that is, a member of the community who form the sovereignty, although he exercises no share of the political power, and is incapacitated from holding particular offices. Women and minors, who form a part of the political family, cannot vote; and when a property qualification is required to vote or hold a particular office, those who have not the necessary qualification cannot vote or hold the office, yet they are citizens.

So, too, a person may be entitled to vote by the law of the State, who is not a citizen even of the State itself. And in some of the States of the Union foreigners not naturalized are allowed to vote. And the State may give the right to free negroes and mulattoes, but that does not make them citizens of the State, and still less of the United States. And the provision in the Constitution giving privileges and immunities in other States, does not apply to them.

Neither does it apply to a person who, being the citizen of a State, migrates to another State. For then he becomes subject to the laws of the State in which he lives, and he is no longer a citizen of the State from which he removed. And the State in which he resides may then, unquestionably, determine his status or condition, and place him among the class of persons who are not recognised as citizens, but belong to an inferior and subject race; and may deny him the privileges and immunities enjoyed by its citizens.

But so far as mere rights of person are concerned, the provision in question is confined to citizens of a State who are temporarily in another State without taking up their residence there. It gives them no political rights in the State, as to voting or holding office, or in any other respect. For a citizen of one State has no right to participate in the government of another. But if he ranks as a citizen in the State to which he belongs, within the meaning of the Constitution of the United States, then, whenever he goes into another State, the Constitution clothes him, as to the rights of person, with all the privileges and immunities which belong to citizens of the [60 U.S. 393, 423] State. And if persons of the African race are citizens of a State, and of the United States, they would be entitled to all of these privileges and immunities in every State, and the State could not restrict them; for they would hold these privileges and immunities under the paramount authority of the Federal Government, and its courts would be bound to maintain and enforce them, the Constitution and laws of the State to the contrary notwithstanding. And if the States could limit or restrict them, or place the party in an inferior grade, this clause of the Constitution would be unmeaning, and could have no operation; and would give no rights to the citizen when in another State. He would have none but what the State itself chose to allow him. This is evidently not the construction or meaning of the clause in question. It guaranties rights to the citizen, and the State cannot withhold them. And these rights are of a character and would lead to consequences which make it absolutely certain that the African race were not included under the name of citizens of a State, and were not in the contemplation of the framers of the Constitution when these privileges and immunities were provided for the protection of the citizen in other States.

The case of Legrand v. Darnall (2 Peters, 664) has been referred to for the purpose of showing that this court has decided that the descendant of a slave may sue as a citizen in a court of the United States; but the case itself shows that the question did not arise and could not have arisen in the case.

It appears from the report, that Darnall was born in Maryland, and was the son of a white man by one of his slaves, and his father executed certain instruments to manumit him, and devised to him some landed property in the State. This property Darnall afterwards sold to Legrand, the appellant, who gave his notes for the purchase-money. But becoming afterwards apprehensive that the appellee had not been emancipated according to the laws of Maryland, he refused to pay the notes until he could be better satisfied as to Darnall's right to convey. Darnall, in the mean time, had taken up his residence in Pennsylvania, and brought suit on the notes, and recovered judgment in the Circuit Court for the district of Maryland.

The whole proceeding, as appears by the report, was an amicable one; Legrand being perfectly willing to pay the money, if he could obtain a title, and Darnall not wishing him to pay unless he could make him a good one. In point of fact, the whole proceeding was under the direction of the counsel who argued the case for the appellee, who was the mutual friend of the parties, and confided in by both of them, and whose only [60 U.S. 393, 424] object was to have the rights of both parties established by judicial decision in the most speedy and least expensive manner.

Legrand, therefore, raised no objection to the jurisdiction of the court in the suit at law, because he was himself anxious to obtain the judgment of the court upon his title. Consequently, there was nothing in the record before the court to show that Darnall was of African descent, and the usual judgment and award of execution was entered. And Legrand thereupon filed his bill on the equity side of the Circuit Court, stating that Darnall was born a slave, and had not been legally emancipated, and could not therefore take the land devised to him, nor make Legrand a good title; and praying an injunction to restrain Darnall from proceeding to execution on the judgment, which was granted. Darnall answered, averring in his answer that he was a free man, and capable of conveying a good title. Testimony was taken on this point, and at the hearing the Circuit Court was of opinion that Darnall was a free man and his title good, and dissolved the injunction and dismissed the bill; and that decree was affirmed here, upon the appeal of Legrand.

Now, it is difficult to imagine how any question about the citizenship of Darnall, or his right to sue in that character, can be supposed to have arisen or been decided in that case. The fact that he was of African descent was first brought before the court upon the bill in equity. The suit at law had then passed into judgment and award of execution, and the Circuit Court, as a court of law, had no longer any authority over it. It was a valid and legal judgment, which the court that rendered it had not the power to reverse or set aside. And unless it had jurisdiction as a court of equity to restrain him from using its process as a court of law, Darnall, if he thought proper, would have been at liberty to proceed on his judgment, and compel the payment of the money, although the allegations in the bill were true, and he was incapable of making a title. No other court could have enjoined him, for certainly no State equity court could interfere in that way with the judgment of a Circuit Court of the United States.

But the Circuit Court as a court of equity certainly had equity jurisdiction over its own judgment as a court of law, without regard to the character of the parties; and had not only the right, but it was its duty—no matter who were the parties in the judgment-to prevent them from proceeding to enforce it by execution, if the court was satisfied that the money was not justly and equitably due. The ability of Darnall to convey did not depend upon his citizenship, but upon his title to freedom. And if he was free, he could hold and [60 U.S. 393, 425] convey property, by the laws of Maryland, although he was not a citizen. But if he was by law still a slave, he could not. It was therefore the duty of the court, sitting as a court of equity in the latter case, to prevent him from using its process, as a court of common law, to compel the payment of the purchase-money, when it was evident that the purchaser must lose the land. But if he was free, and could make a title, it was equally the duty of the court not to suffer Legrand to keep the land, and refuse the payment of the money, upon the ground that Darnall was incapable of suing or being sued as a citizen in a court of the United States. The character or citizenship of the parties had no connection with the question of jurisdiction, and the matter in dispute had no relation to the citizenship of Darnall. Nor is such a question alluded to in the opinion of the court.

Besides, we are by no means prepared to say that there are not many cases, civil as well as criminal, in which a Circuit Court of the United States may exercise jurisdiction, although one of the African race is a party; that broad question is not before the court. The question with which we are now dealing is, whether a person of the African race can be a citizen of the United States, and become thereby entitled to a special privilege, by virtue of his title to that character, and which, under the Constitution, no one but a citizen can claim. It is manifest that the case of Legrand and Darnall has no bearing on that question, and can have no application to the case now before the court.

This case, however, strikingly illustrates the consequences that would follow the construction of the Constitution which would give the power contended for to a State. It would in effect give it also to an individual. For if the father of young Darnall had manumitted him in his lifetime, and sent him to reside in a State which recognised him as a citizen, he might have visited and sojourned in Maryland when he pleased, and as long as he pleased, as a citizen of the United States; and the State officers and tribunals would be compelled, by the paramount authority of the Constitution, to receive him and treat him as one of its citizens, exempt from the laws and police of the State in relation to a person of that description, and allow him to enjoy all the rights and privileges of citizenship, without respect to the laws of Maryland, although such laws were deemed by it absolutely essential to its own safety.

The only two provisions which point to them and include them, treat them as property, and make it the duty of the Government to protect it; no other power, in relation to this race, is to be found in the Constitution; and as it is a Government [60 U.S. 393, 426] of special, delegated, powers, no authority beyond these two provisions can be constitutionally exercised. The Government of the United States had no right to interfere for any other purpose but that of protecting the rights of the owner, leaving it altogether with the several States to deal with this race, whether emancipated or not, as each State may think justice, humanity, and the interests and safety of society, require. The States evidently intended to reserve this power exclusively to themselves.

No one, we presume, supposes that any change in public opinion or feeling, in relation to this unfortunate race, in the civilized nations of Europe or in this country, should induce the court to give to the words of the Constitution a more liberal construction in their favor than they were intended to bear when the instrument was framed and adopted.

Such an argument would be altogether inadmissible in any tribunal called on to interpret it. If any of its provisions are deemed unjust, there is a mode prescribed in the instrument itself by which it may be amended; but while it remains unaltered, it must be construed now as it was understood at the time of its adoption. It is not only the same in words, but the same in meaning, and delegates the same powers to the Government, and reserves and secures the same rights and privileges to the citizen; and as long as it continues to exist in its present form, it speaks not only in the same words, but with the same meaning and intent with which it spoke when it came from the hands of its framers, and was voted on and adopted by the people of the United States. Any other rule of construction would abrogate the judicial character of this court, and make it the mere reflex of the popular opinion or passion of the day. This court was not created by the Constitution for such purposes. Higher and graver trusts have been confided to it, and it must not falter in the path of duty.

What the construction was at that time, we think can hardly admit of doubt. We have the language of the Declaration of Independence and of the Articles of Confederation, in addition to the plain words of the Constitution itself; we have the legislation of the different States, before, about the time, and since, the Constitution was adopted; we have the legislation of Congress, from the time of its adoption to a recent period; and we have the constant and uniform action of the Executive Department, all concurring together, and leading to the same result. And if anything in relation to the construction of the Constitution can be regarded as settled, it is that which we now give to the word "citizen" and the word "people."

And upon a full and careful consideration of the subject, [60 U.S. 393, 427] the court is of opinion, that, upon the facts stated in the plea in abatement, Dred Scott was not a citizen of Missouri within the meaning of the Constitution of the United States, and not entitled as such to sue in its courts; and, consequently, that the Circuit Court had no jurisdiction of the case, and that the judgment on the plea in abatement is erroneous.

We are aware that doubts are entertained by some of the members of the court, whether the plea in abatement is legally before the court upon this writ of error; but if that plea is regarded as waived, or out of the case upon any other ground, yet the question as to the jurisdiction of the Circuit Court is presented on the face of the bill of exception itself, taken by the plaintiff at the trial; for he admits that he and his wife were born slaves, but endeavors to make out his title to freedom and citizenship by showing that they were taken by their owner to certain places, hereinafter mentioned, where slavery could not by law exist, and that they thereby became free, and upon their return to Missouri became citizens of that State.

Now, if the removal of which he speaks did not give them their freedom, then by his own admission he is still a slave; and whatever opinions may be entertained in favor of the citizenship of a free person of the African race, no one supposes that a slave is a citizen of the State or of the United States. If, therefore, the acts done by his owner did not make them free persons, he is still a slave, and certainly incapable of suing in the character of a citizen.

The principle of law is too well settled to be disputed, that a court can give no judgment for either party, where it has no jurisdiction; and if, upon the showing of Scott himself, it appeared that he was still a slave, the case ought to have been dismissed, and the judgment against him and in favor of the defendant for costs, is, like that on the plea in abatement, erroneous, and the suit ought to have been dismissed by the Circuit Court for want of jurisdiction in that court.

But, before we proceed to examine this part of the case, it may be proper to notice an objection taken to the judicial authority of this court to decide it; and it has been said, that as this court has decided against the jurisdiction of the Circuit Court on the plea in abatement, it has no right to examine any question presented by the exception; and that anything it may say upon that part of the case will be extra-judicial, and mere obiter dicta.

This is a manifest mistake; there can be no doubt as to the jurisdiction of this court to revise the judgment of a Circuit Court, and to reverse it for any error apparent on the record, [60 U.S. 393, 428] whether it be the error of giving judgment in a case over which it had no jurisdiction, or any other material error; and this, too, whether there is a plea in abatement or not.

The objection appears to have arisen from confounding writs of error to a State court, with writs of error to a Circuit Court of the United States. Undoubtedly, upon a writ of error to a State court, unless the record shows a case that gives jurisdiction, the case must be dismissed for want of jurisdiction in this court. And if it is dismissed on that ground, we have no right to examine and decide upon any question presented by the bill of exceptions, or any other part of the record. But writs of error to a State court, and to a Circuit Court of the United States, are regulated by different laws, and stand upon entirely different principles. And in a writ of error to a Circuit Court of the United States, the whole record is before this court for examination and decision; and if the sum in controversy is large enough to give jurisdiction, it is not only the right, but it is the judicial duty of the court, to examine the whole case as presented by the record; and if it appears upon its face that any material error or errors have been committed by the court below, it is the duty of this court to reverse the judgment, and remand the case. And certainly an error in passing a judgment upon the merits in favor of either party, in a case which it was not authorized to try, and over which it had no jurisdiction, is as grave an error as a court can commit.

The plea in abatement is not a plea to the jurisdiction of this court, but to the jurisdiction of the Circuit Court. And it appears by the record before us, that the Circuit Court committed an error, in deciding that it had jurisdiction, upon the facts in the case, admitted by the pleadings. It is the duty of the appellate tribunal to correct this error; but that could not be done by dismissing the case for want of jurisdiction here—for that would leave the erroneous judgment in full force, and the injured party without remedy. And the appellate court therefore exercises the power for which alone appellate courts are constituted, by reversing the judgment of the court below for this error. It exercises its proper and appropriate jurisdiction over the judgment and proceedings of the Circuit Court, as they appear upon the record brought up by the writ of error.

The correction of one error in the court below does not deprive the appellate court of the power of examining further into the record, and correcting any other material errors which may have been committed by the inferior court. There is certainly no rule of law—nor any practice-nor any decision of a [60 U.S. 393, 429] court—which even questions this power in the appellate tribunal. On the contrary, it is the daily practice of this court, and of all appellate courts where they reverse the judgment of an inferior court for error, to correct by its opinions whatever errors may appear on the record material to the case; and they have always held it to be their duty to do so where the silence of the court might lead to misconstruction or future controversy, and the point has been relied on by either side, and argued before the court.

In the case before us, we have already decided that the Circuit Court erred in deciding that it had jurisdiction upon the facts admitted by the pleadings. And it appears that, in the further progress of the case, it acted upon the erroneous principle it had decided on the pleadings, and gave judgment for the defendant, where, upon the facts admitted in the exception, it had no jurisdiction.

We are at a loss to understand upon what principle of law, applicable to appellate jurisdiction, it can be supposed that this court has not judicial authority to correct the last-mentioned error, because they had before corrected the former; or by what process of reasoning it can be made out, that the error of an inferior court in actually pronouncing judgment for one of the parties, in a case in which it had no jurisdiction, cannot be looked into or corrected by this court, because we have decided a similar question presented in the pleadings. The last point is distinctly presented by the facts contained in the plaintiff's own bill of exceptions, which he himself brings here by this writ of error. It was the point which chiefly occupied the attention of the counsel on both sides in the argument—and the judgment which this court must render upon both errors is precisely the same. It must, in each of them, exercise jurisdiction over the judgment, and reverse it for the errors committed by the court below; and issue a mandate to the Circuit Court to conform its judgment to the opinion pronounced by this court, by dismissing the case for want of jurisdiction in the Circuit Court. This is the constant and invariable practice of this court, where it reverses a judgment for want of jurisdiction in the Circuit Court.

It can scarcely be necessary to pursue such a question further. The want of jurisdiction in the court below may appear on the record without any plea in abatement. This is familiarly the case where a court of chancery has exercised jurisdiction in a case where the plaintiff had a plain and adequate remedy at law, and it so appears by the transcript when brought here by appeal. So also where it appears that a court of admiralty has exercised jurisdiction in a case belonging exclusively [60 U.S. 393, 430] to a court of common law. In these cases there is no plea in abatement. And for the same reason, and upon the same principles, where the defect of jurisdiction is patent on the record, this court is bound to reverse the judgment, although the defendant has not pleaded in abatement to the jurisdiction of the inferior court.

The cases of Jackson v. Ashton and of Capron v. Van Noorden, to which we have referred in a previous part of this opinion, are directly in point. In the last-mentioned case, Capron brought an action against Van Noorden in a Circuit Court of the United States, without showing, by the usual averments of citizenship, that the court had jurisdiction. There was no plea in abatement put in, and the parties went to trial upon the merits. The court gave judgment in favor of the defendant with costs. The plaintiff thereupon brought his writ of error, and this court reversed the judgment given in favor of the defendant, and remanded the case with directions to dismiss it, because it did not appear by the transcript that the Circuit Court had jurisdiction.

The case before us still more strongly imposes upon this court the duty of examining whether the court below has not committed an error, in taking jurisdiction and giving a judgment for costs in favor of the defendant; for in Capron v. Van Noorden the judgment was reversed, because it did not appear that the parties were citizens of different States. They might or might not be. But in this case it does appear that the plaintiff was born a slave; and if the facts upon which he relies have not made him free, then it appears affirmatively on the record that he is not a citizen, and consequently his suit against Sandford was not a suit between citizens of different States, and the court had no authority to pass any judgment between the parties. The suit ought, in this view of it, to have been dismissed by the Circuit Court, and its judgment in favor of Sandford is erroneous, and must be reversed.

It is true that the result either way, by dismissal or by a judgment for the defendant, makes very little, if any, difference in a pecuniary or personal point of view to either party. But the fact that the result would be very nearly the same to the parties in either form of judgment, would not justify this court in sanctioning an error in the judgment which is patent on the record, and which, if sanctioned, might be drawn into precedent, and lead to serious mischief and injustice in some future suit.

We proceed, therefore, to inquire whether the facts relied on by the plaintiff entitled him to his freedom. [60 U.S. 393, 431] The case, as he himself states it, on the record brought here by his writ of error, is this:

The plaintiff was a negro slave, belonging to Dr. Emerson, who was a surgeon in the army of the United States. In the year 1834, he took the plaintiff from the State of Missouri to the military post at Rock Island, in the State of Illinois, and held him there as a slave until the month of April or May, 1836. At the time last mentioned, said Dr. Emerson removed the plaintiff from said military post at Rock Island to the military post at Fort Snelling, situate on the west bank of the Mississippi river, in the Territory known as Upper Louisiana, acquired by the United States of France, and situate north of the latitude of thirty-six degrees thirty minutes north, and north of the State of Missouri. Said Dr. Emerson held the plaintiff in slavery at said Fort Snelling, from said last-mentioned date until the year 1838.

In the year 1835, Harriet, who is named in the second count of the plaintiff's declaration, was the negro slave of Major Taliaferro, who belonged to the army of the United States. In that year, 1835, said Major Taliaferro took said Harriet to said Fort Snelling, a military post, situated as hereinbefore stated, and kept her there as a slave until the year 1836, and then sold and delivered her as a slave, at said Fort Snelling, unto the said Dr. Emerson hereinbefore named. Said Dr. Emerson held said Harriet in slavery at said Fort Snelling until the year 1838.

In the year 1836, the plaintiff and Harriet intermarried, at Fort Snelling, with the consent of Dr. Emerson, who then claimed to be their master and owner. Eliza and Lizzie, named in the third count of the plaintiff's declaration, are the fruit of that marriage. Eliza is about fourteen years old, and was born on board the steamboat Gipsey, north of the north line of the State of Missouri, and upon the river Mississippi. Lizzie is about seven years old, and was born in the State of Missouri, at the military post called Jefferson Barracks.

In the year 1838, said Dr. Emerson removed the plaintiff and said Harriet, and their said daughter Eliza, from said Fort Snelling to the State of Missouri, where they have ever since resided.

Before the commencement of this suit, said Dr. Emerson sold and conveyed the plaintiff, and Harriet, Eliza, and Lizzie, to the defendant, as slaves, and the defendant has ever since claimed to hold them, and each of them, as slaves.

In considering this part of the controversy, two questions arise: 1. Was he, together with his family, free in Missouri by reason of the stay in the territory of the United States hereinbefore [60 U.S. 393, 432] mentioned? And 2. If they were not, is Scott himself free by reason of his removal to Rock Island, in the State of Illinois, as stated in the above admissions?

We proceed to examine the first question.

The act of Congress, upon which the plaintiff relies, declares that slavery and involuntary servitude, except as a punishment for crime, shall be forever prohibited in all that part of the territory ceded by France, under the name of Louisiana, which lies north of thirty-six degrees thirty minutes north latitude, and not included within the limits of Missouri. And the difficulty which meets us at the threshold of this part of the inquiry is, whether Congress was authorized to pass this law under any of the powers granted to it by the Constitution; for if the authority is not given by that instrument, it is the duty of this court to declare it void and inoperative, and incapable of conferring freedom upon any one who is held as a slave under the have of any one of the States.

The counsel for the plaintiff has laid much stress upon that article in the Constitution which confers on Congress the power "to dispose of and make all needful rules and regulations respecting the territory or other property belonging to the United States;" but, in the judgment of the court, that provision has no bearing on the present controversy, and the power there given, whatever it may be, is confined, and was intended to be confined, to the territory which at that time belonged to, or was claimed by, the United States, and was within their boundaries as settled by the treaty with Great Britain, and can have no influence upon a territory afterwards acquired from a foreign Government. It was a special provision for a known and particular territory, and to meet a present emergency, and nothing more.

A brief summary of the history of the times, as well as the careful and measured terms in which the article is framed, will show the correctness of this proposition.

It will be remembered that, from the commencement of the Revolutionary war, serious difficulties existed between the States, in relation to the disposition of large and unsettled territories which were included in the chartered limits of some of the States. And some of the other States, and more especially Maryland, which had no unsettled lands, insisted that as the unoccupied lands, if wrested from Great Britain, would owe their preservation to the common purse and the common

sword, the money arising from them ought to be applied in just proportion among the several States to pay the expenses of the war, and ought
not to be appropriated to the use of the State in whose chartered limits
they might happen [60 U.S. 393, 433] to lie, to the exclusion of the other
States, by whose combined efforts and common expense the territory
was defended and preserved against the claim of the British Government.

These difficulties caused much uneasiness during the war, while the
issue was in some degree doubtful, and the future boundaries of the
United States yet to be defined by treaty, if we achieved our independence.

The majority of the Congress of the Confederation obviously concurred in opinion with the State of Maryland, and desired to obtain from
the States which claimed it a cession of this territory, in order that
Congress might raise money on this security to carry on the war. This
appears by the resolution passed on the 6th of September, 1780, strongly
urging the States to cede these lands to the United States, both for the
sake of peace and union among themselves, and to maintain the public
credit; and this was followed by the resolution of October 10th, 1780, by
which Congress pledged itself, that if the lands were ceded, as recommended by the resolution above mentioned, they should be disposed of
for the common benefit of the United States, and be settled and formed
into distinct republican States, which should become members of the
Federal Union, and have the same rights of sovereignty, and freedom, and
independence, as other States.

But these difficulties became much more serious after peace took
place, and the boundaries of the United States were established. Every
State, at that time, felt severely the pressure of its war debt; but in
Virginia, and some other States, there were large territories of unsettled
lands, the sale of which would enable them to discharge their obligations
without much inconvenience; while other States, which had no such
resource, saw before them many years of heavy and burdensome taxation;
and the latter insisted, for the reasons before stated, that these unsettled
lands should be treated as the common property of the States, and the
proceeds applied to their common benefit.

The letters from the statesmen of that day will show how much this
controversy occupied their thoughts, and the dangers that were apprehended from it. It was the disturbing element of the time, and fears were
entertained that it might dissolve the Confederation by which the States
were then united.

These fears and dangers were, however, at once removed, when the
State of Virginia, in 1784, voluntarily ceded to the United States the
immense tract of country lying northwest of the river Ohio, and which
was within the acknowledged limits of the State. The only object of the
State, in making [60 U.S. 393, 434] this cession, was to put an end to the

threatening and exciting controversy, and to enable the Congress of that time to dispose of the lands, and appropriate the proceeds as a common fund for the common benefit of the States. It was not ceded, because it was inconvenient to the State to hold and govern it, nor from any expectation that it could be better or more conveniently governed by the United States.

The example of Virginia was soon afterwards followed by other States, and, at the time of the adoption of the Constitution, all of the States, similarly situated, had ceded their unappropriated lands, except North Carolina and Georgia. The main object for which these cessions were desired and made, was on account of their money value, and to put an end to a dangerous controversy, as to who was justly entitled to the proceeds when the lands should be sold. It is necessary to bring this part of the history of these cessions thus distinctly into view, because it will enable us the better to comprehend the phraseology of the article in the Constitution, so often referred to in the argument.

Undoubtedly the powers of sovereignty and the eminent domain were ceded with the land. This was essential, in order to make it effectual, and to accomplish its objects. But it must be remembered that, at that time, there was no Government of the United States in existence with enumerated and limited powers; what was then called the United States, were thirteen separate, sovereign, independent States, which had entered into a league or confederation for their mutual protection and advantage, and the Congress of the United States was composed of the representatives of these separate sovereignties, meeting together, as equals, to discuss and decide on certain measures which the States, by the Articles of Confederation, had agreed to submit to their decision. But this Confederation had none of the attributes of sovereignty in legislative, executive, or judicial power. It was little more than a congress of ambassadors, authorized to represent separate nations, in matters in which they had a common concern.

It was this Congress that accepted the cession from Virginia. They had no power to accept it under the Articles of Confederation. But they had an undoubted right, as independent sovereignties, to accept any cession of territory for their common benefit, which all of them assented to; and it is equally clear, that as their common property, and having no superior to control them, they had the right to exercise absolute dominion over it, subject only to the restrictions which Virginia had imposed in her act of cession. There was, as we have said, no Government of the United States then in existence [60 U.S. 393, 435] with special enumerated and limited powers. The territory belonged to sovereignties, who, subject to the limitations above mentioned, had a right to establish any form of government they pleased, by compact or treaty among themselves, and to regulate rights of person and rights of property in the territory, as they might deem proper. It was by a Congress, representing the authority of these several and separate sovereignties, and acting under their authority and command, (but not from any authority derived from the Articles of Confederation,) that the instrument usually called the ordinance of 1787 was adopted; regulating in much detail the principles and the laws by which this territory should be governed; and among other provisions, slavery is prohibited in it. We do not question the power of the States, by agreement among themselves, to pass this ordinance, nor its obligatory force in the territory, while the confederation or league of the States in their separate sovereign character continued to exist.

This was the state of things when the Constitution of the United States was formed. The territory ceded by Virginia belonged to the several confederated States as common property, and they had united in establishing in it a system of government and jurisprudence, in order to prepare it for admission as States, according to the terms of the cession. They were about to dissolve this federative Union, and to surrender a portion of their independent sovereignty to a new Government, which, for certain purposes, would make the people of the several States one people, and which was to be supreme and controlling within its sphere of action throughout the United States; but this Government was to be carefully limited in its powers, and to exercise no authority beyond those expressly granted by the Constitution, or necessarily to be implied from the language of the instrument, and the objects it was intended to accomplish; and as this league of States would, upon the adoption of the new Government, cease to have any power over the territory, and the ordinance they had agreed upon be incapable of execution, and a mere nullity, it was obvious that some provision was necessary to give the new Government sufficient power to enable it to carry into effect the objects for which it was ceded, and the compacts and agreements which the States had made with each other in the exercise of their powers of sovereignty. It was necessary that the lands should be sold to pay the war debt; that a Government and system of jurisprudence should be maintained in it, to protect the citizens of the United States who should migrate to the territory, in their rights of person and of property. It was also necessary that the new Government, about to be [60 U.S. 393, 436] adopted, should be authorized to maintain the claim of the United States to the unappropriated lands in North Carolina and Georgia, which had not then been ceded, but the cession of which was confidently anticipated upon some terms that would be arranged between the General Government and these two States. And, moreover, there were many articles of value besides this property in land, such as arms, military stores, munitions, and ships of war, which were the common property of the

States, when acting in their independent characters as confederates, which neither the new Government nor any one else would have a right to take possession of, or control, without authority from them; and it was to place these things under the guardianship and protection of the new Government, and to clothe it with the necessary powers, that the clause was inserted in the Constitution which give Congress the power "to dispose of and make all needful rules and regulations respecting the territory or other property belonging to the United States." It was intended for a specific purpose, to provide for the things we have mentioned. It was to transfer to the new Government the property then held in common by the States, and to give to that Government power to apply it to the objects for which it had been destined by mutual agreement among the States before their league was dissolved. It applied only to the property which the States held in common at that time, and has no reference whatever to any territory or other property which the new sovereignty might afterwards itself acquire.

The language used in the clause, the arrangement and combination of the powers, and the somewhat unusual phraseology it uses, when it speaks of the political power to be exercised in the government of the territory, all indicate the design and meaning of the clause to be such as we have mentioned. It does not speak of any territory, nor of Territories, but uses language which, according to its legitimate meaning, points to a particular thing. The power is given in relation only to the territory of the United States—that is, to a territory then in existence, and then known or claimed as the territory of the United States. It begins its enumeration of powers by that of disposing, in other words, making sale of the lands, or raising money from them, which, as we have already said, was the main object of the cession, and which is accordingly the first thing provided for in the article. It then gives the power which was necessarily associated with the disposition and sale of the lands—that is, the power of making needful rules and regulations respecting the territory. And whatever construction may now be given to these words, every one, we think, [60 U.S. 393, 437] must admit that they are not the words usually employed by statesmen in giving supreme power of legislation. They are certainly very unlike the words used in the power granted to legislate over territory which the new Government might afterwards itself obtain by cession from a State, either for its seat of Government, or for forts, magazines, arsenals, dock yards, and other needful buildings.

And the same power of making needful rules respecting the territory is, in precisely the same language, applied to the other property belonging to the United States—associating the power over the territory in this respect with the power over movable or personal property—that is, the ships, arms, and munitions of war, which then belonged in common to the State sovereignties. And it will hardly be said, that this power, in relation to the last-mentioned objects, was deemed necessary to be thus specially given to the new Government, in order to authorize it to make needful rules and regulations respecting the ships it might itself build, or arms and munitions of war it might itself manufacture or provide for the public service.

No one, it is believed, would think a moment of deriving the power of Congress to make needful rules and regulations in relation to property of this kind from this clause of the Constitution. Nor can it, upon any fair construction, be applied to any property but that which the new Government was about to receive from the confederated States. And if this be true as to this property, it must be equally true and limited as to the territory, which is so carefully and precisely coupled with it—and like it referred to as property in the power granted. The concluding words of the clause appear to render this construction irresistible; for, after the provisions we have mentioned, it proceeds to say, "that nothing in the Constitution shall be so construed as to prejudice any claims of the United States, or of any particular State."

Now, as we have before said, all of the States, except North Carolina and Georgia, had made the cession before the Constitution was adopted, according to the resolution of Congress of October 10, 1780. The claims of other States, that the unappropriated lands in these two States should be applied to the common benefit, in like manner, was still insisted on, but refused by the States. And this member of the clause in question evidently applies to them, and can apply to nothing else. It was to exclude the conclusion that either party, by adopting the Constitution, would surrender what they deemed their rights. And when the latter provision relates so obviously to the unappropriated lands not yet ceded by the States, and the first clause makes provision for those then actually ceded, it is [60 U.S. 393, 438] impossible, by any just rule of construction, to make the first provision general, and extend to all territories, which the Federal Government might in any way afterwards acquire, when the latter is plainly and unequivocally confined to a particular territory; which was a part of the same controversy, and involved in the same dispute, and depended upon the same principles. The union of the two provisions in the same clause shows that they were kindred subjects; and that the whole clause is local, and relates only to lands, within the limits of the United States, which had been or then were claimed by a State; and that no other territory was in the mind of the framers of the Constitution, or intended to be embraced in it. Upon any other construction it would be impossible to account for the insertion of the last provision in the place where it is found, or to comprehend why, or for what object, it was associated with the previous provision.

This view of the subject is confirmed by the manner in which the present Government of the United States dealt with the subject as soon as it came into existence. It must be borne in mind that the same States that formed the Confederation also formed and adopted the new Government, to which so large a portion of their former sovereign powers were surrendered. It must also be borne in mind that all of these same States which had then ratified the new Constitution were represented in the Congress which passed the first law for the government of this territory; and many of the members of that legislative body had been deputies from the States under the Confederation—had united in adopting the ordinance of 1787, and assisted in forming the new Government under which they were then acting, and whose powers they were then exercising. And it is obvious from the law they passed to carry into effect the principles and provisions of the ordinance, that they regarded it as the act of the States done in the exercise of their legitimate powers at the time. The new Government took the territory as it found it, and in the condition in which it was transferred, and did not attempt to undo anything that had been done. And, among the earliest laws passed under the new Government, is one reviving the ordinance of 1787, which had become inoperative and a nullity upon the adoption of the Constitution. This law introduces no new form or principles for its government, but recites, in the preamble, that it is passed in order that this ordinance may continue to have full effect, and proceeds to make only those rules and regulations which were needful to adapt it to the new Government, into whose hands the power had fallen. It appears, therefore, that this Congress regarded the purposes [60 U.S. 393, 439] to which the land in this Territory was to be applied, and the form of government and principles of jurisprudence which were to prevail there, while it remained in the Territorial state, as already determined on by the States when they had full power and right to make the decision; and that the new Government, having received it in this condition, ought to carry substantially into effect the plans and principles which had been previously adopted by the States, and which no doubt the States anticipated when they surrendered their power to the new Government. And if we regard this clause of the Constitution as pointing to this Territory, with a Territorial Government already established in it, which had been ceded to the States for the purposes hereinbefore mentioned—every word in it is perfectly appropriate and easily understood, and the provisions it contains are in perfect harmony with the objects for which it was ceded, and with the condition of its government as a Territory at the time. We can, then, easily account for the manner in which the first Congress legislated on the subject—and can also understand why this power over the territory was associated in the same clause with the other property of the

United States, and subjected to the like power of making needful rules and regulations. But if the clause is construed in the expanded sense contended for, so as to embrace any territory acquired from a foreign nation by the present Government, and to give it in such territory a despotic and unlimited power over persons and property, such as the confederated States might exercise in their common property, it would be difficult to account for the phraseology used, when compared with other grants of power—and also for its association with the other provisions in the same clause.

The Constitution has always been remarkable for the felicity of its arrangement of different subjects, and the perspicuity and appropriateness of the language it uses. But if this clause is construed to extend to territory acquired by the present Government from a foreign nation, outside of the limits of any charter from the British Government to a colony, it would be difficult to say, why it was deemed necessary to give the Government the power to sell any vacant lands belonging to the sovereignty which might be found within it; and if this was necessary, why the grant of this power should precede the power to legislate over it and establish a Government there; and still more difficult to say, why it was deemed necessary so specially and particularly to grant the power to make needful rules and regulations in relation to any personal or movable property it might acquire there. For the words, other property necessarily, by every known rule of interpretation, must mean [60 U.S. 393, 440] property of a different description from territory or land. And the difficulty would perhaps be insurmountable in endeavoring to account for the last member of the sentence, which provides that "nothing in this Constitution shall be so construed as to prejudice any claims of the United States or any particular State," or to say how any particular State could have claims in or to a territory ceded by a foreign Government, or to account for associating this provision with the preceding provisions of the clause, with which it would appear to have no connection.

The words "needful rules and regulations" would seem, also, to have been cautiously used for some definite object. They are not the words usually employed by statesmen, when they mean to give the powers of sovereignty, or to establish a Government, or to authorize its establishment. Thus, in the law to renew and keep alive the ordinance of 1787, and to re-establish the Government, the title of the law is: "An act to provide for the government of the territory northwest of the river Ohio." And in the Constitution, when granting the power to legislate over the territory that may be selected for the seat of Government independently of a State, it does not say Congress shall have power "to make all needful rules and regulations respecting the territory;" but it declares that "Congress shall have power to exercise exclusive legislation in all cases whatsoever over such District (not exceeding ten miles square) as may, by cession of particular States and the acceptance of Congress, become the seat of the Government of the United States.

The words "rules and regulations" are usually employed in the Constitution in speaking of some particular specified power which it means to confer on the Government, and not, as we have seen, when granting general powers of legislation. As, for example, in the particular power to Congress "to make rules for the government and regulation of the land and naval forces, or the particular and specific power to regulate commerce;" "to establish an uniform rule of naturalization;" "to coin money and regulate the value thereof." And to construe the words of which we are speaking as a general and unlimited grant of sovereignty over territories which the Government might afterwards acquire, is to use them in a sense and for a purpose for which they were not used in any other part of the instrument. But if confined to a particular Territory, in which a Government and laws had already been established, but which would require some alterations to adapt it to the new Government, the words are peculiarly applicable and appropriate for that purpose. [60 U.S. 393, 441] The necessity of this special provision in relation to property and the rights or property held in common by the confederated States, is illustrated by the first clause of the sixth article. This clause provides that "all debts, contracts, and engagements entered into before the adoption of this Constitution, shall be as valid against the United States under this Government as under the Confederation." This provision, like the one under consideration, was indispensable if the new Constitution was adopted. The new Government was not a mere change in a dynasty, or in a form of government, leaving the nation or sovereignty the same, and clothed with all the rights, and bound by all the obligations of the preceding one. But, when the present United States came into existence under the new Government, it was a new political body, a new nation, then for the first time taking its place in the family of nations. It took nothing by succession from the Confederation. It had no right, as its successor, to any property or rights of property which it had acquired, and was not liable for any of its obligations. It was evidently viewed in this light by the framers of the Constitution. And as the several States would cease to exist in their former confederated character upon the adoption of the Constitution, and could not, in that character, again assemble together, special provisions were indispensable to transfer to the new Government the property and rights which at that time they held in common; and at the same time to authorize it to lay taxes and appropriate money to pay the common debt which they had contracted; and this power could only be given to it by special provisions in the Constitution. The clause in relation to the territory and other property of the United States provided for the first, and the clause last quoted provided for the other. They have no connection with the general powers and rights of sovereignty delegated to the new Government, and can neither enlarge nor diminish them. They were inserted to meet a present emergency, and not to regulate its powers as a Government.

Indeed, a similar provision was deemed necessary, in relation to treaties made by the Confederation; and when in the clause next succeeding the one of which we have last spoken, it is declared that treaties shall be the supreme law of the land, care is taken to include, by express words, the treaties made by the confederated States. The language is: "and all treaties made, or which shall be made, under the authority of the United States, shall be the supreme law of the land."

Whether, therefore, we take the particular clause in question, by itself, or in connection with the other provisions of the Constitution, we think it clear, that it applies only to the particular [60 U.S. 393, 442] territory of which we have spoken, and cannot, by any just rule of interpretation, be extended to territory which the new Government might afterwards obtain from a foreign nation. Consequently, the power which Congress may have lawfully exercised in this Territory, while it remained under a Territorial Government, and which may have been sanctioned by judicial decision, can furnish no justification and no argument to support a similar exercise of power over territory afterwards acquired by the Federal Government. We put aside, therefore, any argument, drawn from precedents, showing the extent of the power which the General Government exercised over slavery in this Territory, as altogether inapplicable to the case before us.

But the case of the American and Ocean Insurance Companies v. Canter (1 Pet., 511) has been quoted as establishing a different construction of this clause of the Constitution. There is, however, not the slightest conflict between the opinion now given and the one referred to; and it is only by taking a single sentence out of the latter and separating it from the context, that even an appearance of conflict can be shown. We need not comment on such a mode of expounding an opinion of the court. Indeed it most commonly misrepresents instead of expounding it. And this is fully exemplified in the case referred to, where, if one sentence is taken by itself, the opinion would appear to be in direct conflict with that now given; but the words which immediately follow that sentence show that the court did not mean to decide the point, but merely affirmed the power of Congress to establish a Government in the Territory, leaving it an open question, whether that power was derived from this clause in the Constitution, or was to be necessarily inferred from a power to acquire territory by cession from a foreign Government. The opinion on this part of the case is short, and we give the whole of it to show how well the selection of a single sentence is calculated to mislead.

The passage referred to is in page 542, in which the court, in speaking of the power of Congress to establish a Territorial Government in Florida until it should become a State, uses the following language:

> "In the mean time Florida continues to be a Territory of the United States, governed by that clause of the Constitution which empowers Congress to make all needful rules and regulations respecting the territory or other property of the United States. Perhaps the power of governing a Territory belonging to the United States, which has not, by becoming a State, acquired the means of self-government, may result, necessarily, from the facts that it is not within the jurisdiction of any particular [60 U.S. 393, 443] State, and is within the power and jurisdiction of the United States. The right to govern may be the inevitable consequence of the right to acquire territory. Whichever may be the source from which the power is derived, the possession of it is unquestionable."

It is thus clear, from the whole opinion on this point, that the court did not mean to decide whether the power was derived from the clause in the Constitution, or was the necessary consequence of the right to acquire. They do decide that the power in Congress is unquestionable, and in this we entirely concur, and nothing will be found in this opinion to the contrary. The power stands firmly on the latter alternative put by the court—that is, as "the inevitable consequence of the right to acquire territory."

And what still more clearly demonstrates that the court did not mean to decide the question, but leave it open for future consideration, is the fact that the case was decided in the Circuit Court by Mr. Justice Johnson, and his decision was affirmed by the Supreme Court. His opinion at the circuit is given in full in a note to the case, and in that opinion he states, in explicit terms, that the clause of the Constitution applies only to the territory then within the limits of the United States, and not to Florida, which had been acquired by cession from Spain. This part of his opinion will be found in the note in page 517 of the report. But he does not dissent from the opinion of the Supreme Court; thereby showing that, in his judgment, as well as that of the court, the case before them did not call for a decision on that particular point, and the court abstained from deciding it. And in a part of its opinion subsequent to the passage we have quoted, where the court speak of the legislative power of Congress in Florida, they still speak with the same reserve. And in page 546, speaking of the power of Congress to authorize the Territorial

Legislature to establish courts there, the court say: "They are legislative courts, created in virtue of the general right of sovereignty which exists in the Government, or in virtue of that clause which enables Congress to make all needful rules and regulations respecting the territory belonging to the United States."

It has been said that the construction given to this clause is new, and now for the first time brought forward. The case of which we are speaking, and which has been so much discussed, shows that the fact is otherwise. It shows that precisely the same question came before Mr. Justice Johnson, at his circuit, thirty years ago—was fully considered by him, and the same construction given to the clause in the Constitution which is now given by this court. And that upon an appeal [60 U.S. 393, 444] from his decision the same question was brought before this court, but was not decided because a decision upon it was not required by the case before the court.

There is another sentence in the opinion which has been commented on, which even in a still more striking manner shows how one may mislead or be misled by taking out a single sentence from the opinion of a court, and leaving out of view what precedes and follows. It is in page 546, near the close of the opinion, in which the court say: "In legislating for them," (the territories of the United States,) "Congress exercises the combined powers of the General and of a State Government." And it is said, that as a State may unquestionably prohibit slavery within its territory, this sentence decides in effect that Congress may do the same in a Territory of the United States, exercising there the powers of a State, as well as the power of the General Government.

The examination of this passage in the case referred to, would be more appropriate when we come to consider in another part of this opinion what power Congress can constitutionally exercise in a Territory, over the rights of person or rights of property of a citizen. But, as it is in the same case with the passage we have before commented on, we dispose of it now, as it will save the court from the necessity of referring again to the case. And it will be seen upon reading the page in which this sentence is found, that it has no reference whatever to the power of Congress over rights of person or rights of property—but relates altogether to the power of establishing judicial tribunals to administer the laws constitutionally passed, and defining the jurisdiction they may exercise.

The law of Congress establishing a Territorial Government in Florida, provided that the Legislature of the Territory should have legislative powers over "all rightful objects of legislation; but no law should be valid which was inconsistent with the laws and Constitution of the United States."

Under the power thus conferred, the Legislature of Florida passed an act, erecting a tribunal at Key West to decide cases of salvage. And in the case of which we are speaking, the question arose whether the Territorial Legislature could be authorized by Congress to establish such a tribunal, with such powers; and one of the parties, among other objections, insisted that Congress could not under the Constitution authorize the Legislature of the Territory to establish such a tribunal with such powers, but that it must be established by Congress itself; and that a sale of cargo made under its order, to pay salvors, was void, as made without legal authority, and passed no property to the purchaser. [60 U.S. 393, 445] It is in disposing of this objection that the sentence relied on occurs, and the court begin that part of the opinion by stating with great precision the point which they are about to decide.

They say: "It has been contended that by the Constitution of the United States, the judicial power of the United States extends to all cases of admiralty and maritime jurisdiction; and that the whole of the judicial power must be vested "in one Supreme Court, and in such inferior courts as Congress shall from time to time ordain and establish." Hence it has been argued that Congress cannot vest admiralty jurisdiction in courts created by the Territorial Legislature."

And after thus clearly stating the point before them, and which they were about to decide, they proceed to show that these Territorial tribunals were not constitutional courts, but merely legislative, and that Congress might, therefore, delegate the power to the Territorial Government to establish the court in question; and they conclude that part of the opinion in the following words: "Although admiralty jurisdiction can be exercised in the States in those courts only which are established in pursuance of the third article of the Constitution, the same limitation does not extend to the Territories. In legislating for them, Congress exercises the combined powers of the General and State Governments."

Thus it will be seen by these quotations from the opinion, that the court, after stating the question it was about to decide in a manner too plain to be misunderstood, proceeded to decide it, and announced, as the opinion of the tribunal, that in organizing the judicial department of the Government in a Territory of the United States, Congress does not act under, and is not restricted by, the third article in the Constitution, and is not bound, in a Territory, to ordain and establish courts in which the judges hold their offices during good behaviour, but may exercise the discretionary power which a State exercises in establishing its judicial department, and regulating the jurisdiction of its courts, and may authorize the Territorial Government to establish, or may itself establish, courts in which the judges hold their offices for a term of years only; and may vest in them judicial power upon subjects confided to the judiciary of the United States. And in doing this, Congress undoubtedly exercises the combined power of the General and a State Government. It exercises the discretionary power of a State Government in authorizing the establishment of a court in which the judges hold their appointments for a term of years only, and not during good behaviour; and it exercises the power of the General Government in investing that [60 U.S. 393, 446] court with admiralty jurisdiction, over which the General Government had exclusive jurisdiction in the Territory.

No one, we presume, will question the correctness of that opinion; nor is there anything in conflict with it in the opinion now given. The point decided in the case cited has no relation to the question now before the court. That depended on the construction of the third article of the Constitution, in relation to the judiciary of the United States, and the power which Congress might exercise in a Territory in organizing the judicial department of the Government. The case before us depends upon other and different provisions of the Constitution, altogether separate and apart from the one above mentioned. The question as to what courts Congress may ordain or establish in a Territory to administer laws which the Constitution authorizes it to pass, and what laws it is or is not authorized by the Constitution to pass, are widely different—are regulated by different and separate articles of the Constitution, and stand upon different principles. And we are satisfied that no one who reads attentively the page in Peters's Reports to which we have referred, can suppose that the attention of the court was drawn for a moment to the question now before this court, or that it meant in that case to say that Congress had a right to prohibit a citizen of the United States from taking any property which he lawfully held into a Territory of the United States.

This brings us to examine by what provision of the Constitution the present Federal Government, under its delegated and restricted powers, is authorized to acquire territory outside of the original limits of the United States, and what powers it may exercise therein over the person or property of a citizen of the United States, while it remains a Territory, and until it shall be admitted as one of the States of the Union.

There is certainly no power given by the Constitution to the Federal Government to establish or maintain colonies bordering on the United States or at a distance, to be ruled and governed at its own pleasure; nor to enlarge its territorial limits in any way, except by the admission of new States. That power is plainly given; and if a new State is admitted, it needs no further legislation by Congress, because the Constitution itself defines the relative rights and powers, and duties of the State, and the citizens of the State, and the Federal Government. But no power is given to acquire a Territory to be held and governed permanently in that character.

And indeed the power exercised by Congress to acquire territory and establish a Government there, according to its own unlimited discretion, was viewed with great jealousy by the [60 U.S. 393, 447] leading statesmen of the day. And in the Federalist, (No. 38,) written by Mr. Madison, he speaks of the acquisition of the Northwestern Territory by the confederated States, by the cession from Virginia, and the establishment of a Government there, as an exercise of power not warranted by the Articles of Confederation, and dangerous to the liberties of the people. And he urges the adoption of the Constitution as a security and safeguard against such an exercise of power.

We do not mean, however, to question the power of Congress in this respect. The power to expand the territory of the United States by the admission of new States is plainly given; and in the construction of this power by all the departments of the Government, it has been held to authorize the acquisition of territory, not fit for admission at the time, but to be admitted as soon as its population and situation would entitle it to admission. It is acquired to become a State, and not to be held as a colony and governed by Congress with absolute authority; and as the propriety of admitting a new State is committed to the sound discretion of Congress, the power to acquire territory for that purpose, to be held by the United States until it is in a suitable condition to become a State upon an equal footing with the other States, must rest upon the same discretion. It is a question for the political department of the Government, and not the judicial; and whatever the political department of the Government shall recognise as within the limits of the United States, the judicial department is also bound to recognise, and to administer in it the laws of the United States, so far as they apply, and to maintain in the Territory the authority and rights of the Government, and also the personal rights and rights of property of individual citizens, as secured by the Constitution. All we mean to say on this point is, that, as there is no express regulation in the Constitution defining the power which the General Government may exercise over the person or property of a citizen in a Territory thus acquired, the court must necessarily look to the provisions and principles of the Constitution, and its distribution of powers, for the rules and principles by which its decision must be governed.

Taking this rule to guide us, it may be safely assumed that citizens of the United States who migrate to a Territory belonging to the people of the United States, cannot be ruled as mere colonists, dependent upon the will of the General Government, and to be governed by any laws it may think proper to impose. The principle upon which our Governments rest, and upon which alone they continue to exist, is the union of States, sovereign and independent within their own limits in [60 U.S. 393, 448] their internal and domestic concerns, and bound together as one people by a General Government, possessing certain enumerated and restricted powers, delegated to it by the people of the several States, and exercising

supreme authority within the scope of the powers granted to it, throughout the dominion of the United States. A power, therefore, in the
General Government to obtain and hold colonies and dependent territories, over which they might legislate without restriction, would be
inconsistent with its own existence in its present form. Whatever it
acquires, it acquires for the benefit of the people of the several States who
created it. It is their trustee acting for them, and charged with the duty
of promoting the interests of the whole people of the Union in the exercise of the powers specifically granted.

At the time when the Territory in question was obtained by cession
from France, it contained no population fit to be associated together and
admitted as a State; and it therefore was absolutely necessary to hold
possession of it, as a Territory belonging to the United States, until
it was settled and inhabited by a civilized community capable of self-
government, and in a condition to be admitted on equal terms with the
other States as a member of the Union. But, as we have before said, it was
acquired by the General Government, as the representative and trustee of
the people of the United States, and it must therefore be held in that
character for their common and equal benefit; for it was the people of
the several States, acting through their agent and representative, the
Federal Government, who in fact acquired the Territory in question, and
the Government holds it for their common use until it shall be associated with the other States as a member of the Union.

But until that time arrives, it is undoubtedly necessary that some
Government should be established, in order to organize society, and to
protect the inhabitants in their persons and property; and as the people of
the United States could act in this matter only through the Government
which represented them, and through which they spoke and acted when
the Territory was obtained, it was not only within the scope of its powers, but it was its duty to pass such laws and establish such a Government
as would enable those by whose authority they acted to reap the advantages anticipated from its acquisition, and to gather there a population
which would enable it to assume the position to which it was destined
among the States of the Union. The power to acquire necessarily carries
with it the power to preserve and apply to the purposes for which it was
acquired. The form of government to be established [60 U.S. 393, 449] necessarily rested in the discretion of Congress. It was their duty to establish
the one that would be best suited for the protection and security of the
citizens of the United States, and other inhabitants who might be authorized to take up their abode there, and that must always depend upon the
existing condition of the Territory, as to the number and character of its
inhabitants, and their situation in the Territory. In some cases a Government,
consisting of persons appointed by the Federal Government, would best

subserve the interests of the Territory, when the inhabitants were few and scattered, and new to one another. In other instances, it would be more advisable to commit the powers of self-government to the people who had settled in the Territory, as being the most competent to determine what was best for their own interests. But some form of civil authority would be absolutely necessary to organize and preserve civilized society, and prepare it to become a State; and what is the best form must always depend on the condition of the Territory at the time, and the choice of the mode must depend upon the exercise of a discretionary power by Congress, acting within the scope of its constitutional authority, and not infringing upon the rights of person or rights of property of the citizen who might go there to reside, or for any other lawful purpose. It was acquired by the exercise of this discretion, and it must be held and governed in like manner, until it is fitted to be a State.

But the power of Congress over the person or property of a citizen can never be a mere discretionary power under our Constitution and form of Government. The powers of the Government and the rights and privileges of the citizen are regulated and plainly defined by the Constitution itself. And when the Territory becomes a part of the United States, the Federal Government enters into possession in the character impressed upon it by those who created it. It enters upon it with its powers over the citizen strictly defined, and limited by the Constitution, from which it derives its own existence, and by virtue of which alone it continues to exist and act as a Government and sovereignty. It has no power of any kind beyond it; and it cannot, when it enters a Territory of the United States, put off its character, and assume discretionary or despotic powers which the Constitution has denied to it. It cannot create for itself a new character separated from the citizens of the United States, and the duties it owes them under the provisions of the Constitution. The Territory being a part of the United States, the Government and the citizen both enter it under the authority of the Constitution, with their respective rights defined and marked out; and the Federal Government [60 U.S. 393, 450] can exercise no power over this person or property, beyond what that instrument confers, nor lawfully deny any right which it has reserved.

A reference to a few of the provisions of the Constitution will illustrate this proposition.

For example, no one, we presume, will contend that Congress can make any law in a Territory respecting the establishment of religion, or the free exercise thereof, or abridging the freedom of speech or of the press, or the right of the people of the Territory peaceably to assemble, and to petition the Government for the redress of grievances.

Nor can Congress deny to the people the right to keep and bear arms, nor the right to trial by jury, nor compel any one to be a witness against himself in a criminal proceeding.

These powers, and others, in relation to rights of person, which it is not necessary here to enumerate, are, in express and positive terms, denied to the General Government; and the rights of private property have been guarded with equal care. Thus the rights of property are united with the rights of person, and placed on the same ground by the fifth amendment to the Constitution, which provides that no person shall be deprived of life, liberty, and property, without due process of law. And an act of Congress which deprives a citizen of the United States of his liberty or property, merely because he came himself or brought his property into a particular Territory of the United States, and who had committed no offence against the laws, could hardly be dignified with the name of due process of law.

So, too, it will hardly be contended that Congress could by law quarter a soldier in a house in a Territory without the consent of the owner, in time of peace; nor in time of war, but in a manner prescribed by law. Nor could they by law forfeit the property of a citizen in a Territory who was convicted of treason, for a longer period than the life of the person convicted; nor take private property for public use without just compensation.

The powers over person and property of which we speak are not only not granted to Congress, but are in express terms denied, and they are forbidden to exercise them. And this prohibition is not confined to the States, but the words are general, and extend to the whole territory over which the Constitution gives it power to legislate, including those portions of it remaining under Territorial Government, as well as that covered by States. It is a total absence of power everywhere within the dominion of the United States, and places the citizens of a Territory, so far as these rights are [60 U.S. 393, 451] concerned, on the same footing with citizens of the States, and guards them as firmly and plainly against any inroads which the General Government might attempt, under the plea of implied or incidental powers. And if Congress itself cannot do this—if it is beyond the powers conferred on the Federal Government— it will be admitted, we presume, that it could not authorize a Territorial Government to exercise them. It could confer no power on any local Government, established by its authority, to violate the provisions of the Constitution.

It seems, however, to be supposed, that there is a difference between property in a slave and other property, and that different rules may be applied to it in expounding the Constitution of the United States. And the laws and usages of nations, and the writings of eminent jurists upon the relation of master and slave and their mutual rights and duties, and the powers which Governments may exercise over it, have been dwelt upon in the argument.

But in considering the question before us, it must be borne in mind that there is no law of nations standing between the people of the United States and their Government, and interfering with their relation to each other. The powers of the Government, and the rights of the citizen under it, are positive and practical regulations plainly written down. The people of the United States have delegated to it certain enumerated powers, and forbidden it to exercise others. It has no power over the person or property of a citizen but what the citizens of the United States have granted. And no laws or usages of other nations, or reasoning of statesmen or jurists upon the relations of master and slave, can enlarge the powers of the Government, or take from the citizens the rights they have reserved. And if the Constitution recognises the right of property of the master in a slave, and makes no distinction between that description of property and other property owned by a citizen, no tribunal, acting under the authority of the United States, whether it be legislative, executive, or judicial, has a right to draw such a distinction, or deny to it the benefit of the provisions and guarantees which have been provided for the protection of private property against the encroachments of the Government.

Now, as we have already said in an earlier part of this opinion, upon a different point, the right of property in a slave is distinctly and expressly affirmed in the Constitution. The right to traffic in it, like an ordinary article of merchandise and property, was guarantied to the citizens of the United States, in every State that might desire it, for twenty years. And the Government in express terms is pledged to protect [60 U.S. 393, 452] it in all future time, if the slave escapes from his owner. This is done in plain words-too plain to be misunderstood. And no word can be found in the Constitution which gives Congress a greater power over slave property, or which entitles property of that kind to less protection than property of any other description. The only power conferred is the power coupled with the duty of guarding and protecting the owner in his rights.

Upon these considerations, it is the opinion of the court that the act of Congress which prohibited a citizen from holding and owning property of this kind in the territory of the United States north of the line therein mentioned, is not warranted by the Constitution, and is therefore void; and that neither Dred Scott himself, nor any of his family, were made free by being carried into this territory; even if they had been carried there by the owner, with the intention of becoming a permanent resident.

We have so far examined the case, as it stands under the Constitution of the United States, and the powers thereby delegated to the Federal Government.

But there is another point in the case which depends on State power and State law. And it is contended, on the part of the plaintiff, that he is made free by being taken to Rock Island, in the State of Illinois, independently of his residence in the territory of the United States; and being so made free, he was not again reduced to a state of slavery by being brought back to Missouri.

Our notice of this part of the case will be very brief; for the principle on which it depends was decided in this court, upon much consideration, in the case of Strader et al. v. Graham, reported in 10th Howard, 82. In that case, the slaves had been taken from Kentucky to Ohio, with the consent of the owner, and afterwards brought back to Kentucky. And this court held that their status or condition, as free or slave, depended upon the laws of Kentucky, when they were brought back into that State, and not of Ohio; and that this court had no jurisdiction to revise the judgment of a State court upon its own laws. This was the point directly before the court, and the decision that this court had not jurisdiction turned upon it, as will be seen by the report of the case.

So in this case. As Scott was a slave when taken into the State of Illinois by his owner, and was there held as such, and brought back in that character, his status, as free or slave, depended on the laws of Missouri, and not of Illinois.

It has, however, been urged in the argument, that by the laws of Missouri he was free on his return, and that this case, [60 U.S. 393, 453] therefore, cannot be governed by the case of Strader et al. v. Graham, where it appeared, by the laws of Kentucky, that the plaintiffs continued to be slaves on their return from Ohio. But whatever doubts or opinions may, at one time, have been entertained upon this subject, we are satisfied, upon a careful examination of all the cases decided in the State courts of Missouri referred to, that it is now firmly settled by the decisions of the highest court in the State, that Scott and his family upon their return were not free, but were, by the laws of Missouri, the property of the defendant; and that the Circuit Court of the United States had no jurisdiction, when, by the laws of the State, the plaintiff was a slave, and not a citizen.

Moreover, the plaintiff, it appears, brought a similar action against the defendant in the State court of Missouri, claiming the freedom of himself and his family upon the same grounds and the same evidence upon which he relies in the case before the court. The case was carried before the Supreme Court of the State; was fully argued there; and that court decided that neither the plaintiff nor his family were entitled to freedom, and were still the slaves of the defendant; and reversed the judgment of the inferior

State court, which had given a different decision. If the plaintiff supposed that this judgment of the Supreme Court of the State was erroneous, and that this court had jurisdiction to revise and reverse it, the only mode by which he could legally bring it before this court was by writ of error directed to the Supreme Court of the State, requiring it to transmit the record to this court. If this had been done, it is too plain for argument that the writ must have been dismissed for want of jurisdiction in this court. The case of Strader and others v. Graham is directly in point; and, indeed, independent of any decision, the language of the 25th section of the act of 1789 is too clear and precise to admit of controversy.

But the plaintiff did not pursue the mode prescribed by law for bringing the judgment of a State court before this court for revision, but suffered the case to be remanded to the inferior State court, where it is still continued, and is, by agreement of parties, to await the judgment of this court on the point. All of this appears on the record before us, and by the printed report of the case.

And while the case is yet open and pending in the inferior State court, the plaintiff goes into the Circuit Court of the United States, upon the same case and the same evidence, and against the same party, and proceeds to judgment, and then brings here the same case from the Circuit Court, which the law would not have permitted him to bring directly from the [60 U.S. 393, 454] State court. And if this court takes jurisdiction in this form, the result, so far as the rights of the respective parties are concerned, is in every respect substantially the same as if it had in open violation of law entertained jurisdiction over the judgment of the State court upon a writ of error, and revised and reversed its judgment upon the ground that its opinion upon the question of law was erroneous. It would ill become this court to sanction such an attempt to evade the law, or to exercise an appellate power in this circuitous way, which it is forbidden to exercise in the direct and regular and invariable forms of judicial proceedings.

Upon the whole, therefore, it is the judgment of this court, that it appears by the record before us that the plaintiff in error is not a citizen of Missouri, in the sense in which that word is used in the Constitution; and that the Circuit Court of the United States, for that reason, had no jurisdiction in the case, and could give no judgment in it. Its judgment for the defendant must, consequently, be reversed, and a mandate issued, directing the suit to be dismissed for want of jurisdiction.

Mr. Justice McLEAN and Mr. Justice CURTIS dissented.

Mr. Justice McLEAN dissenting.

This case is before us on a writ of error from the Circuit Court for the district of Missouri.

An action of trespass was brought, which charges the defendant with an assault and imprisonment of the plaintiff, and also of Harriet Scott, his wife, Eliza and Lizzie, his two children, on the ground that they were his slaves, which was without right on his part, and against law.

The defendant filed a plea in abatement, "that said causes of action, and each and every of them, if any such accrued to the said Dred Scott, accrued out of the jurisdiction of this court, and exclusively within the jurisdiction of the courts of the State of Missouri, for that to wit, said plaintiff, Dred Scott, is not a citizen of the State of Missouri, as alleged in his declaration, because he is a negro of African descent, his ancestors were of pure African blood, and were brought into this country and sold as negro slaves; and this the said Sandford is ready to verify; wherefore he prays judgment whether the court can or will take further cognizance of the action aforesaid."

To this a demurrer was filed, which, on argument, was sustained by the court, the plea in abatement being held insufficient; the defendant was ruled to plead over. Under this rule he pleaded: 1. Not guilty; 2. That Dred Scott was a negro slave, the property of the defendant; and 3. That Harriet, the wife, and Eliza and Lizzie, the daughters of the plaintiff, were the lawful slaves of the defendant.

Issue was joined on the first plea, and replications of de injuria were filed to the other pleas.

The parties agreed to the following facts: In the year 1834, the plaintiff was a negro slave belonging to Dr. Emerson, who was a surgeon in the army of the United States. In that year, Dr. Emerson took the plaintiff from the State of Missouri to [60 U.S. 393, 530] the post of Rock Island, in the State of Illinois, and held him there as a slave until the month of April or May, 1836. At the time last mentioned, Dr. Emerson removed the plaintiff from Rock Island to the military post at Fort Snelling, situate on the west bank of the Mississippi river, in the territory Known as Upper Louisiana, acquired by the United States of France, and situate north of latitude thirty-six degrees thirty minutes north, and north of the State of Missouri. Dr. Emerson held the plaintiff in slavery, at Fort Snelling, from the last-mentioned date until the year 1838.

In the year 1835, Harriet, who is named in the second count of the plaintiff's declaration, was the negro slave of Major Taliaferro, who belonged to the army of the United States. In that year, Major Taliaferro took Harriet to Fort Snelling, a military post situated as hereinbefore stated, and kept her there as a slave until the year 1836, and then sold and delivered her as a slave, at Fort Snelling, unto Dr. Emerson, who held her in slavery, at that place, until the year 1838.

In the year 1836, the plaintiff and Harriet were married at Fort Snelling, with the consent of Dr. Emerson, who claimed to be their master and owner. Eliza and Lizzie, named in the third count of the plaintiff's declaration, are the fruit of that marriage. Eliza is about four-teen years old, and was born on board the steamboat Gipsey, north of the north line of the State of Missouri, and upon the river Mississippi. Lizzie is about seven years old, and was born in the State of Missouri, at the mil-itary post called Jefferson Barracks.

In the year 1838, Dr. Emerson removed the plaintiff and said Harriet and their daughter Eliza from Fort Snelling to the State of Missouri, where they have ever since resided.

Before the commencement of the suit, Dr. Emerson sold and con-veyed the plaintiff, Harriet, Eliza, and Lizzie, to the defendant, as slaves, and he has ever since claimed to hold them as slaves.

At the times mentioned in the plaintiff's declaration, the defendant, claiming to be the owner, laid his hands upon said plaintiff, Harriet, Eliza, and Lizzie, and imprisoned them; doing in this respect, however, no more than he might lawfully do, if they were of right his slaves at such times.

In the first place, the plea to the jurisdiction is not before us, on this writ of error. A demurrer to the plea was sustained, which ruled the plea bad, and the defendant, on leave, pleaded over.

The decision on the demurrer was in favor of the plaintiff; and as the plaintiff prosecutes this writ of error, he does not complain of the decision on the demurrer. The defendant [60 U.S. 393, 531] might have complained of this decision, as against him, and have prosecuted a writ of error, to reverse it. But as the case, under the instruction of the court to the jury, was decided in his favor, of course he had no ground of complaint.

But it is said, if the court, on looking at the record, shall clearly per-ceive that the Circuit Court had no jurisdiction, it is a ground for the dis-missal of the case. This may be characterized as rather a sharp practice, and one which seldom, if ever, occurs. No case was cited in the argument as authority, and not a single case precisely in point is recollected in our reports. The pleadings do not show a want of jurisdiction. This want of jurisdiction can only be ascertained by a judgment on the demurrer to the special plea. No such case, it is believed, can be cited. But if this rule of practice is to be applied in this case, and the plaintiff in error is required to answer and maintain as well the points ruled in his favor, as to show the error of those ruled against him, he has more than an ordinary duty to perform. Under such circumstances, the want of jurisdiction in the Circuit Court must be so clear as not to admit of doubt. Now, the plea which raises the question of jurisdiction, in my judgment, is radically defective. The gravamen of the plea is this: "That the plaintiff is a negro of African descent, his ancestors being of pure African blood, and were brought into this country, and sold as negro slaves."

There is no averment in this plea which shows or conduces to show an inability in the plaintiff to sue in the Circuit Court. It does not allege that the plaintiff had his domicil in any other State, nor that he is not a free man in Missouri. He is averred to have had a negro ancestry, but this does not show that he is not a citizen of Missouri, within the meaning of the act of Congress authorizing him to sue in the Circuit Court. It has never been held necessary, to constitute a citizen within the act, that he should have the qualifications of an elector. Females and minors may sue in the Federal courts, and so may any individual who has a permanent domicil in the State under whose laws his rights are protected, and to which he owes allegiance.

Being born under our Constitution and laws, no naturalization is required, as one of foreign birth, to make him a citizen. The most general and appropriate definition of the term citizen is "a freeman." Being a freeman, and having his domicil in a State different from that of the defendant, he is a citizen within the act of Congress, and the courts of the Union are open to him.

It has often been held, that the jurisdiction, as regards parties, can only be exercised between citizens of different States, [60 U.S. 393, 532] and that a mere residence is not sufficient; but this has been said to distinguish a temporary from a permanent residence.

To constitute a good plea to the jurisdiction, it must negative those qualities and rights which enable an individual to sue in the Federal courts. This has not been done; and on this ground the plea was defective, and the demurrer was properly sustained. No implication can aid a plea in abatement or in bar; it must be complete in itself; the facts stated, if true, must abate or bar the right of the plaintiff to sue. This is not the character of the above plea. The facts stated, if admitted, are not inconsistent with other facts, which may be presumed, and which bring the plaintiff within the act of Congress.

The pleader has not the boldness to allege that the plaintiff is a slave, as that would assume against him the matter in controversy, and embrace the entire merits of the case in a plea to the jurisdiction. But beyond the facts set out in the plea, the court, to sustain it, must assume the plaintiff to be a slave, which is decisive on the merits. This is a short and an effectual mode of deciding the cause; but I am yet to learn that it is sanctioned by any known rule of pleading.

The defendant's counsel complain, that if the court take jurisdiction on the ground that the plaintiff is free, the assumption is against the right of the master. This argument is easily answered. In the first place, the plea does not show him to be a slave; it does not follow that a man is not free whose ancestors were slaves. The reports of the Supreme Court of Missouri show that this assumption has many exceptions; and there is no averment in the plea that the plaintiff is not within them.

By all the rules of pleading, this is a fatal defect in the plea. If there be doubt, what rule of construction has been established in the slave States? In Jacob v. Sharp, (Meigs's Rep., Tennessee, 114,) the court held, when there was doubt as to the construction of a will which emancipated a slave, "it must be construed to be subordinate to the higher and more important right of freedom."

No injustice can result to the master, from an exercise of jurisdiction in this cause. Such a decision does not in any degree affect the merits of the case; it only enables the plaintiff to assert his claims to freedom before this tribunal. If the jurisdiction be ruled against him, on the ground that he is a slave, it is decisive of his fate.

It has been argued that, if a colored person be made a citizen of a State, he cannot sue in the Federal court. The Constitution declares that Federal jurisdiction "may be exercised between citizens of different States," and the same is provided [60 U.S. 393, 533] in the act of 1789. The above argument is properly met by saying that the Constitution was intended to be a practical instrument; and where its language is too plain to be misunderstood, the argument ends."

In Chirae v. Chirae, (2 Wheat., 261; 4 Curtis, 99,) this court says: "That the power of naturalization is exclusively in Congress does not seem to be, and certainly ought not to be, controverted." No person can legally be made a citizen of a State, and consequently a citizen of the United States, of foreign birth, unless he be naturalized under the acts of Congress. Congress has power "to establish a uniform rule of naturalization."

It is a power which belongs exclusively to Congress, as intimately connected with our Federal relations. A State may authorize foreigners to hold real estate within its jurisdiction, but it has no power to naturalize foreigners, and give them the rights of citizens. Such a right is opposed to the acts of Congress on the subject of naturalization, and subversive of the Federal powers. I regret that any countenance should be given from this bench to a practice like this in some of the States, which has no warrant in the Constitution.

In the argument, it was said that a colored citizen would not be an agreeable member of society. This is more a matter of taste than of law. Several of the States have admitted persons of color to the right of suffrage, and in this view have recognised them as citizens; and this has been done in the slave as well as the free States. On the question of citizenship, it must be admitted that we have not been very fastidious. Under the late treaty with Mexico, we have made citizens of all grades, combinations, and colors. The same was done in the admission of Louisiana and Florida. No one ever doubted, and no court ever held, that the people of these Territories did not become citizens under the treaty. They have exercised all the rights of citizens, without being naturalized under the acts of Congress.

There are several important principles involved in this case, which have been argued, and which may be considered under the following heads:

1. The locality of slavery, as settled by this court and the courts of the States. 2. The relation which the Federal Government bears to slavery in the States. 3. The power of Congress to establish Territorial Governments, and to prohibit the introduction of slavery therein. 4. The effect of taking slaves into a new State or Territory, and so holding them, where slavery is prohibited. 5. Whether the return of a slave under the control of his [60 U.S. 393, 534] master, after being entitled to his freedom, reduces him to his former condition.

6. Are the decisions of the Supreme Court of Missouri, on the questions before us, binding on this court, within the rule adopted.

In the course of my judicial duties, I have had occasion to consider and decide several of the above points.

1. As to the locality of slavery. The civil law throughout the Continent of Europe, it is believed, without an exception, is, that slavery can exist only within the territory where it is established; and that, if a slave escapes, or is carried beyond such territory, his master cannot reclaim him, unless by virtue of some express stipulation. (Grotius, lib. 2, chap. 15, 5, 1; lib. 10, chap. 10, 2, 1; Wicqueposts Ambassador, lib. 1, p. 418; 4 Martin, 385; Case of the Creole in the House of Lords, 1842; 1 Phillimore on International Law, 316, 335.)

There is no nation in Europe which considers itself bound to return to his master a fugitive slave, under the civil law or the law of nations. On the contrary, the slave is held to be free where there is no treaty obligation, or compact in some other form, to return him to his master. The Roman law did not allow freedom to be sold. An ambassador or any other public functionary could not take a slave to France, Spain, or any other country of Europe, without emancipating him. A number of slaves escaped from a Florida plantation, and were received on board of ship by Admiral Cochrane; by the King's Bench, they were held to be free. (2 Barn. and Cres., 440.)

In the great and leading case of Prigg v. The State of Pennsylvania, (16 Peters, 594; 14 Curtis, 421,) this court say that, by the general law of nations, no nation is bound to recognise the state of slavery, as found within its territorial dominions, where it is in opposition to its own policy and institutions, in favor of the subjects of other nations where slavery is organized. If it does it, it is as a matter of comity, and not as a matter of international right. The state of slavery is deemed to be a mere municipal regulation, founded upon and limited to the range of the territorial laws. This was fully recognised in Somersett's case, (Lafft's Rep., 1; 20 Howell's State Trials, 79,) which was decided before the American Revolution.

There was some contrariety of opinion among the judges on certain points ruled in Prigg's case, but there was none in regard to the great principle, that slavery is limited to the range of the laws under which it is sanctioned.

No case in England appears to have been more thoroughly examined than that of Somersett. The judgment pronounced [60 U.S. 393, 535] by Lord Mansfield was the judgment of the Court of King's Bench. The cause was argued at great length, and with great ability, by Hargrave and others, who stood among the most eminent counsel in England. It was held under advisement from term to term, and a due sense of its importance was felt and expressed by the Bench.

In giving the opinion of the court, Lord Mansfield said:

"The state of slavery is of such a nature that it is incapable of being introduced on any reasons, moral or political, but only by positive law, which preserves its force long after the reasons, occasion, and time itself, from whence it was created, is erased from the memory; it is of a nature that nothing can be suffered to support it but positive law."

He referred to the contrary opinion of Lord Hardwicke, in October, 1749, as Chancellor: "That he and Lord Talbot, when Attorney and Solicitor General, were of opinion that no such claim, as here presented, for freedom, was valid."

The weight of this decision is sought to be impaired, from the terms in which it was described by the exuberant imagination of Curran. The words of Lord Mansfield, in giving the opinion of the court, were such as were fit to be used by a great judge, in a most important case. It is a sufficient answer to all objections to that judgment, that it was pronounced before the Revolution, and that it was considered by this court as the highest authority. For near a century, the decision in Somersett's case has remained the law of England. The case of the slave Grace, decided by Lord Stowell in 1827, does not, as has been supposed, overrule the judgment of Lord Mansfield. Lord Stowell held that, during the residence of the slave in England, "No dominion, authority, or coercion, can be exercised over him." Under another head, I shall have occasion to examine the opinion in the case of Grace.

To the position, that slavery can only exist except under the authority of law, it is objected, that in few if in any instances has it been established by statutory enactment. This is no answer to the doctrine laid down by the court. Almost all the principles of the common law had their foundation in usage. Slavery was introduced into the colonies of this country by Great Britain at an early period of their history, and it was protected and cherished, until it became incorporated into the colonial policy. It is immaterial whether a system of slavery was introduced by express law, or otherwise, if it have the authority of law. There is no slave State where the institution is not recognised and protected by statutory enactments and judicial decisions. Slaves are made property by the laws of the slave States, and as such are liable to the claims of creditors; [60 U.S. 393, 536] they descend to heirs, are taxed, and in the South they are a subject of commerce.

In the case of Rankin v. Lydia, (2 A. K. Marshall's Rep.,) Judge Mills, speaking for the Court of Appeals of Kentucky, says: "In deciding the question, (of slavery,) we disclaim the influence of the general principles of liberty, which we all admire, and conceive it ought to be decided by the law as it is, and not as it ought to be. Slavery is sanctioned by the laws of this State, and the right to hold slaves under our municipal regulations is unquestionable. But we view this as a right existing by positive law of a municipal character, without foundation in the law of nature, or the unwritten and common law."

I will now consider the relation which the Federal Government bears to slavery in the States:

Slavery is emphatically a State institution. In the ninth section of the first article of the Constitution, it is provided "that the migration or importation of such persons as any of the States now existing shall think proper to admit, shall not be prohibited by the Congress prior to the year 1808, but a tax or duty may be imposed on such importation, not exceeding ten dollars for each person."

In the Convention, it was proposed by a committee of eleven to limit the importation of slaves to the year 1800, when Mr. Pinckney moved to extend the time to the year 1808. This motion was carried—New Hampshire, Massachusetts, Connecticut, Maryland, North Carolina, South carolina, and Georgia, voting in the affirmative; and New Jersey, Pennsylvania, and Virginia, in the negative. In opposition to the motion, Mr. Madison said: "Twenty years will produce all the mischief that can be apprehended from the liberty to import slaves; so long a term will be more dishonorable to the American character than to say nothing about it in the Constitution." (Madison Papers.)

The provision in regard to the slave trade shows clearly that Congress considered slavery a State institution, to be continued and regulated by its individual sovereignty; and to conciliate that interest, the slave trade was continued twenty years, not as a general measure, but for the "benefit of such States as shall think proper to encourage it."

In the case of Groves v. Slaughter, (15 Peters, 499; 14 Curtis, 137,) Messrs. Clay and Webster contended that, under the commercial power, Congress had a right to regulate the slave trade among the several States; but the court held that Congress had no power to interfere with slavery as it exists in the States, or to regulate what is called the slave trade among [60 U.S. 393, 537] them. If this trade were subject to the commercial power, it would follow that Congress could abolish or establish slavery in every State of the Union.

The only connection which the Federal Government holds with slaves in a State, arises from that provision of the Constitution which declares that "No person held to service or labor in one State, under the laws thereof, escaping into another, shall, in consequence of any law or regulation therein, be discharged from such service or labor, but shall be delivered up, on claim of the party to whom such service or labor may be due."

This being a fundamental law of the Federal Government, it rests mainly for its execution, as has been held, on the judicial power of the Union; and so far as the rendition of fugitives from labor has become a subject of judicial action, the Federal obligation has been faithfully discharged.

In the formation of the Federal Constitution, care was taken to confer no power on the Federal Government to interfere with this institution in the States. In the provision respecting the slave trade, in fixing the ratio of representation, and providing for the reclamation of fugitives from labor, slaves were referred to as persons, and in no other respect are they considered in the Constitution.

We need not refer to the mercenary spirit which introduced the infamous traffic in slaves, to show the degradation of negro slavery in our country. This system was imposed upon our colonial settlements by the mother country, and it is due to truth to say that the commercial colonies and States were chiefly engaged in the traffic. But we know as a historical fact, that James Madison, that great and good man, a leading member in the Federal Convention, was solicitous to guard the language of that instrument so as not to convey the idea that there could be property in man.

I prefer the lights of Madison, Hamilton, and Jay, as a means of construing the Constitution in all its bearings, rather than to look behind that period, into a traffic which is now declared to be piracy, and punished with death by Christian nations. I do not like to draw the sources of our domestic relations from so dark a ground. Our independence was a great epoch in the history of freedom; and while I admit the Government was not made especially for the colored race, yet many of them were citizens of the New England States, and exercised, the rights of suffrage when the Constitution was adopted, and it was not doubted by any intelligent person that its tendencies would greatly ameliorate their condition.

Many of the States, on the adoption of the Constitution, or [60 U.S. 393, 538] shortly afterward, took measures to abolish slavery within their respective jurisdictions; and it is a well-known fact that a belief was cherished by the leading men, South as well as North, that the institution of slavery would gradually decline, until it would become extinct. The increased value of slave labor, in the culture of cotton and sugar, prevented the realization of this expectation. Like all other communities and States, the South were influenced by what they considered to be their own interests.

But if we are to turn our attention to the dark ages of the world, why confine our view to colored slavery? On the same principles, white men were made slaves. All slavery has its origin in power, and is against right.

The power of Congress to establish Territorial Governments, and to prohibit the introduction of slavery therein, is the next point to be considered.

After the cession of western territory by Virginia and other States, to the United States, the public attention was directed to the best mode of disposing of it for the general benefit. While in attendance on the Federal Convention, Mr. Madison, in a letter to Edmund Randolph, dated the 22d April, 1787, says: "Congress are deliberating on the plan most eligible for disposing of the western territory not yet surveyed. Some alteration will probably be made in the ordinance on that subject." And in the same letter he says: "The inhabitants of the Illinois complain of the land jobbers, &c., who are purchasing titles among them. Those of St. Vincent's complain of the defective criminal and civil justice among them, as well as of military protection." And on the next day he writes to Mr. Jefferson: "The government of the settlements on the Illinois and Wabash is a subject very perplexing in itself, and rendered more so by our ignorance of the many circumstances on which a right judgment depends. The inhabitants at those places claim protection against the savages, and some provision for both civil and criminal justice."

In May, 1787, Mr. Edmund Randolph submitted to the Federal Convention certain propositions, as the basis of a Federal Government, among which was the following:

"Resolved, That provision ought to be made for the admission of States lawfully arising within the limits of the United States, whether from a voluntary junction of government and territory or otherwise, with the consent of a number of voices in the National Legislature less than the whole."

Afterward, Mr. Madison submitted to the Convention, in order to be referred to the committee of detail, the following powers, as proper to be added to those of general legislation: [60 U.S. 393, 539] "To dispose of the unappropriated lands of the United States. To institute temporary Governments for new States arising therein. To regulate affairs with the Indians, as well within as without the limits of the United States."

Other propositions were made in reference to the same subjects, which it would be tedious to enumerate. Mr. Gouverneur Morris proposed the following:

> "The Legislature shall have power to dispose of and make all needful rules and regulations respecting the territory or other property belonging to the United States; and nothing in this Constitution contained shall be so construed as to prejudice any claims either of the United States or of any particular State."

This was adopted as a part of the Constitution, with two verbal alterations—Congress was substituted for Legislature, and the word either was stricken out.

In the organization of the new Government, but little revenue for a series of years was expected from commerce. The public lands were considered as the principal resource of the country for the payment of the Revolutionary debt. Direct taxation was the means relied on to pay the current expenses of the Government. The short period that occurred between the cession of western lands to the Federal Government by Virginia and other States, and the adoption of the Constitution, was sufficient to show the necessity of a proper land system and a temporary Government. This was clearly seen by propositions and remarks in the Federal Convention, some of which are above cited, by the passage of the Ordinance of 1787, and the adoption of that instrument by Congress, under the Constitution, which gave to it validity.

It will be recollected that the deed of cession of western territory was made to the United States by Virginia in 1784, and that it required the territory ceded to be laid out into States, that the land should be disposed of for the common benefit of the States, and that all right, title, and claim, as well of soil as of jurisdiction, were ceded; and this was the form of cession from other States.

On the 13th of July, the Ordinance of 1787 was passed, "for the government of the United States territory northwest of the river Ohio," with but one dissenting vote. This instrument provided there should be organized in the territory not less than three nor more than five States, designating their boundaries. It passed while the Federal Convention was in session, about two months before the Constitution was adopted by the Convention. The members of the Convention must therefore have been well acquainted with the provisions of the [60 U.S. 393, 540] Ordinance. It provided for a temporary Government, as initiatory to the formation of State Governments. Slavery was prohibited in the territory.

Can any one suppose that the eminent men of the Federal Convention could have overlooked or neglected a matter so vitally important to the country, in the organization of temporary Governments for the vast territory northwest of the river Ohio? In the 3d section of the 4th article of the Constitution, they did make provision for the admission of new States, the sale of the public lands, and the temporary Government of the territory. Without a temporary Government, new States could not have been formed, nor could the public lands have been sold.

If the third section were before us now for consideration for the first time, under the facts stated, I could not hesitate to say there was adequate legislative power given in it. The power to make all needful rules and regulations is a power to legislate. This no one will controvert, as Congress cannot make "rules and regulations," except by legislation. But it is argued that the word territory is used as synonymous with the word land; and that the rules and regulations of Congress are limited to the disposition of lands and other property belonging to the United States. That this is not the true construction of the section appears from the fact that in the first line of the section "the power to dispose of the public lands" is given expressly, and, in addition, to make all needful rules and regulations. The power to dispose of is complete in itself, and requires nothing more. It authorizes Congress to use the proper means within its discretion, and any further provision for this purpose would be a useless verbiage. As a composition, the Constitution is remarkably free from such a charge.

In the discussion of the power of Congress to govern a Territory, in the case of the Atlantic Insurance Company v. Canter, (1 Peters, 511; 7 Curtis, 685,) Chief Justice Marshall, speaking for the court, said, in regard to the people of Florida, "they do not, however, participate in political power; they do not share in the Government till Florida shall become a State; in the mean time, Florida continues to be a Territory of the United States, governed by virtue of that clause in the Constitution which empowers Congress "to make all needful rules and regulations respecting the territory or other property belonging to the United States."

And he adds, "perhaps the power of governing a Territory belonging to the United States, which has not, by becoming a State, acquired the means of self-government, may result [60 U.S. 393, 541] necessarily from the fact that it is not within the jurisdiction of any particular State, and is within the power and jurisdiction of the United States. The right to govern may be the inevitable consequence of the right to acquire territory; whichever may be the source whence the power is derived, the possession of it is unquestioned." And in the close of the opinion, the court say, "in legislating for them [the Territories,] Congress exercises the combined powers of the General and State Governments."

Some consider the opinion to be loose and inconclusive; others, that it is obiter dicta; and the last sentence is objected to as recognising absolute power in Congress over Territories. The learned and eloquent Wirt, who, in the argument of a cause before the court, had occasion to cite a few sentences from an opinion of the Chief Justice, observed, "no one can mistake the style, the words so completely match the thought."

I can see no want of precision in the language of the Chief Justice; his meaning cannot be mistaken. He states, first, the third section as giving power to Congress to govern the Territories, and two other grounds from which the power may also be implied. The objection seems to be, that the Chief Justice did not say which of the grounds stated he considered the source of the power. He did not specifically state this, but he did say, "whichever may be the source whence the power is derived, the possession of it is unquestioned." No opinion of the court could have been expressed with a stronger emphasis; the power in Congress is unquestioned. But those who have undertaken to criticise the opinion, consider it without authority, because the Chief Justice did not designate specially the power. This is a singular objection. If the power be unquestioned, it can be a matter of no importance on which ground it is exercised.

The opinion clearly was not obiter dicta. The turning point in the case was, whether Congress had power to authorize the Territorial Legislature of Florida to pass the law under which the Territorial court was established, whose decree was brought before this court for revision. The power of Congress, therefore, was the point in issue.

The word "territory," according to Worcester, "means land, country, a district of country under a temporary Government." The words "territory or other property," as used, do imply, from the use of the pronoun other, that territory was used as descriptive of land; but does it follow that it was not used also as descriptive of a district of country? In both of these senses it belonged to the United States–as land, for the purpose of sale; as territory, for the purpose of government. [60 U.S. 393, 542] But, if it be admitted that the word territory as used means land, and nothing but land, the power of Congress to organize a temporary Government is clear. It has power to make all needful regulations respecting the public lands, and the extent of those "needful regulations" depends upon the direction of Congress, where the means are appropriate to the end, and do not conflict with any of the prohibitions of the Constitution. If a temporary Government be deemed needful, necessary, requisite, or is wanted, Congress has power to establish it. This court says, in McCulloch v. The State of Maryland, (4 Wheat., 316,) "If a certain means to carry into effect any of the powers expressly given by the Constitution to the Government of the Union be an appropriate measure, not prohibited by the Constitution, the degree of its necessity is a question of legislative discretion, not of judicial cognizance."

The power to establish post offices and post roads gives power to Congress to make contracts for the transportation of the mail, and to punish all who commit depredations upon it in its transit, or at its places of distribution. Congress has power to regulate commerce, and, in the exercise of its discretion, to lay an embargo, which suspends commerce; so, under the same power, harbors, lighthouses, breakwaters, &c., are constructed.

Did Chief Justice Marshall, in saying that Congress governed a Territory, by exercising the combined powers of the Federal and State Governments, refer to unlimited discretion? A Government which can make white men slaves? Surely, such a remark in the argument must have been inadvertently uttered. On the contrary, there is no power in the Constitution by which Congress can make either white or black men slaves. In organizing the Government of a Territory, Congress is limited to means appropriate to the attainment of the constitutional object. No powers can be exercised which are prohibited by the Constitution, or which are contrary to its spirit; so that, whether the object may be the protection of the persons and property of purchasers of the public lands, or of communities who have been annexed to the Union by conquest or purchase, they are initiatory to the establishment of State Governments, and no more power can be claimed or exercised than is necessary to the attainment of the end. This is the limitation of all the Federal powers.

But Congress has no power to regulate the internal concerns of a State, as of a Territory; consequently, in providing for the Government of a Territory, to some extent, the combined powers of the Federal and State Governments are necessarily exercised. [60 U.S. 393, 543] If Congress should deem slaves or free colored persons injurious to the population of a free Territory, as conducing to lessen the value of the public lands, or on any other ground connected with the public interest, they have the power to prohibit them from becoming settlers in it. This can be sustained on the ground of a sound national policy, which is so clearly shown in our history by practical results, that it would seem no considerate individual can question it. And, as regards any unfairness of such a policy to our Southern brethren, as urged in the argument, it is only necessary to say that, with one-fourth of the Federal population of the Union, they have in the slave States a larger extent of fertile territory than is included in the free States; and it is submitted, if masters of slaves be restricted from bringing them into free territory, that the restriction on the free citizens of non-slaveholding States, by bringing slaves into free territory, is four times greater than that complained of by the South. But, not only so; some three or four hundred thousand holders of slaves, by bringing them into free territory, impose a restriction on twenty millions of the free States. The repugnancy to slavery would probably prevent fifty or a hundred freemen from settling in a slave Territory, where one slaveholder would be prevented from settling in a free Territory.

This remark is made in answer to the argument urged, that a prohibition of slavery in the free Territories is inconsistent with the continuance of the Union. Where a Territorial Government is established in a slave Territory, it has uniformly remained in that condition until the people form a State Constitution; the same course where the Territory is free, both parties acting in good faith, would be attended with satisfactory results.

The sovereignty of the Federal Government extends to the entire limits of our territory. Should any foreign power invade our jurisdiction, it would be repelled. There is a law of Congress to punish our citizens for crimes committed in districts of country where there is no organized Government. Criminals are brought to certain Territories or States, designated in the law, for punishment. Death has been inflicted in Arkansas and in Missouri, on individuals, for murders committed beyond the limit of any organized Territory or State; and no one doubts that such a jurisdiction was rightfully exercised. If there be a right to acquire territory, there necessarily must be an implied power to govern it. When the military force of the Union shall conquer a country, may not Congress provide for the government of such country? This would be an implied power essential to the acquisition of new territory. [60 U.S. 393, 544] This power has been exercised, without doubt of its constitutionality, over territory acquired by conquest and purchase.

And when there is a large district of country within the United States, and not within any State Government, if it be necessary to establish a temporary Government to carry out a power expressly vested in Congress—as the disposition of the public lands—may not such Government be instituted by Congress? How do we read the Constitution? Is it not a practical instrument?

In such cases, no implication of a power can arise which is inhibited by the Constitution, or which may be against the theory of its construction. As my opinion rests on the third section, these remarks are made as an intimation that the power to establish a temporary Government may arise, also, on the other two grounds stated in the opinion of the court in the insurance case, without weakening the third section.

I would here simply remark, that the Constitution was formed for our whole country. An expansion or contraction of our territory required no change in the fundamental law. When we consider the men who laid the foundation of our Government and carried it into operation, the men who occupied the bench, who filled the halls of legislation and the Chief Magistracy, it would seem, if any question could be settled clear of all doubt, it was the power of Congress to establish Territorial Governments. Slavery was prohibited in the entire Northwestern Territory, with the approbation of leading men, South and North; but this prohibition was not retained when this ordinance was adopted for the government of Southern Territories, where slavery existed. In a late republication of a letter of Mr. Madison, dated November 27, 1819, speaking of this power of Congress to prohibit slavery in a Territory, he infers there is no such power, from the fact that it has not been exercised. This is not a very satisfactory argument against any power, as there are but few, if any, subjects on which the constitutional powers of Congress are exhausted. It is true, as Mr. Madison states, that Congress, in the act to establish a Government in the Mississippi Territory, prohibited the importation of slaves into it from foreign parts; but it is equally true, that in the act erecting Louisiana into two Territories, Congress declared, "it shall not be lawful for any person to bring into Orleans Territory, from any port or place within the limits of the United States, any slave which shall have been imported since 1798, or which may hereafter be imported, except by a citizen of the United States who settles in the Territory, under the penalty of the freedom of such slave." The inference of Mr. Madison, therefore, against the power of [60 U.S. 393, 545] Congress, is of no force, as it was founded on a fact supposed, which did not exist.

It is refreshing to turn to the early incidents of our history, and learn wisdom from the acts of the great men who have gone to their account. I refer to a report in the House of Representatives, by John Randolph, of Roanoke, as chairman of a committee, in March, 1803—fifty-four years ago. From the Convention held at Vincennes, in Indiana, by their President, and from the people of the Territory, a petition was presented to Congress, praying the suspension of the provision which prohibited slavery in that Territory. The report stated "that the rapid population of the State of Ohio sufficiently evinces, in the opinion of your committee, that the labor of slaves is not necessary to promote the growth and settlement of colonies in that region. That this labor, demonstrably the dearest of any, can only be employed to advantage in the cultivation of products more valuable than any known to that quarter of the United States; that the committee deem it highly dangerous and inexpedient to impair a provision wisely calculated to promote the happiness and prosperity of the Northwestern country, and to give strength and security to that extensive frontier. In the salutary operation of this sagacious and benevolent restraint, it is believed that the inhabitants will, at no very distant day, find ample remuneration for a temporary privation of labor and of emigration." (1 vol. State Papers, Public Lands, 160.)

The judicial mind of this country, State and Federal, has agreed on no subject, within its legitimate action, with equal unanimity, as on the power of Congress to establish Territorial Governments. No court, State or Federal, no judge or statesman, is known to have had any doubts on this question for nearly sixty years after the power was exercised. Such Governments have been established from the sources of the Ohio to the Gulf of Mexico, extending to the Lakes on the north and the Pacific Ocean on the west, and from the lines of Georgia to Texas.

Great interests have grown up under the Territorial laws over a country more than five times greater in extent than the original thirteen States; and these interests, corporate or otherwise, have been cherished and consolidated by a benign policy, without any one supposing the law- making power had united with the Judiciary, under the universal sanction of the whole country, to usurp a jurisdiction which did not belong to them. Such a discovery at this late date is more extraordinary than anything which has occurred in the judicial history of this or any other country. Texas, under a previous organization, [60 U.S. 393, 546] was admitted as a State; but no State can be admitted into the Union which has not been organized under some form of government. Without temporary Governments, our public lands could not have been sold, nor our wildernesses reduced to cultivation, and the population protected; nor could our flourishing States, West and South, have been formed.

What do the lessons of wisdom and experience teach, under such circumstances, if the new light, which has so suddenly and unexpectedly burst upon us, be true? Acquiescence; acquiescence under a settled construction of the Constitution for sixty years, though it may be erroneous; which has secured to the country an advancement and prosperity beyond the power of computation.

An act of James Madison, when President, forcibly illustrates this policy. He had made up his opinion that Congress had no power under the Constitution to establish a National Bank. In 1815, Congress passed a bill to establish a bank. He vetoed the bill, on objections other than constitutional. In his message, he speaks as a wise statesman and Chief Magistrate, as follows:

> "Waiving the question of the constitutional authority of the Legislature to establish an incorporated bank, as being precluded, in my judgment, by the repeated recognitions under varied circumstances of the validity of such an institution, in acts of the Legislative, Executive, and Judicial branches of the Government, accompanied by indications, in different modes, of a concurrence of the general will of the nation."

Has this impressive lesson of practical wisdom become lost to the present generation?

If the great and fundamental principles of our Government are never to be settled, there can be no lasting prosperity. The Constitution will become a floating waif on the billows of popular excitement.

The prohibition of slavery north of thirty-six degrees thirty minutes, and of the State of Missouri, contained in the act admitting that State into the Union, was passed by a vote of 134, in the House of Representatives, to 42. Before Mr. Monroe signed the act, it was submitted by him to his Cabinet, and they held the restriction of slavery in a Territory to be within the constitutional powers of Congress. It would be singular, if in 1804 Congress had power to prohibit the introduction of slaves in Orleans Territory from any other part of the Union, under the penalty of freedom to the slave, if the same power, embodied in the Missouri compromise, could not be exercised in 1820.

But this law of Congress, which prohibits slavery north of [60 U.S. 393, 547] Missouri and of thirty-six degrees thirty minutes, is declared to have been null and void by my brethren. And this opinion is founded mainly, as I understand, on the distinction drawn between the ordinance of 1787 and the Missouri compromise line. In what does the distinction consist? The ordinance, it is said, was a compact entered into by the confederated States before the adoption of the Constitution; and that in the cession of territory authority was given to establish a Territorial Government.

It is clear that the ordinance did not go into operation by virtue of the authority of the Confederation, but by reason of its modification and adoption by Congress under the Constitution. It seems to be supposed, in the opinion of the court, that the articles of cession placed it on a different footing from territories subsequently acquired. I am unable to perceive the force of this distinction. That the ordinance was intended for the government of the Northwestern Territory, and was limited to such Territory, is admitted. It was extended to Southern Territories, with modifications, by acts of Congress, and to some Northern Territories. But the ordinance was made valid by the act of Congress, and without such act could have been of no force. It rested for its validity on the act of Congress, the same, in my opinion, as the Missouri compromise line.

If Congress may establish a Territorial Government in the exercise of its discretion, it is a clear principle that a court cannot control that discretion. This being the case, I do not see on what ground the act is held to be void. It did not purport to forfeit property, or take it for public purposes. It only prohibited slavery; in doing which, it followed the ordinance of 1787.

I will now consider the fourth head, which is: "The effect of taking slaves into a State or Territory, and so holding them, where slavery is prohibited."

If the principle laid down in the case of Prigg v. The State of Pennsylvania is to be maintained, and it is certainly to be maintained until overruled, as the law of this court, there can be no difficulty on this point. In that case, the court says: "The state of slavery is deemed to be a mere municipal regulation, founded upon and limited to the range of the territorial laws." If this be so, slavery can exist nowhere except under the authority of law, founded on usage having the force of law, or by statutory recognition. And the court further says: "It is manifest, from this consideration, that if the Constitution had not contained the clause requiring the rendition of fugitives from labor, every non-slaveholding State in the Union would have been at liberty to have declared free all runaway slaves [60 U.S. 393, 548] coming within its limits, and to have given them entire immunity and protection against the claims of their masters."

Now, if a slave abscond, he may be reclaimed; but if he accompany his master into a State or Territory where slavery is prohibited, such slave cannot be said to have left the service of his master where his services were legalized. And if slavery be limited to the range of the territorial laws, how can the slave be coerced to serve in a State or Territory, not only without the authority of law, but against its express provisions? What gives the master the right to control the will of his slave? The local law, which exists in some form. But where there is no such law, can the master control the will of the slave by force? Where no slavery exists, the presumption, without regard to color, is in favor of freedom. Under such a jurisdiction, may the colored man be levied on as the property of his master by a creditor? On the decease of the master, does the slave descend to his heirs as property? Can the master sell him? Any one or all of these acts may be done to the slave, where he is legally held to service. But where the law does not confer this power, it cannot be exercised.

Lord Mansfield held that a slave brought into England was free. Lord Stowell agreed with Lord Mansfield in this respect, and that the slave could not be coerced in England; but on her voluntary return to Antigua, the place of her slave domicil, her former status attached. The law of England did not prohibit slavery, but did not authorize it. The jurisdiction which prohibits slavery is much stronger in behalf of the slave within it, than where it only does not authorize it.

By virtue of what law is it, that a master may take his slave into free territory, and exact from him the duties of a slave? The law of the Territory does not sanction it. No authority can be claimed under the Constitution of the United States, or any law of Congress. Will it be said that the slave is taken as property, the same as other property which the master may own? To this I answer, that colored persons are made property by the law of the State, and no such power has been given to Congress. Does the master carry with him the law of the State from which he removes into the Territory? and does that enable him to coerce his slave in the Territory? Let us test this theory. If this may be done by a master from one slave State, it may be done by a master from every other slave State. This right is supposed to be connected with the person of the master, by virtue of the local law. Is it transferable? May it be negotiated, as a promissory note or bill of exchange? If it be assigned to a man from a free State, may he coerce the slave by virtue of it? What shall this thing be [60 U.S. 393, 549] denominated? Is it personal or real property? Or is it an indefinable fragment of sovereignty, which every person carries with him from his late domicil? One thing is certain, that its origin has been very recent, and it is unknown to the laws of any civilized country.

A slave is brought to England from one of its islands, where slavery was introduced and maintained by the mother country. Although there is no law prohibiting slavery in England, yet there is no law authorizing it; and, for near a century, its courts have declared that the slave there is free from the coercion of the master. Lords Mansfield and Stowell agree upon this point, and there is no dissenting authority.

There is no other description of property which was not protected in England, brought from one of its slave islands. Does not this show that property in a human being does not arise from nature or from the common law, but, in the language of this court, "it is a mere municipal regulation, founded upon and limited to the range of the territorial laws?" This decision is not a mere argument, but it is the end of the law, in regard to the extent of slavery. Until it shall be overturned, it is not a point for argument; it is obligatory on myself and my brethren, and on all judicial tribunals over which this court exercises an appellate power.

It is said the Territories are common property of the States, and that every man has a right to go there with his property. This is not controverted. But the court say a slave is not property beyond the operation of the local law which makes him such. Never was a truth more authoritatively and justly uttered by man. Suppose a master of a slave in a British island owned a million of property in England; would that authorize him to take his slaves with him to England? The Constitution, in express terms, recognises the status of slavery as founded on the municipal law: "No person held to service or labor in one State, under the laws thereof, escaping into another, shall," &c. Now, unless the fugitive escape from a place where, by the municipal law, he is held to labor, this provision affords no remedy to the master. What can be more conclusive than this? Suppose a slave escape from a Territory where slavery is not authorized by law, can he be reclaimed?

In this case, a majority of the court have said that a slave may be taken by his master into a Territory of the United States, the same as a horse, or any other kind of property. It is true, this was said by the court, as also many other things, which are of no authority. Nothing that has been said by them, which has not a direct bearing on the jurisdiction of the court, against which they decided, can be considered as [60 U.S. 393, 550] authority. I shall certainly not regard it as such. The question of jurisdiction, being before the court, was decided by them authoritatively, but nothing beyond that question. A slave is not a mere chattel. He bears the impress of his Maker, and is amenable to the laws of God and man; and he is destined to an endless existence.

Under this head I shall chiefly rely on the decisions of the Supreme Courts of the Southern States, and especially of the State of Missouri.

In the first and second sections of the sixth article of the Constitution of Illinois, it is declared that neither slavery nor involuntary servitude shall hereafter be introduced into this State, otherwise than for the punishment of crimes whereof the party shall have been duly convicted; and in the second section it is declared that any violation of this article shall effect the emancipation of such person from his obligation to service. In Illinois, a right of transit through the State is given the master with his slaves. This is a matter which, as I suppose, belongs exclusively to the State.

The Supreme Court of Illinois, in the case of Jarrot v. Jarrot, (2 Gilmer, 7,) said:

> "After the conquest of this Territory by Virginia, she ceded it to the United States, and stipulated that the titles and possessions, rights and liberties, of the French settlers, should be guarantied to them. This, it has been contended, secured them in the possession of those negroes as slaves which they held before that time, and that neither Congress nor the Convention had power to deprive them of it; or, in other words, that the ordinance and Constitution should not be so interpreted and understood as applying to such slaves, when it is therein declared that there shall be neither slavery nor involuntary servitude in the Northwest Territory, nor in the State of Illinois, otherwise than in the punishment of crimes. But it was held that those rights could not be thus protected, but must yield to the ordinance and Constitution."

The first slave case decided by the Supreme Court of Missouri, contained in the reports, was Winny v. Whitesides, (1 Missouri Rep., 473,) at October term, 1824. It appeared that, more than twenty-five years before, the defendant, with her husband, had removed from Carolina to

Illinois, and brought with them the plaintiff; that they continued to reside in Illinois three or four years, retaining the plaintiff as a slave; after which, they removed to Missouri, taking her with them.

The court held, that if a slave be detained in Illinois until he be entitled to freedom, the right of the owner does not revive when he finds the negro in a slave State. [60 U.S. 393, 551] That when a slave is taken to Illinois by his owner, who takes up his residence there, the slave is entitled to freedom.

In the case of Lagrange v. Chouteau, (2 Missouri Rep., 20, at May term, 1828,) it was decided that the ordinance of 1787 was intended as a fundamental law for those who may choose to live under it, rather than as a penal statute.

That any sort of residence contrived or permitted by the legal owner of the slave, upon the faith of secret trusts or contracts, in order to defeat or evade the ordinance, and thereby introduce slavery de facto, would entitle such slave to freedom.

In Julia v. McKinney, (3 Missouri Rep., 279,) it was held, where a slave was settled in the State of Illinois, but with an intention on the part of the owner to be removed at some future day, that hiring said slave to a person to labor for one or two days, and receiving the pay for the hire, the slave is entitled to her freedom, under the second section of the sixth article of the Constitution of Illinois.

Rachel v. Walker (4 Missouri Rep., 350, June term, 1836) is a case involving, in every particular, the principles of the case before us. Rachel sued for her freedom; and it appeared that she had been bought as a slave in Missouri, by Stockton, an officer of the army, taken to Fort Snelling, where he was stationed, and she was retained there as a slave a year; and then Stockton removed to Prairie du Chien, taking Rachel with him as a slave, where he continued to hold her three years, and then he took her to the State of Missouri, and sold her as a slave.

> "Fort Snelling was admitted to be on the west side of the Mississippi river, and north of the State of Missouri, in the territory of the United States. That Prairie du Chien was in the Michigan Territory, on the east side of the Mississippi river. Walker, the defendant, held Rachel under Stockton."

The court said, in this case:

> "The officer lived in Missouri Territory, at the time he bought the slave; he sent to a slaveholding country and procured her; this was his voluntary act, done without any other reason than that of his convenience; and he and those claiming under him must be holden to

abide the consequences of introducing slavery both in Missouri Territory and Michigan, contrary to law; and on that ground Rachel was declared to be entitled to freedom." In answer to the argument that, as an officer of the army, the master had a right to take his slave into free territory, the court said no authority of law or the Government compelled him to keep the plaintiff there as a slave. "Shall it be said, that because an officer of the army owns [60 U.S. 393, 552] slaves in Virginia, that when, as officer and soldier, he is required to take the command of a fort in the non-slaveholding States or Territories, he thereby has a right to take with him as many slaves as will suit his interests or convenience? It surely cannot be law. If this be true, the court say, then it is also true that the convenience or supposed convenience of the officer repeals, as to him and others who have the same character, the ordinance and the act of 1821, admitting Missouri into the Union, and also the prohibition of the several laws and Constitutions of the non-slaveholding States."

In Wilson v. Melvin, (4 Missouri R., 592,) it appeared the defendant left Tennessee with an intention of residing in Illinois, taking his negroes with him. After a month's stay in Illinois, he took his negroes to St. Louis, and hired them, then returned to Illinois. On these facts, the inferior court instructed the jury that the defendant was a sojourner in Illinois. This the Supreme Court held was error, and the judgment was reversed.

The case of Dred Scott v. Emerson (15 Missouri R., 682, March term, 1852) will now be stated. This case involved the identical question before us, Emerson having, since the hearing, sold the plaintiff to Sandford, the defendant.

Two of the judges ruled the case, the Chief Justice dissenting. It cannot be improper to state the grounds of the opinion of the court, and of the dissent.

The court say: "Cases of this kind are not strangers in our court. Persons have been frequently here adjudged to be entitled to their freedom, on the ground that their masters held them in slavery in Territories or States in which that institution is prohibited. From the first case decided in our court, it might be inferred that this result was brought about by a presumed assent of the master, from the fact of having voluntarily taken his slave to a place where the relation of master and slave did not exist. But subsequent cases base the right to "exact the forfeiture of emancipation," as they term it, on the ground, it would seem, that it was the duty of the courts of this State to carry into effect the Constitution and laws of other States and Territories, regardless of the rights, the policy, or the institutions, of the people of this State."

And the court say that the States of the Union, in their municipal concerns, are regarded as foreign to each other; that the courts of one State do not take notice of the laws of other States, unless proved as facts, and that every State has the right to determine how far its comity to other States shall extend; and it is laid down, that when there is no act of manumission decreed to the free State, the courts of the slave States [60 U.S. 393, 553] cannot be called to give effect to the law of the free State. Comity, it alleges, between States, depends upon the discretion of both, which may be varied by circumstances. And it is declared by the court, "that times are not as they were when the former decisions on this subject were made." Since then, not only individuals but States have been possession with a dark and fell spirit in relation to slavery, whose gratification is sought in the pursuit of measures whose inevitable consequence must be the overthrow and destruction of our Government. Under such circumstances, it does not behoove the State of Missouri to show the least countenance to any measure which might gratify this spirit. She is willing to assume her full responsibility for the existence of slavery within her limits, nor does she seek to share or divide it with others.

Chief Justice Gamble dissented from the other two judges. He says:

> "In every slaveholding State in the Union, the subject of emancipation is regulated by statute; and the forms are prescribed in which it shall be effected. Whenever the forms required by the laws of the State in which the master and slave are resident are complied with, the emancipation is complete, and the slave is free. If the right of the person thus emancipated is subsequently drawn in question in another State, it will be ascertained and determined by the law of the State in which the slave and his former master resided; and when it appears that such law has been complied with, the right to freedom will be fully sustained in the courts of all the slaveholding States, although the act of emancipation may not be in the form required by law in which the court sits.
>
> "In all such cases, courts continually administer the law of the country where the right was acquired; and when that law becomes known to the court, it is just as much a matter of course to decide the rights of the parties according to its requirements, as it is to settle the title of real estate situated in our State by its own laws."

This appears to me a most satisfactory answer to the argument of the court. Chief Justice continues:

> "The perfect equality of the different States lies at the foundation of the Union. As the institution of slavery in the States is one over

which the Constitution of the United States gives no power to the General Government, it is left to be adopted or rejected by the several States, as they think best; nor can any one State, or number of States, claim the right to interfere with any other State upon the question of admitting or excluding this institution.

"A citizen of Missouri, who removes with his slave to Illinois, [60 U.S. 393, 554] has no right to complain that the fundamental law of that State to which he removes, and in which he makes his residence, dissolves the relation between him and his slave. It is as much his own voluntary act, as if he had executed a deed of emancipation. No one can pretend ignorance of this constitutional provision, and," he says, "the decisions which have heretofore been made in this State, and in many other slaveholding States, give effect to this and other similar provisions, on the ground that the master, by making the free State the residence of his slave, has submitted his right to the operation of the law of such State; and this," he says, "is the same in law as a regular deed of emancipation."

He adds:

"I regard the question as conclusively settled by repeated adjudications of this court, and, if I doubted or denied the propriety of those decisions, I would not feel myself any more at liberty to overturn them, than I would any other series of decisions by which the law of any other question was settled. There is with me," he says, "nothing in the law relating to slavery which distinguishes it from the law on any other subject, or allows any more accommodation to the temporary public excitements which are gathered around it."

"In this State," he says, "it has been recognised from the beginning of the Government as a correct position in law, that a master who takes his slave to reside in a State or Territory where slavery is prohibited, thereby emancipates his slave." These decisions, which come down to the year 1837, seemed to have so fully settled the question, that since that time there has been no case bringing it before the court for any reconsideration, until the present. In the case of Winny v. Whitesides, the question was made in the argument, "whether one nation would execute the penal laws of another," and the court replied in this language, (Huberus, quoted in 4 Dallas,) which says, "personal rights or disabilities obtained or communicated by the laws of any particular place are of a nature which accompany the person wherever he goes;" and the Chief Justice observed, in the case of Rachel v. Walker, the act of Congress called the Missouri compromise was held as operative as the ordinance of 1787.

When Dred Scott, his wife and children, were removed from Fort Snelling to Missouri, in 1838, they were free, as the law was then settled, and continued for fourteen years afterwards, up to 1852, when the above decision was made. Prior to this, for nearly thirty years, as Chief Justice Gamble declares, the residence of a master with his slave in the State of Illinois, or in the Territory north of Missouri, where slavery was prohibited [60 U.S. 393, 555] by the act called the Missouri compromise, would manumit the slave as effectually as if he had executed a deed of emancipation; and that an officer of the army who takes his slave into that State or Territory, and holds him there as a slave, liberates him the same as any other citizen—and down to the above time it was settled by numerous and uniform decisions, and that on the return of the slave to Missouri, his former condition of slavery did not attach. Such was the settled law of Missouri until the decision of Scott and Emerson.

In the case of Sylvia v. Kirby, (17 Misso. Rep., 434,) the court followed the above decision, observing it was similar in all respects to the case of Scott and Emerson.

This court follows the established construction of the statutes of a State by its Supreme Court. Such a construction is considered as a part of the statute, and we follow it to avoid two rules of property in the same State. But we do not follow the decisions of the Supreme Court of a State beyond a statutory construction as a rule of decision for this court. State decisions are always viewed with respect and treated as authority; but we follow the settled construction of the statutes, not because it is of binding authority, but in pursuance of a rule of judicial policy.

But there is no pretence that the case of Dred Scott v. Emerson turned upon the construction of a Missouri statute; nor was there any established rule of property which could have rightfully influenced the decision. On the contrary, the decision overruled the settled law for near thirty years.

This is said by my brethren to be a Missouri question; but there is nothing which gives it this character, except that it involves the right to persons claimed as slaves who reside in Missouri, and the decision was made by the Supreme Court of that State. It involves a right claimed under an act of Congress and the Constitution of Illinois, and which cannot be decided without the consideration and construction of those laws. But the Supreme Court of Missouri held, in this case, that it will not regard either of those laws, without which there was no case before it; and Dred Scott, having been a slave, remains a slave. In this respect it is admitted this is a Missouri question—a case which has but one side, if the act of Congress and the Constitution of Illinois are not recognised.

And does such a case constitute a rule of decision for this court—a case to be followed by this court? The course of decision so long and so uniformly maintained established a comity or law between Missouri and the free States and Territories where slavery was prohibited, which must be somewhat regarded in this case. Rights sanctioned for twenty-eight years [60 U.S. 393, 556] ought not and cannot be repudiated, with any semblance of justice, by one or two decisions, influenced, as declared, by a determination to counteract the excitement against slavery in the free States.

The courts of Louisiana having held, for a series of years, that where a master took his slave to France, or any free State, he was entitled to freedom, and that on bringing him back the status of slavery did not attach, the Legislature of Louisiana declared by an act that the slave should not be made free under such circumstances. This regulated the rights of the master from the time the act took effect. But the decision of the Missouri court, reversing a former decision, affects all previous decisions, technically, made on the same principles, unless such decisions are protected by the lapse of time or the statute of limitations. Dred Scott and his family, beyond all controversy, were free under the decisions made for twenty-eight years, before the case of Scott v. Emerson. This was the undoubted law of Missouri for fourteen years after Scott and his family were brought back to that State. And the grave question arises, whether this law may be so disregarded as to enslave free persons. I am strongly inclined to think that a rule of decision so well settled as not to be questioned, cannot be annulled by a single decision of the court. Such rights may be inoperative under the decision in future; but I cannot well perceive how it can have the same effect in prior cases.

It is admitted, that when a former decision is reversed, the technical effect of the judgment is to make all previous adjudications on the same question erroneous. But the case before us was not that the law had been erroneously construed, but that, under the circumstances which then existed, that law would not be recognised; and the reason for this is declared to be the excitement against the institution of slavery in the free States. While I lament this excitement as much as any one, I cannot assent that it shall be made a basis of judicial action.

In 1816, the common law, by statute, was made a part of the law of Missouri; and that includes the great principles of international law. These principles cannot be abrogated by judicial decisions. It will require the same exercise of power to abolish the common law, as to introduce it. International law is founded in the opinions generally received and acted on by civilized nations, and enforced by moral sanctions. It becomes a more authoritative system when it results from special compacts, founded on modified rules, adapted to the exigencies of human society; it is in fact an international morality, adapted to the best interests of nations. And in regard to the States [60 U.S. 393, 557] of this Union, on the subject of slavery, it is eminently fitted for a rule of action, subject to the Federal Constitution. "The laws of nations are but the natural rights of man applied to nations." (Vattel.)

If the common law have the force of a statutory enactment in Missouri, it is clear, as it seems to me, that a slave who, by a residence in Illinois in the service of his master, becomes entitled to his freedom, cannot again be reduced to slavery by returning to his former domicil in a slave State. It is unnecessary to say what legislative power might do by a general act in such a case, but it would be singular if a freeman could be made a slave by the exercise of a judicial discretion. And it would be still more extraordinary if this could be done, not only in the absence of special legislation, but in a State where the common law is in force.

It is supposed by some, that the third article in the treaty of cession of Louisiana to this country, by France, in 1803, may have some bearing on this question. The article referred to provides, "that the inhabitants of the ceded territory shall be incorporated into the Union, and enjoy all the advantages of citizens of the United States, and in the mean time they shall be maintained and protected in the free enjoyment of their liberty, property, and the religion they profess."

As slavery existed in Louisiana at the time of the cession, it is supposed this is a guaranty that there should be no change in its condition.

The answer to this is, in the first place, that such a subject does not belong to the treaty-making power; and any such arrangement would have been nugatory. And, in the second place, by no admissible construction can the guaranty be carried further than the protection of property in slaves at that time in the ceded territory. And this has been complied with. The organization of the slave States of Louisiana, Missouri, and Arkansas, embraced every slave in Louisiana at the time of the cession. This removes every ground of objection under the treaty. There is therefore no pretence, growing out of the treaty, that any part of the territory of Louisiana, as ceded, beyond the organized States, is slave territory.

Under the fifth head, we were to consider whether the status of slavery attached to the plaintiff and wife, on their return to Missouri.

This doctrine is not asserted in the late opinion of the Supreme Court of Missouri, and up to 1852 the contrary doctrine was uniformly maintained by that court.

In its late decision, the court say that it will not give effect in Missouri to the laws of Illinois, or the law of Congress [60 U.S. 393, 558] called the Missouri compromise. This was the effect of the decision, though its terms were, that the court would not take notice, judicially, of those laws.

In 1851, the Court of Appeals of South Carolina recognised the principle, that a slave, being taken to a free State, became free. (Commonwealth v. Pleasants, 10 Leigh Rep., 697.) In Betty v. Horton, the Court of Appeals held that the freedom of the slave was acquired by the action of the laws of Massachusetts, by the said slave being taken there. (5 Leigh Rep., 615.)

The slave States have generally adopted the rule, that where the master, by a residence with his slave in a State or Territory where slavery is prohibited, the slave was entitled to his freedom everywhere. This was the settled doctrine of the Supreme Court of Missouri. It has been so held in Mississippi, in Virginia, in Louisiana, formerly in Kentucky, Maryland, and in other States.

The law, where a contract is made and is to be executed, governs it. This does not depend upon comity, but upon the law of the contract. And if, in the language of the Supreme Court of Missouri, the master, by taking his slave to Illinois, and employing him there as a slave, emancipates him as effectually as by a deed of emancipation, is it possible that such an act is not matter for adjudication in any slave State where the master may take him? Does not the master assent to the law, when he places himself under it in a free State?

The States of Missouri and Illinois are bounded by a common line. The one prohibits slavery, the other admits it. This has been done by the exercise of that sovereign power which appertains to each. We are bound to respect the institutions of each, as emanating from the voluntary action of the people. Have the people of either any right to disturb the relations of the other? Each State rests upon the basis of its own sovereignty, protected by the Constitution. Our Union has been the foundation of our prosperity and national glory. Shall we not cherish and maintain it? This can only be done by respecting the legal rights of each State.

If a citizen of a free State shall entice or enable a slave to escape from the service of his master, the law holds him responsible, not only for the loss of the slave, but he is liable to be indicted and fined for the misdemeanor. And I am bound here to say, that I have never found a jury in the four States which constitute my circuit, which have not sustained this law, where the evidence required them to sustain it. And it is proper that I should also say, that more cases have arisen in my circuit, by reason of its extent and locality, than in all [60 U.S. 393, 559] other parts of the Union. This has been done to vindicate the sovereign rights of the Southern States, and protect the legal interests of our brethren of the South.

Let these facts be contrasted with the case now before the court. Illinois has declared in the most solemn and impressive form that there shall be neither slavery nor involuntary servitude in that State, and that any slave brought into it, with a view of becoming a resident, shall be emancipated. And effect has been given to this provision of the Constitution by the decision of the Supreme Court of that State. With a full knowledge of these facts, a slave is brought from Missouri to Rock Island, in the State of Illinois, and is retained there as a slave for two years, and then taken to Fort Snelling, where slavery is prohibited by the Missouri compromise act, and there he is detained two years longer in a state of slavery. Harriet, his wife, was also kept at the same place four years as a slave, having been purchased in Missouri. They were then removed to the State of Missouri, and sold as slaves, and in the action before us they are not only claimed as slaves, but a majority of my brethren have held that on their being returned to Missouri the status of slavery attached to them.

I am not able to reconcile this result with the respect due to the State of Illinois. Having the same rights of sovereignty as the State of Missouri in adopting a Constitution, I can perceive no reason why the institutions of Illinois should not receive the same consideration as those of Missouri. Allowing to my brethren the same right of judgment that I exercise myself, I must be permitted to say that it seems to me the principle laid down will enable the people of a slave State to introduce slavery into a free State, for a longer or shorter time, as may suit their convenience; and by returning the slave to the State whence he was brought, by force or otherwise, the status of slavery attaches, and protects the rights of the master, and defies the sovereignty of the free State. There is no evidence before us that Dred Scott and his family returned to Missouri voluntarily. The contrary is inferable from the agreed case: "In the year 1838, Dr. Emerson removed the plaintiff and said Harriet, and their daughter Eliza, from Fort Snelling to the State of Missouri, where they have ever since resided." This is the agreed case; and can it be inferred from this that Scott and family returned to Missouri voluntarily? He was removed; which shows that he was passive, as a slave, having exercised no volition on the subject. He did not resist the master by absconding or force. But that was not sufficient to bring him within Lord Stowell's decision; he must have acted voluntarily. It would be a [60 U.S. 393, 560] mockery of law and an outrage on his rights to coerce his return, and then claim that it was voluntary, and on that ground that his former status of slavery attached.

If the decision be placed on this ground, it is a fact for a jury to decide, whether the return was voluntary, or else the fact should be distinctly admitted. A presumption against the plaintiff in this respect, I say with confidence, is not authorized from the facts admitted.

In coming to the conclusion that a voluntary return by Grace to her former domicil, slavery attached, Lord Stowell took great pains to show that England forced slavery upon her colonies, and that it was maintained by numerous acts of Parliament and public policy, and, in short, that the system of slavery was not only established by Great Britain in her West Indian colonies, but that it was popular and profitable to many of the wealthy and influential people of England, who were engaged in trade, or owned and cultivated plantations in the colonies. No one can read his elaborate views, and not be struck with the great difference between England and her colonies, and the free and slave States of this Union. While slavery in the colonies of England is subject to the power of the mother country, our States, especially in regard to slavery, are independent, resting upon their own sovereignties, and subject only to international laws, which apply to independent States.

In the case of Williams, who was a slave in Granada, having run away, came to England, Lord Stowell said: "The four judges all concur in this— that he was a slave in Granada, though a free man in England, and he would have continued a free man in all other parts of the world except Granada."

Strader v. Graham (10 Howard, 82, and 18 Curtis, 305) has been cited as having a direct bearing in the case before us. In that case the court say: "It was exclusively in the power of Kentucky to determine, for itself, whether the employment of slaves in another State should or should not make them free on their return." No question was before the court in that case, except that of jurisdiction. And any opinion given on any other point is obiter dictum, and of no authority. In the conclusion of his opinion, the Chief Justice said: "In every view of the subject, therefore, this court has no jurisdiction of the case, and the writ of error must on that ground be dismissed."

In the case of Spencer v. Negro Dennis, (8 Gill's Rep., 321,) the court say: "Once free, and always free, is the maxim of Maryland law upon the subject. Freedom having once vested, by no compact between the master and the liberated slave, [60 U.S. 393, 561] nor by any condition subsequent, attached by the master to the gift of freedom, can a state of slavery be reproduced."

In Hunter v. Bulcher, (1 Leigh, 172:)

"By a statute of Maryland of 1796, all slaves brought into that State to reside are declared free; a Virginian-born slave is carried by his master to Maryland; the master settled there, and keeps the slave there in bondage for twelve years, the statute in force all the time; then he brings him as a slave to Virginia, and sells him there. Adjudged, in an action brought by the man against the purchaser, that he is free."

Judge Kerr, in the case, says:

"Agreeing, as I do, with the general view taken in this case by my brother Green, I would not add a word, but to mark the exact extent to which I mean to go. The law of Maryland having enacted that slaves carried into that State for sale or to reside shall be free, and the owner of the slave here having carried him to Maryland, and voluntarily submitting himself and the slave to that law, it governs the case."

In every decision of a slave case prior to that of Dred Scott v. Emerson, the Supreme Court of Missouri considered it as turning upon the Constitution of Illinois, the ordinance of 1787, or the Missouri compromise act of 1820. The court treated these acts as in force, and held itself bound to execute them, by declaring the slave to be free who had acquired a domicil under them with the consent of his master.

The late decision reversed this whole line of adjudication, and held that neither the Constitution and laws of the States, nor acts of Congress in relation to Territories, could be judicially noticed by the Supreme Court of Missouri. This is believed to be in conflict with the decisions of all the courts in the Southern States, with some exceptions of recent cases.

In Marie Louise v. Morat et al., (9 Louisiana Rep., 475,) it was held, where a slave having been taken to the kingdom of France or other country by the owner, where slavery is not tolerated, operates on the condition of the slave, and produces immediate emancipation; and that, where a slave thus becomes free, the master cannot reduce him again to slavery. Josephine v. Poultney, (Louisiana Annual Rep., 329,) "where the owner removes with a slave into a State in which slavery is prohibited, with the intention of residing there, the slave will be thereby emancipated, and their subsequent return to the State of Louisiana cannot restore the relation of master and slave." To the same import are the cases of Smith v. Smith, (13 Louisiana Rep., 441; Thomas v. Generis, Louisiana Rep., 483; Harry et al. v. Decker and Hopkins, Walker's Mississippi Rep., 36.) It was held that, "slaves within the jurisdiction [60 U.S. 393, 562] of the Northwestern Territory became freemen by virtue of the ordinance of 1787, and can assert their claim to freedom in the courts of Mississippi." (Griffith v. Fanny, 1 Virginia Rep., 143.) It was decided that a negro held in servitude in Ohio, under a deed executed in Virginia, is entitled to freedom by the Constitution of Ohio.

The case of Rhodes v. Bell (2 Howard, 307; 15 Curtis, 152) involved the main principle in the case before us. A person residing in Washington city purchased a slave in Alexandria, and brought him to Washington. Washington continued under the law of Maryland, Alexandria under the law of Virginia. The act of Maryland of November, 1796, (2 Maxcy's Laws, 351,) declared any one who shall bring any negro, mulatto, or other slave, into Maryland, such slave should be free. The above slave, by reason of his being brought into Washington city, was declared by this court to be free. This, it appears to me, is a much stronger case against the slave than the facts in the case of Scott.

In Bush v. White, (3 Monroe, 104,) the court say:

"That the ordinance was paramount to the Territorial laws, and restrained the legislative power there as effectually as a Constitution in an organized State. It was a public act of the Legislature of the Union, and a part of the supreme law of the land; and, as such, this court is as much bound to take notice of it as it can be of any other law."

In the case of Rankin v. Lydia, before cited, Judge Mills, speaking for the Court of Appeals of Kentucky, says:

"If, by the positive provision in our code, we can and must hold our slaves in the one case, and statutory provisions equally positive decide against that right in the other, and liberate the slave, he must, by an authority equally imperious, be declared free. Every argument which supports the right of the master on one side, based upon the force of written law, must be equally conclusive in favor of the slave, when he can point out in the statute the clause which secures his freedom."

And he further said:

"Free people of color in all the States are, it is believed, quasi citizens, or, at least, denizens. Although none of the States may allow them the privilege of office and suffrage, yet all other civil and conventional rights are secured to them; at least, such rights were evidently secured to them by the ordinance in question for the government of Indiana. If these rights are vested in that or any other portion of the United States, can it be compatible with the spirit of our confederated Government to deny their existence in any other part? Is there less comity existing between State and State, or State [60 U.S. 393, 563] and Territory, than exists between the despotic Governments of Europe?"

These are the words of a learned and great judge, born and educated in a slave State.

I now come to inquire, under the sixth and last head, "whether the decisions of the Supreme Court of Missouri, on the question before us, are binding on this court."

While we respect the learning and high intelligence of the State courts, and consider their decisions, with others, as authority, we follow them only where they give a construction to the State statutes. On this head, I consider myself fortunate in being able to turn to the decision of this court, given by Mr. Justice Grier, in Pease v. Peck, a case from the State of Michigan, (18 Howard, 589,) decided in December term, 1855. Speaking for the court, Judge Grier said:

> "We entertain the highest respect for that learned court, (the Supreme Court of Michigan,) and in any question affecting the construction of their own laws, where we entertain any doubt, would be glad to be relieved from doubt and responsibility by reposing on their decision. There are, it is true, many dicta to be found in our decisions, averring that the courts of the United States are bound to follow the decisions of the State courts on the construction of their own laws. But although this may be correct, yet a rather strong expression of a general rule, it cannot be received as the annunciation of a maxim of universal application. Accordingly, our reports furnish many cases of exceptions to it. In all cases where there is a settled construction of the laws of the State, by its highest judicature established by admitted precedent, it is the practice of the courts of the United States to receive and adopt it, without criticism or further inquiry. When the decisions of the State court are not consistent, we do not feel bound to follow the last, if it is contrary to our own convictions; and much more is this the case where, after a long course of consistent decisions, some new light suddenly springs up, or an excited public opinion has elicited new doctrines subversive of former safe precedent."

These words, it appears to me, have a stronger application to the case before us than they had to the cause in which they were spoken as the opinion of this court; and I regret that they do not seem to be as fresh in the recollection of some of my brethren as in my own. For twenty-eight years, the decisions of the Supreme Court of Missouri were consistent on all the points made in this case. But this consistent course was suddenly terminated, whether by some new light suddenly springing up, or an excited public opinion, or both, it is not [60 U.S. 393, 564] necessary to say. In the case of Scott v. Emerson, in 1852, they were overturned and repudiated.

This, then, is the very case in which seven of my brethren declared they would not follow the last decision. On this authority I may well repose. I can desire no other or better basis.

But there is another ground which I deem conclusive, and which I will re-state.

The Supreme Court of Missouri refused to notice the act of Congress or the Constitution of Illinois, under which Dred Scott, his wife and children, claimed that they are entitled to freedom.

This being rejected by the Missouri court, there was no case before it, or least it was a case with only one side. And this is the case which, in the opinion of this court, we are bound to follow. The Missouri court disregards the express provisions of an act of Congress and the Constitution of a sovereign State, both of which laws for twenty-eight years it had not only regarded, but carried into effect.

If a State court may do this, on a question involving the liberty of a human being, what protection do the laws afford? So far from this being a Missouri question, it is a question, as it would seem, within the twenty-fifth section of the judiciary act, where a right to freedom being set up under the act of Congress, and the decision being against such right, it may be brought for revision before this court, from the Supreme Court of Missouri. I think the judgment of the court below should be reversed.

Mr. Justice CURTIS dissenting.

I dissent from the opinion pronounced by the Chief Justice, and from the judgment which the majority of the court think it proper to render in this case. The plaintiff alleged, in his declaration, that he was a citizen of the State of Missouri, and that the defendant was a citizen of the State of New York. It is not doubted that it was necessary to make each of these allegations, to sustain the jurisdiction of the Circuit Court. The defendant denied, by a plea to the jurisdiction, either sufficient or insufficient, that the plaintiff was a citizen of the State of Missouri. The plaintiff demurred to that plea. The Circuit Court adjudged the plea insufficient, and the first question for our consideration is, whether the sufficiency of that plea is before this court for judgment, upon this writ of error. The part of the judicial power of the United States, conferred by Congress on the Circuit Courts, being limited to certain described cases and controversies, the question whether a particular [60 U.S. 393, 565] case is within the cognizance of a Circuit Court, may be raised by a plea to the jurisdiction of such court. When that question has been raised, the Circuit Court must, in the first instance, pass upon and determine it. Whether its determination be final, or subject to review by this appellate court, must depend upon the will of Congress; upon which body the Constitution has conferred the power, with certain restrictions, to establish inferior courts, to determine their jurisdiction, and to regulate the appellate power of this court. The twenty-second section of the judiciary act of 1789, which allows a writ of error from final judgments of Circuit Courts, provides that there shall be no reversal in this court, on such writ of error, for error in ruling any plea in abatement, other than a plea to the jurisdiction of the court. Accordingly it has been held, from the origin of the court to the present day, that Circuit Courts have not been made by Congress the final judges of their own jurisdiction in civil cases. And that when a record comes here upon a writ of error or appeal, and, on its inspection, it appears to this court that the Circuit Court had not jurisdiction, its judgment must be reversed, and the cause remanded, to be dismissed for want of jurisdiction.

It is alleged by the defendant in error, in this case, that the plea to the jurisdiction was a sufficient plea; that it shows, on inspection of its allegations, confessed by the demurrer, that the plaintiff was not a citizen of the State of Missouri; that upon this record, it must appear to this court that the case was not within the judicial power of the United States, as defined and granted by the Constitution, because it was not a suit by a citizen of one State against a citizen of another State.

To this it is answered, first, that the defendant, by pleading over, after the plea to the jurisdiction was adjudged insufficient, finally waived all benefit of that plea.

When that plea was adjudged insufficient, the defendant was obliged to answer over. He held no alternative. He could not stop the further progress of the case in the Circuit Court by a writ of error, on which the sufficiency of his plea to the jurisdiction could be tried in this court, because the judgment on that plea was not final, and no writ of error would lie. He was forced to plead to the merits. It cannot be true, then, that he waived the benefit of his plea to the jurisdiction by answering over. Waiver includes consent. Here, there was no consent. And if the benefit of the plea was finally lost, it must be, not by any waiver, but because the laws of the United States have not provided any mode of reviewing the decision of the Circuit Court on such a plea, when that decision is against the defendant. This is not the [60 U.S. 393, 566] law. Whether the decision of the Circuit Court on a plea to the jurisdiction be against the plaintiff, or against the defendant, the losing party may have any alleged error in law, in ruling such a plea, examined in this court on a writ of error, when the matter in controversy exceeds the sum or value of two thousand dollars. If the decision be against the plaintiff, and his suit dismissed for want of jurisdiction, the judgment is technically final, and he may at once sue out his writ of error. (Mollan v. Torrance, 9 Wheat., 537.) If the decision be against the defendant, though he must answer over, and wait for a final judgment in the cause, he may then have his writ of error, and upon it obtain the judgment of this court on any question of law apparent on the record, touching the jurisdiction. The fact that he pleaded over to the merits, under compulsion, can have no effect on his right to object to the jurisdiction. If this were not so, the condition of the two parties would be grossly unequal. For if a plea to the jurisdiction were ruled against the plaintiff, he could at once take his writ of error, and have the ruling reviewed here; while, if the same plea were ruled against the defendant, he must not only wait for a final judgment, but could in no event have the ruling of the Circuit Court upon the plea reviewed by this court. I know of no ground for saying that the laws of the United States have thus discriminated between the parties to a suit in its courts.

It is further objected, that as the judgment of the Circuit Court was in favor of the defendant, and the writ of error in this cause was sued out by the plaintiff, the defendant is not in a condition to assign any error in the record, and therefore this court is precluded from considering the question whether the Circuit Court had jurisdiction.

The practice of this court does not require a technical assignment of errors. (See the rule.) Upon a writ of error, the whole record is open for inspection; and if any error be found in it, the judgment is reversed. (Bank of U. S. v. Smith, 11 Wheat., 171.)

It is true, as a general rule, that the court will not allow a party to rely on anything as cause for reversing a judgment, which was for his advantage. In this, we follow an ancient rule of the common law. But so careful was that law of the preservation of the course of its courts, that it made an exception out of that general rule, and allowed a party to assign for error that which was for his advantage, if it were a departure by the court itself from its settled course of procedure. The cases on this subject are collected in Bac. Ab., Error H. 4. And this court followed this practice in Capron v. Van Noorden, [60 U.S. 393, 567] (2 Cranch, 126), where the plaintiff below procured the reversal of a judgment for the defendant, on the ground that the plaintiff's allegations of citizenship had not shown jurisdiction.

But it is not necessary to determine whether the defendant can be allowed to assign want of jurisdiction as an error in a judgment in his own favor. The true question is, not what either of the parties may be allowed to do, but whether this court will affirm or reverse a judgment of the Circuit Court on the merits, when it appears on the record, by a plea to the jurisdiction, that it is a case to which the judicial power of the United States does not extend. The course of the court is, where no motion is made by either party, on its own motion, to reverse such a judgment for want of jurisdiction, not only in cases where it is shown, negatively, by a plea to the jurisdiction, that jurisdiction does not exist, but even where it does not appear, affirmatively, that it does exist. (Pequignot v. The Pennsylvania R. R. Co., 16 How., 104.) It acts upon the principle that the judicial power of the United States must not be exerted in a case to which it does not extend, even if both parties desire to have it exerted. (Cutler v. Rae, 7 How., 729.) I consider, therefore, that when there was a plea to the jurisdiction of the Circuit Court in a case brought here by a writ of error, the first duty of this court is, sua sponte, if not moved to it by either party, to examine the sufficiency of that plea; and thus to take care that neither the Circuit Court nor this court shall use the judicial power of the United States in a case to which the Constitution and laws of the United States have not extended that power.

I proceed, therefore, to examine the plea to the jurisdiction.

I do not perceive any sound reason why it is not to be judged by the rules of the common law applicable to such pleas. It is true, where the jurisdiction of the Circuit Court depends on the citizenship of the parties, it is incumbent on the plaintiff to allege on the record the necessary citizenship; but when he has done so, the defendant must interpose a plea in abatement, the allegations whereof show that the court has not jurisdiction; and it is incumbent on him to prove the truth of his plea.

In Sheppard v. Graves, (14 How., 27,) the rules on this subject are thus stated in the opinion of the court: "That although, in the courts of the United States, it is necessary to set forth the grounds of their cognizance as courts of limited jurisdiction, yet wherever jurisdiction shall be averred in the pleadings, in conformity with the laws creating those courts, it must be taken, prima facie, as existing; and it is incumbent [60 U.S. 393, 568] on him who would impeach that jurisdiction for causes dehors the pleading, to allege and prove such causes; that the necessity for the allegation, and the burden of sustaining it by proof, both rest upon the party taking the exception." These positions are sustained by the authorities there cited, as well as by Wickliffe v. Owings, (17 How., 47.)

When, therefore, as in this case, the necessary averments as to citizenship are made on the record, and jurisdiction is assumed to exist, and the defendant comes by a plea to the jurisdiction to displace that presumption, he occupies, in my judgment, precisely the position described in Bacon Ab., Abatement: "Abatement, in the general acceptation of the word, signifies a plea, put in by the defendant, in which he shows cause to the court why he should not be impleaded; or, if at all, not in the manner and form he now is."

This being, then, a plea in abatement, to the jurisdiction of the court, I must judge of its sufficiency by those rules of the common law applicable to such pleas.

The plea was as follows: "And the said John F. A. Sandford, in his own proper person, comes and says that this court ought not to have or take further cognizance of the action aforesaid, because he says that said cause of action, and each and every of them, (if any such have accrued to the said Dred Scott,) accrued to the said Dred Scott out of the jurisdiction of this court, and exclusively within the jurisdiction of the courts of the State of Missouri; for that, to wit, the said plaintiff, Dred Scott, is not a citizen of the State of Missouri, as alleged in his declaration, because he is a negro of African descent; his ancestors were of pure African blood, and were brought into this country and sold as negro slaves, and this the said Sandford is ready to verify. Wherefore, he prays judgment whether this court can or will take further cognizance of the action aforesaid."

The plaintiff demurred, and the judgment of the Circuit Court was, that the plea was insufficient.

I cannot treat this plea as a general traverse of the citizenship alleged by the plaintiff. Indeed, if it were so treated, the plea was clearly bad, for it concludes with a verification, and not to the country, as a general traverse should. And though this defect in a plea in bar must be pointed out by a special demurrer, it is never necessary to demur specially to a plea in abatement; all matters, though of form only, may be taken advantage of upon a general demurrer to such a plea. (Chitty on Pl., 465.)

The truth is, that though not drawn with the utmost technical accuracy, it is a special traverse of the plaintiff's allegation [60 U.S. 393, 569] of citizenship, and was a suitable and proper mode of traverse under the circumstances. By reference to Mr. Stephen's description of the uses of such a traverse, contained in his excellent analysis of pleadings, (Steph. on Pl., 176,) it will be seen how precisely this plea meets one of his descriptions. No doubt the defendant might have traversed, by a common or general traverse, the plaintiff's allegation that he was a citizen of the State of Missouri, concluding to the country. The issue thus presented being joined, would have involved matter of law, on which the jury must have passed, under the direction of the court. But by traversing the plaintiff's citizenship specially—that is, averring those facts on which the defendant relied to show that in point of law the plaintiff was not a citizen, and basing the traverse on those facts as a deduction therefrom—opportunity was given to do, what was done; that is, to present directly to the court, by a demurrer, the sufficiency of those facts to negative, in point of law, the plaintiff's allegation of citizenship. This, then, being a special, and not a general or common traverse, the rule is settled, that the facts thus set out in the plea, as the reason or ground of the traverse, must of themselves constitute, in point of law, a negative of the allegation thus traversed. (Stephen on Pl., 183; Ch. on Pl., 620.) And upon a demurrer to this plea, the question which arises is, whether the facts, that the plaintiff is a negro, of African descent, whose ancestors were of pure African blood, and were brought into this country and sold as negro slaves, may all be true, and yet the plaintiff be a citizen of the State of Missouri, within the meaning of the Constitution and laws of the United States, which confer on citizens of one State the right to sue citizens of another State in the Circuit Courts. Undoubtedly, if these facts, taken together, amount to an allegation that, at the time of action brought, the plaintiff was himself a slave, the plea is sufficient. It has been suggested that the plea, in legal effect, does so aver, because, if his ancestors were sold as slaves, the presumption is they continued slaves; and if so, the presumption is, the plaintiff was born a slave; and if so, the presumption is, he continued to be a slave to the time of action brought.

I cannot think such presumptions can be resorted to, to help out defective averments in pleading; especially, in pleading in abatement, where the utmost certainty and precision are required. (Chitty on Pl., 457.) That the plaintiff himself was a slave at the time of action brought, is a substantive fact, having no necessary connection with the fact that his parents were sold as slaves. For they might have been sold after he was born; or the plaintiff himself, if once a slave, might have [60 U.S. 393, 570] became a freeman before action brought. To aver that his ancestors were sold as slaves, is not equivalent, in point of law, to an averment that he was a slave. If it were, he could not even confess and avoid the averment of the slavery of his ancestors, which would be monstrous; and if it be not equivalent in point of law, it cannot be treated as amounting thereto when demurred to; for a demurrer confesses only those substantive facts which are well pleaded, and not other distinct substantive facts which might be inferred therefrom by a jury. To treat an averment that the plaintiff's ancestors were Africans, brought to this country and sold as slaves, as amounting to an averment on the record that he was a slave, because it may lay some foundation for presuming so, is to hold that the facts actually alleged may be treated as intended as evidence of another distinct facts not alleged. But it is a cardinal rule of pleading, laid down in Dowman's case, (9 Rep., 9 b,) and in even earlier authorities therein referred to, "that evidence shall never be pleaded, for it only tends to prove matter of fact; and therefore the matter of fact shall be pleaded." Or, as the rule is sometimes stated, pleadings must not be argumentative. (Stephen on Pleading, 384, and authorities cited by him.) In Com. Dig., Pleader E. 3, and Bac. Abridgement, Pleas I, 5, and Stephen on Pl., many decisions under this rule are collected. In trover, for an indenture whereby A granted a manor, it is no plea that A did not grant the manor, for it does not answer the declaration except by argument. (Yelv., 223.)

So in trespass for taking and carrying away the plaintiff's goods, the defendant pleaded that the plaintiff never had any goods. The court said, "this is an infallible argument that the defendant is not guilty, but it is no plea." (Dyer, a 43.)

In ejectment, the defendant pleaded a surrender of a copyhold by the hand of Fosset, the steward. The plaintiff replied, that Fosset was not steward. The court held this no issue, for it traversed the surrender only argumentatively. (Cro. Elis., 260.)

In these cases, and many others reported in the books, the inferences from the facts stated were irresistible. But the court held they did not, when demurred to, amount to such inferable facts. In the case at bar, the inference that the defendant was a slave at the time of action brought, even if it can be made at all, from the fact that his parents were slaves, is certainly not a necessary inference. This case, therefore, is like that of Digby v. Alexander, (8 Bing., 116.) In that case, the defendant pleaded many facts strongly tending to show that he was once Earl of Stirling; but as there was no positive allegation [60 U.S. 393, 571] that he was so at the time of action brought, and as every fact averred might be true, and yet the defendant not have been Earl of Stirling at the time of action brought, the plea was held to be insufficient.

A lawful seizing of land is presumed to continue. But if, in an action of trespass quare clausum, the defendant were to plead that he was lawfully seized of the locus in quo, one month before the time of the alleged trespass, I should have no doubt it would be a bad plea. (See Mollan v. Torrance, 9 Wheat., 537.) So if a plea to the jurisdiction, instead of alleging that the plaintiff was a citizen of the same State as the defendant, were to allege that the plaintiff's ancestors were citizens of that State, I think the plea could not be supported. My judgment would be, as it is in this case, that if the defendant meant to aver a particular substantive fact, as existing at the time of action brought, he must do it directly and explicitly, and not by way of inference from certain other averments, which are quite consistent with the contrary hypothesis. I cannot, therefore, treat this plea as containing an averment that the plaintiff himself was a slave at the time of action brought; and the inquiry recurs, whether the facts, that he is of African descent, and that his parents were once slaves, are necessarily inconsistent with his own citizenship in the State of Missouri, within the meaning of the Constitution and laws of the United States.

In Gassies v. Ballon, (6 Pet., 761,) the defendant was described on the record as a naturalized citizen of the United States, residing in Louisiana. The court held this equivalent to an averment that the defendant was a citizen of Louisiana; because a citizen of the United States, residing in any State of the Union, is, for purposes of jurisdiction, a citizen of that State. Now, the plea to the jurisdiction in this case does not controvert the fact that the plaintiff resided in Missouri at the date of the writ. If he did then reside there, and was also a citizen of the United States, no provisions contained in the Constitution or laws of Missouri can deprive the plaintiff of his right to sue citizens of States other than Missouri, in the courts of the United States.

So that, under the allegations contained in this plea, and admitted by the demurrer, the question is, whether any person of African descent, whose ancestors were sold as slaves in the United States, can be a citizen of the United States. If any such person can be a citizen, this plaintiff has the right to the judgment of the court that he is so; for no cause is shown by the plea why he is not so, except his descent and the slavery of his ancestors.

The first section of the second article of the Constitution [60 U.S. 393, 572] uses the language, "a citizen of the United States at the time of the adoption of the Constitution." One mode of approaching this question is, to inquire who were citizens of the United States at the time of the adoption of the Constitution.

Citizens of the United States at the time of the adoption of the Constitution can have been no other than citizens of the United States under the Confederation. By the Articles of Confederation, a Government was organized, the style whereof was, "The United States of America." This Government was in existence when the Constitution was framed and proposed for adoption, and was to be superseded by the new Government of the United States of America, organized under the Constitution. When, therefore, the Constitution speaks of citizenship of the United States, existing at the time of the adoption of the Constitution, it must necessarily refer to citizenship under the Government which existed prior to and at the time of such adoption.

Without going into any question concerning the powers of the Confederation to govern the territory of the United States out of the limits of the States, and consequently to sustain the relation of Government and citizen in respect to the inhabitants of such territory, it may safely be said that the citizens of the several States were citizens of the United States under the Confederation.

That Government was simply a confederacy of the several States, possessing a few defined powers over subjects of general concern, each State retaining every power, jurisdiction, and right, not expressly delegated to the United States in Congress assembled. And no power was thus delegated to the Government of the Confederation, to act on any question of citizenship, or to make any rules in respect thereto. The whole matter was left to stand upon the action of the several States, and to the natural consequence of such action, that the citizens of each State should be citizens of that Confederacy into which that State had entered, the style whereof was, "The United States of America."

To determine whether any free persons, descended from Africans held in slavery, were citizens of the United States under the Confederation, and consequently at the time of the adoption of the Constitution of the United States, it is only necessary to know whether any such persons were citizens of either of the States under the Confederation, at the time of the adoption of the Constitution.

Of this there can be no doubt. At the time of the ratification of the Articles of Confederation, all free native-born inhabitants of the States of New Hampshire, Massachusetts, New [60 U.S. 393, 573] York, New Jersey, and North Carolina, though descended from African slaves, were not only citizens of those States, but such of them as had the other necessary qualifications possessed the franchise of electors, on equal terms with other citizens.

The Supreme Court of North Carolina, in the case of the State v. Manuel, (4 Dev. and Bat., 20,) has declared the law of that State on this subject, in terms which I believe to be as sound law in the other States I have enumerated, as it was in North Carolina.

"According to the laws of this State," says Judge Gaston, in delivering the opinion of the court, "all human beings within it, who are not slaves, fall within one of two classes. Whatever distinctions may have existed in the Roman laws between citizens and free inhabitants, they are unknown to our institutions. Before our Revolution, all free persons born within the dominions of the King of Great Britain, whatever their color or complexion, were native-born British subjects—those born out of his allegiance were aliens. Slavery did not exist in England, but it did in the British colonies. Slaves were not in legal parlance persons, but property. The moment the incapacity, the disqualification of slavery, was removed, they became persons, and were then either British subjects, or not British subjects, according as they were or were not born within the allegiance of the British King. Upon the Revolution, no other change took place in the laws of North Carolina than was consequent on the transition from a colony dependent on a European King, to a free and sovereign State. Slaves remained slaves. British subjects in North Carolina became North Carolina freemen. Foreigners, until made members of the State, remained aliens. Slaves, manumitted here, became freemen, and therefore, if born within North Carolina, are citizens of North Carolina, and all free persons born within the State are born citizens of the State. The Constitution extended the elective franchise to every freeman who had arrived at the age of twenty-one, and paid a public tax; and it is a matter of universal notoriety, that, under it, free persons, without regard to color, claimed and exercised the franchise, until it was taken from free men of color a few years since by our amended Constitution."

In the State v. Newcomb, (5 Iredell's R., 253,) decided in 1844, the same court referred to this case of the State v. Manuel, and said: "That case underwent a very laborious investigation, both by the bar and the bench. The case was brought here by appeal, and was felt to be one of great importance in principle. It was considered with an anxiety and care worthy of the principle involved, and which give it a controlling [60 U.S. 393, 574] influence and authority on all questions of a similar character."

An argument from speculative premises, however well chosen, that the then state of opinion in the Commonwealth of Massachusetts was not consistent with the natural rights of people of color who were born on that soil, and that they were not, by the Constitution of 1780 of that State, admitted to the condition of citizens, would be received with surprise by the people of that State, who know their own political history. It is true, beyond all controversy, that persons of color, descended from African slaves, were by that Constitution made citizens of the State; and such of them as have had the necessary qualifications, have held and exercised the elective franchise, as citizens, from that time to the present. (See Com. v. Aves, 18 Pick. R., 210.)

The Constitution of New Hampshire conferred the elective franchise upon "every inhabitant of the State having the necessary qualifications," of which color or descent was not one.

The Constitution of New York gave the right to vote to "every male inhabitant, who shall have resided," &c.; making no discrimination between free colored persons and others. (See Con. of N. Y., Art. 2, Rev. Stats. of N. Y., vol. 1, p. 126.)

That of New Jersey, to "all inhabitants of this colony, of full age, who are worth œ50 proclamation money, clear estate."

New York, by its Constitution of 1820, required colored persons to have some qualifications as prerequisites for voting, which white persons need not possess. And New Jersey, by its present Constitution, restricts the right to vote to white male citizens. But these changes can have no other effect upon the present inquiry, except to show, that before they were made, no such restrictions existed; and colored in common with white persons, were not only citizens of those States, but entitled to the elective franchise on the same qualifications as white persons, as they now are in New Hampshire and Massachusetts. I shall not enter into an examination of the existing opinions of that period respecting the African race, nor into any discussion concerning the meaning of those who asserted, in the Declaration of Independence, that all men are created equal; that they are endowed by their Creator with certain inalienable rights; that among these are life, liberty, and the pursuit of happiness. My own opinion is, that a calm comparison of these assertions of universal abstract truths, and of their own individual opinions and acts, would not leave [60 U.S. 393, 575] these men under any reproach of inconsistency; that the great truths they asserted on that solemn occasion, they were ready and anxious to make effectual, wherever a necessary regard to circumstances, which no statesman can disregard without producing more evil than good, would allow; and that it would not be just to them, nor true in itself, to allege that they intended to say that the Creator of all men had endowed the white race, exclusively, with the great natural rights which the Declaration of Independence asserts. But this is not the place to vindicate their memory. As I conceive, we should deal here, not with such disputes, if there can be a dispute concerning this subject, but with those substantial facts evinced by the written Constitutions of States, and by the notorious practice under them. And they show, in a manner which no argument can obscure, that in some of the original thirteen States, free colored persons, before and at the time of the formation of the Constitution, were citizens of those States.

The fourth of the fundamental articles of the Confederation was as follows: "The free inhabitants of each of these States, paupers, vagabonds, and fugitives from justice, excepted, shall be entitled to all the privileges and immunities of free citizens in the several States."

The fact that free persons of color were citizens of some of the several States, and the consequence, that this fourth article of the Confederation would have the effect to confer on such persons the privileges and immunities of general citizenship, were not only known to those who framed and adopted those articles, but the evidence is decisive, that the fourth article was intended to have that effect, and that more restricted language, which would have excluded such persons, was deliberately and purposely rejected.

On the 25th of June, 1778, the Articles of Confederation being under consideration by the Congress, the delegates from South Carolina moved to amend this fourth article, by inserting after the word "free," and before the word "inhabitants," the word "white," so that the privileges and immunities of general citizenship would be secured only to white persons. Two States voted for the amendment, eight States against it, and the vote of one State was divided. The language of the article stood unchanged, and both by its terms of inclusion, "free inhabitants," and the strong implication from its terms of exclusion, "paupers, vagabonds, and fugitives from justice," who alone were excepted, it is clear, that under the Confederation, and at the time of the adoption of the Constitution, free colored persons of African descent might be, and, by reason of their citizenship in certain States, were entitled to the [60 U.S. 393, 576] privileges and immunities of general citizenship of the United States.

Did the Constitution of the United States deprive them or their descendants of citizenship?

That Constitution was ordained and established by the people of the United States, through the action, in each State, of those persons who were qualified by its laws to act thereon, in behalf of themselves and all other citizens of that State. In some of the States, as we have seen, colored persons were among those qualified by law to act on this subject. These colored persons were not only included in the body of "the people of the United States," by whom the Constitution was ordained and established, but in at least five of the States they had the power to act, and doubtless did act, by their suffrages, upon the question of its adoption. It would be strange, if we were to find in that instrument anything which deprived of their citizenship any part of the people of the United States who were among those by whom it was established.

I can find nothing in the Constitution which, proprio vigore, deprives of their citizenship any class of persons who were citizens of the United States at the time of its adoption, or who should be native-born citizens of any State after its adoption; nor any power enabling Congress to disfranchise persons born on the soil of any State, and entitled to citizenship of such State by its Constitution and laws. And my opinion is, that, under the Constitution of the United States, every free person born on the soil of a State, who is a citizen of that State by force of its Constitution or laws, is also a citizen of the United States.

I will proceed to state the grounds of that opinion.

The first section of the second article of the Constitution uses the language, "a natural-born citizen." It thus assumes that citizenship may be acquired by birth. Undoubtedly, this language of the Constitution was used in reference to that principle of public law, well understood in this country at the time of the adoption of the Constitution, which referred citizenship to the place of birth. At the Declaration of Independence, and ever since, the received general doctrine has been, in conformity with the common law, that free persons born within either of the colonies were subjects of the King; that by the Declaration of Independence, and the consequent acquisition of sovereignty by the several States, all such persons ceased to be subjects, and became citizens of the several States, except so far as some of them were disfranchised by the legislative power of the States, or availed themselves, seasonably, of the right to adhere to the British Crown in the civil contest, [60 U.S. 393, 577] and thus to continue British subjects. (McIlvain v. Coxe's Lessee, 4 Cranch, 209; Inglis v. Sailors' Snug Harbor, 3 Peters, p. 99; Shanks v. Dupont, Ibid, p. 242.)

The Constitution having recognised the rule that persons born within the several States are citizens of the United States, one of four things must be true:

First. That the Constitution itself has described what native-born persons shall or shall not be citizens of the United States; or, Second. That it has empowered Congress to do so; or, Third. That all free persons, born within the several States, are citizens of the United States; or, Fourth. That it is left to each State to determine what free persons, born within its limits, shall be citizens of such State, and thereby be citizens of the United States.

If there be such a thing as citizenship of the United States acquired by birth within the States, which the Constitution expressly recognises, and no one denies, then these four alternatives embrace the entire subject, and it only remains to select that one which is true.

That the Constitution itself has defined citizenship of the United States by declaring what persons, born within the several States, shall or shall not be citizens of the United States, will not be pretended. It contains no such declaration. We may dismiss the first alternative, as without doubt unfounded.

Has it empowered Congress to enact what free persons, born within the several States, shall or shall not be citizens of the United States?

Before examining the various provisions of the Constitution which may relate to this question, it is important to consider for a moment the substantial nature of this inquiry. It is, in effect, whether the Constitution has empowered Congress to create privileged classes within the States, who alone can be entitled to the franchises and powers of citizenship of the United States. If it be admitted that the Constitution has enabled Congress to declare what free persons, born within the several States, shall be citizens of the United States, it must at the same time be admitted that it is an unlimited power. If this subject is within the control of Congress, it must depend wholly on its discretion. For, certainly, no limits of that discretion can be found in the Constitution, which is wholly silent concerning it; and the necessary consequence is, that the Federal Government may select classes of persons within the several States who alone can be entitled to the political privileges of citizenship of the United States. If this power exists, what persons born within the States may be President or Vice President [60 U.S. 393, 578] of the United States, or members of either House of Congress, or hold any office or enjoy any privilege whereof citizenship of the United States is a necessary qualification, must depend solely on the will of Congress. By virtue of it, though Congress can grant no title of nobility, they may create an oligarchy, in whose hands would be concentrated the entire power of the Federal Government.

It is a substantive power, distinct in its nature from all others; capable of affecting not only the relations of the States to the General Government, but of controlling the political condition of the people of the United States. Certainly we ought to find this power granted by the Constitution, at least by some necessary inference, before we can say it does not remain to the States or the people. I proceed therefore to examine all the provisions of the Constitution which may have some bearing on this subject.

Among the powers expressly granted to Congress is "the power to establish a uniform rule of naturalization." It is not doubted that this is a power to prescribe a rule for the removal of the disabilities consequent on foreign birth. To hold that it extends further than this, would do violence to the meaning of the term naturalization, fixed in the common law, (Co. Lit., 8 a, 129 a; 2 Ves., sen., 286; 2 Bl. Com., 293,) and in the minds of those who concurred in framing and adopting the Constitution. It was in this sense of conferring on an alien and his issue the rights and powers of a native-born citizen, that it was employed in the Declaration of Independence. It was in this sense it was expounded in the Federalist, (No. 42,) has been understood by Congress, by the Judiciary, (2 Wheat., 259, 269; 3 Wash. R., 313, 322; 12 Wheat., 277,) and by commentators on the Constitution. (3 Story's Com. on Con., 1-3; 1 Rawle on Con., 84-88; 1 Tucker's Bl. Com. App., 255-259.)

It appears, then, that the only power expressly granted to Congress to legislate concerning citizenship, is confined to the removal of the disabilities of foreign birth.

Whether there be anything in the Constitution from which a broader power may be implied, will best be seen when we come to examine the two other alternatives, which are, whether all free persons, born on the soil of the several States, or only such of them as may be citizens of each State, respectively, are thereby citizens of the United States. The last of these alternatives, in my judgment, contains the truth.

Undoubtedly, as has already been said, it is a principle of public law, recognised by the Constitution itself, that birth on the soil of a country both creates the duties and confers the rights of citizenship. But it must be remembered, that though [60 U.S. 393, 579] the Constitution was to form a Government, and under it the United States of America were to be one united sovereign nation, to which loyalty and obedience on the one side, and from which protection and privileges on the other, would be due, yet the several sovereign States, whose people were then citizens, were not only to continue in existence, but with powers unimpaired, except so far as they were granted by the people to the National Government.

Among the powers unquestionably possessed by the several States, was that of determining what persons should and what persons should not be citizens. It was practicable to confer on the Government of the Union this entire power. It embraced what may, well enough for the purpose now in view, be divided into three parts. First: The power to remove the disabilities of alienage, either by special acts in reference to each individual case, or by establishing a rule of naturalization to be administered and applied by the courts. Second: Determining what persons should enjoy the privileges of citizenship, in respect to the internal affairs of the several States. Third: What native-born persons should be citizens of the United States.

The first-named power, that of establishing a uniform rule of naturalization, was granted; and here the grant, according to its terms, stopped. Construing a Constitution containing only limited and defined powers of government, the argument derived from this definite and restricted power to establish a rule of naturalization, must be admitted to be exceedingly strong. I do not say it is necessarily decisive. It might be controlled by other parts of the Constitution. But when this particular subject of citizenship was under consideration, and, in the clause specially intended to define the extent of power concerning it, we find a particular part of this entire power separated from the residue, and conferred on the General Government, there arises a strong presumption that this is all which is granted, and that the residue is left to the States and to the people. And this presumption is, in my opinion, converted into a certainty, by an examination of all such other clauses of the Constitution as touch this subject.

It will examine each which can have any possible bearing on this question.

The first clause of the second section of the third article of the Constitution is, "The judicial power shall extend to controversies between a State and citizens of another State; between citizens of different States; between citizens of the same State, claiming lands under grants of different States; and between States, or the citizens thereof, and foreign States, [60 U.S. 393, 580] citizens, or subjects." I do not think this clause has any considerable bearing upon the particular inquiry now under consideration. Its purpose was, to extend the judicial power to those controversies into which local feelings or interests might to enter as to disturb the course of justice, or give rise to suspicions that they had done so, and thus possibly give occasion to jealousy or ill will between different States, or a particular State and a foreign nation. At the same time, I would remark, in passing, that it has never been held, I do not know that it has ever been supposed, that any citizen of a State could bring himself under this clause and the eleventh and twelfth sections of the judiciary act of 1789, passed in pursuance of it, who was not a citizen of the United States. But I have referred to the clause, only because it is one of the places where citizenship is mentioned by the Constitution. Whether it is entitled to any weight in this inquiry or not, it refers only to citizenship of the several States; it recognises that; but it does not recognise citizenship of the United States as something distinct therefrom.

As has been said, the purpose of this clause did not necessarily connect it with citizenship of the United States, even if that were something distinct from citizenship of the several States, in the contemplation of the Constitution. This cannot be said of other clauses of the Constitution, which I now proceed to refer to.

"The citizens of each State shall be entitled to all the privileges and immunities of citizens of the several States." Nowhere else in the Constitution is there anything concerning a general citizenship; but here, privileges and immunities to be enjoyed throughout the United States, under and by force of the national compact, are granted and secured. In selecting those who are to enjoy these national rights of citizenship, how are they described? As citizens of each State. It is to them these national rights are secured. The qualification for them is not to be looked for in any provision of the Constitution or laws of the United States. They are to be citizens of the several States, and, as such, the privileges and immunities of general citizenship, derived from and guarantied by the Constitution, are to be enjoyed by them. It would seem that if it had been intended to constitute a class of native-born persons within the States, who should derive their citizenship of the United States from the action of the Federal Government, this was an occasion for referring to them. It cannot be supposed that it was the purpose of this article to confer the privileges and immunities of citizens in all the States upon persons not citizens of the United States. [60 U.S. 393, 581] And if it was intended to secure these rights only to citizens of the United States, how has the Constitution here described such persons? Simply as citizens of each State.

But, further: though, as I shall presently more fully state, I do not think the enjoyment of the elective franchise essential to citizenship, there can be no doubt it is one of the chiefest attributes of citizenship under the American Constitutions; and the just and constitutional possession of this right is decisive evidence of citizenship. The provisions made by a Constitution on this subject must therefore be looked to as bearing directly on the question what persons are citizens under that Constitution; and as being decisive, to this extent, that all such persons as are allowed by the Constitution to exercise the elective franchise, and thus to participate in the Government of the United States, must be deemed citizens of the United States.

Here, again, the consideration presses itself upon us, that if there was designed to be a particular class of native-born persons within the States, deriving their citizenship from the Constitution and laws of the United States, they should at least have been referred to as those by whom the President and House of Representatives were to be elected, and to whom they should be responsible.

Instead of that, we again find this subject referred to the laws of the several States. The electors of President are to be appointed in such manner as the Legislature of each State may direct, and the qualifications of electors of members of the House of Representatives shall be the same as for electors of the most numerous branch of the State Legislature.

Laying aside, then, the case of aliens, concerning which the Constitution of the United States has provided, and confining our view to free persons born within the several States, we find that the Constitution has recognised the general principle of public law, that allegiance and citizenship depend on the place of birth; that it has not attempted practically to apply this principle by designating the particular classes of persons who should or should not come under it; that when we turn to the Constitution for an answer to the question, what free persons, born within the several States, are citizens of the United States, the only answer we can receive from any of its express provisions is, the citizens of the several States are to enjoy the privileges and immunities of citizens in every State, and their franchise as electors under the Constitution depends on their citizenship in the several States. Add to this, that the Constitution was ordained by the citizens of the several States; that they were "the people of the United States," for whom [60 U.S. 393, 582] and whose posterity the Government was declared in the preamble of the Constitution to be made; that each of them was "a citizen of the United States at the time of the adoption of the Constitution," within the meaning of those words in that instrument; they by them the Government was to be and was in fact organized; and that no power is conferred on the Government of the Union to discriminate between them, or to disfranchise any of them—the necessary conclusion is, that those persons born within the several States, who, by force of their respective Constitutions and laws, are citizens of the State, are thereby citizens of the United States.

It may be proper here to notice some supposed objections to this view of the subject.

It has been often asserted that the Constitution was made exclusively by and for the white race. It has already been shown that in five of the thirteen original States, colored persons then possessed the elective franchise, and were among those by whom the Constitution was ordained and established. If so, it is not true, in point of fact, that the Constitution was made exclusively by the white race. And that it was made exclusively for the white race is, in my opinion, not only an assumption not warranted by anything in the Constitution, but contradicted by its opening declaration, that it was ordained and established by the people of the United States, for themselves and their posterity. And as free colored persons were then citizens of at least five States, and so in every sense part of the people of the United States, they were among those for whom and whose posterity the Constitution was ordained and established.

Again, it has been objected, that if the Constitution has left to the several States the rightful power to determine who of their inhabitants shall be citizens of the United States, the States may make aliens citizens.

The answer is obvious. The Constitution has left to the States the determination what persons, born within their respective limits, shall acquire by birth citizenship of the United States; it has not left to them any power to prescribe any rule for the removal of the disabilities of alienage. This power is exclusively in Congress.

It has been further objected, that if free colored persons, born within a particular State, and made citizens of that State by its Constitution and laws, are thereby made citizens of the United States, then, under the second section of the fourth article of the Constitution, such persons would be entitled to all the privileges and immunities of citizens in the several States; and if so, then colored persons could vote, and be [60 U.S. 393, 583] eligible to not only Federal offices, but offices even in those States whose Constitution and laws disqualify colored persons from voting or being elected to office.

But this position rests upon an assumption which I deem untenable. Its basis is, that no one can be deemed a citizen of the United States who is not entitled to enjoy all the privileges and franchises which are conferred on any citizen. (See 1 Lit. Kentucky R., 326.) That this is not true, under the Constitution of the United States, seems to me clear.

A naturalized citizen cannot be President of the United States, nor a Senator till after the lapse of nine years, nor a Representative till after the lapse of seven years, from his naturalization. Yet, as soon as naturalized, he is certainly a citizen of the United States. Nor is any inhabitant of the District of Columbia, or of either of the Territories, eligible to the office of Senator or Representative in Congress, though they may be citizens of the United States. So, in all the States, numerous persons, though citizens, cannot vote, or cannot hold office, either on account of their age, or sex, or the want of the necessary legal qualifications. The truth is, that citizenship, under the Constitution of the United States, is not dependent on the possession of any particular political or even of all civil rights; and any attempt so to define it must lead to error. To what citizens the elective franchise shall be confided, is a question to be determined by each State, in accordance with its own views of the necessities or expediencies of its condition. What civil rights shall be enjoyed by its citizens, and whether all shall enjoy the same, or how they may be gained or lost, are to be determined in the same way.

One may confine the right of suffrage to white male citizens; another may extend it to colored persons and females; one may allow all persons above a prescribed age to convey property and transact business; another may exclude married women. But whether native-born women, or persons under age, or under guardianship because insane or spendthrifts, be excluded from voting or holding office, or allowed to do so, I apprehend no one will deny that they are citizens of the United States. Besides, this clause of the Constitution does not confer on the citizens of one State, in all other States, specific and enumerated privileges and immunities. They are entitled to such as belong to citizenship, but not to such as belong to particular citizens attended by other qualifications. Privileges and immunities which belong to certain citizens of a State, by reason of the operation of causes other than mere citizenship, are not conferred. Thus, if the laws of a State require, in addition to [60 U.S. 393, 584] citizenship of the State, some qualification for office, or the exercise of the elective franchise, citizens of all other States, coming thither to reside, and not possessing those qualifications, cannot enjoy those privileges, not because they are not to be deemed entitled to the privileges of citizens of the State in which they reside, but because they, in common with the native-born citizens of that State, must have the qualifications prescribed by law for the enjoyment of such privileges, under its Constitution and laws. It rests with the States themselves so to frame their Constitutions and laws as not to attach a particular privilege or immunity to mere naked citizenship. If one of the States will not deny to any of its own citizens a particular privilege or immunity, if it confer it on all of them by reason of mere naked citizenship, then it may be claimed by every citizen of each State by force of the Constitution; and it must be borne in mind, that the difficulties which attend the allowance of the claims of colored persons to be citizens of the United States are not avoided by saying that, though each State may make them its citizens, they are not thereby made citizens of the United States, because the privileges of general citizenship are secured to the citizens of each State. The language of the Constitution is, "The citizens of each State shall be entitled to all privileges and immunities of citizens in the several States." If each State may make such persons its citizens, they became, as such, entitled to the benefits of this article, if there be a native-born citizenship of the United States distinct from a native-born citizenship of the several States.

There is one view of this article entitled to consideration in this connection. It is manifestly copied from the fourth of the Articles of Confederation, with only slight changes of phraseology, which render its meaning more precise, and dropping the clause which excluded paupers, vagabonds, and fugitives from justice, probably because these cases, could be dealt with under the police powers of the States, and a special provision therefor was not necessary. It has been suggested, that in adopting it into the Constitution, the words "free inhabitants" were changed for the word "citizens." An examination of the forms of expression commonly used in the State papers of that day, and an attention to the substance of this article of the Confederation, will show that the words "free inhabitants," as then used, were synonymous with citizens. When the Articles of Confederation were adopted, we were in the midst of the war of the Revolution, and there were very few persons then embraced in the words "free inhabitants," who were not born on our soil. It was not a time when many, save the [60 U.S. 393, 585] children of the soil, were willing to embark their fortunes in our cause; and though there might be an inaccuracy in the uses of words to call free inhabitants citizens, it was then a technical rather than a substantial difference. If we look into the Constitutions and State papers of that period, we find the inhabitants or people of these colonies, or the inhabitants of this State, or Commonwealth, employed to designate those whom we should now denominate citizens. The substance and purpose of the article prove it was in this sense it used these words: it secures to the free inhabitants of each State the privileges and immunities of free citizens in every State. It is not conceivable that the States should have agreed to extend the privileges of citizenship to persons not entitled to enjoy the privileges of citizens in the States where they dwelt; that under this article there was a class of persons in some of the States, not citizens, to whom were secured all the privileges and immunities of citizens when they went into other States; and the just conclusion is, that though the Constitution cured an inaccuracy of language, it left the substance of this article in the National Constitution the same as it was in the Articles of Confederation.

The history of this fourth article, respecting the attempt to exclude free persons of color from its operation, has been already stated. It is reasonable to conclude that this history was known to those who framed and adopted the Constitution. That under this fourth article of the Confederation, free persons of color might be entitled to the privileges of general citizenship, if otherwise entitled thereto, is clear. When this article was, in substance, placed in and made part of the Constitution of the United States, with no change in its language calculated to exclude free colored persons from the benefit of its provisions, the presumption is, to say the least, strong, that the practical effect which it was designed to have, and did have, under the former Government, it was designed to have, and should have, under the new Government.

It may be further objected, that if free colored persons may be citizens of the United States, it depends only on the will of a master whether he will emancipate his slave, and thereby make him a citizen. Not so. The master is subject to the will of the State. Whether he shall be allowed to emancipate his slave at all; if so, on what conditions; and what is to be the political status of the freed man, depend, not on the will of the master, but on the will of the State, upon which the political status of all its native-born inhabitants depends. Under the Constitution of the United States, each State has retained this power of determining the political status of its native-born [60 U.S. 393, 586] inhabitants, and no exception thereto can be found in the Constitution. And if a master in a slave-holding State should carry his slave into a free State, and there emancipate him, he would not thereby make him a native- born citizen of that State, and consequently no privileges could be claimed by such emancipated slave as a citizen of the United States. For, whatever powers the States may exercise to confer privileges of citizenship on persons not born on their soil, the Constitution of the United States does not recognise such citizens. As has already been said, it recognises the great principle of public law, that allegiance and citizenship spring from the place of birth. It leaves to the States the application of that principle to individual cases. It secured to the citizens of each State the privileges and immunities of citizens in every other State. But it does not allow to the States the power to make aliens citizens, or permit one State to take persons born on the soil of another State, and, contrary to the laws and policy of the State where they were born, make them its citizens, and so citizens of the United States. No such deviation from the great rule of public law was contemplated by the Constitution; and when any such attempt shall be actually made, it is to be met by applying to it those rules of law and those principles of good faith which will be sufficient to decide it, and not, in my judgment, by denying that all the free native-born inhabitants of a State, who are its citizens under its Constitution and laws, are also citizens of the United States.

It has sometimes been urged that colored persons are shown not to be citizens of the United States by the fact that the naturalization laws apply only to white persons. But whether a person born in the United States be or be not a citizen, cannot depend on laws which refer only to aliens, and do not affect the status of persons born in the United States. The utmost effect which can be attributed to them is, to show that Congress has not deemed it expedient generally to apply the rule to colored aliens. That they might do so, if thought fit, is clear. The Constitution has not excluded them. And since that has conferred the power on Congress to naturalize colored aliens, it certainly shows color is not a necessary qualification for citizenship under the Constitution of the United States. It may be added, that the power to make colored persons citizens of the United States, under the Constitution, has been actually exercised in repeated and important instances. (See the Treaties with the Choctaws, of September 27, 1830, art. 14; with the Cherokees, of May 23, 1836, art. 12, Treaty of Guadalupe Hidalgo, February 2, 1848, art. 8.)

I do not deem it necessary to review at length the legislation [60 U.S. 393, 587] of Congress having more or less bearing on the citizenship of colored persons. It does not seem to me to have any considerable tendency to prove that it has been considered by the legislative department of the Government, that no such persons are citizens of the United States. Undoubtedly they have been debarred from the exercise of particular rights or privileges extended to white persons, but, I believe, always in terms which, by implication, admit they may be citizens. Thus the act of May 17, 1792, for the organization of the militia, directs the enrolment of "every free, able-bodied, white male citizen." An assumption that none but white persons are citizens, would be as inconsistent with the just import of this language, as that all citizens are able-bodied, or males.

So the act of February 28, 1803, (2 Stat. at Large, 205,) to prevent the importation of certain persons into States, when by the laws thereof their admission is prohibited, in its first section forbids all masters of vessels to import or bring "any negro, mulatto, or other person of color, not being a native, a citizen, or registered seaman of the United States," &c.

The acts of March 3, 1813, section 1, (2 Stat. at Large, 809,) and March 1, 1817, section 3, (3 Stat. at Large, 351,) concerning seamen, certainly imply there may be persons of color, natives of the United States, who are not citizens of the United States. This implication is undoubtedly in accordance with the fact. For not only slaves, but free persons of color, born in some of the States, are not citizens. But there is nothing in these laws inconsistent with the citizenship of persons of color in others of the States, nor with their being citizens of the United States.

Whether much or little weight should be attached to the particular phraseology of these and other laws, which were not passed with any direct reference to this subject, I consider their tendency to be, as already indicated, to show that, in the apprehension of their framers, color was not a necessary qualification of citizenship. It would be strange, if laws were found on our statute book to that effect, when, by solemn treaties, large bodies of Mexican and North American Indians as well as free colored inhabitants of Louisiana have been admitted to citizenship of the United States.

In the legislative debates which preceded the admission of the State of Missouri into the Union, this question was agitated. Its result is found in the resolution of Congress, of March 5, 1821, for the admission of that State into the Union. The Constitution of Missouri, under which that State applied for admission into the Union, provided, that it should be the duty [60 U.S. 393, 588] of the Legislature "to pass laws to prevent free negroes and mulattoes from coming to and settling in the State, under any pretext whatever." One ground of objection to the admission of the State under this Constitution was, that it would require the Legislature to exclude free persons of color, who would be entitled, under the second section of the fourth article of the Constitution, not only to come within the State, but to enjoy there the privileges and immunities of citizens. The resolution of Congress admitting the State was upon the fundamental condition, "that the Constitution of Missouri shall never be construed to authorize the passage of any law, and that no law shall be passed in conformity thereto, by which any citizen of either of the States of this Union shall be excluded from the enjoyment of any of the privileges and immunities to which such citizen is entitled under the Constitution of the United States." It is true, that neither this legislative declaration, nor anything in the Constitution or laws of Missouri, could confer or take away any privilege or immunity granted by the Constitution. But it is also true, that it expresses the then conviction of the legislative power of the United States, that free negroes, as citizens of some of the States, might be entitled to the privileges and immunities of citizens in all the States.

The conclusions at which I have arrived on this part of the case are:

First. That the free native-born citizens of each State are citizens of the United States.

Second. That as free colored persons born within some of the States are citizens of those States, such persons are also citizens of the United States.

Third. That every such citizen, residing in any State, has the right to sue and is liable to be sued in the Federal courts, as a citizen of that State in which he resides.

Fourth. That as the plea to the jurisdiction in this case shows no facts, except that the plaintiff was of African descent, and his ancestors were sold as slaves, and as these facts are not inconsistent with his citizenship of the United States, and his residence in the State of Missouri, the plea to the jurisdiction was bad, and the judgment of the Circuit Court overruling it was correct.

I dissent, therefore, from that part of the opinion of the majority of the court, in which it is held that a person of African descent cannot be a citizen of the United States; and I regret I must go further, and dissent both from what I deem their assumption of authority to examine the constitutionality of the act of Congress commonly called the Missouri compromise [60 U.S. 393, 589] act, and the grounds and conclusions announced in their opinion.

Having first decided that they were bound to consider the sufficiency of the plea to the jurisdiction of the Circuit Court, and having decided that this plea showed that the Circuit Court had not jurisdiction, and consequently that this is a case to which the judicial power of the United States does not extend, they have gone on to examine the merits of the case as they appeared on the trial before the court and jury, on the issues joined on the pleas in bar, and so have reached the question of the power of Congress to pass the act of 1820. On so grave a subject as this, I feel obliged to say that, in my opinion, such an exertion of judicial power transcends the limits of the authority of the court, as described by its repeated decisions, and, as I understand, acknowledged in this opinion of the majority of the court.

In the course of that opinion, it became necessary to comment on the case of Legrand v. Darnall, (reported in 2 Peters's R., 664.) In that case, a bill was filed, by one alleged to be a citizen of Maryland, against one alleged to be a citizen of Pennsylvania. The bill stated that the defendant was the son of a white man by one of his slaves; and that the defendant's father devised to him certain lands, the title to which was put in controversy by the bill. These facts were admitted in the answer, and upon these and other facts the court made its decree, founded on the principle that a devise of land by a master to a slave was by implication also a bequest of his freedom. The facts that the defendant was of African descent, and was born a slave, were not only before the court, but entered into the entire substance of its inquiries. The opinion of the majority of my brethren in this case disposes of the case of Legrand v. Darnall, by saying, among other things, that as the fact that the defendant was born a slave only came before this court on the bill and answer, it was then too late to raise the question of the personal disability of the party, and therefore that decision is altogether inapplicable in this case.

In this I concur. Since the decision of this court in Livingston v. Story, (11 Pet., 351,) the law has been settled, that when the declaration or bill contains the necessary averments of citizenship, this court cannot look at the record, to see whether those averments are true, except so far as they are put in issue by a plea to the jurisdiction. In that case, the defendant denied by his answer that Mr. Livingston was a citizen of New York, as he had alleged in the bill. Both parties went into proofs. The court refused to examine those proofs, with reference to the personal disability of the plaintiff. This is the [60 U.S. 393, 590] settled law of the court, affirmed so lately as Shepherd v. Graves, (14 How., 27,) and Wickliff v. Owings, (17 How., 51.) (See also De Wolf v. Rabaud, 1 Pet., 476.) But I do not understand this to be a rule which the court may depart from at its pleasure. If it be a rule, it is as binding on the court as on the suitors. If it removes from the latter the power to take any objection to the personal disability of a party alleged by the record to be competent, which is not shown by a plea to the jurisdiction, it is because the court are forbidden by law to consider and decide on objections so taken. I do not consider it to be within the scope of the judicial power of the majority of the court to pass upon any question respecting the plaintiff's citizenship in Missouri, save that raised by the plea to the jurisdiction; and I do not hold any opinion of this court, or any court, binding, when expressed on a question not legitimately before it. (Carroll v. Carroll, 16 How., 275.) The judgment of this court is, that the case is to be dismissed for want of jurisdiction, because the plaintiff was not a citizen of Missouri, as he alleged in his declaration. Into that judgment, according to the settled course of this court, nothing appearing after a plea to the merits can enter. A great question of constitutional law, deeply affecting the peace and welfare of the country, is not, in my opinion, a fit subject to be thus reached.

But as, in my opinion, the Circuit Court had jurisdiction, I am obliged to consider the question whether its judgment on the merits of the case should stand or be reversed.

The residence of the plaintiff in the State of Illinois, and the residence of himself and his wife in the territory acquired from France lying north of latitude thirty-six degrees thirty minutes, and north of the State of Missouri, are each relied on by the plaintiff in error. As the residence in the territory affects the plaintiff's wife and children as well as himself, I must inquire what was its effect.

The general question may be stated to be, whether the plaintiff's status, as a slave, was so changed by his residence within that territory, that he was not a slave in the State of Missouri, at the time this action was brought.

In such cases, two inquiries arise, which may be confounded, but should be kept distinct.

The first is, what was the law of the Territory into which the master and slave went, respecting the relation between them?

The second is, whether the State of Missouri recognises and allows the effect of that law of the Territory, on the status of the slave, on his return within its jurisdiction.

As to the first of these questions, the will of States and nations, [60 U.S. 393, 591] by whose municipal law slavery is not recognised, has been manifested in three different ways.

One is, absolutely to dissolve the relation, and terminate the rights of the master existing under the law of the country whence the parties came. This is said by Lord Stowell, in the case of the slave Grace, (2 Hag. Ad. R., 94,) and by the Supreme Court of Louisiana in the case of Maria Louise v. Marot, (9 Louis. R., 473,) to be the law of France; and it has been the law of several States of this Union, in respect to slaves introduced under certain conditions. (Wilson v. Isabel, 5 Call's R., 430; Hunter v. Hulcher, 1 Leigh, 172; Stewart v. Oaks, 5 Har. and John., 107.)

The second is, where the municipal law of a country not recognising slavery, it is the will of the State to refuse the master all aid to exercise any control over his slave; and if he attempt to do so, in a manner justifiable only by that relation, to prevent the exercise of that control. But no law exists, designed to operate directly on the relation of master and slave, and put an end to that relation. This is said by Lord Stowell, in the case above mentioned, to be the law of England, and by Mr. Chief Justice Shaw, in the case of the Commonwealth v. Aves, (18 Pick., 193,) to be the law of Massachusetts.

The third is, to make a distinction between the case of a master and his slave only temporarily in the country, *animo non manendi*, and those who are there to reside for permanent or indefinite purposes. This is said by Mr. Wheaton to be the law of Prussia, and was formerly the statute law of several States of our Union. It is necessary in this case to keep in view this distinction between those countries whose laws are designed to act directly on the status of a slave, and make him a freeman, and those where his master can obtain no aid from the laws to enforce his rights.

It is to the last case only that the authorities, out of Missouri, relied on by defendant, apply, when the residence in the nonslaveholding Territory was permanent. In the Commonwealth v. Aves, (18 Pick., 218,) Mr. Chief Justice Shaw said: "From the principle above stated, on which a slave brought here becomes free, to wit: that he becomes entitled to the protection of our laws, it would seem to follow, as a necessary conclusion, that if the slave waives the protection of those laws, and returns to the State where he is held as a slave, his condition is not changed." It was upon this ground, as is apparent from his whole reasoning, that Sir William Scott rests his opinion in the case of the slave Grace. To use one of his expressions, the effect of the law of England was to put the liberty of the slave into a parenthesis. If there had been an [60 U.S. 393, 592] act of Parliament declaring that a slave coming to England with his master should thereby be deemed no longer to be a slave, it is easy to see that the learned judge could not have arrived at the same conclusion. This distinction is very clearly stated and shown by President Tucker, in his opinion in the case of Betty v. Horton, (5 Leigh's Virginia R., 615.) (See also Hunter v. Fletcher, 1 Leigh's Va. R., 172; Maria Louise v. Marot, 9 Louisiana R.; Smith v. Smith, 13 Ib., 441; Thomas v. Genevieve, 16 Ib., 483; Rankin v. Lydia, 2 A. K. Marshall, 467; Davies v. Tingle, 8 B. Munroe, 539; Griffeth v. Fanny, Gilm. Va. R., 143; Lumford v. Coquillon, 14 Martin's La. R., 405; Josephine v. Poultney, 1 Louis. Ann. R., 329.)

But if the acts of Congress on this subject are valid, the law of the Territory of Wisconsin, within whose limits the residence of the plaintiff and his wife, and their marriage and the birth of one or both of their children, took place, falls under the first category, and is a law operating directly on the status of the slave. By the eighth section of the act of March 6, 1820, (3 Stat. at Large, 548,) it was enacted that, within this Territory, "slavery and involuntary servitude, otherwise than in the punishment of crimes, whereof the parties shall have been duly convicted, shall be, and is hereby, forever prohibited: Provided, always, that any person escaping into the same, from whom labor or service is lawfully claimed in any State or Territory of the United States, such fugitive may be lawfully reclaimed, and conveyed to the person claiming his or her labor or service, as aforesaid."

By the act of April 20, 1836, (4 Stat. at Large, 10,) passed in the same month and year of the removal of the plaintiff to Fort Snelling, this part of the territory ceded by France, where Fort Snelling is, together with so much of the territory of the United States east of the Mississippi as now constitutes the State of Wisconsin, was brought under a Territorial Government, under the name of the Territory of Wisconsin. By the eighteenth section of this act, it was enacted, "That the inhabitants of this Territory shall be entitled to and enjoy all and singular the rights, privileges, and advantages, granted and secured to the people of the Territory of the United States northwest of the river Ohio, by the articles of compact contained in the ordinance for the government of said Territory, passed on the 13th day of July, 1787; and shall be subject to all the restrictions and prohibitions in said articles of compact imposed upon the people of the said Territory." The sixth article of that compact is, "there shall be neither slavery nor involuntary servitude in the said Territory, otherwise than in [60 U.S. 393, 593] the punishment of crimes, whereof the party shall have been duly convicted. Provided, always, that any person escaping into the same, from whom labor or service is lawfully claimed in any one of the original States, such fugitive may be lawfully reclaimed, and conveyed to the person claiming his or her labor or service, as aforesaid." By other provisions of this act establishing the Territory of Wisconsin, the laws of the United States, and the then existing laws of the State of Michigan, are extended over the Territory; the latter being subject to alteration and repeal by the legislative power of the Territory created by the act.

Fort Snelling was within the Territory of Wisconsin, and these laws were extended over it. The Indian title to that site for a military post had been acquired from the Sioux nation as early as September 23, 1805, (Am. State Papers, Indian Affairs, vol. 1, p. 744,) and until the erection of the Territorial Government, the persons at that post were governed by the rules and articles of war, and such laws of the United States, including the eighth section of the act of March 6, 1820, prohibiting slavery, as were applicable to their condition; but after the erection of the Territory, and the extension of the laws of the United States and the laws of Michigan over the whole of the Territory, including this military post, the persons residing there were under the dominion of those laws in all particulars to which the rules and articles of war did not apply.

It thus appears that, by these acts of Congress, not only was a general system of municipal law borrowed from the State of Michigan, which did not tolerate slavery, but it was positively enacted that slavery and involuntary servitude, with only one exception, specifically described, should not exist there. It is not simply that slavery is not recognised and cannot be aided by the municipal law. It is recognised for the purpose of being absolutely prohibited, and declared incapable of existing within the Territory, save in the instance of a fugitive slave.

It would not be easy for the Legislature to employ more explicit language to signify its will that the status of slavery should not exist within the Territory, than the words found in the act of 1820, and in the ordinance of 1787; and if any doubt could exist concerning their application to cases of masters coming into the Territory with their slaves to reside, that doubt must yield to the inference required by the words of exception. That exception is, of cases of fugitive slaves. An exception from a prohibition marks the extent of the prohibition; for it would be absurd, as well as useless, to except from a prohibition [60 U.S. 393, 594] a case not contained within it. (9 Wheat., 200.) I must conclude, therefore, that it was the will of Congress that the state of involuntary servitude of a slave, coming into the Territory with his master, should cease to exist. The Supreme Court of Missouri so held in Rachel v. Walker, (4 Misso. R., 350,) which was the case of a military officer going into the Territory with two slaves.

But it is a distinct question, whether the law of Missouri recognised and allowed effect to the change wrought in the status of the plaintiff, by force of the laws of the Territory of Wisconsin.

I say the law of Missouri, because a judicial tribunal, in one State or nation, can recognise personal rights acquired by force of the law of any other State or nation, only so far as it is the law of the former State that those rights should be recognised. But, in the absence of positive law to the contrary, the will of every civilized State must be presumed to be to allow such effect to foreign laws as is in accordance with the settled rules of international law. And legal tribunals are bound to act on this presumption. It may be assumed that the motive of the State in allowing such operation to foreign laws is what has been termed comity. But, as has justly been said, (per Chief Justice Taney, 13 Pet., 589,) it is the comity of the State, not of the court. The judges have nothing to do with the motive of the State. Their duty is simply to ascertain and give effect to its will. And when it is found by them that its will to depart from a rule of international law has not been manifested by the State, they are bound to assume that its will is to give effect to it. Undoubtedly, every sovereign State may refuse to recognise a change, wrought by the law of a foreign State, on the status of a person, while within such foreign State, even in cases where the rules of international law require that recognition. Its will to refuse such recognition may be manifested by what we term statute law, or by the customary law of the State. It is within the province of its judicial tribunals to inquire and adjudge whether it appears, from the statute or customary law of the State, to be the will of the State to refuse to recognise such changes of status by force of foreign law, as the rules of the law of nations require to be recognised. But, in my opinion, it is not within the province of any judicial tribunal to refuse such recognition from any political considerations, or any view it may take of the exterior political relations between the State and one or more foreign States, or any impressions it may have that a change of foreign opinion and action on the subject of slavery may afford a reason why the State should change its own action. To understand and give [60 U.S. 393, 595] just effect to such considerations, and to change the action of the State in consequence of them, are functions of diplomatists and legislators, not of judges.

The inquiry to be made on this part of the case is, therefore, whether the State of Missouri has, by its statute, or its customary law, manifested its will to displace any rule of international law, applicable to a change of the status of a slave, by foreign law.

I have not heard it suggested that there was any statute of the State of Missouri bearing on this question. The customary law of Missouri is the common law, introduced by statute in 1816. (1 Ter. Laws, 436.) And the common law, as Blackstone says, (4 Com., 67,) adopts, in its full extent, the law of nations, and holds it to be a part of the law of the land.

I know of no sufficient warrant for declaring that any rule of international law, concerning the recognition, in that State, of a change of status, wrought by an extra-territorial law, has been displaced or varied by the will of the State of Missouri.

I proceed then to inquire what the rules of international law prescribe concerning the change of status of the plaintiff wrought by the law of the Territory of Wisconsin.

It is generally agreed by writers upon international law, and the rule has been judicially applied in a great number of cases, that wherever any question may arise concerning the status of a person, it must be determined according to that law which has next previously rightfully operated on and fixed that status. And, further, that the laws of a country do not rightfully operate upon and fix the status of persons who are within its limits in itinere, or who are abiding there for definite temporary purposes, as for health, curiosity, or occasional business; that these laws, known to writers on public and private international law as personal statutes, operate only on the inhabitants of the country. Not that it is or can be denied that each independent nation may, if it thinks fit, apply them to all persons within their limits. But when this is done, not in conformity with the principles of international law, other States are not understood to be willing to recognise or allow effect to such applications of personal statutes.

It becomes necessary, therefore, to inquire whether the operation of the laws of the Territory of Wisconsin upon the status of the plaintiff was or was not such an operation as these principles of international law require other States to recognise and allow effect to.

And this renders it needful to attend to the particular facts and circumstances of this case. [60 U.S. 393, 596] It appears that this case came on for trial before the Circuit Court and a jury, upon an issue, in substance, whether the plaintiff, together with his wife and children, were the slaves of the defendant.

The court instructed the jury that, "upon the facts in this case, the law is with the defendant." This withdrew from the jury the consideration and decision of every matter of fact. The evidence in the case consisted of written admissions, signed by the counsel of the parties. If the case had been submitted to the judgment of the court, upon an agreed statement of facts, entered of record, in place of a special verdict, it would have been necessary for the court below, and for this court, to pronounce its judgment solely on those facts, thus agreed, without inferring any other facts therefrom. By the rules of the common law applicable to such a case, and by force of the seventh article of the amendments of the Constitution, this court is precluded from finding any fact not agreed to by the parties on the record. No submission to the court on a statement of facts was made. It was a trial by jury, in which certain admissions, made by the parties, were the evidence. The jury were not only competent, but were bound to draw from that evidence every inference which, in their judgment, exercised according to the rules of law, it would warrant. The Circuit Court took from the jury the power to draw any inferences from the admissions made by the parties, and decided the case for the defendant. This course can be justified here, if at all, only by its appearing that upon the facts agreed, and all such inferences of fact favorable to the plaintiff's case, as the jury might have been warranted in drawing from those admissions, the law was with the defendant. Otherwise, the plaintiff would be deprived of the benefit of his trial by jury, by whom, for aught we can know, those inferences favorable to his case would have been drawn.

The material facts agreed, bearing on this part of the case, are, that Dr. Emerson, the plaintiff's master, resided about two years at the military post of Fort Snelling, being a surgeon in the army of the United States, his domicil of origin being unknown; and what, if anything, he had done, to preserve or change his domicil prior to his residence at Rock Island, being also unknown.

Now, it is true, that under some circumstances the residence of a military officer at a particular place, in the discharge of his official duties, does not amount to the acquisition of a technical domicil. But it cannot be affirmed, with correctness, that it never does. There being actual residence, and this being presumptive evidence of domicil, all the circumstances [60 U.S. 393, 597] of the case must be considered, before a legal conclusion can be reached, that his place of residence is not his domicil. If a military officer stationed at a particular post should entertain an expectation that his residence there would be indefinitely protracted, and in consequence should remove his family to the place where his duties were to be discharged, form a permanent domestic establishment there, exercise there the civil rights and discharge the civil duties of an inhabitant, while he did not act and manifested no intent to have a domicil elsewhere, I think no one would say that the mere fact that he was himself liable to be called away by the orders of the Government would prevent his acquisition of a technical domicil at the place of the residence of himself and his family. In other words, I do not think a military officer incapable of acquiring a domicil. (Bruce v. Bruce, 2 Bos. and Pul., 230; Munroe v. Douglass, 5 Mad. Ch. R., 232.) This being so, this case stands thus: there was evidence before the jury that Emerson resided about two years at Fort Snelling, in the Territory of Wisconsin. This may or may not have been with such intent as to make it his technical domicil. The presumption is that it was. It is so laid down by this court, in Ennis v. Smith, (14 How.,) and the authorities in support of the position are there referred to. His intent was a question of fact for the jury. (Fitchburg v. Winchendon, 4 Cush., 190.)

The case was taken from the jury. If they had power to find that the presumption of the necessary intent had not been rebutted, we cannot say, on this record, that Emerson had not his technical domicil at Fort Snelling. But, for reasons which I shall now proceed to give, I do not deem it necessary in this case to determine the question of the technical domicil of Dr. Emerson.

It must be admitted that the inquiry whether the law of a particular country has rightfully fixed the status of a person, so that in accordance with the principles of international law that status should be recognised in other jurisdictions, ordinarily depends on the question whether the person was domiciled in the country whose laws are asserted to have fixed his status. But, in the United States, questions of this kind may arise, where an attempt to decide solely with reference to technical domicil, tested by the rules which are applicable to changes of places of abode from one country to another, would not be consistent with sound principles. And, in my judgment, this is one of those cases.

The residence of the plaintiff, who was taken by his master, Dr. Emerson, as a slave, from Missouri to the State of Illinois, and thence to the Territory of Wisconsin, must be deemed to [60 U.S. 393, 598] have been for the time being, and until he asserted his own separate intention, the same as the residence of his master; and the inquiry, whether the personal statutes of the Territory were rightfully extended over the plaintiff, and ought, in accordance with the rules of international law, to be allowed to fix his status, must depend upon the circumstances under which Dr. Emerson went into that Territory, and remained there; and upon the further question, whether anything was there rightfully done by the plaintiff to cause those personal statutes to operate on him.

Dr. Emerson was an officer in the army of the United States. He went into the Territory to discharge his duty to the United States. The place was out of the jurisdiction of any particular State, and within the exclusive jurisdiction of the United States. It does not appear where the domicil of origin of Dr. Emerson was, nor whether or not he had lost it, and gained another domicil, nor of what particular State, if any, he was a citizen.

On what ground can it be denied that all valid laws of the United States, constitutionally enacted by Congress for the government of the Territory, rightfully extended over an officer of the United States and his servant who went into the Territory to remain there for an indefinite length of time, to take part in its civil or military affairs? They were not foreigners, coming from abroad. Dr. Emerson was a citizen of the country which had exclusive jurisdiction over the Territory; and not only a citizen, but he went there in a public capacity, in the service of the same sovereignty which made the laws. Whatever those laws might be, whether of the kind denominated personal statutes, or not, so far as they were intended by the legislative will, constitutionally expressed, to operate on him and his servant, and on the relations between them, they had a rightful operation, and no other State or country can refuse to allow that those laws might rightfully operate on the plaintiff and his servant, because such a refusal would be a denial that the United States could, by laws constitutionally enacted, govern their own servants, residing on their own Territory, over which the United States had the exclusive control, and in respect to which they are an independent sovereign power. Whether the laws now in question were constitutionally enacted, I repeat once more, is a separate question. But, assuming that they were, and that they operated directly on the status of the plaintiff, I consider that no other State or country could question the rightful power of the United States so to legislate, or, consistently with the settled rules of international law, could refuse to recognise the effects [60 U.S. 393, 599] of such legislation upon the status of their officers and servants, as valid everywhere.

This alone would, in my apprehension, be sufficient to decide this question.

But there are other facts stated on the record which should not be passed over. It is agreed that, in the year 1836, the plaintiff, while residing in the Territory, was married, with the consent of Dr. Emerson, to Harriet, named in the declaration as his wife, and that Eliza and Lizzie were the children of that marriage, the first named having been born on the Mississippi river, north of the line of Missouri, and the other having been born after their return to Missouri. And the inquiry is, whether, after the marriage of the plaintiff in the Territory, with the consent of Dr. Emerson, any other State or country can, consistently with the settled rules of international law, refuse to recognise and treat him as a free man, when suing for the liberty of himself, his wife, and the children of the marriage. It is in reference to his status, as viewed in other States and countries, that the contract of marriage and the birth of children becomes strictly material. At the same time, it is proper to observe that the female to whom he was married having been taken to the same military post of Fort Snelling as a slave, and Dr. Emerson claiming also to be her master at the time of her marriage, her status, and that of the children of the marriage, are also affected by the same considerations.

If the laws of Congress governing the Territory of Wisconsin were constitutional and valid laws, there can be no doubt these parties were capable of contracting a lawful marriage, attended with all the usual civil rights and obligations of that condition. In that Territory they were absolutely free persons, having full capacity to enter into the civil contract of marriage.

It is a principle of international law, settled beyond controversy in England and America, that a marriage, valid by the law of the place where it was contracted, and not in fraud of the law of any other place, is valid everywhere; and that no technical domicil at the place of the contract is necessary to make it so. (See Bishop on Mar. and Div., 125–129, where the cases are collected.)

If, in Missouri, the plaintiff were held to be a slave, the validity and operation of his contract of marriage must be denied. He can have no legal rights; of course, not those of a husband and father. And the same is true of his wife and children. The denial of his rights is the denial of theirs. So that, though lawfully married in the Territory, when they came out of it, into the State of Missouri, they were no longer [60 U.S. 393, 600] husband and wife; and a child of that lawful marriage, though born under the same dominion where its parents contracted a lawful marriage, is not the fruit of that marriage, nor the child of its father, but subject to the maxim, partus sequitur ventrem.

It must be borne in mind that in this case there is no ground for the inquiry, whether it be the will of the State of Missouri not to recognise the validity of the marriage of a fugitive slave, who escapes into a State or country where slavery is not allowed, and there contracts a marriage; or the validity of such a marriage, where the master, being a citizen of the State of Missouri, voluntarily goes with his slave, in itinere, into a State or country which does not permit slavery to exist, and the slave there contracts marriage without the consent of his master; for in this case, it is agreed, Dr. Emerson did consent; and no further question can arise concerning his rights, so far as their assertion is inconsistent with the validity of the marriage. Nor do I know of any ground for the assertion that this marriage was in fraud of any law of Missouri. It has been held by this court, that a bequest of property by a master to his slave, by necessary implication entitles the slave to his freedom; because, only as a freeman could he take and hold the bequest. (Legrand v. Darnall, 2 Pet. R., 664.) It has also been held, that when a master goes with his slave to reside for an indefinite period in a State where slavery is not tolerated, this operates as an act of manumission; because it is sufficiently expressive of the consent of the master that the slave should be free. (2 Marshall's Ken. R., 470; 14 Martin's Louis. R., 401.)

What, then, shall we say of the consent of the master, that the slave may contract a lawful marriage, attended with all the civil rights and duties which belong to that relation; that he may enter into a relation which none but a free man can assume—a relation which involves not only the rights and duties of the slave, but those of the other party to the contract, and of their descendants to the remotest generation? In my judgment, there can be no more effectual abandonment of the legal rights of a master over his slave, than by the consent of the master that the slave should enter into a contract of marriage, in a free State, attended by all the civil rights and obligations which belong to that condition.

And any claim by Dr. Emerson, or any one claiming under him, the effect of which is to deny the validity of this marriage, and the lawful paternity of the children born from it, wherever asserted, is, in my judgment, a claim inconsistent with good faith and sound reason, as well as with the rules of international law. And I go further: in my opinion, a law of the State [60 U.S. 393, 601] of Missouri, which should thus annul a marriage, lawfully contracted by these parties while resident in Wisconsin, not in fraud of any law of Missouri, or of any right of Dr. Emerson, who consented thereto, would be a law impairing the obligation of a contract, and within the prohibition of the Constitution of the United States. (See 4 Wheat., 629, 695, 696.)

To avoid misapprehension on this important and difficult subject, I will state, distinctly, the conclusions at which I have arrived. They are:

First. The rules of international law respecting the emancipation of slaves, by the rightful operation of the laws of another State or country upon the status of the slave, while resident in such foreign State or country, are part of the common law of Missouri, and have not been abrogated by any statute law of that State.

Second. The laws of the United States, constitutionally enacted, which operated directly on and changed the status of a slave coming into the

Territory of Wisconsin with his master, who went thither to reside for an indefinite length of time, in the performance of his duties as an officer of the United States, had a rightful operation on the status of the slave, and it is in conformity with the rules of international law that this change of status should be recognised everywhere.

Third. The laws of the United States, in operation in the Territory of Wisconsin at the time of the plaintiff's residence there, did act directly on the status of the plaintiff, and change his status to that of a free man.

Fourth. The plaintiff and his wife were capable of contracting, and, with the consent of Dr. Emerson, did contract a marriage in that Territory, valid under its laws; and the validity of this marriage cannot be questioned in Missouri, save by showing that it was in fraud of the laws of that State, or of some right derived from them; which cannot be shown in this case, because the master consented to it.

Fifth. That the consent of the master that his slave, residing in a country which does not tolerate slavery, may enter into a lawful contract of marriage, attended with the civil rights and duties which being to that condition, is an effectual act of emancipation. And the law does not enable Dr. Emerson, or any one claiming under him, to assert a title to the married persons as slaves, and thus destroy the obligation of the contract of marriage, and bastardize their issue, and reduce them to slavery.

But it is insisted that the Supreme Court of Missouri has settled this case by its decision in Scott v. Emerson, (15 Missouri Reports, 576;) and that this decision is in conformity [60 U.S. 393, 602] with the weight of authority elsewhere, and with sound principles. If the Supreme Court of Missouri had placed its decision on the ground that it appeared Dr. Emerson never became domiciled in the Territory, and so its laws could not rightfully operate on him and his slave; and the facts that he went there to reside indefinitely, as an officer of the United States, and that the plaintiff was lawfully married there, with Dr. Emerson's consent, were left out of view, the decision would find support in other cases, and I might not be prepared to deny its correctness. But the decision is not rested on this ground. The domicil of Dr. Emerson in that Territory is not questioned in that decision; and it is placed on a broad denial of the operation, in Missouri, of the law of any foreign State or country upon the status of a slave, going with his master from Missouri into such foreign State or country, even though they went thither to become, and actually became, permanent inhabitants of such foreign State or country, the laws whereof acted directly on the status of the slave, and changed his status to that of a freeman.

To the correctness of such a decision I cannot assent. In my judgment, the opinion of the majority of the court in that case is in conflict with its previous decisions, with a great weight of judicial authority in other slaveholding States, and with fundamental principles of private international law. Mr. Chief Justice Gamble, in his dissenting opinion in that case, said:

> "I regard the question as conclusively settled by repeated adjudications of this court; and if I doubted or denied the propriety of those decisions, I would not feel myself any more at liberty to overturn them, than I would any other series of decisions by which the law upon any other question had been settled. There is with me nothing in the law of slavery which distinguishes it from the law on any other subject, or allows any more accommodation to the temporary excitements which have gathered around it. . . . But in the midst of all such excitement, it is proper that the judicial mind, calm and self-balanced, should adhere to principles established when there was no feeling to disturb the view of the legal questions upon which the rights of parties depend."

> "In this State, it has been recognized from the beginning of the Government as a correct position in law, that the master who takes his slave to reside in a State or Territory where slavery is prohibited, thereby emancipates his slave." (Winney v. Whitesides, 1 Mo., 473; Le Grange v. Chouteau, 2 Mo., 20; Milley v. Smith, Ib., 36; Ralph v. Duncan, 3 Mo., 194; Julia v. McKinney, Ib., 270; Nat v. Ruddle, Ib., 400; Rachel v. Walker, 4 Mo., 350; Wilson v. Melvin, 592.) [60 U.S. 393, 603] Chief Justice Gamble has also examined the decisions of the courts of other States in which slavery is established, and finds them in accordance with these preceding decisions of the Supreme Court of Missouri to which he refers.

It would be a useless parade of learning for me to go over the ground which he has so fully and ably occupied.

But it is further insisted we are bound to follow this decision. I do not think so. In this case, it is to be determined what laws of the United States were in operation in the Territory of Wisconsin, and what was their effect on the status of the plaintiff. Could the plaintiff contract a lawful marriage there? Does any law of the State of Missouri impair the obligation of that contract of marriage, destroy his rights as a husband, bastardize the issue of the marriage, and reduce them to a state of slavery?

These questions, which arise exclusively under the Constitution and laws of the United States, this court, under the Constitution and laws of the United States, has the rightful authority finally to decide. And if we look beyond these questions, we come to the consideration whether the rules of international law, which are part of the laws of Missouri until displaced by some statute not alleged to exist, do or do not require the status of the plaintiff, as fixed by the laws of the Territory of Wisconsin, to be recognised in Missouri. Upon such a question, not depending on any statute or local usage, but on principles of universal jurisprudence, this court has repeatedly asserted it could not hold itself bound by the decisions of State courts, however great respect might be felt for their learning, ability, and impartiality. (See Swift v. Tyson, 16 Peters's R., 1; Carpenter v. The Providence Ins. Co., Ib., 495; Foxcroft v. Mallet, 4 How., 353; Rowan v. Runnels, 5 How., 134.)

Some reliance has been placed on the fact that the decision in the Supreme Court of Missouri was between these parties, and the suit there was abandoned to obtain another trial in the courts of the United States.

In Homer v. Brown, (16 How., 354,) this court made a decision upon the construction of a devise of lands, in direct opposition to the unanimous opinion of the Supreme Court of Massachusetts, between the same parties, respecting the same subject-matter—the claimant having become nonsuit in the State court, in order to bring his action in the Circuit Court of the United States. I did not sit in that case, having been of counsel for one of the parties while at the bar; but, on examining the report of the argument of the counsel for the plaintiff in error, I find they made the point, that this court ought to give effect to the construction put upon the will by the State [60 U.S. 393, 604] court, to the end that rights respecting lands may be governed by one law, and that the law of the place where the lands are situated; that they referred to the State decision of the case, reported in 3 Cushing, 390, and to many decisions of this court. But this court does not seem to have considered the point of sufficient importance to notice it in their opinions. In Millar v. Austin, (13 How., 218,) an action was brought by the endorsee of a written promise. The question was, whether it was negotiable under a statute of Ohio. The Supreme Court of that State having decided it was not negotiable, the plaintiff became nonsuit, and brought his action in the Circuit Court of the United States. The decision of the Supreme Court of the State, reported in 4 Ves., L. J., 527, was relied on. This court unanimously held the paper to be negotiable.

When the decisions of the highest court of a State are directly in conflict with each other, it has been repeatedly held, here, that the last decision is not necessarily to be taken as the rule. (State Bank v. Knoop, 16 How., 369; Pease v. Peck, 18 How., 599.)

To these considerations I desire to add, that it was not made known to the Supreme Court of Missouri, so far as appears, that the plaintiff was married in Wisconsin with the consent of Dr. Emerson, and it is not made known to us that Dr. Emerson was a citizen of Missouri, a fact to which that court seem to have attached much importance.

Sitting here to administer the law between these parties, I do not feel at liberty to surrender my own convictions of what the law requires, to the authority of the decision in 15 Missouri Reports.

I have thus far assumed, merely for the purpose of the argument, that the laws of the United States, respecting slavery in this Territory, were constitutionally enacted by Congress. It remains to inquire whether they are constitutional and binding laws.

In the argument of this part of the case at bar, it was justly considered by all the counsel to be necessary to ascertain the source of the power of Congress over the territory belonging to the United States. Until this is ascertained, it is not possible to determine the extent of that power. On the one side it was maintained that the Constitution contains no express grant of power to organize and govern what is now known to the laws of the United States as a Territory. That whatever power of this kind exists, is derived by implication from the capacity of the United States to hold and acquire territory out of the limits of any State, and the necessity for its having some government. [60 U.S. 393, 605] On the other side, it was insisted that the Constitution has not failed to make an express provision for this end, and that it is found in the third section of the fourth article of the Constitution.

To determine which of these is the correct view, it is needful to advert to some facts respecting this subject, which existed when the Constitution was framed and adopted. It will be found that these facts not only shed much light on the question, whether the framers of the Constitution omitted to make a provision concerning the power of Congress to organize and govern Territories, but they will also aid in the construction of any provision which may have been made respecting this subject.

Under the Confederation, the unsettled territory within the limits of the United States had been a subject of deep interest. Some of the States insisted that these lands were within their chartered boundaries, and that they had succeeded to the title of the Crown to the soil. On the other hand, it was argued that the vacant lands had been acquired by the United States, by the war carried on by them under a common Government and for the common interest.

This dispute was further complicated by unsettled questions of boundary among several States. It not only delayed the accession of Maryland to the Confederation, but at one time seriously threatened its existence. (5 Jour. of Cong., 208, 442.) Under the pressure of these circumstances, Congress earnestly recommended to the several States a cession of their claims and rights to the United States. (5 Jour. of Cong., 442.) And before the Constitution was framed, it had been begun. That by New York had been made on the 1st day of March, 1781; that of Virginia on the 1st day of March, 1784; that of Massachusetts on the 19th day of April, 1785; that of Connecticut on the 14th day of September, 1786; that of South Carolina on the 8th day of August, 1787, while the Convention for framing the Constitution was in session.

It is very material to observe, in this connection, that each of these acts cedes, in terms, to the United States, as well the jurisdiction as the soil.

It is also equally important to note that, when the Constitution was framed and adopted, this plan of vesting in the United States, for the common good, the great tracts of ungranted lands claimed by the several States, in which so deep an interest was felt, was yet incomplete. It remained for North Carolina and Georgia to cede their extensive and valuable claims. These were made, by North Carolina on the 25th day of February, 1790, and by Georgia on the 24th day of April, [60 U.S. 393, 606] 1802. The terms of these last-mentioned cessions will hereafter be noticed in another connection; but I observe here that each of them distinctly shows, upon its face, that they were not only in execution of the general plan proposed by the Congress of the Confederation, but of a formed purpose of each of these States, existing when the assent of their respective people was given to the Constitution of the United States.

It appears, then, that when the Federal Constitution was framed, and presented to the people of the several States for their consideration, the unsettled territory was viewed as justly applicable to the common benefit, so far as it then had or might attain thereafter a pecuniary value; and so far as it might become the seat of new States, to be admitted into the Union upon an equal footing with the original States. And also that the relations of the United States to that unsettled territory were of different kinds. The titles of the States of New York, Virginia, Massachusetts, Connecticut, and South Carolina, as well of soil as of jurisdiction, had been transferred to the United States. North Carolina and Georgia had not actually made transfers, but a confident expectation, founded on their appreciation of the justice of the general claim, and fully justified by the results, was entertained, that these cessions would be made. The ordinance of 1787 had made provision for the temporary government of so much of the territory actually ceded as lay northwest of the river Ohio.

But it must have been apparent, both to the framers of the Constitution and the people of the several States who were to act upon it, that the Government thus provided for could not continue, unless the Constitution should confer on the United States the necessary powers to continue it. That temporary Government, under the ordinance, was to consist of certain officers, to be appointed by and responsible to the Congress of the Confederation; their powers had been conferred and defined by the ordinance. So far as it provided for the temporary government of the Territory, it was an ordinary act of legislation, deriving its force from the legislative power of Congress, and depending for its vitality upon the continuance of that legislative power. But the officers to be appointed for the Northwestern Territory, after the adoption of the Constitution, must necessarily be officers of the United States, and not of the Congress of the Confederation; appointed and commissioned by the President, and exercising powers derived from the United States under the Constitution.

Such was the relation between the United States and the North-western Territory, which all reflecting men must have foreseen would exist, when the Government created by the [60 U.S. 393, 607] Constitution should supersede that of the Confederation. That if the new Government should be without power to govern this Territory, it could not appoint and commission officers, and send them into the Territory, to exercise there legislative, judicial, and executive power; and that this Territory, which was even then foreseen to be so important, both politically and financially, to all the existing States, must be left not only without the control of the General Government, in respect to its future political relations to the rest of the States, but absolutely without any Government, save what its inhabitants, acting in their primary capacity, might from time to time create for themselves.

But this Northwestern Territory was not the only territory, the soil and jurisdiction whereof were then understood to have been ceded to the United States. The cession by South Carolina, made in August, 1787, was of "all the territory included within the river Mississippi, and a line beginning at that part of the said river which is intersected by the southern boundary of North Carolina, and continuing along the said boundary line until it intersects the ridge or chain of mountains which divides the Eastern from the Western waters; then to be continued along the top of the said ridge of mountains, until it intersects a line to be drawn due west from the head of the southern branch of the Tugaloo river, to the said mountains; and thence to run a due west course to the river Mississippi."

It is true that by subsequent explorations it was ascertained that the source of the Tugaloo river, upon which the title of South Carolina depended, was so far to the northward, that the transfer conveyed only a narrow slip of land, about twelve miles wide, lying on the top of the ridge of mountains, and extending from the northern boundary of Georgia to the southern boundary of North Carolina. But this was a discovery made long after the cession, and there can be no doubt that the State of South Carolina, in making the cession, and the Congress in accepting it, viewed it as a transfer to the United States of the soil and jurisdiction of an extensive and important part of the unsettled territory ceded by the Crown of Great Britain by the treaty of peace, though its quantity or extent then remained to be ascertained.[1]

It must be remembered also, as has been already stated, that not only was there a confident expectation entertained by the [60 U.S. 393, 608] other States, that North Carolina and Georgia would complete the plan already so far executed by New York, Virginia, Massachusetts, Connecticut, and South Carolina, but that the opinion was in no small degree prevalent, that the just title to this "back country," as it was termed, had vested in the United States by the treaty of peace, and could not rightfully be claimed by any individual State.

There is another consideration applicable to this part of the subject, and entitled, in my judgment, to great weight.

The Congress of the Confederation had assumed the power not only to dispose of the lands ceded, but to institute Governments and make laws for their inhabitants. In other words, they had proceeded to act under the cession, which, as we have seen, was as well of the jurisdiction as of the soil. This ordinance was passed on the 13th of July, 1787. The Convention for framing the Constitution was then in session at Philadelphia. The proof is direct and decisive, that it was known to the Convention.[2] It is equally clear that it was admitted and understood not to be within the legitimate powers of the Confederation to pass this ordinance. (Jefferson's Works, vol. 9, pp. 251, 276; Federalist, Nos. 38, 43.)

The importance of conferring on the new Government regular powers commensurate with the objects to be attained, and thus avoiding the alternative of a failure to execute the trust assumed by the acceptance of the cessions made and expected, or its execution by usurpation, could scarcely fail to be perceived. That it was in fact perceived, is clearly shown by the Federalist, (No. 38,) where this very argument is made use of in commendation of the Constitution.

Keeping these facts in view, it may confidently be asserted that there is very strong reason to believe, before we examine the Constitution itself, that the necessity for a competent grant of power to hold, dispose of, and govern territory, ceded and expected to be ceded, could not have escaped the attention of those who framed or adopted the Constitution; and that if it did not escape their attention, it could not fail to be adequately provided for.

Any other conclusion would involve the assumption that a subject of the gravest national concern, respecting which the small States felt so much jealousy that it had been almost an insurmountable obstacle to the formation of the Confederation, and as to which all the States had deep pecuniary and political interests, and which had been so recently and constantly agitated, [60 U.S. 393, 609] was nevertheless overlooked; or that such a subject was not overlooked, but designedly left unprovided for, though it was manifestly a subject of common concern, which belonged to the care of the General Government, and adequate provision for which could not fail to be deemed necessary and proper.

The admission of new States, to be framed out of the ceded territory, early attracted the attention of the Convention. Among the resolutions introduced by Mr. Randolph, on the 29th of May, was one on this subject, (Res. No. 10, 5 Elliot, 128,) which, having been affirmed in Committee of the Whole, on the 5th of June, (5 Elliot, 156,) and reported to the Convention on the 13th of June, (5 Elliot, 190,) was referred to the Committee of Detail, to prepare the Constitution, on the 26th of July, (5 Elliot, 376.) This committee reported an article for the admission of new States "lawfully constituted or established." Nothing was said concerning the power of Congress to prepare or form such States. This omission struck Mr. Madison, who, on the 18th of August, (5 Elliot, 439,) moved for the insertion of power to dispose of the unappropriated lands of the United States, and to institute temporary Governments for new States arising therein.

On the 29th of August, (5 Elliot, 492,) the report of the committee was taken up, and after debate, which exhibited great diversity of views concerning the proper mode of providing for the subject, arising out of the supposed diversity of interests of the large and small States, and between those which had and those which had not unsettled territory, but no difference of opinion respecting the propriety and necessity of some adequate provision for the subject, Gouverneur Morris moved the clause as it stands in the Constitution. This met with general approbation, and was at once adopted. The whole section is as follows:

> "New States may be admitted by the Congress into this Union; but no new State shall be formed or erected within the jurisdiction of any other State, nor any State be formed by the junction of two or more States, or parts of States, without the consent of the Legislatures of the States concerned, as well as of Congress.
>
> "The Congress shall have power to dispose of and make all needful rules and regulations respecting the territory or other property belonging to the United States; and nothing in this Constitution shall be so construed as to prejudice any claims of the United States or any particular State."

That Congress has some power to institute temporary Governments over the territory, I believe all agree; and, if it be admitted that the necessity of some power to govern the territory [60 U.S. 393, 610] of the United States could not and did not escape the attention of the Convention and the people, and that the necessity is so great, that, in the absence of any express grant, it is strong enough to raise an implication of the existence of that power, it would seem to follow that it is also strong enough to afford material aid in construing an express grant of power respecting that territory; and that they who maintain the existence of the power, without finding any words at all in which it is conveyed, should be willing to receive a reasonable interpretation of language of the Constitution, manifestly intended to relate to the territory, and to convey to Congress some authority concerning it.

It would seem, also, that when we find the subject-matter of the growth and formation and admission of new States, and the disposal of the territory for these ends, were under consideration, and that some provision therefor was expressly made, it is improbable that it would be, in its terms, a grossly inadequate provision; and that an indispensably necessary power to institute temporary Governments, and to legislate for the inhabitants of the territory, was passed silently by, and left to be deduced from the necessity of the case.

In the argument at the bar, great attention has been paid to the meaning of the word "territory."

Ordinarily, when the territory of a sovereign power is spoken of, it refers to that tract of country which is under the political jurisdiction of that sovereign power. Thus Chief Justice Marshall (in United States v. Bevans, 3 Wheat., 386) says: "What, then, is the extent of jurisdiction which a State possesses? We answer, without hesitation, the jurisdiction of a State is coextensive with its territory." Examples might easily be multiplied of this use of the word, but they are unnecessary, because it is familiar. But the word "territory" is not used in this broad and general sense in this clause of the Constitution.

At the time of the adoption of the Constitution, the United States held a great tract of country northwest of the Ohio; another tract, then of unknown extent, ceded by South Carolina; and a confident expectation was then entertained, and afterwards realized, that they then were or would become the owners of other great tracts, claimed by North Carolina and Georgia. These ceded tracts lay within the limits of the United States, and out of the limits of any particular State; and the cessions embraced the civil and political jurisdiction, and so much of the soil as had not previously been granted to individuals.

These words, "territory belonging to the United States," [60 U.S. 393, 611] were not used in the Constitution to describe an abstraction, but to identify and apply to these actual subjects matter then existing and belonging to the United States, and other similar subjects which might afterwards be acquired; and this being so, all the essential qualities and incidents attending such actual subjects are embraced within the words "territory belonging to the United States," as fully as if each of those essential qualities and incidents had been specifically described.

I say, the essential qualities and incidents. But in determining what were the essential qualities and incidents of the subject with which they were dealing, we must take into consideration not only all the particular facts which were immediately before them, but the great consideration, ever present to the minds of those who framed and adopted the Constitution, that they were making a frame of government for the people of the United States and their posterity, under which they hoped the United States might be, what they have now become, a great and powerful nation, possessing the power to make war and to conclude treaties, and thus to acquire territory. (See Cerre v. Pitot, 6 Cr., 336; Am. Ins. Co. v. Canter, 1 Pet., 542.) With these in view, I turn to examine the clause of the article now in question.

It is said this provision has no application to any territory save that then belonging to the United States. I have already shown that, when the Constitution was framed, a confident expectation was entertained, which was speedily realized, that North Carolina and Georgia would cede their claims to that great territory which lay west of those States. No doubt has been suggested that the first clause of this same article, which enabled Congress to admit new States, refers to and includes new States to be formed out of this territory, expected to be thereafter ceded by North Carolina and Georgia, as well as new States to be formed out of territory northwest of the Ohio, which then had been ceded by Virginia. It must have been seen, therefore, that the same necessity would exist for an authority to dispose of and make all needful regulations respecting this territory, when ceded, as existed for a like authority respecting territory which had been ceded.

No reason has been suggested why any reluctance should have been felt, by the framers of the Constitution, to apply this provision to all the territory which might belong to the United States, or why any distinction should have been made, founded on the accidental circumstance of the dates of the cessions; a circumstance in no way material as respects the necessity for rules and regulations, or the propriety of conferring [60 U.S. 393, 612] on the Congress power to make them. And if we look at the course of the debates in the Convention on this article, we shall find that the then unceded lands, so far from having been left out of view in adopting this article, constituted, in the minds of members, a subject of even paramount importance.

Again, in what an extraordinary position would the limitation of this clause to territory then belonging to the United States, place the territory which lay within the chartered limits of North Carolina and Georgia. The title to that territory was then claimed by those States, and by the United States; their respective claims are purposely left unsettled by the express words of this clause; and when cessions were made by those States, they were merely of their claims to this territory, the United States neither admitting nor denying the validity of those claims; so that it was impossible then, and has ever since remained impossible, to know whether this territory did or did not then belong to the United States; and, consequently, to know whether it was within or without the authority conferred by this clause, to dispose of and make rules and regulations respecting the territory of the United States. This attributes to the eminent men who acted on this subject a want of ability and forecast, or a want of attention to the known facts upon which they were acting, in which I cannot concur.

There is not, in my judgment, anything in the language, the history, or the subject-matter of this article, which restricts its operation to territory owned by the United States when the Constitution was adopted.

But it is also insisted that provisions of the Constitution respecting territory belonging to the United States do not apply to territory acquired by treaty from a foreign nation. This objection must rest upon the position that the Constitution did not authorize the Federal Government to acquire foreign territory, and consequently has made no provision for its government when acquired; or, that though the acquisition of foreign territory was contemplated by the Constitution, its provisions concerning the admission of new States, and the making of all needful rules and regulations respecting territory belonging to the United States, were not designed to be applicable to territory acquired from foreign nations.

It is undoubtedly true, that at the date of the treaty of 1803, between the United States and France, for the cession of Louisiana, it was made a question, whether the Constitution had conferred on the executive department of the Government of the United States power to acquire foreign territory by a treaty. [60 U.S. 393, 613] There is evidence that very grave doubts were then entertained concerning the existence of this power. But that there was then a settled opinion in the executive and legislative branches of the Government, that this power did not exist, cannot be admitted, without at the same time imputing to those who negotiated and ratified the treaty, and passed the laws necessary to carry it into execution, a deliberate and known violation of their oaths to support the Constitution; and whatever doubts may then have existed, the question must now be taken to have been settled. Four distinct acquisitions of foreign territory have been made by as many different treaties, under as many different Administrations. Six States, formed on such territory, are now in the Union. Every branch of this Government, during a period of more than fifty years, has participated in these transactions. To question their validity now, is vain. As was said by Mr. Chief Justice Marshall, in the American Insurance Company v. Canter, (1 Peters, 542,) "the Constitution confers absolutely on the Government of the Union the powers of making war and of making treaties; consequently, sequently, that Government possesses the power of acquiring territory, either by conquest or treaty." (See Cerre v. Pitot, 6 Cr., 336.) And I add, it also possesses the power of governing it, when acquired, not by resorting to supposititious powers, nowhere found described in the Constitution, but expressly granted in the authority to make all needful rules and regulations respecting the territory of the United States.

There was to be established by the Constitution a frame of government, under which the people of the United States and their posterity were to continue indefinitely. To take one of its provisions, the language of which is broad enough to extend throughout the existence of the Government, and embrace all territory belonging to the United States throughout all time, and the purposes and objects of which apply to all territory of the United States, and narrow it down to territory belonging to the United States when the Constitution was framed, while at the same time it is admitted that the Constitution contemplated and authorized the acquisition, from time to time, of other and foreign territory, seems to me to be an interpretation as inconsistent with the nature and purposes of the instrument, as it is with its language, and I can have no hesitation in rejecting it.

I construe this clause, therefore, as if it had read, Congress shall have power to make all needful rules and regulations respecting those tracts of country, out of the limits of the several States, which the United States have acquired, or may hereafter acquire, by cessions, as well of the jurisdiction as of the [60 U.S. 393, 614] soil, so far as the soil may be the property of the party making the cession, at the time of making it.

It has been urged that the words "rules and regulations" are not appropriate terms in which to convey authority to make laws for the government of the territory.

But it must be remembered that this is a grant of power to the Congress-that it is therefore necessarily a grant of power to legislate—and, certainly, rules and regulations respecting a particular subject, made by the legislative power of a country, can be nothing but laws. Nor do the particular terms employed, in my judgment, tend in any degree to restrict this legislative power. Power granted to a Legislature to make all needful rules and regulations respecting the territory, is a power to pass all needful laws respecting it.

The word regulate, or regulation, is several times used in the Constitution. It is used in the fourth section of the first article to describe those laws of the States which prescribe the times, places, and manner, of choosing Senators and Representatives; in the second section of the fourth article, to designate the legislative action of a State on the subject of fugitives from service, having a very close relation to the matter of our present inquiry; in the second section of the third article, to empower Congress to fix the extent of the appellate jurisdiction of this court; and, finally, in the eighth section of the first article are the words, "Congress shall have power to regulate commerce."

It is unnecessary to describe the body of legislation which has been enacted under this grant of power; its variety and extent are well known. But it may be mentioned, in passing, that under this power to regulate commerce, Congress has enacted a great system of municipal laws, and extended it over the vessels and crews of the United States on the high seas and in foreign ports, and even over citizens of the United States resident in China; and has established judicatures, with power to inflict even capital punishment within that country.

If, then, this clause does contain a power to legislate respecting the territory, what are the limits of that power?

To this I answer, that, in common with all the other legislative powers of Congress, it finds limits in the express prohibitions on Congress not to do certain things; that, in the exercise of the legislative power, Congress cannot pass an ex post facto law or bill of attainder; and so in respect to each of the other prohibitions contained in the Constitution.

Besides this, the rules and regulations must be needful. But undoubtedly the question whether a particular rule or regulation be needful, must be finally determined by Congress itself. Whether a law be needful, is a legislative or political, [60 U.S. 393, 615] not a judicial, question. Whatever Congress deems needful is so, under the grant of power.

Nor am I aware that it has ever been questioned that laws providing for the temporary government of the settlers on the public lands are needful, not only to prepare them for admission to the Union as States, but even to enable the United States to dispose of the lands.

Without government and social order, there can be no property; for without law, its ownership, its use, and the power of disposing of it, cease to exist, in the sense in which those words are used and understood in all civilized States.

Since, then, this power was manifestly conferred to enable the United States to dispose of its public lands to settlers, and to admit them into the Union as States, when in the judgment of Congress they should be fitted therefor, since these were the needs provided for, since it is confessed that Government is indispensable to provide for those needs, and the power is, to make all needful rules and regulations respecting the territory, I cannot doubt that this is a power to govern the inhabitants of the territory, by such laws as Congress deems needful, until they obtain admission as States.

Whether they should be thus governed solely by laws enacted by Congress, or partly by laws enacted by legislative power conferred by Congress, is one of those questions which depend on the judgment of Congress—a question which of these is needful.

But it is insisted, that whatever other powers Congress may have respecting the territory of the United States, the subject of negro slavery forms an exception.

The Constitution declares that Congress shall have power to make "all needful rules and regulations" respecting the territory belonging to the United States.

The assertion is, though the Constitution says all, it does not mean all—though it says all, without qualification, it means all except such as allow or prohibit slavery. It cannot be doubted that it is incumbent on those who would thus introduce an exception not found in the language of the instrument, to exhibit some solid and satisfactory reason, drawn from the subject-matter or the purposes and objects of the clause, the context, or from other provisions of the Constitution, showing that the words employed in this clause are not to be understood according to their clear, plain, and natural signification.

The subject-matter is the territory of the United States out of the limits of every State, and consequently under the exclusive power of the people of the United States. Their [60 U.S. 393, 616] will respecting it, manifested in the Constitution, can be subject to no restriction. The purposes and objects of the clause were the enactment of laws concerning the disposal of the public lands, and the temporary government of the settlers thereon until new States should be formed. It will not be questioned that, when the Constitution of the United States was framed and adopted, the allowance and the prohibition of negro slavery were recognised subjects of municipal legislation; every State had in some measure acted thereon; and the only legislative act concerning the territory—the ordinance of 1787, which had then so recently been passed—contained a prohibition of slavery. The purpose and object of the clause being to enable Congress to provide a body of municipal law for the government of the settlers, the allowance or the prohibition of slavery comes within the known and recognised scope of that purpose and object.

There is nothing in the context which qualifies the grant of power. The regulations must be "respecting the territory." An enactment that slavery may or may not exist there, is a regulation respecting the territory. Regulations must be needful; but it is necessarily left to the legislative discretion to determine whether a law be needful. No other clause of the Constitution has been referred to at the bar, or has been seen by me, which imposes any restriction or makes any exception concerning the power of Congress to allow or prohibit slavery in the territory belonging to the United States.

A practical construction, nearly contemporaneous with the adoption of the Constitution, and continued by repeated instances through a long series of years, may always influence, and in doubtful cases should determine, the judicial mind, on a question of the interpretation of the Constitution. (Stuart v. Laird, 1 Cranch, 269; Martin v. Hunter, 1 Wheat., 304; Cohens v. Virginia, 6 Wheat., 264; Prigg v. Pennsylvania, 16 Pet., 621; Cooley v. Port Wardens, 12 How., 315.)

In this view, I proceed briefly to examine the practical construction placed on the clause now in question, so far as it respects the inclusion therein of power to permit or prohibit slavery in the Territories.

It has already been stated, that after the Government of the United States was organized under the Constitution, the temporary Government of the Territory northwest of the river Ohio could no longer exist, save under the powers conferred on Congress by the Constitution. Whatever legislative, judicial, or executive authority should be exercised therein could be derived only from the people of the United States under the Constitution. And, accordingly, an act was passed on the [60 U.S. 393, 617] 7th day of August, 1789, (1 Stat. at Large, 50,) which recites: "Whereas, in order that the ordinance of the United States in Congress assembled, for the government of the territory northwest of the river Ohio, may continue to have full effect, it is required that certain provisions should be made, so as to adapt the same to the present Constitution of the United States." It then provides for the appointment by the President of all officers, who, by force of the ordinance, were to have been appointed by the Congress of the Confederation, and their commission in the manner required by the Constitution; and empowers the Secretary of the Territory to exercise the powers of the Governor in case of the death or necessary absence of the latter.

Here is an explicit declaration of the will of the first Congress, of which fourteen members, including Mr. Madison, had been members of the Convention which framed the Constitution, that the ordinance, one article of which prohibited slavery, "should continue to have full effect." Gen. Washington, who signed this bill, as President, was the President of that Convention.

It does not appear to me to be important, in this connection, that that clause in the ordinance which prohibited slavery was one of a series of articles of what is therein termed a compact. The Congress of the Confederation had no power to make such a compact, nor to act at all on the subject; and after what had been so recently said by Mr. Madison on this subject, in the thirty-eighth number of the Federalist, I cannot suppose that he, or any others who voted for this bill, attributed any intrinsic effect to what was denominated in the ordinance a compact between "the original States and the people and States in the new territory;" there being no new States then in existence in the territory, with whom a compact could be made, and the few scattered inhabitants, unorganized into a political body, not being capable of becoming a party to a treaty, even if the Congress of the Confederation had had power to make one touching the government of that territory.

I consider the passage of this law to have been an assertion by the first Congress of the power of the United States to prohibit slavery within this part of the territory of the United States; for it clearly shows that slavery was thereafter to be prohibited there, and it could be prohibited only by an exertion of the power of the United States, under the Constitution; no other power being capable of operating within that territory after the Constitution took effect.

On the 2d of April, 1790, (1 Stat. at Large, 106,) the first Congress passed an act accepting a deed of cession by North [60 U.S. 393, 618] Carolina of that territory afterwards erected into the State of Tennessee. The fourth express condition contained in this deed of cession, after providing that the inhabitants of the Territory shall be temporarily governed in the same manner as those beyond the Ohio, is followed by these words: "Provided, always, that no regulations made or to be made by Congress shall tend to emancipate slaves."

This provision shows that it was then understood Congress might make a regulation prohibiting slavery, and that Congress might also allow it to continue to exist in the Territory; and accordingly, when, a few days later, Congress passed the act of May 20th, 1790, (1 Stat. at Large, 123,) for the government of the Territory south of the river Ohio, it provided, "and the Government of the Territory south of the Ohio shall be similar to that now exercised in the Territory northwest of the Ohio, except so far as is otherwise provided in the conditions expressed in an act of Congress of the present session, entitled, "An act to accept a cession of the claims of the State of North Carolina to a certain district of western territory." Under the Government thus established, slavery existed until the Territory became the State of Tennessee.

On the 7th of April, 1798, (1 Stat. at Large, 649,) an act was passed to establish a Government in the Mississippi Territory in all respects like that exercised in the Territory northwest of the Ohio, "excepting and excluding the last article of the ordinance made for the government thereof by the late Congress, on the 13th day of July, 1787." When the limits of this Territory had been amicably settled with Georgia, and the latter ceded all its claim thereto, it was one stipulation in the compact of cession, that the ordinance of July 13th, 1787, "shall in all its parts extend to the Territory contained in the present act of cession, that article only excepted which forbids slavery." The Government of this Territory was subsequently established and organized under the act of May 10th, 1800; but so much of the ordinance as prohibited slavery was not put in operation there.

Without going minutely into the details of each case, I will now give reference to two classes of acts, in one of which Congress has extended the ordinance of 1787, including the article prohibiting slavery, over different Territories, and thus exerted its power to prohibit it; in the other, Congress has erected Governments over Territories acquired from France and Spain, in which slavery already existed, but refused to apply to them that part of the Government under the ordinance which excluded slavery.

Of the first class are the act of May 7th, 1800, (2 Stat. at [60 U.S. 393, 619] Large, 58,) for the government of the Indiana Territory; the act of January 11th, 1805, (2 Stat. at Large, 309,) for the government of Michigan Territory; the act of May 3d, 1809, (2 Stat. at Large, 514,) for the government of the Illinois Territory; the act of April 20th, 1836, (5 Stat. at Large, 10,) for the government of the Territory of Wisconsin; the act of June 12th, 1838, for the government of the Territory of Iowa; the act of August 14th, 1848, for the government of the Territory of Oregon. To these instances should be added the act of March 6th, 1820, (3 Stat. at Large, 548,) prohibiting slavery in the territory acquired from France, being northwest of Missouri, and north of thirty-six degrees thirty minutes north latitude.

Of the second class, in which Congress refused to interfere with slavery already existing under the municipal law of France or Spain, and established Governments by which slavery was recognised and allowed, are: the act of March 26th, 1804, (2 Stat. at Large, 283,) for the government of Louisiana; the act of March 2d, 1805, (2 Stat. at Large, 322,) for the government of the Territory of Orleans; the act of June 4th, 1812, (2 Stat. at Large, 743,) for the government of the Missouri Territory; the act of March 30th, 1822, (3 Stat. at Large, 654,) for the government of the Territory of Florida. Here are eight distinct instances, beginning with the first Congress, and coming down to the year 1848, in which Congress has excluded slavery from the territory of the United States; and six distinct instances in which Congress organized Governments of Territories by which slavery was recognised and continued, beginning also with the first Congress, and coming down to the year 1822. These acts were severally signed by seven Presidents of the United States, beginning with General Washington, and coming regularly down as far as Mr. John Quincy Adams, thus including all who were in public life when the Constitution was adopted.

If the practical construction of the Constitution contemporaneously with its going into effect, by men intimately acquainted with its history from their personal participation in framing and adopting it, and continued by them through a long series of acts of the gravest importance, be entitled to weight in the judicial mind on a question of construction, it would seem to be difficult to resist the force of the acts above adverted to.

It appears, however, from what has taken place at the bar, that notwithstanding the language of the Constitution, and the long line of legislative and executive precedents under it, three different and opposite views are taken of the power of Congress respecting slavery in the Territories. [60 U.S. 393, 620] One is, that though Congress can make a regulation prohibiting slavery in a Territory, they cannot make a regulation allowing it; another is, that it can neither be established nor prohibited by Congress, but that the people of a Territory, when organized by Congress, can establish or prohibit slavery; while the third is, that the Constitution itself secures to every citizen who holds slaves, under the laws of any State, the indefeasible right to carry them into any Territory, and there hold them as property.

No particular clause of the Constitution has been referred to at the bar in support of either of these views. The first seems to be rested upon general considerations concerning the social and moral evils of slavery, its relations to republican Governments, its inconsistency with the Declaration of Independence and with natural right.

The second is drawn from consideration equally general, concerning the right of self-government, and the nature of the political institutions which have been established by the people of the United States.

While the third is said to rest upon the equal right of all citizens to go with their property upon the public domain, and the inequality of a regulation which would admit the property of some and exclude the property of other citizens; and, inasmuch as slaves are chiefly held by citizens of those particular States where slavery is established, it is insisted that a regulation excluding slavery from a Territory operates, practically, to make an unjust discrimination between citizens of different States, in respect to their use and enjoyment of the territory of the United States.

With the weight of either of these considerations, when presented to Congress to influence its action, this court has no concern. One or the other may be justly entitled to guide or control the legislative judgment upon what is a needful regulation. The question here is, whether they are sufficient to authorize this court to insert into this clause of the Constitution an exception of the exclusion or allowance of slavery, not found therein, nor in any other part of that instrument. To engraft on any instrument a substantive exception not found in it, must be admitted to be a matter attended with great difficulty. And the difficulty increases with the importance of the instrument, and the magnitude and complexity of the interests involved in its construction. To allow this to be done with the Constitution, upon reasons purely political, renders its judicial interpretation impossible—because judicial tribunals, as such, cannot decide upon political considerations. Political reasons have not the requisite certainty to afford rules of juridical [60 U.S. 393, 621] interpretation. They are different in different men. They are different in the same men at different times. And when a strict interpretation of the Constitution, according to the fixed rules which govern the interpretation of laws, is abandoned, and the theoretical opinions of individuals are allowed to control its meaning, we have no longer a Constitution; we are under the government of individual men, who for the time being have power to declare what the Constitution is, according to their own views of what it ought to mean. When such a method of interpretation of the Constitution obtains, in place of a republican Government, with limited and defined powers, we have a Government which is merely an exponent of the will of Congress; or what, in my opinion, would not be preferable, an exponent of the individual political opinions of the members of this court.

If it can be shown, by anything in the Constitution itself, that when it confers on Congress the power to make all needful rules and regulations respecting the territory belonging to the United States, the exclusion or the allowance of slavery was excepted; or if anything in the history of this provision tends to show that such an exception was intended by those who framed and adopted the Constitution to be introduced into it, I hold it to be my duty carefully to consider, and to allow just weight to such considerations in interpreting the positive text of the Constitution. But where the Constitution has said all needful rules and regulations, I must find something more than theoretical reasoning to induce me to say it did not mean all.

There have been eminent instances in this court closely analogous to this one, in which such an attempt to introduce an exception, not found in the Constitution itself, has failed of success.

By the eighth section of the first article, Congress has the power of exclusive legislation in all cases whatsoever within this District.

In the case of Loughborough v. Blake, (5 Whea., 324,) the question arose, whether Congress has power to impose direct taxes on persons and property in this District. It was insisted, that though the grant of power was in its terms broad enough to include direct taxation, it must be limited by the principle, that taxation and representation are inseparable. It would not be easy to fix on any political truth, better established or more fully admitted in our country, than that taxation and representation must exist together. We went into the war of the Revolution to assert it, and it is incorporated as fundamental into all American Governments. But however true and important [60 U.S. 393, 622] this maxim may be, it is not necessarily of universal application. It was for the people of the United States, who ordained the Constitution, to decide whether it should or should not be permitted to operate within this District. Their decision was embodied in the words of the Constitution; and as that contained no such exception as would permit the maxim to operate in this District, this court, interpreting that language, held that the exception did not exist.

Again, the Constitution confers on Congress power to regulate commerce with foreign nations. Under this, Congress passed an act on the 22d of December, 1807, unlimited in duration, laying an embargo on all ships and vessels in the ports or within the limits and jurisdiction of the United States. No law of the United States ever pressed so severely upon particular States. Though the constitutionality of the law was contested with an earnestness and zeal proportioned to the ruinous effects which were felt from it, and though, as Mr. Chief Justice Marshall has said, (9 Wheat., 192,) "a want of acuteness in discovering objections to a measure to which they felt the most deep-rooted hostility will not be imputed to those who were arrayed in opposition to this," I am not aware that the fact that it prohibited the use of a particular species of property, belonging almost exclusively to citizens of a few States, and this indefinitely, was ever supposed to show that it was unconstitutional. Something much more stringent, as a ground of legal judgment, was relied on—that the power to regulate commerce did not include the power to annihilate commerce.

But the decision was, that under the power to regulate commerce, the power of Congress over the subject was restricted only by those exceptions and limitations contained in the Constitution; and as neither the clause in question, which was a general grant of power to regulate commerce, nor any other clause of the Constitution, imposed any restrictions as to the duration of an embargo, an unlimited prohibition of the use of the shipping of the country was within the power of Congress. On this subject, Mr. Justice Daniel, speaking for the court in the case of United States v. Marigold, (9 How., 560,) says: "Congress are, by the Constitution, vested with the power to regulate commerce with foreign nations; and however, at periods of high excitement, an application of the terms "to regulate commerce," such as would embrace absolute prohibition, may have been questioned, yet, since the passage of the embargo and nonintercourse laws, and the repeated judicial sanctions these statutes have received, it can scarcely at this day be open to doubt, that every subject falling legitimately [60 U.S. 393, 623] within the sphere of commercial regulation may be partially or wholly excluded, when either measure shall be demanded by the safety or the important interests of the entire nation. The power once conceded, it may operate on any and every subject of commerce to which the legislative discretion may apply it."

If power to regulate commerce extends to an indefinite prohibition of the use of all vessels belonging to citizens of the several States, and may operate, without exception, upon every subject of commerce to which the legislative discretion may apply it, upon what grounds can I say that power to make all needful rules and regulations respecting the territory of the United States is subject to an exception of the allowance or prohibition of slavery therein?

While the regulation is one "respecting the territory," while it is, in the judgment of Congress, "a needful regulation," and is thus completely within the words of the grant, while no other clause of the Constitution can be shown, which requires the insertion of an exception respecting slavery, and while the practical construction for a period of upwards of fifty years forbids such an exception, it would, in my opinion, violate every sound rule of interpretation to force that exception into the Constitution upon the strength of abstract political reasoning, which we are bound to believe the people of the United States thought insufficient to induce them to limit the power of Congress, because what they have said contains no such limitation.

Before I proceed further to notice some other grounds of supposed objection to this power of Congress, I desire to say, that if it were not for my anxiety to insist upon what I deem a correct exposition of the Constitution, if I looked only to the purposes of the argument, the source of the power of Congress asserted in the opinion of the majority of the court would answer those purposes equally well. For they admit that Congress has power to organize and govern the Territories until they arrive at a suitable condition for admission to the Union; they admit, also, that the kind of Government which shall thus exist should be regulated by the condition and wants of each Territory, and that it is necessarily committed to the discretion of Congress to enact such laws for that purpose as that discretion may dictate; and no limit to that discretion has been shown, or even suggested, save those positive prohibitions to legislate, which are found in the Constitution.

I confess myself unable to perceive any difference whatever between my own opinion of the general extent of the power of Congress and the opinion of the majority of the court, save [60 U.S. 393, 624] that I consider it derivable from the express language of the Constitution, while they hold it to be silently implied from the power to acquire territory. Looking at the power of Congress over the Territories as of the extent just described, what positive prohibition exists in the Constitution, which restrained Congress from enacting a law in 1820 to prohibit slavery north of thirty-six degrees thirty minutes north latitude?

The only one suggested is that clause in the fifth article of the amendments of the Constitution which declares that no person shall be deprived of his life, liberty, or property, without due process of law. I will now proceed to examine the question, whether this clause is entitled to the effect thus attributed to it. It is necessary, first, to have a clear view of the nature and incidents of that particular species of property which is now in question.

Slavery, being contrary to natural right, is created only by municipal law. This is not only plain in itself, and agreed by all writers on the subject, but is inferable from the Constitution, and has been explicitly declared by this court. The Constitution refers to slaves as "persons held to service in one State, under the laws thereof." Nothing can more clearly describe a status created by municipal law. In Prigg v. Pennsylvania, (10 Pet., 611,) this court said: "The state of slavery is deemed to be a mere municipal regulation, founded on and limited to the range of territorial laws." In Rankin v. Lydia, (2 Marsh., 12, 470,) the Supreme Court of Appeals of Kentucky said: "Slavery is sanctioned by the laws of this State, and the right to hold them under our municipal regulations is unquestionable. But we view this as a right existing by positive law of a municipal character, without foundation in the law of nature or the unwritten common law." I am not acquainted with any case or writer questioning the correctness of this doctrine. (See also 1 Burge, Col. and For. Laws, 738-741, where the authorities are collected.)

The status of slavery is not necessarily always attended with the same powers on the part of the master. The master is subject to the supreme power of the State, whose will controls his action towards his slave, and this control must be defined and regulated by the municipal law. In one State, as at one period of the Roman law, it may put the life of the slave into the hand of the master; others, as those of the United States, which tolerate slavery, may treat the slave as a person, when the master takes his life; while in others, the law may recognise a right of the slave to be protected from cruel treatment. In other words, the status of slavery embraces every condition, from that in which the slave is known to the law simply as a [60 U.S. 393, 625] chattel, with no civil rights, to that in which he is recognised as a person for all purposes, save the compulsory power of directing and receiving the fruits of his labor. Which of these conditions shall attend the status of slavery, must depend on the municipal law which creates and upholds it.

And not only must the status of slavery be created and measured by municipal law, but the rights, powers, and obligations, which grow out of that status, must be defined, protected, and enforced, by such laws. The liability of the master for the torts and crimes of his slave, and of third persons for assaulting or injuring or harboring or kidnapping him, the forms and modes of emancipation and sale, their subjection to the debts of the master, succession by death of the master, suits for freedom, the capacity of the slave to be party to a suit, or to be a witness, with such police regulations as have existed in all civilized States where slavery has been tolerated, are among the subjects upon which municipal legislation becomes necessary when slavery is introduced.

Is it conceivable that the Constitution has conferred the right on every citizen to become a resident on the territory of the United States with his slaves, and there to hold them as such, but has neither made nor provided for any municipal regulations which are essential to the existence of slavery?

Is it not more rational to conclude that they who framed and adopted the constitution were aware that persons held to service under the laws of a State are property only to the extent and under the conditions fixed by those laws; that they must cease to be available as property, when their owners voluntarily place them permanently within another jurisdiction, where no municipal laws on the subject of slavery exist; and that, being aware of these principles, and having said nothing to interfere with or displace them, or to compel Congress to legislate in any particular manner on the subject, and having empowered Congress to make all needful rules and regulations respecting the territory of the United States, it was their intention to leave to the discretion of Congress what regulations, if any, should be made concerning slavery therein? Moreover, if the right exists, what are its limits, and what are its conditions? If citizens of the United States have the right to take their slaves to a Territory, and hold them there as slaves, without regard to the laws of the Territory, I suppose this right is not to be restricted to the citizens of slaveholding States. A citizen of a State which does not tolerate slavery can hardly be denied the power of doing the same thing. And what law of slavery does either take with him to the Territory? If it be said to be those laws respecting [60 U.S. 393, 626] slavery which existed in the particular State from which each slave last came, what an anomaly is this? Where else can we find, under the law of any civilized country, the power to introduce and permanently continue diverse systems of foreign municipal law, for holding persons in slavery? I say, not merely to introduce, but permanently to continue, these anomalies. For the offspring of the female must be governed by the foreign municipal laws to which the mother was subject; and when any slave is sold or passes by succession on the death of the owner, there must pass with him, by a species of subrogation, and as a kind of unknown jus in re, the foreign municipal laws which constituted, regulated, and preserved, the status of the slave before his exportation. Whatever theoretical importance may be now supposed to belong to the maintenance of such a right, I feel a perfect conviction that it would, if ever tried, prove to be as impracticable in fact, as it is, in my judgment, monstrous in theory.

I consider the assumption which lies at the basis of this theory to be unsound; not in its just sense, and when properly understood, but in the sense which has been attached to it. That assumption is, that the territory ceded by France was acquired for the equal benefit of all the citizens of the United States. I agree to the position. But it was acquired for their benefit in their collective, not their individual, capacities. It was acquired for their benefit, as an organized political society, subsisting as "the people of the United States," under the Constitution of the United States; to be administered justly and impartially, and as nearly as possible for the equal benefit of every individual citizen, according to the best judgment and discretion of the Congress; to whose power, as the Legislature of the nation which acquired it, the people of the United States have committed its administration. Whatever individual claims may be founded on local circumstances, or sectional differences of condition, cannot, in my opinion, be recognised in this court, without arrogating to the judicial branch of the Government powers not committed to it; and which, with all the unaffected respect I feel for it, when acting in its proper sphere, I do not think it fitted to wield.

Nor, in my judgment, will the position, that a prohibition to bring slaves into a Territory deprives any one of his property without due process of law, bear examination.

It must be remembered that this restriction on the legislative power is not peculiar to the Constitution of the United States; it was borrowed from Magna Charta; was brought to America by our ancestors, as part of their inherited liberties, and has existed in all the States, usually in the very words of [60 U.S. 393, 627] the great charter. It existed in every political community in America in 1787, when the ordinance prohibiting slavery north and west of the Ohio was passed.

And if a prohibition of slavery in a Territory in 1820 violated this principle of Magna Charta, the ordinance of 1787 also violated it; and what power had, I do not say the Congress of the Confederation alone, but the Legislature of Virginia, or the Legislature of any or all the States of the Confederacy, to consent to such a violation? The people of the States had conferred no such power. I think I may at least say, if the Congress did then violate Magna Charta by the ordinance, no one discovered that violation. Besides, if the prohibition upon all persons, citizens as well as others, to bring slaves into a Territory, and a declaration that if brought they shall be free, deprives citizens of their property without due process of law, what shall we say of the legislation of many of the slaveholding States which have enacted the same prohibition? As early as October, 1778, a law was passed in Virginia, that thereafter no slave should be imported into that Commonwealth by sea or by land, and that every slave who should be imported should become free. A citizen of Virginia purchased in Maryland a slave who belonged to another citizen of Virginia, and removed with the slave to Virginia. The slave sued for her freedom, and recovered it; as may be seen in Wilson v. Isabel, (5 Call's R., 425.) See also Hunter v. Hulsher, (1 Leigh, 172;) and a similar law has been recognised as valid in Maryland, in Stewart v. Oaks, (5 Har.

and John., 107.) I am not aware that such laws, though they exist in many States, were ever supposed to be in conflict with the principle of Magna Charta incorporated into the State Constitutions. It was certainly understood by the Convention which framed the Constitution, and has been so understood ever since, that, under the power to regulate commerce, Congress could prohibit the importation of slaves; and the exercise of the power was restrained till 1808. A citizen of the United States owns slaves in Cuba, and brings them to the United States, where they are set free by the legislation of Congress. Does this legislation deprive him of his property without due process of law? If so, what becomes of the laws prohibiting the slave trade? If not, how can similar regulation respecting a Territory violate the fifth amendment of the Constitution?

Some reliance was placed by the defendant's counsel upon the fact that the prohibition of slavery in this territory was in the words, "that slavery, &c., shall be and is hereby forever prohibited." But the insertion of the word forever can have no legal effect. Every enactment not expressly limited in its [60 U.S. 393, 628] duration continues in force until repealed or abrogated by some competent power, and the use of the word "forever" can give to the law no more durable operation. The argument is, that Congress cannot so legislate as to bind the future States formed out of the territory, and that in this instance it has attempted to do so. Of the political reasons which may have induced the Congress to use these words, and which caused them to expect that subsequent Legislatures would conform their action to the then general opinion of the country that it ought to be permanent, this court can take no cognizance.

However fit such considerations are to control the action of Congress, and however reluctant a statesman may be to disturb what has been settled, every law made by Congress may be repealed, and, saving private rights, and public rights gained by States, its repeal is subject to the absolute will of the same power which enacted it. If Congress had enacted that the crime of murder, committed in this Indian Territory, north of thirty-six degrees thirty minutes, by or on any white man, should forever be punishable with death, it would seem to me an insufficient objection to an indictment, found while it was a Territory, that at some future day States might exist there, and so the law was invalid, because, by its terms, it was to continue in force forever. Such an objection rests upon a misapprehension of the province and power of courts respecting the constitutionality of laws enacted by the Legislature.

If the Constitution prescribe one rule, and the law another and different rule, it is the duty of courts to declare that the Constitution, and not the law, governs the case before them for judgment. If the law include no case save those for which the Constitution has furnished a different rule, or no case which the Legislature has the power to govern, then the law can have no operation. If it includes cases which the Legislature has power to govern, and concerning which the Constitution does not pre-scribe a different rule, the law governs those cases, though it may, in its terms, attempt to include others, on which it cannot operate. In other words, this court cannot declare void an act of Congress which consti-tutionally embraces some cases, though other cases, within its terms, are beyond the control of Congress, or beyond the reach of that particular law. If, therefore, Congress had power to make a law excluding slavery from this territory while under the exclusive power of the United States, the use of the word "forever" does not invalidate the law, so long as Congress has the exclusive legislative power in the territory. [60 U.S. 393, 629] But it is further insisted that the treaty of 1803, between the United States and France, by which this territory was acquired, has so restrained the constitutional powers of Congress, that it cannot, by law, prohibit the introduction of slavery into that part of this territory north and west of Missouri, and north of thirty-six degrees thirty minutes north latitude.

By a treaty with a foreign nation, the United States may rightfully stip-ulate that the Congress will or will not exercise its legislative power in some particular manner, on some particular subject. Such promises, when made, should be voluntarily kept, with the most scrupulous good faith. But that a treaty with a foreign nation can deprive the Congress of any part of the legislative power conferred by the people, so that it no longer can leg-islate as it was empowered by the Constitution to do, I more than doubt.

The powers of the Government do and must remain unimpaired. The responsibility of the Government to a foreign nation, for the exercise of those powers, is quite another matter. That responsibility is to be met, and justified to the foreign nation, according to the requirements of the rules of public law; but never upon the assumption that the United States had parted with or restricted any power of acting according to its own free will, governed solely by its own appreciation of its duty.

The second section of the fourth article is, "This Constitution, and the laws of the United States which shall be made in pursuance thereof, and all treaties made or which shall be made under the authority of the United States, shall be the supreme law of the land." This has made treaties part of our municipal law; but it has not assigned to them any particular degree of authority, nor declared that laws so enacted shall be irrepealable. No supremacy is assigned to treaties over acts of Congress. That they are not perpetual, and must be in some way repealable, all will agree.

If the President and the Senate alone possess the power to repeal or modify a law found in a treaty, inasmuch as they can change or abrogate one treaty only by making another inconsistent with the first, the Government of the United States could not act at all, to that effect, with-out the consent of some foreign Government. I do not consider, I am not aware it has ever been considered, that the Constitution has placed our country in this helpless condition. The action of Congress in repealing the treaties with France by the act of July 7th, 1798, (1 Stat. at Large, 578,) was in conformity with these views. In the case of Taylor et al. v. Morton, (2 Curtis's Cir. Ct. R., [60 U.S. 393, 630] 454,) I had occasion to consider this subject, and I adhere to the views there expressed.

If, therefore, it were admitted that the treaty between the United States and France did contain an express stipulation that the United States would not exclude slavery from so much of the ceded territory as is now in question, this court could not declare that an act of Congress excluding it was void by force of the treaty. Whether or no a case existed sufficient to justify a refusal to execute such a stipulation, would not be a judicial, but a political and legislative question, wholly beyond the authority of this court to try and determine. It would belong to diplomacy and legislation, and not to the administration of existing laws. Such a stipulation in a treaty, to legislate or not to legislate in a particular way, has been repeatedly held in this court to address itself to the political or the legislative power, by whose action thereon this court is bound. (Foster v. Nicolson, 2 Peters, 314; Garcia v. Lee, 12 Peters, 519.)

But, in my judgment, this treaty contains no stipulation in any manner affecting the action of the United States respecting the territory in question. Before examining the language of the treaty, it is material to bear in mind that the part of the ceded territory lying north of thirty-six degrees thirty minutes, and west and north of the present State of Missouri, was then a wilderness, uninhabited save by savages, whose possessory title had not then been extinguished.

It is impossible for me to conceive on what ground France could have advanced a claim, or could have desired to advance a claim, to restrain the United States from making any rules and regulations respecting this territory, which the United States might think fit to make; and still less can I conceive of any reason which would have induced the United States to yield to such a claim. It was to be expected that France would desire to make the change of sovereignty and jurisdiction as little burdensome as possible to the then inhabitants of Louisiana, and might well exhibit even an anxious solicitude to protect their property and persons, and secure to them and their posterity their religious and political rights; and the United States, as a just Government, might readily accede to all proper stipulations respecting those who were about to have their allegiance transferred. But what interest France could have in uninhabited territory, which, in the language of the treaty, was to be transferred "forever, and in full sovereignty," to the United States, or how the United States could consent to allow a foreign nation to interfere in its purely internal affairs, in which that foreign nation had no concern [60 U.S. 393, 631] whatever, is difficult for me to conjecture. In my judgment, this treaty contains nothing of the kind.

The third article is supposed to have a bearing on the question. It is as follows: "The inhabitants of the ceded territory shall be incorporated in the Union of the United States, and admitted as soon as possible, according to the principles of the Federal Constitution, to the enjoyment of all the rights, advantages, and immunities, of citizens of the United States; and in the mean time they shall be maintained and protected in the enjoyment of their liberty, property, and the religion they profess."

There are two views of this article, each of which, I think, decisively shows that it was not intended to restrain the Congress from excluding slavery from that part of the ceded territory then uninhabited. The first is, that, manifestly, its sole object was to protect individual rights of the then inhabitants of the territory. They are to be "maintained and protected in the free enjoyment of their liberty, property, and the religion they profess." But this article does not secure to them the right to go upon the public domain ceded by the treaty, either with or without their slaves. The right or power of doing this did not exist before or at the time the treaty was made. The French and Spanish Governments while they held the country, as well as the United States when they acquired it, always exercised the undoubted right of excluding inhabitants from the Indian country, and of determining when and on what conditions it should be opened to settlers. And a stipulation, that the then inhabitants of Louisiana should be protected in their property, can have no reference to their use of that property, where they had no right, under the treaty, to go with it, save at the will of the United States. If one who was an inhabitant of Louisiana at the time of the treaty had afterwards taken property then owned by him, consisting of fire-arms, ammunition, and spirits, and had gone into the Indian country north of thirty-six degrees thirty minutes, to sell them to the Indians, all must agree the third article of the treaty would not have protected him from indictment under the act of Congress of March 30, 1802, (2 Stat. at Large, 139,) adopted and extended to this territory by the act of March 26, 1804, (2 Stat. at Large, 283.)

Besides, whatever rights were secured were individual rights. If Congress should pass any law which violated such rights of any individual, and those rights were of such a character as not to be within the lawful control of Congress under the Constitution, that individual could complain, and the act of Congress, as to such rights of his, would be inoperative; but it [60 U.S. 393, 632] would be valid and operative as to all other persons, whose individual rights did not come under the protection of the treaty. And inasmuch as it does not appear that any inhabitant of Louisiana, whose rights were secured by treaty, had been injured, it would be wholly inadmissible for this court to assume, first, that one or more such cases may have existed; and, second, that if any did exist, the entire law was void—not only as to those cases, if any, in which it could not rightfully operate, but as to all others, wholly unconnected with the treaty, in which such law could rightfully operate.

But it is quite unnecessary, in my opinion, to pursue this inquiry further, because it clearly appears from the language of the article, and it has been decided by this court, that the stipulation was temporary, and ceased to have any effect when the then inhabitants of the Territory of Louisiana, in whose behalf the stipulation was made, were incorporated into the Union.

In the cases of New Orleans v. De Armas et al., (9 Peters, 223,) the question was, whether a title to property, which existed at the date of the treaty, continued to be protected by the treaty after the State of Louisiana was admitted to the Union. The third article of the treaty was relied on. Mr. Chief Justice Marshall said: "This article obviously contemplates two objects. One, that Louisiana shall be admitted into the Union as soon as possible, on an equal footing with the other States; and the other, that, till such admission, the inhabitants of the ceded territory shall be protected in the free enjoyment of their liberty, property, and religion. Had any one of these rights been violated while these stipulations continued in force, the individual supposing himself to be injured might have brought his case into this court, under the twenty-fifth section of the judicial act. But this stipulation ceased to operate when Louisiana became a member of the Union, and its inhabitants were "admitted to the enjoyment of all the rights, advantages, and immunities, of citizens of the United States."

The cases of Chouteau v. Marguerita, (12 Peters, 507,) and Permoli v. New Orleans, (3 How., 589,) are in conformity with this view of the treaty.

To convert this temporary stipulation of the treaty, in behalf of French subjects who then inhabited a small portion of Louisiana, into a permanent restriction upon the power of Congress to regulate territory then uninhabited, and to assert that it not only restrains Congress from affecting the rights of property of the then inhabitants, but enabled them and all other citizens of the United States to go into any part of the [60 U.S. 393, 633] ceded territory with their slaves, and hold them there, is a construction of this treaty so opposed to its natural meaning, and so far beyond its subject-matter and the evident design of the parties, that I cannot assent to it. In my opinion, this treaty has no bearing on the present question.

For these reasons, I am of opinion that so much of the several acts of Congress as prohibited slavery and involuntary servitude within that part of the Territory of Wisconsin lying north of thirty-six degrees thirty minutes north latitude, and west of the river Mississippi, were constitutional and valid laws.

I have expressed my opinion, and the reasons therefor, at far greater length than I could have wished, upon the different questions on which I have found it necessary to pass, to arrive at a judgment on the case at bar. These questions are numerous, and the grave importance of some of them required me to exhibit fully the grounds of my opinion. I have touched no question which, in the view I have taken, it was not absolutely necessary for me to pass upon, to ascertain whether the judgment of the Circuit Court should stand or be reversed. I have avoided no question on which the validity of that judgment depends. To have done either more or less, would have been inconsistent with my views of my duty.

In my opinion, the judgment of the Circuit Court should be reversed, and the cause remanded for a new trial.

FOOTNOTES

[1] Note by Mr. Justice Curtis. This statement that some territory did actually pass by this cession, is taken from the opinion of the court, delivered by Mr. Justice Wayne, in the case of Howard v. Ingersoll, reported in 13 How., 405. It is an obscure matter, and, on some examination of it, I have been led to doubt whether any territory actually passed by this cession. But as the fact is not important to the argument, I have not thought it necessary further to investigate it.

[2] It was published in a newspaper at Philadelphia, in May, and a copy of it was sent by R. H. Lee to Gen. Washington, on the 15th of July. (See p. 261, Cor. of Am. Rev., vol. 4, and Writings of Washington, vol. 9, p. 174.)

Plessy v. Ferguson
1896

After the end of Reconstruction in 1877, many southern states began passing what were commonly called "Jim Crow" laws, designed to create complete segregation between blacks and whites. This segregation extended to all areas of public life, including bathrooms, restaurants, buses, trains, etc. On June 7, 1892, Homer Plessy, a man of ⅛ black ancestry, boarded a "whites only" car on a train headed from New Orleans to Covington, Louisiana. Though he had purchased a first-class ticket, Plessy was promptly arrested and imprisoned for violating Louisiana's "Jim Crow" law. During his trial at the criminal district court of Orleans Parish, Plessy petitioned the Louisiana Supreme Court for a writ of prohibition against Judge John H. Ferguson, which would have ordered the lower court not to exercise jurisdiction in the case. When the Louisiana Supreme Court denied his petition, Plessy petitioned the U.S. Supreme Court, which accepted the jurisdiction.

Despite counsel Albion Tourgee's famous argument that separate but equal was equal only in theory—thus violating the Fourteenth Amendment—the court ruled 8 to 1 against Plessy, upholding Louisiana's segregationist policies. This led to an increase in "Jim Crow" laws throughout the South, until this case was finally overruled by *Brown v. Board of Education* in 1954.

U.S. SUPREME COURT

PLESSY V. FERGUSON, 163 U.S. 537 (1896)

163 U.S. 537

PLESSY
V.
FERGUSON.

No. 210.

MAY 18, 1896. [163 U.S. 537, 538] This was a petition for writs of prohibition and certiorari originally filed in the supreme court of the state by Plessy, the plaintiff in error, against the Hon. John H. Ferguson, judge of the criminal district court for the parish of Orleans, and setting forth, in substance, the following facts:

That petitioner was a citizen of the United States and a resident of the state of Louisiana, of mixed descent, in the proportion of seven-eighths Caucasian and one-eighth African blood; that the mixture of colored blood was not discernible in him, and that he was entitled to every recognition, right, privilege, and immunity secured to the citizens of the United States of the white race by its constitution and laws; that on June 7, 1892, he engaged and paid for a first-class passage on the East Louisiana Railway, from New Orleans to Covington, in the same state, and thereupon entered a passenger train, and took possession of a vacant seat in a coach where passengers of the white race were accommodated; that such railroad company was incorporated by the laws of Louisiana as a common carrier, and was not authorized to distinguish between citizens according to their race, but, notwithstanding this, petitioner was required by the conductor, under penalty of ejection from said train and imprisonment, to vacate said coach, and occupy another seat, in a coach assigned by said company for persons not of the white race, and for no other reason than that petitioner was of the colored race; that, upon petitioner's refusal to comply with such order, he was, with the aid of a police officer, forcibly ejected from said coach, and hurried off to, and imprisoned in, the parish jail of [163 U.S. 537, 539] New Orleans, and there held to answer a charge made by such officer to the effect that he was guilty of having criminally violated an act of the general assembly of the state, approved July 10, 1890, in such case made and provided.

The petitioner was subsequently brought before the recorder of the city for preliminary examination, and committed for trial to the criminal district court for the parish of Orleans, where an information was filed against him in the matter above set forth, for a violation of the above act, which act the petitioner affirmed to be null and void, because in conflict with the constitution of the United States; that petitioner interposed a plea to such information, based upon the unconstitutionality of the act of the general assembly, to which the district attorney, on behalf of the state, filed a demurrer; that, upon issue being joined upon such demurrer and plea, the court sustained the demurrer, overruled the plea, and ordered petitioner to plead over to the facts set forth in the information, and that, unless the judge of the said court be enjoined by a writ of prohibition from further proceeding in such case, the court will proceed to fine and sentence petitioner to imprisonment, and thus deprive him of his constitutional rights set forth in his said plea, notwithstanding the unconstitutionality of the act under which he was being prosecuted; that no appeal lay from such sentence, and petitioner was without relief or remedy except by writs of prohibition and certiorari. Copies of the information and other proceedings in the criminal district court were annexed to the petition as an exhibit.

Upon the filing of this petition, an order was issued upon the respondent to show cause why a writ of prohibition should not issue, and be made perpetual, and a further order that the record of the proceedings had in the criminal cause be certified and transmitted to the supreme court.

To this order the respondent made answer, transmitting a certified copy of the proceedings, asserting the constitutionality of the law, and averring that, instead of pleading or admitting that he belonged to the colored race, the said Plessy declined and refused, either by pleading or otherwise, to admit [163 U.S. 537, 540] that he was in any sense or in any proportion a colored man.

The case coming on for hearing before the supreme court, that court was of opinion that the law under which the prosecution was had was constitutional and denied the relief prayed for by the petitioner (Ex parte Plessy, 45 La. Ann. 80, 11 South. 948); whereupon petitioner prayed for a writ of error from this court, which was allowed by the chief justice of the supreme court of Louisiana.

Mr. Justice Harlan dissenting.

A. W. Tourgee and S. F. Phillips, for plaintiff in error.

Alex. Porter Morse, for defendant in error.

Mr. Justice BROWN, after stating the facts in the foregoing language, delivered the opinion of the court.

This case turns upon the constitutionality of an act of the general assembly of the state of Louisiana, passed in 1890, providing for separate railway carriages for the white and colored races. Acts 1890, No. 111, p. 152.

The first section of the statute enacts "that all railway companies carrying passengers in their coaches in this state, shall provide equal but separate accommodations for the white, and colored races, by providing two or more passenger coaches for each passenger train, or by dividing the passenger coaches by a partition so as to secure separate accommodations: provided, that this section shall not be construed to apply to street railroads. No person or persons shall be permitted to occupy seats in coaches, other than the ones assigned to them, on account of the race they belong to."

By the second section it was enacted "that the officers of such passenger trains shall have power and are hereby required [163 U.S. 537, 541] to assign each passenger to the coach or compartment used for the race to which such passenger belongs; any passenger insisting on going into a coach or compartment to which by race he does not belong, shall be liable to a fine of twenty-five dollars, or in lieu thereof to imprisonment for a period of not more than twenty days in the parish prison, and any officer of any railroad insisting on assigning a passenger to a coach or compartment other than the one set aside for the race to which said passenger belongs, shall be liable to a fine of twenty-five dollars, or in lieu thereof to imprisonment for a period of not more than twenty days in the parish prison; and should any passenger refuse to occupy the coach or compartment to which he or she is assigned by the officer of such railway, said officer shall have power to refuse to carry such passenger on his train, and for such refusal neither he nor the railway company which he represents shall be liable for damages in any of the courts of this state."

The third section provides penalties for the refusal or neglect of the officers, directors, conductors, and employees of railway companies to comply with the act, with a proviso that "nothing in this act shall be construed as applying to nurses attending children of the other race." The fourth section is immaterial.

The information filed in the criminal district court charged, in substance, that Plessy, being a passenger between two stations within the state of Louisiana, was assigned by officers of the company to the coach used for the race to which he belonged, but he insisted upon going into a coach used by the race to which he did not belong. Neither in the information nor plea was his particular race or color averred.

The petition for the writ of prohibition averred that petitioner was seven-eighths Caucasian and one-eighth African blood; that the mixture of colored blood was not discernible in him; and that he was entitled to every right, privilege, and immunity secured to citizens of the United States of the white race; and that, upon such theory, he took possession of a vacant seat in a coach where passengers of the white race were accommodated, and was ordered by the conductor to vacate [163 U.S. 537, 542] said coach, and take a seat in another, assigned to persons of the colored race, and, having refused to comply with such demand, he was forcibly ejected, with the aid of a police officer, and imprisoned in the parish jail to answer a charge of having violated the above act.

The constitutionality of this act is attacked upon the ground that it conflicts both with the thirteenth amendment of the constitution, abolishing slavery, and the fourteenth amendment, which prohibits certain restrictive legislation on the part of the states.

1. That it does not conflict with the thirteenth amendment, which abolished slavery and involuntary servitude, except a punishment for crime, is too clear for argument. Slavery implies involuntary servitude,— a state of bondage; the ownership of mankind as a chattel, or, at least, the control of the labor and services of one man for the benefit of another, and the absence of a legal right to the disposal of his own person, property, and services. This amendment was said in the Slaughter-House Cases, 16 Wall. 36, to have been intended primarily to abolish slavery, as it had been previously known in this country, and that it equally forbade Mexican peonage or the Chinese coolie trade, when they amounted to slavery or involuntary servitude, and that the use of the word "servitude" was intended to prohibit the use of all forms of involuntary slavery, of whatever class or name. It was intimated, however, in that case, that this amendment was regarded by the statesmen of that day as insufficient to protect the colored race from certain laws which had been enacted in the Southern states, imposing upon the colored race onerous disabilities and burdens, and curtailing their rights in the pursuit of life, liberty, and property to such an extent that their freedom was of little value; and that the fourteenth amendment was devised to meet this exigency.

So, too, in the Civil Rights Cases, 109 U.S. 3, 3 Sup. Ct. 18, it was said that the act of a mere individual, the owner of an inn, a public conveyance or place of amusement, refusing accommodations to colored people, cannot be justly regarded as imposing any badge of slavery or servitude upon the applicant, but [163 U.S. 537, 543] only as involving an ordinary civil injury, properly cognizable by the laws of the state, and presumably subject to redress by those laws until the contrary appears. "It would be running the slavery question into the ground," said Mr. Justice Bradley, "to make it apply to every act of discrimination which a person may see fit to make as to the guests he will entertain, or as to the people he will take into his coach or cab or car, or admit to his concert or theater, or deal with in other matters of intercourse or business."

A statute which implies merely a legal distinction between the white and colored races—a distinction which is founded in the color of the two races, and which must always exist so long as white men are distinguished from the other race by color—has no tendency to destroy the legal equality of the two races, or re-establish a state of involuntary servitude. Indeed, we do not understand that the thirteenth amendment is strenuously relied upon by the plaintiff in error in this connection.

2. By the fourteenth amendment, all persons born or naturalized in the United States, and subject to the jurisdiction thereof, are made citizens of the United States and of the state wherein they reside; and the states are forbidden from making or enforcing any law which shall abridge the privileges or immunities of citizens of the United States, or shall deprive any person of life, liberty, or property without due process of law, or deny to any person within their jurisdiction the equal protection of the laws.

The proper construction of this amendment was first called to the attention of this court in the Slaughter-House Cases, 16 Wall. 36, which involved, however, not a question of race, but one of exclusive privileges. The case did not call for any expression of opinion as to the exact rights it was intended to secure to the colored race, but it was said generally that its main purpose was to establish the citizenship of the negro, to give definitions of citizenship of the United States and of the states, and to protect from the hostile legislation of the states the privileges and immunities of citizens of the United States, as distinguished from those of citizens of the states. [163 U.S. 537, 544] The object of the amendment was undoubtedly to enforce the absolute equality of the two races before the law, but, in the nature of things, it could not have been intended to abolish distinctions based upon color, or to enforce social, as distinguished from political, equality, or a commingling of the two races upon terms unsatisfactory to either. Laws permitting, and even requiring, their separation, in places where they are liable to be brought into contact, do not necessarily imply the inferiority of either race to the other, and have been generally, if not universally, recognized as within the competency of the state legislatures in the exercise of their police power. The most common instance of this is connected with the establishment of separate schools for white and colored children, which have been held to be a valid exercise of the legislative power even by courts of states where the political rights of the colored race have been longest and most earnestly enforced.

One of the earliest of these cases is that of Roberts v. City of Boston, 5 Cush. 198, in which the supreme judicial court of Massachusetts held that the general school committee of Boston had power to make provision for the instruction of colored children in separate schools established exclusively for them, and to prohibit their attendance upon the other schools. "The great principle," said Chief Justice Shaw, "advanced by the learned and eloquent advocate for the plaintiff [Mr. Charles Sumner], is that, by the constitution and laws of Massachusetts, all persons, without distinction of age or sex, birth or color, origin or condition, are equal before the law. . . . But, when this great principle comes to be applied to the actual and various conditions of persons in society, it will not warrant the assertion that men and women are legally clothed with the same civil and political powers, and that children and adults are legally to have the same functions and be subject to the same treatment; but only that the rights of all, as they are settled and regulated by law, are equally entitled to the paternal consideration and protection of the law for their maintenance and security." It was held that the powers of the committee extended to the establishment [163 U.S. 537, 545] of separate schools for children of different ages, sexes and colors, and that they might also establish special schools for poor and neglected children, who have become too old to attend the primary school, and yet have not acquired the rudiments of learning, to enable them to enter the ordinary schools. Similar laws have been enacted by congress under its general power of legislation over the District of Columbia (sections 281–283, 310, 319, Rev. St. D. C.), as well as by the legislatures of many of the states, and have been generally, if not uniformly, sustained by the courts. State v. McCann, 21 Ohio St. 210; Lehew v. Brummell (Mo. Sup.) 15 S. W. 765; Ward v. Flood, 48 Cal. 36; Bertonneau v. Directors of City Schools, 3 Woods, 177, Fed. Cas. No. 1,361; People v. Gallagher, 93 N. Y. 438; Cory v. Carter, 48 Ind. 337; Dawson v. Lee, 83 Ky. 49.

Laws forbidding the intermarriage of the two races may be said in a technical sense to interfere with the freedom of contract, and yet have been universally recognized as within the police power of the state. State v. Gibson, 36 Ind. 389.

The distinction between laws interfering with the political equality of the negro and those requiring the separation of the two races in schools, theaters, and railway carriages has been frequently drawn by this court. Thus, in Strauder v. West Virginia, 100 U.S. 303, it was held that a law of West Virginia limiting to white male persons 21 years of age, and citizens of the state, the right to sit upon juries, was a discrimination which implied a legal inferiority in civil society, which lessened the security of the right of the colored race, and was a step towards reducing them to a condition of servility. Indeed, the right of a colored man that, in the selection of jurors to pass upon his life, liberty, and property, there shall be no exclusion of his race, and no discrimination against them because of color, has been asserted in a number of cases. Virginia v. Rivers, 100 U.S. 313; Neal v. Delaware, 103 U.S. 370; ush v. Com., 107 U.S. 110, 1 Sup. Ct. 625; Gibson v. Mississippi, 162 U.S. 565, 16 Sup. Ct. 904. So, where the laws of a particular locality or the charter of a particular railway corporation has provided that no person shall be excluded from the cars on account of [163 U.S. 537, 546] color, we have held that this meant that persons of color should travel in the same car as white ones, and that the enactment was not satisfied by the company providing cars assigned exclusively to people of color, though they were as good as those which they assigned exclusively to white persons. Railroad Co. v. Brown, 17 Wall. 445.

Upon the other hand, where a statute of Louisiana required those engaged in the transportation of passengers among the states to give to all persons traveling within that state, upon vessels employed in that business, equal rights and privileges in all parts of the vessel, without distinction on account of race or color, and subjected to an action for damages the owner of such a vessel who excluded colored passengers on account of their color from the cabin set aside by him for the use of whites, it was held to be, so far as it applied to interstate commerce, unconstitutional and void. Hall v. De Cuir, 95 U.S. 485. The court in this case, however, expressly disclaimed that it had anything whatever to do with the statute as a regulation of internal commerce, or affecting anything else than commerce among the states.

In the Civil Rights Cases, 109 U.S. 3, 3 Sup. Ct. 18, it was held that an act of congress entitling all persons within the jurisdiction of the United States to the full and equal enjoyment of the accommodations, advantages, facilities, and privileges of inns, public conveyances, on land or water, theaters, and other places of public amusement, and made applicable to citizens of every race and color, regardless of any previous condition of servitude, was unconstitutional and void, upon the ground that the fourteenth amendment was prohibitory upon the states only, and the legislation authorized to be adopted by congress for enforcing it was not direct legislation on matters respecting which the states were prohibited from making or enforcing certain laws, or doing certain acts, but was corrective legislation, such as might be necessary or proper for counteracting and redressing the effect of such laws or acts. In delivering the opinion of the court, Mr. Justice Bradley observed that the fourteenth amendment "does not invest congress with power to legislate upon subjects that are within the [163 U.S. 537, 547] domain of state legislation, but to provide modes of relief against state legislation or state action of the kind referred to. It does not authorize congress to create a code of municipal law for the regulation of private rights, but to provide modes of redress against the operation of state laws, and the action of state officers, executive or judicial, when these are subversive of the fundamental rights specified in the amendment. Positive rights and privileges are undoubtedly secured by the fourteenth amendment; but they are secured by way of prohibition against state laws and state proceedings affecting those rights and privileges, and by power given to congress to legislate for the purpose of carrying such prohibition into effect; and such legislation must necessarily be predicated upon such supposed state laws or state proceedings, and be directed to the correction of their operation and effect."

Much nearer, and, indeed, almost directly in point, is the case of the Louisville, N. O. & T. Ry. Co. v. State, 133 U.S. 587, 10 Sup. Ct. 348, wherein the railway company was indicted for a violation of a statute of Mississippi, enacting that all railroads carrying passengers should provide equal, but separate, accommodations for the white and colored races, by providing two or more passenger cars for each passenger train, or by dividing the passenger cars by a partition, so as to secure separate accommodations. The case was presented in a different aspect from the one under consideration, inasmuch as it was an indictment against the railway company for failing to provide the separate accommodations, but the question considered was the constitutionality of the law. In that case, the supreme court of Mississippi (66 Miss. 662, 6 South. 203) had held that the statute applied solely to commerce within the state, and, that being the construction of the state statute by its highest court, was accepted as conclusive. "If it be a matter," said the court (page 591, 133 U. S., and page 348, 10 Sup. Ct.), "respecting commerce wholly within a state, and not interfering with commerce between the states, then, obviously, there is no violation of the commerce clause of the federal constitution. . . . No question arises under this section as to the power of the state to separate in different compartments interstate passengers, [163 U.S. 537, 548] or affect, in any manner, the privileges and rights of such passengers. All that we can consider is whether the state has the power to require that railroad trains within her limits shall have separate accommodations for the two races. That affecting only commerce within the state is no invasion of the power given to congress by the commerce clause."

A like course of reasoning applies to the case under consideration, since the supreme court of Louisiana, in the case of State v. Judge, 44 La. Ann. 770, 11 South. 74, held that the statute in question did not apply to interstate passengers, but was confined in its application to passengers traveling exclusively within the borders of the state. The case was decided largely upon the authority of Louisville, N. O. & T. Ry. Co. v. State, 66 Miss. 662, 6 South, 203, and affirmed by this court in 133 U.S. 587, 10 Sup. Ct. 348. In the present case no question of interference with interstate commerce can possibly arise, since the East Louisiana Railway appears to have been purely a local line, with both its termini within the state of Louisiana. Similar statutes for the separation of the two races upon public conveyances were held to be constitutional in Railroad v. Miles, 55 Pa. St. 209; Day v. Owen, 5 Mich. 520; Railway Co. v. Williams,

55 Ill. 185; Railroad Co. v. Wells, 85 Tenn. 613; 4 S. W. 5; Railroad Co.
v. Benson, 85 Tenn. 627, 4 S. W. 5; The Sue, 22 Fed. 843; Logwood v.
Railroad Co., 23 Fed. 318; McGuinn v. Forbes, 37 Fed. 639; People v.
King (N. Y. App.) 18 N. E. 245; Houck v. Railway Co., 38 Fed. 226;
Heard v. Railroad Co., 3 Inter St. Commerce Com. R. 111, 1 Inter St.
Commerce Com. R. 428.

While we think the enforced separation of the races, as applied to the
internal commerce of the state, neither abridges the privileges or immunities of the colored man, deprives him of his property without due
process of law, nor denies him the equal protection of the laws, within
the meaning of the fourteenth amendment, we are not prepared to say
that the conductor, in assigning passengers to the coaches according to
their race, does not act at his peril, or that the provision of the second
section of the act that denies to the passenger compensation [163 U.S. 537,
549] in damages for a refusal to receive him into the coach in which he
properly belongs is a valid exercise of the legislative power. Indeed, we
understand it to be conceded by the state's attorney that such part of the
act as exempts from liability the railway company and its officers is
unconstitutional. The power to assign to a particular coach obviously
implies the power to determine to which race the passenger belongs, as
well as the power to determine who, under the laws of the particular
state, is to be deemed a white, and who a colored, person. This question,
though indicated in the brief of the plaintiff in error, does not properly
arise upon the record in this case, since the only issue made is as to the
unconstitutionality of the act, so far as it requires the railway to provide
separate accommodations, and the conductor to assign passengers
according to their race.

It is claimed by the plaintiff in error that, in a mixed community, the
reputation of belonging to the dominant race, in this instance the white
race, is "property," in the same sense that a right of action or of inheritance is property. Conceding this to be so, for the purposes of this case,
we are unable to see how this statute deprives him of, or in any way affects
his right to, such property. If he be a white man, and assigned to a colored
coach, he may have his action for damages against the company for being
deprived of his so-called "property." Upon the other hand, if he be a colored man, and be so assigned, he has been deprived of no property, since
he is not lawfully entitled to the reputation of being a white man.

In this connection, it is also suggested by the learned counsel for the
plaintiff in error that the same argument that will justify the state legislature in requiring railways to provide separate accommodations for the
two races will also authorize them to require separate cars to be provided
for people whose hair is of a certain color, or who are aliens, or who
belong to certain nationalities, or to enact laws requiring colored people

to walk upon one side of the street, and white people upon the other, or requiring white men's houses to be painted white, and colored men's black, or their vehicles or business signs to be of different colors, upon the theory that one side [163 U.S. 537, 550] of the street is as good as the other, or that a house or vehicle of one color is as good as one of another color. The reply to all this is that every exercise of the police power must be reasonable, and extend only to such laws as are enacted in good faith for the promotion of the public good, and not for the annoyance or oppression of a particular class. Thus, in Yick Wo v. Hopkins, 118 U.S. 356, 6 Sup. Ct. 1064, it was held by this court that a municipal ordinance of the city of San Francisco, to regulate the carrying on of public laundries within the limits of the municipality, violated the provisions of the constitution of the United States, if it conferred upon the municipal authorities arbitrary power, at their own will, and without regard to discretion, in the legal sense of the term, to give or withhold consent as to persons or places, without regard to the competency of the persons applying or the propriety of the places selected for the carrying on of the business. It was held to be a covert attempt on the part of the municipality to make an arbitrary and unjust discrimination against the Chinese race. While this was the case of a municipal ordinance, a like principle has been held to apply to acts of a state legislature passed in the exercise of the police power. Railroad Co. v. Husen, 95 U.S. 465; Louisville & N. R. Co. v. Kentucky, 161 U.S. 677, 16 Sup. Ct. 714, and cases cited on page 700, 161 U. S., and page 714, 16 Sup. Ct.; Daggett v. Hudson, 43 Ohio St. 548, 3 N. E. 538; Capen v. Foster, 12 Pick. 485; State v. Baker, 38 Wis. 71; Monroe v. Collins, 17 Ohio St. 665; Hulseman v. Rems, 41 Pa. St. 396; Osman v. Riley, 15 Cal. 48.

So far, then, as a conflict with the fourteenth amendment is concerned, the case reduces itself to the question whether the statute of Louisiana is a reasonable regulation, and with respect to this there must necessarily be a large discretion on the part of the legislature. In determining the question of reasonableness, it is at liberty to act with reference to the established usages, customs, and traditions of the people, and with a view to the promotion of their comfort, and the preservation of the public peace and good order. Gauged by this standard, we cannot say that a law which authorizes or even requires the separation of the two races in public conveyances [163 U.S. 537, 551] is unreasonable, or more obnoxious to the fourteenth amendment than the acts of congress requiring separate schools for colored children in the District of Columbia, the constitutionality of which does not seem to have been questioned, or the corresponding acts of state legislatures.

We consider the underlying fallacy of the plaintiff's argument to consist in the assumption that the enforced separation of the two races stamps the colored race with a badge of inferiority. If this be so, it is not by reason of anything found in the act, but solely because the colored race chooses to put that construction upon it. The argument necessarily assumes that if, as has been more than once the case, and is not unlikely to be so again, the colored race should become the dominant power in the state legislature, and should enact a law in precisely similar terms, it would thereby relegate the white race to an inferior position. We imagine that the white race, at least, would not acquiesce in this assumption. The argument also assumes that social prejudices may be overcome by legislation, and that equal rights cannot be secured to the negro except by an enforced commingling of the two races. We cannot accept this proposition. If the two races are to meet upon terms of social equality, it must be the result of natural affinities, a mutual appreciation of each other's merits, and a voluntary consent of individuals. As was said by the court of appeals of New York in People v. Gallagher, 93 N. Y. 438, 448: "This end can neither be accomplished nor promoted by laws which conflict with the general sentiment of the community upon whom they are designed to operate. When the government, therefore, has secured to each of its citizens equal rights before the law, and equal opportunities for improvement and progress, it has accomplished the end for which it was organized, and performed all of the functions respecting social advantages with which it is endowed." Legislation is powerless to eradicate racial instincts, or to abolish distinctions based upon physical differences, and the attempt to do so can only result in accentuating the difficulties of the present situation. If the civil and political rights of both races be equal, one cannot be inferior to the other civilly [163 U.S. 537, 552] or politically. If one race be inferior to the other socially, the constitution of the United States cannot put them upon the same plane.

It is true that the question of the proportion of colored blood necessary to constitute a colored person, as distinguished from a white person, is one upon which there is a difference of opinion in the different states; some holding that any visible admixture of black blood stamps the person as belonging to the colored race (State v. Chavers, 5 Jones [N. C.] 1); others, that it depends upon the preponderance of blood (Gray v. State, 4 Ohio, 354; Monroe v. Collins, 17 Ohio St. 665); and still others, that the predominance of white blood must only be in the proportion of three-fourths (People v. Dean, 14 Mich. 406; Jones v. Com., 80 Va. 544). But these are questions to be determined under the laws of each state, and are not properly put in issue in this case. Under the allegations of his petition, it may undoubtedly become a question of importance whether, under the laws of Louisiana, the petitioner belongs to the white or colored race.

The judgment of the court below is therefore affirmed.

Mr. Justice BREWER did not hear the argument or participate in the decision of this case.

Mr. Justice HARLAN dissenting.

By the Louisiana statute the validity of which is here involved, all railway companies (other than street-railroad companies) carry passengers in that state are required to have separate but equal accommodations for white and colored persons, "by providing two or more passenger coaches for each passenger train, or by dividing the passenger coaches by a partition so as to secure separate accommodations." Under this statute, no colored person is permitted to occupy a seat in a coach assigned to white persons; nor any white person to occupy a seat in a coach assigned to colored persons. The managers of the railroad are not allowed to exercise any discretion in the premises, but are required to assign each passenger to some coach or compartment set apart for the exclusive use of his race. If a passenger insists upon going into a coach or compartment not set apart for persons of his race, [163 U.S. 537, 553] he is subject to be fined, or to be imprisoned in the parish jail. Penalties are prescribed for the refusal or neglect of the officers, directors, conductors, and employees of railroad companies to comply with the provisions of the act.

Only "nurses attending children of the other race" are excepted from the operation of the statute. No exception is made of colored attendants traveling with adults. A white man is not permitted to have his colored servant with him in the same coach, even if his condition of health requires the constant personal assistance of such servant. If a colored maid insists upon riding in the same coach with a white woman whom she has been employed to serve, and who may need her personal attention while traveling, she is subject to be fined or imprisoned for such an exhibition of zeal in the discharge of duty.

While there may be in Louisiana persons of different races who are not citizens of the United States, the words in the act "white and colored races" necessarily include all citizens of the United States of both races residing in that state. So that we have before us a state enactment that compels, under penalties, the separation of the two races in railroad passenger coaches, and makes it a crime for a citizen of either race to enter a coach that has been assigned to citizens of the other race.

Thus, the state regulates the use of a public highway by citizens of the United States solely upon the basis of race.

However apparent the injustice of such legislation may be, we have only to consider whether it is consistent with the constitution of the United States.

That a railroad is a public highway, and that the corporation which owns or operates it is in the exercise of public functions, is not, at this day, to be disputed. Mr. Justice Nelson, speaking for this court in New Jersey Steam Nav. Co. v. Merchants' Bank, 6 How. 344, 382, said that a common carrier was in the exercise "of a sort of public office, and has public duties to perform, from which he should not be permitted to exonerate himself without the assent of the parties concerned." Mr. Justice Strong, delivering the judgment of [163 U.S. 537, 554] this court in Olcott v. Supervisors, 16 Wall. 678, 694, said: "That railroads, though constructed by private corporations, and owned by them, are public highways, has been the doctrine of nearly all the courts ever since such conveniences for passage and transportation have had any existence. Very early the question arose whether a state's right of eminent domain could be exercised by a private corporation created for the purpose of constructing a railroad. Clearly, it could not, unless taking land for such a purpose by such an agency is taking land for public use. The right of eminent domain nowhere justifies taking property for a private use. Yet it is a doctrine universally accepted that a state legislature may authorize a private corporation to take land for the construction of such a road, making compensation to the owner. What else does this doctrine mean if not that building a railroad, though it be built by a private corporation, is an act done for a public use?" So, in Township of Pine Grove v. Talcott, 19 Wall. 666, 676: "Though the corporation [a railroad company] was private, its work was public, as much so as if it were to be constructed by the state." So, in Inhabitants of Worcester v. Western R. Corp., 4 Metc. (Mass.) 564: "The establishment of that great thoroughfare is regarded as a public work, established by public authority, intended for the public use and benefit, the use of which is secured to the whole community, and constitutes, therefore, like a canal, turnpike, or highway, a public easement." "It is true that the real and personal property, necessary to the establishment and management of the railroad, is vested in the corporation; but it is in trust for the public."

In respect of civil rights, common to all citizens, the constitution of the United States does not, I think, permit any public authority to know the race of those entitled to be protected in the enjoyment of such rights. Every true man has pride of race, and under appropriate circumstances, when the rights of others, his equals before the law, are not to be affected, it is his privilege to express such pride and to take such action based upon it as to him seems proper. But I deny that any legislative body or judicial tribunal may have regard to the [163 U.S. 537, 555] race of citizens when the civil rights of those citizens are involved. Indeed, such legislation as that here in question is inconsistent not only with that equality of rights which pertains to citizenship, national and state, but with the personal liberty enjoyed by every one within the United States.

The thirteenth amendment does not permit the withholding or the deprivation of any right necessarily inhering in freedom. It not only struck down the institution of slavery as previously existing in the United States, but it prevents the imposition of any burdens or disabilities that constitute badges of slavery or servitude. It decreed universal civil freedom in this country. This court has so adjudged. But, that amendment having been found inadequate to the protection of the rights of those who had been in slavery, it was followed by the fourteenth amendment, which added greatly to the dignity and glory of American citizenship, and to the security of personal liberty, by declaring that "all persons born or naturalized in the United States, and subject to the jurisdiction thereof, are citizens of the United States and of the state wherein they reside," and that "no state shall make or enforce any law which shall abridge the privileges or immunities of citizens of the United States; nor shall any state deprive any person of life, liberty or property without due process of law, nor deny to any person within its jurisdiction the equal protection of the laws." These two amendments, if enforced according to their true intent and meaning, will protect all the civil rights that pertain to freedom and citizenship. Finally, and to the end that no citizen should be denied, on account of his race, the privilege of participating in the political control of his country, it was declared by the fifteenth amendment that "the right of citizens of the United States to vote shall not be denied or abridged by the United States or by any state on account of race, color or previous condition of servitude."

These notable additions to the fundamental law were welcomed by the friends of liberty throughout the world. They removed the race line from our governmental systems. They had, as this court has said, a common purpose, namely, to secure "to a race recently emancipated, a race that through [163 U.S. 537, 556] many generations have been held in slavery, all the civil rights that the superior race enjoy." They declared, in legal effect, this court has further said, "that the law in the states shall be the same for the black as for the white; that all persons, whether colored or white, shall stand equal before the laws of the states; and in regard to the colored race, for whose protection the amendment was primarily designed, that no discrimination shall be made against them by law because of their color." We also said: "The words of the amendment, it is true, are prohibitory, but they contain a necessary implication of a positive immunity or right, most valuable to the colored race,—the right to exemption from unfriendly legislation against them distinctively as colored; exemption from legal discriminations, implying inferiority in civil society, lessening the security of their enjoyment of the rights which others enjoy; and discriminations which are steps towards reducing them to the condition of a subject race." It was, consequently, adjudged that a state law that excluded citizens of the colored race from juries, because of their race, however well qualified in other respects to discharge the duties of jurymen, was repugnant to the fourteenth amendment. Strauder v. West Virginia, 100 U.S. 303, 306, 307 S.; Virginia v. Rives, Id. 313; Ex parte Virginia, Id. 339; Neal v. Delaware, 103 U.S. 370, 386; Bush v. Com., 107 U.S. 110, 116, 1 S. Sup. Ct. 625. At the present term, referring to the previous adjudications, this court declared that "underlying all of those decisions is the principle that the constitution of the United States, in its present form, forbids, so far as civil and political rights are concerned, discrimination by the general government or the states against any citizen because of his race. All citizens are equal before the law." Gibson v. State, 162 U.S. 565, 16 Sup. Ct. 904.

The decisions referred to show the scope of the recent amendments of the constitution. They also show that it is not within the power of a state to prohibit colored citizens, because of their race, from participating as jurors in the administration of justice.

It was said in argument that the statute of Louisiana does [163 U.S. 537, 557] not discriminate against either race, but prescribes a rule applicable alike to white and colored citizens. But this argument does not meet the difficulty. Every one knows that the statute in question had its origin in the purpose, not so much to exclude white persons from railroad cars occupied by blacks, as to exclude colored people from coaches occupied by or assigned to white persons. Railroad corporations of Louisiana did not make discrimination among whites in the matter of acommodation for travelers. The thing to accomplish was, under the guise of giving equal accommodation for whites and blacks, to compel the latter to keep to themselves while traveling in railroad passenger coaches. No one would be so wanting in candor as to assert the contrary. The fundamental objection, therefore, to the statute, is that it interferes with the personal freedom of citizens. "Personal liberty," it has been well said, "consists in the power of locomotion, of changing situation, or removing one's person to whatsoever places one's own inclination may direct, without imprisonment or restraint, unless by due course of law." 1 Bl. Comm. *134. If a white man and a black man choose to occupy the same public conveyance on a public highway, it is their right to do so; and no government, proceeding alone on grounds of race, can prevent it without infringing the personal liberty of each.

It is one thing for railroad carriers to furnish, or to be required by law to furnish, equal accommodations for all whom they are under a legal duty to carry. It is quite another thing for government to forbid citizens of the white and black races from traveling in the same public conveyance, and to punish officers of railroad companies for permitting persons of the two races to occupy the same passenger coach. If a state can prescribe, as a rule of civil conduct, that whites and blacks shall not travel as passengers in the same railroad coach, why may it not so regulate the use of the streets of its cities and towns as to compel white citizens to keep on one side of a street, and black citizens to keep on the other?

Why may it not, upon like grounds, punish whites and blacks who ride together in street cars or in open vehicles on a public road [163 U.S. 537, 558] or street? Why may it not require sheriffs to assign whites to one side of a court room, and blacks to the other? And why may it not also prohibit the commingling of the two races in the galleries of legislative halls or in public assemblages convened for the consideration of the political questions of the day? Further, if this statute of Louisiana is consistent with the personal liberty of citizens, why may not the state require the separation in railroad coaches of native and naturalized citizens of the United States, or of Protestants and Roman Catholics?

The answer given at the argument to these questions was that regulations of the kind they suggest would be unreasonable, and could not, therefore, stand before the law. Is it meant that the determination of questions of legislative power depends upon the inquiry whether the statute whose validity is questioned is, in the judgment of the courts, a reasonable one, taking all the circumstances into consideration? A statute may be unreasonable merely because a sound public policy forbade its enactment. But I do not understand that the courts have anything to do with the policy or expediency of legislation. A statute may be valid, and yet, upon grounds of public policy, may well be characterized as unreasonable. Mr. Sedgwick correctly states the rule when he says that, the legislative intention being clearly ascertained, "the courts have no other duty to perform than to execute the legislative will, without any regard to their views as to the wisdom or justice of the particular enactment." Sedg. St. & Const. Law, 324. There is a dangerous tendency in these latter days to enlarge the functions of the courts, by means of judicial interference with the will of the people as expressed by the legislature. Our institutions have the distinguishing characteristic that the three departments of government are co-ordinate and separate. Each must keep within the limits defined by the constitution. And the courts best discharge their duty by executing the will of the law-making power, constitutionally expressed, leaving the results of legislation to be dealt with by the people through their representatives. Statutes must always have a reasonable construction. Sometimes they are to be construed strictly, sometimes literally, in order to carry out the legislative [163 U.S. 537, 559] will. But, however construed, the intent of the legislature is to be respected if the particular statute in question is valid, although the courts, looking at the public interests, may conceive the statute to be both unreasonable and impolitic. If the power exists to enact a statute, that ends the matter so far as the courts are concerned. The adjudged cases in which statutes have been held to be void, because unreasonable, are those in which the means employed by the legislature were not at all germane to the end to which the legislature was competent.

The white race deems itself to be the dominant race in this country.

And so it is, in prestige, in achievements, in education, in wealth, and in power. So, I doubt not, it will continue to be for all time, if it remains true to its great heritage, and holds fast to the principles of constitutional liberty. But in view of the constitution, in the eye of the law, there is in this country no superior, dominant, ruling class of citizens. There is no caste here. Our constitution is color-blind, and neither knows nor tolerates classes among citizens. In respect of civil rights, all citizens are equal before the law. The humblest is the peer of the most powerful. The law regards man as man, and takes no account of his surroundings or of his color when his civil rights as guarantied by the supreme law of the land are involved. It is therefore to be regretted that this high tribunal, the final expositor of the fundamental law of the land, has reached the conclusion that it is competent for a state to regulate the enjoyment by citizens of their civil rights solely upon the basis of race.

In my opinion, the judgment this day rendered will, in time, prove to be quite as pernicious as the decision made by this tribunal in the Dred Scott Case.

It was adjudged in that case that the descendants of Africans who were imported into this country, and sold as slaves, were not included nor intended to be included under the word "citizens" in the constitution, and could not claim any of the rights and privileges which that instrument provided for and secured to citizens of the United States; that, at time of the adoption of the constitution, they were "considered as a subordinate and inferior class of beings, who had been subjugated by the dominant [163 U.S. 537, 560] race, and, whether emancipated or not, yet remained subject to their authority, and had no rights or privileges but such as those who held the power and the government might choose to grant them." 17 How. 393, 404. The recent amendments of the constitution, it was supposed, had eradicated these principles from our institutions. But it seems that we have yet, in some of the states, a dominant race,—a superior class of citizens,—which assumes to regulate the enjoyment of civil rights, common to all citizens, upon the basis of race. The present decision, it may well be apprehended, will not only stimulate aggressions, more or less brutal and irritating, upon the admitted rights of colored citizens, but will encourage the belief that it is possible, by means of state enactments, to defeat the beneficent purposes which the people of the United States had in view when they adopted the recent amendments of the constitution, by one of which the blacks of this country were made citizens of the United States and of the states in which they respectively reside, and whose privileges and immunities, as citizens, the states are forbidden to abridge. Sixty millions of whites are in no danger from the presence here of eight millions of blacks. The destinies of the two races, in this country, are indissolubly linked together, and the interests of both require that the common government of all shall not permit the seeds of race hate to be planted under the sanction of law. What can more certainly arouse race hate, what more certainly create and perpetuate a feeling of distrust between these races, than state enactments which, in fact, proceed on the ground that colored citizens are so inferior and degraded that they cannot be allowed to sit in public coaches occupied by white citizens? That, as all will admit, is the real meaning of such legislation as was enacted in Louisiana.

The sure guaranty of the peace and security of each race is the clear, distinct, unconditional recognition by our governments, national and state, of every right that inheres in civil freedom, and of the equality before the law of all citizens of the United States, without regard to race. State enactments regulating the enjoyment of civil rights upon the basis of race, and cunningly devised to defeat legitimate results of the [163 U.S. 537, 561] war, under the pretense of recognizing equality of rights, can have no other result than to render permanent peace impossible, and to keep alive a conflict of races, the continuance of which must do harm to all concerned. This question is not met by the suggestion that social equality cannot exist between the white and black races in this country. That argument, if it can be properly regarded as one, is scarcely worthy of consideration; for social equality no more exists between two races when traveling in a passenger coach or a public highway than when members of the same races sit by each other in a street car or in the jury box, or stand or sit with each other in a political assembly, or when they use in common the streets of a city or town, or when they are in the same room for the purpose of having their names placed on the registry of voters, or when they approach the ballot box in order to exercise the high privilege of voting.

There is a race so different from our own that we do not permit those belonging to it to become citizens of the United States. Persons belonging to it are, with few exceptions, absolutely excluded from our country. I allude to the Chinese race. But, by the statute in question, a Chinaman can ride in the same passenger coach with white citizens of the United States, while citizens of the black race in Louisiana, many of whom, perhaps, risked their lives for the preservation of the Union, who are entitled, by law, to participate in the political control of the state and nation, who are not excluded, by law or by reason of their race, from public stations of any kind, and who have all the legal rights that belong to white citizens, are yet declared to be criminals, liable to imprisonment, if they ride in a public coach occupied by citizens of the white race. It is scarcely just to say that a colored citizen should not object to occupying a public coach assigned to his own race. He does not object, nor, perhaps, would he object to separate coaches for his race if his rights under the law were recognized. But he does object, and he ought never to cease objecting, that citizens of the white and black races can be adjudged criminals because they sit, or claim the right to sit, in the same public coach on a public highway. [163 U.S. 537, 562] The arbitrary separation of citizens, on the basis of race, while they are on a public highway, is a badge of servitude wholly inconsistent with the civil freedom and the equality before the law established by the constitution. It cannot be justified upon any legal grounds.

If evils will result from the commingling of the two races upon public highways established for the benefit of all, they will be infinitely less than those that will surely come from state legislation regulating the enjoyment of civil rights upon the basis of race. We boast of the freedom enjoyed by our people above all other peoples. But it is difficult to reconcile that boast with a state of the law which, practically, puts the brand of servitude and degradation upon a large class of our fellow citizens,—our equals before the law. The thin disguise of "equal" accommodations for passengers in railroad coaches will not mislead any one, nor atone for the wrong this day done.

The result of the whole matter is that while this court has frequently adjudged, and at the present term has recognized the doctrine, that a state cannot, consistently with the constitution of the United States, prevent white and black citizens, having the required qualifications for jury service, from sitting in the same jury box, it is now solemnly held that a state may prohibit white and black citizens from sitting in the same passenger coach on a public highway, or may require that they be separated by a "partition" when in the same passenger coach. May it not now be reasonably expected that astute men of the dominant race, who affect to be disturbed at the possibility that the integrity of the white race may be corrupted, or that its supremacy will be imperiled, by contact on public highways with black people, will endeavor to procure statutes requiring white and black jurors to be separated in the jury box by a "partition," and that, upon retiring from the court room to consult as to their verdict, such partition, if it be a movable one, shall be taken to their consultation room, and set up in such way as to prevent black jurors from coming too close to their brother jurors of the white race. If the "partition" used in the court room happens to be stationary, provision could be made for screens with openings through [163 U.S. 537, 563] which jurors of the two races could confer as to their verdict without coming into personal contact with each other. I cannot see but that, according to the principles this day announced, such state legislation, although conceived in hostility to, and enacted for the purpose of humiliating, citizens of the United States of a particular race, would be held to be consistent with the constitution.

I do not deem it necessary to review the decisions of state courts to which reference was made in argument. Some, and the most important, of them, are wholly inapplicable, because rendered prior to the adoption of the last amendments of the constitution, when colored people had very few rights which the dominant race felt obliged to respect. Others were made at a time when public opinion, in many localities, was dominated by the institution of slavery; when it would not have been safe to do justice to the black man; and when, so far as the rights of blacks were concerned, race prejudice was, practically, the supreme law of the land. Those decisions cannot be guides in the era introduced by the recent amendments of the supreme law, which established universal civil freedom, gave citizenship to all born or naturalized in the United States, and residing here, obliterated the race line from our systems of governments, national and state, and placed our free institutions upon the broad and sure foundation of the equality of all men before the law.

I am of opinion that the state of Louisiana is inconsistent with the personal liberty of citizens, white and black, in that state, and hostile to both the spirit and letter of the constitution of the United States. If laws of like character should be enacted in the several states of the Union, the effect would be in the highest degree mischievous. Slavery, as an institution tolerated by law, would, it is true, have disappeared from our country; but there would remain a power in the states, by sinister legislation, to interfere with the full enjoyment of the blessings of freedom, to regulate civil rights, common to all citizens, upon the basis of race, and to place in a condition of legal inferiority a large body of American citizens, now constituting a part of the political community, called the [163 U.S. 537, 564] "People of the United States," for whom, and by whom through representatives, our government is administered. Such a system is inconsistent with the guaranty given by the constitution to each state of a republican form of government, and may be stricken down by congressional action, or by the courts in the discharge of their solemn duty to maintain the supreme law of the land, anything in the constitution or laws of any state to the contrary notwithstanding.

For the reason stated, I am constrained to withhold my assent from the opinion and judgment of the majority.

Brown v. Board of Education
1954, 1955

More than fifty years after *Plessy v. Ferguson* legitimized the "separate but equal" doctrine of segregation, separate schools for blacks and whites were the norm in much of the country, with seventeen states requiring educational segregation, and only sixteen states prohibiting the practice. Linda Brown was a third grader in Topeka, Kansas, who had to walk six blocks to catch a bus to her segregated black school over a mile away, while there was a white school only six blocks from her home. When Linda's father, Oliver Brown, attempted to enroll her at the more convenient white school, he was refused and directed back to the segregated black school. Thus, with the backing of the NAACP and along with eleven other plaintiffs, Brown filed a class action suit in the U.S. District Court against the Board of Education of Topeka, Kansas. When that case failed, due to the judges" citation of the Supreme Court's *Plessy v. Ferguson* decision, Brown et al. appealed to the U.S. Supreme Court. In taking up *Brown v. Board of Ed.*, the Supreme Court decided to combine it with four other NAACP-sponsored cases on similar issues, so as to hear and decide on all five of them together. These other cases were: *Briggs v. Elliott, Davis et al. v. County School Board of Prince Edward County, Virginia, et al., Gebhart et al. v. Belton et al.*, and *Bolling v. Sharp.*

The Court's decision was delivered in two parts: the first, delivered on May 17, 1954, refuted the "separate but equal" doctrine in education, stating that segregation was inherently unequal and thus a violation of the Fourteenth Amendment; the second part, delivered on April 11, 1955, directed the lower courts to see to it that schools be desegregated "with all deliberate speed." This case was the first of many that, over the next twenty years, eradicated nearly all legally sanctioned discrimination against blacks in the United States.

U.S. SUPREME COURT

BROWN v. BOARD OF EDUCATION, 347 U.S. 483 (1954)

347 U.S. 483

BROWN ET AL. v. BOARD OF EDUCATION OF TOPEKA ET AL.

APPEAL FROM THE UNITED STATES DISTRICT COURT FOR THE DISTRICT OF KANSAS. *NO. 1.

Argued December 9, 1952. Reargued December 8, 1953. Decided May 17, 1954.

SEGREGATION of white and Negro children in the public schools of a State solely on the basis of race, pursuant to state laws permitting or requiring such segregation, denies to Negro children the equal protection of the laws guaranteed by the Fourteenth Amendment—even though the physical facilities and other "tangible" factors of white and Negro schools may be equal. Pp. 486–496.

(a) The history of the Fourteenth Amendment is inconclusive as to its intended effect on public education. Pp. 489–490.

(b) The question presented in these cases must be determined, not on the basis of conditions existing when the Fourteenth

---

*Together with No. 2, Briggs et al. v. Elliott et al., on appeal from the United States District Court for the Eastern District of South Carolina, argued December 9–10, 1952, reargued December 7–8, 1953; No. 4, Davis et al. v. County School Board of Prince Edward County, Virginia, et al., on appeal from the United States District Court for the Eastern District of Virginia, argued December 10, 1952, reargued December 7–8, 1953; and No. 10, Gebhart et al. v. Belton et al., on certiorari to the Supreme Court of Delaware, argued December 11, 1952, reargued December 9, 1953.

Amendment was adopted, but in the light of the full development of public education and its present place in American life throughout the Nation. Pp. 492–493.

(c) Where a State has undertaken to provide an opportunity for an education in its public schools, such an opportunity is a right which must be made available to all on equal terms. P. 493.

(d) Segregation of children in public schools solely on the basis of race deprives children of the minority group of equal educational opportunities, even though the physical facilities and other "tangible" factors may be equal. Pp. 493–494.

(e) The "separate but equal" doctrine adopted in Plessy v. Ferguson, 163 U.S. 537, has no place in the field of public education. P. 495. [347 U.S. 483, 484]

(f) The cases are restored to the docket for further argument on specified questions relating to the forms of the decrees. Pp. 495–496.

Robert L. Carter argued the cause for appellants in No. 1 on the original argument and on the reargument. Thurgood Marshall argued the cause for appellants in No. 2 on the original argument and Spottswood W. Robinson, III, for appellants in No. 4 on the original argument, and both argued the causes for appellants in Nos. 2 and 4 on the reargument. Louis L. Redding and Jack Greenberg argued the cause for respondents in No. 10 on the original argument and Jack Greenberg and Thurgood Marshall on the reargument.

On the briefs were Robert L. Carter, Thurgood Marshall, Spottswood W. Robinson, III, Louis L. Redding, Jack Greenberg, George E. C. Hayes, William R. Ming, Jr., Constance Baker Motley, James M. Nabrit, Jr., Charles S. Scott, Frank D. Reeves, Harold R. Boulware and Oliver W. Hill for appellants in Nos. 1, 2 and 4 and respondents in No. 10; George M. Johnson for appellants in Nos. 1, 2 and 4; and Loren Miller for appellants in Nos. 2 and 4. Arthur D. Shores and A. T. Walden were on the Statement as to Jurisdiction and a brief opposing a Motion to Dismiss or Affirm in No. 2.

Paul E. Wilson, Assistant Attorney General of Kansas, argued the cause for appellees in No. 1 on the original argument and on the reargument. With him on the briefs was Harold R. Fatzer, Attorney General.

John W. Davis argued the cause for appellees in No. 2 on the original argument and for appellees in Nos. 2 and 4 on the reargument. With him on the briefs in No. 2 were T. C. Callison, Attorney General of South Carolina, Robert McC. Figg, Jr., S. E. Rogers, William R. Meagher and Taggart Whipple. [347 U.S. 483, 485]

J. Lindsay Almond, Jr., Attorney General of Virginia, and T. Justin Moore argued the cause for appellees in No. 4 on the original argument and for appellees in Nos. 2 and 4 on the reargument. On the briefs in No. 4 were J. Lindsay Almond, Jr., Attorney General, and Henry T. Wickham, Special Assistant Attorney General, for the State of Virginia, and T. Justin Moore, Archibald G. Robertson, John W. Riely and T. Justin Moore, Jr. for the Prince Edward County School Authorities, appellees.

H. Albert Young, Attorney General of Delaware, argued the cause for petitioners in No. 10 on the original argument and on the reargument. With him on the briefs was Louis J. Finger, Special Deputy Attorney General.

By special leave of Court, Assistant Attorney General Rankin argued the cause for the United States on the reargument, as amicus curiae, urging reversal in Nos. 1, 2 and 4 and affirmance in No. 10. With him on the brief were Attorney General Brownell, Philip Elman, Leon Ulman, William J. Lamont and M. Magdelena Schoch. James P. McGranery, then Attorney General, and Philip Elman filed a brief for the United States on the original argument, as amicus curiae, urging reversal in Nos. 1, 2 and 4 and affirmance in No. 10.

Briefs of amici curiae supporting appellants in No. 1 were filed by Shad Polier, Will Maslow and Joseph B. Robison for the American Jewish Congress; by Edwin J. Lukas, Arnold Forster, Arthur Garfield Hays, Frank E. Karelsen, Leonard Haas, Saburo Kido and Theodore Leskes for the American Civil Liberties Union et al.; and by John Ligtenberg and Selma M. Borchardt for the American Federation of Teachers. Briefs of amici curiae supporting appellants in No. 1 and respondents in No. 10 were filed by Arthur J. Goldberg and Thomas E. Harris [347 U.S. 483, 486] for the Congress of Industrial Organizations and by Phineas Indritz for the American Veterans Committee, Inc.

MR. CHIEF JUSTICE WARREN delivered the opinion of the Court.

These cases come to us from the States of Kansas, South Carolina, Virginia, and Delaware. They are premised on different facts and different local conditions, but a common legal question justifies their consideration together in this consolidated opinion.[1] [347 U.S. 483, 487]

In each of the cases, minors of the Negro race, through their legal representatives, seek the aid of the courts in obtaining admission to the public schools of their community on a nonsegregated basis. In each instance, [347 U.S. 483, 488] they had been denied admission to schools attended by white children under laws requiring or permitting segregation according to race. This segregation was alleged to deprive the plaintiffs of the equal protection of the laws under the Fourteenth Amendment. In each of the cases other than the Delaware case, a three-judge federal district court denied relief to the plaintiffs on the so-called "separate but equal" doctrine announced by this Court in Plessy v. Ferguson, 163 U.S. 537. Under that doctrine, equality of treatment is accorded when the races are provided substantially equal facilities, even though these facilities be separate. In the Delaware case, the Supreme Court of Delaware adhered to that doctrine, but ordered that the plaintiffs be admitted to the white schools because of their superiority to the Negro schools.

The plaintiffs contend that segregated public schools are not "equal" and cannot be made "equal," and that hence they are deprived of the equal protection of the laws. Because of the obvious importance of the question presented, the Court took jurisdiction.[2] Argument was heard in the 1952 Term, and reargument was heard this Term on certain questions propounded by the Court.[3] [347 U.S. 483, 489]

Reargument was largely devoted to the circumstances surrounding the adoption of the Fourteenth Amendment in 1868. It covered exhaustively consideration of the Amendment in Congress, ratification by the states, then existing practices in racial segregation, and the views of proponents and opponents of the Amendment. This discussion and our own investigation convince us that, although these sources cast some light, it is not enough to resolve the problem with which we are faced. At best, they are inconclusive. The most avid proponents of the post–War Amendments undoubtedly intended them to remove all legal distinctions among "all persons born or naturalized in the United States." Their opponents, just as certainly, were antagonistic to both the letter and the spirit of the Amendments and wished them to have the most limited effect. What others in Congress and the state legislatures had in mind cannot be determined with any degree of certainty.

An additional reason for the inconclusive nature of the Amendment's history, with respect to segregated schools, is the status of public education at that time.[4] In the South, the movement toward free common schools, supported [347 U.S. 483, 490] by general taxation, had not yet taken hold. Education of white children was largely in the hands of private groups. Education of Negroes was almost nonexistent, and practically all of the race were illiterate. In fact, any education of Negroes was forbidden by law in some states. Today, in contrast, many Negroes have achieved outstanding success in the arts and sciences as well as in the business and professional world. It is true that public school education at the time of the Amendment had advanced further in the North, but the effect of the Amendment on Northern States was generally ignored in the congressional debates. Even in the North, the conditions of public education did not approximate those existing today. The curriculum was usually rudimentary; ungraded schools were common in rural areas; the school term was but three months a year in many states; and compulsory school attendance was virtually unknown. As a consequence, it is not surprising that there should be so little in the history of the Fourteenth Amendment relating to its intended effect on public education.

In the first cases in this Court construing the Fourteenth Amendment, decided shortly after its adoption, the Court interpreted it as proscribing all state-imposed discriminations against the Negro race.[5] The doctrine of [347 U.S. 483, 491] "separate but equal" did not make its appearance in this Court until 1896 in the case of Plessy v. Ferguson, supra, involving not education but transportation.[6] American courts have since labored with the doctrine for over half a century. In this Court, there have been six cases involving the "separate but equal" doctrine in the field of public education.[7] In Cumming v. County Board of Education, 175 U.S. 528, and Gong Lum v. Rice, 275 U.S. 78, the validity of the doctrine itself was not challenged.[8] In more recent cases, all on the graduate school [347 U.S. 483, 492] level, inequality was found in that specific benefits enjoyed by white students were denied to Negro students of the same educational qualifications. Missouri ex rel. Gaines v. Canada, 305 U.S. 337; Sipuel v. Oklahoma, 332 U.S. 631; Sweatt v. Painter, 339 U.S. 629; McLaurin v. Oklahoma State Regents, 339 U.S. 637. In none of these cases was it necessary to re-examine the doctrine to grant relief to the Negro plaintiff. And in Sweatt v. Painter, supra, the Court expressly reserved decision on the question whether Plessy v. Ferguson should be held inapplicable to public education.

In the instant cases, that question is directly presented. Here, unlike Sweatt v. Painter, there are findings below that the Negro and white schools involved have been equalized, or are being equalized, with respect to buildings, curricula, qualifications and salaries of teachers, and other "tangible" factors.[9] Our decision, therefore, cannot turn on merely a comparison of these tangible factors in the Negro and white schools involved in each of the cases. We must look instead to the effect of segregation itself on public education.

In approaching this problem, we cannot turn the clock back to 1868 when the Amendment was adopted, or even to 1896 when Plessy v. Ferguson was written. We must consider public education in the light of its full development and its present place in American life throughout [347 U.S. 483, 493] the Nation. Only in this way can it be determined if segregation in public schools deprives these plaintiffs of the equal protection of the laws.

Today, education is perhaps the most important function of state and local governments. Compulsory school attendance laws and the great expenditures for education both demonstrate our recognition of the importance of education to our democratic society. It is required in the performance of our most basic public responsibilities, even service in the armed forces. It is the very foundation of good citizenship. Today it is a principal instrument in awakening the child to cultural values, in preparing him for later professional training, and in helping him to adjust normally to his environment. In these days, it is doubtful that any child may reasonably be expected to succeed in life if he is denied the opportunity of an education. Such an opportunity, where the state has undertaken to provide it, is a right which must be made available to all on equal terms.

We come then to the question presented: Does segregation of children in public schools solely on the basis of race, even though the physical facilities and other "tangible" factors may be equal, deprive the children of the minority group of equal educational opportunities? We believe that it does.

In Sweatt v. Painter, supra, in finding that a segregated law school for Negroes could not provide them equal educational opportunities, this Court relied in large part on "those qualities which are incapable of objective measurement but which make for greatness in a law school." In McLaurin v. Oklahoma State Regents, supra, the Court, in requiring that a Negro admitted to a white graduate school be treated like all other students, again resorted to intangible considerations: ". . . his ability to study, to engage in discussions and exchange views with other students, and, in general, to learn his profession." [347 U.S. 483, 494] Such considerations apply with added force to children in grade and high schools. To separate them from others of similar age and qualifications solely because of their race generates a feeling of inferiority as to their status in the community that may affect their hearts and minds in a way unlikely ever to be undone. The effect of this separation on their educational opportunities was well stated by a finding in the Kansas case by a court which nevertheless felt compelled to rule against the Negro plaintiffs:

> "Segregation of white and colored children in public schools has a detrimental effect upon the colored children. The impact is greater when it has the sanction of the law; for the policy of separating the races is usually interpreted as denoting the inferiority of the negro group. A sense of inferiority affects the motivation of a child to learn. Segregation with the sanction of law, therefore, has a tendency to [retard] the educational and mental development of negro children and to deprive them of some of the benefits they would receive in a racial[ly] integrated school system."[10]

Whatever may have been the extent of psychological knowledge at the time of Plessy v. Ferguson, this finding is amply supported by modern authority.[11] Any language [347 U.S. 483, 495] in Plessy v. Ferguson contrary to this finding is rejected.

We conclude that in the field of public education the doctrine of "separate but equal" has no place. Separate educational facilities are inherently unequal. Therefore, we hold that the plaintiffs and others similarly situated for whom the actions have been brought are, by reason of the segregation complained of, deprived of the equal protection of the laws guaranteed by the Fourteenth Amendment. This disposition makes unnecessary any discussion whether such segregation also violates the Due Process Clause of the Fourteenth Amendment.[12]

Because these are class actions, because of the wide applicability of this decision, and because of the great variety of local conditions, the formulation of decrees in these cases presents problems of considerable complexity. On reargument, the consideration of appropriate relief was necessarily subordinated to the primary question—the constitutionality of segregation in public education. We have now announced that such segregation is a denial of the equal protection of the laws. In order that we may have the full assistance of the parties in formulating decrees, the cases will be restored to the docket, and the parties are requested to present further argument on Questions 4 and 5 previously propounded by the Court for the reargument this Term.[13] The Attorney General [347 U.S. 483, 496] of the United States is again invited to participate. The Attorneys General of the states requiring or permitting segregation in public education will also be permitted to appear as amici curiae upon request to do so by September 15, 1954, and submission of briefs by October 1, 1954.[14]

It is so ordered.

FOOTNOTES

[1] In the Kansas case, Brown v. Board of Education, the plaintiffs are Negro children of elementary school age residing in Topeka. They brought this action in the United States District Court for the District of Kansas to enjoin enforcement of a Kansas statute which permits, but does not require, cities of more than 15,000 population to maintain separate school facilities for Negro and white students. Kan. Gen. Stat. 72–1724 (1949). Pursuant to that authority, the Topeka Board of Education elected to establish segregated elementary schools. Other public schools in the community, however, are operated on a nonsegregated basis. The three-judge District Court, convened under 28 U.S.C. 2281 and 2284, found that segregation in public education has a detrimental effect upon Negro children, but denied relief on the ground that the Negro and white schools were substantially equal with respect to buildings, transportation, curricula, and educational qualifications of teachers. 98 F. Supp. 797. The case is here on direct appeal under 28 U.S.C. 1253. In the South Carolina case, Briggs v. Elliott, the plaintiffs are Negro children of both elementary and high school age residing in Clarendon County. They brought this action in the United States District Court for the Eastern District of South Carolina to enjoin enforcement of provisions in the state constitution and statutory code which require the segregation of Negroes and whites in public schools. S. C. Const., Art. XI, 7; S. C. Code 5377 (1942). The three-judge District Court, convened under 28 U.S.C. 2281 and 2284, denied the requested relief. The court found that the Negro schools

were inferior to the white schools and ordered the defendants to begin immediately to equalize the facilities. But the court sustained the validity of the contested provisions and denied the plaintiffs admission [347 U.S. 483, 487] to the white schools during the equalization program. 98 F. Supp. 529. This Court vacated the District Court's judgment and remanded the case for the purpose of obtaining the court's views on a report filed by the defendants concerning the progress made in the equalization program. 342 U.S. 350. On remand, the District Court found that substantial equality had been achieved except for buildings and that the defendants were proceeding to rectify this inequality as well. 103 F. Supp. 920. The case is again here on direct appeal under 28 U.S.C. 1253. In the Virginia case, Davis v. County School Board, the plaintiffs are Negro children of high school age residing in Prince Edward county. They brought this action in the United States District Court for the Eastern District of Virginia to enjoin enforcement of provisions in the state constitution and statutory code which require the segregation of Negroes and whites in public schools. Va. Const., 140; Va. Code 22–221 (1950). The three-judge District Court, convened under 28 U.S.C. 2281 and 2284, denied the requested relief. The court found the Negro school inferior in physical plant, curricula, and transportation, and ordered the defendants forthwith to provide substantially equal curricula and transportation and to "proceed with all reasonable diligence and dispatch to remove" the inequality in physical plant. But, as in the South Carolina case, the court sustained the validity of the contested provisions and denied the plaintiffs admission to the white schools during the equalization program. 103 F. Supp. 337. The case is here on direct appeal under 28 U.S.C. 1253. In the Delaware case, Gebhart v. Belton, the plaintiffs are Negro children of both elementary and high school age residing in New Castle County. They brought this action in the Delaware Court of Chancery to enjoin enforcement of provisions in the state constitution and statutory code which require the segregation of Negroes and whites in public schools. Del. Const., Art. X, 2; Del. Rev. Code 2631 (1935). The Chancellor gave judgment for the plaintiffs and ordered their immediate admission to schools previously attended only by white children, on the ground that the Negro schools were inferior with respect to teacher training, pupil-teacher ratio, extracurricular activities, physical plant, and time and distance involved [347 U.S. 483, 488] in travel. 87 A. 2d 862. The Chancellor also found that segregation itself results in an inferior education for Negro children (see note 10, infra), but did not rest his decision on that ground. Id., at 865. The Chancellor's decree was affirmed by the Supreme Court of Delaware, which intimated, however, that the defendants might be able to obtain a modification of the decree after equalization of the Negro and white schools had been accomplished. 91 A. 2d 137, 152. The defendants, contending only that the Delaware courts had erred in ordering the immediate admission of the Negro plaintiffs to the white schools, applied to this Court for certiorari. The writ was granted, 344 U.S. 891. The plaintiffs, who were successful below, did not submit a cross-petition.

[2] 344 U.S. 1, 141, 891.

[3] 345 U.S. 972. The Attorney General of the United States participated both Terms as amicus curiae.

[4] For a general study of the development of public education prior to the Amendment, see Butts and Cremin, A History of Education in American Culture (1953), Pts. I, II; Cubberley, Public Education in the United States (1934 ed.), cc. II–XII. School practices current at the time of the adoption of the Fourteenth Amendment are described in Butts and Cremin, supra, at 269–275; Cubberley, supra, at 288–339, 408–431; Knight, Public Education in the South (1922), cc. VIII, IX. See also H. Ex. Doc. No. 315, 41st Cong., 2d Sess. (1871). Although the demand for free public schools followed substantially the same pattern in both the North and the South, the development in the South did not begin to gain momentum until about 1850, some twenty years after that in the

North. The reasons for the somewhat slower development in the South (e. g., the rural character of the South and the different regional attitudes toward state assistance) are well explained in Cubberley, supra, at 408–423. In the country as a whole, but particularly in the South, the War [347 U.S. 483, 490] virtually stopped all progress in public education. Id., at 427–428. The low status of Negro education in all sections of the country, both before and immediately after the War, is described in Beale, A History of Freedom of Teaching in American Schools (1941), 112–132, 175–195. Compulsory school attendance laws were not generally adopted until after the ratification of the Fourteenth Amendment, and it was not until 1918 that such laws were in force in all the states. Cubberley, supra, at 563–565.

[5] Slaughter-House Cases, 16 Wall. 36, 67–72 (1873); Strauder v. West Virginia, 100 U.S. 303, 307–308 (1880): "It ordains that no State shall deprive any person of life, liberty, or property, without due process of law, or deny to any person within its jurisdiction the equal protection of the laws. What is this but [347 U.S. 483, 491] declaring that the law in the States shall be the same for the black as for the white; that all persons, whether colored or white, shall stand equal before the laws of the States, and, in regard to the colored race, for whose protection the amendment was primarily designed, that no discrimination shall be made against them by law because of their color? The words of the amendment, it is true, are prohibitory, but they contain a necessary implication of a positive immunity, or right, most valuable to the colored race,—the right to exemption from unfriendly legislation against them distinctively as colored,—exemption from legal discriminations, implying inferiority in civil society, lessening the security of their enjoyment of the rights which others enjoy, and discriminations which are steps towards reducing them to the condition of a subject race." See also Virginia v. Rives, 100 U.S. 313, 318 (1880); Ex parte Virginia, 100 U.S. 339, 344–345 (1880).

[6] The doctrine apparently originated in Roberts v. City of Boston, 59 Mass. 198, 206 (1850), upholding school segregation against attack as being violative of a state constitutional guarantee of equality. Segregation in Boston public schools was eliminated in 1855. Mass. Acts 1855, c. 256. But elsewhere in the North segregation in public education has persisted in some communities until recent years. It is apparent that such segregation has long been a nationwide problem, not merely one of sectional concern.

[7] See also Berea College v. Kentucky, 211 U.S. 45 (1908).

[8] In the Cumming case, Negro taxpayers sought an injunction requiring the defendant school board to discontinue the operation of a high school for white children until the board resumed operation of a high school for Negro children. Similarly, in the Gong Lum case, the plaintiff, a child of Chinese descent, contended only that state authorities had misapplied the doctrine by classifying him with Negro children and requiring him to attend a Negro school.

[9] In the Kansas case, the court below found substantial equality as to all such factors. 98 F. Supp. 797, 798. In the South Carolina case, the court below found that the defendants were proceeding "promptly and in good faith to comply with the court's decree." 103 F. Supp. 920, 921. In the Virginia case, the court below noted that the equalization program was already "afoot and progressing" (103 F. Supp. 337, 341); since then, we have been advised, in the Virginia Attorney General's brief on reargument, that the program has now been completed. In the Delaware case, the court below similarly noted that the state's equalization program was well under way. 91 A. 2d 137, 149.

[10] A similar finding was made in the Delaware case: "I conclude from the testimony that in our Delaware society, State-imposed segregation in education itself results in the Negro children, as a class, receiving educational opportunities which are substantially inferior to those available to white children otherwise similarly situated." 87 A. 2d 862, 865.

[11] K. B. Clark, Effect of Prejudice and Discrimination on Personality Development

(Midcentury White House Conference on Children and Youth, 1950); Witmer and Kotinsky, Personality in the Making (1952), c. VI; Deutscher and Chein, The Psychological Effects of Enforced Segregation: A Survey of Social Science Opinion, 26 J. Psychol. 259 (1948); Chein, What are the Psychological Effects of [347 U.S. 483, 495] Segregation Under Conditions of Equal Facilities?, 3 Int. J. Opinion and Attitude Res. 229 (1949); Brameld, Educational Costs, in Discrimination and National Welfare (MacIver, ed., (1949), 44–48; Frazier, The Negro in the United States (1949), 674–681. And see generally Myrdal, An American Dilemma (1944).

[12] See Bolling v. Sharpe, post, p. 497, concerning the Due Process Clause of the Fifth Amendment.

[13] "4. Assuming it is decided that segregation in public schools violates the Fourteenth Amendment "(a) would a decree necessarily follow providing that, within the [347 U.S. 483, 496] limits set by normal geographic school districting, Negro children should forthwith be admitted to schools of their choice, or "(b) may this Court, in the exercise of its equity powers, permit an effective gradual adjustment to be brought about from existing segregated systems to a system not based on color distinctions? "5. On the assumption on which questions 4 (a) and (b) are based, and assuming further that this Court will exercise its equity powers to the end described in question 4 (b), "(a) should this Court formulate detailed decrees in these cases; "(b) if so, what specific issues should the decrees reach; "(c) should this Court appoint a special master to hear evidence with a view to recommending specific terms for such decrees; "(d) should this Court remand to the courts of first instance with directions to frame decrees in these cases, and if so what general directions should the decrees of this Court include and what procedures should the courts of first instance follow in arriving at the specific terms of more detailed decrees?"

[14] See Rule 42, Revised Rules of this Court (effective July 1, 1954). [347 U.S. 483, 497].

U.S. SUPREME COURT

BROWN v. BOARD OF EDUCATION, 349 U.S. 294 (1955)

349 U.S. 294

BROWN ET AL. V. BOARD OF EDUCATION OF TOPEKA ET AL.

APPEAL FROM THE UNITED STATES DISTRICT COURT FOR THE DISTRICT OF KANSAS.

*No. 1. Reargued on the question of relief April 11–14, 1955. Opinion and judgments announced May 31, 1955.

1. Racial discrimination in public education is unconstitutional, 347 U.S. 483, 497, and all provisions of federal, state or local law requiring or permitting such discrimination must yield to this principle. P. 298.

2. The judgments below (except that in the Delaware case) are reversed and the cases are remanded to the District Courts to take such proceedings and enter such orders and decrees consistent with this opinion as are necessary and proper to admit the parties to these cases to public schools on a racially nondiscriminatory basis with all deliberate speed. P. 301.

(a) School authorities have the primary responsibility for elucidating, assessing and solving the varied local school problems which may require solution in fully implementing the governing constitutional principles. P. 299.

---

*Together with No. 2, Briggs et al. v. Elliott et al., on appeal from the United States District Court for the Eastern District of South Carolina; No. 3, Davis et al. v. County School Board of Prince Edward County, Virginia, et al., on appeal from the United States District Court for the Eastern District of Virginia; No. 4, Bolling et al. v. Sharpe et al., on certiorari to the United States Court of Appeals for the District of Columbia Circuit; and No. 5, Gebhart et al. v. Belton et al., on certiorari to the Supreme Court of Delaware. [349 U.S. 294, 296]

(b) Courts will have to consider whether the action of school authorities constitutes good faith implementation of the governing constitutional principles. P. 299.

(c) Because of their proximity to local conditions and the possible need for further hearings, the courts which originally heard these cases can best perform this judicial appraisal. P. 299.

(d) In fashioning and effectuating the decrees, the courts will be guided by equitable principles—characterized by a practical flexibility in shaping remedies and a facility for adjusting and reconciling public and private needs. P. 300. [349 U.S. 294, 295]

(e) At stake is the personal interest of the plaintiffs in admission to public schools as soon as practicable on a nondiscriminatory basis. P. 300.

(f) Courts of equity may properly take into account the public interest in the elimination in a systematic and effective manner of a variety of obstacles in making the transition to school systems operated in accordance with the constitutional principles enunciated in 347 U.S. 483, 497; but the vitality of these constitutional principles cannot be allowed to yield simply because of disagreement with them. P. 300.

(g) While giving weight to these public and private considerations, the courts will require that the defendants make a prompt and reasonable start toward full compliance with the ruling of this Court. P. 300.

(h) Once such a start has been made, the courts may find that additional time is necessary to carry out the ruling in an effective manner. P. 300.

(i) The burden rests on the defendants to establish that additional time is necessary in the public interest and is consistent with good faith compliance at the earliest practicable date. P. 300.

(j) The courts may consider problems related to administration, arising from the physical condition of the school plant, the school transportation system, personnel, revision of school districts and attendance areas into compact units to achieve a system of determining admission to the public schools on a nonracial basis, and revision of local laws and regulations which may be necessary in solving the foregoing problems. Pp. 300–301.

(k) The courts will also consider the adequacy of any plans the defendants may propose to meet these problems and to effectuate a transition to a racially nondiscriminatory school system. P. 301.

(l) During the period of transition, the courts will retain jurisdiction of these cases. P. 301.

3. The judgment in the Delaware case, ordering the immediate admission of the plaintiffs to schools previously attended only by white children, is affirmed on the basis of the principles stated by this Court in its opinion, 347 U.S. 483; but the case is remanded to the Supreme Court

of Delaware for such further proceedings as that Court may deem necessary in the light of this opinion. P. 301.

98 F. Supp. 797, 103 F. Supp. 920, 103 F. Supp. 337 and judgment in No. 4, reversed and remanded.

91 A. 2d 137, affirmed and remanded.

Robert L. Carter argued the cause for appellants in No. 1. Spottswood W. Robinson, III, argued the causes for appellants in Nos. 2 and 3. George E. C. Hayes and James M. Nabrit, Jr. argued the cause for petitioners in No. 4. Louis L. Redding argued the cause for respondents in No. 5. Thurgood Marshall argued the causes for appellants in Nos. 1, 2 and 3, petitioners in No. 4 and respondents in No. 5.

On the briefs were Harold Boulware, Robert L. Carter, Jack Greenberg, Oliver W. Hill, Thurgood Marshall, Louis L. Redding, Spottswood W. Robinson, III, Charles S. Scott, William T. Coleman, Jr., Charles T. Duncan, George E. C. Hayes, Loren Miller, William R. Ming, Jr., Constance Baker Motley, James M. Nabrit, Jr., Louis H. Pollak and Frank D. Reeves for appellants in Nos. 1, 2 and 3, and respondents in No. 5; and George E. C. Hayes, James M. Nabrit, Jr., George M. Johnson, Charles W. Quick, Herbert O. Reid, Thurgood Marshall and Robert L. Carter for petitioners in No. 4.

Harold R. Fatzer, Attorney General of Kansas, argued the cause for appellees in No. 1. With him on the brief was Paul E. Wilson, Assistant Attorney General. Peter F. Caldwell filed a brief for the Board of Education of Topeka, Kansas, appellee.

S. E. Rogers and Robert McC. Figg, Jr. argued the cause and filed a brief for appellees in No. 2.

J. Lindsay Almond, Jr., Attorney General of Virginia, and Archibald G. Robertson argued the cause for appellees in No. 3. With them on the brief were Henry T. Wickham, Special Assistant to the Attorney General, T. Justin Moore, John W. Riely and T. Justin Moore, Jr.

Milton D. Korman argued the cause for respondents in No. 4. With him on the brief were Vernon E. West, Chester H. Gray and Lyman J. Umstead. [349 U.S. 294, 297]

Joseph Donald Craven, Attorney General of Delaware, argued the cause for petitioners in No. 5. On the brief were H. Albert Young, then Attorney General, Clarence W. Taylor, Deputy Attorney General, and Andrew D. Christie, Special Deputy to the Attorney General.

In response to the Court's invitation, 347 U.S. 483, 495–496, Solicitor General Sobeloff participated in the oral argument for the United States. With him on the brief were Attorney General Brownell, Assistant Attorney General Rankin, Philip Elman, Ralph S. Spritzer and Alan S. Rosenthal.

By invitation of the Court, 347 U.S. 483, 496, the following State officials presented their views orally as amici curiae: Thomas J. Gentry, Attorney General of Arkansas, with whom on the brief were James L. Sloan, Assistant Attorney General, and Richard B. McCulloch, Special Assistant Attorney General. Richard W. Ervin, Attorney General of Florida, and Ralph E. Odum, Assistant Attorney General, both of whom were also on a brief. C. Ferdinand Sybert, Attorney General of Maryland, with whom on the brief were Edward D. E. Rollins, then Attorney General, W. Giles Parker, Assistant Attorney General, and James H. Norris, Jr., Special Assistant Attorney General. I. Beverly Lake, Assistant Attorney General of North Carolina, with whom on the brief were Harry McMullan, Attorney General, and T. Wade Bruton, Ralph Moody and Claude L. Love, Assistant Attorneys General. Mac Q. Williamson, Attorney General of Oklahoma, who also filed a brief. John Ben Shepperd, Attorney General of Texas, and Burnell Waldrep, Assistant Attorney General, with whom on the brief were Billy E. Lee, J. A. Amis, Jr., L. P. Lollar, J. Fred Jones, John Davenport, John Reeves and Will Davis.

Phineas Indritz filed a brief for the American Veterans Committee, Inc., as amicus curiae. [349 U.S. 294, 298]

MR. CHIEF JUSTICE WARREN delivered the opinion of the Court.

These cases were decided on May 17, 1954. The opinions of that date,[1] declaring the fundamental principle that racial discrimination in public education is unconstitutional, are incorporated herein by reference. All provisions of federal, state, or local law requiring or permitting such discrimination must yield to this principle. There remains for consideration the manner in which relief is to be accorded.

Because these cases arose under different local conditions and their disposition will involve a variety of local problems, we requested further argument on the question of relief.[2] In view of the nationwide importance of the decision, we invited the Attorney General of the United [349 U.S. 294, 299] States and the Attorneys General of all states requiring or permitting racial discrimination in public education to present their views on that question. The parties, the United States, and the States of Florida, North Carolina, Arkansas, Oklahoma, Maryland, and Texas filed briefs and participated in the oral argument.

These presentations were informative and helpful to the Court in its consideration of the complexities arising from the transition to a system of public education freed of racial discrimination. The presentations also demonstrated that substantial steps to eliminate racial discrimination in public schools have already been taken, not only in some of the communities in which these cases arose, but in some of the states appearing as amici curiae, and in other states as well. Substantial progress has been made in the District of Columbia and in the communities in Kansas and Delaware involved in this litigation. The defendants in the cases coming to us from South Carolina and Virginia are awaiting the decision of this Court concerning relief.

Full implementation of these constitutional principles may require solution of varied local school problems. School authorities have the primary responsibility for elucidating, assessing, and solving these problems; courts will have to consider whether the action of school authorities constitutes good faith implementation of the governing constitutional principles. Because of their proximity to local conditions and the possible need for further hearings, the courts which originally heard these cases can best perform this judicial appraisal. Accordingly, we believe it appropriate to remand the cases to those courts.[3] [349 U.S. 294, 300]

In fashioning and effectuating the decrees, the courts will be guided by equitable principles. Traditionally, equity has been characterized by a practical flexibility in shaping its remedies[4] and by a facility for adjusting and reconciling public and private needs.[5] These cases call for the exercise of these traditional attributes of equity power. At stake is the personal interest of the plaintiffs in admission to public schools as soon as practicable on a nondiscriminatory basis. To effectuate this interest may call for elimination of a variety of obstacles in making the transition to school systems operated in accordance with the constitutional principles set forth in our May 17, 1954, decision. Courts of equity may properly take into account the public interest in the elimination of such obstacles in a systematic and effective manner. But it should go without saying that the vitality of these constitutional principles cannot be allowed to yield simply because of disagreement with them.

While giving weight to these public and private considerations, the courts will require that the defendants make a prompt and reasonable start toward full compliance with our May 17, 1954, ruling. Once such a start has been made, the courts may find that additional time is necessary to carry out the ruling in an effective manner. The burden rests upon the defendants to establish that such time is necessary in the public interest and is consistent with good faith compliance at the earliest practicable date. To that end, the courts may consider problems related to administration, arising from the physical condition of the school plant, the school transportation system, personnel, revision of school districts and attendance areas into compact units to achieve a system of determining admission to the public schools [349 U.S. 294, 301] on a nonracial basis, and revision of local laws and regulations which may be necessary in solving the foregoing problems. They will also consider the adequacy of any plans the defendants may propose to meet these problems and to effectuate a transition to a racially nondiscriminatory school system. During this period of transition, the courts will retain jurisdiction of these cases.

The judgments below, except that in the Delaware case, are accordingly reversed and the cases are remanded to the District Courts to take such proceedings and enter such orders and decrees consistent with this opinion as are necessary and proper to admit to public schools on a racially nondiscriminatory basis with all deliberate speed the parties to these cases. The judgment in the Delaware case—ordering the immediate admission of the plaintiffs to schools previously attended only by white children—is affirmed on the basis of the principles stated in our May 17, 1954, opinion, but the case is remanded to the Supreme Court of Delaware for such further proceedings as that Court may deem necessary in light of this opinion.

It is so ordered.

FOOTNOTES

[1] 347 U.S. 483; 347 U.S. 497.

[2] Further argument was requested on the following questions, 347 U.S. 483, 495–496, n. 13, previously propounded by the Court: "4. Assuming it is decided that segregation in public schools violates the Fourteenth Amendment "(a) would a decree necessarily follow providing that, within the limits set by normal geographic school districting, Negro children should forthwith be admitted to schools of their choice, or "(b) may this Court, in the exercise of its equity powers, permit an effective gradual adjustment to be brought about from existing segregated systems to a system not based on color distinctions? "5. On the assumption on which questions 4 (a) and (b) are based, and assuming further that this Court will exercise its equity powers to the end described in question 4 (b), "(a) should this Court formulate detailed decrees in these cases; "(b) if so, what specific issues should the decrees reach; "(c) should this Court appoint a special master to hear evidence with a view to recommending specific terms for such decrees; "(d) should this Court remand to the courts of first instance with directions to frame decrees in these cases, and if so what general directions should the decrees of this Court include and what procedures should the courts of first instance follow in arriving at the specific terms of more detailed decrees?"

[3] The cases coming to us from Kansas, South Carolina, and Virginia were originally heard by three-judge District Courts convened under 28 U.S.C. 2281 and 2284. These cases will accordingly be remanded to those three-judge courts. See Briggs v. Elliott, 342 U.S. 350.

[4] See Alexander v. Hillman, 296 U.S. 222, 239.

[5] See Hecht Co. v. Bowles, 321 U.S. 321, 329–330. [349 U.S. 294, 302]

Engel v. Vitale
1962

In 1951 the New York State Board of Regents authorized a brief, "nondenominational" prayer to be included in the opening ceremonies of all New York public schools. Though the prayer was nondenominational and optional, parents of ten children in New Hyde Park, New York, objected to its use of the phrase "Almighty God." In an attempt to stop the prayer, these parents filed suit against their school board president, William Vitale, and the New York State Board of Regents, claiming that such a practice contradicted their beliefs and violated the First Amendment. After losing their case in the trial court of New York, the parents appealed unsuccessfully to both the Appellate Division and the Court of Appeals of New York, before finally bringing their suit to the U.S. Supreme Court.

Led by Justice Hugo Black, the Supreme Court found that the state-sponsored twenty-two-word prayer was in fact a religious activity, and thus a violation of the First Amendment's ban against the establishment of a religion. Although there was an intense firestorm of criticism from the public in response to this decision, the precedent set by *Engel v. Vitale* has remained intact to this day.

U.S. SUPREME COURT

ENGEL V. VITALE, 370 U.S. 421 (1962)

370 U.S. 421

ENGEL ET AL. V. VITALE ET AL.
CERTIORARI TO THE COURT OF APPEALS
OF NEW YORK.
No. 468.
Argued April 3, 1962.
Decided June 25, 1962.

BECAUSE of the prohibition of the First Amendment against the enactment of any law "respecting an establishment of religion," which is made applicable to the States by the Fourteenth Amendment, state officials may not compose an official state prayer and require that it be recited in the public schools of the State at the beginning of each school day— even if the prayer is denominationally neutral and pupils who wish to do so may remain silent or be excused from the room while the prayer is being recited. Pp. 422–436.

10 N. Y. 2d 174, 176 N. E. 2d 579, reversed.

William J. Butler argued the cause for petitioners. With him on the briefs was Stanley Geller.

Bertram B. Daiker argued the cause for respondents. With him on the briefs was Wilford E. Neier.

Porter R. Chandler argued the cause for intervenors–respondents. With him on the briefs were Thomas J. Ford and Richard E. Nolan.

Charles A. Brind filed a brief for the Board of Regents of the University of the State of New York, as amicus curiae, in opposition to the petition for certiorari.

Briefs of amici curiae, urging reversal, were filed by Herbert A. Wolff, Leo Rosen and Nancy Wechsler for the American Ethical Union; Louis Caplan, Edwin J. Lukas, Paul Hartman, Theodore Leskes and Sol Rabkin for the American Jewish Committee et al.; and Leo Pfeffer, Lewis H.

Weinstein, Albert Wald, Shad Polier and Samuel Lawrence Brennglass for the Synagogue Council of America et al.

A brief of amici curiae, urging affirmance, was filed by Roger D. Foley, Attorney General of Nevada, Robert [370 U.S. 421, 422] Pickrell, Attorney General of Arizona, Frank Holt, Attorney General of Arkansas, Albert L. Coles, Attorney General of Connecticut, Richard W. Ervin, Attorney General of Florida, Eugene Cook, Attorney General of Georgia, Frank Benson, Attorney General of Idaho, Edwin K. Steers, Attorney General of Indiana, William M. Ferguson, Attorney General of Kansas, Jack P. F. Gremillion, Attorney General of Louisiana, Thomas B. Finan, Attorney General of Maryland, Joe T. Patterson, Attorney General of Mississippi, William Maynard, Attorney General of New Hampshire, Arthur J. Sills, Attorney General of New Jersey, Earl E. Hartley, Attorney General of New Mexico, Leslie R. Burgum, Attorney General of North Dakota, David Stahl, Attorney General of Pennsylvania, J. Joseph Nugent, Attorney General of Rhode Island, Daniel R. McLeod, Attorney General of South Carolina, A. C. Miller, Attorney General of South Dakota, Will Wilson, Attorney General of Texas, and C. Donald Robertson, Attorney General of West Virginia.

MR. JUSTICE BLACK delivered the opinion of the Court.

The respondent Board of Education of Union Free School District No. 9, New Hyde Park, New York, acting in its official capacity under state law, directed the School District's principal to cause the following prayer to be said aloud by each class in the presence of a teacher at the beginning of each school day:

> "Almighty God, we acknowledge our dependence upon Thee, and we beg Thy blessings upon us, our parents, our teachers and our Country."

This daily procedure was adopted on the recommendation of the State Board of Regents, a governmental agency created by the State Constitution to which the New York Legislature has granted broad supervisory, executive, and [370 U.S. 421, 423] legislative powers over the State's public school system.[1] These state officials composed the prayer which they recommended and published as a part of their "Statement on Moral and Spiritual Training in the Schools," saying: "We believe that this Statement will be subscribed to by all men and women of good will, and we call upon all of them to aid in giving life to our program."

Shortly after the practice of reciting the Regents" prayer was adopted by the School District, the parents of ten pupils brought this action in a New York State Court insisting that use of this official prayer in the public schools was contrary to the beliefs, religions, or religious practices of both themselves and their children. Among other things, these parents challenged the constitutionality of both the state law authorizing the School District to direct the use of prayer in public schools and the School District's regulation ordering the recitation of this particular prayer on the ground that these actions of official governmental agencies violate that part of the First Amendment of the Federal Constitution which commands that "Congress shall make no law respecting an establishment of religion"—a command which was "made applicable to the State of New York by the Fourteenth Amendment of the said Constitution." The New York Court of Appeals, over the dissents of Judges Dye and Fuld, sustained an order of the lower state courts which had upheld the power of New York to use the Regents" prayer as a part of the daily procedures of its public schools so long as the schools did not compel any pupil to join in the prayer over his or his parents" objection.[2] [370 U.S. 421, 424] We granted certiorari to review this important decision involving rights protected by the First and Fourteenth Amendments.[3]

We think that by using its public school system to encourage recitation of the Regents" prayer, the State of New York has adopted a practice wholly inconsistent with the Establishment Clause. There can, of course, be no doubt that New York's program of daily classroom invocation of God's blessings as prescribed in the Regents" prayer is a religious activity. It is a solemn avowal of divine faith and supplication for the blessings of the Almighty. The nature of such a prayer has always been [370 U.S. 421, 425] religious, none of the respondents has denied this and the trial court expressly so found:

> "The religious nature of prayer was recognized by Jefferson and has been concurred in by theological writers, the United States Supreme Court and State courts and administrative officials, including New York's Commissioner of Education. A committee of the New York Legislature has agreed.
>
> "The Board of Regents as amicus curiae, the respondents and intervenors all concede the religious nature of prayer, but seek to distinguish this prayer because it is based on our spiritual heritage. . . ."[4]

The petitioners contend among other things that the state laws requiring or permitting use of the Regents" prayer must be struck down as a violation of the Establishment Clause because that prayer was composed by governmental officials as a part of a governmental program to further religious beliefs. For this reason, petitioners argue, the State's use of the Regents" prayer in its public school system breaches the constitutional wall of separation between Church and State. We agree with that contention since we think that the constitutional prohibition against laws respecting an establishment of religion must at least mean that in this country it is no part of the business of government to compose official prayers for any group of the American people to recite as a part of a religious program carried on by government.

It is a matter of history that this very practice of establishing governmentally composed prayers for religious services was one of the reasons which caused many of our early colonists to leave England and seek religious freedom in America. The Book of Common Prayer, [370 U.S. 421, 426] which was created under governmental direction and which was approved by Acts of Parliament in 1548 and 1549,[5] set out in minute detail the accepted form and content of prayer and other religious ceremonies to be used in the established, tax-supported Church of England.[6] The controversies over the Book and what should be its content repeatedly threatened to disrupt the peace of that country as the accepted forms of prayer in the established church changed with the views of the particular ruler that happened to be in control at the time.[7] Powerful groups representing some of the varying religious views of the people struggled among themselves to impress their particular views upon the Government and [370 U.S. 421, 427] obtain amendments of the Book more suitable to their respective notions of how religious services should be conducted in order that the official religious establishment would advance their particular religious beliefs.[8] Other groups, lacking the necessary political power to influence the Government on the matter, decided to leave England and its established church and seek freedom in America from England's governmentally ordained and supported religion.

It is an unfortunate fact of history that when some of the very groups which had most strenuously opposed the established Church of England found themselves sufficiently in control of colonial governments in this country to write their own prayers into law, they passed laws making their own religion the official religion of their respective colonies.[9] Indeed, as late as the time of the Revolutionary [370 U.S. 421, 428] War, there were established churches in at least eight of the thirteen former colonies and established religions in at least four of the other five.[10] But the successful Revolution against English political domination was shortly followed by intense opposition to the practice of establishing religion by law. This opposition crystallized rapidly into an effective political force in Virginia where the minority religious groups such as Presbyterians, Lutherans, Quakers and Baptists had gained such strength that the adherents to the established Episcopal Church were actually a minority themselves. In 1785–1786, those opposed to the established Church, led by James Madison and Thomas Jefferson, who, though themselves not members of any of these dissenting religious groups, opposed all religious establishments by law on grounds of principle, obtained the enactment of the famous "Virginia Bill for Religious Liberty" by which all religious groups were placed on an equal footing so far as the State was concerned.[11] Similar though less far-reaching [370 U.S. 421, 429] legislation was being considered and passed in other States.[12]

By the time of the adoption of the Constitution, our history shows that there was a widespread awareness among many Americans of the dangers of a union of Church and State. These people knew, some of them from bitter personal experience, that one of the greatest dangers to the freedom of the individual to worship in his own way lay in the Government's placing its official stamp of approval upon one particular kind of prayer or one particular form of religious services. They knew the anguish, hardship and bitter strife that could come when zealous religious groups struggled with one another to obtain the Government's stamp of approval from each King, Queen, or Protector that came to temporary power. The Constitution was intended to avert a part of this danger by leaving the government of this country in the hands of the people rather than in the hands of any monarch. But this safeguard was not enough. Our Founders were no more willing to let the content of their prayers and their privilege of praying whenever they pleased be influenced by the ballot box than they were to let these vital matters of personal conscience depend upon the succession of monarchs. The First Amendment was added to the Constitution to stand as a guarantee that neither the power nor the prestige of the Federal Government would be used to control, support or influence the kinds of prayer the American people can say—[370 U.S. 421, 430] that the people's religions must not be subjected to the pressures of government for change each time a new political administration is elected to office. Under that Amendment's prohibition against governmental establishment of religion, as reinforced by the provisions of the Fourteenth Amendment, government in this country, be it state or federal, is without power to prescribe by law any particular form of prayer which is to be used as an official prayer in carrying on any program of governmentally sponsored religious activity.

There can be no doubt that New York's state prayer program officially establishes the religious beliefs embodied in the Regents" prayer. The respondents" argument to the contrary, which is largely based upon the contention that the Regents" prayer is "non-denominational" and the fact that the program, as modified and approved by state courts, does not require all pupils to recite the prayer but permits those who wish to do so to remain silent or be excused from the room, ignores the essential nature of the program's constitutional defects. Neither the fact that the prayer may be denominationally neutral nor the fact that its observance on the part of the students is voluntary can serve to free it from the limitations of the Establishment Clause, as it might from the Free Exercise

Clause, of the First Amendment, both of which are operative against the States by virtue of the Fourteenth Amendment. Although these two clauses may in certain instances overlap, they forbid two quite different kinds of governmental encroachment upon religious freedom. The Establishment Clause, unlike the Free Exercise Clause, does not depend upon any showing of direct governmental compulsion and is violated by the enactment of laws which establish an official religion whether those laws operate directly to coerce nonobserving individuals or not. This is not to say, of course, that [370 U.S. 421, 431] laws officially prescribing a particular form of religious worship do not involve coercion of such individuals. When the power, prestige and financial support of government is placed behind a particular religious belief, the indirect coercive pressure upon religious minorities to conform to the prevailing officially approved religion is plain. But the purposes underlying the Establishment Clause go much further than that. Its first and most immediate purpose rested on the belief that a union of government and religion tends to destroy government and to degrade religion. The history of governmentally established religion, both in England and in this country, showed that whenever government had allied itself with one particular form of religion, the inevitable result had been that it had incurred the hatred, disrespect and even contempt of those who held contrary beliefs.[13] That same history showed that many people had lost their respect for any religion that had relied upon the support of government to spread its faith.[14] The Establishment Clause [370 U.S. 421, 432] thus stands as an expression of principle on the part of the Founders of our Constitution that religion is too personal, too sacred, too holy, to permit its "unhallowed perversion" by a civil magistrate.[15] Another purpose of the Establishment Clause rested upon an awareness of the historical fact that governmentally established religions and religious persecutions go hand in hand.[16] The Founders knew that only a few years after the Book of Common Prayer became the only accepted form of religious services in the established Church of England, an Act of Uniformity was passed to compel all Englishmen to attend those services and to make it a criminal offense to conduct or attend religious gatherings of any other kind[17]—a law [370 U.S. 421, 433] which was consistently flouted by dissenting religious groups in England and which contributed to widespread persecutions of people like John Bunyan who persisted in holding "unlawful [religious] meetings . . . to the great disturbance and distraction of the good subjects of this kingdom . . . ."[18] And they knew that similar persecutions had received the sanction of law in several of the colonies in this country soon after the establishment of official religions in those colonies.[19] It was in large part to get completely away from this sort of systematic religious persecution that the Founders brought into being our Nation, our

Constitution, and our Bill of Rights with its prohibition against any governmental establishment of religion. The New York laws officially prescribing the Regents" prayer are inconsistent both with the purposes of the Establishment Clause and with the Establishment Clause itself.

It has been argued that to apply the Constitution in such a way as to prohibit state laws respecting an [370 U.S. 421, 434] establishment of religious services in public schools is to indicate a hostility toward religion or toward prayer. Nothing, of course, could be more wrong. The history of man is inseparable from the history of religion. And perhaps it is not too much to say that since the beginning of that history many people have devoutly believed that "More things are wrought by prayer than this world dreams of." It was doubtless largely due to men who believed this that there grew up a sentiment that caused men to leave the cross-currents of officially established state religions and religious persecution in Europe and come to this country filled with the hope that they could find a place in which they could pray when they pleased to the God of their faith in the language they chose.[20] And there were men of this same faith in the [370 U.S. 421, 435] power of prayer who led the fight for adoption of our Constitution and also for our Bill of Rights with the very guarantees of religious freedom that forbid the sort of governmental activity which New York has attempted here. These men knew that the First Amendment, which tried to put an end to governmental control of religion and of prayer, was not written to destroy either. They knew rather that it was written to quiet well-justified fears which nearly all of them felt arising out of an awareness that governments of the past had shackled men's tongues to make them speak only the religious thoughts that government wanted them to speak and to pray only to the God that government wanted them to pray to. It is neither sacrilegious nor antireligious to say that each separate government in this country should stay out of the business of writing or sanctioning official prayers and leave that purely religious function to the people themselves and to those the people choose to look to for religious guidance.[21] [370 U.S. 421, 436]

It is true that New York's establishment of its Regents" prayer as an officially approved religious doctrine of that State does not amount to a total establishment of one particular religious sect to the exclusion of all others—that, indeed, the governmental endorsement of that prayer seems relatively insignificant when compared to the governmental encroachments upon religion which were commonplace 200 years ago. To those who may subscribe to the view that because the Regents" official prayer is so brief and general there can be no danger to religious freedom in its governmental establishment, however, it may be appropriate to say in the words of James Madison, the author of the First Amendment:

"[I]t is proper to take alarm at the first experiment on our liberties. ... Who does not see that the same authority which can establish Christianity, in exclusion of all other Religions, may establish with the same ease any particular sect of Christians, in exclusion of all other Sects? That the same authority which can force a citizen to contribute three pence only of his property for the support of any one establishment, may force him to conform to any other establishment in all cases whatsoever?"[22]

The judgment of the Court of Appeals of New York is reversed and the cause remanded for further proceedings not inconsistent with this opinion.

Reversed and remanded.

MR. JUSTICE FRANKFURTER took no part in the decision of this case.

MR. JUSTICE WHITE took no part in the consideration or decision of this case.

FOOTNOTES

[1] See New York Constitution, Art. V, 4; New York Education Law, 101, 120 et seq., 202, 214–219, 224, 245 et seq., 704, and 801 et seq.

[2] 10 N. Y. 2d 174, 176 N. E. 2d 579. The trial court's opinion, which is reported at 18 Misc. 2d 659, 191 N. Y. S. 2d 453, had made it clear that the Board of Education must set up some sort [370 U.S. 421, 424] of procedures to protect those who objected to reciting the prayer: "This is not to say that the rights accorded petitioners and their children under the 'free exercise' clause do not mandate safeguards against such embarrassments and pressures. It is enough on this score, however, that regulations, such as were adopted by New York City's Board of Education in connection with its released time program, be adopted, making clear that neither teachers nor any other school authority may comment on participation or nonparticipation in the exercise nor suggest or require that any posture or language be used or dress be worn or be not used or not worn. Nonparticipation may take the form either of remaining silent during the exercise, or if the parent or child so desires, of being excused entirely from the exercise. Such regulations must also make provision for those nonparticipants who are to be excused from the prayer exercise. The exact provision to be made is a matter for decision by the board, rather than the court, within the framework of constitutional requirements. Within that framework would fall a provision that prayer participants proceed to a common assembly while nonparticipants attend other rooms, or that nonparticipants are permitted to arrive at school a few minutes late or to attend separate opening exercises, or any other method which treats with equality both participants and nonparticipants." 18 Misc. 2d, at 696, 191 N. Y. S. 2d, at 492–493. See also the opinion of the Appellate Division affirming that of the trial court, reported at 11 App. Div. 2d 340, 206 N. Y. S. 2d 183.

[3] 368 U.S. 924.

[4] 18 Misc. 2d, at 671–672, 191 N. Y. S. 2d, at 468–469.

⁵ 2 & 3 Edward VI, c. 1, entitled "An Act for Uniformity of Service and Administration of the Sacraments throughout the Realm"; 3 & 4 Edward VI, c. 10, entitled "An Act for the abolishing and putting away of divers Books and Images."

⁶ The provisions of the various versions of the Book of Common Prayer are set out in broad outline in the Encyclopedia Britannica, Vol. 18 (1957 ed.), pp. 420–423. For a more complete description, see Pullan, The History of the Book of Common Prayer (1900).

⁷ The first major revision of the Book of Common Prayer was made in 1552 during the reign of Edward VI. 5 & 6 Edward VI, c. 1. In 1553, Edward VI died and was succeeded by Mary who abolished the Book of Common Prayer entirely. 1 Mary, c. 2. But upon the accession of Elizabeth in 1558, the Book was restored with important alterations from the form it had been given by Edward VI. 1 Elizabeth, c. 2. The resentment to this amended form of the Book was kept firmly under control during the reign of Elizabeth but, upon her death in 1603, a petition signed by more than 1,000 Puritan ministers was presented to King James I asking for further alterations in the Book. Some alterations were made and the Book retained substantially this form until it was completely suppressed again in 1645 as a result of the successful Puritan Revolution. Shortly after the restoration in 1660 of Charles II, the Book was again reintroduced, 13 & 14 Charles II, c. 4, and again with alterations. Rather than accept this form of the Book some 2,000 Puritan ministers vacated their benefices. See generally Pullan, The History of the Book of Common Prayer (1900), pp. vii–xvi; Encyclopaedia Britannica (1957 ed.), Vol. 18, pp. 421–422.

⁸ For example, the Puritans twice attempted to modify the Book of Common Prayer and once attempted to destroy it. The story of their struggle to modify the Book in the reign of Charles I is vividly summarized in Pullan, History of the Book of Common Prayer, at p. xiii: "The King actively supported those members of the Church of England who were anxious to vindicate its Catholic character and maintain the ceremonial which Elizabeth had approved. Laud, Archbishop of Canterbury, was the leader of this school. Equally resolute in his opposition to the distinctive tenets of Rome and of Geneva, he enjoyed the hatred of both Jesuit and Calvinist. He helped the Scottish bishops, who had made large concessions to the uncouth habits of Presbyterian worship, to draw up a Book of Common Prayer for Scotland. It contained a Communion Office resembling that of the book of 1549. It came into use in 1637, and met with a bitter and barbarous opposition. The vigour of the Scottish Protestants strengthened the hands of their English sympathisers. Laud and Charles were executed, Episcopacy was abolished, the use of the Book of Common Prayer was prohibited."

⁹ For a description of some of the laws enacted by early theocratic governments in New England, see Parrington, Main Currents in American Thought (1930), Vol. 1, pp. 5–50; Whipple, Our Ancient Liberties (1927), pp. 63–78; Wertenbaker, The Puritan Oligarchy (1947).

¹⁰ The Church of England was the established church of at least five colonies: Maryland, Virginia, North Carolina, South Carolina and Georgia. There seems to be some controversy as to whether that church was officially established in New York and New Jersey but there is no doubt that it received substantial support from those States. See Cobb, The Rise of Religious Liberty in America (1902), pp. 338, 408. In Massachusetts, New Hampshire and Connecticut, the Congregationalist Church was officially established. In Pennsylvania and Delaware, all Christian sects were treated equally in most situations but Catholics were discriminated against in some respects. See generally Cobb, The Rise of Religious Liberty in America (1902). In Rhode Island all Protestants enjoyed equal privileges but it is not clear whether Catholics were allowed to vote. Compare Fiske, The Critical Period in American History (1899), p. 76 with Cobb, The Rise of Religious Liberty in America (1902), pp. 437–438.

[11] 12 Hening, Statutes of Virginia (1823), 84, entitled "An act for establishing religious freedom." The story of the events surrounding the enactment of this law was reviewed in Everson v. Board of Education, 330 U.S. 1, both by the Court, at pp. 11–13, and in the [370 U.S. 421, 429] dissenting opinion of Mr. Justice Rutledge, at pp. 33–42. See also Fiske, The Critical Period in American History (1899), pp. 78–82; James, The Struggle for Religious Liberty in Virginia (1900); Thom, The Struggle for Religious Freedom in Virginia: The Baptists (1900); Cobb, The Rise of Religious Liberty in America (1902), pp. 74–115, 482–499.

[12] See Cobb, The Rise of Religious Liberty in America (1902), pp. 482–509.

[13] "[A]ttempts to enforce by legal sanctions, acts obnoxious to so great a proportion of Citizens, tend to enervate the laws in general, and to slacken the bands of Society. If it be difficult to execute any law which is not generally deemed necessary or salutary, what must be the case where it is deemed invalid and dangerous? and what may be the effect of so striking an example of impotency in the Government, on its general authority." Memorial and Remonstrance against Religious Assessments, II Writings of Madison 183, 190.

[14] "It is moreover to weaken in those who profess this Religion a pious confidence in its innate excellence, and the patronage of its Author; and to foster in those who still reject it, a suspicion that its friends are too conscious of its fallacies, to trust it to its own merits. . . . [E]xperience witnesseth that ecclesiastical establishments, instead of maintaining the purity and efficacy of Religion, have had a contrary operation. During almost fifteen centuries, has the legal establishment of Christianity been on trial. What have been its fruits? More or less in all places, pride and indolence in the Clergy; ignorance and servility in the laity; in both, superstition, [370 U.S. 421, 432] bigotry and persecution. Enquire of the Teachers of Christianity for the ages in which it appeared in its greatest lustre; those of every sect, point to the ages prior to its incorporation with Civil policy." Id., at 187.

[15] Memorial and Remonstrance against Religious Assessments, II Writings of Madison, at 187.

[16] "[T]he proposed establishment is a departure from that generous policy, which, offering an asylum to the persecuted and oppressed of every Nation and Religion, promised a lustre to our country, and an accession to the number of its citizens. What a melancholy mark is the Bill of sudden degeneracy? Instead of holding forth an asylum to the persecuted, it is itself a signal of persecution. . . . Distant as it may be, in its present form, from the Inquisition it differs from it only in degree. The one is the first step, the other the last in the career of intolerance. The magnanimous sufferer under this cruel scourge in foreign Regions, must view the Bill as a Beacon on our Coast, warning him to seek some other haven, where liberty and philanthropy in their due extent may offer a more certain repose from his troubles." Id., at 188.

[17] 5 & 6 Edward VI, c. 1, entitled "An Act for the Uniformity of Service and Administration of Sacraments throughout the Realm." This Act was repealed during the reign of Mary but revived upon the accession of Elizabeth. See note 7, supra. The reasons which led to the enactment of this statute were set out in its preamble: "Where there hath been a very godly Order set forth by the Authority of Parliament, for Common Prayer and Administration of the Sacraments [370 U.S. 421, 433] to be used in the Mother Tongue within the Church of England, agreeable to the Word of God and the Primitive Church, very comfortable to all good People desiring to live in Christian Conversation, and most profitable to the Estate of this Realm, upon the which the Mercy, Favour and Blessing of Almighty God is in no wise so readily and plenteously poured as by Common Prayers, due using of the Sacraments, and often preaching of the Gospel, with the Devotion of the Hearers: (1) And yet this notwithstanding, a great Number of People in divers Parts of this Realm, following their own Sensuality, and liv-

ing either without Knowledge or due Fear of God, do wilfully and damnably before Almighty God abstain and refuse to come to their Parish Churches and other Places where Common Prayer, Administration of the Sacraments, and Preaching of the Word of God, is used upon Sundays and other Days ordained to be Holydays."

[18] Bunyan's own account of his trial is set forth in A Relation of the Imprisonment of Mr. John Bunyan, reprinted in Grace Abounding and The Pilgrim's Progress (Brown ed. 1907), at 103–132.

[19] For a vivid account of some of these persecutions, see Wertenbaker, The Puritan Oligarchy (1947).

[20] Perhaps the best example of the sort of men who came to this country for precisely that reason is Roger Williams, the founder of Rhode Island, who has been described as "the truest Christian amongst many who sincerely desired to be Christian." Parrington, Main Currents in American Thought (1930), Vol. 1, at p. 74. Williams, who was one of the earliest exponents of the doctrine of separation of church and state, believed that separation was necessary in order to protect the church from the danger of destruction which he thought inevitably flowed from control by even the best-intentioned civil authorities: "The unknowing zeale of Constantine and other Emperours, did more hurt to Christ Jesus his Crowne and Kingdome, then the raging fury of the most bloody Neroes. In the persecutions of the later, Christians were sweet and fragrant, like spice pounded and beaten in morters: But those good Emperours, persecuting some erroneous persons, Arrius, & c. and advancing the professours of some Truths of Christ (for there was no small number of Truths lost in those times) and maintaining their Religion by the materiall Sword, I say by this meanes Christianity was ecclipsed, and the Professors of it fell asleep. . . ." Williams, The Bloudy Tenent, of Persecution, for cause of Conscience, discussed in A Conference between Truth and Peace (London, 1644), reprinted in Narragansett Club Publications, Vol. III, p. 184. To Williams, it was no part of the business or competence of a civil magistrate to interfere in religious matters: "[W]hat imprudence and indiscretion is it in the most common [370 U.S. 421, 435] affaires of Life, to conceive that Emperours, Kings and Rulers of the earth must not only be qualified with politicall and state abilities to make and execute such Civill Lawes which may concerne the common rights, peace and safety (which is worke and businesse, load and burthen enough for the ablest shoulders in the Commonweal) but also furnished with such Spirituall and heavenly abilities to governe the Spirituall and Christian Commonweale. . . ." Id., at 366. See also id., at 136–137.

[21] There is of course nothing in the decision reached here that is inconsistent with the fact that school children and others are officially encouraged to express love for our country by reciting historical documents such as the Declaration of Independence which contain references to the Deity or by singing officially espoused anthems which include the composer's professions of faith in a Supreme Being, or with the fact that there are many manifestations in our public life of belief in God. Such patriotic or ceremonial occasions bear no true resemblance to the unquestioned religious exercise that the State of New York has sponsored in this instance.

[22] Memorial and Remonstrance against Religious Assessments, II Writings of Madison 183, at 185–186. [370 U.S. 421, 437]

MR. JUSTICE STEWART, dissenting.

A local school board in New York has provided that those pupils who wish to do so may join in a brief prayer at the beginning of each school day, acknowledging their dependence upon God and asking His blessing upon them [370 U.S. 421, 445] and upon their parents, their teachers, and their country. The Court today decides that in permitting this brief nondenominational prayer the school board has violated the Constitution of the United States. I think this decision is wrong.

The Court does not hold, nor could it, that New York has interfered with the free exercise of anybody's religion. For the state courts have made clear that those who object to reciting the prayer must be entirely free of any compulsion to do so, including any "embarrassments and pressures." Cf. West Virginia State Board of Education v. Barnette, 319 U.S. 624. But the Court says that in permitting school children to say this simple prayer, the New York authorities have established "an official religion."

With all respect, I think the Court has misapplied a great constitutional principle. I cannot see how an "official religion" is established by letting those who want to say a prayer say it. On the contrary, I think that to deny the wish of these school children to join in reciting this prayer is to deny them the opportunity of sharing in the spiritual heritage of our Nation.

The Court's historical review of the quarrels over the Book of Common Prayer in England throws no light for me on the issue before us in this case. England had then and has now an established church. Equally unenlightening, I think, is the history of the early establishment and later rejection of an official church in our own States. For we deal here not with the establishment of a state church, which would, of course, be constitutionally impermissible, but with whether school children who want to begin their day by joining in prayer must be prohibited from doing so. Moreover, I think that the Court's task, in this as in all areas of constitutional adjudication, is not responsibly aided by the uncritical invocation of metaphors like the "wall of separation," a phrase nowhere to [370 U.S. 421, 446] be found in the Constitution. What is relevant to the issue here is not the history of an established church in sixteenth century England or in eighteenth century America, but the history of the religious traditions of our people, reflected in countless practices of the institutions and officials of our government.

At the opening of each day's Session of this Court we stand, while one of our officials invokes the protection of God. Since the days of John Marshall our Crier has said, "God save the United States and this Honorable Court."[1] Both the Senate and the House of Representatives open their daily Sessions with prayer.[2] Each of our Presidents, from George Washington to John F. Kennedy, has upon assuming his Office asked the protection and help of God.[3] [370 U.S. 421, 447]

The Court today says that the state and federal governments are without constitutional power to prescribe any particular form of words to be recited by any group of the American people on any subject touching religion.[4] One of the stanzas of "The Star-Spangled Banner," made our National Anthem by Act of Congress in 1931,[5] contains these verses:

"Blest with victory and peace, may the heav'n rescued land
Praise the Pow'r that hath made and preserved us a nation!
Then conquer we must, when our cause it is just, And this be our
    motto "In God is our Trust.""

In 1954 Congress added a phrase to the Pledge of Allegiance to the
Flag so that it now contains the words "one Nation under God, indivis-
ible, with liberty and justice for all."[6] In 1952 Congress enacted legislation calling upon the President each year to proclaim a National Day
of Prayer.[7] Since 1865 the words "IN GOD WE TRUST" have been
impressed on our coins.[8] [370 U.S. 421, 450]

Countless similar examples could be listed, but there is no need to
belabor the obvious.[9] It was all summed up by this Court just ten years
ago in a single sentence: "We are a religious people whose institutions
presuppose a Supreme Being." Zorach v. Clauson, 343 U.S. 306, 313.

I do not believe that this Court, or the Congress, or the President has
by the actions and practices I have mentioned established an "official religion" in violation of the Constitution. And I do not believe the State of
New York has done so in this case. What each has done has been to recognize and to follow the deeply entrenched and highly cherished spiritual traditions of our Nation—traditions which come down to us from
those who almost two hundred years ago avowed their "firm Reliance
on the Protection of divine Providence" when they proclaimed the freedom and independence of this brave new world.[10]

I dissent.

FOOTNOTES

[1] See Warren, The Supreme Court in United States History, Vol. 1, p. 469.
[2] See Rule III, Senate Manual, S. Doc. No. 2, 87th Cong., 1st Sess. See Rule VII, Rules
of the House of Representatives, H. R. Doc. No. 459, 86th Cong., 2d Sess.
[3] For example:

On April 30, 1789, President George Washington said:
". . . it would be peculiarly improper to omit in this first official act my fervent
supplications to that Almighty Being who rules over the universe, who presides
in the councils of nations, and whose providential aids can supply every human
defect, that His benediction may consecrate to the liberties and happiness of the
people of the United States a Government instituted by themselves for these
essential purposes, and may enable every instrument employed in its administration to execute with success the functions allotted to his charge. In tendering this
homage to the Great Author of every public and private good, I assure myself
that it expresses your sentiments not less than my own, nor those of my fellow-
citizens at large less than either. No people can be bound to acknowledge and
adore the Invisible Hand which conducts the affairs of men more than those of
the United States. . . .

"Having thus imparted to you my sentiments as they have been awakened by the occasion which brings us together, I shall [370 U.S. 421, 447] take my present leave; but not without resorting once more to the benign Parent of the Human Race in humble supplication that, since He has been pleased to favor the American people with opportunities for deliberating in perfect tranquillity, and dispositions for deciding with unparalleled unanimity on a form of government for the security of their union and the advancement of their happiness, so His divine blessing may be equally conspicuous in the enlarged views, the temperate consultations, and the wise measures on which the success of this Government must depend."

On March 4, 1797, President John Adams said:

"And may that Being who is supreme over all, the Patron of Order, the Fountain of Justice, and the Protector in all ages of the world of virtuous liberty, continue His blessing upon this nation and its Government and give it all possible success and duration consistent with the ends of His providence."

On March 4, 1805, President Thomas Jefferson said:

". . . I shall need, too, the favor of that Being in whose hands we are, who led our fathers, as Israel of old, from their native land and planted them in a country flowing with all the necessaries and comforts of life; who has covered our infancy with His providence and our riper years with His wisdom and power, and to whose goodness I ask you to join in supplications with me that He will so enlighten the minds of your servants, guide their councils, and prosper their measures that whatsoever they do shall result in your good, and shall secure to you the peace, friendship, and approbation of all nations."

On March 4, 1809, President James Madison said:

"But the source to which I look . . . is in . . . my fellow-citizens, and in the counsels of those representing them in the other departments associated in the care of the national interests. In these my confidence will under every difficulty be best placed, next to that which we have all been encouraged to feel in the guardianship and guidance of that Almighty Being whose power regulates the destiny of nations, whose blessings have been so conspicuously dispensed to this rising Republic, and to whom we are bound to address our devout gratitude for the past, as well as our fervent supplications and best hopes for the future." [370 U.S. 421, 448]

On March 4, 1865, President Abraham Lincoln said:

". . . Fondly do we hope, fervently do we pray, that this mighty scourge of war may speedily pass away. Yet, if God wills that it continue until all the wealth piled by the bondsman's two hundred and fifty years of unrequited toil shall be sunk, and until every drop of blood drawn with the lash shall be paid by another drawn with the sword, as was said three thousand years ago, so still it must be said 'the judgments of the Lord are true and righteous altogether."

"With malice toward none, with charity for all, with firmness in the right as God gives us to see the right, let us strive on to finish the work we are in, to bind up the nation's wounds, to care for him who shall have borne the battle and for his widow and his orphan, to do all which may achieve and cherish a just and lasting peace among ourselves and with all nations."

On March 4, 1885, President Grover Cleveland said:

". . . And let us not trust to human effort alone, but humbly acknowledging the power and goodness of Almighty God, who presides over the destiny of nations, and who has at all times been revealed in our country's history, let us invoke His aid and His blessing upon our labors."

On March 5, 1917, President Woodrow Wilson said:

". . . I pray God I may be given the wisdom and the prudence to do my duty in the true spirit of this great people."

On March 4, 1933, President Franklin D. Roosevelt said:

"In this dedication of a Nation we humbly ask the blessing of God. May He protect each and every one of us. May He guide me in the days to come."

On January 21, 1957, President Dwight D. Eisenhower said:

"Before all else, we seek, upon our common labor as a nation, the blessings of Almighty God. And the hopes in our hearts fashion the deepest prayers of our whole people."

On January 20, 1961, President John F. Kennedy said:

"The world is very different now. . . . And yet the same revolutionary beliefs for which our forebears fought are still at issue around the globe—the belief that the rights of man come [370 U.S. 421, 449] not from the generosity of the state but from the hand of God.

"With a good conscience our only sure reward, with history the final judge of our deeds, let us go forth to lead the land we love, asking His blessing and His help, but knowing that here on earth God's work must truly be our own."

[4] My brother DOUGLAS says that the only question before us is whether government "can constitutionally finance a religious exercise." The official chaplains of Congress are paid with public money. So are military chaplains. So are state and federal prison chaplains.

[5] 36 U.S.C. 170.

[6] 36 U.S.C. 172.

[7] 36 U.S.C. 185.

[8] 13 Stat. 517, 518; 17 Stat. 427; 35 Stat. 164; 69 Stat. 290. The current provisions are embodied in 31 U.S.C. 324, 324a.

[9] I am at a loss to understand the Court's unsupported ipse dixit that these official expressions of religious faith in and reliance upon a Supreme Being "bear no true resemblance to the unquestioned religious exercise that the State of New York has sponsored in this instance." See ante, p. 435, n. 21. I can hardly think that the Court means to say that the First Amendment imposes a lesser restriction upon the Federal Government than does the Fourteenth Amendment upon the States. Or is the Court suggesting that the Constitution permits judges and Congressmen and Presidents to join in prayer, but prohibits school children from doing so?

[10] The Declaration of Independence ends with this sentence: "And for the support of this Declaration, with a firm reliance on the protection of divine Providence, we mutually pledge to each other our Lives, our Fortunes and our sacred Honor." [370 U.S. 421, 451]

New York Times Co. v. Sullivan
1964

On March 29, 1960, The *New York Times* ran a full-page advertisement, paid for by supporters of Martin Luther King, Jr., entitled "Heed Their Rising Voices." This advertisement reported on instances of civil rights abuse that had taken place in Montgomery, Alabama at the hands of the Montgomery Police Department. Upset by this ad, Montgomery City Commissioner L. B. Sullivan filed a libel action against the *New York Times* in the circuit court of Montgomery County, claiming that the advertisement constituted defamation against him, as it contained untrue statements about the police department that he personally oversaw. After losing in the Alabama State court, The *New York Times* appealed their case to the U. S. Supreme Court, claiming that the ruling violated the First and Fourteenth Amendments.

In a unanimous decision, the Supreme Court reversed the state court's decision, holding that Alabama's libel law was unconstitutional, as it would unfairly discourage a "good-faith" critic of the government. Furthermore, the court contended that for a statement to be considered libelous under the law, it must be proven to have been made with "actual malice" or, "with reckless disregard as to whether it was false or not." This ruling proved instrumental in the eventual abolition of state defamation laws, allowing all areas of media a far greater measure of freedom to criticize the government without fear of retribution.

U.S. SUPREME COURT

NEW YORK TIMES CO. V. SULLIVAN, 376 U.S. 254 (1964)

376 U.S. 254

NEW YORK TIMES CO. V. SULLIVAN. CERTIORARI TO THE SUPREME COURT OF ALABAMA.
NO. 39.

Argued January 6, 1964.
Decided March 9, 1964.★

RESPONDENT, an elected official in Montgomery, Alabama, brought suit in a state court alleging that he had been libeled by an advertisement in corporate petitioner's newspaper, the text of which appeared over the names of the four individual petitioners and many others. The advertisement included statements, some of which were false, about police action allegedly directed against students who participated in a civil rights demonstration and against a leader of the civil rights movement; respondent claimed the statements referred to him because his duties included supervision of the police department. The trial judge instructed the jury that such statements were "libelous per se," legal injury being implied without proof of actual damages, and that for the purpose of compensatory damages malice was presumed, so that such damages could be awarded against petitioners if the statements were found to have been published by them and to have related to respondent. As to punitive damages, the judge instructed that mere negligence was not evidence of actual malice and would not justify an award of punitive damages; he refused to instruct that actual intent to harm or recklessness had to be

---

★Together with No. 40, Abernathy et al. v. Sullivan, also on certiorari to the same court, argued January 7, 1964.

found before punitive damages could be awarded, or that a verdict for respondent should differentiate between compensatory and punitive damages. The jury found for respondent and the State Supreme Court affirmed. Held: A State cannot under the First and Fourteenth Amendments award damages to a public official for defamatory falsehood relating to his official conduct unless he proves "actual malice"— that the statement was made with knowledge of its falsity or with reckless disregard of whether it was true or false. Pp. 265–292.

(a) Application by state courts of a rule of law, whether statutory or not, to award a judgment in a civil action, is "state action" under the Fourteenth Amendment. P. 265.

(b) Expression does not lose constitutional protection to which it would otherwise be entitled because it appears in the form of a paid advertisement. Pp. 265–266. [376 U.S. 254, 255]

(c) Factual error, content defamatory of official reputation, or both, are insufficient to warrant an award of damages for false statements unless "actual malice"—knowledge that statements are false or in reckless disregard of the truth—is alleged and proved. Pp. 279–283.

(d) State court judgment entered upon a general verdict which does not differentiate between punitive damages, as to which under state law actual malice must be proved, and general damages, as to which it is "presumed," precludes any determination as to the basis of the verdict and requires reversal, where presumption of malice is inconsistent with federal constitutional requirements. P. 284.

(e) The evidence was constitutionally insufficient to support the judgment for respondent, since it failed to support a finding that the statements were made with actual malice or that they related to respondent. Pp. 285–292.

273 Ala. 656, 144 So.2d 25, reversed and remanded.

Herbert Wechsler argued the cause for petitioner in No. 39. With him on the brief were Herbert Brownell, Thomas F. Daly, Louis M. Loeb, T. Eric Embry, Marvin E. Frankel, Ronald S. Diana and Doris Wechsler.

William P. Rogers and Samuel R. Pierce, Jr. argued the cause for petitioners in No. 40. With Mr. Pierce on the brief were I. H. Wachtel, Charles S. Conley, Benjamin Spiegel, Raymond S. Harris, Harry H. Wachtel, Joseph B. Russell, David N. Brainin, Stephen J. Jelin and Charles B. Markham.

M. Roland Nachman, Jr. argued the cause for respondent in both cases. With him on the brief were Sam Rice Baker and Calvin Whitesell.

Briefs of amici curiae, urging reversal, were filed in No. 39 by William P. Rogers, Gerald W. Siegel and Stanley Godofsky for the Washington

Post Company, and by Howard Ellis, Keith Masters and Don H. Reuben for the Tribune Company. Brief of amici curiae, urging reversal, was filed in both cases by Edward S. Greenbaum, Harriet F. Pilpel, Melvin L. Wulf, Nanette Dembitz and Nancy F. Wechsler for the American Civil Liberties Union et al. [376 U.S. 254, 256]

MR. JUSTICE BRENNAN delivered the opinion of the Court.

We are required in this case to determine for the first time the extent to which the constitutional protections for speech and press limit a State's power to award damages in a libel action brought by a public official against critics of his official conduct.

Respondent L. B. Sullivan is one of the three elected Commissioners of the City of Montgomery, Alabama. He testified that he was "Commissioner of Public Affairs and the duties are supervision of the Police Department, Fire Department, Department of Cemetery and Department of Scales." He brought this civil libel action against the four individual petitioners, who are Negroes and Alabama clergymen, and against petitioner the New York Times Company, a New York corporation which publishes the New York Times, a daily newspaper. A jury in the Circuit Court of Montgomery County awarded him damages of $500,000, the full amount claimed, against all the petitioners, and the Supreme Court of Alabama affirmed. 273 Ala. 656, 144 So.2d 25.

Respondent's complaint alleged that he had been libeled by statements in a full-page advertisement that was carried in the New York Times on March 29, 1960.[1] Entitled "Heed Their Rising Voices," the advertisement began by stating that "As the whole world knows by now, thousands of Southern Negro students are engaged in widespread non-violent demonstrations in positive affirmation of the right to live in human dignity as guaranteed by the U.S. Constitution and the Bill of Rights." It went on to charge that "in their efforts to uphold these guarantees, they are being met by an unprecedented wave of terror by those who would deny and negate that document which the whole world looks upon as setting the pattern for modern freedom. . . ." Succeeding [376 U.S. 254, 257] paragraphs purported to illustrate the "wave of terror" by describing certain alleged events. The text concluded with an appeal for funds for three purposes: support of the student movement, "the struggle for the right-to-vote," and the legal defense of Dr. Martin Luther King, Jr., leader of the movement, against a perjury indictment then pending in Montgomery.

The text appeared over the names of 64 persons, many widely known for their activities in public affairs, religion, trade unions, and the performing arts. Below these names, and under a line reading "We in the south who are struggling daily for dignity and freedom warmly endorse this appeal," appeared the names of the four individual petitioners and of

16 other persons, all but two of whom were identified as clergymen in various Southern cities. The advertisement was signed at the bottom of the page by the "Committee to Defend Martin Luther King and the Struggle for Freedom in the South," and the officers of the Committee were listed.

Of the 10 paragraphs of text in the advertisement, the third and a portion of the sixth were the basis of respondent's claim of libel. They read as follows:

Third paragraph:

"In Montgomery, Alabama, after students sang 'My Country, 'Tis of Thee' on the State Capitol steps, their leaders were expelled from school, and truckloads of police armed with shotguns and tear-gas ringed the Alabama State College Campus. When the entire student body protested to state authorities by refusing to re-register, their dining hall was padlocked in an attempt to starve them into submission."

Sixth paragraph:

"Again and again the Southern violators have answered Dr. King's peaceful protests with intimidation and violence. They have bombed his home almost killing his wife and child. They have [376 U.S. 254, 258] assaulted his person. They have arrested him seven times—for "speeding," "loitering" and similar "offenses." And now they have charged him with "perjury'—a felony under which they could imprison him for ten years. . . ."

Although neither of these statements mentions respondent by name, he contended that the word "police" in the third paragraph referred to him as the Montgomery Commissioner who supervised the Police Department, so that he was being accused of "ringing" the campus with police. He further claimed that the paragraph would be read as imputing to the police, and hence to him, the padlocking of the dining hall in order to starve the students into submission.[2] As to the sixth paragraph, he contended that since arrests are ordinarily made by the police, the statement "They have arrested [Dr. King] seven times" would be read as referring to him; he further contended that the "They" who did the arresting would be equated with the "They" who committed the other described acts and with the "Southern violators." Thus, he argued, the paragraph would be read as accusing the Montgomery police, and hence him, of answering Dr. King's protests with "intimidation and violence," bombing his home, assaulting his person, and charging him with perjury. Respondent and six other Montgomery residents testified that they read some or all of the statements as referring to him in his capacity as Commissioner.

It is uncontroverted that some of the statements contained in the paragraphs were not accurate descriptions of events which occurred in Montgomery. Although Negro students staged a demonstration on the State Capitol steps, they sang the National Anthem and not "My [376 U.S. 254, 259] Country, 'Tis of Thee." Although nine students were expelled by the State Board of Education, this was not for leading the demonstration at the Capitol, but for demanding service at a lunch counter in the Montgomery County Courthouse on another day. Not the entire student body, but most of it, had protested the expulsion, not by refusing to register, but by boycotting classes on a single day; virtually all the students did register for the ensuing semester. The campus dining hall was not padlocked on any occasion, and the only students who may have been barred from eating there were the few who had neither signed a preregistration application nor requested temporary meal tickets. Although the police were deployed near the campus in large numbers on three occasions, they did not at any time "ring" the campus, and they were not called to the campus in connection with the demonstration on the State Capitol steps, as the third paragraph implied. Dr. King had not been arrested seven times, but only four; and although he claimed to have been assaulted some years earlier in connection with his arrest for loitering outside a courtroom, one of the officers who made the arrest denied that there was such an assault.

On the premise that the charges in the sixth paragraph could be read as referring to him, respondent was allowed to prove that he had not participated in the events described. Although Dr. King's home had in fact been bombed twice when his wife and child were there, both of these occasions antedated respondent's tenure as Commissioner, and the police were not only not implicated in the bombings, but had made every effort to apprehend those who were. Three of Dr. King's four arrests took place before respondent became Commissioner. Although Dr. King had in fact been indicted (he was subsequently acquitted) on two counts of perjury, each of which carried a possible five-year sentence, respondent had nothing to do with procuring the indictment. [376 U.S. 254, 260]

Respondent made no effort to prove that he suffered actual pecuniary loss as a result of the alleged libel.[3] One of his witnesses, a former employer, testified that if he had believed the statements, he doubted whether he "would want to be associated with anybody who would be a party to such things that are stated in that ad," and that he would not re-employ respondent if he believed "that he allowed the Police Department to do the things that the paper say he did." But neither this witness nor any of the others testified that he had actually believed the statements in their supposed reference to respondent.

The cost of the advertisement was approximately $4800, and it was published by the Times upon an order from a New York advertising agency acting for the signatory Committee. The agency submitted the advertisement with a letter from A. Philip Randolph, Chairman of the Committee, certifying that the persons whose names appeared on the advertisement had given their permission. Mr. Randolph was known to the Times" Advertising Acceptability Department as a responsible person, and in accepting the letter as sufficient proof of authorization it followed its established practice. There was testimony that the copy of the advertisement which accompanied the letter listed only the 64 names appearing under the text, and that the statement, "We in the south . . . warmly endorse this appeal," and the list of names thereunder, which included those of the individual petitioners, were subsequently added when the first proof of the advertisement was received. Each of the individual petitioners testified that he had not authorized the use of his name, and that he had been unaware of its use until receipt of respondent's demand for a retraction. The manager of the Advertising Acceptability [376 U.S. 254, 261] Department testified that he had approved the advertisement for publication because he knew nothing to cause him to believe that anything in it was false, and because it bore the endorsement of "a number of people who are well known and whose reputation" he "had no reason to question." Neither he nor anyone else at the Times made an effort to confirm the accuracy of the advertisement, either by checking it against recent Times news stories relating to some of the described events or by any other means.

Alabama law denies a public officer recovery of punitive damages in a libel action brought on account of a publication concerning his official conduct unless he first makes a written demand for a public retraction and the defendant fails or refuses to comply. Alabama Code, Tit. 7, 914. Respondent served such a demand upon each of the petitioners. None of the individual petitioners responded to the demand, primarily because each took the position that he had not authorized the use of his name on the advertisement and therefore had not published the statements that respondent alleged had libeled him. The Times did not publish a retraction in response to the demand, but wrote respondent a letter stating, among other things, that "we . . . are somewhat puzzled as to how you think the statements in any way reflect on you," and "you might, if you desire, let us know in what respect you claim that the statements in the advertisement reflect on you." Respondent filed this suit a few days later without answering the letter. The Times did, however, subsequently publish a retraction of the advertisement upon the demand of Governor John Patterson of Alabama, who asserted that the publication charged him with "grave misconduct and . . . improper actions and omissions as Governor of Alabama and Ex-Officio Chairman of the State Board of Education of

Alabama." When asked to explain why there had been a retraction for the Governor but not for respondent, the [376 U.S. 254, 262] Secretary of the Times testified: "We did that because we didn't want anything that was published by The Times to be a reflection on the State of Alabama and the Governor was, as far as we could see, the embodiment of the State of Alabama and the proper representative of the State and, furthermore, we had by that time learned more of the actual facts which the ad purported to recite and, finally, the ad did refer to the action of the State authorities and the Board of Education presumably of which the Governor is the ex-officio chairman . . . ." On the other hand, he testified that he did not think that "any of the language in there referred to Mr. Sullivan."

The trial judge submitted the case to the jury under instructions that the statements in the advertisement were "libelous per se" and were not privileged, so that petitioners might be held liable if the jury found that they had published the advertisement and that the statements were made "of and concerning" respondent. The jury was instructed that, because the statements were libelous per se, "the law . . . implies legal injury from the bare fact of publication itself," "falsity and malice are presumed," "general damages need not be alleged or proved but are presumed," and "punitive damages may be awarded by the jury even though the amount of actual damages is neither found nor shown." An award of punitive damages—as distinguished from "general" damages, which are compensatory in nature—apparently requires proof of actual malice under Alabama law, and the judge charged that "mere negligence or carelessness is not evidence of actual malice or malice in fact, and does not justify an award of exemplary or punitive damages." He refused to charge, however, that the jury must be "convinced" of malice, in the sense of "actual intent" to harm or "gross negligence and recklessness," to make such an award, and he also refused to require that a verdict for respondent differentiate between compensatory and punitive damages. The judge rejected petitioners" contention [376 U.S. 254, 263] that his rulings abridged the freedoms of speech and of the press that are guaranteed by the First and Fourteenth Amendments.

In affirming the judgment, the Supreme Court of Alabama sustained the trial judge's rulings and instructions in all respects. 273 Ala. 656, 144 So.2d 25. It held that "where the words published tend to injure a person libeled by them in his reputation, profession, trade or business, or charge him with an indictable offense, or tend to bring the individual into public contempt," they are "libelous per se"; that "the matter complained of is, under the above doctrine, libelous per se, if it was published of and concerning the plaintiff"; and that it was actionable without "proof of pecuniary injury . . . , such injury being implied." Id., at 673, 676, 144 So.2d, at 37, 41. It approved the trial court's ruling that the jury could find the statements to have been made "of and concerning" respondent, stating: "We think it common knowledge that the average person knows that municipal agents, such as police and firemen, and others, are under the control and direction of the city governing body, and more particularly under the direction and control of a single commissioner. In measuring the performance or deficiencies of such groups, praise or criticism is usually attached to the official in complete control of the body." Id., at 674–675, 144 So.2d at 39. In sustaining the trial court's determination that the verdict was not excessive, the court said that malice could be inferred from the Times" "irresponsibility" in printing the advertisement while "the Times in its own files had articles already published which would have demonstrated the falsity of the allegations in the advertisement"; from the Times" failure to retract for respondent while retracting for the Governor, whereas the falsity of some of the allegations was then known to the Times and "the matter contained in the advertisement was equally false as to both parties"; and from the testimony of the Times" Secretary that, [376 U.S. 254, 264] apart from the statement that the dining hall was pad-locked, he thought the two paragraphs were "substantially correct." Id., at 686–687, 144 So.2d at 50–51. The court reaffirmed a statement in an earlier opinion that "There is no legal measure of damages in cases of this character." Id., at 686, 144 So.2d, at 50. It rejected petitioners" constitutional contentions with the brief statements that "The First Amendment of the U.S. Constitution does not protect libelous publications" and "The Fourteenth Amendment is directed against State action and not private action." Id., at 676, 144 So.2d, at 40.

Because of the importance of the constitutional issues involved, we granted the separate petitions for certiorari of the individual petitioners and of the Times. 371 U.S. 946. We reverse the judgment. We hold that the rule of law applied by the Alabama courts is constitutionally deficient for failure to provide the safeguards for freedom of speech and of the press that are required by the First and Fourteenth Amendments in a libel action brought by a public official against critics of his official conduct.[4] We [376 U.S. 254, 265] further hold that under the proper safeguards the evidence presented in this case is constitutionally insufficient to support the judgment for respondent.

I.

We may dispose at the outset of two grounds asserted to insulate the judgment of the Alabama courts from constitutional scrutiny. The first is the proposition relied on by the State Supreme Court—that "The

Fourteenth Amendment is directed against State action and not private action." That proposition has no application to this case. Although this is a civil lawsuit between private parties, the Alabama courts have applied a state rule of law which petitioners claim to impose invalid restrictions on their constitutional freedoms of speech and press. It matters not that that law has been applied in a civil action and that it is common law only, though supplemented by statute. See, e. g., Alabama Code, Tit. 7, 908–917. The test is not the form in which state power has been applied but, whatever the form, whether such power has in fact been exercised. See Ex parte Virginia, 100 U.S. 339, 346–347; American Federation of Labor v. Swing, 312 U.S. 321.

The second contention is that the constitutional guarantees of freedom of speech and of the press are inapplicable here, at least so far as the Times is concerned, because the allegedly libelous statements were published as part of a paid, "commercial" advertisement. The argument relies on Valentine v. Chrestensen, 316 U.S. 52, where the Court held that a city ordinance forbidding street distribution of commercial and business advertising matter did not abridge the First Amendment freedoms, even as applied to a handbill having a commercial message on one side but a protest against certain official action on the other. The reliance is wholly misplaced. The Court in Chrestensen reaffirmed the constitutional protection for "the freedom of communicating [376 U.S. 254, 266] information and disseminating opinion"; its holding was based upon the factual conclusions that the handbill was "purely commercial advertising" and that the protest against official action had been added only to evade the ordinance.

The publication here was not a "commercial" advertisement in the sense in which the word was used in Chrestensen. It communicated information, expressed opinion, recited grievances, protested claimed abuses, and sought financial support on behalf of a movement whose existence and objectives are matters of the highest public interest and concern. See N. A. A. C. P. v. Button, 371 U.S. 415, 435. That the Times was paid for publishing the advertisement is as immaterial in this connection as is the fact that newspapers and books are sold. Smith v. California, 361 U.S. 147, 150; cf. Bantam Books, Inc., v. Sullivan, 372 U.S. 58, 64, n. 6. Any other conclusion would discourage newspapers from carrying "editorial advertisements" of this type, and so might shut off an important outlet for the promulgation of information and ideas by persons who do not themselves have access to publishing facilities—who wish to exercise their freedom of speech even though they are not members of the press. Cf. Lovell v. Griffin, 303 U.S. 444, 452; Schneider v. State, 308 U.S. 147, 164. The effect would be to shackle the First Amendment in its attempt to secure "the widest possible dissemination of information from diverse and antagonistic sources." Associated Press v. United States, 326 U.S. 1, 20. To avoid placing such a handicap upon the freedoms of expression, we hold that if the allegedly libelous statements would otherwise be constitutionally protected from the present judgment, they do not forfeit that protection because they were published in the form of a paid advertisement.[5] [376 U.S. 254, 267]

II.

Under Alabama law as applied in this case, a publication is "libelous per se" if the words "tend to injure a person . . . in his reputation" or to "bring [him] into public contempt"; the trial court stated that the standard was met if the words are such as to "injure him in his public office, or impute misconduct to him in his office, or want of official integrity, or want of fidelity to a public trust . . . ." The jury must find that the words were published "of and concerning" the plaintiff, but where the plaintiff is a public official his place in the governmental hierarchy is sufficient evidence to support a finding that his reputation has been affected by statements that reflect upon the agency of which he is in charge. Once "libel per se" has been established, the defendant has no defense as to stated facts unless he can persuade the jury that they were true in all their particulars. Alabama Ride Co. v. Vance, 235 Ala. 263, 178 So. 438 (1938); Johnson Publishing Co. v. Davis, 271 Ala. 474, 494–495, 124 So.2d 441, 457–458 (1960). His privilege of "fair comment" for expressions of opinion depends on the truth of the facts upon which the comment is based. Parsons v. Age-Herald Publishing Co., 181 Ala. 439, 450, 61 So. 345, 350 (1913). Unless he can discharge the burden of proving truth, general damages are presumed, and may be awarded without proof of pecuniary injury. A showing of actual malice is apparently a prerequisite to recovery of punitive damages, and the defendant may in any event forestall a punitive award by a retraction meeting the statutory requirements. Good motives and belief in truth do not negate an inference of malice, but are relevant only in mitigation of punitive damages if the jury chooses to accord them weight. Johnson Publishing Co. v. Davis, supra, 271 Ala., at 495, 124 So.2d, at 458. [376 U.S. 254, 268]

The question before us is whether this rule of liability, as applied to an action brought by a public official against critics of his official conduct, abridges the freedom of speech and of the press that is guaranteed by the First and Fourteenth Amendments.

Respondent relies heavily, as did the Alabama courts, on statements of this Court to the effect that the Constitution does not protect libelous publications.[6] Those statements do not foreclose our inquiry here. None of the cases sustained the use of libel laws to impose sanctions upon expression critical of the official conduct of public officials. The dictum in Pennekamp v. Florida, 328 U.S. 331, 348–349, that "when the statements amount to defamation, a judge has such remedy in damages for libel as do other public servants," implied no view as to what remedy might constitutionally be afforded to public officials. In Beauharnais v. Illinois, 343 U.S. 250, the Court sustained an Illinois criminal libel statute as applied to a publication held to be both defamatory of a racial group and "liable to cause violence and disorder." But the Court was careful to note that it "retains and exercises authority to nullify action which encroaches on freedom of utterance under the guise of punishing libel"; for "public men, are, as it were, public property," and "discussion cannot be denied and the right, as well as the duty, of criticism must not be stifled." Id., at 263–264, and n. 18. In the only previous case that did present the question of constitutional limitations upon the power to award damages for libel of a public official, the Court was equally divided and the question was not decided. Schenectady Union Pub. Co. v. Sweeney, 316 U.S. 642. [376 U.S. 254, 269] In deciding the question now, we are compelled by neither precedent nor policy to give any more weight to the epithet "libel" than we have to other "mere labels" of state law. N. A. A. C. P. v. Button, 371 U.S. 415, 429. Like insurrection,[7] contempt,[8] advocacy of unlawful acts,[9] breach of the peace,[10] obscenity,[11] solicitation of legal business,[12] and the various other formulae for the repression of expression that have been challenged in this court, libel can claim no talismanic immunity from constitutional limitations. It must be measured by standards that satisfy the First Amendment.

The general proposition that freedom of expression upon public questions is secured by the First Amendment has long been settled by our decisions. The constitutional safeguard, we have said, "was fashioned to assure unfettered interchange of ideas for the bringing about of political and social changes desired by the people." Roth v. United States, 354 U.S. 476, 484. "The maintenance of the opportunity for free political discussion to the end that government may be responsive to the will of the people and that changes may be obtained by lawful means, an opportunity essential to the security of the Republic, is a fundamental principle of our constitutional system." Stromberg v. California, 283 U.S. 359, 369. "[I]t is a prized American privilege to speak one's mind, although not always with perfect good taste, on all public institutions," Bridges v. California, 314 U.S. 252, 270, and this opportunity is to be afforded for "vigorous advocacy" no less than "abstract discussion." N. A. A. C. P. v. Button, 371 U.S. 415, 429. [376 U.S. 254, 270] The First Amendment, said Judge Learned Hand, "presupposes that right conclusions are more likely to be gathered out of a multitude of tongues, than through any kind of authoritative selection. To many this is, and always will be, folly; but we have staked upon it our all." United States v. Associated Press, 52 F. Supp. 362, 372 (D.C. S. D. N. Y. 1943). Mr. Justice Brandeis, in his concurring opinion in Whitney v. California, 274 U.S. 357, 375–376, gave the principle its classic formulation:

> "Those who won our independence believed . . . that public discussion is a political duty; and that this should be a fundamental principle of the American government. They recognized the risks to which all human institutions are subject. But they knew that order cannot be secured merely through fear of punishment for its infraction; that it is hazardous to discourage thought, hope and imagination; that fear breeds repression; that repression breeds hate; that hate menaces stable government; that the path of safety lies in the opportunity to discuss freely supposed grievances and proposed remedies; and that the fitting remedy for evil counsels is good ones. Believing in the power of reason as applied through public discussion, they eschewed silence coerced by law—the argument of force in its worst form. Recognizing the occasional tyrannies of governing majorities, they amended the Constitution so that free speech and assembly should be guaranteed."

Thus we consider this case against the background of a profound national commitment to the principle that debate on public issues should be uninhibited, robust, and wide-open, and that it may well include vehement, caustic, and sometimes unpleasantly sharp attacks on government and public officials. See Terminiello v. Chicago, 337 U.S. 1, 4; De Jonge v. Oregon, 299 U.S. 353, [376 U.S. 254, 271] 365. The present advertisement, as an expression of grievance and protest on one of the major public issues of our time, would seem clearly to qualify for the constitutional protection. The question is whether it forfeits that protection by the falsity of some of its factual statements and by its alleged defamation of respondent.

Authoritative interpretations of the First Amendment guarantees have consistently refused to recognize an exception for any test of truth—whether administered by judges, juries, or administrative officials—and especially one that puts the burden of proving truth on the speaker. Cf. Speiser v. Randall, 357 U.S. 513, 525–526. The constitutional protection does not turn upon "the truth, popularity, or social utility of the ideas and beliefs which are offered." N. A. A. C. P. v. Button, 371 U.S. 415, 445. As Madison said, "Some degree of abuse is inseparable from the proper use of every thing; and in no instance is this more true than in that of the press." 4 Elliot's Debates on the Federal Constitution (1876), p. 571. In Cantwell v. Connecticut, 310 U.S. 296, 310, the Court declared:

"In the realm of religious faith, and in that of political belief, sharp differences arise. In both fields the tenets of one man may seem the rankest error to his neighbor. To persuade others to his own point of view, the pleader, as we know, at times, resorts to exaggeration, to vilification of men who have been, or are, prominent in church or state, and even to false statement. But the people of this nation have ordained in the light of history, that, in spite of the probability of excesses and abuses, these liberties are, in the long view, essential to enlightened opinion and right conduct on the part of the citizens of a democracy."

That erroneous statement is inevitable in free debate, and that it must be protected if the freedoms of expression [376 U.S. 254, 272] are to have the "breathing space" that they "need . . . to survive," N. A. A. C. P. v. Button, 371 U.S. 415, 433, was also recognized by the Court of Appeals for the District of Columbia Circuit in Sweeney v. Patterson, 76 U.S. App. D.C. 23, 24, 128 F.2d 457, 458 (1942), cert. denied, 317 U.S. 678. Judge Edgerton spoke for a unanimous court which affirmed the dismissal of a Congressman's libel suit based upon a newspaper article charging him with anti-Semitism in opposing a judicial appointment. He said:

"Cases which impose liability for erroneous reports of the political conduct of officials reflect the obsolete doctrine that the governed must not criticize their governors. . . . The interest of the public here outweighs the interest of appellant or any other individual. The protection of the public requires not merely discussion, but information. Political conduct and views which some respectable people approve, and others condemn, are constantly imputed to Congressmen. Errors of fact, particularly in regard to a man's mental states and processes, are inevitable. . . . Whatever is added to the field of libel is taken from the field of free debate."[13]

Injury to official reputation affords no more warrant for repressing speech that would otherwise be free than does factual error. Where judicial officers are involved, this Court has held that concern for the dignity and [376 U.S. 254, 273] reputation of the courts does not justify the punishment as criminal contempt of criticism of the judge or his decision. Bridges v. California, 314 U.S. 252. This is true even though the utterance contains "half-truths" and "misinformation." Pennekamp v. Florida, 328 U.S. 331, 342, 343, n. 5, 345. Such repression can be justified, if at all, only by a clear and present danger of the obstruction of justice. See also Craig v. Harney, 331 U.S. 367; Wood v. Georgia, 370 U.S. 375. If judges are to be treated as "men of fortitude, able to thrive in a hardy climate,"

Craig v. Harney, supra, 331 U.S., at 376, surely the same must be true of other government officials, such as elected city commissioners.[14] Criticism of their official conduct does not lose its constitutional protection merely because it is effective criticism and hence diminishes their official reputations.

If neither factual error nor defamatory content suffices to remove the constitutional shield from criticism of official conduct, the combination of the two elements is no less inadequate. This is the lesson to be drawn from the great controversy over the Sedition Act of 1798, 1 Stat. 596, which first crystallized a national awareness of the central meaning of the First Amendment. See Levy, Legacy of Suppression (1960), at 258 et seq.; Smith, Freedom's Fetters (1956), at 426, 431, and passim. That statute made it a crime, punishable by a $5,000 fine and five years in prison, "if any person shall write, print, utter or publish . . . any false, scandalous and malicious [376 U.S. 254, 274] writing or writings against the government of the United States, or either house of the Congress . . . , or the President . . . , with intent to defame . . . or to bring them, or either of them, into contempt or disrepute; or to excite against them, or either or any of them, the hatred of the good people of the United States." The Act allowed the defendant the defense of truth, and provided that the jury were to be judges both of the law and the facts. Despite these qualifications, the Act was vigorously condemned as unconstitutional in an attack joined in by Jefferson and Madison. In the famous Virginia Resolutions of 1798, the General Assembly of Virginia resolved that it

> "doth particularly protest against the palpable and alarming infractions of the Constitution, in the two late cases of the "Alien and Sedition Acts," passed at the last session of Congress . . . . [The Sedition Act] exercises . . . a power not delegated by the Constitution, but, on the contrary, expressly and positively forbidden by one of the amendments thereto—a power which, more than any other, ought to produce universal alarm, because it is levelled against the right of freely examining public characters and measures, and of free communication among the people thereon, which has ever been justly deemed the only effectual guardian of every other right." 4 Elliot's Debates, supra, pp. 553–554.

Madison prepared the Report in support of the protest. His premise was that the Constitution created a form of government under which "The people, not the government, possess the absolute sovereignty." The structure of the government dispersed power in reflection of the people's distrust of concentrated power, and of power itself at all levels. This form of government was "altogether different" from the British form, under which the Crown was sovereign and the people were subjects. "Is [376 U.S. 254, 275] it not natural and necessary, under such different circumstances," he asked, "that a different degree of freedom in the use of the press should be contemplated?" Id., pp. 569–570. Earlier, in a debate in the House of Representatives, Madison had said: "If we advert to the nature of Republican Government, we shall find that the censorial power is in the people over the Government, and not in the Government over the people." 4 Annals of Congress, p. 934 (1794). Of the exercise of that power by the press, his Report said: "In every state, probably, in the Union, the press has exerted a freedom in canvassing the merits and measures of public men, of every description, which has not been confined to the strict limits of the common law. On this footing the freedom of the press has stood; on this foundation it yet stands . . . ." 4 Elliot's Debates, supra, p. 570. The right of free public discussion of the stewardship of public officials was thus, in Madison's view, a fundamental principle of the American form of government.[15] [376 U.S. 254, 276]

Although the Sedition Act was never tested in this Court,[16] the attack upon its validity has carried the day in the court of history. Fines levied in its prosecution were repaid by Act of Congress on the ground that it was unconstitutional. See, e. g., Act of July 4, 1840, c. 45, 6 Stat. 802, accompanied by H. R. Rep. No. 86, 26th Cong., 1st Sess. (1840). Calhoun, reporting to the Senate on February 4, 1836, assumed that its invalidity was a matter "which no one now doubts." Report with Senate bill No. 122, 24th Cong., 1st Sess., p. 3. Jefferson, as President, pardoned those who had been convicted and sentenced under the Act and remitted their fines, stating: "I discharged every person under punishment or prosecution under the sedition law, because I considered, and now consider, that law to be a nullity, as absolute and as palpable as if Congress had ordered us to fall down and worship a golden image." Letter to Mrs. Adams, July 22, 1804, 4 Jefferson's Works (Washington ed.), pp. 555, 556. The invalidity of the Act has also been assumed by Justices of this Court. See Holmes, J., dissenting and joined by Brandeis, J., in Abrams v. United States, 250 U.S. 616, 630; Jackson, J., dissenting in Beauharnais v. Illinois, 343 U.S. 250, 288–289; Douglas, The Right of the People (1958), p. 47. See also Cooley, Constitutional Limitations (8th ed., Carrington, 1927), pp. 899–900; Chafee, Free Speech in the United States (1942), pp. 27–28. These views reflect a broad consensus that the Act, because of the restraint it imposed upon criticism of government and public officials, was inconsistent with the First Amendment.

There is no force in respondent's argument that the constitutional limitations implicit in the history of the Sedition Act apply only to Congress and not to the States. It is true that the First Amendment was originally addressed only to action by the Federal Government, and [376

U.S. 254, 277] that Jefferson, for one, while denying the power of Congress "to controul the freedom of the press," recognized such a power in the States. See the 1804 Letter to Abigail Adams quoted in Dennis v. United States, 341 U.S. 494, 522, n. 4 (concurring opinion). But this distinction was eliminated with the adoption of the Fourteenth Amendment and the application to the States of the First Amendment's restrictions. See, e. g., Gitlow v. New York, 268 U.S. 652, 666; Schneider v. State, 308 U.S. 147, 160; Bridges v. California, 314 U.S. 252, 268; Edwards v. South Carolina, 372 U.S. 229, 235.

What a State may not constitutionally bring about by means of a criminal statute is likewise beyond the reach of its civil law of libel.[17] The fear of damage awards under a rule such as that invoked by the Alabama courts here may be markedly more inhibiting than the fear of prosecution under a criminal statute. See City of Chicago v. Tribune Co., 307 Ill. 595, 607, 139 N. E. 86, 90 (1923). Alabama, for example, has a criminal libel law which subjects to prosecution "any person who speaks, writes, or prints of and concerning another any accusation falsely and maliciously importing the commission by such person of a felony, or any other indictable offense involving moral turpitude," and which allows as punishment upon conviction a fine not exceeding $500 and a prison sentence of six months. Alabama Code, Tit. 14, 350. Presumably a person charged with violation of this statute enjoys ordinary criminal-law safeguards such as the requirements of an indictment and of proof beyond a reasonable doubt. These safeguards are not available to the defendant in a civil action. The judgment awarded in this case—without the need for any proof of actual pecuniary loss—was one thousand times greater than the maximum fine provided by the Alabama criminal statute, and one hundred times greater than that provided by the Sedition Act. [376 U.S. 254, 278] And since there is no double-jeopardy limitation applicable to civil lawsuits, this is not the only judgment that may be awarded against petitioners for the same publication.[18] Whether or not a newspaper can survive a succession of such judgments, the pall of fear and timidity imposed upon those who would give voice to public criticism is an atmosphere in which the First Amendment freedoms cannot survive. Plainly the Alabama law of civil libel is "a form of regulation that creates hazards to protected freedoms markedly greater than those that attend reliance upon the criminal law." Bantam Books, Inc., v. Sullivan, 372 U.S. 58, 70.

The state rule of law is not saved by its allowance of the defense of truth. A defense for erroneous statements honestly made is no less essential here than was the requirement of proof of guilty knowledge which, in Smith v. California, 361 U.S. 147, we held indispensable to a valid conviction of a bookseller for possessing obscene writings for sale. We said:

"For if the bookseller is criminally liable without knowledge of the contents, . . . he will tend to restrict the books he sells to those he has inspected; and thus the State will have imposed a restriction upon the distribution of constitutionally protected as well as obscene literature. . . . And the bookseller's burden would become the public's burden, for by restricting him the public's access to reading matter would be restricted. . . . [H]is timidity in the face of his absolute criminal liability, thus would tend to restrict the public's access to forms of the printed word which the State could not constitutionally [376 U.S. 254, 279] suppress directly. The bookseller's self-censorship, compelled by the State, would be a censorship affecting the whole public, hardly less virulent for being privately administered. Through it, the distribution of all books, both obscene and not obscene, would be impeded." (361 U.S. 147, 153–154.)

A rule compelling the critic of official conduct to guarantee the truth of all his factual assertions—and to do so on pain of libel judgments virtually unlimited in amount—leads to a comparable "self-censorship." Allowance of the defense of truth, with the burden of proving it on the defendant, does not mean that only false speech will be deterred.[19] Even courts accepting this defense as an adequate safeguard have recognized the difficulties of adducing legal proofs that the alleged libel was true in all its factual particulars. See, e. g., Post Publishing Co. v. Hallam, 59 F. 530, 540 (C. A. 6th Cir. 1893); see also Noel, Defamation of Public Officers and Candidates. 49 Col. L. Rev. 875, 892 (1949). Under such a rule, would-be critics of official conduct may be deterred from voicing their criticism, even though it is believed to be true and even though it is in fact true, because of doubt whether it can be proved in court or fear of the expense of having to do so. They tend to make only statements which "steer far wider of the unlawful zone." Speiser v. Randall, supra, 357 U.S., at 526. The rule thus dampens the vigor and limits the variety of public debate. It is inconsistent with the First and Fourteenth Amendments.

The constitutional guarantees require, we think, a federal rule that prohibits a public official from recovering damages for a defamatory falsehood relating to his official conduct unless he proves that the statement was made [376 U.S. 254, 280] with "actual malice"—that is, with knowledge that it was false or with reckless disregard of whether it was false or not. An oft-cited statement of a like rule, which has been adopted by a number of state courts,[20] is found in the Kansas case of Coleman v. MacLennan, 78 Kan. 711, 98 P. 281 (1908). The State Attorney General, a candidate for re-election and a member of the commission charged with the management and control of the state school fund, sued a newspaper publisher for alleged libel in an article purporting to state facts relating to his official conduct in connection with a school-fund transaction. The defendant pleaded privilege and the trial judge, over the plaintiff's objection, instructed the jury that

> "where an article is published and circulated among voters for the sole purpose of giving what the defendant [376 U.S. 254, 281] believes to be truthful information concerning a candidate for public office and for the purpose of enabling such voters to cast their ballot more intelligently, and the whole thing is done in good faith and without malice, the article is privileged, although the principal matters contained in the article may be untrue in fact and derogatory to the character of the plaintiff; and in such a case the burden is on the plaintiff to show actual malice in the publication of the article."

In answer to a special question, the jury found that the plaintiff had not proved actual malice, and a general verdict was returned for the defendant. On appeal the Supreme Court of Kansas, in an opinion by Justice Burch, reasoned as follows (78 Kan., at 724, 98 P., at 286):

> "It is of the utmost consequence that the people should discuss the character and qualifications of candidates for their suffrages. The importance to the state and to society of such discussions is so vast, and the advantages derived are so great, that they more than counterbalance the inconvenience of private persons whose conduct may be involved, and occasional injury to the reputations of individuals must yield to the public welfare, although at times such injury may be great. The public benefit from publicity is so great, and the chance of injury to private character so small, that such discussion must be privileged."

The court thus sustained the trial court's instruction as a correct statement of the law, saying:

> "In such a case the occasion gives rise to a privilege, qualified to this extent: any one claiming to be defamed by the communication must show actual malice or go remediless. This privilege extends to a great variety of subjects, and includes matters of [376 U.S. 254, 282] public concern, public men, and candidates for office." 78 Kan., at 723, 98 P., at 285.

Such a privilege for criticism of official conduct[21] is appropriately analogous to the protection accorded a public official when he is sued for libel by a private citizen. In Barr v. Matteo, 360 U.S. 564, 575, this Court held the utterance of a federal official to be absolutely privileged if made "within the outer perimeter" of his duties. The States accord the same immunity to statements of their highest officers, although some differentiate their lesser officials and qualify the privilege they enjoy.[22] But all hold that all officials are protected unless actual malice can be proved. The reason for the official privilege is said to be that the threat of damage suits would otherwise "inhibit the fearless, vigorous, and effective administration of policies of government" and "dampen the ardor of all but the most resolute, or the most irresponsible, in the unflinching discharge of their duties." Barr v. Matteo, supra, 360 U.S., at 571. Analogous considerations support the privilege for the citizen-critic of government. It is as much his duty to criticize as it is the official's duty to administer. See Whitney v. California, 274 U.S. 357, 375 (concurring opinion of Mr. Justice Brandeis), quoted supra, p. 270. As Madison said, see supra, p. 275, "the censorial power is in the people over the Government, and not in the Government over the people." It would give public servants an unjustified preference over the public they serve, if critics of official conduct [376 U.S. 254, 283] did not have a fair equivalent of the immunity granted to the officials themselves.

We conclude that such a privilege is required by the First and Fourteenth Amendments.

III.

We hold today that the Constitution delimits a State's power to award damages for libel in actions brought by public officials against critics of their official conduct. Since this is such an action,[23] the rule requiring proof of actual malice is applicable. While Alabama law apparently requires proof of actual malice for an award of punitive damages,[24] where general damages are concerned malice is "presumed." Such a presumption is inconsistent [376 U.S. 254, 284] with the federal rule. "The power to create presumptions is not a means of escape from constitutional restrictions," Bailey v. Alabama, 219 U.S. 219, 239; "the showing of malice required for the forfeiture of the privilege is not presumed but is a matter for proof by the plaintiff . . . ." Lawrence v. Fox, 357 Mich. 134, 146, 97 N. W. 2d 719, 725 (1959).[25] Since the trial judge did not instruct the jury to differentiate between general and punitive damages, it may be that the verdict was wholly an award of one or the other. But it is impossible to know, in view of the general verdict returned. Because of this uncertainty, the judgment must be reversed and the case remanded. Stromberg v. California, 283 U.S. 359, 367–368; Williams v. North Carolina, 317

U.S. 287, 291–292; see Yates v. United States, 354 U.S. 298, 311–312; Cramer v. United States, 325 U.S. 1, 36, n. 45.

Since respondent may seek a new trial, we deem that considerations of effective judicial administration require us to review the evidence in the present record to determine [376 U.S. 254, 285] whether it could constitutionally support a judgment for respondent. This Court's duty is not limited to the elaboration of constitutional principles; we must also in proper cases review the evidence to make certain that those principles have been constitutionally applied. This is such a case, particularly since the question is one of alleged trespass across "the line between speech unconditionally guaranteed and speech which may legitimately be regulated." Speiser v. Randall, 357 U.S. 513, 525. In cases where that line must be drawn, the rule is that we "examine for ourselves the statements in issue and the circumstances under which they were made to see . . . whether they are of a character which the principles of the First Amendment, as adopted by the Due Process Clause of the Fourteenth Amendment, protect." Pennekamp v. Florida, 328 U.S. 331, 335; see also One, Inc., v. Olesen, 355 U.S. 371; Sunshine Book Co. v. Summerfield, 355 U.S. 372. We must "make an independent examination of the whole record," Edwards v. South Carolina, 372 U.S. 229, 235, so as to assure ourselves that the judgment does not constitute a forbidden intrusion on the field of free expression.[26]

Applying these standards, we consider that the proof presented to show actual malice lacks the convincing [376 U.S. 254, 286] clarity which the constitutional standard demands, and hence that it would not constitutionally sustain the judgment for respondent under the proper rule of law. The case of the individual petitioners requires little discussion. Even assuming that they could constitutionally be found to have authorized the use of their names on the advertisement, there was no evidence whatever that they were aware of any erroneous statements or were in any way reckless in that regard. The judgment against them is thus without constitutional support.

As to the Times, we similarly conclude that the facts do not support a finding of actual malice. The statement by the Times" Secretary that, apart from the padlocking allegation, he thought the advertisement was "substantially correct," affords no constitutional warrant for the Alabama Supreme Court's conclusion that it was a "cavalier ignoring of the falsity of the advertisement [from which] the jury could not have but been impressed with the bad faith of The Times, and its maliciousness inferable therefrom." The statement does not indicate malice at the time of the publication; even if the advertisement was not "substantially correct"— although respondent's own proofs tend to show that it was—that opinion was at least a reasonable one, and there was no evidence to impeach the witness' good faith in holding it. The Times' failure to retract upon respondent's demand, although it later retracted upon the demand of Governor Patterson, is likewise not adequate evidence of malice for constitutional purposes. Whether or not a failure to retract may ever constitute such evidence, there are two reasons why it does not here. First, the letter written by the Times reflected a reasonable doubt on its part as to whether the advertisement could reasonably be taken to refer to respondent at all. Second, it was not a final refusal, since it asked for an explanation on this point—a request that respondent chose to ignore. Nor does the retraction upon the demand of the Governor supply the [376 U.S. 254, 287] necessary proof. It may be doubted that a failure to retract which is not itself evidence of malice can retroactively become such by virtue of a retraction subsequently made to another party. But in any event that did not happen here, since the explanation given by the Times' Secretary for the distinction drawn between respondent and the Governor was a reasonable one, the good faith of which was not impeached.

Finally, there is evidence that the Times published the advertisement without checking its accuracy against the news stories in the Times' own files. The mere presence of the stories in the files does not, of course, establish that the Times "knew" the advertisement was false, since the state of mind required for actual malice would have to be brought home to the persons in the Times' organization having responsibility for the publication of the advertisement. With respect to the failure of those persons to make the check, the record shows that they relied upon their knowledge of the good reputation of many of those whose names were listed as sponsors of the advertisement, and upon the letter from A. Philip Randolph, known to them as a responsible individual, certifying that the use of the names was authorized. There was testimony that the persons handling the advertisement saw nothing in it that would render it unacceptable under the Times' policy of rejecting advertisements containing "attacks of a personal character";[27] their failure to reject it on this ground was not unreasonable. We think [376 U.S. 254, 288] the evidence against the Times supports at most a finding of negligence in failing to discover the misstatements, and is constitutionally insufficient to show the recklessness that is required for a finding of actual malice. Cf. Charles Parker Co. v. Silver City Crystal Co., 142 Conn. 605, 618, 116 A. 2d 440, 446 (1955); Phoenix Newspapers, Inc., v. Choisser, 82 Ariz. 271, 277–278, 312 P.2d 150, 154–155 (1957).

We also think the evidence was constitutionally defective in another respect: it was incapable of supporting the jury's finding that the allegedly libelous statements were made "of and concerning" respondent. Respondent relies on the words of the advertisement and the testimony of six witnesses to establish a connection between it and himself. Thus, in his brief to this Court, he states:

"The reference to respondent as police commissioner is clear from the ad. In addition, the jury heard the testimony of a newspaper editor . . .; a real estate and insurance man . . .; the sales manager of a men's clothing store . . .; a food equipment man . . .; a service station operator . . .; and the operator of a truck line for whom respondent had formerly worked . . . . Each of these witnesses stated that he associated the statements with respondent . . . ." (Citations to record omitted.)

There was no reference to respondent in the advertisement, either by name or official position. A number of the allegedly libelous statements—the charges that the dining hall was padlocked and that Dr. King's home was bombed, his person assaulted, and a perjury prosecution instituted against him—did not even concern the police; despite the ingenuity of the arguments which would attach this significance to the word "They," it is plain that these statements could not reasonably be read as accusing respondent of personal involvement in the acts [376 U.S. 254, 289] in question. The statements upon which respondent principally relies as referring to him are the two allegations that did concern the police or police functions: that "truckloads of police . . . ringed the Alabama State College Campus" after the demonstration on the State Capitol steps, and that Dr. King had been "arrested . . . seven times." These statements were false only in that the police had been "deployed near" the campus but had not actually "ringed" it and had not gone there in connection with the State Capitol demonstration, and in that Dr. King had been arrested only four times. The ruling that these discrepancies between what was true and what was asserted were sufficient to injure respondent's reputation may itself raise constitutional problems, but we need not consider them here. Although the statements may be taken as referring to the police, they did not on their face make even an oblique reference to respondent as an individual. Support for the asserted reference must, therefore, be sought in the testimony of respondent's witnesses. But none of them suggested any basis for the belief that respondent himself was attacked in the advertisement beyond the bare fact that he was in overall charge of the Police Department and thus bore official responsibility for police conduct; to the extent that some of the witnesses thought respondent to have been charged with ordering or approving the conduct or otherwise being personally involved in it, they based this notion not on any statements in the advertisement, and not on any evidence that he had in fact been so involved, but solely on the unsupported assumption that, because of his official position, he must have been.[28] This reliance on the bare [376 U.S. 254, 290] fact of respondent's official position[29] was made explicit by the Supreme Court of Alabama. That court, in holding that the trial court "did not err in overruling the demurrer [of the Times] in the aspect that the libelous [376 U.S. 254, 291] matter was not of and concerning the [plaintiff,]" based its ruling on the proposition that:

> "We think it common knowledge that the average person knows that municipal agents, such as police and firemen, and others, are under the control and direction of the city governing body, and more particularly under the direction and control of a single commissioner. In measuring the performance or deficiencies of such groups, praise or criticism is usually attached to the official in complete control of the body." 273 Ala., at 674–675, 144 So.2d. at 39.

This proposition has disquieting implications for criticism of governmental conduct. For good reason, "no court of last resort in this country has ever held, or even suggested, that prosecutions for libel on government have any place in the American system of jurisprudence." City of Chicago v. Tribune Co., 307 Ill. 595, 601, 139 N. E. [376 U.S. 254, 292] 86, 88 (1923). The present proposition would sidestep this obstacle by transmuting criticism of government, however impersonal it may seem on its face, into personal criticism, and hence potential libel, of the officials of whom the government is composed. There is no legal alchemy by which a State may thus create the cause of action that would otherwise be denied for a publication which, as respondent himself said of the advertisement. "reflects not only on me but on the other Commissioners and the community." Raising as it does the possibility that a good-faith critic of government will be penalized for his criticism, the proposition relied on by the Alabama courts strikes at the very center of the constitutionally protected area of free expression.[30] We hold that such a proposition may not constitutionally be utilized to establish that an otherwise impersonal attack on governmental operations was a libel of an official responsible for those operations. Since it was relied on exclusively here, and there was no other evidence to connect the statements with respondent, the evidence was constitutionally insufficient to support a finding that the statements referred to respondent.

The judgment of the Supreme Court of Alabama is reversed and the case is remanded to that court for further proceedings not inconsistent with this opinion.

Reversed and remanded.

FOOTNOTES

[1] A copy of the advertisement is printed in the Appendix.
[2] Respondent did not consider the charge of expelling the students to be applicable to him, since "that responsibility rests with the State Department of Education."

[3] Approximately 394 copies of the edition of the Times containing the advertisement were circulated in Alabama. Of these, about 35 copies were distributed in Montgomery County. The total circulation of the Times for that day was approximately 650,000 copies.

[4] Since we sustain the contentions of all the petitioners under the First Amendment's guarantees of freedom of speech and of the press as applied to the State by the Fourteenth Amendment, we do not decide the questions presented by the other claims of violation of the Fourteenth Amendment. The individual petitioners contend that the judgment against them offends the Due Process Clause because there was no evidence to show that they had published or authorized the publication of the alleged libel, and that the Due Process and Equal Protection Clauses were violated by racial segregation and racial bias in the courtroom. The Times contends that the assumption of jurisdiction over its corporate person by the Alabama courts overreaches the territorial limits of the Due Process Clause. The latter claim is foreclosed from our review by the ruling of the Alabama courts that the Times entered a general appearance in the action and thus waived its jurisdictional objection; we cannot say that this ruling lacks "fair or substantial support" in prior Alabama decisions. See Thompson v. Wilson, 224 Ala. 299, 140 So. 439 (1932); compare N. A. A. C. P. v. Alabama, 357 U.S. 449, 454–458.

[5] See American Law Institute, Restatement of Torts, 593, Comment b (1938).

[6] Konigsberg v. State Bar of California, 366 U.S. 36, 49, and n. 10; Times Film Corp. v. City of Chicago, 365 U.S. 43, 48; Roth v. United States, 354 U.S. 476, 486–487; Beauharnais v. Illinois, 343 U.S. 250, 266; Pennekamp v. Florida, 328 U.S. 331, 348–349; Chaplinsky v. New Hampshire, 315 U.S. 568, 572; Near v. Minnesota, 283 U.S. 697, 715.

[7] Herndon v. Lowry, 301 U.S. 242.

[8] Bridges v. California, 314 U.S. 252; Pennekamp v. Florida, 328 U.S. 331.

[9] De Jonge v. Oregon, 299 U.S. 353.

[10] Edwards v. South Carolina, 372 U.S. 229.

[11] Roth v. United States, 354 U.S. 476.

[12] N. A. A. C. P. v. Button, 371 U.S. 415.

[13] See also Mill, On Liberty (Oxford: Blackwell, 1947), at 47: ". . . [T]o argue sophistically, to suppress facts or arguments, to misstate the elements of the case, or misrepresent the opposite opinion . . . all this, even to the most aggravated degree, is so continually done in perfect good faith, by persons who are not considered, and in many other respects may not deserve to be considered, ignorant or incompetent, that it is rarely possible, on adequate grounds, conscientiously to stamp the misrepresentation as morally culpable; and still less could law presume to interfere with this kind of controversial misconduct."

[14] The climate in which public officials operate, especially during a political campaign, has been described by one commentator in the following terms: "Charges of gross incompetence, disregard of the public interest, communist sympathies, and the like usually have filled the air; and hints of bribery, embezzlement, and other criminal conduct are not infrequent." Noel, Defamation of Public Officers and Candidates, 49 Col. L. Rev. 875 (1949). For a similar description written 60 years earlier, see Chase, Criticism of Public Officers and Candidates for Office, 23 Am. L. Rev. 346 (1889).

[15] The Report on the Virginia Resolutions further stated: "[I]t is manifestly impossible to punish the intent to bring those who administer the government into disrepute or contempt, without striking at the right of freely discussing public characters and measures; . . . which, again, is equivalent to a protection of those who administer the government, if they should at any time deserve the contempt or hatred of the people, against being exposed to it, by free animadversions on their characters and conduct. Nor can there be a doubt . . . that a government thus intrenched in penal statutes against the just and natural effects of a culpable administration, will easily evade the responsibility which is essential to a faithful discharge of its duty. "Let it be recollected, lastly, that

the right of electing the members of the government constitutes more particularly the essence of a free and responsible government. The value and efficacy of this right depends on the knowledge of the comparative merits and demerits of the candidates for public trust, and on the equal freedom, consequently, of examining and discussing these merits and demerits of the candidates respectively." 4 Elliot's Debates, supra, p. 575.

[16] The Act expired by its terms in 1801.

[17] Cf. Farmers Union v. WDAY, 360 U.S. 525, 535.

[18] The Times states that four other libel suits based on the advertisement have been filed against it by others who have served as Montgomery City Commissioners and by the Governor of Alabama: that another $500,000 verdict has been awarded in the only one of these cases that has yet gone to trial; and that the damages sought in the other three total $2,000,000.

[19] Even a false statement may be deemed to make a valuable contribution to public debate, since it brings about "the clearer perception and livelier impression of truth, produced by its collision with error." Mill, On Liberty (Oxford: Blackwell, 1947), at 15; see also Milton, Areopagitica, in Prose Works (Yale, 1959), Vol. II, at 561.

[20] E. g., Ponder v. Cobb, 257 N.C. 281, 299, 126 S. E. 2d 67, 80 (1962); Lawrence v. Fox, 357 Mich. 134, 146, 97 N. W. 2d 719, 725 (1959); Stice v. Beacon Newspaper Corp., 185 Kan. 61, 65–67, 340 P.2d 396, 400–401 (1959); Bailey v. Charleston Mail Assn., 126 W. Va. 292, 307, 27 S. E. 2d 837, 844 (1943); Salinger v. Cowles, 195 Iowa 873, 889, 191 N. W. 167, 174 (1922); Snively v. Record Publishing Co., 185 Cal. 565, 571–576, 198 P. 1 (1921); McLean v. Merriman, 42 S. D. 394, 175 N. W. 878 (1920). Applying the same rule to candidates for public office, see, e. g., Phoenix Newspapers v. Choisser, 82 Ariz. 271, 276–277, 312 P.2d 150, 154 (1957); Friedell v. Blakely Printing Co., 163 Minn. 226, 230, 203 N. W. 974, 975 (1925). And see Chagnon v. Union-Leader Corp., 103 N. H. 426, 438, 174 A. 2d 825, 833 (1961), cert. denied, 369 U.S. 830. The consensus of scholarly opinion apparently favors the rule that is here adopted. E. g., 1 Harper and James, Torts, 5.26, at 449–450 (1956); Noel, Defamation of Public Officers and Candidates, 49 Col. L. Rev. 875, 891–895, 897, 903 (1949); Hallen, Fair Comment, 8 Tex. L. Rev. 41; 61 (1929); Smith, Charges Against Candidates, 18 Mich. L. Rev. 1, 115 (1919); Chase, Criticism of Public Officers and Candidates for Office, 23 Am. L. Rev. 346, 367–371 (1889); Cooley, Constitutional Limitations (7th ed., Lane, 1903), at 604, 616–628. But see, e. g., American Law Institute, Restatement of Torts, 598, Comment a (1938) (reversing the position taken in Tentative Draft 13, 1041 (2) (1936)); Veeder, Freedom of Public Discussion, 23 Harv. L. Rev. 413, 419 (1910).

[21] The privilege immunizing honest misstatements of fact is often referred to as a "conditional" privilege to distinguish it from the "absolute" privilege recognized in judicial, legislative, administrative and executive proceedings. See, e. g., Prosser, Torts (2d ed., 1955), 95.

[22] See 1 Harper and James, Torts, 5.23, at 429–430 (1956): Prosser, Torts (2d ed., 1955), at 612–613; American Law Institute, Restatement of Torts (1938), 591.

[23] We have no occasion here to determine how far down into the lower ranks of government employees the "public official" designation would extend for purposes of this rule, or otherwise to specify categories of persons who would or would not be included. Cf. Barr v. Matteo, 360 U.S. 564, 573–575. Nor need we here determine the boundaries of the "official conduct" concept. It is enough for the present case that respondent's position as an elected city commissioner clearly made him a public official, and that the allegations in the advertisement concerned what was allegedly his official conduct as Commissioner in charge of the Police Department. As to the statements alleging the assaulting of Dr. King and the bombing of his home, it is immaterial that they might not be considered to involve respondent's official conduct if he himself had been

accused of perpetrating the assault and the bombing. Respondent does not claim that the statements charged him personally with these acts; his contention is that the advertisement connects him with them only in his official capacity as the Commissioner supervising the police, on the theory that the police might be equated with the "They" who did the bombing and assaulting. Thus, if these allegations can be read as referring to respondent at all, they must be read as describing his performance of his official duties.

[24] Johnson Publishing Co. v. Davis, 271 Ala. 474, 487, 124 So.2d 441, 450 (1960). Thus, the trial judge here instructed the jury that "mere negligence or carelessness is not evidence of actual malice or malice in fact, and does not justify an award of exemplary or punitive damages in an action for libel." [376 U.S. 254, 284] The court refused, however, to give the following instruction which had been requested by the Times: "I charge you . . . that punitive damages, as the name indicates, are designed to punish the defendant, the New York Times Company, a corporation, and the other defendants in this case, . . . and I further charge you that such punitive damages may be awarded only in the event that you, the jury, are convinced by a fair preponderance of the evidence that the defendant . . . was motivated by personal ill will, that is actual intent to do the plaintiff harm, or that the defendant . . . was guilty of gross negligence and recklessness and not of just ordinary negligence or carelessness in publishing the matter complained of so as to indicate a wanton disregard of plaintiff's rights." The trial court's error in failing to require any finding of actual malice for an award of general damages makes it unnecessary for us to consider the sufficiency under the federal standard of the instructions regarding actual malice that were given as to punitive damages.

[25] Accord, Coleman v. MacLennan, supra, 78 Kan., at 741, 98 P., at 292; Gough v. Tribune-Journal Co., 75 Idaho 502, 510, 275 P.2d 663, 668 (1954).

[26] The Seventh Amendment does not, as respondent contends, preclude such an examination by this Court. That Amendment, providing that "no fact tried by a jury, shall be otherwise reexamined in any Court of the United States, than according to the rules of the common law," is applicable to state cases coming here. Chicago, B. & Q. R. Co. v. Chicago, 166 U.S. 226, 242–243; cf. The Justices v. Murray. 9 Wall. 274. But its ban on re-examination of facts does not preclude us from determining whether governing rules of federal law have been properly applied to the facts. "[T]his Court will review the finding of facts by a State court . . . where a conclusion of law as to a Federal right and a finding of fact are so intermingled as to make it necessary, in order to pass upon the Federal question, to analyze the facts." Fiske v. Kansas, 274 U.S. 380, 385–386. See also Haynes v. Washington, 373 U.S. 503, 515–516.

[27] The Times has set forth in a booklet its "Advertising Acceptability Standards." Listed among the classes of advertising that the newspaper does not accept are advertisements that are "fraudulent or deceptive," that are "ambiguous in wording and . . . may mislead," and that contain "attacks of a personal character." In replying to respondent's interrogatories before the trial, the Secretary of the Times stated that "as the advertisement made no attacks of a personal character upon any individual and otherwise met the advertising acceptability standards promulgated," it had been approved for publication.

[28] Respondent's own testimony was that "as Commissioner of Public Affairs it is part of my duty to supervise the Police Department and I certainly feel like it [a statement] is associated with me when it describes police activities." He thought that "by virtue of being [376 U.S. 254, 290] Police Commissioner and Commissioner of Public Affairs," he was charged with "any activity on the part of the Police Department." "When it describes police action, certainly I feel it reflects on me as an individual." He added that "It is my feeling that it reflects not only on me but on the other Commissioners and the community." Grover C. Hall testified that to him the third paragraph of the advertisement called to mind "the City government—the Commissioners," and that "now

that you ask it I would naturally think a little more about the police Commissioner because his responsibility is exclusively with the constabulary." It was "the phrase about starvation" that led to the association; "the other didn't hit me with any particular force." Arnold D. Blackwell testified that the third paragraph was associated in his mind with "the Police Commissioner and the police force. The people on the police force." If he had believed the statement about the padlocking of the dining hall, he would have thought "that the people on our police force or the heads of our police force were acting without their jurisdiction and would not be competent for the position." "I would assume that the Commissioner had ordered the police force to do that and therefore it would be his responsibility." Harry W. Kaminsky associated the statement about "truck-loads of police" with respondent "because he is the Police Commissioner." He thought that the reference to arrests in the sixth paragraph "implicates the Police Department, I think, or the authorities that would do that—arrest folks for speeding and loitering and such as that." Asked whether he would associate with respondent a newspaper report that the police had "beat somebody up or assaulted them on the streets of Montgomery," he replied: "I still say he is the Police Commissioner and those men are working directly under him and therefore I would think that he would have something to do with it." In general, he said, "I look at Mr. Sullivan when I see the Police Department." H. M. Price, Sr., testified that he associated the first sentence of the third paragraph with respondent because: "I would just automatically consider that the Police Commissioner in Montgomery [376 U.S. 254, 291] would have to put his approval on those kind of things as an individual." William M. Parker, Jr., testified that he associated the statements in the two paragraphs with "the Commissioners of the City of Montgomery," and since respondent "was the Police Commissioner," he "thought of him first." He told the examining counsel: "I think if you were the Police Commissioner I would have thought it was speaking of you." Horace W. White, respondent's former employer, testified that the statement about "truck-loads of police" made him think of respondent "as being the head of the Police Department." Asked whether he read the statement as charging respondent himself with ringing the campus or having shotguns and tear-gas, he replied: "Well, I thought of his department being charged with it, yes, sir. He is the head of the Police Department as I understand it." He further said that the reason he would have been unwilling to re-employ respondent if he had believed the advertisement was "the fact that he allowed the Police Department to do the things that the paper say he did."

[29] Compare Ponder v. Cobb, 257 N.C. 281, 126 S. E. 2d 67 (1962).

[30] Insofar as the proposition means only that the statements about police conduct libeled respondent by implicitly criticizing his ability to run the Police Department, recovery is also precluded in this case by the doctrine of fair comment. See American Law Institute, Restatement of Torts (1938), 607. Since the Fourteenth Amendment requires recognition of the conditional privilege for honest misstatements of fact, it follows that a defense of fair comment must be afforded for honest expression of opinion based upon privileged, as well as true, statements of fact. Both defenses are of course defeasible if the public official proves actual malice, as was not done here. [376 U.S. 254, 293]

Miranda v. Arizona
1966

The case known as *Miranda v. Arizona* was in fact a consolidation of four similar cases—*Miranda v. Arizona, Westover v. United States, Virginia v. New York,* and *California v. Stewart*—taken up by the Supreme Court during a period in which it was ruling on numerous issues of criminal procedure, usually with the effect of expanding procedural safeguards for criminal defendants. *Miranda v. Arizona* was the case of Ernesto Miranda, an Arizona man convicted of rape and kidnapping based solely on a confession made to police while under interrogation; the other three cases similarly involved criminal defendants whose confessions had been made under interrogation wherein no discernible effort was made by the interrogators to inform the defendants of their rights.

The Supreme Court ruled that prosecution may not use confessions made by a defendant unless it can show that actions were taken to inform the defendant of his or her Fifth Amendment rights against self-incrimination prior to the confession. Furthermore, Chief Justice Earl Warren's opinion went on to clearly define exactly how a suspect should be informed of his or her rights, laying out what would come to be known as the "Miranda warning." While civil libertarians praised the *Miranda* decision for upholding the principles of the Constitution, many advocates of law enforcement harshly criticized the ruling for valuing the rights of suspected criminals more than the rights of society.

U.S. SUPREME COURT

MIRANDA V. ARIZONA, 384 U.S. 436 (1966)

384 U.S. 436

MIRANDA V. ARIZONA.
CERTIORARI TO THE SUPREME COURT
OF ARIZONA.
NO. 759.

Argued February 28–March 1, 1966.
Decided June 13, 1966.★

IN each of these cases the defendant while in police custody was questioned by police officers, detectives, or a prosecuting attorney in a room in which he was cut off from the outside world. None of the defendants was given a full and effective warning of his rights at the outset of the interrogation process. In all four cases the questioning elicited oral admissions, and in three of them signed statements as well, which were admitted at their trials. All defendants were convicted and all convictions, except in No. 584, were affirmed on appeal. Held:

1. The prosecution may not use statements, whether exculpatory or inculpatory, stemming from questioning initiated by law enforcement officers after a person has been taken into custody or otherwise deprived of his freedom of action in any significant way, unless it demonstrates the use of procedural safeguards effective to secure the Fifth Amendment's privilege against self-incrimination. Pp. 444–491.

★Together with No. 760, Vignera v. New York, on certiorari to the Court of Appeals of New York and No. 761, Westover v. United States, on certiorari to the United States Court of Appeals for the Ninth Circuit, both argued February 28–March 1, 1966; and No. 584, California v. Stewart, on certiorari to the Supreme Court of California, argued February 28–March 2, 1966.

(a) The atmosphere and environment of incommunicado interrogation as it exists today is inherently intimidating and works to undermine the privilege against self-incrimination. Unless adequate preventive measures are taken to dispel the compulsion inherent in custodial surroundings, no statement obtained from the defendant can truly be the product of his free choice. Pp. 445–458.

(b) The privilege against self-incrimination, which has had a long and expansive historical development, is the essential mainstay of our adversary system and guarantees to the individual the "right to remain silent unless he chooses to speak in the unfettered exercise of his own will," during a period of custodial interrogation [384 U.S. 436, 437] as well as in the courts or during the course of other official investigations. Pp. 458–465.

(c) The decision in Escobedo v. Illinois, 378 U.S. 478, stressed the need for protective devices to make the process of police interrogation conform to the dictates of the privilege. Pp. 465–466.

(d) In the absence of other effective measures the following procedures to safeguard the Fifth Amendment privilege must be observed: The person in custody must, prior to interrogation, be clearly informed that he has the right to remain silent, and that anything he says will be used against him in court; he must be clearly informed that he has the right to consult with a lawyer and to have the lawyer with him during interrogation, and that, if he is indigent, a lawyer will be appointed to represent him. Pp. 467–473.

(e) If the individual indicates, prior to or during questioning, that he wishes to remain silent, the interrogation must cease; if he states that he wants an attorney, the questioning must cease until an attorney is present. Pp. 473–474.

(f) Where an interrogation is conducted without the presence of an attorney and a statement is taken, a heavy burden rests on the Government to demonstrate that the defendant knowingly and intelligently waived his right to counsel. P. 475.

(g) Where the individual answers some questions during incustody interrogation he has not waived his privilege and may invoke his right to remain silent thereafter. Pp. 475–476.

(h) The warnings required and the waiver needed are, in the absence of a fully effective equivalent, prerequisites to the admissibility of any statement, inculpatory or exculpatory, made by a defendant. Pp. 476–477.

2. The limitations on the interrogation process required for the protection of the individual's constitutional rights should not cause an undue interference with a proper system of law enforcement, as

260 Landmark Decisions of the U.S. Supreme Court

demonstrated by the procedures of the FBI and the safeguards afforded in other jurisdictions. Pp. 479–491.

3. In each of these cases the statements were obtained under circumstances that did not meet constitutional standards for protection of the privilege against self-incrimination. Pp. 491–499.

98 Ariz. 18, 401 P.2d 721; 15 N. Y. 2d 970, 207 N. E. 2d 527; 16 N. Y. 2d 614, 209 N. E. 2d 110; 342 F.2d 684, reversed; 62 Cal. 2d 571, 400 P.2d 97, affirmed. [384 U.S. 436, 438]

John J. Flynn argued the cause for petitioner in No. 759. With him on the brief was John P. Frank. Victor M. Earle III argued the cause and filed a brief for petitioner in No. 760. F. Conger Fawcett argued the cause and filed a brief for petitioner in No. 761. Gordon Ringer, Deputy Attorney General of California, argued the cause for petitioner in No. 584. With him on the briefs were Thomas C. Lynch, Attorney General, and William E. James, Assistant Attorney General.

Gary K. Nelson, Assistant Attorney General of Arizona, argued the cause for respondent in No. 759. With him on the brief was Darrell F. Smith, Attorney General. William I. Siegel argued the cause for respondent in No. 760. With him on the brief was Aaron E. Koota. Solicitor General Marshall argued the cause for the United States in No. 761. With him on the brief were Assistant Attorney General Vinson, Ralph S. Spritzer, Nathan Lewin, Beatrice Rosenberg and Ronald L. Gainer. William A. Norris, by appointment of the Court, 382 U.S. 952, argued the cause and filed a brief for respondent in No. 584.

Telford Taylor, by special leave of Court, argued the cause for the State of New York, as amicus curiae, in all cases. With him on the brief were Louis J. Lefkowitz, Attorney General of New York, Samuel A. Hirshowitz, First Assistant Attorney General, and Barry Mahoney and George D. Zuckerman, Assistant Attorneys General, joined by the Attorneys General for their respective States and jurisdictions as follows: Richmond M. Flowers of Alabama, Darrell F. Smith of Arizona, Bruce Bennett of Arkansas, Duke W. Dunbar of Colorado, David P. Buckson of Delaware, Earl Faircloth of Florida, Arthur K. Bolton of Georgia, Allan G. Shepard of Idaho, William G. Clark of Illinois, Robert C. Londerholm of Kansas, Robert Matthews of Kentucky, Jack P. F. [384 U.S. 436, 439] Gremillion of Louisiana, Richard J. Dubord of Maine, Thomas B. Finan of Maryland, Norman H. Anderson of Missouri, Forrest H. Anderson of Montana, Clarence A. H. Meyer of Nebraska, T. Wade Bruton of North Carolina, Helgi Johanneson of North Dakota, Robert Y. Thornton of Oregon, Walter E. Alessandroni of Pennsylvania, J. Joseph Nugent of Rhode Island, Daniel R. McLeod of South Carolina, Waggoner Carr of Texas, Robert Y. Button of Virginia, John J.

O'Connell of Washington, C. Donald Robertson of West Virginia, John F. Raper of Wyoming, Rafael Hernandez Colon of Puerto Rico and Francisco Corneiro of the Virgin Islands.

Duane R. Nedrud, by special leave of Court, argued the cause for the National District Attorneys Association, as amicus curiae, urging affirmance in Nos. 759 and 760, and reversal in No. 584. With him on the brief was Marguerite D. Oberto.

Anthony G. Amsterdam, Paul J. Mishkin, Raymond L. Bradley, Peter Hearn and Melvin L. Wulf filed a brief for the American Civil Liberties Union, as amicus curiae, in all cases.

MR. CHIEF JUSTICE WARREN delivered the opinion of the Court.

The cases before us raise questions which go to the roots of our concepts of American criminal jurisprudence: the restraints society must observe consistent with the Federal Constitution in prosecuting individuals for crime. More specifically, we deal with the admissibility of statements obtained from an individual who is subjected to custodial police interrogation and the necessity for procedures which assure that the individual is accorded his privilege under the Fifth Amendment to the Constitution not to be compelled to incriminate himself. [384 U.S. 436, 440]

We dealt with certain phases of this problem recently in Escobedo v. Illinois, 378 U.S. 478 (1964). There, as in the four cases before us, law enforcement officials took the defendant into custody and interrogated him in a police station for the purpose of obtaining a confession. The police did not effectively advise him of his right to remain silent or of his right to consult with his attorney. Rather, they confronted him with an alleged accomplice who accused him of having perpetrated a murder. When the defendant denied the accusation and said "I didn't shoot Manuel, you did it," they handcuffed him and took him to an interrogation room. There, while handcuffed and standing, he was questioned for four hours until he confessed. During this interrogation, the police denied his request to speak to his attorney, and they prevented his retained attorney, who had come to the police station, from consulting with him. At his trial, the State, over his objection, introduced the confession against him. We held that the statements thus made were constitutionally inadmissible.

This case has been the subject of judicial interpretation and spirited legal debate since it was decided two years ago. Both state and federal courts, in assessing its implications, have arrived at varying conclusions.[1] A wealth of scholarly material has been written tracing its ramifications and underpinnings.[2] Police and prosecutor [384 U.S. 436, 441] have speculated on its range and desirability.[3] We granted certiorari in these cases, 382 U.S. 924, 925, 937, in order further to explore some facets of the problems, thus exposed, of applying the privilege against self-incrimination to in-custody interrogation, and to give [384 U.S. 436, 442] concrete constitutional guidelines for law enforcement agencies and courts to follow.

We start here, as we did in Escobedo, with the premise that our holding is not an innovation in our jurisprudence, but is an application of principles long recognized and applied in other settings. We have undertaken a thorough re-examination of the Escobedo decision and the principles it announced, and we reaffirm it. That case was but an explication of basic rights that are enshrined in our Constitution—that "No person . . . shall be compelled in any criminal case to be a witness against himself," and that "the accused shall . . . have the Assistance of Counsel"— rights which were put in jeopardy in that case through official overbearing. These precious rights were fixed in our Constitution only after centuries of persecution and struggle. And in the words of Chief Justice Marshall, they were secured "for ages to come, and . . . designed to approach immortality as nearly as human institutions can approach it," Cohens v. Virginia, 6 Wheat. 264, 387 (1821).

Over 70 years ago, our predecessors on this Court eloquently stated:

"The maxim nemo tenetur seipsum accusare had its origin in a protest against the inquisitorial and manifestly unjust methods of interrogating accused persons, which [have] long obtained in the continental system, and, until the expulsion of the Stuarts from the British throne in 1688, and the erection of additional barriers for the protection of the people against the exercise of arbitrary power, [were] not uncommon even in England. While the admissions or confessions of the prisoner, when voluntarily and freely made, have always ranked high in the scale of incriminating evidence, if an accused person be asked to explain his apparent connection with a crime under investigation, the ease with which the [384 U.S. 436, 443] questions put to him may assume an inquisitorial character, the temptation to press the witness unduly, to browbeat him if he be timid or reluctant, to push him into a corner, and to entrap him into fatal contradictions, which is so painfully evident in many of the earlier state trials, notably in those of Sir Nicholas Throckmorton, and Udal, the Puritan minister, made the system so odious as to give rise to a demand for its total abolition. The change in the English criminal procedure in that particular seems to be founded upon no statute and no judicial opinion, but upon a general and silent acquiescence of the courts in a popular demand. But, however adopted, it has become firmly embedded in English, as well as in American jurisprudence. So deeply did the iniquities of the ancient system impress themselves upon the minds of the American colonists that the States, with one accord, made a denial of the right to question an accused person a part of their fundamental law, so that a maxim, which in England was a mere rule of evidence, became clothed in this country with the impregnability of a constitutional enactment." Brown v. Walker, 161 U.S. 591, 596–597 (1896).

In stating the obligation of the judiciary to apply these constitutional rights, this Court declared in Weems v. United States, 217 U.S. 349, 373 (1910):

". . . our contemplation cannot be only of what has been but of what may be. Under any other rule a constitution would indeed be as easy of application as it would be deficient in efficacy and power. Its general principles would have little value and be converted by precedent into impotent and lifeless formulas. Rights declared in words might be lost in reality. And this has been recognized. The [384 U.S. 436, 444] meaning and vitality of the Constitution have developed against narrow and restrictive construction."

This was the spirit in which we delineated, in meaningful language, the manner in which the constitutional rights of the individual could be enforced against overzealous police practices. It was necessary in Escobedo, as here, to insure that what was proclaimed in the Constitution had not become but a "form of words," Silverthorne Lumber Co. v. United States, 251 U.S. 385, 392 (1920), in the hands of government officials. And it is in this spirit, consistent with our role as judges, that we adhere to the principles of Escobedo today.

Our holding will be spelled out with some specificity in the pages which follow but briefly stated it is this: the prosecution may not use statements, whether exculpatory or inculpatory, stemming from custodial interrogation of the defendant unless it demonstrates the use of procedural safeguards effective to secure the privilege against self-incrimination. By custodial interrogation, we mean questioning initiated by law enforcement officers after a person has been taken into custody or otherwise deprived of his freedom of action in any significant way.[4] As for the procedural safeguards to be employed, unless other fully effective means are devised to inform accused persons of their right of silence and to assure a continuous opportunity to exercise it, the following measures are required. Prior to any questioning, the person must be warned that he has a right to remain silent, that any statement he does make may be used as evidence against him, and that he has a right to the presence of an attorney, either retained or appointed. The defendant may waive effectuation of these rights, provided the waiver is made voluntarily, knowingly and intelligently. If, however, he indicates in any manner and at any stage of the [384 U.S. 436, 445] process that he wishes to consult with an attorney before speaking there can be no questioning. Likewise, if the individual is alone and indicates in any manner that he does not wish to be interrogated, the police may not question him. The mere fact that he may have answered some questions or volunteered some statements on his own does not deprive him of the right to refrain from answering any further inquiries until he has consulted with an attorney and thereafter consents to be questioned.

I.

The constitutional issue we decide in each of these cases is the admissibility of statements obtained from a defendant questioned while in custody or otherwise deprived of his freedom of action in any significant way. In each, the defendant was questioned by police officers, detectives, or a prosecuting attorney in a room in which he was cut off from the outside world. In none of these cases was the defendant given a full and effective warning of his rights at the outset of the interrogation process. In all the cases, the questioning elicited oral admissions, and in three of them, signed statements as well which were admitted at their trials. They all thus share salient features—incommunicado interrogation of individuals in a police-dominated atmosphere, resulting in self-incriminating statements without full warnings of constitutional rights.

An understanding of the nature and setting of this in-custody interrogation is essential to our decisions today. The difficulty in depicting what transpires at such interrogations stems from the fact that in this country they have largely taken place incommunicado. From extensive factual studies undertaken in the early 1930's, including the famous Wickersham Report to Congress by a Presidential Commission, it is clear that police violence and the "third degree" flourished at that time.[5] [384 U.S. 436, 446] In a series of cases decided by this Court long after these studies, the police resorted to physical brutality—beating, hanging, whipping—and to sustained and protracted questioning incommunicado in order to extort confessions.[6] The Commission on Civil Rights in 1961 found much evidence to indicate that "some policemen still resort to physical force to obtain confessions," 1961 Comm'n on Civil Rights Rep., Justice, pt. 5, 17. The use of physical brutality and violence is not, unfortunately, relegated to the past or to any part of the country. Only recently in Kings County, New York, the police brutally beat, kicked and placed lighted cigarette butts on the back of a potential witness under interrogation for the purpose of securing a statement incriminating a third party. People v. Portelli, 15 N. Y. 2d 235, 205 N. E. 2d 857, 257 N. Y. S. 2d 931 (1965).[7] [384 U.S. 436, 447]

The examples given above are undoubtedly the exception now, but they are sufficiently widespread to be the object of concern. Unless a proper limitation upon custodial interrogation is achieved—such as these decisions will advance—there can be no assurance that practices of this nature will be eradicated in the foreseeable future. The conclusion of the Wickersham Commission Report, made over 30 years ago, is still pertinent:

> "To the contention that the third degree is necessary to get the facts, the reporters aptly reply in the language of the present Lord Chancellor of England (Lord Sankey): 'It is not admissible to do a great right by doing a little wrong. . . . It is not sufficient to do justice by obtaining a proper result by irregular or improper means.' Not only does the use of the third degree involve a flagrant violation of law by the officers of the law, but it involves also the dangers of false confessions, and it tends to make police and prosecutors less zealous in the search for objective evidence. As the New York prosecutor quoted in the report said, 'It is a short cut and makes the police lazy and unenterprising.' Or, as another official quoted remarked: 'If you use your fists, you [384 U.S. 436, 448] are not so likely to use your wits.' We agree with the conclusion expressed in the report, that 'The third degree brutalizes the police, hardens the prisoner against society, and lowers the esteem in which the administration of justice is held by the public.'" IV National Commission on Law Observance and Enforcement, Report on Lawlessness in Law Enforcement 5 (1931).

Again we stress that the modern practice of in-custody interrogation is psychologically rather than physically oriented. As we have stated before, "Since Chambers v. Florida, 309 U.S. 227, this Court has recognized that coercion can be mental as well as physical, and that the blood of the accused is not the only hallmark of an unconstitutional inquisition." Blackburn v. Alabama, 361 U.S. 199, 206 (1960). Interrogation still takes place in privacy. Privacy results in secrecy and this in turn results in a gap in our knowledge as to what in fact goes on in the interrogation rooms. A valuable source of information about present police practices, however, may be found in various police manuals and texts which document procedures employed with success in the past, and which recommend various other effective tactics.[8] These [384 U.S. 436, 449] texts are used by law enforcement agencies themselves as guides.[9] It should be noted that these texts professedly present the most enlightened and effective means presently used to obtain statements through custodial interrogation. By considering these texts and other data, it is possible to describe procedures observed and noted around the country.

The officers are told by the manuals that the "principal psychological factor contributing to a successful interrogation is privacy—being alone with the person under interrogation."[10] The efficacy of this tactic has been explained as follows:

"If at all practicable, the interrogation should take place in the investigator's office or at least in a room of his own choice. The subject should be deprived of every psychological advantage. In his own home he may be confident, indignant, or recalcitrant. He is more keenly aware of his rights and [384 U.S. 436, 450] more reluctant to tell of his indiscretions or criminal behavior within the walls of his home. Moreover his family and other friends are nearby, their presence lending moral support. In his own office, the investigator possesses all the advantages. The atmosphere suggests the invincibility of the forces of the law."[11]

To highlight the isolation and unfamiliar surroundings, the manuals instruct the police to display an air of confidence in the suspect's guilt and from outward appearance to maintain only an interest in confirming certain details. The guilt of the subject is to be posited as a fact. The interrogator should direct his comments toward the reasons why the subject committed the act, rather than court failure by asking the subject whether he did it. Like other men, perhaps the subject has had a bad family life, had an unhappy childhood, had too much to drink, had an unrequited desire for women. The officers are instructed to minimize the moral seriousness of the offense,[12] to cast blame on the victim or on society.[13] These tactics are designed to put the subject in a psychological state where his story is but an elaboration of what the police purport to know already—that he is guilty. Explanations to the contrary are dismissed and discouraged.

The texts thus stress that the major qualities an interrogator should possess are patience and perseverance. [384 U.S. 436, 451] One writer describes the efficacy of these characteristics in this manner:

"In the preceding paragraphs emphasis has been placed on kindness and stratagems. The investigator will, however, encounter many situations where the sheer weight of his personality will be the deciding factor. Where emotional appeals and tricks are employed to no avail, he must rely on an oppressive atmosphere of dogged persistence. He must interrogate steadily and without relent, leaving the subject no prospect of surcease. He must dominate his subject and overwhelm him with his inexorable will to obtain the truth. He should interrogate for a spell of several hours pausing only for the subject's necessities in acknowledgment of the need to avoid a charge of duress that can be technically substantiated. In a serious case, the interrogation may continue for days, with the required intervals for food and sleep, but with no respite from the atmosphere of domination. It is possible in this way to induce the subject to talk without resorting to duress or coercion. The method should be used only when the guilt of the subject appears highly probable."[14]

The manuals suggest that the suspect be offered legal excuses for his actions in order to obtain an initial admission of guilt. Where there is a suspected revenge-killing, for example, the interrogator may say:

"Joe, you probably didn't go out looking for this fellow with the purpose of shooting him. My guess is, however, that you expected something from him and that's why you carried a gun—for your own protection. You knew him for what he was, no good. Then when you met him he probably started using foul, abusive language and he gave some indication [384 U.S. 436, 452] that he was about to pull a gun on you, and that's when you had to act to save your own life. That's about it, isn't it, Joe?"[15]

Having then obtained the admission of shooting, the interrogator is advised to refer to circumstantial evidence which negates the self-defense explanation. This should enable him to secure the entire story. One text notes that "Even if he fails to do so, the inconsistency between the subject's original denial of the shooting and his present admission of at least doing the shooting will serve to deprive him of a self-defense 'out' at the time of trial."[16]

When the techniques described above prove unavailing, the texts recommend they be alternated with a show of some hostility. One ploy often used has been termed the "friendly-unfriendly" or the "Mutt and Jeff" act:

". . . In this technique, two agents are employed. Mutt, the relentless investigator, who knows the subject is guilty and is not going to waste any time. He's sent a dozen men away for this crime and he's going to send the subject away for the full term. Jeff, on the other hand, is obviously a kindhearted man. He has a family himself. He has a brother who was involved in a little scrape like this. He disapproves of Mutt and his tactics and will arrange to get him off the case if the subject will cooperate. He can't hold Mutt off for very long. The subject would be wise to make a quick decision. The technique is applied by having both investigators present while Mutt acts out his role. Jeff may stand by quietly and demur at some of Mutt's tactics. When Jeff makes his plea for cooperation, Mutt is not present in the room."[17] [384 U.S. 436, 453]

The interrogators sometimes are instructed to induce a confession out of trickery. The technique here is quite effective in crimes which require identification or which run in series. In the identification situation, the interrogator may take a break in his questioning to place the subject among a group of men in a line-up. "The witness or complainant (previously coached, if necessary) studies the line-up and confidently points out the subject as the guilty party."[18] Then the questioning resumes "as though there were now no doubt about the guilt of the subject." A variation on this technique is called the "reverse line-up":

> "The accused is placed in a line-up, but this time he is identified by several fictitious witnesses or victims who associated him with different offenses. It is expected that the subject will become desperate and confess to the offense under investigation in order to escape from the false accusations."[19]

The manuals also contain instructions for police on how to handle the individual who refuses to discuss the matter entirely, or who asks for an attorney or relatives. The examiner is to concede him the right to remain silent. "This usually has a very undermining effect. First of all, he is disappointed in his expectation of an unfavorable reaction on the part of the interrogator. Secondly, a concession of this right to remain silent impresses [384 U.S. 436, 454] the subject with the apparent fairness of his interrogator."[20] After this psychological conditioning, however, the officer is told to point out the incriminating significance of the suspect's refusal to talk:

> "Joe, you have a right to remain silent. That's your privilege and I'm the last person in the world who'll try to take it away from you. If that's the way you want to leave this, O. K. But let me ask you this. Suppose you were in my shoes and I were in yours and you called me in to ask me about this and I told you, 'I don't want to answer any of your questions.' You'd think I had something to hide, and you'd probably be right in thinking that. That's exactly what I'll have to think about you, and so will everybody else. So let's sit here and talk this whole thing over."[21]

Few will persist in their initial refusal to talk, it is said, if this mono-
logue is employed correctly.

In the event that the subject wishes to speak to a relative or an attorney, the following advice is tendered:

> "[T]he interrogator should respond by suggesting that the subject
> first tell the truth to the interrogator himself rather than get anyone
> else involved in the matter. If the request is for an attorney, the inter-
> rogator may suggest that the subject save himself or his family the
> expense of any such professional service, particularly if he is innocent
> of the offense under investigation. The interrogator may also add,
> "Joe, I'm only looking for the truth, and if you're telling the truth,
> that's it. You can handle this by yourself.'"[22] [384 U.S. 436, 455]

From these representative samples of interrogation techniques, the setting prescribed by the manuals and observed in practice becomes clear. In
essence, it is this: To be alone with the subject is essential to prevent distraction and to deprive him of any outside support. The aura of confidence in his guilt undermines his will to resist. He merely confirms the
preconceived story the police seek to have him describe. Patience and
persistence, at times relentless questioning, are employed. To obtain a confession, the interrogator must "patiently maneuver himself or his quarry
into a position from which the desired objective may be attained."[23]
When normal procedures fail to produce the needed result, the police
may resort to deceptive stratagems such as giving false legal advice. It is
important to keep the subject off balance, for example, by trading on his
insecurity about himself or his surroundings. The police then persuade,
trick, or cajole him out of exercising his constitutional rights.

Even without employing brutality, the "third degree" or the specific
stratagems described above, the very fact of custodial interrogation exacts
a heavy toll on individual liberty and trades on the weakness of individuals.[24] [384 U.S. 436, 456] This fact may be illustrated simply by referring
to three confession cases decided by this Court in the Term immediately
preceding our Escobedo decision. In Townsend v. Sain, 372 U.S. 293
(1963), the defendant was a 19–year–old heroin addict, described as a
"near mental defective," id., at 307–310. The defendant in Lynumn v.
Illinois, 372 U.S. 528 (1963), was a woman who confessed to the arresting officer after being importuned to "cooperate" in order to prevent her
children from being taken by relief authorities. This Court as in those
cases reversed the conviction of a defendant in Haynes v. Washington,
373 U.S. 503 (1963), whose persistent request during his interrogation
was to phone his wife or attorney.[25] In other settings, these individuals

might have exercised their constitutional rights. In the incommunicado police-dominated atmosphere, they succumbed.

In the cases before us today, given this background, we concern ourselves primarily with this interrogation atmosphere and the evils it can bring. In No. 759, Miranda v. Arizona, the police arrested the defendant and took him to a special interrogation room where they secured a confession. In No. 760, Vignera v. New York, the defendant made oral admissions to the police after interrogation in the afternoon, and then signed an inculpatory statement upon being questioned by an assistant district attorney later the same evening. In No. 761, Westover v. United States, the defendant was handed over to the Federal Bureau of Investigation by [384 U.S. 436, 457] local authorities after they had detained and interrogated him for a lengthy period, both at night and the following morning. After some two hours of questioning, the federal officers had obtained signed statements from the defendant. Lastly, in No. 584, California v. Stewart, the local police held the defendant five days in the station and interrogated him on nine separate occasions before they secured his inculpatory statement.

In these cases, we might not find the defendants' statements to have been involuntary in traditional terms. Our concern for adequate safeguards to protect precious Fifth Amendment rights is, of course, not lessened in the slightest. In each of the cases, the defendant was thrust into an unfamiliar atmosphere and run through menacing police interrogation procedures. The potentiality for compulsion is forcefully apparent, for example, in Miranda, where the indigent Mexican defendant was a seriously disturbed individual with pronounced sexual fantasies, and in Stewart, in which the defendant was an indigent Los Angeles Negro who had dropped out of school in the sixth grade. To be sure, the records do not evince overt physical coercion or patent psychological ploys. The fact remains that in none of these cases did the officers undertake to afford appropriate safeguards at the outset of the interrogation to insure that the statements were truly the product of free choice.

It is obvious that such an interrogation environment is created for no purpose other than to subjugate the individual to the will of his examiner. This atmosphere carries its own badge of intimidation. To be sure, this is not physical intimidation, but it is equally destructive of human dignity.[26] The current practice of incommunicado interrogation is at odds with one of our [384 U.S. 436, 458] Nation's most cherished principles—that the individual may not be compelled to incriminate himself. Unless adequate protective devices are employed to dispel the compulsion inherent in custodial surroundings, no statement obtained from the defendant can truly be the product of his free choice.

From the foregoing, we can readily perceive an intimate connection between the privilege against self-incrimination and police custodial questioning. It is fitting to turn to history and precedent underlying the Self-Incrimination Clause to determine its applicability in this situation.

II.

We sometimes forget how long it has taken to establish the privilege against self-incrimination, the sources from which it came and the fervor with which it was defended. Its roots go back into ancient times.[27] Perhaps [384 U.S. 436, 459] the critical historical event shedding light on its origins and evolution was the trial of one John Lilburn, a vocal anti-Stuart Leveller, who was made to take the Star Chamber Oath in 1637. The oath would have bound him to answer to all questions posed to him on any subject. The Trial of John Lilburn and John Wharton, 3 How. St. Tr. 1315 (1637). He resisted the oath and declaimed the proceedings, stating:

> "Another fundamental right I then contended for, was, that no man's conscience ought to be racked by oaths imposed, to answer to questions concerning himself in matters criminal, or pretended to be so." Haller & Davies, The Leveller Tracts 1647–1653, p. 454 (1944).

On account of the Lilburn Trial, Parliament abolished the inquisitorial Court of Star Chamber and went further in giving him generous reparation. The lofty principles to which Lilburn had appealed during his trial gained popular acceptance in England.[28] These sentiments worked their way over to the Colonies and were implanted after great struggle into the Bill of Rights.[29] Those who framed our Constitution and the Bill of Rights were ever aware of subtle encroachments on individual liberty. They knew that "illegitimate and unconstitutional practices get their first footing . . . by silent approaches and slight deviations from legal modes of procedure." Boyd v. United States, 116 U.S. 616, 635 (1886). The privilege was elevated to constitutional status and has always been "as broad as the mischief [384 U.S. 436, 460] against which it seeks to guard." Counselman v. Hitchcock, 142 U.S. 547, 562 (1892). We cannot depart from this noble heritage.

Thus we may view the historical development of the privilege as one which groped for the proper scope of governmental power over the citizen. As a "noble principle often transcends its origins," the privilege has come rightfully to be recognized in part as an individual's substantive right, a "right to a private enclave where he may lead a private life. That right is the hallmark of our democracy." United States v. Grunewald, 233 F.2d 556, 579, 581–582 (Frank, J., dissenting), rev'd, 353

U.S. 391 (1957). We have recently noted that the privilege against self-incrimination—the essential mainstay of our adversary system—is founded on a complex of values, Murphy v. Waterfront Comm'n, 378 U.S. 52, 55–57, n. 5 (1964); Tehan v. Shott, 382 U.S. 406, 414–415, n. 12 (1966). All these policies point to one overriding thought: the constitutional foundation underlying the privilege is the respect a government—state or federal—must accord to the dignity and integrity of its citizens. To maintain a "fair state-individual balance," to require the government "to shoulder the entire load," 8 Wigmore, Evidence 317 (McNaughton rev. 1961), to respect the inviolability of the human personality, our accusatory system of criminal justice demands that the government seeking to punish an individual produce the evidence against him by its own independent labors, rather than by the cruel, simple expedient of compelling it from his own mouth. Chambers v. Florida, 309 U.S. 227, 235–238 (1940). In sum, the privilege is fulfilled only when the person is guaranteed the right "to remain silent unless he chooses to speak in the unfettered exercise of his own will." Malloy v. Hogan, 378 U.S. 1, 8 (1964).

The question in these cases is whether the privilege is fully applicable during a period of custodial interrogation. [384 U.S. 436, 461] In this Court, the privilege has consistently been accorded a liberal construction. Albertson v. SACB, 382 U.S. 70, 81 (1965); Hoffman v. United States, 341 U.S. 479, 486 (1951); Arndstein v. McCarthy, 254 U.S. 71, 72 –73 (1920); Counselman v. Hitchcock, 142 U.S. 547, 562 (1892). We are satisfied that all the principles embodied in the privilege apply to informal compulsion exerted by law-enforcement officers during in-custody questioning. An individual swept from familiar surroundings into police custody, surrounded by antagonistic forces, and subjected to the techniques of persuasion described above cannot be otherwise than under compulsion to speak. As a practical matter, the compulsion to speak in the isolated setting of the police station may well be greater than in courts or other official investigations, where there are often impartial observers to guard against intimidation or trickery.[30]

This question, in fact, could have been taken as settled in federal courts almost 70 years ago, when, in Bram v. United States, 168 U.S. 532, 542 (1897), this Court held:

> "In criminal trials, in the courts of the United States, wherever a question arises whether a confession is incompetent because not voluntary, the issue is controlled by that portion of the Fifth Amendment . . . commanding that no person 'shall be compelled in any criminal case to be a witness against himself.'"

In Bram, the Court reviewed the British and American history and case law and set down the Fifth Amendment standard for compulsion which we implement today:

> "Much of the confusion which has resulted from the effort to deduce from the adjudged cases what [384 U.S. 436, 462] would be a sufficient quantum of proof to show that a confession was or was not voluntary, has arisen from a misconception of the subject to which the proof must address itself. The rule is not that in order to render a statement admissible the proof must be adequate to establish that the particular communications contained in a statement were voluntarily made, but it must be sufficient to establish that the making of the statement was voluntary; that is to say, that from the causes, which the law treats as legally sufficient to engender in the mind of the accused hope or fear in respect to the crime charged, the accused was not involuntarily impelled to make a statement, when but for the improper influences he would have remained silent. . . ." 168 U.S., at 549. And see, id., at 542.

The Court has adhered to this reasoning. In 1924, Mr. Justice Brandeis wrote for a unanimous Court in reversing a conviction resting on a compelled confession, Wan v. United States, 266 U.S. 1. He stated:

> "In the federal courts, the requisite of voluntariness is not satisfied by establishing merely that the confession was not induced by a promise or a threat. A confession is voluntary in law if, and only if, it was, in fact, voluntarily made. A confession may have been given voluntarily, although it was made to police officers, while in custody, and in answer to an examination conducted by them. But a confession obtained by compulsion must be excluded whatever may have been the character of the compulsion, and whether the compulsion was applied in a judicial proceeding or otherwise. Bram v. United States, 168 U.S. 532." 266 U.S., at 14–15.

In addition to the expansive historical development of the privilege and the sound policies which have nurtured [384 U.S. 436, 463] its evolution, judicial precedent thus clearly establishes its application to incommunicado interrogation. In fact, the Government concedes this point as well established in No. 761, Westover v. United States, stating: "We have no doubt . . . that it is possible for a suspect's Fifth Amendment right to be violated during in-custody questioning by a law-enforcement officer."[31]

Because of the adoption by Congress of Rule 5 (a) of the Federal Rules of Criminal Procedure, and this Court's effectuation of that Rule in McNabb v. United States, 318 U.S. 332 (1943), and Mallory v. United States, 354 U.S. 449 (1957), we have had little occasion in the past quarter century to reach the constitutional issues in dealing with federal interrogations. These supervisory rules, requiring production of an arrested person before a commissioner "without unnecessary delay" and excluding evidence obtained in default of that statutory obligation, were nonetheless responsive to the same considerations of Fifth Amendment policy that unavoidably face us now as to the States. In McNabb, 318 U.S., at 343–344, and in Mallory, 354 U.S., at 455–456, we recognized both the dangers of interrogation and the appropriateness of prophylaxis stemming from the very fact of interrogation itself.[32]

Our decision in Malloy v. Hogan, 378 U.S. 1 (1964), necessitates an examination of the scope of the privilege in state cases as well. In Malloy, we squarely held the [384 U.S. 436, 464] privilege applicable to the States, and held that the substantive standards underlying the privilege applied with full force to state court proceedings. There, as in Murphy v. Waterfront Comm'n, 378 U.S. 52 (1964), and Griffin v. California, 380 U.S. 609 (1965), we applied the existing Fifth Amendment standards to the case before us. Aside from the holding itself, the reasoning in Malloy made clear what had already become apparent—that the substantive and procedural safeguards surrounding admissibility of confessions in state cases had become exceedingly exacting, reflecting all the policies embedded in the privilege, 378 U.S., at 7–8.[33] The voluntariness doctrine in the state cases, as Malloy indicates, encompasses all interrogation practices which are likely to exert such pressure upon an individual as to disable him from [384 U.S. 436, 465] making a free and rational choice.[34] The implications of this proposition were elaborated in our decision in Escobedo v. Illinois, 378 U.S. 478, decided one week after Malloy applied the privilege to the States.

Our holding there stressed the fact that the police had not advised the defendant of his constitutional privilege to remain silent at the outset of the interrogation, and we drew attention to that fact at several points in the decision, 378 U.S., at 483, 485, 491. This was no isolated factor, but an essential ingredient in our decision. The entire thrust of police interrogation there, as in all the cases today, was to put the defendant in such an emotional state as to impair his capacity for rational judgment. The abdication of the constitutional privilege—the choice on his part to speak to the police—was not made knowingly or competently because of the failure to apprise him of his rights; the compelling atmosphere of the in-custody interrogation, and not an independent decision on his part, caused the defendant to speak.

A different phase of the Escobedo decision was significant in its attention to the absence of counsel during the questioning. There, as in the cases today, we sought a protective device to dispel the compelling atmosphere of the interrogation. In Escobedo, however, the police did not relieve the defendant of the anxieties which they had created in the interrogation rooms. Rather, they denied his request for the assistance of counsel, 378 U.S., at 481, 488, 491.[35] This heightened his dilemma, and [384 U.S. 436, 466] made his later statements the product of this compulsion. Cf. Haynes v. Washington, 373 U.S. 503, 514 (1963). The denial of the defendant's request for his attorney thus undermined his ability to exercise the privilege—to remain silent if he chose or to speak without any intimidation, blatant or subtle. The presence of counsel, in all the cases before us today, would be the adequate protective device necessary to make the process of police interrogation conform to the dictates of the privilege. His presence would insure that statements made in the government-established atmosphere are not the product of compulsion.

It was in this manner that Escobedo explicated another facet of the pre-trial privilege, noted in many of the Court's prior decisions: the protection of rights at trial.[36] That counsel is present when statements are taken from an individual during interrogation obviously enhances the integrity of the fact-finding processes in court. The presence of an attorney, and the warnings delivered to the individual, enable the defendant under otherwise compelling circumstances to tell his story without fear, effectively, and in a way that eliminates the evils in the interrogation process. Without the protections flowing from adequate warnings and the rights of counsel, "all the careful safeguards erected around the giving of testimony, whether by an accused or any other witness, would become empty formalities in a procedure where the most compelling possible evidence of guilt, a confession, would have already been obtained at the unsupervised pleasure of the police." Mapp v. Ohio, 367 U.S. 643, 685 (1961) (HARLAN, J., dissenting). Cf. Pointer v. Texas, 380 U.S. 400 (1965). [384 U.S. 436, 467]

III.

Today, then, there can be no doubt that the Fifth Amendment privilege is available outside of criminal court proceedings and serves to protect persons in all settings in which their freedom of action is curtailed in any significant way from being compelled to incriminate themselves. We have concluded that without proper safeguards the process of in-custody interrogation of persons suspected or accused of crime contains inherently compelling pressures which work to undermine the individual's will to resist and to compel him to speak where he would not otherwise do so freely. In order to combat these pressures and to permit a full opportunity to exercise the privilege against self-incrimination, the accused must be adequately and effectively apprised of his rights and the exercise of those rights must be fully honored.

It is impossible for us to foresee the potential alternatives for protecting the privilege which might be devised by Congress or the States in the exercise of their creative rule-making capacities. Therefore we cannot say that the Constitution necessarily requires adherence to any particular solution for the inherent compulsions of the interrogation process as it is presently conducted. Our decision in no way creates a constitutional straitjacket which will handicap sound efforts at reform, nor is it intended to have this effect. We encourage Congress and the States to continue their laudable search for increasingly effective ways of protecting the rights of the individual while promoting efficient enforcement of our criminal laws. However, unless we are shown other procedures which are at least as effective in apprising accused persons of their right of silence and in assuring a continuous opportunity to exercise it, the following safeguards must be observed.

At the outset, if a person in custody is to be subjected to interrogation, he must first be informed in clear and [384 U.S. 436, 468] unequivocal terms that he has the right to remain silent. For those unaware of the privilege, the warning is needed simply to make them aware of it—the threshold requirement for an intelligent decision as to its exercise. More important, such a warning is an absolute prerequisite in overcoming the inherent pressures of the interrogation atmosphere. It is not just the subnormal or woefully ignorant who succumb to an interrogator's imprecations, whether implied or expressly stated, that the interrogation will continue until a confession is obtained or that silence in the face of accusation is itself damning and will bode ill when presented to a jury.[37] Further, the warning will show the individual that his interrogators are prepared to recognize his privilege should he choose to exercise it.

The Fifth Amendment privilege is so fundamental to our system of constitutional rule and the expedient of giving an adequate warning as to the availability of the privilege so simple, we will not pause to inquire in individual cases whether the defendant was aware of his rights without a warning being given. Assessments of the knowledge the defendant possessed, based on information [384 U.S. 436, 469] as to his age, education, intelligence, or prior contact with authorities, can never be more than speculation;[38] a warning is a clearcut fact. More important, whatever the background of the person interrogated, a warning at the time of the interrogation is indispensable to overcome its pressures and to insure that the individual knows he is free to exercise the privilege at that point in time.

The warning of the right to remain silent must be accompanied by the explanation that anything said can and will be used against the individual in court. This warning is needed in order to make him aware not only of the privilege, but also of the consequences of forgoing it. It is only through an awareness of these consequences that there can be any assurance of real understanding and intelligent exercise of the privilege. Moreover, this warning may serve to make the individual more acutely aware that he is faced with a phase of the adversary system—that he is not in the presence of persons acting solely in his interest.

The circumstances surrounding in-custody interrogation can operate very quickly to overbear the will of one merely made aware of his privilege by his interrogators. Therefore, the right to have counsel present at the interrogation is indispensable to the protection of the Fifth Amendment privilege under the system we delineate today. Our aim is to assure that the individual's right to choose between silence and speech remains unfettered throughout the interrogation process. A once-stated warning, delivered by those who will conduct the interrogation, cannot itself suffice to that end among those who most require knowledge of their rights. A mere [384 U.S. 436, 470] warning given by the interrogators is not alone sufficient to accomplish that end. Prosecutors themselves claim that the admonishment of the right to remain silent without more "will benefit only the recidivist and the professional." Brief for the National District Attorneys Association as amicus curiae, p. 14. Even preliminary advice given to the accused by his own attorney can be swiftly overcome by the secret interrogation process. Cf. Escobedo v. Illinois, 378 U.S. 478, 485, n. 5. Thus, the need for counsel to protect the Fifth Amendment privilege comprehends not merely a right to consult with counsel prior to questioning, but also to have counsel present during any questioning if the defendant so desires.

The presence of counsel at the interrogation may serve several significant subsidiary functions as well. If the accused decides to talk to his interrogators, the assistance of counsel can mitigate the dangers of untrustworthiness. With a lawyer present the likelihood that the police will practice coercion is reduced, and if coercion is nevertheless exercised the lawyer can testify to it in court. The presence of a lawyer can also help to guarantee that the accused gives a fully accurate statement to the police and that the statement is rightly reported by the prosecution at trial. See Crooker v. California, 357 U.S. 433, 443–448 (1958) (DOUGLAS, J., dissenting).

An individual need not make a pre-interrogation request for a lawyer. While such request affirmatively secures his right to have one, his failure to ask for a lawyer does not constitute a waiver. No effective waiver of the right to counsel during interrogation can be recognized unless specifically made after the warnings we here delineate have been given.

The accused who does not know his rights and therefore does not make a request [384 U.S. 436, 471] may be the person who most needs counsel. As the California Supreme Court has aptly put it:

> "Finally, we must recognize that the imposition of the requirement for the request would discriminate against the defendant who does not know his rights. The defendant who does not ask for counsel is the very defendant who most needs counsel. We cannot penalize a defendant who, not understanding his constitutional rights, does not make the formal request and by such failure demonstrates his helplessness. To require the request would be to favor the defendant whose sophistication or status had fortuitously prompted him to make it." People v. Dorado, 62 Cal. 2d 338, 351, 398 P.2d 361, 369–370, 42 Cal. Rptr. 169, 177–178 (1965) (Tobriner, J.).

In Carnley v. Cochran, 369 U.S. 506, 513 (1962), we stated: "[I]t is settled that where the assistance of counsel is a constitutional requisite, the right to be furnished counsel does not depend on a request." This proposition applies with equal force in the context of providing counsel to protect an accused's Fifth Amendment privilege in the face of interrogation.[39] Although the role of counsel at trial differs from the role during interrogation, the differences are not relevant to the question whether a request is a prerequisite.

Accordingly we hold that an individual held for interrogation must be clearly informed that he has the right to consult with a lawyer and to have the lawyer with him during interrogation under the system for protecting the privilege we delineate today. As with the warnings of the right to remain silent and that anything stated can be used in evidence against him, this warning is an absolute prerequisite to interrogation. No amount of [384 U.S. 436, 472] circumstantial evidence that the person may have been aware of this right will suffice to stand in its stead: Only through such a warning is there ascertainable assurance that the accused was aware of this right.

If an individual indicates that he wishes the assistance of counsel before any interrogation occurs, the authorities cannot rationally ignore or deny his request on the basis that the individual does not have or cannot afford a retained attorney. The financial ability of the individual has no relationship to the scope of the rights involved here. The privilege against self-incrimination secured by the Constitution applies to all individuals. The need for counsel in order to protect the privilege exists for the indigent as well as the affluent. In fact, were we to limit these constitutional rights to those who can retain an attorney, our decisions today would be of little significance. The cases before us as well as the vast majority of confession cases with which we have dealt in the past involve those unable to retain counsel.[40] While authorities are not required to relieve the accused of his poverty, they have the obligation not to take advantage of indigence in the administration of justice.[41] Denial [384 U.S. 436, 473] of counsel to the indigent at the time of interrogation while allowing an attorney to those who can afford one would be no more supportable by reason or logic than the similar situation at trial and on appeal struck down in Gideon v. Wainwright, 372 U.S. 335 (1963), and Douglas v. California, 372 U.S. 353 (1963).

In order fully to apprise a person interrogated of the extent of his rights under this system then, it is necessary to warn him not only that he has the right to consult with an attorney, but also that if he is indigent a lawyer will be appointed to represent him. Without this additional warning, the admonition of the right to consult with counsel would often be understood as meaning only that he can consult with a lawyer if he has one or has the funds to obtain one. The warning of a right to counsel would be hollow if not couched in terms that would convey to the indigent—the person most often subjected to interrogation—the knowledge that he too has a right to have counsel present.[42] As with the warnings of the right to remain silent and of the general right to counsel, only by effective and express explanation to the indigent of this right can there be assurance that he was truly in a position to exercise it.[43]

Once warnings have been given, the subsequent procedure is clear. If the individual indicates in any manner, [384 U.S. 436, 474] at any time prior to or during questioning, that he wishes to remain silent, the interrogation must cease.[44] At this point he has shown that he intends to exercise his Fifth Amendment privilege; any statement taken after the person invokes his privilege cannot be other than the product of compulsion, subtle or otherwise. Without the right to cut off questioning, the setting of in-custody interrogation operates on the individual to overcome free choice in producing a statement after the privilege has been once invoked. If the individual states that he wants an attorney, the interrogation must cease until an attorney is present. At that time, the individual must have an opportunity to confer with the attorney and to have him present during any subsequent questioning. If the individual cannot obtain an attorney and he indicates that he wants one before speaking to police, they must respect his decision to remain silent.

This does not mean, as some have suggested, that each police station must have a "station house lawyer" present at all times to advise prisoners. It does mean, however, that if police propose to interrogate a person they must make known to him that he is entitled to a lawyer and that if he cannot afford one, a lawyer will be provided for him prior to any interrogation. If authorities conclude that they will not provide counsel during a reasonable period of time in which investigation in the field is carried out, they may refrain from doing so without violating the person's Fifth Amendment privilege so long as they do not question him during that time. [384 U.S. 436, 475]

If the interrogation continues without the presence of an attorney and a statement is taken, a heavy burden rests on the government to demonstrate that the defendant knowingly and intelligently waived his privilege against self-incrimination and his right to retained or appointed counsel. Escobedo v. Illinois, 378 U.S. 478, 490, n. 14. This Court has always set high standards of proof for the waiver of constitutional rights, Johnson v. Zerbst, 304 U.S. 458 (1938), and we re-assert these standards as applied to in-custody interrogation. Since the State is responsible for establishing the isolated circumstances under which the interrogation takes place and has the only means of making available corroborated evidence of warnings given during incommunicado interrogation, the burden is rightly on its shoulders.

An express statement that the individual is willing to make a statement and does not want an attorney followed closely by a statement could constitute a waiver. But a valid waiver will not be presumed simply from the silence of the accused after warnings are given or simply from the fact that a confession was in fact eventually obtained. A statement we made in Carnley v. Cochran, 369 U.S. 506, 516 (1962), is applicable here:

> "Presuming waiver from a silent record is impermissible. The record must show, or there must be an allegation and evidence which show, that an accused was offered counsel but intelligently and understandingly rejected the offer. Anything less is not waiver."

See also Glasser v. United States, 315 U.S. 60 (1942). Moreover, where in-custody interrogation is involved, there is no room for the contention that the privilege is waived if the individual answers some questions or gives [384 U.S. 436, 476] some information on his own prior to invoking his right to remain silent when interrogated.[45]

Whatever the testimony of the authorities as to waiver of rights by an accused, the fact of lengthy interrogation or incommunicado incarceration before a statement is made is strong evidence that the accused did not validly waive his rights. In these circumstances the fact that the individual eventually made a statement is consistent with the conclusion that the compelling influence of the interrogation finally forced him to do so. It is inconsistent with any notion of a voluntary relinquishment of the privilege. Moreover, any evidence that the accused was threatened, tricked, or cajoled into a waiver will, of course, show that the defendant did not voluntarily waive his privilege. The requirement of warnings and waiver of rights is a fundamental with respect to the Fifth Amendment privilege and not simply a preliminary ritual to existing methods of interrogation.

The warnings required and the waiver necessary in accordance with our opinion today are, in the absence of a fully effective equivalent, prerequisites to the admissibility of any statement made by a defendant. No distinction can be drawn between statements which are direct confessions and statements which amount to "admissions" of part or all of an offense. The privilege against self-incrimination protects the individual from being compelled to incriminate himself in any manner; it does not distinguish degrees of incrimination. Similarly, [384 U.S. 436, 477] for precisely the same reason, no distinction may be drawn between inculpatory statements and statements alleged to be merely "exculpatory." If a statement made were in fact truly exculpatory it would, of course, never be used by the prosecution. In fact, statements merely intended to be exculpatory by the defendant are often used to impeach his testimony at trial or to demonstrate untruths in the statement given under interrogation and thus to prove guilt by implication. These statements are incriminating in any meaningful sense of the word and may not be used without the full warnings and effective waiver required for any other statement. In Escobedo itself, the defendant fully intended his accusation of another as the slayer to be exculpatory as to himself.

The principles announced today deal with the protection which must be given to the privilege against self-incrimination when the individual is first subjected to police interrogation while in custody at the station or otherwise deprived of his freedom of action in any significant way. It is at this point that our adversary system of criminal proceedings commences, distinguishing itself at the outset from the inquisitorial system recognized in some countries. Under the system of warnings we delineate today or under any other system which may be devised and found effective, the safeguards to be erected about the privilege must come into play at this point.

Our decision is not intended to hamper the traditional function of police officers in investigating crime. See Escobedo v. Illinois, 378 U.S. 478, 492. When an individual is in custody on probable cause, the police may, of course, seek out evidence in the field to be used at trial against him. Such investigation may include inquiry of persons not under restraint. General on-the-scene questioning as to facts surrounding a crime or other general questioning of citizens in the fact-finding process is not affected by our holding. It is an act of [384 U.S. 436, 478] responsible citizenship for individuals to give whatever information they may have to aid in law enforcement. In such situations the compelling atmosphere inherent in the process of in-custody interrogation is not necessarily present.[46]

In dealing with statements obtained through interrogation, we do not purport to find all confessions inadmissible. Confessions remain a proper element in law enforcement. Any statement given freely and voluntarily without any compelling influences is, of course, admissible in evidence. The fundamental import of the privilege while an individual is in custody is not whether he is allowed to talk to the police without the benefit of warnings and counsel, but whether he can be interrogated. There is no requirement that police stop a person who enters a police station and states that he wishes to confess to a crime,[47] or a person who calls the police to offer a confession or any other statement he desires to make. Volunteered statements of any kind are not barred by the Fifth Amendment and their admissibility is not affected by our holding today.

To summarize, we hold that when an individual is taken into custody or otherwise deprived of his freedom by the authorities in any significant way and is subjected to questioning, the privilege against self-incrimination is jeopardized. Procedural safeguards must be employed to [384 U.S. 436, 479] protect the privilege, and unless other fully effective means are adopted to notify the person of his right of silence and to assure that the exercise of the right will be scrupulously honored, the following measures are required. He must be warned prior to any questioning that he has the right to remain silent, that anything he says can be used against him in a court of law, that he has the right to the presence of an attorney, and that if he cannot afford an attorney one will be appointed for him prior to any questioning if he so desires. Opportunity to exercise these rights must be afforded to him throughout the interrogation. After such warnings have been given, and such opportunity afforded him, the individual may knowingly and intelligently waive these rights and agree to answer questions or make a statement. But unless and until such warnings and waiver are demonstrated by the prosecution at trial, no evidence obtained as a result of interrogation can be used against him.[48]

IV.

A recurrent argument made in these cases is that society's need for interrogation outweighs the privilege. This argument is not unfamiliar to this Court. See, e. g., Chambers v. Florida, 309 U.S. 227, 240–241 (1940). The whole thrust of our foregoing discussion demonstrates that the Constitution has prescribed the rights of the individual when confronted with the power of government when it provided in the Fifth Amendment that an individual cannot be compelled to be a witness against himself. That right cannot be abridged. As Mr. Justice Brandeis once observed:

"Decency, security and liberty alike demand that government officials shall be subjected to the same [384 U.S. 436, 480] rules of conduct that are commands to the citizen. In a government of laws,
existence of the government will be imperilled if it fails to observe
the law scrupulously. Our Government is the potent, the omnipresent
teacher. For good or for ill, it teaches the whole people by its
example. Crime is contagious. If the Government becomes a law-
breaker, it breeds contempt for law; it invites every man to become
a law unto himself; it invites anarchy. To declare that in the administration of the criminal law the end justifies the means . . . would
bring terrible retribution. Against that pernicious doctrine this
Court should resolutely set its face." Olmstead v. United States, 277
U.S. 438, 485 (1928) (dissenting opinion).[49]

In this connection, one of our country's distinguished jurists has
pointed out: "The quality of a nation's civilization can be largely measured by the methods it uses in the enforcement of its criminal law."[50]

If the individual desires to exercise his privilege, he has the right to do
so. This is not for the authorities to decide. An attorney may advise his
client not to talk to police until he has had an opportunity to investigate
the case, or he may wish to be present with his client during any police
questioning. In doing so an attorney is merely exercising the good professional judgment he has been taught. This is not cause for considering
the attorney a menace to law enforcement. He is merely carrying out
what he is sworn to do under his oath—to protect to the extent of his
ability the rights of his [384 U.S. 436, 481] client. In fulfilling this responsibility the attorney plays a vital role in the administration of criminal
justice under our Constitution.

In announcing these principles, we are not unmindful of the burdens
which law enforcement officials must bear, often under trying circumstances. We also fully recognize the obligation of all citizens to aid in
enforcing the criminal laws. This Court, while protecting individual
rights, has always given ample latitude to law enforcement agencies in the
legitimate exercise of their duties. The limits we have placed on the
interrogation process should not constitute an undue interference with a
proper system of law enforcement. As we have noted, our decision does
not in any way preclude police from carrying out their traditional investigatory functions. Although confessions may play an important role in
some convictions, the cases before us present graphic examples of the
overstatement of the "need" for confessions. In each case authorities
conducted interrogations ranging up to five days in duration despite the
presence, through standard investigating practices, of considerable evidence against each defendant.[51] Further examples are chronicled in our

prior cases. See, e. g., Haynes v. Washington, 373 U.S. 503, 518–519 (1963); Rogers v. Richmond, 365 U.S. 534, 541 (1961); Malinski v. New York, 324 U.S. 401, 402 (1945).[52] [384 U.S. 436, 482]

It is also urged that an unfettered right to detention for interrogation should be allowed because it will often redound to the benefit of the person questioned. When police inquiry determines that there is no reason to believe that the person has committed any crime, it is said, he will be released without need for further formal procedures. The person who has committed no offense, however, will be better able to clear himself after warnings with counsel present than without. It can be assumed that in such circumstances a lawyer would advise his client to talk freely to police in order to clear himself.

Custodial interrogation, by contrast, does not necessarily afford the innocent an opportunity to clear themselves. A serious consequence of the present practice of the interrogation alleged to be beneficial for the innocent is that many arrests "for investigation" subject large numbers of innocent persons to detention and interrogation. In one of the cases before us, No. 584, California v. Stewart, police held four persons, who were in the defendant's house at the time of the arrest, in jail for five days until defendant confessed. At that time they were finally released. Police stated that there was "no evidence to connect them with any crime." Available statistics on the extent of this practice where it is condoned indicate that these four are far from alone in being subjected to arrest, prolonged detention, and interrogation without the requisite probable cause.[53] [384 U.S. 436, 483]

Over the years the Federal Bureau of Investigation has compiled an exemplary record of effective law enforcement while advising any suspect or arrested person, at the outset of an interview, that he is not required to make a statement, that any statement may be used against him in court, that the individual may obtain the services of an attorney of his own choice and, more recently, that he has a right to free counsel if he is unable to pay.[54] A letter received from the Solicitor General in response to a question from the Bench makes it clear that the present pattern of warnings and respect for the [384 U.S. 436, 484] rights of the individual followed as a practice by the FBI is consistent with the procedure which we delineate today. It states:

> "At the oral argument of the above cause, Mr. Justice Fortas asked whether I could provide certain information as to the practices followed by the Federal Bureau of Investigation. I have directed these questions to the attention of the Director of the Federal Bureau of Investigation and am submitting herewith a statement of the questions and of the answers which we have received.

"'(1) When an individual is interviewed by agents of the Bureau, what warning is given to him?

"'The standard warning long given by Special Agents of the FBI to both suspects and persons under arrest is that the person has a right to say nothing and a right to counsel, and that any statement he does make may be used against him in court. Examples of this warning are to be found in the Westover case at 342 F.2d 684 (1965), and Jackson v. U.S., 337 F.2d 136 (1964), cert. den. 380 U.S. 935.

"'After passage of the Criminal Justice Act of 1964, which provides free counsel for Federal defendants unable to pay, we added to our instructions to Special Agents the requirement that any person who is under arrest for an offense under FBI jurisdiction, or whose arrest is contemplated following the interview, must also be advised of his right to free counsel if he is unable to pay, and the fact that such counsel will be assigned by the Judge. At the same time, we broadened the right to counsel warning [384 U.S. 436, 485] to read counsel of his own choice, or anyone else with whom he might wish to speak.

"'(2) When is the warning given?

"'The FBI warning is given to a suspect at the very outset of the interview, as shown in the Westover case, cited above. The warning may be given to a person arrested as soon as practicable after the arrest, as shown in the Jackson case, also cited above, and in U.S. v. Konigsberg, 336 F.2d 844 (1964), cert. den. 379 U.S. 933, but in any event it must precede the interview with the person for a confession or admission of his own guilt.

"'(3) What is the Bureau's practice in the event that (a) the individual requests counsel and (b) counsel appears?

"'When the person who has been warned of his right to counsel decides that he wishes to consult with counsel before making a statement, the interview is terminated at that point, Shultz v. U.S., 351 F.2d 287 (1965). It may be continued, however, as to all matters other than the person's own guilt or innocence. If he is indecisive in his request for counsel, there may be some question on whether he did or did not waive counsel. Situations of this kind must necessarily be left to the judgment of the interviewing Agent. For example, in Hiram v. U.S., 354 F.2d 4 (1965), the Agent's conclusion that the person arrested had waived his right to counsel was upheld by the courts.

"'A person being interviewed and desiring to consult counsel by telephone must be permitted to do so, as shown in Caldwell v. U.S., 351 F.2d 459 (1965). When counsel appears in person, he is permitted to confer with his client in private. [384 U.S. 436, 486]

"'(4) What is the Bureau's practice if the individual requests counsel, but cannot afford to retain an attorney?

"'If any person being interviewed after warning of counsel decides that he wishes to consult with counsel before proceeding further the interview is terminated, as shown above. FBI Agents do not pass judgment on the ability of the person to pay for counsel. They do, however, advise those who have been arrested for an offense under FBI jurisdiction, or whose arrest is contemplated following the interview, of a right to free counsel if they are unable to pay, and the availability of such counsel from the Judge.'"[55]

The practice of the FBI can readily be emulated by state and local enforcement agencies. The argument that the FBI deals with different crimes than are dealt with by state authorities does not mitigate the significance of the FBI experience.[56]

The experience in some other countries also suggests that the danger to law enforcement in curbs on interrogation is overplayed. The English procedure since 1912 under the Judges" Rules is significant. As recently [384 U.S. 436, 487] strengthened, the Rules require that a cautionary warning be given an accused by a police officer as soon as he has evidence that affords reasonable grounds for suspicion; they also require that any statement made be given by the accused without questioning by police.[57] [384 U.S. 436, 488] The right of the individual to consult with an attorney during this period is expressly recognized.[58]

The safeguards present under Scottish law may be even greater than in England. Scottish judicial decisions bar use in evidence of most confessions obtained through police interrogation.[59] In India, confessions made to police not in the presence of a magistrate have been excluded [384 U.S. 436, 489] by rule of evidence since 1872, at a time when it operated under British law.[60] Identical provisions appear in the Evidence Ordinance of Ceylon, enacted in 1895.[61] Similarly, in our country the Uniform Code of Military Justice has long provided that no suspect may be interrogated without first being warned of his right not to make a statement and that any statement he makes may be used against him.[62] Denial of the right to consult counsel during interrogation has also been proscribed by military tribunals.[63] There appears to have been no marked detrimental effect on criminal law enforcement in these jurisdictions as a result of these rules. Conditions of law enforcement in our country are sufficiently similar to permit reference to this experience as assurance that lawlessness will not result from warning an individual of his rights or allowing him to exercise them. Moreover, it is consistent with our legal system that we give at least as much protection to these rights as is given in the jurisdictions described. We deal in our country with rights grounded in a specific requirement of the Fifth Amendment of the Constitution, [384 U.S. 436, 490] whereas other jurisdictions arrived at their conclusions on the basis of principles of justice not so specifically defined.[64]

It is also urged upon us that we withhold decision on this issue until state legislative bodies and advisory groups have had an opportunity to deal with these problems by rule making.[65] We have already pointed out that the Constitution does not require any specific code of procedures for protecting the privilege against self-incrimination during custodial interrogation. Congress and the States are free to develop their own safeguards for the privilege, so long as they are fully as effective as those described above in informing accused persons of their right of silence and in affording a continuous opportunity to exercise it. In any event, however, the issues presented are of constitutional dimensions and must be determined by the courts. The admissibility of a statement in the face of a claim that it was obtained in violation of the defendant's constitutional rights is an issue the resolution of which has long since been undertaken by this Court. See Hopt v. Utah, 110 U.S. 574 (1884). Judicial solutions to problems of constitutional dimension have evolved decade by decade. As courts have been presented with the need to enforce constitutional rights, they have found means of doing so. That was our responsibility when Escobedo was before us and it is our [384 U.S. 436, 491] responsibility today. Where rights secured by the Constitution are involved, there can be no rule making or legislation which would abrogate them.

V.

Because of the nature of the problem and because of its recurrent significance in numerous cases, we have to this point discussed the relationship of the Fifth Amendment privilege to police interrogation without specific concentration on the facts of the cases before us. We turn now to these facts to consider the application to these cases of the constitutional principles discussed above. In each instance, we have concluded that statements were obtained from the defendant under circumstances that did not meet constitutional standards for protection of the privilege.

No. 759. Miranda v. Arizona.

On March 13, 1963, petitioner, Ernesto Miranda, was arrested at his home and taken in custody to a Phoenix police station. He was there identified by the complaining witness. The police then took him to "Interrogation Room No. 2" of the detective bureau. There he was questioned by two police officers. The officers admitted at trial that Miranda was not advised that he had a right to have an attorney present.[66] Two hours later, the [384 U.S. 436, 492] officers emerged from the interrogation room with a written confession signed by Miranda. At the top of the statement was a typed paragraph stating that the confession was made voluntarily, without threats or promises of immunity and "with full knowledge of my legal rights, understanding any statement I make may be used against me."[67]

At his trial before a jury, the written confession was admitted into evidence over the objection of defense counsel, and the officers testified to the prior oral confession made by Miranda during the interrogation. Miranda was found guilty of kidnapping and rape. He was sentenced to 20 to 30 years" imprisonment on each count, the sentences to run concurrently. On appeal, the Supreme Court of Arizona held that Miranda's constitutional rights were not violated in obtaining the confession and affirmed the conviction. 98 Ariz. 18, 401 P.2d 721. In reaching its decision, the court emphasized heavily the fact that Miranda did not specifically request counsel.

We reverse. From the testimony of the officers and by the admission of respondent, it is clear that Miranda was not in any way apprised of his right to consult with an attorney and to have one present during the interrogation, nor was his right not to be compelled to incriminate himself effectively protected in any other manner. Without these warnings the statements were inadmissible. The mere fact that he signed a statement which contained a typed-in clause stating that he had "full knowledge" of his "legal rights" does not approach the knowing and intelligent waiver required to relinquish constitutional rights. Cf. Haynes v. Washington, 373 U.S. 503, [384 U.S. 436, 493] 512–513 (1963); Haley v. Ohio, 332 U.S. 596, 601 (1948) (opinion of MR. JUSTICE DOUGLAS).

No. 760. Vignera v. New York.

Petitioner, Michael Vignera, was picked up by New York police on October 14, 1960, in connection with the robbery three days earlier of a Brooklyn dress shop. They took him to the 17th Detective Squad headquarters in Manhattan. Sometime thereafter he was taken to the 66th Detective Squad. There a detective questioned Vignera with respect to the robbery. Vignera orally admitted the robbery to the detective. The detective was asked on cross-examination at trial by defense counsel whether Vignera was warned of his right to counsel before being interrogated. The prosecution objected to the question and the trial judge sustained the objection. Thus, the defense was precluded from making any showing that warnings had not been given. While at the 66th Detective Squad, Vignera was identified by the store owner and a saleslady as the man who robbed the dress shop. At about 3 p. m. he was formally arrested. The police then transported him to still another station, the 70th Precinct in Brooklyn, "for detention." At 11 p. m. Vignera was questioned by an assistant district attorney in the presence of a hearing reporter who transcribed the questions and Vignera's answers. This verbatim account of these proceedings contains no statement of any warnings given by the assistant district attorney. At Vignera's trial on a charge of first degree robbery, the detective testified as to the oral confession. The transcription of the statement taken was also introduced in evidence. At the conclusion of the testimony, the trial judge charged the jury in part as follows:

> "The law doesn't say that the confession is void or invalidated because the police officer didn't advise the defendant as to his rights. Did you hear what [384 U.S. 436, 494] I said? I am telling you what the law of the State of New York is."

Vignera was found guilty of first degree robbery. He was subsequently adjudged a third-felony offender and sentenced to 30 to 60 years" imprisonment.[68] The conviction was affirmed without opinion by the Appellate Division, Second Department, 21 App. Div. 2d 752, 252 N. Y. S. 2d 19, and by the Court of Appeals, also without opinion, 15 N. Y. 2d 970, 207 N. E. 2d 527, 259 N. Y. S. 2d 857, remittitur amended, 16 N. Y. 2d 614, 209 N. E. 2d 110, 261 N. Y. S. 2d 65. In argument to the Court of Appeals, the State contended that Vignera had no constitutional right to be advised of his right to counsel or his privilege against self-incrimination.

We reverse. The foregoing indicates that Vignera was not warned of any of his rights before the questioning by the detective and by the assistant district attorney. No other steps were taken to protect these rights. Thus he was not effectively apprised of his Fifth Amendment privilege or of his right to have counsel present and his statements are inadmissible.

No. 761. Westover v. United States.

At approximately 9:45 p. m. on March 20, 1963, petitioner, Carl Calvin Westover, was arrested by local police in Kansas City as a suspect in two Kansas City robberies. A report was also received from the FBI that he was wanted on a felony charge in California. The local authorities took him to a police station and placed him in a line-up on the local charges, and at about 11:45 p. m. he was booked. Kansas City police interrogated Westover [384 U.S. 436, 495] on the night of his arrest. He denied any knowledge of criminal activities. The next day local officers interrogated him again throughout the morning. Shortly before noon they informed the FBI that they were through interrogating Westover and that the FBI could proceed to interrogate him. There is nothing in the record to indicate that Westover was ever given any warning as to his rights by local police. At noon, three special agents of the FBI continued the interrogation in a private interview room of the Kansas City Police Department, this time with respect to the robbery of a savings and loan association and a bank in Sacramento, California. After two or two and one-half hours, Westover signed separate confessions to each of these two robberies which had been prepared by one of the agents during the interrogation. At trial one of the agents testified, and a paragraph on each of the statements states, that the agents advised Westover that he did not have to make a statement, that any statement he made could be used against him, and that he had the right to see an attorney.

Westover was tried by a jury in federal court and convicted of the California robberies. His statements were introduced at trial. He was sentenced to 15 years imprisonment on each count, the sentences to run consecutively. On appeal, the conviction was affirmed by the Court of Appeals for the Ninth Circuit. 342 F.2d 684.

We reverse. On the facts of this case we cannot find that Westover knowingly and intelligently waived his right to remain silent and his right to consult with counsel prior to the time he made the statement.[69] At the [384 U.S. 436, 496] time the FBI agents began questioning Westover, he had been in custody for over 14 hours and had been interrogated at length during that period. The FBI interrogation began immediately upon the conclusion of the interrogation by Kansas City police and was conducted in local police headquarters. Although the two law enforcement authorities are legally distinct and the crimes for which they interrogated Westover were different, the impact on him was that of a continuous period of questioning. There is no evidence of any warning given prior to the FBI interrogation nor is there any evidence of an articulated waiver of rights after the FBI commenced its interrogation. The record simply shows that the defendant did in fact confess a short time after being turned over to the FBI following interrogation by local police. Despite the fact that the FBI agents gave warnings at the outset of their interview, from Westover's point of view the warnings came at the end of the interrogation process. In these circumstances an intelligent waiver of constitutional rights cannot be assumed.

We do not suggest that law enforcement authorities are precluded from questioning any individual who has been held for a period of time by other authorities and interrogated by them without appropriate warnings. A different case would be presented if an accused were taken into custody by the second authority, removed both in time and place from his original surroundings, and then adequately advised of his rights and given an opportunity to exercise them. But here the FBI interrogation was conducted immediately following the state interrogation in the same police station—in the same compelling surroundings. Thus, in obtaining a confession from Westover [384 U.S. 436, 497] the federal authorities were the beneficiaries of the pressure applied by the local in-custody interrogation. In these circumstances the giving of warnings alone was not sufficient to protect the privilege.

No. 584. California v. Stewart.

In the course of investigating a series of purse-snatch robberies in which one of the victims had died of injuries inflicted by her assailant, respondent, Roy Allen Stewart, was pointed out to Los Angeles police as the endorser of dividend checks taken in one of the robberies. At about 7:15 p. m., January 31, 1963, police officers went to Stewart's house and arrested him. One of the officers asked Stewart if they could search the house, to which he replied, "Go ahead." The search turned up various items taken from the five robbery victims. At the time of Stewart's arrest, police also arrested Stewart's wife and three other persons who were visiting him. These four were jailed along with Stewart and were interrogated. Stewart was taken to the University Station of the Los Angeles Police Department where he was placed in a cell. During the next five days, police interrogated Stewart on nine different occasions. Except during the first interrogation session, when he was confronted with an accusing witness, Stewart was isolated with his interrogators.

During the ninth interrogation session, Stewart admitted that he had robbed the deceased and stated that he had not meant to hurt her. Police then brought Stewart before a magistrate for the first time. Since there was no evidence to connect them with any crime, the police then released the other four persons arrested with him.

Nothing in the record specifically indicates whether Stewart was or was not advised of his right to remain silent or his right to counsel. In a number of instances, [384 U.S. 436, 498] however, the interrogating officers were asked to recount everything that was said during the interrogations. None indicated that Stewart was ever advised of his rights.

Stewart was charged with kidnapping to commit robbery, rape, and murder. At his trial, transcripts of the first interrogation and the confession at the last interrogation were introduced in evidence. The jury found Stewart guilty of robbery and first degree murder and fixed the penalty as death. On appeal, the Supreme Court of California reversed. 62 Cal. 2d 571, 400 P.2d 97, 43 Cal. Rptr. 201. It held that under this Court's decision in Escobedo, Stewart should have been advised of his right to remain silent and of his right to counsel and that it would not presume in the face of a silent record that the police advised Stewart of his rights.[70]

We affirm.[71] In dealing with custodial interrogation, we will not presume that a defendant has been effectively apprised of his rights and that his privilege against self-incrimination has been adequately safeguarded on a record that does not show that any warnings have been given or that any effective alternative has been employed. Nor can a knowing and intelligent waiver of [384 U.S. 436, 499] these rights be assumed on a silent record. Furthermore, Stewart's steadfast denial of the alleged offenses through eight of the nine interrogations over a period of five days is subject to no other construction than that he was compelled by persistent interrogation to forgo his Fifth Amendment privilege.

Therefore, in accordance with the foregoing, the judgments of the Supreme Court of Arizona in No. 759, of the New York Court of Appeals in No. 760, and of the Court of Appeals for the Ninth Circuit in No. 761 are reversed. The judgment of the Supreme Court of California in No. 584 is affirmed.

It is so ordered.

FOOTNOTES

[1] Compare United States v. Childress, 347 F.2d 448 (C. A. 7th Cir. 1965), with Collins v. Beto, 348 F.2d 823 (C. A. 5th Cir. 1965). Compare People v. Dorado, 62 Cal. 2d 338, 398 P.2d 361, 42 Cal. Rptr. 169 (1964) with People v. Hartgraves, 31 Ill. 2d 375, 202 N. E. 2d 33 (1964).

[2] See, e. g., Enker & Elsen, Counsel for the Suspect: Massiah v. United States and Escobedo v. Illinois, 49 Minn. L. Rev. 47 (1964); Herman, The Supreme Court and Restrictions on Police Interrogation, 25 Ohio St. L. J. 449 (1964); Kamisar, Equal Justice in the Gatehouses and Mansions of American Criminal Procedure, in Criminal Justice in Our Time 1 (1965); Dowling, Escobedo and [384 U.S. 436, 441] Beyond: The Need for a Fourteenth Amendment Code of Criminal Procedure, 56 J. Crim. L., C. & P. S. 143, 156 (1965).

The complex problems also prompted discussions by jurists. Compare Bazelon, Law, Morality, and Civil Liberties, 12 U. C. L. A. L. Rev. 13 (1964), with Friendly, The Bill of Rights as a Code of Criminal Procedure, 53 Calif. L. Rev. 929 (1965).

[3] For example, the Los Angeles Police Chief stated that "If the police are required . . . to . . . establish that the defendant was apprised of his constitutional guarantees of silence and legal counsel prior to the uttering of any admission or confession, and that he intelligently waived these guarantees . . . a whole Pandora's box is opened as to under what circumstances . . . can a defendant intelligently waive these rights. . . . Allegations that modern criminal investigation can compensate for the lack of a confession or admission in every criminal case is totally absurd!" Parker, 40 L. A. Bar Bull. 603, 607, 642 (1965). His prosecutorial counterpart, District Attorney Younger, stated that "[I]t begins to appear that many of these seemingly restrictive decisions are going to contribute directly to a more effective, efficient and professional level of law enforcement." L. A. Times, Oct. 2, 1965, p. 1. The former Police Commissioner of New York, Michael J. Murphy, stated of Escobedo: "What the Court is doing is akin to requiring one boxer to fight by Marquis of Queensbury rules while permitting the other to butt, gouge and bite." N. Y. Times, May 14, 1965, p. 39. The former United States Attorney for the District of Columbia, David C. Acheson, who is presently Special Assistant to the Secretary of the Treasury (for Enforcement), and directly in charge of the Secret Service and the Bureau of Narcotics, observed that "Prosecution procedure has, at most, only the most remote causal connection with crime. Changes in court decisions and prosecution procedure would have about the same effect on the crime rate as an aspirin would have on a tumor of the brain." Quoted in Herman, supra, n. 2, at 500, n. 270. Other views on the subject in general are collected in Weisberg, Police Interrogation of Arrested Persons: A Skeptical View, 52 J. Crim. L., C. & P. S. 21 (1961).

[4] This is what we meant in Escobedo when we spoke of an investigation which had focused on an accused.

[5] See, for example, IV National Commission on Law Observance and Enforcement, Report on Lawlessness in Law Enforcement (1931) [384 U.S. 436, 446] [Wickersham Report]; Booth, Confessions, and Methods Employed in Procuring Them, 4 So. Calif. L. Rev. 83 (1930); Kauper, Judicial Examination of the Accused—A Remedy for the Third Degree, 30 Mich. L. Rev. 1224 (1932). It is significant that instances of third-degree treatment of prisoners almost invariably took place during the period between arrest and preliminary examination. Wickersham Report, at 169; Hall, The Law of Arrest in Relation to Contemporary Social Problems, 3 U. Chi. L. Rev. 345, 357 (1936). See also Foote, Law and Police Practice: Safeguards in the Law of Arrest, 52 Nw. U. L. Rev. 16 (1957).

[6] Brown v. Mississippi, 297 U.S. 278 (1936); Chambers v. Florida, 309 U.S. 227 (1940); Canty v. Alabama, 309 U.S. 629 (1940); White v. Texas, 310 U.S. 530 (1940); Vernon v. Alabama, 313 U.S. 547 (1941); Ward v. Texas, 316 U.S. 547 (1942); Ashcraft v. Tennessee, 322 U.S. 143 (1944); Malinski v. New York, 324 U.S. 401 (1945); Leyra v. Denno, 347 U.S. 556 (1954). See also Williams v. United States, 341 U.S. 97 (1951).

[7] In addition, see People v. Wakat, 415 Ill. 610, 114 N. E. 2d 706 (1953); Wakat v. Harlib, 253 F.2d 59 (C. A. 7th Cir. 1958) (defendant suffering from broken bones, multiple bruises and injuries sufficiently serious to require eight months" medical treatment after being manhandled by five policemen); Kier v. State, 213 Md. 556, 132 A. 2d 494 (1957) (police doctor told accused, who was [384 U.S. 436, 447] strapped to a chair completely nude, that he proposed to take hair and skin scrapings from anything that looked like blood or sperm from various parts of his body); Bruner v. People, 113 Colo. 194, 156 P.2d 111 (1945) (defendant held in custody over two months, deprived of food for 15 hours, forced to submit to a lie detector test when he wanted to go to the toilet); People v. Matlock, 51 Cal. 2d 682, 336 P.2d 505 (1959) (defendant questioned incessantly over an evening's time, made to lie on cold board and to answer questions whenever it appeared he was getting sleepy). Other cases are documented in American Civil Liberties Union, Illinois Division, Secret Detention by the Chicago Police (1959); Potts, The Preliminary Examination and "The Third Degree," 2 Baylor L. Rev. 131 (1950); Sterling, Police Interrogation and the Psychology of Confession, 14 J. Pub. L. 25 (1965).

[8] The manuals quoted in the text following are the most recent and representative of the texts currently available. Material of the same nature appears in Kidd, Police Interrogation (1940); Mulbar, Interrogation (1951); Dienstein, Technics for the Crime Investigator 97–115 (1952). Studies concerning the observed practices of the police appear in LaFave, Arrest: The Decision To Take a Suspect Into Custody 244–437, 490–521 (1965); LaFave, Detention for Investigation by the Police: An Analysis of Current Practices, 1962 Wash. U. L. Q. 331; Barrett, Police Practices and the Law—From Arrest to Release or Charge, 50 Calif. L. Rev. 11 (1962); Sterling, supra, n. 7, at 47–65.

[9] The methods described in Inbau & Reid, Criminal Interrogation and Confessions (1962), are a revision and enlargement of material presented in three prior editions of a predecessor text, Lie Detection and Criminal Interrogation (3d ed. 1953). The authors and their associates are officers of the Chicago Police Scientific Crime Detection Laboratory and have had extensive experience in writing, lecturing and speaking to law enforcement authorities over a 20-year period. They say that the techniques portrayed in their manuals reflect their experiences and are the most effective psychological stratagems to employ during interrogations. Similarly, the techniques described in O'Hara, Fundamentals of Criminal Investigation (1956), were gleaned from long service as observer, lecturer in police science, and work as a federal criminal investigator. All these texts have had rather extensive use among law enforcement agencies and among students of police science, with total sales and circulation of over 44,000.

[10] Inbau & Reid, Criminal Interrogation and Confessions (1962), at 1.

[11] O'Hara, supra, at 99.

[12] Inbau & Reid, supra, at 34–43, 87. For example, in Leyra v. Denno, 347 U.S. 556 (1954),

the interrogator–psychiatrist told the accused, "We do sometimes things that are not right, but in a fit of temper or anger we sometimes do things we aren't really responsible for, id., at 562, and again, "We know that morally you were just in anger. Morally, you are not to be condemned," id., at 582.

[13] Inbau & Reid, supra, at 43–55.

[14] O'Hara, supra, at 112.

[15] Inbau & Reid, supra, at 40.

[16] Ibid.

[17] O'Hara, supra, at 104, Inbau & Reid, supra, at 58–59. See Spano v. New York, 360 U.S. 315 (1959). A variant on the technique [384 U.S. 436, 453] of creating hostility is one of engendering fear. This is perhaps best described by the prosecuting attorney in Malinski v. New York, 324 U.S. 401, 407 (1945): "Why this talk about being undressed? Of course, they had a right to undress him to look for bullet scars, and keep the clothes off him. That was quite proper police procedure. That is some more psychology—let him sit around with a blanket on him, humiliate him there for a while; let him sit in the corner, let him think he is going to get a shellacking."

[18] O'Hara, supra, at 105–106.

[19] Id., at 106.

[20] Inbau & Reid, supra, at 111.

[21] Ibid.

[22] Inbau & Reid, supra, at 112.

[23] Inbau & Reid, Lie Detection and Criminal Interrogation 185 (3d ed. 1953).

[24] Interrogation procedures may even give rise to a false confession. The most recent conspicuous example occurred in New York, in 1964, when a Negro of limited intelligence confessed to two brutal murders and a rape which he had not committed. When this was discovered, the prosecutor was reported as saying: "Call it what you want—brainwashing, hypnosis, fright. They made him give an untrue confession. The only thing I don't believe is that Whitmore was beaten." N. Y. Times, Jan. 28, 1965, p. 1, col. 5. In two other instances, similar events had occurred. N. Y. Times, Oct. 20, 1964, p. 22, col. 1; N. Y. Times, Aug. 25, 1965, p. 1, col. 1. In general, see Borchard, Convicting the Innocent (1932); Frank & Frank, Not Guilty (1957).

[25] In the fourth confession case decided by the Court in the 1962 Term, Fay v. Noia, 372 U.S. 391 (1963), our disposition made it unnecessary to delve at length into the facts. The facts of the defendant's case there, however, paralleled those of his co-defendants, whose confessions were found to have resulted from continuous and coercive interrogation for 27 hours, with denial of requests for friends or attorney. See United States v. Murphy, 222 F.2d 698 (C. A. 2d Cir. 1955) (Frank, J.); People v. Bonino, 1 N. Y. 2d 752, 135 N. E. 2d 51 (1956).

[26] The absurdity of denying that a confession obtained under these circumstances is compelled is aptly portrayed by an example in Professor [384 U.S. 436, 458] Sutherland's recent article, Crime and Confession, 79 Harv. L. Rev. 21, 37 (1965):

"Suppose a well-to-do testatrix says she intends to will her property to Elizabeth. John and James want her to bequeath it to them instead. They capture the testatrix, put her in a carefully designed room, out of touch with everyone but themselves and their convenient "witnesses," keep her secluded there for hours while they make insistent demands, weary her with contradictions of her assertions that she wants to leave her money to Elizabeth, and finally induce her to execute the will in their favor. Assume that John and James are deeply and correctly convinced that Elizabeth is unworthy and will make base use of the property if she gets her hands on it, whereas John and James have the noblest and most righteous intentions. Would any judge of probate accept the will so procured as the "voluntary" act of the testatrix?"

[27] Thirteenth century commentators found an analogue to the privilege grounded in the Bible. "To sum up the matter, the principle that no man is to be declared guilty on his own admission is a divine decree." Maimonides, Mishneh Torah (Code of Jewish Law), Book of Judges, Laws of the Sanhedrin, c. 18, □ 6, III Yale Judaica Series 52–53. See also Lamm, The Fifth Amendment and Its Equivalent in the Halakhah, 5 Judaism 53 (Winter 1956).

[28] See Morgan, The Privilege Against Self-Incrimination, 34 Minn. L. Rev. 1, 9–11 (1949); 8 Wigmore, Evidence 289–295 (McNaughton rev. 1961). See also Lowell, The Judicial Use of Torture, Parts I and II, 11 Harv. L. Rev. 220, 290 (1897).

[29] See Pittman, The Colonial and Constitutional History of the Privilege Against Self-Incrimination in America, 21 Va. L. Rev. 763 (1935); Ullmann v. United States, 350 U.S. 422, 445–449 (1956) (DOUGLAS, J., dissenting).

[30] Compare Brown v. Walker, 161 U.S. 591 (1896); Quinn v. United States, 349 U.S. 155 (1955).

[31] Brief for the United States, p. 28. To the same effect, see Brief for the United States, pp. 40–49, n. 44, Anderson v. United States, 318 U.S. 350 (1943); Brief for the United States, pp. 17–18, McNabb v. United States, 318 U.S. 332 (1943).

[32] Our decision today does not indicate in any manner, of course, that these rules can be disregarded. When federal officials arrest an individual, they must as always comply with the dictates of the congressional legislation and cases thereunder. See generally, Hogan & Snee, The McNabb-Mallory Rule: Its Rise, Rationale and Rescue, 47 Geo. L. J. 1 (1958).

[33] The decisions of this Court have guaranteed the same procedural protection for the defendant whether his confession was used in a federal or state court. It is now axiomatic that the defendant's constitutional rights have been violated if his conviction is based, in whole or in part, on an involuntary confession, regardless of its truth or falsity. Rogers v. Richmond, 365 U.S. 534, 544 (1961); Wan v. United States, 266 U.S. 1 (1924). This is so even if there is ample evidence aside from the confession to support the conviction, e. g., Malinski v. New York, 324 U.S. 401, 404 (1945); Bram v. United States, 168 U.S. 532, 540–542 (1897). Both state and federal courts now adhere to trial procedures which seek to assure a reliable and clear-cut determination of the voluntariness of the confession offered at trial, Jackson v. Denno, 378 U.S. 368 (1964); United States v. Carignan, 342 U.S. 36, 38 (1951); see also Wilson v. United States, 162 U.S. 613, 624 (1896). Appellate review is exacting, see Haynes v. Washington, 373 U.S. 503 (1963); Blackburn v. Alabama, 361 U.S. 199 (1960). Whether his conviction was in a federal or state court, the defendant may secure a post-conviction hearing based on the alleged involuntary character of his confession, provided he meets the procedural requirements, Fay v. Noia, 372 U.S. 391 (1963); Townsend v. Sain, 372 U.S. 293 (1963). In addition, see Murphy v. Waterfront Comm'n, 378 U.S. 52 (1964).

[34] See Lisenba v. California, 314 U.S. 219, 241 (1941); Ashcraft v. Tennessee, 322 U.S. 143 (1944); Malinski v. New York, 324 U.S. 401 (1945); Spano v. New York, 360 U.S. 315 (1959); Lynumn v. Illinois, 372 U.S. 528 (1963); Haynes v. Washington, 373 U.S. 503 (1963).

[35] The police also prevented the attorney from consulting with his client. Independent of any other constitutional proscription, this action constitutes a violation of the Sixth Amendment right to the assistance of counsel and excludes any statement obtained in its [384 U.S. 436, 466] wake. See People v. Donovan, 13 N. Y. 2d 148, 193 N. E. 2d 628, 243 N. Y. S. 2d 841 (1963) (Fuld, J.).

[36] In re Groban, 352 U.S. 330, 340–352 (1957) (BLACK, J., dissenting); Note, 73 Yale L. J. 1000, 1048–1051 (1964); Comment, 31 U. Chi. L. Rev. 313, 320 (1964) and authorities cited.

[37] See p. 454, supra. Lord Devlin has commented:

"It is probable that even today, when there is much less ignorance about these matters than formerly, there is still a general belief that you must answer all questions put to you by a policeman, or at least that it will be the worse for you if you do not." Devlin, The Criminal Prosecution in England 32 (1958).

In accord with our decision today, it is impermissible to penalize an individual for exercising his Fifth Amendment privilege when he is under police custodial interrogation. The prosecution may not, therefore, use at trial the fact that he stood mute or claimed his privilege in the face of accusation. Cf. Griffin v. California, 380 U.S. 609 (1965); Malloy v. Hogan, 378 U.S. 1, 8 (1964); Comment, 31 U. Chi. L. Rev. 556 (1964); Developments in the Law—Confessions, 79 Harv. L. Rev. 935, 1041–1044 (1966). See also Bram v. United States, 168 U.S. 532, 562 (1897).

[38] Cf. Betts v. Brady, 316 U.S. 455 (1942), and the recurrent inquiry into special circumstances it necessitated. See generally, Kamisar, Betts v. Brady Twenty Years Later: The Right to Counsel and Due Process Values, 61 Mich. L. Rev. 219 (1962).

[39] See Herman, The Supreme Court and Restrictions on Police Interrogation, 25 Ohio St. L. J. 449, 480 (1964).

[40] Estimates of 50–90% indigency among felony defendants have been reported. Pollock, Equal Justice in Practice, 45 Minn. L. Rev. 737, 738–739 (1961); Birzon, Kasanof & Forma, The Right to Counsel and the Indigent Accused in Courts of Criminal Jurisdiction in New York State, 14 Buffalo L. Rev. 428, 433 (1965).

[41] See Kamisar, Equal Justice in the Gatehouses and Mansions of American Criminal Procedure, in Criminal Justice in Our Time 1, 64–81 (1965). As was stated in the Report of the Attorney General's Committee on Poverty and the Administration of Federal Criminal Justice 9 (1963):

"When government chooses to exert its powers in the criminal area, its obligation is surely no less than that of taking reasonable measures to eliminate those factors that are irrelevant to just administration of the law but which, nevertheless, may occasionally affect determinations of the accused's liability or penalty. While government [384 U.S. 436, 473] may not be required to relieve the accused of his poverty, it may properly be required to minimize the influence of poverty on its administration of justice."

[42] Cf. United States ex rel. Brown v. Fay, 242 F. Supp. 273, 277 (D.C. S. D. N. Y. 1965); People v. Witenski, 15 N. Y. 2d 392, 207 N. E. 2d 358, 259 N. Y. S. 2d 413 (1965).

[43] While a warning that the indigent may have counsel appointed need not be given to the person who is known to have an attorney or is known to have ample funds to secure one, the expedient of giving a warning is too simple and the rights involved too important to engage in ex post facto inquiries into financial ability when there is any doubt at all on that score.

[44] If an individual indicates his desire to remain silent, but has an attorney present, there may be some circumstances in which further questioning would be permissible. In the absence of evidence of overbearing, statements then made in the presence of counsel might be free of the compelling influence of the interrogation process and might fairly be construed as a waiver of the privilege for purposes of these statements.

[45] Although this Court held in Rogers v. United States, 340 U.S. 367 (1951), over strong dissent, that a witness before a grand jury may not in certain circumstances decide to answer some questions and then refuse to answer others, that decision has no application to the interrogation situation we deal with today. No legislative or judicial fact-finding authority is involved here, nor is there a possibility that the individual might make self-serving statements of which he could make use at trial while refusing to answer incriminating statements.

[46] The distinction and its significance has been aptly described in the opinion of a Scottish court:

"In former times such questioning, if undertaken, would be conducted by police officers visiting the house or place of business of the suspect and there questioning him, probably in the presence of a relation or friend. However convenient the modern practice may be, it must normally create a situation very unfavorable to the suspect." Chalmers v. H. M. Advocate, 1954. Sess. Cas. 66, 78 (J. C.).

[47] See People v. Dorado, 62 Cal. 2d 338, 354, 398 P.2d 361, 371, 42 Cal. Rptr. 169, 179 (1965).

[48] In accordance with our holdings today and in Escobedo v. Illinois, 378 U.S. 478, 492, Crooker v. California, 357 U.S. 433 (1958) and Cicenia v. Lagay, 357 U.S. 504 (1958) are not to be followed.

[49] In quoting the above from the dissenting opinion of Mr. Justice Brandeis we, of course, do not intend to pass on the constitutional questions involved in the Olmstead case.

[50] Schaefer, Federalism and State Criminal Procedure, 70 Harv. L. Rev. 1, 26 (1956).

[51] Miranda, Vignera, and Westover were identified by eyewitnesses. Marked bills from the bank robbed were found in Westover's car. Articles stolen from the victim as well as from several other robbery victims were found in Stewart's home at the outset of the investigation.

[52] Dealing as we do here with constitutional standards in relation to statements made, the existence of independent corroborating evidence produced at trial is, of course, irrelevant to our decisions. Haynes v. Washington, 373 U.S. 503, 518–519 (1963); Lynumn v. [384 U.S. 436, 482] Illinois, 372 U.S. 528, 537–538 (1963); Rogers v. Richmond, 365 U.S. 534, 541 (1961); Blackburn v. Alabama, 361 U.S. 199, 206 (1960).

[53] See, e. g., Report and Recommendations of the [District of Columbia] Commissioners" Committee on Police Arrests for Investigation (1962); American Civil Liberties Union, Secret Detention by the Chicago Police (1959). An extreme example of this practice occurred in the District of Columbia in 1958. Seeking three "stocky" young Negroes who had robbed a restaurant, police rounded up 90 persons of that general description. Sixty-three were held overnight [384 U.S. 436, 483] before being released for lack of evidence. A man not among the 90 arrested was ultimately charged with the crime. Washington Daily News, January 21, 1958, p. 5, col. 1; Hearings before a Subcommittee of the Senate Judiciary Committee on H. R. 11477, S. 2970, S. 3325, and S. 3355, 85th Cong., 2d Sess. (July 1958), pp. 40, 78.

[54] In 1952, J. Edgar Hoover, Director of the Federal Bureau of Investigation, stated:
"Law enforcement, however, in defeating the criminal, must maintain inviolate the historic liberties of the individual. To turn back the criminal, yet, by so doing, destroy the dignity of the individual, would be a hollow victory.

"We can have the Constitution, the best laws in the land, and the most honest reviews by courts—but unless the law enforcement profession is steeped in the democratic tradition, maintains the highest in ethics, and makes its work a career of honor, civil liberties will continually—and without end—be violated.... The best protection of civil liberties is an alert, intelligent and honest law enforcement agency. There can be no alternative.

". . . Special Agents are taught that any suspect or arrested person, at the outset of an interview, must be advised that he is not required to make a statement and that any statement given can be used against him in court. Moreover, the individual must be informed that, if he desires, he may obtain the services of an attorney of his own choice."
Hoover, Civil Liberties and Law Enforcement: The Role of the FBI, 37 Iowa L. Rev. 175, 177–182 (1952).

[55] We agree that the interviewing agent must exercise his judgment in determining whether the individual waives his right to counsel. Because of the constitutional basis of the right, however, the standard for waiver is necessarily high. And, of course, the ultimate responsibility for resolving this constitutional question lies with the courts.

[56] Among the crimes within the enforcement jurisdiction of the FBI are kidnapping, 18 U.S.C. 1201 (1964 ed.), white slavery, 18 U.S.C. 2421–2423 (1964 ed.), bank robbery, 18 U.S.C. 2113 (1964 ed.), interstate transportation and sale of stolen property, 18 U.S.C. 2311–2317 (1964 ed.), all manner of conspiracies, 18 U.S.C. 371 (1964 ed.), and violations of civil rights, 18 U.S.C. 241–242 (1964 ed.). See also 18 U.S.C. 1114 (1964 ed.) (murder of officer or employee of the United States).

[57] 1964. Crim. L. Rev., at 166–170. These Rules provide in part:

> "II. As soon as a police officer has evidence which would afford reasonable grounds for suspecting that a person has committed an offence, he shall caution that person or cause him to be cautioned before putting to him any questions, or further questions, relating to that offence.
> "The caution shall be in the following terms:
> "'You are not obliged to say anything unless you wish to do so but what you say may be put into writing and given in evidence.'"
> "When after being cautioned a person is being questioned, or elects to make a statement, a record shall be kept of the time and place at which any such questioning or statement began and ended and of the persons present.

> "III. . . .
> "(b) It is only in exceptional cases that questions relating to the offence should be put to the accused person after he has been charged or informed that he may be prosecuted.

> "IV. All written statements made after caution shall be taken in the following manner:
> "(a) If a person says that he wants to make a statement he shall be told that it is intended to make a written record of what he says.
> "He shall always be asked whether he wishes to write down himself what he wants to say; if he says that he cannot write or that he would like someone to write it for him, a police officer may offer to write the statement for him. . . .
> "(b) Any person writing his own statement shall be allowed to do so without any prompting as distinct from indicating to him what matters are material.
> "(d) Whenever a police officer writes the statement, he shall take down the exact words spoken by the person making the statement, without putting any questions other than such as may be needed to [384 U.S. 436, 488] make the statement coherent, intelligible and relevant to the material matters: he shall not prompt him."

The prior Rules appear in Devlin, The Criminal Prosecution in England 137–141 (1958). Despite suggestions of some laxity in enforcement of the Rules and despite the fact some discretion as to admissibility is invested in the trial judge, the Rules are a significant influence in the English criminal law enforcement system. See, e. g., 1964. Crim. L. Rev., at 182; and articles collected in 1960. Crim. L. Rev., at 298–356.

[58] The introduction to the Judges" Rules states in part:

"These Rules do not affect the principles

(c) "That every person at any stage of an investigation should be able to communicate and to consult privately with a solicitor. This is so even if he is in custody
provided that in such a case no unreasonable delay or hindrance is caused to the
processes of investigation or the administration of justice by his doing so . . . ." 1964.
Crim. L. Rev., at 166–167.

[59] As stated by the Lord Justice General in Chalmers v. H. M. Advocate, 1954. Sess. Cas.
66, 78 (J. C.):

"The theory of our law is that at the stage of initial investigation the police may
question anyone with a view to acquiring information which may lead to the
detection of the criminal; but that, when the stage has been reached at which suspicion, or more than suspicion, has in their view centred upon some person as
the likely perpetrator of the crime, further interrogation of that person becomes
very dangerous, and, if carried too far, e. g., to the point of extracting a confession by what amounts to cross-examination, the evidence of that confession will
almost certainly be excluded. Once the accused has been apprehended and
charged he has the statutory right to a private interview with a solicitor and to
be brought before a magistrate with all convenient speed so that he may, if so
advised, emit a declaration in presence of his solicitor under conditions which
safeguard him against prejudice."

[60] "No confession made to a police officer shall be proved as against a person accused of
any offence." Indian Evidence Act 25.

"No confession made by any person whilst he is in the custody of a police officer
unless it be made in the immediate presence of a Magistrate, shall be proved as
against such person." Indian Evidence Act 26. See 1 Ramaswami & Rajagopalan,
Law of Evidence in India 553–569 (1962). To avoid any continuing effect of police
pressure or inducement, the Indian Supreme Court has invalidated a confession
made shortly after police brought a suspect before a magistrate, suggesting: "[I]t
would, we think, be reasonable to insist upon giving an accused person at least 24
hours to decide whether or not he should make a confession." Sarwan Singh v.
State of Punjab, 44 All India Rep. 1957, Sup. Ct. 637, 644.

[61] I Legislative Enactments of Ceylon 211 (1958).

[62] 10 U.S.C. 831 (b) (1964 ed.).

[63] United States v. Rose, 24 CMR 251 (1957); United States v. Gunnels, 23 CMR 354
(1957).

[64] Although no constitution existed at the time confessions were excluded by rule of evidence in 1872, India now has a written constitution which includes the provision that
"No person accused of any offence shall be compelled to be a witness against himself."
Constitution of India, Article 20 (3). See Tope, The Constitution of India 63–67
(1960).

[65] Brief for United States in No. 761, Westover v. United States, pp. 44–47; Brief for the
State of New York as amicus curiae, pp. 35–39. See also Brief for the National District
Attorneys Association as amicus curiae, pp. 23–26.

[66] Miranda was also convicted in a separate trial on an unrelated robbery charge not presented here for review. A statement introduced at that trial was obtained from Miranda
during the same interrogation which resulted in the confession involved here. At the
robbery trial, one officer testified that during the interrogation he did not tell Miranda
that anything he said would be held against him or that he could consult with an attor-

ney. The other officer stated that they had both told Miranda that anything he said would be used against him and that he was not required by law to tell them anything.

[67] One of the officers testified that he read this paragraph to Miranda. Apparently, however, he did not do so until after Miranda had confessed orally.

[68] Vignera thereafter successfully attacked the validity of one of the prior convictions, Vignera v. Wilkins, Civ. 9901 (D.C. W. D. N. Y. Dec. 31, 1961) (unreported), but was then resentenced as a second-felony offender to the same term of imprisonment as the original sentence. R. 31–33.

[69] The failure of defense counsel to object to the introduction of the confession at trial, noted by the Court of Appeals and emphasized by the Solicitor General, does not preclude our consideration of the issue. Since the trial was held prior to our decision in Escobedo and, of course, prior to our decision today making the [384 U.S. 436, 496] objection available, the failure to object at trial does not constitute a waiver of the claim. See, e. g., United States ex rel. Angelet v. Fay, 333 F.2d 12, 16 (C. A. 2d Cir. 1964), aff'd, 381 U.S. 654 (1965). Cf. Ziffrin, Inc. v. United States, 318 U.S. 73, 78 (1943).

[70] Because of this disposition of the case, the California Supreme Court did not reach the claims that the confession was coerced by police threats to hold his ailing wife in custody until he confessed, that there was no hearing as required by Jackson v. Denno, 378 U.S. 368 (1964), and that the trial judge gave an instruction condemned by the California Supreme Court's decision in People v. Morse, 60 Cal. 2d 631, 388 P.2d 33, 36 Cal. Rptr. 201 (1964).

[71] After certiorari was granted in this case, respondent moved to dismiss on the ground that there was no final judgment from which the State could appeal since the judgment below directed that he be retried. In the event respondent was successful in obtaining an acquittal on retrial, however, under California law the State would have no appeal. Satisfied that in these circumstances the decision below constituted a final judgment under 28 U.S.C. 1257 (3) (1964 ed.), we denied the motion. 383 U.S. 903.

MR. JUSTICE CLARK, dissenting in Nos. 759, 760, and 761, and concurring in the result in No. 584.

It is with regret that I find it necessary to write in these cases. However, I am unable to join the majority because its opinion goes too far on too little, while my dissenting brethren do not go quite far enough. Nor can I join in the Court's criticism of the present practices of police and investigatory agencies as to custodial interrogation. The materials it refers to as "police manuals"[1] are, as I read them, merely writings in this field by professors and some police officers. Not one is shown by the record here to be the official manual of any police department, much less in universal use in crime detection. Moreover, the examples of police brutality mentioned by the Court[2] are rare exceptions to the thousands of cases [384 U.S. 436, 500] that appear every year in the law reports. The police agencies—all the way from municipal and state forces to the federal bureaus—are responsible for law enforcement and public safety in this country. I am proud of their efforts, which in my view are not fairly characterized by the Court's opinion.

I.

The ipse dixit of the majority has no support in our cases. Indeed, the Court admits that "we might not find the defendants'" statements [here] to have been involuntary in traditional terms." Ante, p. 457. In short, the Court has added more to the requirements that the accused is entitled to consult with his lawyer and that he must be given the traditional warning that he may remain silent and that anything that he says may be used against him. Escobedo v. Illinois, 378 U.S. 478, 490–491 (1964). Now, the Court fashions a constitutional rule that the police may engage in no custodial interrogation without additionally advising the accused that he has a right under the Fifth Amendment to the presence of counsel during interrogation and that, if he is without funds, counsel will be furnished him. When at any point during an interrogation the accused seeks affirmatively or impliedly to invoke his rights to silence or counsel, interrogation must be forgone or postponed. The Court further holds that failure to follow the new procedures requires inexorably the exclusion of any statement by the accused, as well as the fruits thereof. Such a strict constitutional specific inserted at the nerve center of crime detection may well kill the patient.[3] [384 U.S. 436, 501] Since there is at this time a paucity of information and an almost total lack of empirical knowledge on the practical operation of requirements truly comparable to those announced by the majority, I would be more restrained lest we go too far too fast.

II.

Custodial interrogation has long been recognized as "undoubtedly an essential tool in effective law enforcement." Haynes v. Washington, 373 U.S. 503, 515 (1963). Recognition of this fact should put us on guard against the promulgation of doctrinaire rules. Especially is this true where the Court finds that "the Constitution has prescribed" its holding and where the light of our past cases, from Hopt v. Utah, 110 U.S. 574, (1884), down to Haynes v. Washington, supra, is to [384 U.S. 436, 502] the contrary. Indeed, even in Escobedo the Court never hinted that an affirmative "waiver" was a prerequisite to questioning; that the burden of proof as to waiver was on the prosecution; that the presence of counsel—absent a waiver—during interrogation was required; that a waiver can be withdrawn at the will of the accused; that counsel must be furnished during an accusatory stage to those unable to pay; nor that admissions and exculpatory statements are "confessions." To require all those things at one gulp should cause the Court to choke over more cases than Crooker

v. California, 357 U.S. 433 (1958), and Cicenia v. Lagay, 357 U.S. 504 (1958), which it expressly overrules today.

The rule prior to today—as Mr. Justice Goldberg, the author of the Court's opinion in Escobedo, stated it in Haynes v. Washington—depended upon "a totality of circumstances evidencing an involuntary . . . admission of guilt." 373 U.S., at 514. And he concluded:

> "Of course, detection and solution of crime is, at best, a difficult and arduous task requiring determination and persistence on the part of all responsible officers charged with the duty of law enforcement. And, certainly, we do not mean to suggest that all interrogation of witnesses and suspects is impermissible. Such questioning is undoubtedly an essential tool in effective law enforcement. The line between proper and permissible police conduct and techniques and methods offensive to due process is, at best, a difficult one to draw, particularly in cases such as this where it is necessary to make fine judgments as to the effect of psychologically coercive pressures and inducements on the mind and will of an accused. . . . We are here impelled to the conclusion, from all of the facts presented, that the bounds of due process have been exceeded." Id., at 514–515. [384 U.S. 436, 503]

III.

I would continue to follow that rule. Under the "totality of circumstances" rule of which my Brother Goldberg spoke in Haynes, I would consider in each case whether the police officer prior to custodial interrogation added the warning that the suspect might have counsel present at the interrogation and, further, that a court would appoint one at his request if he was too poor to employ counsel. In the absence of warnings, the burden would be on the State to prove that counsel was knowingly and intelligently waived or that in the totality of the circumstances, including the failure to give the necessary warnings, the confession was clearly voluntary.

Rather than employing the arbitrary Fifth Amendment rule[4] which the Court lays down I would follow the more pliable dictates of the Due Process Clauses of the Fifth and Fourteenth Amendments which we are accustomed to administering and which we know from our cases are effective instruments in protecting persons in police custody. In this way we would not be acting in the dark nor in one full sweep changing the traditional rules of custodial interrogation which this Court has for so long recognized as a justifiable and proper tool in balancing individual rights against the rights of society. It will be soon enough to go further when we are able to appraise with somewhat better accuracy the effect of such a holding.

I would affirm the convictions in Miranda v. Arizona, No. 759; Vignera v. New York, No. 760; and Westover v. United States, No. 761. In each of those cases I find from the circumstances no warrant for reversal. In [384 U.S. 436, 504] California v. Stewart, No. 584, I would dismiss the writ of certiorari for want of a final judgment, 28 U.S.C. 1257 (3) (1964 ed.); but if the merits are to be reached I would affirm on the ground that the State failed to fulfill its burden, in the absence of a showing that appropriate warnings were given, of proving a waiver or a totality of circumstances showing voluntariness. Should there be a retrial, I would leave the State free to attempt to prove these elements.

FOOTNOTES

[1] E. g., Inbau & Reid, Criminal Interrogation and Confessions (1962); O'Hara, Fundamentals of Criminal Investigation (1956); Dienstein, Technics for the Crime Investigator (1952); Mulbar, Interrogation (1951); Kidd, Police Interrogation (1940).

[2] As developed by my Brother HARLAN, post, pp. 506–514, such cases, with the exception of the long-discredited decision in Bram v. United States, 168 U.S. 532 (1897), were adequately treated in terms of due process.

[3] The Court points to England, Scotland, Ceylon and India as having equally rigid rules. As my Brother HARLAN points out, post, pp. 521–523, the Court is mistaken in this regard, for it overlooks counterbalancing prosecutorial advantages. Moreover, the requirements of the Federal Bureau of Investigation do not appear from the Solicitor General's letter, ante, pp. 484–486, to be as strict as [384 U.S. 436, 501] those imposed today in at least two respects: (1) The offer of counsel is articulated only as "a right to counsel"; nothing is said about a right to have counsel present at the custodial interrogation. (See also the examples cited by the Solicitor General, Westover v. United States, 342 F.2d 684, 685 (1965) ("right to consult counsel"); Jackson v. United States, 337 F.2d 136, 138 (1964) (accused "entitled to an attorney").) Indeed, the practice is that whenever the suspect "decides that he wishes to consult with counsel before making a statement, the interview is terminated at that point . . . . When counsel appears in person, he is permitted to confer with his client in private." This clearly indicates that the FBI does not warn that counsel may be present during custodial interrogation. (2) The Solicitor General's letter states: "[T]hose who have been arrested for an offense under FBI jurisdiction, or whose arrest is contemplated following the interview, [are advised] of a right to free counsel if they are unable to pay, and the availability of such counsel from the Judge." So phrased, this warning does not indicate that the agent will secure counsel. Rather, the statement may well be interpreted by the suspect to mean that the burden is placed upon himself and that he may have counsel appointed only when brought before the judge or at trial—but not at custodial interrogation. As I view the FBI practice, it is not as broad as the one laid down today by the Court.

[4] In my view there is "no significant support" in our cases for the holding of the Court today that the Fifth Amendment privilege, in effect, forbids custodial interrogation. For a discussion of this point see the dissenting opinion of my Brother WHITE, post, pp. 526–531.

MR. JUSTICE HARLAN, whom MR. JUSTICE STEWART and MR. JUSTICE WHITE join, dissenting.

I believe the decision of the Court represents poor constitutional law and entails harmful consequences for the country at large. How serious these consequences may prove to be only time can tell. But the basic flaws in the Court's justification seem to me readily apparent now once all sides of the problem are considered.

I. INTRODUCTION.

At the outset, it is well to note exactly what is required by the Court's new constitutional code of rules for confessions. The foremost requirement, upon which later admissibility of a confession depends, is that a fourfold warning be given to a person in custody before he is questioned, namely, that he has a right to remain silent, that anything he says may be used against him, that he has a right to have present an attorney during the questioning, and that if indigent he has a right to a lawyer without charge. To forgo these rights, some affirmative statement of rejection is seemingly required, and threats, tricks, or cajolings to obtain this waiver are forbidden. If before or during questioning the suspect seeks to invoke his right to remain silent, interrogation must be forgone or cease; a request for counsel [384 U.S. 436, 505] brings about the same result until a lawyer is procured. Finally, there are a miscellany of minor directives, for example, the burden of proof of waiver is on the State, admissions and exculpatory statements are treated just like confessions, withdrawal of a waiver is always permitted, and so forth.[1]

While the fine points of this scheme are far less clear than the Court admits, the tenor is quite apparent. The new rules are not designed to guard against police brutality or other unmistakably banned forms of coercion. Those who use third-degree tactics and deny them in court are equally able and destined to lie as skillfully about warnings and waivers. Rather, the thrust of the new rules is to negate all pressures, to reinforce the nervous or ignorant suspect, and ultimately to discourage any confession at all. The aim in short is toward "voluntariness" in a utopian sense, or to view it from a different angle, voluntariness with a vengeance.

To incorporate this notion into the Constitution requires a strained reading of history and precedent and a disregard of the very pragmatic concerns that alone may on occasion justify such strains. I believe that reasoned examination will show that the Due Process Clauses provide an adequate tool for coping with confessions and that, even if the Fifth Amendment privilege against self-incrimination be invoked, its precedents taken as a whole do not sustain the present rules. Viewed as a choice based on pure policy, these new rules prove to be a highly debatable, if not one-sided, appraisal of the competing interests, imposed over widespread objection, at the very time when judicial restraint is most called for by the circumstances. [384 U.S. 436, 506]

II. CONSTITUTIONAL PREMISES.

It is most fitting to begin an inquiry into the constitutional precedents by surveying the limits on confessions the Court has evolved under the Due Process Clause of the Fourteenth Amendment. This is so because these cases show that there exists a workable and effective means of dealing with confessions in a judicial manner; because the cases are the baseline from which the Court now departs and so serve to measure the actual as opposed to the professed distance it travels; and because examination of them helps reveal how the Court has coasted into its present position.

The earliest confession cases in this Court emerged from federal prosecutions and were settled on a nonconstitutional basis, the Court adopting the common-law rule that the absence of inducements, promises, and threats made a confession voluntary and admissible. Hopt v. Utah, 110 U.S. 574; Pierce v. United States, 160 U.S. 355. While a later case said the Fifth Amendment privilege controlled admissibility, this proposition was not itself developed in subsequent decisions.[2] The Court did, however, heighten the test of admissibility in federal trials to one of voluntariness "in fact," Wan v. [384 U.S. 436, 507] United States, 266 U.S. 1, 14 (quoted, ante, p. 462), and then by and large left federal judges to apply the same standards the Court began to derive in a string of state court cases.

This new line of decisions, testing admissibility by the Due Process Clause, began in 1936 with Brown v. Mississippi, 297 U.S. 278, and must now embrace somewhat more than 30 full opinions of the Court.[3] While the voluntariness rubric was repeated in many instances, e. g., Lyons v. Oklahoma, 322 U.S. 596, the Court never pinned it down to a single meaning but on the contrary infused it with a number of different values. To travel quickly over the main themes, there was an initial emphasis on reliability, e. g., Ward v. Texas, 316 U.S. 547, supplemented by concern over the legality and fairness of the police practices, e. g., Ashcraft v. Tennessee, 322 U.S. 143, in an "accusatorial" system of law enforcement, Watts v. Indiana, 338 U.S. 49, 54, and eventually by close attention to the individual's state of mind and capacity for effective choice, e. g., Gallegos v. Colorado, 370 U.S. 49. The outcome was a continuing re-evaluation on the facts of each case of how much pressure on the suspect was permissible.[4] [384 U.S. 436, 508]

Among the criteria often taken into account were threats or imminent danger, e. g., Payne v. Arkansas, 356 U.S. 560, physical deprivations such as lack of sleep or food, e. g., Reck v. Pate, 367 U.S. 433, repeated or extended interrogation, e. g., Chambers v. Florida, 309 U.S. 227, limits on access to counsel or friends, Crooker v. California, 357 U.S. 433; Cicenia v. Lagay, 357 U.S. 504, length and illegality of detention under state law, e. g., Haynes v. Washington, 373 U.S. 503, and individual weakness or incapacities, Lynumn v. Illinois, 372 U.S. 528. Apart from direct physical coercion, however, no single default or fixed combination of defaults guaranteed exclusion, and synopses of the cases would serve little use because the overall gauge has been steadily changing, usually in the direction of restricting admissibility. But to mark just what point had been reached before the Court jumped the rails in Escobedo v. Illinois, 378 U.S. 478, it is worth capsulizing the then-recent case of Haynes v. Washington, 373 U.S. 503. There, Haynes had been held some 16 or more hours in violation of state law before signing the disputed confession, had received no warnings of any kind, and despite requests had been refused access to his wife or to counsel, the police indicating that access would be allowed after a confession. Emphasizing especially this last inducement and rejecting some contrary indicia of voluntariness, the Court in a 5–to–4 decision held the confession inadmissible.

There are several relevant lessons to be drawn from this constitutional history. The first is that with over 25 years of precedent the Court has developed an elaborate, sophisticated, and sensitive approach to admissibility of confessions. It is "judicial" in its treatment of one case at a time, see Culombe v. Connecticut, 367 U.S. 568, 635 (concurring opinion of THE CHIEF JUSTICE), flexible in its ability to respond to the endless mutations of fact presented, and ever more familiar to the lower courts. [384 U.S. 436, 509] Of course, strict certainty is not obtained in this developing process, but this is often so with constitutional principles, and disagreement is usually confined to that borderland of close cases where it matters least.

The second point is that in practice and from time to time in principle, the Court has given ample recognition to society's interest in suspect questioning as an instrument of law enforcement. Cases countenancing quite significant pressures can be cited without difficulty,[5] and the lower courts may often have been yet more tolerant. Of course the limitations imposed today were rejected by necessary implication in case after case, the right to warnings having been explicitly rebuffed in this Court many years ago. Powers v. United States, 223 U.S. 303; Wilson v. United States, 162 U.S. 613. As recently as Haynes v. Washington, 373 U.S. 503, 515, the Court openly acknowledged that questioning of witnesses and suspects "is undoubtedly an essential tool in effective law enforcement." Accord, Crooker v. California, 357 U.S. 433, 441.

Finally, the cases disclose that the language in many of the opinions overstates the actual course of decision. It has been said, for example, that an admissible confession must be made by the suspect "in the unfettered exercise of his own will," Malloy v. Hogan, 378 U.S. 1, 8, and that "a prisoner is not 'to be made the deluded instrument of his own conviction,'" Culombe v. Connecticut, 367 U.S. 568, 581 (Frankfurter, J., announcing the Court's judgment and an opinion). Though often repeated, such principles are rarely observed in full measure. Even the word "voluntary" may be deemed somewhat [384 U.S. 436, 510] misleading, especially when one considers many of the confessions that have been brought under its umbrella. See, e. g., supra, n. 5. The tendency to overstate may be laid in part to the flagrant facts often before the Court; but in any event one must recognize how it has tempered attitudes and lent some color of authority to the approach now taken by the Court.

I turn now to the Court's asserted reliance on the Fifth Amendment, an approach which I frankly regard as a trompe l'oeil. The Court's opinion in my view reveals no adequate basis for extending the Fifth Amendment's privilege against self-incrimination to the police station. Far more important, it fails to show that the Court's new rules are well supported, let alone compelled, by Fifth Amendment precedents. Instead, the new rules actually derive from quotation and analogy drawn from precedents under the Sixth Amendment, which should properly have no bearing on police interrogation.

The Court's opening contention, that the Fifth Amendment governs police station confessions, is perhaps not an impermissible extension of the law but it has little to commend itself in the present circumstances. Historically, the privilege against self-incrimination did not bear at all on the use of extra-legal confessions, for which distinct standards evolved; indeed, "the history of the two principles is wide apart, differing by one hundred years in origin, and derived through separate lines of precedents. . . ."[8] Wigmore, Evidence 2266, at 401 (McNaughton rev. 1961). Practice under the two doctrines has also differed in a number of important respects.[6] [384 U.S. 436, 511] Even those who would readily enlarge the privilege must concede some linguistic difficulties since the Fifth Amendment in terms proscribes only compelling any person "in any criminal case to be a witness against himself." Cf. Kamisar, Equal Justice in the Gatehouses and Mansions of American Criminal Procedure, in Criminal Justice in Our Time 1, 25–26 (1965).

Though weighty, I do not say these points and similar ones are conclusive, for, as the Court reiterates, the privilege embodies basic principles always capable of expansion.[7] Certainly the privilege does represent a protective concern for the accused and an emphasis upon accusatorial rather than inquisitorial values in law enforcement, although this is similarly true of other limitations such as the grand jury requirement and the reasonable doubt standard. Accusatorial values, however, have openly been absorbed into the due process standard governing confessions; this indeed is why at present "the kinship of the two rules [governing confessions and self-incrimination] is too apparent for denial." McCormick, Evidence 155 (1954). Since extension of the general principle has already occurred, to insist that the privilege applies as such serves only to carry over inapposite historical details and engaging rhetoric and to obscure the policy choices to be made in regulating confessions.

Having decided that the Fifth Amendment privilege does apply in the police station, the Court reveals that the privilege imposes more exacting restrictions than does the Fourteenth Amendment's voluntariness test.[8] [384 U.S. 436, 512] It then emerges from a discussion of Escobedo that the Fifth Amendment requires for an admissible confession that it be given by one distinctly aware of his right not to speak and shielded from "the compelling atmosphere" of interrogation. See ante, pp. 465–466. From these key premises, the Court finally develops the safeguards of warning, counsel, and so forth. I do not believe these premises are sustained by precedents under the Fifth Amendment.[9]

The more important premise is that pressure on the suspect must be eliminated though it be only the subtle influence of the atmosphere and surroundings. The Fifth Amendment, however, has never been thought to forbid all pressure to incriminate one's self in the situations covered by it. On the contrary, it has been held that failure to incriminate one's self can result in denial of removal of one's case from state to federal court, Maryland v. Soper, 270 U.S. 9; in refusal of a military commission, Orloff v. Willoughby, 345 U.S. 83; in denial of a discharge in bankruptcy, Kaufman v. Hurwitz, 176 F.2d 210; and in numerous other adverse consequences. See 8 Wigmore, Evidence 2272, at 441–444, n. 18 (McNaughton rev. 1961); Maguire, Evidence of Guilt 2.062 (1959). This is not to say that short of jail or torture any sanction is permissible in any case; policy and history alike may impose sharp limits. See, e. g., [384 U.S. 436, 513] Griffin v. California, 380 U.S. 609. However, the Court's unspoken assumption that any pressure violates the privilege is not supported by the precedents and it has failed to show why the Fifth Amendment prohibits that relatively mild pressure the Due Process Clause permits.

The Court appears similarly wrong in thinking that precise knowledge of one's rights is a settled prerequisite under the Fifth Amendment to the loss of its protections. A number of lower federal court cases have held that grand jury witnesses need not always be warned of their privilege, e. g., United States v. Scully, 225 F.2d 113, 116, and Wigmore states this to be the better rule for trial witnesses. See 8 Wigmore, Evidence 2269 (McNaughton rev. 1961). Cf. Henry v. Mississippi, 379 U.S. 443, 451–452 (waiver of constitutional rights by counsel despite defendant's ignorance held allowable). No Fifth Amendment precedent is cited for the Court's contrary view. There might of course be reasons apart from Fifth Amendment precedent for requiring warning or any other safeguard on questioning but that is a different matter entirely. See infra, pp. 516–517.

A closing word must be said about the Assistance of Counsel Clause of the Sixth Amendment, which is never expressly relied on by the Court but whose judicial precedents turn out to be linchpins of the confession rules announced today. To support its requirement of a knowing and intelligent waiver, the Court cites Johnson v. Zerbst, 304 U.S. 458, ante, p. 475; appointment of counsel for the indigent suspect is tied to Gideon v. Wainwright, 372 U.S. 335, and Douglas v. California, 372 U.S. 353, ante, p. 473; the silent-record doctrine is borrowed from Carnley v. Cochran, 369 U.S. 506, ante, p. 475, as is the right to an express offer of counsel, ante, p. 471. All these cases imparting glosses to the Sixth Amendment concerned counsel at trial or on appeal. While the Court finds no pertinent difference between judicial proceedings and police interrogation, I believe [384 U.S. 436, 514] the differences are so vast as to disqualify wholly the Sixth Amendment precedents as suitable analogies in the present cases.[10]

The only attempt in this Court to carry the right to counsel into the station house occurred in Escobedo, the Court repeating several times that that stage was no less "critical" than trial itself. See 378 U.S., 485–488. This is hardly persuasive when we consider that a grand jury inquiry, the filing of a certiorari petition, and certainly the purchase of narcotics by an undercover agent from a prospective defendant may all be equally "critical" yet provision of counsel and advice on that score have never been thought compelled by the Constitution in such cases. The sound reason why this right is so freely extended for a criminal trial is the severe injustice risked by confronting an untrained defendant with a range of technical points of law, evidence, and tactics familiar to the prosecutor but not to himself. This danger shrinks markedly in the police station where indeed the lawyer in fulfilling his professional responsibilities of necessity may become an obstacle to truthfinding. See infra, n. 12. The Court's summary citation of the Sixth Amendment cases here seems to me best described as "the domino method of constitutional adjudication . . . wherein every explanatory statement in a previous opinion is made the basis for extension to a wholly different situation." Friendly, supra, n. 10, at 950.

III. POLICY CONSIDERATIONS.

Examined as an expression of public policy, the Court's new regime proves so dubious that there can be no due [384 U.S. 436, 515] compensation for its weakness in constitutional law. The foregoing discussion has shown, I think, how mistaken is the Court in implying that the Constitution has struck the balance in favor of the approach the Court takes. Ante, p. 479. Rather, precedent reveals that the Fourteenth Amendment in practice has been construed to strike a different balance, that the Fifth Amendment gives the Court little solid support in this context, and that the Sixth Amendment should have no bearing at all. Legal history has been stretched before to satisfy deep needs of society. In this instance, however, the Court has not and cannot make the powerful showing that its new rules are plainly desirable in the context of our society, something which is surely demanded before those rules are engrafted onto the Constitution and imposed on every State and county in the land.

Without at all subscribing to the generally black picture of police conduct painted by the Court, I think it must be frankly recognized at the outset that police questioning allowable under due process precedents may inherently entail some pressure on the suspect and may seek advantage in his ignorance or weaknesses. The atmosphere and questioning techniques, proper and fair though they be, can in themselves exert a tug on the suspect to confess, and in this light "[t]o speak of any confessions of crime made after arrest as being "voluntary" or "uncoerced" is somewhat inaccurate, although traditional. A confession is wholly and incontestably voluntary only if a guilty person gives himself up to the law and becomes his own accuser." Ashcraft v. Tennessee, 322 U.S. 143, 161 (Jackson, J., dissenting). Until today, the role of the Constitution has been only to sift out undue pressure, not to assure spontaneous confessions.[11] [384 U.S. 436, 516]

The Court's new rules aim to offset these minor pressures and disadvantages intrinsic to any kind of police interrogation. The rules do not serve due process interests in preventing blatant coercion since, as I noted earlier, they do nothing to contain the policeman who is prepared to lie from the start. The rules work for reliability in confessions almost only in the Pickwickian sense that they can prevent some from being given at all.[12] In short, the benefit of this new regime is simply to lessen or wipe out the inherent compulsion and inequalities to which the Court devotes some nine pages of description. Ante, pp. 448–456.

What the Court largely ignores is that its rules impair, if they will not eventually serve wholly to frustrate, an instrument of law enforcement that has long and quite reasonably been thought worth the price paid for it.[13] There can be little doubt that the Court's new code would markedly decrease the number of confessions. To warn the suspect that he may remain silent and remind him that his confession may be used in court are minor obstructions. To require also an express waiver by the suspect and an end to questioning whenever he demurs [384 U.S. 436, 517] must heavily handicap questioning. And to suggest or provide counsel for the suspect simply invites the end of the interrogation. See, supra, n. 12.

How much harm this decision will inflict on law enforcement cannot fairly be predicted with accuracy. Evidence on the role of confessions is notoriously incomplete, see Developments, supra, n. 2, at 941–944, and little is added by the Court's reference to the FBI experience and the resources believed wasted in interrogation. See infra, n. 19, and text. We do know that some crimes cannot be solved without confessions, that ample expert testimony attests to their importance in crime control,[14] and that the Court is taking a real risk with society's welfare in imposing its new regime on the country. The social costs of crime are too great to call the new rules anything but a hazardous experimentation.

While passing over the costs and risks of its experiment, the Court portrays the evils of normal police questioning in terms which I think are exaggerated. Albeit stringently confined by the due process standards interrogation is no doubt often inconvenient and unpleasant for the suspect. However, it is no less so for a man to be arrested and jailed, to have his house searched, or to stand trial in court, yet all this may properly happen to the most innocent given probable cause, a warrant, or an indictment. Society has always paid a stiff price for law and order, and peaceful interrogation is not one of the dark moments of the law.

This brief statement of the competing considerations seems to me ample proof that the Court's preference is highly debatable at best and therefore not to be read into [384 U.S. 436, 518] the Constitution. However, it may make the analysis more graphic to consider the actual facts of one of the four cases reversed by the Court. Miranda v. Arizona serves best, being neither the hardest nor easiest of the four under the Court's standards.[15]

On March 3, 1963, an 18-year-old girl was kidnapped and forcibly raped near Phoenix, Arizona. Ten days later, on the morning of March 13, petitioner Miranda was arrested and taken to the police station. At this time Miranda was 23 years old, indigent, and educated to the extent of completing half the ninth grade. He had "an emotional illness" of the schizophrenic type, according to the doctor who eventually examined him; the doctor's report also stated that Miranda was "alert and oriented as to time, place, and person," intelligent within normal limits, compe-

tent to stand trial, and sane within the legal definition. At the police station, the victim picked Miranda out of a lineup, and two officers then
took him into a separate room to interrogate him, starting about 11:30
a. m. Though at first denying his guilt, within a short time Miranda gave
a detailed oral confession and then wrote out in his own hand and signed
a brief statement admitting and describing the crime. All this was
accomplished in two hours or less without any force, threats or promises
and—I will assume this though the record is uncertain, ante, 491–492
and nn. 66–67—without any effective warnings at all.

Miranda's oral and written confessions are now held inadmissible
under the Court's new rules. One is entitled to feel astonished that the
Constitution can be read to produce this result. These confessions were
obtained [384 U.S. 436, 519] during brief, daytime questioning conducted
by two officers and unmarked by any of the traditional indicia of coercion. They assured a conviction for a brutal and unsettling crime, for
which the police had and quite possibly could obtain little evidence other
than the victim's identifications, evidence which is frequently unreliable.
There was, in sum, a legitimate purpose, no perceptible unfairness, and
certainly little risk of injustice in the interrogation. Yet the resulting confessions, and the responsible course of police practice they represent, are
to be sacrificed to the Court's own finespun conception of fairness which
I seriously doubt is shared by many thinking citizens in this country.[16]

The tenor of judicial opinion also falls well short of supporting the
Court's new approach. Although Escobedo has widely been interpreted
as an open invitation to lower courts to rewrite the law of confessions, a
significant heavy majority of the state and federal decisions in point have
sought quite narrow interpretations.[17] Of [384 U.S. 436, 520] the courts
that have accepted the invitation, it is hard to know how many have felt
compelled by their best guess as to this Court's likely construction; but
none of the state decisions saw fit to rely on the state privilege against
self-incrimination, and no decision at all has gone as far as this Court
goes today.[18]

It is also instructive to compare the attitude in this case of those
responsible for law enforcement with the official views that existed
when the Court undertook three major revisions of prosecutorial practice prior to this case, Johnson v. Zerbst, 304 U.S. 458, Mapp v. Ohio,
367 U.S. 643, and Gideon v. Wainwright, 372 U.S. 335. In Johnson,
which established that appointed counsel must be offered the indigent
in federal criminal trials, the Federal Government all but conceded the
basic issue, which had in fact been recently fixed as Department of
Justice policy. See Beaney, Right to Counsel 29–30, 36–42 (1955). In
Mapp, which imposed the exclusionary rule on the States for Fourth

Amendment violations, more than half of the States had themselves already adopted some such rule. See 367 U.S., at 651. In Gideon, which extended Johnson v. Zerbst to the States, an amicus brief was filed by 22 States and Commonwealths urging that course; only two States besides that of the respondent came forward to protest. See 372 U.S., at 345. By contrast, in this case new restrictions on police [384 U.S. 436, 521] questioning have been opposed by the United States and in an amicus brief signed by 27 States and Commonwealths, not including the three other States which are parties. No State in the country has urged this Court to impose the newly announced rules, nor has any State chosen to go nearly so far on its own.

The Court in closing its general discussion invokes the practice in federal and foreign jurisdictions as lending weight to its new curbs on confessions for all the States. A brief resume will suffice to show that none of these jurisdictions has struck so one-sided a balance as the Court does today. Heaviest reliance is placed on the FBI practice. Differing circumstances may make this comparison quite untrustworthy,[19] but in any event the FBI falls sensibly short of the Court's formalistic rules. For example, there is no indication that FBI agents must obtain an affirmative "waiver" before they pursue their questioning. Nor is it clear that one invoking his right to silence may not be prevailed upon to change his mind. And the warning as to appointed counsel apparently indicates only that one will be assigned by the judge when the suspect appears before him; the thrust of the Court's rules is to induce the suspect to obtain appointed counsel before continuing the interview. See ante, pp. 484–486. Apparently American military practice, briefly mentioned by the Court, has these same limits and is still less favorable to the suspect than the FBI warning, making no mention of appointed counsel. Developments, supra, n. 2, at 1084–1089.

The law of the foreign countries described by the Court also reflects a more moderate conception of the rights of [384 U.S. 436, 522] the accused as against those of society when other data are considered. Concededly, the English experience is most relevant. In that country, a caution as to silence but not counsel has long been mandated by the "Judges" Rules," which also place other somewhat imprecise limits on police cross-examination of suspects. However, in the court's discretion confessions can be and apparently quite frequently are admitted in evidence despite disregard of the Judges" Rules, so long as they are found voluntary under the common-law test. Moreover, the check that exists on the use of pretrial statements is counterbalanced by the evident admissibility of fruits of an illegal confession and by the judge's often-used authority to comment adversely on the defendant's failure to testify.[20]

India, Ceylon and Scotland are the other examples chosen by the

Court. In India and Ceylon the general ban on police-adduced confessions cited by the Court is subject to a major exception: if evidence is uncovered by police questioning, it is fully admissible at trial along with the confession itself, so far as it relates to the evidence and is not blatantly coerced. See Developments, supra, n. 2, at 1106–1110; Reg. v. Ramasamy 1965. A. C. 1 (P. C.). Scotland's limits on interrogation do measure up to the Court's; however, restrained comment at trial on the defendant's failure to take the stand is allowed the judge, and in many other respects Scotch law redresses the prosecutor's disadvantage in ways not permitted in this country.[21] The Court ends its survey by imputing [384 U.S. 436, 523] added strength to our privilege against self-incrimination since, by contrast to other countries, it is embodied in a written Constitution. Considering the liberties the Court has today taken with constitutional history and precedent, few will find this emphasis persuasive.

In closing this necessarily truncated discussion of policy considerations attending the new confession rules, some reference must be made to their ironic untimeliness. There is now in progress in this country a massive re-examination of criminal law enforcement procedures on a scale never before witnessed. Participants in this undertaking include a Special Committee of the American Bar Association, under the chairmanship of Chief Judge Lumbard of the Court of Appeals for the Second Circuit; a distinguished study group of the American Law Institute, headed by Professors Vorenberg and Bator of the Harvard Law School; and the President's Commission on Law Enforcement and Administration of Justice, under the leadership of the Attorney General of the United States.[22] Studies are also being conducted by the District of Columbia Crime Commission, the Georgetown Law Center, and by others equipped to do practical research.[23] There are also signs that legislatures in some of the States may be preparing to re-examine the problem before us.[24] [384 U.S. 436, 524]

It is no secret that concern has been expressed lest long-range and lasting reforms be frustrated by this Court's too rapid departure from existing constitutional standards. Despite the Court's disclaimer, the practical effect of the decision made today must inevitably be to handicap seriously sound efforts at reform, not least by removing options necessary to a just compromise of competing interests. Of course legislative reform is rarely speedy or unanimous, though this Court has been more patient in the past.[25] But the legislative reforms when they come would have the vast advantage of empirical data and comprehensive study, they would allow experimentation and use of solutions not open to the courts, and they would restore the initiative in criminal law reform to those forums where it truly belongs.

IV. CONCLUSIONS.

All four of the cases involved here present express claims that confessions were inadmissible, not because of coercion in the traditional due process sense, but solely because of lack of counsel or lack of warnings concerning counsel and silence. For the reasons stated in this opinion, I would adhere to the due process test and reject the new requirements inaugurated by the Court. On this premise my disposition of each of these cases can be stated briefly.

In two of the three cases coming from state courts, Miranda v. Arizona (No. 759) and Vignera v. New York (No. 760), the confessions were held admissible and no other errors worth comment are alleged by petitioners. [384 U.S. 436, 525] I would affirm in these two cases. The other state case is California v. Stewart (No. 584), where the state supreme court held the confession inadmissible and reversed the conviction. In that case I would dismiss the writ of certiorari on the ground that no final judgment is before us, 28 U.S.C. 1257 (1964 ed.); putting aside the new trial open to the State in any event, the confession itself has not even been finally excluded since the California Supreme Court left the State free to show proof of a waiver. If the merits of the decision in Stewart be reached, then I believe it should be reversed and the case remanded so the state supreme court may pass on the other claims available to respondent.

In the federal case, Westover v. United States (No. 761), a number of issues are raised by petitioner apart from the one already dealt with in this dissent. None of these other claims appears to me tenable, nor in this context to warrant extended discussion. It is urged that the confession was also inadmissible because not voluntary even measured by due process standards and because federal-state cooperation brought the McNabb-Mallory rule into play under Anderson v. United States, 318 U.S. 350. However, the facts alleged fall well short of coercion in my view, and I believe the involvement of federal agents in petitioner's arrest and detention by the State too slight to invoke Anderson. I agree with the Government that the admission of the evidence now protested by petitioner was at most harmless error, and two final contentions—one involving weight of the evidence and another improper prosecutor comment—seem to me without merit. I would therefore affirm Westover's conviction.

In conclusion: Nothing in the letter or the spirit of the Constitution or in the precedents squares with the heavy-handed and one-sided action that is so precipitously [384 U.S. 436, 526] taken by the Court in the name of fulfilling its constitutional responsibilities. The foray which the Court makes today brings to mind the wise and farsighted words of Mr. Justice Jackson in Douglas v. Jeannette, 319 U.S. 157, 181 (separate opinion):

"This Court is forever adding new stories to the temples of constitutional law, and the temples have a way of collapsing when one story too many is added."

FOOTNOTES

[1] My discussion in this opinion is directed to the main questions decided by the Court and necessary to its decision; in ignoring some of the collateral points, I do not mean to imply agreement.

[2] The case was Bram v. United States, 168 U.S. 532 (quoted, ante, p. 461). Its historical premises were afterwards disproved by Wigmore, who concluded "that no assertions could be more unfounded." 3 Wigmore, Evidence 823, at 250, n. 5 (3d ed. 1940). The Court in United States v. Carignan, 342 U.S. 36, 41, declined to choose between Bram and Wigmore, and Stein v. New York, 346 U.S. 156, 191, n. 35, cast further doubt on Bram. There are, however, several Court opinions which assume in dicta the relevance of the Fifth Amendment privilege to confessions. Burdeau v. McDowell, 256 U.S. 465, 475; see Shotwell Mfg. Co. v. United States, 371 U.S. 341, 347. On Bram and the federal confession cases generally, see Developments in the Law—Confessions, 79 Harv. L. Rev. 935, 959–961 (1966).

[3] Comment, 31 U. Chi. L. Rev. 313 & n. 1 (1964), states that by the 1963 Term 33 state coerced-confession cases had been decided by this Court, apart from per curiams. Spano v. New York, 360 U.S. 315, 321, n. 2, collects 28 cases.

[4] Bator & Vorenberg, Arrest, Detention, Interrogation and the Right to Counsel, 66 Col. L. Rev. 62, 73 (1966): "In fact, the concept of involuntariness seems to be used by the courts as a shorthand to refer to practices which are repellent to civilized standards of decency or which, under the circumstances, are thought to apply a degree of pressure to an individual which unfairly impairs his capacity to make a rational choice." See Herman, The Supreme Court and Restrictions on Police Interrogation, 25 Ohio St. L. J. 449, 452–458 (1964); Developments, supra, n. 2, at 964–984.

[5] See the cases synopsized in Herman, supra, n. 4, at 456, nn. 36–39. One not too distant example is Stroble v. California, 343 U.S. 181, in which the suspect was kicked and threatened after his arrest, questioned a little later for two hours, and isolated from a lawyer trying to see him; the resulting confession was held admissible.

[6] Among the examples given in 8 Wigmore, Evidence 2266, at 401 (McNaughton rev. 1961), are these: the privilege applies to any witness, civil or criminal, but the confession rule protects only criminal defendants; the privilege deals only with compulsion, while the confession rule may exclude statements obtained by trick or promise; and where the privilege has been nullified—as by the English Bankruptcy Act—the confession rule may still operate.

[7] Additionally, there are precedents and even historical arguments that can be arrayed in favor of bringing extra-legal questioning within the privilege. See generally Maguire, Evidence of Guilt 2.03, at 15–16 (1959).

[8] This, of course, is implicit in the Court's introductory announcement that "[o]ur decision in Malloy v. Hogan, 378 U.S. 1 (1964) [extending the Fifth Amendment privilege to the States] necessitates [384 U.S. 436, 512] an examination of the scope of the privilege in state cases as well." Ante, p. 463. It is also inconsistent with Malloy itself, in which extension of the Fifth Amendment to the States rested in part on the view that the Due Process Clause restriction on state confessions has in recent years been "the same standard" as that imposed in federal prosecutions assertedly by the Fifth Amendment. 378 U.S., at 7.

⁹ I lay aside Escobedo itself; it contains no reasoning or even general conclusions addressed to the Fifth Amendment and indeed its citation in this regard seems surprising in view of Escobedo's primary reliance on the Sixth Amendment.

¹⁰ Since the Court conspicuously does not assert that the Sixth Amendment itself warrants its new police-interrogation rules, there is no reason now to draw out the extremely powerful historical and precedential evidence that the Amendment will bear no such meaning. See generally Friendly, The Bill of Rights as a Code of Criminal Procedure, 53 Calif. L. Rev. 929, 943–948 (1965).

¹¹ See supra, n. 4, and text. Of course, the use of terms like voluntariness involves questions of law and terminology quite as much as questions of fact. See Collins v. Beto, 348 F.2d 823, 832 (concurring opinion); Bator & Vorenberg, supra, n. 4, at 72–73.

¹² The Court's vision of a lawyer "mitigat[ing] the dangers of untrustworthiness" (ante, p. 470) by witnessing coercion and assisting accuracy in the confession is largely a fancy; for if counsel arrives, there is rarely going to be a police station confession. Watts v. Indiana, 338 U.S. 49, 59 (separate opinion of Jackson, J.): "[A]ny lawyer worth his salt will tell the suspect in no uncertain terms to make no statement to police under any circumstances." See Enker & Elsen, Counsel for the Suspect, 49 Minn. L. Rev. 47, 66–68 (1964).

¹³ This need is, of course, what makes so misleading the Court's comparison of a probate judge readily setting aside as involuntary the will of an old lady badgered and beleaguered by the new heirs. Ante, pp. 457–458, n. 26. With wills, there is no public interest save in a totally free choice; with confessions, the solution of crime is a countervailing gain, however the balance is resolved.

¹⁴ See, e. g., the voluminous citations to congressional committee testimony and other sources collected in Culombe v. Connecticut, 367 U.S. 568, 578–579 (Frankfurter, J., announcing the Court's judgment and an opinion).

¹⁵ In Westover, a seasoned criminal was practically given the Court's full complement of warnings and did not heed them. The Stewart case, on the other hand, involves long detention and successive questioning. In Vignera, the facts are complicated and the record somewhat incomplete.

¹⁶ "[J]ustice, though due to the accused, is due to the accuser also. The concept of fairness must not be strained till it is narrowed to a filament. We are to keep the balance true." Snyder v. Massachusetts, 291 U.S. 97, 122 (Cardozo, J.).

¹⁷ A narrow reading is given in: United States v. Robinson, 354 F.2d 109 (C. A. 2d Cir.); Davis v. North Carolina, 339 F.2d 770 (C. A. 4th Cir.); Edwards v. Holman, 342 F.2d 679 (C. A. 5th Cir.); United States ex rel. Townsend v. Ogilvie, 334 F.2d 837 (C. A. 7th Cir.); People v. Hartgraves, 31 Ill. 2d 375, 202 N. E. 2d 33; State v. Fox, ___ Iowa ___, 131 N. W. 2d 684; Rowe v. Commonwealth, 394 S. W. 2d 751 (Ky.); Parker v. Warden, 236 Md. 236, 203 A. 2d 418; State v. Howard, 383 S. W. 2d 701 (Mo.); Bean v. State, ___ Nev. ___, 398 P.2d 251; State v. Hodgson, 44 N. J. 151, 207 A. 2d 542; People v. Gunner, 15 N. Y. 2d 226, 205 N. E. 2d 852; Commonwealth ex rel. Linde v. Maroney, 416 Pa. 331, 206 A. 2d 288; Browne v. State, 24 Wis. 2d 491, 131 N. W. 2d 169.

An ample reading is given in: United States ex rel. Russo v. New Jersey, 351 F.2d 429 (C. A. 3d Cir.); Wright v. Dickson, [384 U.S. 436, 520] 336 F.2d 878 (C. A. 9th Cir.); People v. Dorado, 62 Cal. 2d 338, 398 P.2d 361; State v. Dufour, ___ R. I. ___, 206 A. 2d 82; State v. Neely, 239 Ore. 487, 395 P.2d 557, modified, 398 P.2d 482.

The cases in both categories are those readily available; there are certainly many others.

¹⁸ For instance, compare the requirements of the catalytic case of People v. Dorado, 62 Cal. 2d 338, 398 P.2d 361, with those laid down today. See also Traynor, The Devils of Due Process in Criminal Detection, Detention, and Trial, 33 U. Chi. L. Rev. 657, 670.

¹⁹ The Court's obiter dictum notwithstanding, ante, p. 486, there is some basis for believ-

ing that the staple of FBI criminal work differs importantly from much crime within the ken of local police. The skill and resources of the FBI may also be unusual.

[20] For citations and discussion covering each of these points, see Developments, supra, n. 2, at 1091–1097, and Enker & Elsen, supra, n. 12, at 80 & n. 94.

[21] On comment, see Hardin, Other Answers: Search and Seizure, Coerced Confession, and Criminal Trial in Scotland, 113 U. Pa. L. Rev. 165, 181 and nn. 96–97 (1964). Other examples are less stringent search and seizure rules and no automatic exclusion for violation of them, id., at 167–169; guilt based on majority jury verdicts, id., at 185; and pre-trial discovery of evidence on both sides, id., at 175.

[22] Of particular relevance is the ALI's drafting of a Model Code of Pre-Arraignment Procedure, now in its first tentative draft. While the ABA and National Commission studies have wider scope, the former is lending its advice to the ALI project and the executive director of the latter is one of the reporters for the Model Code.

[23] See Brief for the United States in Westover, p. 45. The N. Y. Times, June 3, 1966, p. 41 (late city ed.) reported that the Ford Foundation has awarded $1,100,000 for a five-year study of arrests and confessions in New York.

[24] The New York Assembly recently passed a bill to require certain warnings before an admissible confession is taken, though the rules are less strict than are the Court's. N. Y. Times, May 24, 1966, p. 35 (late city ed.).

[25] The Court waited 12 years after Wolf v. Colorado, 338 U.S. 25, declared privacy against improper state intrusions to be constitutionally safeguarded before it concluded in Mapp v. Ohio, 367 U.S. 643, that adequate state remedies had not been provided to protect this interest so the exclusionary rule was necessary.

MR. JUSTICE WHITE, with whom MR. JUSTICE HARLAN and MR. JUSTICE STEWART join, dissenting.

I.

The proposition that the privilege against self-incrimination forbids in-custody interrogation without the warnings specified in the majority opinion and without a clear waiver of counsel has no significant support in the history of the privilege or in the language of the Fifth Amendment. As for the English authorities and the common-law history, the privilege, firmly established in the second half of the seventeenth century, was never applied except to prohibit compelled judicial interrogations. The rule excluding coerced confessions matured about 100 years later, "[b]ut there is nothing in the reports to suggest that the theory has its roots in the privilege against self-incrimination. And so far as the cases reveal, the privilege, as such, seems to have been given effect only in judicial proceedings, including the preliminary examinations by authorized magistrates." Morgan, The Privilege Against Self-Incrimination, 34 Minn. L. Rev. 1, 18 (1949).

Our own constitutional provision provides that no person "shall be compelled in any criminal case to be a witness against himself." These words, when "[c]onsidered in the light to be shed by grammar and the dictionary . . . appear to signify simply that nobody shall be [384 U.S. 436, 527] compelled to give oral testimony against himself in a criminal proceeding under way in which he is defendant." Corwin, The Supreme Court's Construction of the Self-Incrimination Clause, 29 Mich. L. Rev. 1, 2. And there is very little in the surrounding circumstances of the adoption of the Fifth Amendment or in the provisions of the then existing state constitutions or in state practice which would give the constitutional provision any broader meaning. Mayers, The Federal Witness" Privilege Against Self-Incrimination: Constitutional or Common-Law? 4 American Journal of Legal History 107 (1960). Such a construction, however, was considerably narrower than the privilege at common law, and when eventually faced with the issues, the Court extended the constitutional privilege to the compulsory production of books and papers, to the ordinary witness before the grand jury and to witnesses generally. Boyd v. United States, 116 U.S. 616, and Counselman v. Hitchcock, 142 U.S. 547. Both rules had solid support in common-law history, if not in the history of our own constitutional provision.

A few years later the Fifth Amendment privilege was similarly extended to encompass the then well-established rule against coerced confessions: "In criminal trials, in the courts of the United States, wherever a question arises whether a confession is incompetent because not voluntary, the issue is controlled by that portion of the Fifth Amendment to the Constitution of the United States, commanding that no person "shall be compelled in any criminal case to be a witness against himself." Bram v. United States, 168 U.S. 532, 542. Although this view has found approval in other cases, Burdeau v. McDowell, 256 U.S. 465, 475; Powers v. United States, 223 U.S. 303, 313; Shotwell v. United States, 371 U.S. 341, 347, it has also been questioned, see Brown v. Mississippi, 297 U.S. 278, 285; United States v. Carignan, [384 U.S. 436, 528] 342 U.S. 36, 41; Stein v. New York, 346 U.S. 156, 191, n. 35, and finds scant support in either the English or American authorities, see generally Regina v. Scott, Dears. & Bell 47; 3 Wigmore, Evidence 823 (3d ed. 1940), at 249 ("a confession is not rejected because of any connection with the privilege against self-crimination"), and 250, n. 5 (particularly criticizing Bram); 8 Wigmore, Evidence 2266, at 400–401 (McNaughton rev. 1961). Whatever the source of the rule excluding coerced confessions, it is clear that prior to the application of the privilege itself to state courts, Malloy v. Hogan, 378 U.S. 1, the admissibility of a confession in a state criminal prosecution was tested by the same standards as were applied in federal prosecutions. Id., at 6–7, 10.

Bram, however, itself rejected the proposition which the Court now espouses. The question in Bram was whether a confession, obtained during custodial interrogation, had been compelled, and if such interrogation was to be deemed inherently vulnerable the Court's inquiry could have ended there. After examining the English and American authorities, however, the Court declared that:

> "In this court also it has been settled that the mere fact that the confession is made to a police officer, while the accused was under arrest in or out of prison, or was drawn out by his questions, does not necessarily render the confession involuntary, but, as one of the circumstances, such imprisonment or interrogation may be taken into account in determining whether or not the statements of the prisoner were voluntary." 168 U.S., at 558.

In this respect the Court was wholly consistent with prior and subsequent pronouncements in this Court.

Thus prior to Bram the Court, in Hopt v. Utah, 110 U.S. 574, 583–587, had upheld the admissibility of a [384 U.S. 436, 529] confession made to police officers following arrest, the record being silent concerning what conversation had occurred between the officers and the defendant in the short period preceding the confession. Relying on Hopt, the Court ruled squarely on the issue in Sparf and Hansen v. United States, 156 U.S. 51, 55:

> "Counsel for the accused insist that there cannot be a voluntary statement, a free open confession, while a defendant is confined and in irons under an accusation of having committed a capital offence. We have not been referred to any authority in support of that position. It is true that the fact of a prisoner being in custody at the time he makes a confession is a circumstance not to be overlooked, because it bears upon the inquiry whether the confession was voluntarily made or was extorted by threats or violence or made under the influence of fear. But confinement or imprisonment is not in itself sufficient to justify the exclusion of a confession, if it appears to have been voluntary, and was not obtained by putting the prisoner in fear or by promises. Wharton's Cr. Ev. 9th ed. 661, 663, and authorities cited."

Accord, Pierce v. United States, 160 U.S. 355, 357.

And in Wilson v. United States, 162 U.S. 613, 623, the Court had considered the significance of custodial interrogation without any antecedent warnings regarding the right to remain silent or the right to counsel. There the defendant had answered questions posed by a Commissioner, who had failed to advise him of his rights, and his answers were held admissible over his claim of involuntariness. "The fact that [a defendant] is in custody and manacled does not necessarily render his statement involuntary, nor is that necessarily the effect of popular excitement shortly preceding.... And it is laid down [384 U.S. 436, 530] that it is not essential to the admissibility of a confession that it should appear that the person was warned that what he said would be used against him, but on the contrary, if the confession was voluntary, it is sufficient though it appear that he was not so warned."

Since Bram, the admissibility of statements made during custodial interrogation has been frequently reiterated. Powers v. United States, 223 U.S. 303, cited Wilson approvingly and held admissible as voluntary statements the accused's testimony at a preliminary hearing even though he was not warned that what he said might be used against him. Without any discussion of the presence or absence of warnings, presumably because such discussion was deemed unnecessary, numerous other cases have declared that "[t]he mere fact that a confession was made while in the custody of the police does not render it inadmissible," McNabb v. United States, 318 U.S. 332, 346; accord, United States v. Mitchell, 322 U.S. 65, despite its having been elicited by police examination, Wan v. United States, 266 U.S. 1, 14; United States v. Carignan, 342 U.S. 36, 39. Likewise, in Crooker v. California, 357 U.S. 433, 437, the Court said that "the bare fact of police "detention and police examination in private of one in official state custody" does not render involuntary a confession by the one so detained." And finally, in Cicenia v. Lagay, 357 U.S. 504, a confession obtained by police interrogation after arrest was held voluntary even though the authorities refused to permit the defendant to consult with his attorney. See generally Culombe v. Connecticut, 367 U.S. 568, 587–602 (opinion of Frankfurter, J.); 3 Wigmore, Evidence 851, at 313 (3d ed. 1940); see also Joy, Admissibility of Confessions 38, 46 (1842).

Only a tiny minority of our judges who have dealt with the question, including today's majority, have considered in-custody interrogation, without more, to be a violation of the Fifth Amendment. And this Court, as [384 U.S. 436, 531] every member knows, has left standing literally thousands of criminal convictions that rested at least in part on confessions taken in the course of interrogation by the police after arrest.

II.

That the Court's holding today is neither compelled nor even strongly suggested by the language of the Fifth Amendment, is at odds with American and English legal history, and involves a departure from a long line of precedent does not prove either that the Court has exceeded its powers or that the Court is wrong or unwise in its present reinterpretation of the Fifth Amendment. It does, however, underscore the obvious—that the Court has not discovered or found the law in making today's decision, nor has it derived it from some irrefutable sources; what it has done is to make new law and new public policy in much the same way that it has in the course of interpreting other great clauses of the Constitution.[1] This is what the Court historically has done. Indeed, it is what it must do and will continue to do until and unless there is some fundamental change in the constitutional distribution of governmental powers.

But if the Court is here and now to announce new and fundamental policy to govern certain aspects of our affairs, it is wholly legitimate to examine the mode of this or any other constitutional decision in this Court and to inquire into the advisability of its end product in terms of the long-range interest of the country. At the very least the Court's text and reasoning should withstand analysis and be a fair exposition of the constitutional provision which its opinion interprets. Decisions [384 U.S. 436, 532] like these cannot rest alone on syllogism, metaphysics or some ill-defined notions of natural justice, although each will perhaps play its part. In proceeding to such constructions as it now announces, the Court should also duly consider all the factors and interests bearing upon the cases, at least insofar as the relevant materials are available; and if the necessary considerations are not treated in the record or obtainable from some other reliable source, the Court should not proceed to formulate fundamental policies based on speculation alone.

III.

First, we may inquire what are the textual and factual bases of this new fundamental rule. To reach the result announced on the grounds it does, the Court must stay within the confines of the Fifth Amendment, which forbids self-incrimination only if compelled. Hence the core of the Court's opinion is that because of the "compulsion inherent in custodial surroundings, no statement obtained from [a] defendant [in custody] can truly be the product of his free choice," ante, at 458, absent the use of adequate protective devices as described by the Court. However, the Court does not point to any sudden inrush of new knowledge requiring the rejection of 70 years" experience. Nor does it assert that its novel conclusion reflects a changing consensus among state courts, see Mapp v. Ohio, 367 U.S. 643, or that a succession of cases had steadily eroded the old rule and proved it unworkable, see Gideon v. Wainwright, 372 U.S. 335. Rather than asserting new knowledge, the Court concedes that it cannot truly know what occurs during custodial questioning, because of the innate secrecy of such proceedings. It extrapolates a picture of what it conceives to be the norm from police investigatorial manuals, published in 1959 and 1962 or earlier, without any attempt to allow for adjustments in police practices that may [384 U.S. 436, 533] have occurred in the wake of more recent decisions of state appellate tribunals or this Court. But even if the relentless application of the described procedures could lead to involuntary confessions, it most assuredly does not follow that each and every case will disclose this kind of interrogation or this kind of consequence.[2] Insofar as appears from the Court's opinion, it has not examined a single transcript of any police interrogation, let alone the interrogation that took place in any one of these cases which it decides today. Judged by any of the standards for empirical investigation utilized in the social sciences the factual basis for the Court's premise is patently inadequate.

Although in the Court's view in-custody interrogation is inherently coercive, the Court says that the spontaneous product of the coercion of arrest and detention is still to be deemed voluntary. An accused, arrested on probable cause, may blurt out a confession which will be admissible despite the fact that he is alone and in custody, without any showing that he had any notion of his right to remain silent or of the consequences of his admission. Yet, under the Court's rule, if the police ask him a single question such as "Do you have anything to say?" or "Did you kill your wife?" his response, if there is one, has somehow been compelled, even if the accused has [384 U.S. 436, 534] been clearly warned of his right to remain silent. Common sense informs us to the contrary. While one may say that the response was "involuntary" in the sense the question provoked or was the occasion for the response and thus the defendant was induced to speak out when he might have remained silent if not arrested and not questioned, it is patently unsound to say the response is compelled.

Today's result would not follow even if it were agreed that to some extent custodial interrogation is inherently coercive. See Ashcraft v. Tennessee, 322 U.S. 143, 161 (Jackson, J., dissenting). The test has been whether the totality of circumstances deprived the defendant of a "free choice to admit, to deny, or to refuse to answer," Lisenba v. California, 314 U.S. 219, 241, and whether physical or psychological coercion was of such a degree that "the defendant's will was overborne at the time he confessed," Haynes v. Washington, 373 U.S. 503, 513; Lynumn v. Illinois, 372 U.S. 528, 534. The duration and nature of incommunicado custody, the presence or absence of advice concerning the defendant's constitutional rights, and the granting or refusal of requests to communicate with lawyers, relatives or friends have all been rightly regarded as important data bearing on the basic inquiry. See, e. g., Ashcraft v. Tennessee, 322 U.S. 143; Haynes v. Washington, 373 U.S. 503.[3] [384 U.S. 436, 535] But it has never been suggested, until today, that such questioning was so coercive and accused persons so lacking in hardihood that the very first response to the very first question following the commencement of custody must be conclusively presumed to be the product of an overborne will.

If the rule announced today were truly based on a conclusion that all confessions resulting from custodial interrogation are coerced, then it would simply have no rational foundation. Compare Tot v. United States, 319 U.S. 463, 466; United States v. Romano, 382 U.S. 136. A fortiori that would be true of the extension of the rule to exculpatory statements, which the Court effects after a brief discussion of why, in the Court's view, they must be deemed incriminatory but without any discussion of why they must be deemed coerced. See Wilson v. United States, 162 U.S. 613, 624. Even if one were to postulate that the Court's concern is not that all confessions induced by police interrogation are coerced but rather that some such confessions are coerced and present judicial procedures are believed to be inadequate to identify the confessions that are coerced and those that are not, it would still not be essential to impose the rule that the Court has now fashioned. Transcripts or observers could be required, specific time limits, tailored to fit the cause, could be imposed, or other devices could be utilized to reduce the chances that otherwise indiscernible coercion will produce an inadmissible confession.

On the other hand, even if one assumed that there was an adequate factual basis for the conclusion that all confessions obtained during in-custody interrogation are the product of compulsion, the rule propounded by [384 U.S. 436, 536] the Court would still be irrational, for, apparently, it is only if the accused is also warned of his right to counsel and waives both that right and the right against self-incrimination that the inherent compulsiveness of interrogation disappears. But if the defendant may not answer without a warning a question such as "Where were you last night?" without having his answer be a compelled one, how can the Court ever accept his negative answer to the question of whether he wants to consult his retained counsel or counsel whom the court will appoint? And why if counsel is present and the accused nevertheless confesses, or counsel tells the accused to tell the truth, and that is what the accused does, is the situation any less coercive insofar as the accused is concerned? The Court apparently realizes its dilemma of foreclosing questioning without the necessary warnings but at the same time permitting the accused, sitting in the same chair in front of the same policemen, to waive his right to consult an attorney. It expects, however, that the accused will not often waive the right; and if it is claimed that he has, the State faces a severe, if not impossible burden of proof.

All of this makes very little sense in terms of the compulsion which the Fifth Amendment proscribes. That amendment deals with compelling the accused himself. It is his free will that is involved. Confessions and incriminating admissions, as such, are not forbidden evidence; only those which are compelled are banned. I doubt that the Court observes these distinctions today. By considering any answers to any interrogation to be compelled regardless of the content and course of examination and by escalating the requirements to prove waiver, the Court not only prevents the use of compelled confessions but for all practical purposes forbids interrogation except in the presence of counsel. That is, instead of confining itself to protection of the right against compelled [384 U.S. 436, 537] self-incrimination the Court has created a limited Fifth Amendment right to counsel—or, as the Court expresses it, a "need for counsel to protect the Fifth Amendment privilege. . . ." Ante, at 470. The focus then is not on the will of the accused but on the will of counsel and how much influence he can have on the accused. Obviously there is no warrant in the Fifth Amendment for thus installing counsel as the arbiter of the privilege.

In sum, for all the Court's expounding on the menacing atmosphere of police interrogation procedures, it has failed to supply any foundation for the conclusions it draws or the measures it adopts.

IV.

Criticism of the Court's opinion, however, cannot stop with a demonstration that the factual and textual bases for the rule it propounds are, at best, less than compelling. Equally relevant is an assessment of the rule's consequences measured against community values. The Court's duty to assess the consequences of its action is not satisfied by the utterance of the truth that a value of our system of criminal justice is "to respect the inviolability of the human personality" and to require government to produce the evidence against the accused by its own independent labors. Ante, at 460. More than the human dignity of the accused is involved; the human personality of others in the society must also be preserved. Thus the values reflected by the privilege are not the sole desideratum; society's interest in the general security is of equal weight.

The obvious underpinning of the Court's decision is a deep-seated distrust of all confessions. As the Court declares that the accused may not be interrogated without counsel present, absent a waiver of the right to counsel, and as the Court all but admonishes the lawyer to [384 U.S. 436, 538] advise the accused to remain silent, the result adds up to a judicial judgment that evidence from the accused should not be used against him in any way, whether compelled or not. This is the not so subtle overtone of the opinion—that it is inherently wrong for the police to gather evidence from the accused himself. And this is precisely the nub of this dissent. I see nothing wrong or immoral, and certainly nothing unconstitutional, in the police's asking a suspect whom they have reasonable cause to arrest whether or not he killed his wife or in confronting him with the evidence on which the arrest was based, at least where he has been plainly advised that he may remain completely silent, see Escobedo v. Illinois, 378 U.S. 478, 499 (dissenting opinion). Until today, "the admissions or confessions of the prisoner, when voluntarily and freely made, have always ranked high in the scale of incriminating evidence." Brown v. Walker, 161 U.S. 591, 596; see also Hopt v. Utah, 110 U.S. 574, 584–585. Particularly when corroborated, as where the police have confirmed the accused's disclosure of the hiding place of implements or fruits of the crime, such confessions have the highest reliability and significantly contribute to the certitude with which we may believe the accused is guilty. Moreover, it is by no means certain that the process of confessing is injurious to the accused. To the contrary it may provide psychological relief and enhance the prospects for rehabilitation.

This is not to say that the value of respect for the inviolability of the accused's individual personality should be accorded no weight or that all confessions should be indiscriminately admitted. This Court has long read the Constitution to proscribe compelled confessions, a salutary rule from which there should be no retreat. But I see no sound basis, factual or otherwise, and the Court gives none, for concluding that the present rule against the receipt of coerced confessions is inadequate for the [384 U.S. 436, 539] task of sorting out inadmissible evidence and must be replaced by the per se rule which is now imposed. Even if the new concept can be said to have advantages of some sort over the present law, they are far outweighed by its likely undesirable impact on other very relevant and important interests.

The most basic function of any government is to provide for the security of the individual and of his property. Lanzetta v. New Jersey, 306 U.S. 451, 455. These ends of society are served by the criminal laws which for the most part are aimed at the prevention of crime. Without the reasonably effective performance of the task of preventing private violence and retaliation, it is idle to talk about human dignity and civilized values.

The modes by which the criminal laws serve the interest in general security are many. First the murderer who has taken the life of another is removed from the streets, deprived of his liberty and thereby prevented from repeating his offense. In view of the statistics on recidivism in this country[4] and of the number of instances [384 U.S. 436, 540] in which apprehension occurs only after repeated offenses, no one can sensibly claim that this aspect of the criminal law does not prevent crime or contribute significantly to the personal security of the ordinary citizen.

Secondly, the swift and sure apprehension of those who refuse to respect the personal security and dignity of their neighbor unquestionably has its impact on others who might be similarly tempted. That the criminal law is wholly or partly ineffective with a segment of the population or with many of those who have been apprehended and convicted is a very faulty basis for concluding that it is not effective with respect to the great bulk of our citizens or for thinking that without the criminal laws, [384 U.S. 436, 541] or in the absence of their enforcement, there would be no increase in crime. Arguments of this nature are not borne out by any kind of reliable evidence that I have seen to this date.

Thirdly, the law concerns itself with those whom it has confined. The hope and aim of modern penology, fortunately, is as soon as possible to return the convict to society a better and more law-abiding man than when he left. Sometimes there is success, sometimes failure. But at least the effort is made, and it should be made to the very maximum extent of our present and future capabilities.

The rule announced today will measurably weaken the ability of the criminal law to perform these tasks. It is a deliberate calculus to prevent interrogations, to reduce the incidence of confessions and pleas of guilty and to increase the number of trials.[5] Criminal trials, no [384 U.S. 436, 542] matter how efficient the police are, are not sure bets for the prosecution, nor should they be if the evidence is not forthcoming. Under the present law, the prosecution fails to prove its case in about 30% of the criminal cases actually tried in the federal courts. See Federal Offenders: 1964, supra, note 4, at 6 (Table 4), 59 (Table 1); Federal Offenders: 1963, supra, note 4, at 5 (Table 3); District of Columbia Offenders: 1963, supra, note 4, at 2 (Table 1). But it is something else again to remove from the ordinary criminal case all those confessions which heretofore have been held to be free and voluntary acts of the accused and to thus establish a new constitutional barrier to the ascertainment of truth by the judicial process. There is, in my view, every reason to believe that a good many criminal defendants who otherwise would have been convicted on what this Court has previously thought to be the most satisfactory kind of evidence will now, under this new version of the Fifth Amendment, either not be tried at all or will be acquitted if the State's evidence, minus the confession, is put to the test of litigation.

I have no desire whatsoever to share the responsibility for any such impact on the present criminal process.

In some unknown number of cases the Court's rule will return a killer, a rapist or other criminal to the streets and to the environment which produced him, to repeat his crime whenever it pleases him. As a consequence, there will not be a gain, but a loss, in human dignity. The real concern is not the unfortunate consequences of this new decision on the criminal law as an abstract, disembodied series of authoritative proscriptions, but the impact on those who rely on the public authority for protection and who without it can only engage in violent self-help with guns, knives and the help of their neighbors similarly inclined. There is, of [384 U.S. 436, 543] course, a saving factor: the next victims are uncertain, unnamed and unrepresented in this case.

Nor can this decision do other than have a corrosive effect on the criminal law as an effective device to prevent crime. A major component in its effectiveness in this regard is its swift and sure enforcement. The easier it is to get away with rape and murder, the less the deterrent effect on those who are inclined to attempt it. This is still good common sense. If it were not, we should posthaste liquidate the whole law enforcement establishment as a useless, misguided effort to control human conduct.

And what about the accused who has confessed or would confess in response to simple, noncoercive questioning and whose guilt could not otherwise be proved? Is it so clear that release is the best thing for him in every case? Has it so unquestionably been resolved that in each and every case it would be better for him not to confess and to return to his environment with no attempt whatsoever to help him? I think not. It may well be that in many cases it will be no less than a callous disregard for his own welfare as well as for the interests of his next victim.

There is another aspect to the effect of the Court's rule on the person whom the police have arrested on probable cause. The fact is that he may not be guilty at all and may be able to extricate himself quickly and simply if he were told the circumstances of his arrest and were asked to explain. This effort, and his release, must now await the hiring of a lawyer or his appointment by the court, consultation with counsel and then a session with the police or the prosecutor. Similarly, where probable cause exists to arrest several suspects, as where the body of the victim is discovered in a house having several residents, compare Johnson v. State, 238 Md. 140, 207 A. 2d 643 (1965), cert. denied, 382 U.S. 1013, it will often [384 U.S. 436, 544] be true that a suspect may be cleared only through the results of interrogation of other suspects. Here too the release of the innocent may be delayed by the Court's rule.

Much of the trouble with the Court's new rule is that it will operate indiscriminately in all criminal cases, regardless of the severity of the crime or the circumstances involved. It applies to every defendant, whether the professional criminal or one committing a crime of momentary passion who is not part and parcel of organized crime. It will slow down the investigation and the apprehension of confederates in those cases where time is of the essence, such as kidnapping, see Brinegar v. United States, 338 U.S. 160, 183 (Jackson, J., dissenting); People v. Modesto, 62 Cal. 2d 436, 446, 398 P.2d 753, 759 (1965), those involving the national security, see United States v. Drummond, 354 F.2d 132, 147 (C. A. 2d Cir. 1965) (en banc) (espionage case), pet. for cert. pending, No. 1203, Misc., O. T. 1965; cf. Gessner v. United States, 354 F.2d 726, 730, n. 10 (C. A. 10th Cir. 1965) (upholding, in espionage case, trial ruling that Government need not submit classified portions of interrogation transcript), and some of those involving organized crime. In the latter context the lawyer who arrives may also be the lawyer for the defendant's colleagues and can be relied upon to insure that no breach of the organization's security takes place even though the accused may feel that the best thing he can do is to cooperate.

At the same time, the Court's per se approach may not be justified on the ground that it provides a "bright line" permitting the authorities to judge in advance whether interrogation may safely be pursued without jeopardizing the admissibility of any information obtained as a consequence. Nor can it be claimed that judicial time and effort, assuming that is a relevant consideration, [384 U.S. 436, 545] will be conserved because of the ease of application of the new rule. Today's decision leaves open such questions as whether the accused was in custody, whether his statements were spontaneous or the product of interrogation, whether the accused has effectively waived his rights, and whether nontestimonial evidence introduced at trial is the fruit of statements made during a prohibited interrogation, all of which are certain to prove productive of uncertainty during investigation and litigation during prosecution. For all these reasons, if further restrictions on police interrogation are desirable at this time, a more flexible approach makes much more sense than the Court's constitutional straitjacket which forecloses more discriminating treatment by legislative or rule-making pronouncements.

Applying the traditional standards to the cases before the Court, I would hold these confessions voluntary. I would therefore affirm in Nos. 759, 760, and 761, and reverse in No. 584.

FOOTNOTES

[1] Of course the Court does not deny that it is departing from prior precedent; it expressly overrules Crooker and Cicenia, ante, at 479, n. 48, and it acknowledges that in the instant "cases we might not find the defendants" statements to have been involuntary in traditional terms," ante, at 457.

[2] In fact, the type of sustained interrogation described by the Court appears to be the exception rather than the rule. A survey of 399 cases in one city found that in almost

half of the cases the interrogation lasted less than 30 minutes. Barrett, Police Practices and the Law—From Arrest to Release or Charge, 50 Calif. L. Rev. 11, 41–45 (1962). Questioning tends to be confused and sporadic and is usually concentrated on confrontations with witnesses or new items of evidence, as these are obtained by officers conducting the investigation. See generally LaFave, Arrest: The Decision to Take a Suspect into Custody 386 (1965); ALI, A Model Code of Pre-Arraignment Procedure, Commentary 5.01, at 170, n. 4 (Tent. Draft No. 1, 1966).

[3] By contrast, the Court indicates that in applying this new rule it "will not pause to inquire in individual cases whether the defendant was aware of his rights without a warning being given." Ante, at 468. The reason given is that assessment of the knowledge of the defendant based on information as to age, education, intelligence, or prior contact with authorities can never be more than speculation, while a warning is a clear-cut fact. But the officers" claim that they gave the requisite warnings may be disputed, and facts respecting the defendant's prior experience may be undisputed and be of such a nature as to virtually preclude any doubt that the defendant knew of his rights. See United States v. Bolden, 355 F.2d 453 [384 U.S. 436, 535] (C. A. 7th Cir. 1965), petition for cert. pending No. 1146, O. T. 1965 (Secret Service agent); People v. Du Bont, 235 Cal. App. 2d 844, 45 Cal. Rptr. 717, pet. for cert. pending No. 1053, Misc., O. T. 1965 (former police officer).

[4] Precise statistics on the extent of recidivism are unavailable, in part because not all crimes are solved and in part because criminal records of convictions in different jurisdictions are not brought together by a central data collection agency. Beginning in 1963, however, the Federal Bureau of Investigation began collating data on "Careers in Crime," which it publishes in its Uniform Crime Reports. Of 92,869 offenders processed in 1963 and 1964, 76% had a prior arrest record on some charge. Over a period of 10 years the group had accumulated 434,000 charges. FBI, Uniform Crime Reports—1964, 27–28. In 1963 and 1964 between 23% and 25% of all offenders sentenced in 88 federal district courts (excluding the District Court for the District of Columbia) whose criminal records were reported had previously been sentenced to a term of imprisonment of 13 months or more. Approximately an additional 40% had a prior record less than prison (juvenile record, probation record, etc.). Administrative Office of the United States Courts, Federal Offenders in the United States District Courts: 1964, x, 36 (hereinafter cited as Federal Offenders: 1964); Administrative [384 U.S. 436, 540] Office of the United States Courts, Federal Offenders in the United States District Courts: 1963, 25–27 (hereinafter cited as Federal Offenders: 1963). During the same two years in the District Court for the District of Columbia between 28% and 35% of those sentenced had prior prison records and from 37% to 40% had a prior record less than prison. Federal Offenders: 1964, xii, 64, 66; Administrative Office of the United States Courts, Federal Offenders in the United States District Court for the District of Columbia: 1963, 8, 10 (hereinafter cited as District of Columbia Offenders: 1963).

A similar picture is obtained if one looks at the subsequent records of those released from confinement. In 1964, 12.3% of persons on federal probation had their probation revoked because of the commission of major violations (defined as one in which the probationer has been committed to imprisonment for a period of 90 days or more, been placed on probation for over one year on a new offense, or has absconded with felony charges outstanding). Twenty-three and two-tenths percent of parolees and 16.9% of those who had been mandatorily released after service of a portion of their sentence likewise committed major violations. Reports of the Proceedings of the Judicial Conference of the United States and Annual Report of the Director of the Administrative Office of the United States Courts: 1965, 138. See also Mandel et al., Recidivism Studied and Defined, 56 J. Crim. L., C. & P. S. 59 (1965) (within five years of release 62.33% of sample had committed offenses placing them in recidivist category).

[5] Eighty-eight federal district courts (excluding the District Court for the District of Columbia) disposed of the cases of 33,381 criminal defendants in 1964. Only 12.5% of those cases were actually tried. Of the remaining cases, 89.9% were terminated by convictions upon pleas of guilty and 10.1% were dismissed. Stated differently, approximately 90% of all convictions resulted from guilty pleas. Federal Offenders: 1964, supra, note 4, 3–6. In the District Court for the District of Columbia a higher percentage, 27%, went to trial, and the defendant pleaded guilty in approximately 78% of the cases terminated prior to trial. Id., at 58–59. No reliable statistics are available concerning the percentage of cases in which guilty pleas are induced because of the existence of a confession or of physical evidence unearthed as a result of a confession. Undoubtedly the number of such cases is substantial.

Perhaps of equal significance is the number of instances of known crimes which are not solved. In 1964, only 388,946, or 23.9% of 1,626,574 serious known offenses were cleared. The clearance rate ranged from 89.8% for homicides to 18.7% for larceny. FBI, Uniform Crime Reports—1964, 20–22, 101. Those who would replace interrogation as an investigatorial tool by modern scientific investigation techniques significantly overestimate the effectiveness of present procedures, even when interrogation is included. [384 U.S. 436, 546]

Roe v. Wade
1973

In March of 1970, an unmarried and pregnant Norma L. McCorvey (aka "Jane Roe") filed suit in the U.S. District Court for the Northern District of Texas, naming Dallas County district attorney Henry B. Wade as the defendant. In this suit, McCorvey requested that the court declare the Texas abortion statutes—which permitted abortions only when necessary to save the life of the mother—to be unconstitutional, and thus grant an injunction to cease their enforcement. James Hubert Halford, a licensed physician with three pending abortion violations, was permitted by the court to intervene and terminate her pregnancy. Contemporaneously, a childless married couple, "Jane and John Doe" filed a similar suit, claiming that due to the wife's mental illness, they would seek an abortion should she become pregnant in the future. A three-judge panel consolidated these two cases, ruling that the Texas law was in fact unconstitutional, though denying Roe's requested injunction. Failing to win the injunction, both Roe and the Does appealed their case to the U.S. Supreme Court.

The Supreme Court found, most notably, that the Ninth Amendment's guarantee of privacy protects a woman's choice of whether or not to end her own pregnancy. The court went on to rule on a number of other facets of the case, which further defined the individual's rights, while laying out the role of the legislature in regulating abortion. Though *Roe v. Wade* remains one of the most contentious and challenged decisions in the history of the Supreme Court, it has yet to be overturned or significantly revised.

U.S. SUPREME COURT

ROE V. WADE, 410 U.S. 113 (1973)

410 U.S. 113

ROE ET AL. V. WADE, DISTRICT ATTORNEY OF DALLAS COUNTY
APPEAL FROM THE UNITED STATES DISTRICT COURT FOR THE NORTHERN DISTRICT OF TEXAS
NO. 70–18.

Argued December 13, 1971 Reargued October 11, 1972 Decided January 22, 1973.

A PREGNANT single woman (Roe) brought a class action challenging the constitutionality of the Texas criminal abortion laws, which proscribe procuring or attempting an abortion except on medical advice for the purpose of saving the mother's life. A licensed physician (Hallford), who had two state abortion prosecutions pending against him, was permitted to intervene. A childless married couple (the Does), the wife not being pregnant, separately attacked the laws, basing alleged injury on the future possibilities of contraceptive failure, pregnancy, unpreparedness for parenthood, and impairment of the wife's health. A three-judge District Court, which consolidated the actions, held that Roe and Hallford, and members of their classes, had standing to sue and presented justiciable controversies. Ruling that declaratory, though not injunctive, relief was warranted, the court declared the abortion statutes void as vague and overbroadly infringing those plaintiffs" Ninth and Fourteenth Amendment rights. The court ruled the Does" complaint not justiciable. Appellants directly appealed to this Court on the injunctive rulings, and appellee cross-appealed from the District Court's grant of declaratory relief to Roe and Hallford. Held:

  1. While 28 U.S.C. 1253 authorizes no direct appeal to this Court from the grant or denial of declaratory relief alone, review is not

foreclosed when the case is properly before the Court on appeal from specific denial of injunctive relief and the arguments as to both injunctive and declaratory relief are necessarily identical. P. 123.

2. Roe has standing to sue; the Does and Hallford do not. Pp. 123–129.

(a) Contrary to appellee's contention, the natural termination of Roe's pregnancy did not moot her suit. Litigation involving pregnancy, which is "capable of repetition, yet evading review," is an exception to the usual federal rule that an actual controversy [410 U.S. 113, 114] must exist at review stages and not simply when the action is initiated. Pp. 124–125.

(b) The District Court correctly refused injunctive, but erred in granting declaratory, relief to Hallford, who alleged no federally protected right not assertable as a defense against the good-faith state prosecutions pending against him. Samuels v. Mackell, 401 U.S. 66. Pp. 125–127.

(c) The Does' complaint, based as it is on contingencies, any one or more of which may not occur, is too speculative to present an actual case or controversy. Pp. 127–129.

3. State criminal abortion laws, like those involved here, that except from criminality only a life-saving procedure on the mother's behalf without regard to the stage of her pregnancy and other interests involved violate the Due Process Clause of the Fourteenth Amendment, which protects against state action the right to privacy, including a woman's qualified right to terminate her pregnancy. Though the State cannot override that right, it has legitimate interests in protecting both the pregnant woman's health and the potentiality of human life, each of which interests grows and reaches a "compelling" point at various stages of the woman's approach to term. Pp. 147–164.

(a) For the stage prior to approximately the end of the first trimester, the abortion decision and its effectuation must be left to the medical judgment of the pregnant woman's attending physician. Pp. 163, 164.

(b) For the stage subsequent to approximately the end of the first trimester, the State, in promoting its interest in the health of the mother, may, if it chooses, regulate the abortion procedure in ways that are reasonably related to maternal health. Pp. 163, 164.

(c) For the stage subsequent to viability the State, in promoting its interest in the potentiality of human life, may, if it chooses, regulate, and even proscribe, abortion except where necessary, in appropriate medical judgment, for the preservation of the life or health of the mother. Pp. 163–164; 164–165.

4. The State may define the term "physician" to mean only a

physician currently licensed by the State, and may proscribe any abortion by a person who is not a physician as so defined. P. 165.
5. It is unnecessary to decide the injunctive relief issue since the Texas authorities will doubtless fully recognize the Court's ruling [410 U.S. 113, 115] that the Texas criminal abortion statutes are unconstitutional. P. 166.

314 F. Supp. 1217, affirmed in part and reversed in part.

BLACKMUN, J., delivered the opinion of the Court, in which BURGER, C. J., and DOUGLAS, BRENNAN, STEWART, MAR-SHALL, and POWELL, JJ., joined. BURGER, C. J., post, p. 207, DOUGLAS, J., post, p. 209, and STEWART, J., post, p. 167, filed concurring opinions. WHITE, J., filed a dissenting opinion, in which REHNQUIST, J., joined, post, p. 221. REHNQUIST, J., filed a dissenting opinion, post, p. 171.

Sarah Weddington reargued the cause for appellants. With her on the briefs were Roy Lucas, Fred Bruner, Roy L. Merrill, Jr., and Norman Dorsen.

Robert C. Flowers, Assistant Attorney General of Texas, argued the cause for appellee on the reargument. Jay Floyd, Assistant Attorney General, argued the cause for appellee on the original argument. With them on the brief were Crawford C. Martin, Attorney General, Nola White, First Assistant Attorney General, Alfred Walker, Executive Assistant Attorney General, Henry Wade, and John B. Tolle.* [410 U.S. 113, 116]

---

*Briefs of amici curiae were filed by Gary K. Nelson, Attorney General of Arizona, Robert K. Killian, Attorney General of Connecticut, Ed W. Hancock, Attorney General of Kentucky, Clarence A. H. Meyer, Attorney General of Nebraska, and Vernon B. Romney, Attorney General of Utah; by Joseph P. Witherspoon, Jr., for the Association of Texas Diocesan Attorneys; by Charles E. Rice for Americans United for Life; by Eugene J. McMahon for Women for the Unborn et al.; by Carol Ryan for the American College of Obstetricians and Gynecologists et al.; by Dennis J. Horan, Jerome A. Frazel, Jr., Thomas M. Crisham, and Dolores V. Horan for Certain Physicians, Professors and Fellows of the American College of Obstetrics and Gynecology; by Harriet F. Pilpel, Nancy F. Wechsler, and Frederic S. Nathan for Planned Parenthood Federation of America, Inc., et al.; by Alan F. Charles for the National Legal Program on Health Problems of the Poor et al.; by Marttie L. Thompson for State Communities Aid Assn.; by [410 U.S. 113, 116] Alfred L. Scanlan, Martin J. Flynn, and Robert M. Byrn for the National Right to Life Committee; by Helen L. Buttenwieser for the American Ethical Union et al.; by Norma G. Zarky for the American Association of University Women et al.; by Nancy Stearns for New Women Lawyers et al.; by the California Committee to Legalize Abortion et al.; and by Robert E. Dunne for Robert L. Sassone.

MR. JUSTICE BLACKMUN delivered the opinion of the Court.

This Texas federal appeal and its Georgia companion, Doe v. Bolton, post, p. 179, present constitutional challenges to state criminal abortion legislation. The Texas statutes under attack here are typical of those that have been in effect in many States for approximately a century. The Georgia statutes, in contrast, have a modern cast and are a legislative product that, to an extent at least, obviously reflects the influences of recent attitudinal change, of advancing medical knowledge and techniques, and of new thinking about an old issue.

We forthwith acknowledge our awareness of the sensitive and emotional nature of the abortion controversy, of the vigorous opposing views, even among physicians, and of the deep and seemingly absolute convictions that the subject inspires. One's philosophy, one's experiences, one's exposure to the raw edges of human existence, one's religious training, one's attitudes toward life and family and their values, and the moral standards one establishes and seeks to observe, are all likely to influence and to color one's thinking and conclusions about abortion.

In addition, population growth, pollution, poverty, and racial overtones tend to complicate and not to simplify the problem.

Our task, of course, is to resolve the issue by constitutional measurement, free of emotion and of predilection. We seek earnestly to do this, and, because we do, we [410 U.S. 113, 117] have inquired into, and in this opinion place some emphasis upon, medical and medical-legal history and what that history reveals about man's attitudes toward the abortion procedure over the centuries. We bear in mind, too, Mr. Justice Holmes" admonition in his now-vindicated dissent in Lochner v. New York, 198 U.S. 45, 76 (1905):

> "[The Constitution] is made for people of fundamentally differing views, and the accident of our finding certain opinions natural and familiar or novel and even shocking ought not to conclude our judgment upon the question whether statutes embodying them conflict with the Constitution of the United States."

I.

The Texas statutes that concern us here are Arts. 1191–1194 and 1196 of the State's Penal Code.[1] These make it a crime to "procure an abortion," as therein [410 U.S. 113, 118] defined, or to attempt one, except with respect to "an abortion procured or attempted by medical advice for the purpose of saving the life of the mother." Similar statutes are in existence in a majority of the States.[2] [410 U.S. 113, 119]

Texas first enacted a criminal abortion statute in 1854. Texas Laws 1854, c. 49, 1, set forth in 3 H. Gammel, Laws of Texas 1502 (1898). This was soon modified into language that has remained substantially unchanged to the present time. See Texas Penal Code of 1857, c. 7, Arts. 531–536; G. Paschal, Laws of Texas, Arts. 2192–2197 (1866); Texas Rev. Stat., c. 8, Arts. 536–541 (1879); Texas Rev. Crim. Stat., Arts. 1071–1076 (1911). The final article in each of these compilations provided the same exception, as does the present Article 1196, for an abortion by "medical advice for the purpose of saving the life of the mother."[3] [410 U.S. 113, 120]

II.

Jane Roe,[4] a single woman who was residing in Dallas County, Texas, instituted this federal action in March 1970 against the District Attorney of the county. She sought a declaratory judgment that the Texas criminal abortion statutes were unconstitutional on their face, and an injunction restraining the defendant from enforcing the statutes.

Roe alleged that she was unmarried and pregnant; that she wished to terminate her pregnancy by an abortion "performed by a competent, licensed physician, under safe, clinical conditions"; that she was unable to get a "legal" abortion in Texas because her life did not appear to be threatened by the continuation of her pregnancy; and that she could not afford to travel to another jurisdiction in order to secure a legal abortion under safe conditions. She claimed that the Texas statutes were unconstitutionally vague and that they abridged her right of personal privacy, protected by the First, Fourth, Fifth, Ninth, and Fourteenth Amendments. By an amendment to her complaint Roe purported to sue "on behalf of herself and all other women" similarly situated.

James Hubert Hallford, a licensed physician, sought and was granted leave to intervene in Roe's action. In his complaint he alleged that he had been arrested previously for violations of the Texas abortion statutes and [410 U.S. 113, 121] that two such prosecutions were pending against him. He described conditions of patients who came to him seeking abortions, and he claimed that for many cases he, as a physician, was unable to determine whether they fell within or outside the exception recognized by Article 1196. He alleged that, as a consequence, the statutes were vague and uncertain, in violation of the Fourteenth Amendment, and that they violated his own and his patients" rights to privacy in the doctor-patient relationship and his own right to practice medicine, rights he claimed were guaranteed by the First, Fourth, Fifth, Ninth, and Fourteenth Amendments.

John and Mary Doe,[5] a married couple, filed a companion complaint to that of Roe. They also named the District Attorney as defendant, claimed like constitutional deprivations, and sought declaratory and injunctive relief. The Does alleged that they were a childless couple; that Mrs. Doe was suffering from a "neural-chemical" disorder; that her physician had "advised her to avoid pregnancy until such time as her condition has materially improved" (although a pregnancy at the present time would not present "a serious risk" to her life); that, pursuant to medical advice, she had discontinued use of birth control pills; and that if she should become pregnant, she would want to terminate the pregnancy by an abortion performed by a competent, licensed physician under safe, clinical conditions. By an amendment to their complaint, the Does purported to sue "on behalf of themselves and all couples similarly situated."

The two actions were consolidated and heard together by a duly convened three-judge district court. The suits thus presented the situations of the pregnant single woman, the childless couple, with the wife not pregnant, [410 U.S. 113, 122] and the licensed practicing physician, all joining in the attack on the Texas criminal abortion statutes. Upon the filing of affidavits, motions were made for dismissal and for summary judgment. The court held that Roe and members of her class, and Dr. Hallford, had standing to sue and presented justiciable controversies, but that the Does had failed to allege facts sufficient to state a present controversy and did not have standing. It concluded that, with respect to the requests for a declaratory judgment, abstention was not warranted. On the merits, the District Court held that the "fundamental right of single women and married persons to choose whether to have children is protected by the Ninth Amendment, through the Fourteenth Amendment," and that the Texas criminal abortion statutes were void on their face because they were both unconstitutionally vague and constituted an overbroad infringement of the plaintiffs" Ninth Amendment rights. The court then held that abstention was warranted with respect to the requests for an injunction. It therefore dismissed the Does" complaint, declared the abortion statutes void, and dismissed the application for injunctive relief. 314 F. Supp. 1217, 1225 (ND Tex. 1970).

The plaintiffs Roe and Doe and the intervenor Hallford, pursuant to 28 U.S.C. 1253, have appealed to this Court from that part of the District Court's judgment denying the injunction. The defendant District Attorney has purported to cross-appeal, pursuant to the same statute, from the court's grant of declaratory relief to Roe and Hallford. Both sides also have taken protective appeals to the United States Court of Appeals for the Fifth Circuit. That court ordered the appeals held in abeyance pending decision here. We postponed decision on jurisdiction to the hearing on the merits. 402 U.S. 941 (1971). [410 U.S. 113, 123]

III.

It might have been preferable if the defendant, pursuant to our Rule 20, had presented to us a petition for certiorari before judgment in the Court of Appeals with respect to the granting of the plaintiffs'' prayer for declaratory relief. Our decisions in Mitchell v. Donovan, 398 U.S. 427 (1970), and Gunn v. University Committee, 399 U.S. 383 (1970), are to the effect that 1253 does not authorize an appeal to this Court from the grant or denial of declaratory relief alone. We conclude, nevertheless, that those decisions do not foreclose our review of both the injunctive and the declaratory aspects of a case of this kind when it is properly here, as this one is, on appeal under 1253 from specific denial of injunctive relief, and the arguments as to both aspects are necessarily identical. See Carter v. Jury Comm'n, 396 U.S. 320 (1970); Florida Lime Growers v. Jacobsen, 362 U.S. 73, 80–81 (1960). It would be destructive of time and energy for all concerned were we to rule otherwise. Cf. Doe v. Bolton, post, p. 179.

IV.

We are next confronted with issues of justiciability, standing, and abstention. Have Roe and the Does established that "personal stake in the outcome of the controversy," Baker v. Carr, 369 U.S. 186, 204 (1962), that insures that "the dispute sought to be adjudicated will be presented in an adversary context and in a form historically viewed as capable of judicial resolution," Flast v. Cohen, 392 U.S. 83, 101 (1968), and Sierra Club v. Morton, 405 U.S. 727, 732 (1972)? And what effect did the pendency of criminal abortion charges against Dr. Hallford in state court have upon the propriety of the federal court's granting relief to him as a plaintiff-intervenor? [410 U.S. 113, 124]

A. Jane Roe. Despite the use of the pseudonym, no suggestion is made that Roe is a fictitious person. For purposes of her case, we accept as true, and as established, her existence; her pregnant state, as of the inception of her suit in March 1970 and as late as May 21 of that year when she filed an alias affidavit with the District Court; and her inability to obtain a legal abortion in Texas.

Viewing Roe's case as of the time of its filing and thereafter until as late as May, there can be little dispute that it then presented a case or controversy and that, wholly apart from the class aspects, she, as a pregnant single woman thwarted by the Texas criminal abortion laws, had standing to challenge those statutes. Abele v. Markle, 452 F.2d 1121, 1125 (CA2 1971); Crossen v. Breckenridge, 446 F.2d 833, 838–839 (CA6 1971); Poe v. Menghini, 339 F. Supp. 986, 990–991 (Kan. 1972). See

Truax v. Raich, 239 U.S. 33 (1915). Indeed, we do not read the appellee's brief as really asserting anything to the contrary. The "logical nexus between the status asserted and the claim sought to be adjudicated," Flast v. Cohen, 392 U.S., at 102, and the necessary degree of contentiousness, Golden v. Zwickler, 394 U.S. 103 (1969), are both present.

The appellee notes, however, that the record does not disclose that Roe was pregnant at the time of the District Court hearing on May 22, 1970,[6] or on the following June 17 when the court's opinion and judgment were filed. And he suggests that Roe's case must now be moot because she and all other members of her class are no longer subject to any 1970 pregnancy. [410 U.S. 113, 125]

The usual rule in federal cases is that an actual controversy must exist at stages of appellate or certiorari review, and not simply at the date the action is initiated. United States v. Munsingwear, Inc., 340 U.S. 36 (1950); Golden v. Zwickler, supra; SEC v. Medical Committee for Human Rights, 404 U.S. 403 (1972).

But when, as here, pregnancy is a significant fact in the litigation, the normal 266-day human gestation period is so short that the pregnancy will come to term before the usual appellate process is complete. If that termination makes a case moot, pregnancy litigation seldom will survive much beyond the trial stage, and appellate review will be effectively denied. Our law should not be that rigid. Pregnancy often comes more than once to the same woman, and in the general population, if man is to survive, it will always be with us. Pregnancy provides a classic justification for a conclusion of nonmootness. It truly could be "capable of repetition, yet evading review." Southern Pacific Terminal Co. v. ICC, 219 U.S. 498, 515 (1911). See Moore v. Ogilvie, 394 U.S. 814, 816 (1969); Carroll v. Princess Anne, 393 U.S. 175, 178–179 (1968); United States v. W. T. Grant Co., 345 U.S. 629, 632–633 (1953).

We, therefore, agree with the District Court that Jane Roe had standing to undertake this litigation, that she presented a justiciable controversy, and that the termination of her 1970 pregnancy has not rendered her case moot.

B. Dr. Hallford. The doctor's position is different. He entered Roe's litigation as a plaintiff-intervenor, alleging in his complaint that he:

"[I]n the past has been arrested for violating the Texas Abortion Laws and at the present time stands charged by indictment with violating said laws in the Criminal District Court of Dallas County, Texas to-wit: (1) The State of Texas vs. [410 U.S. 113, 126] James H. Hallford, No. C-69-5307-IH, and (2) The State of Texas vs. James H. Hallford, No. C-69-2524-H. In both cases the defendant is charged with abortion . . . ."

In his application for leave to intervene, the doctor made like representations as to the abortion charges pending in the state court. These representations were also repeated in the affidavit he executed and filed in support of his motion for summary judgment.

Dr. Hallford is, therefore, in the position of seeking, in a federal court, declaratory and injunctive relief with respect to the same statutes under which he stands charged in criminal prosecutions simultaneously pending in state court. Although he stated that he has been arrested in the past for violating the State's abortion laws, he makes no allegation of any substantial and immediate threat to any federally protected right that cannot be asserted in his defense against the state prosecutions. Neither is there any allegation of harassment or bad-faith prosecution. In order to escape the rule articulated in the cases cited in the next paragraph of this opinion that, absent harassment and bad faith, a defendant in a pending state criminal case cannot affirmatively challenge in federal court the statutes under which the State is prosecuting him, Dr. Hallford seeks to distinguish his status as a present state defendant from his status as a "potential future defendant" and to assert only the latter for standing purposes here.

We see no merit in that distinction. Our decision in Samuels v. Mackell, 401 U.S. 66 (1971), compels the conclusion that the District Court erred when it granted declaratory relief to Dr. Hallford instead of refraining from so doing. The court, of course, was correct in refusing to grant injunctive relief to the doctor. The reasons supportive of that action, however, are those expressed in Samuels v. Mackell, supra, and in Younger v. [410 U.S. 113, 127] Harris, 401 U.S. 37 (1971); Boyle v. Landry, 401 U.S. 77 (1971); Perez v. Ledesma, 401 U.S. 82 (1971); and Byrne v. Karalexis, 401 U.S. 216 (1971). See also Dombrowski v. Pfister, 380 U.S. 479 (1965). We note, in passing, that Younger and its companion cases were decided after the three-judge District Court decision in this case.

Dr. Hallford's complaint in intervention, therefore, is to be dismissed.[7] He is remitted to his defenses in the state criminal proceedings against him. We reverse the judgment of the District Court insofar as it granted Dr. Hallford relief and failed to dismiss his complaint in intervention.

C. The Does. In view of our ruling as to Roe's standing in her case, the issue of the Does" standing in their case has little significance. The claims they assert are essentially the same as those of Roe, and they attack the same statutes. Nevertheless, we briefly note the Does" posture.

Their pleadings present them as a childless married couple, the woman not being pregnant, who have no desire to have children at this time because of their having received medical advice that Mrs. Doe should avoid pregnancy, and for "other highly personal reasons." But they "fear . . . they may face the prospect of becoming [410 U.S. 113, 128] parents." And if pregnancy ensues, they "would want to terminate" it by an abortion. They assert an inability to obtain an abortion legally in Texas and, consequently, the prospect of obtaining an illegal abortion there or of going outside Texas to some place where the procedure could be obtained legally and competently.

We thus have as plaintiffs a married couple who have, as their asserted immediate and present injury, only an alleged "detrimental effect upon [their] marital happiness" because they are forced to "the choice of refraining from normal sexual relations or of endangering Mary Doe's health through a possible pregnancy." Their claim is that sometime in the future Mrs. Doe might become pregnant because of possible failure of contraceptive measures, and at that time in the future she might want an abortion that might then be illegal under the Texas statutes.

This very phrasing of the Does" position reveals its speculative character. Their alleged injury rests on possible future contraceptive failure, possible future pregnancy, possible future unpreparedness for parenthood, and possible future impairment of health. Any one or more of these several possibilities may not take place and all may not combine. In the Does" estimation, these possibilities might have some real or imagined impact upon their marital happiness. But we are not prepared to say that the bare allegation of so indirect an injury is sufficient to present an actual case or controversy. Younger v. Harris, 401 U.S., at 41–42; Golden v. Zwickler, 394 U.S., at 109–110; Abele v. Markle, 452 F.2d, at 1124–1125; Crossen v. Breckenridge, 446 F.2d, at 839. The Does" claim falls far short of those resolved otherwise in the cases that the Does urge upon us, namely, Investment Co. Institute v. Camp, 401 U.S. 617 (1971); Data Processing Service v. Camp, 397 U.S. 150 (1970); [410 U.S. 113, 129] and Epperson v. Arkansas, 393 U.S. 97 (1968). See also Truax v. Raich, 239 U.S. 33 (1915).

The Does therefore are not appropriate plaintiffs in this litigation. Their complaint was properly dismissed by the District Court, and we affirm that dismissal.

V.

The principal thrust of appellant's attack on the Texas statutes is that they improperly invade a right, said to be possessed by the pregnant woman, to choose to terminate her pregnancy. Appellant would discover this right in the concept of personal "liberty" embodied in the Fourteenth Amendment's Due Process Clause; or in personal, marital, familial, and sexual privacy said to be protected by the Bill of Rights or its penumbras, see Griswold v. Connecticut, 381 U.S. 479 (1965); Eisenstadt v. Baird, 405 U.S. 438 (1972); id., at 460 (WHITE, J., concurring in result);

or among those rights reserved to the people by the Ninth Amendment, Griswold v. Connecticut, 381 U.S., at 486 (Goldberg, J., concurring). Before addressing this claim, we feel it desirable briefly to survey, in several aspects, the history of abortion, for such insight as that history may afford us, and then to examine the state purposes and interests behind the criminal abortion laws.

VI.

It perhaps is not generally appreciated that the restrictive criminal abortion laws in effect in a majority of States today are of relatively recent vintage. Those laws, generally proscribing abortion or its attempt at any time during pregnancy except when necessary to preserve the pregnant woman's life, are not of ancient or even of common-law origin. Instead, they derive from statutory changes effected, for the most part, in the latter half of the 19th century. [410 U.S. 113, 130]

1. Ancient attitudes. These are not capable of precise determination. We are told that at the time of the Persian Empire abortifacients were known and that criminal abortions were severely punished.[8] We are also told, however, that abortion was practiced in Greek times as well as in the Roman Era,[9] and that "it was resorted to without scruple."[10] The Ephesian, Soranos, often described as the greatest of the ancient gynecologists, appears to have been generally opposed to Rome's prevailing free-abortion practices. He found it necessary to think first of the life of the mother, and he resorted to abortion when, upon this standard, he felt the procedure advisable.[11] Greek and Roman law afforded little protection to the unborn. If abortion was prosecuted in some places, it seems to have been based on a concept of a violation of the father's right to his offspring. Ancient religion did not bar abortion.[12]

2. The Hippocratic Oath. What then of the famous Oath that has stood so long as the ethical guide of the medical profession and that bears the name of the great Greek (460(?)–377(?) B. C.), who has been described [410 U.S. 113, 131] as the Father of Medicine, the "wisest and the greatest practitioner of his art," and the "most important and most complete medical personality of antiquity," who dominated the medical schools of his time, and who typified the sum of the medical knowledge of the past?[13] The Oath varies somewhat according to the particular translation, but in any translation the content is clear: "I will give no deadly medicine to anyone if asked, nor suggest any such counsel; and in like manner I will not give to a woman a pessary to produce abortion,"[14] or "I will neither give a deadly drug to anybody if asked for it, nor will I make a suggestion to this effect. Similarly, I will not give to a woman an abortive remedy."[15]

Although the Oath is not mentioned in any of the principal briefs in this case or in Doe v. Bolton, post, p. 179, it represents the apex of the development of strict ethical concepts in medicine, and its influence endures to this day. Why did not the authority of Hippocrates dissuade abortion practice in his time and that of Rome? The late Dr. Edelstein provides us with a theory:[16] The Oath was not uncontested even in Hippocrates" day; only the Pythagorean school of philosophers frowned upon the related act of suicide. Most Greek thinkers, on the other hand, commended abortion, at least prior to viability. See Plato, Republic, V, 461; Aristotle, Politics, VII, 1335b 25. For the Pythagoreans, however, it was a matter of dogma. For them the embryo was animate from the moment of conception, and abortion meant destruction of a living being. The abortion clause of the Oath, therefore, "echoes Pythagorean doctrines," [410 U.S. 113, 132] and "[i]n no other stratum of Greek opinion were such views held or proposed in the same spirit of uncompromising austerity."[17]

Dr. Edelstein then concludes that the Oath originated in a group representing only a small segment of Greek opinion and that it certainly was not accepted by all ancient physicians. He points out that medical writings down to Galen (A. D. 130–200) "give evidence of the violation of almost every one of its injunctions."[18] But with the end of antiquity a decided change took place. Resistance against suicide and against abortion became common. The Oath came to be popular. The emerging teachings of Christianity were in agreement with the Pythagorean ethic. The Oath "became the nucleus of all medical ethics" and "was applauded as the embodiment of truth." Thus, suggests Dr. Edelstein, it is "a Pythagorean manifesto and not the expression of an absolute standard of medical conduct."[19]

This, it seems to us, is a satisfactory and acceptable explanation of the Hippocratic Oath's apparent rigidity. It enables us to understand, in historical context, a long-accepted and revered statement of medical ethics.

3. The common law. It is undisputed that at common law, abortion performed before "quickening"—the first recognizable movement of the fetus in utero, appearing usually from the 16th to the 18th week of pregnancy[20]—was not an indictable offense.[21] The absence [410 U.S. 113, 133] of a common-law crime for pre-quickening abortion appears to have developed from a confluence of earlier philosophical, theological, and civil and canon law concepts of when life begins. These disciplines variously approached the question in terms of the point at which the embryo or fetus became "formed" or recognizably human, or in terms of when a "person" came into being, that is, infused with a "soul" or "animated." A loose consensus evolved in early English law that these events occurred at some point between conception and live birth.[22] This

was "mediate animation." Although [410 U.S. 113, 134] Christian theology and the canon law came to fix the point of animation at 40 days for a male and 80 days for a female, a view that persisted until the 19th century, there was otherwise little agreement about the precise time of formation or animation. There was agreement, however, that prior to this point the fetus was to be regarded as part of the mother, and its destruction, therefore, was not homicide. Due to continued uncertainty about the precise time when animation occurred, to the lack of any empirical basis for the 40–80-day view, and perhaps to Aquinas" definition of movement as one of the two first principles of life, Bracton focused upon quickening as the critical point. The significance of quickening was echoed by later common-law scholars and found its way into the received common law in this country.

Whether abortion of a quick fetus was a felony at common law, or even a lesser crime, is still disputed. Bracton, writing early in the 13th century, thought it homicide.[23] But the later and predominant view, following the great common-law scholars, has been that it was, at most, a lesser offense. In a frequently cited [410 U.S. 113, 135] passage, Coke took the position that abortion of a woman "quick with childe" is "a great misprision, and no murder."[24] Blackstone followed, saying that while abortion after quickening had once been considered manslaughter (though not murder), "modern law" took a less severe view.[25] A recent review of the common-law precedents argues, however, that those precedents contradict Coke and that even post-quickening abortion was never established as a common-law crime.[26] This is of some importance because while most American courts ruled, in holding or dictum, that abortion of an unquickened fetus was not criminal under their received common law,[27] others followed Coke in stating that abortion [410 U.S. 113, 136] of a quick fetus was a "misprision," a term they translated to mean "misdemeanor."[28] That their reliance on Coke on this aspect of the law was uncritical and, apparently in all the reported cases, dictum (due probably to the paucity of common-law prosecutions for post-quickening abortion), makes it now appear doubtful that abortion was ever firmly established as a common-law crime even with respect to the destruction of a quick fetus.

4. The English statutory law. England's first criminal abortion statute, Lord Ellenborough's Act, 43 Geo. 3, c. 58, came in 1803. It made abortion of a quick fetus, 1, a capital crime, but in 2 it provided lesser penalties for the felony of abortion before quickening, and thus preserved the "quickening" distinction. This contrast was continued in the general revision of 1828, 9 Geo. 4, c. 31, 13. It disappeared, however, together with the death penalty, in 1837, 7 Will. 4 & 1 Vict., c. 85. 6, and did not reappear in the Offenses Against the Person Act of 1861, 24 & 25 Vict., c. 100, 59, that

formed the core of English anti-abortion law until the liberalizing reforms of 1967. In 1929, the Infant Life (Preservation) Act, 19 & 20 Geo. 5, c. 34, came into being. Its emphasis was upon the destruction of "the life of a child capable of being born alive." It made a willful act performed with the necessary intent a felony. It contained a proviso that one was not to be [410 U.S. 113, 137] found guilty of the offense "unless it is proved that the act which caused the death of the child was not done in good faith for the purpose only of preserving the life of the mother."

A seemingly notable development in the English law was the case of Rex v. Bourne, 1939. 1 K. B. 687. This case apparently answered in the affirmative the question whether an abortion necessary to preserve the life of the pregnant woman was excepted from the criminal penalties of the 1861 Act. In his instructions to the jury, Judge Macnaghten referred to the 1929 Act, and observed that that Act related to "the case where a child is killed by a wilful act at the time when it is being delivered in the ordinary course of nature." Id., at 691. He concluded that the 1861 Act's use of the word "unlawfully," imported the same meaning expressed by the specific proviso in the 1929 Act, even though there was no mention of preserving the mother's life in the 1861 Act. He then construed the phrase "preserving the life of the mother" broadly, that is, "in a reasonable sense," to include a serious and permanent threat to the mother's health, and instructed the jury to acquit Dr. Bourne if it found he had acted in a good-faith belief that the abortion was necessary for this purpose. Id., at 693–694. The jury did acquit.

Recently, Parliament enacted a new abortion law. This is the Abortion Act of 1967, 15 & 16 Eliz. 2, c. 87. The Act permits a licensed physician to perform an abortion where two other licensed physicians agree (a) "that the continuance of the pregnancy would involve risk to the life of the pregnant woman, or of injury to the physical or mental health of the pregnant woman or any existing children of her family, greater than if the pregnancy were terminated," or (b) "that there is a substantial risk that if the child were born it would suffer from such physical or mental abnormalities as [410 U.S. 113, 138] to be seriously handicapped." The Act also provides that, in making this determination, "account may be taken of the pregnant woman's actual or reasonably foreseeable environment." It also permits a physician, without the concurrence of others, to terminate a pregnancy where he is of the good-faith opinion that the abortion "is immediately necessary to save the life or to prevent grave permanent injury to the physical or mental health of the pregnant woman."

5. The American law. In this country, the law in effect in all but a few States until mid-19th century was the pre-existing English common law. Connecticut, the first State to enact abortion legislation, adopted in 1821 that part of Lord Ellenborough's Act that related to a woman "quick

with child."[29] The death penalty was not imposed. Abortion before quickening was made a crime in that State only in 1860.[30] In 1828, New York enacted legislation[31] that, in two respects, was to serve as a model for early anti-abortion statutes. First, while barring destruction of an unquickened fetus as well as a quick fetus, it made the former only a misdemeanor, but the latter second-degree manslaughter. Second, it incorporated a concept of therapeutic abortion by providing that an abortion was excused if it "shall have been necessary to preserve the life of such mother, or shall have been advised by two physicians to be necessary for such purpose." By 1840, when Texas had received the common law,[32] only eight American States [410 U.S. 113, 139] had statutes dealing with abortion.[33] It was not until after the War Between the States that legislation began generally to replace the common law. Most of these initial statutes dealt severely with abortion after quickening but were lenient with it before quickening. Most punished attempts equally with completed abortions. While many statutes included the exception for an abortion thought by one or more physicians to be necessary to save the mother's life, that provision soon disappeared and the typical law required that the procedure actually be necessary for that purpose.

Gradually, in the middle and late 19th century the quickening distinction disappeared from the statutory law of most States and the degree of the offense and the penalties were increased. By the end of the 1950's, a large majority of the jurisdictions banned abortion, however and whenever performed, unless done to save or preserve the life of the mother.[34] The exceptions, Alabama and the District of Columbia, permitted abortion to preserve the mother's health.[35] Three States permitted abortions that were not "unlawfully" performed or that were not "without lawful justification," leaving interpretation of those standards to the courts.[36] In [410 U.S. 113, 140] the past several years, however, a trend toward liberalization of abortion statutes has resulted in adoption, by about one-third of the States, of less stringent laws, most of them patterned after the ALI Model Penal Code, 230.3,[37] set forth as Appendix B to the opinion in Doe v. Bolton, post, p. 205.

It is thus apparent that at common law, at the time of the adoption of our Constitution, and throughout the major portion of the 19th century, abortion was viewed with less disfavor than under most American statutes currently in effect. Phrasing it another way, a woman enjoyed a substantially broader right to terminate a pregnancy than she does in most States today. At least with respect to the early stage of pregnancy, and very possibly without such a limitation, the opportunity [410 U.S. 113, 141] to make this choice was present in this country well into the 19th century. Even later, the law continued for some time to treat less punitively an abortion procured in early pregnancy.

6. The position of the American Medical Association. The anti-abortion mood prevalent in this country in the late 19th century was shared by the medical profession. Indeed, the attitude of the profession may have played a significant role in the enactment of stringent criminal abortion legislation during that period.

An AMA Committee on Criminal Abortion was appointed in May 1857. It presented its report, 12 Trans. of the Am. Med. Assn. 73–78 (1859), to the Twelfth Annual Meeting. That report observed that the Committee had been appointed to investigate criminal abortion "with a view to its general suppression." It deplored abortion and its frequency and it listed three causes of "this general demoralization":

"The first of these causes is a wide-spread popular ignorance of the true character of the crime—a belief, even among mothers themselves, that the foetus is not alive till after the period of quickening.

"The second of the agents alluded to is the fact that the profession themselves are frequently supposed careless of foetal life . . . .

"The third reason of the frightful extent of this crime is found in the grave defects of our laws, both common and statute, as regards the independent and actual existence of the child before birth, as a living being. These errors, which are sufficient in most instances to prevent conviction, are based, and only based, upon mistaken and exploded medical dogmas. With strange inconsistency, the law fully acknowledges the foetus in utero and its inherent rights, for civil purposes; while personally and as criminally affected, it fails to recognize it, [410 U.S. 113, 142] and to its life as yet denies all protection." Id., at 75–76.

The Committee then offered, and the Association adopted, resolutions protesting "against such unwarrantable destruction of human life," calling upon state legislatures to revise their abortion laws, and requesting the cooperation of state medical societies "in pressing the subject." Id., at 28, 78.

In 1871 a long and vivid report was submitted by the Committee on Criminal Abortion. It ended with the observation, "We had to deal with human life. In a matter of less importance we could entertain no compromise. An honest judge on the bench would call things by their proper names. We could do no less." 22 Trans. of the Am. Med. Assn. 258 (1871). It proffered resolutions, adopted by the Association, id., at 38–39, recommending, among other things, that it "be unlawful and unprofessional for any physician to induce abortion or premature labor, without the concurrent opinion of at least one respectable consulting physician, and then always with a view to the safety of the child—if that be possible," and calling "the attention of the clergy of all denominations to the perverted views of morality entertained by a large class of females—aye, and men also, on this important question."

Except for periodic condemnation of the criminal abortionist, no further formal AMA action took place until 1967. In that year, the Committee on Human Reproduction urged the adoption of a stated policy of opposition to induced abortion, except when there is "documented medical evidence" of a threat to the health or life of the mother, or that the child "may be born with incapacitating physical deformity or mental deficiency," or that a pregnancy "resulting from legally established statutory or forcible rape or incest may constitute a threat to the mental or physical health of the [410 U.S. 113, 143] patient," two other physicians "chosen because of their recognized professional competence have examined the patient and have concurred in writing," and the procedure "is performed in a hospital accredited by the Joint Commission on Accreditation of Hospitals." The providing of medical information by physicians to state legislatures in their consideration of legislation regarding therapeutic abortion was "to be considered consistent with the principles of ethics of the American Medical Association." This recommendation was adopted by the House of Delegates. Proceedings of the AMA House of Delegates 40–51 (June 1967).

In 1970, after the introduction of a variety of proposed resolutions, and of a report from its Board of Trustees, a reference committee noted "polarization of the medical profession on this controversial issue"; division among those who had testified; a difference of opinion among AMA councils and committees; "the remarkable shift in testimony" in six months, felt to be influenced "by the rapid changes in state laws and by the judicial decisions which tend to make abortion more freely available;" and a feeling "that this trend will continue." On June 25, 1970, the House of Delegates adopted preambles and most of the resolutions proposed by the reference committee. The preambles emphasized "the best interests of the patient," "sound clinical judgment," and "informed patient consent," in contrast to "mere acquiescence to the patient's demand." The resolutions asserted that abortion is a medical procedure that should be performed by a licensed physician in an accredited hospital only after consultation with two other physicians and in conformity with state law, and that no party to the procedure should be required to violate personally held moral principles.[38] Proceedings [410 U.S. 113, 144] of the AMA House of Delegates 220 (June 1970). The AMA Judicial Council rendered a complementary opinion.[39]

7. The position of the American Public Health Association. In October 1970, the Executive Board of the APHA adopted Standards for Abortion Services. These were five in number:

a. Rapid and simple abortion referral must be readily available through state and local public [410 U.S. 113, 145] health departments, medical societies, or other nonprofit organizations.

b. An important function of counselling should be to simplify and expedite the provision of abortion services; it should not delay the obtaining of these services.

c. Psychiatric consultation should not be mandatory. As in the case of other specialized medical services, psychiatric consultation should be sought for definite indications and not on a routine basis.

d. A wide range of individuals from appropriately trained, sympathetic volunteers to highly skilled physicians may qualify as abortion counselors.

e. Contraception and/or sterilization should be discussed with each abortion patient." Recommended Standards for Abortion Services, 61 Am. J. Pub. Health 396 (1971).

Among factors pertinent to life and health risks associated with abortion were three that "are recognized as important":

a. the skill of the physician,

b. the environment in which the abortion is performed, and above all

c. the duration of pregnancy, as determined by uterine size and confirmed by menstrual history. Id., at 397.

It was said that "a well-equipped hospital" offers more protection "to cope with unforeseen difficulties than an office or clinic without such resources. . . . The factor of gestational age is of overriding importance." Thus, it was recommended that abortions in the second trimester and early abortions in the presence of existing medical complications be performed in hospitals as inpatient procedures. For pregnancies in the first trimester, [410 U.S. 113, 146] abortion in the hospital with or without overnight stay "is probably the safest practice." An abortion in an extramural facility, however, is an acceptable alternative "provided arrangements exist in advance to admit patients promptly if unforeseen complications develop." Standards for an abortion facility were listed. It was said that at present abortions should be performed by physicians or osteopaths who are licensed to practice and who have "adequate training." Id., at 398.

8. The position of the American Bar Association. At its meeting in February 1972 the ABA House of Delegates approved, with 17 opposing votes, the Uniform Abortion Act that had been drafted and approved the preceding August by the Conference of Commissioners on Uniform

State Laws. 58 A. B. A. J. 380 (1972). We set forth the Act in full in the margin.[40] The [410 U.S. 113, 147] Conference has appended an enlightening Prefatory Note.[41]

VII.

Three reasons have been advanced to explain historically the enactment of criminal abortion laws in the 19th century and to justify their continued existence. [410 U.S. 113, 148]

It has been argued occasionally that these laws were the product of a Victorian social concern to discourage illicit sexual conduct. Texas, however, does not advance this justification in the present case, and it appears that no court or commentator has taken the argument seriously.[42] The appellants and amici contend, moreover, that this is not a proper state purpose at all and suggest that, if it were, the Texas statutes are overbroad in protecting it since the law fails to distinguish between married and unwed mothers.

A second reason is concerned with abortion as a medical procedure. When most criminal abortion laws were first enacted, the procedure was a hazardous one for the woman.[43] This was particularly true prior to the [410 U.S. 113, 149] development of antisepsis. Antiseptic techniques, of course, were based on discoveries by Lister, Pasteur, and others first announced in 1867, but were not generally accepted and employed until about the turn of the century. Abortion mortality was high. Even after 1900, and perhaps until as late as the development of antibiotics in the 1940's, standard modern techniques such as dilation and curettage were not nearly so safe as they are today. Thus, it has been argued that a State's real concern in enacting a criminal abortion law was to protect the pregnant woman, that is, to restrain her from submitting to a procedure that placed her life in serious jeopardy.

Modern medical techniques have altered this situation. Appellants and various amici refer to medical data indicating that abortion in early pregnancy, that is, prior to the end of the first trimester, although not without its risk, is now relatively safe. Mortality rates for women undergoing early abortions, where the procedure is legal, appear to be as low as or lower than the rates for normal childbirth.[44] Consequently, any interest of the State in protecting the woman from an inherently hazardous procedure, except when it would be equally dangerous for her to forgo it, has largely disappeared. Of course, important state interests in the areas of health and medical standards do remain. [410 U.S. 113, 150] The State has a legitimate interest in seeing to it that abortion, like any other medical procedure, is performed under circumstances that insure maximum safety for the patient. This interest obviously extends at least to the performing physician and his staff, to the facilities involved, to the availability of after-care, and to adequate provision for any complication or emergency that might arise. The prevalence of high mortality rates at illegal "abortion mills" strengthens, rather than weakens, the State's interest in regulating the conditions under which abortions are performed. Moreover, the risk to the woman increases as her pregnancy continues. Thus, the State retains a definite interest in protecting the woman's own health and safety when an abortion is proposed at a late stage of pregnancy.

The third reason is the State's interest—some phrase it in terms of duty—in protecting prenatal life. Some of the argument for this justification rests on the theory that a new human life is present from the moment of conception.[45] The State's interest and general obligation to protect life then extends, it is argued, to prenatal life. Only when the life of the pregnant mother herself is at stake, balanced against the life she carries within her, should the interest of the embryo or fetus not prevail. Logically, of course, a legitimate state interest in this area need not stand or fall on acceptance of the belief that life begins at conception or at some other point prior to live birth. In assessing the State's interest, recognition may be given to the less rigid claim that as long as at least potential life is involved, the State may assert interests beyond the protection of the pregnant woman alone. [410 U.S. 113, 151]

Parties challenging state abortion laws have sharply disputed in some courts the contention that a purpose of these laws, when enacted, was to protect prenatal life.[46] Pointing to the absence of legislative history to support the contention, they claim that most state laws were designed solely to protect the woman. Because medical advances have lessened this concern, at least with respect to abortion in early pregnancy, they argue that with respect to such abortions the laws can no longer be justified by any state interest. There is some scholarly support for this view of original purpose.[47] The few state courts called upon to interpret their laws in the late 19th and early 20th centuries did focus on the State's interest in protecting the woman's health rather than in preserving the embryo and fetus.[48] Proponents of this view point out that in many States, including Texas,[49] by statute or judicial interpretation, the pregnant woman herself could not be prosecuted for self-abortion or for cooperating in an abortion performed upon her by another.[50] They claim that adoption of the "quickening" distinction through received common [410 U.S. 113, 152] law and state statutes tacitly recognizes the greater health hazards inherent in late abortion and impliedly repudiates the theory that life begins at conception.

It is with these interests, and the weight to be attached to them, that this case is concerned.

VIII.

The Constitution does not explicitly mention any right of privacy. In a line of decisions, however, going back perhaps as far as Union Pacific R. Co. v. Botsford, 141 U.S. 250, 251 (1891), the Court has recognized that a right of personal privacy, or a guarantee of certain areas or zones of privacy, does exist under the Constitution. In varying contexts, the Court or individual Justices have, indeed, found at least the roots of that right in the First Amendment, Stanley v. Georgia, 394 U.S. 557, 564 (1969); in the Fourth and Fifth Amendments, Terry v. Ohio, 392 U.S. 1, 8–9 (1968), Katz v. United States, 389 U.S. 347, 350 (1967), Boyd v. United States, 116 U.S. 616 (1886), see Olmstead v. United States, 277 U.S. 438, 478 (1928) (Brandeis, J., dissenting); in the penumbras of the Bill of Rights, Griswold v. Connecticut, 381 U.S., at 484–485; in the Ninth Amendment, id., at 486 (Goldberg, J., concurring); or in the concept of liberty guaranteed by the first section of the Fourteenth Amendment, see Meyer v. Nebraska, 262 U.S. 390, 399 (1923). These decisions make it clear that only personal rights that can be deemed "fundamental" or "implicit in the concept of ordered liberty," Palko v. Connecticut, 302 U.S. 319, 325 (1937), are included in this guarantee of personal privacy. They also make it clear that the right has some extension to activities relating to marriage, Loving v. Virginia, 388 U.S. 1, 12 (1967); procreation, Skinner v. Oklahoma, 316 U.S. 535, 541–542 (1942); contraception, Eisenstadt v. Baird, 405 U.S., at 453–454; id., at 460, 463–465 [410 U.S. 113, 153] (WHITE, J., concurring in result); family relationships, Prince v. Massachusetts, 321 U.S. 158, 166 (1944); and child rearing and education, Pierce v. Society of Sisters, 268 U.S. 510, 535 (1925), Meyer v. Nebraska, supra.

This right of privacy, whether it be founded in the Fourteenth Amendment's concept of personal liberty and restrictions upon state action, as we feel it is, or, as the District Court determined, in the Ninth Amendment's reservation of rights to the people, is broad enough to encompass a woman's decision whether or not to terminate her pregnancy. The detriment that the State would impose upon the pregnant woman by denying this choice altogether is apparent. Specific and direct harm medically diagnosable even in early pregnancy may be involved. Maternity, or additional offspring, may force upon the woman a distressful life and future. Psychological harm may be imminent. Mental and physical health may be taxed by child care. There is also the distress, for all concerned, associated with the unwanted child, and there is the problem of bringing a child into a family already unable, psychologically and otherwise, to care for it. In other cases, as in this one, the additional difficulties and continuing stigma of unwed motherhood may be involved.

All these are factors the woman and her responsible physician necessarily will consider in consultation.

On the basis of elements such as these, appellant and some amici argue that the woman's right is absolute and that she is entitled to terminate her pregnancy at whatever time, in whatever way, and for whatever reason she alone chooses. With this we do not agree. Appellant's arguments that Texas either has no valid interest at all in regulating the abortion decision, or no interest strong enough to support any limitation upon the woman's sole determination, are unpersuasive. The [410 U.S. 113, 154] Court's decisions recognizing a right of privacy also acknowledge that some state regulation in areas protected by that right is appropriate. As noted above, a State may properly assert important interests in safeguarding health, in maintaining medical standards, and in protecting potential life. At some point in pregnancy, these respective interests become sufficiently compelling to sustain regulation of the factors that govern the abortion decision. The privacy right involved, therefore, cannot be said to be absolute. In fact, it is not clear to us that the claim asserted by some amici that one has an unlimited right to do with one's body as one pleases bears a close relationship to the right of privacy previously articulated in the Court's decisions. The Court has refused to recognize an unlimited right of this kind in the past. Jacobson v. Massachusetts, 197 U.S. 11 (1905) (vaccination); Buck v. Bell, 274 U.S. 200 (1927) (sterilization).

We, therefore, conclude that the right of personal privacy includes the abortion decision, but that this right is not unqualified and must be considered against important state interests in regulation.

We note that those federal and state courts that have recently considered abortion law challenges have reached the same conclusion. A majority, in addition to the District Court in the present case, have held state laws unconstitutional, at least in part, because of vagueness or because of overbreadth and abridgment of rights. Abele v. Markle, 342 F. Supp. 800 (Conn. 1972), appeal docketed, No. 72–56; Abele v. Markle, 351 F. Supp. 224 (Conn. 1972), appeal docketed, No. 72–730; Doe v. Bolton, 319 F. Supp. 1048 (ND Ga. 1970), appeal decided today, post, p. 179; Doe v. Scott, 321 F. Supp. 1385 (ND Ill. 1971), appeal docketed, No. 70–105; Poe v. Menghini, 339 F. Supp. 986 (Kan. 1972); YWCA v. Kugler, 342 F. Supp. 1048 (NJ 1972); Babbitz v. McCann, [410 U.S. 113, 155] 310 F. Supp. 293 (ED Wis. 1970), appeal dismissed, 400 U.S. 1 (1970); People v. Belous, 71 Cal. 2d 954, 458 P.2d 194 (1969), cert. denied, 397 U.S. 915 (1970); State v. Barquet, 262 So.2d 431 (Fla. 1972).

Others have sustained state statutes. Crossen v. Attorney General, 344 F. Supp. 587 (ED Ky. 1972), appeal docketed, No. 72–256; Rosen

v. Louisiana State Board of Medical Examiners, 318 F. Supp. 1217 (ED La. 1970), appeal docketed, No. 70–42; Corkey v. Edwards, 322 F. Supp. 1248 (WDNC 1971), appeal docketed, No. 71–92; Steinberg v. Brown, 321 F. Supp. 741 (ND Ohio 1970); Doe v. Rampton (Utah 1971), appeal docketed, No. 71–5666; Cheaney v. State, ___ Ind. ___, 285 N. E. 2d 265 (1972); Spears v. State, 257 So.2d 876 (Miss. 1972); State v. Munson, 86 S. D. 663, 201 N. W. 2d 123 (1972), appeal docketed, No. 72–631.

Although the results are divided, most of these courts have agreed that the right of privacy, however based, is broad enough to cover the abortion decision; that the right, nonetheless, is not absolute and is subject to some limitations; and that at some point the state interests as to protection of health, medical standards, and prenatal life, become dominant. We agree with this approach.

Where certain "fundamental rights" are involved, the Court has held that regulation limiting these rights may be justified only by a "compelling state interest," Kramer v. Union Free School District, 395 U.S. 621, 627 (1969); Shapiro v. Thompson, 394 U.S. 618, 634 (1969), Sherbert v. Verner, 374 U.S. 398, 406 (1963), and that legislative enactments must be narrowly drawn to express only the legitimate state interests at stake. Griswold v. Connecticut, 381 U.S., at 485; Aptheker v. Secretary of State, 378 U.S. 500, 508 (1964); Cantwell v. Connecticut, 310 U.S. 296, 307–308 (1940); see [410 U.S. 113, 156] Eisenstadt v. Baird, 405 U.S., at 460, 463–464 (WHITE, J., concurring in result).

In the recent abortion cases, cited above, courts have recognized these principles. Those striking down state laws have generally scrutinized the State's interests in protecting health and potential life, and have concluded that neither interest justified broad limitations on the reasons for which a physician and his pregnant patient might decide that she should have an abortion in the early stages of pregnancy. Courts sustaining state laws have held that the State's determinations to protect health or prenatal life are dominant and constitutionally justifiable.

IX.

The District Court held that the appellee failed to meet his burden of demonstrating that the Texas statute's infringement upon Roe's rights was necessary to support a compelling state interest, and that, although the appellee presented "several compelling justifications for state presence in the area of abortions," the statutes outstripped these justifications and swept "far beyond any areas of compelling state interest." 314 F. Supp., at 1222–1223. Appellant and appellee both contest that holding.

Appellant, as has been indicated, claims an absolute right that bars any state imposition of criminal penalties in the area. Appellee argues that the State's determination to recognize and protect prenatal life from and after conception constitutes a compelling state interest. As noted above, we do not agree fully with either formulation.

A. The appellee and certain amici argue that the fetus is a "person" within the language and meaning of the Fourteenth Amendment. In support of this, they outline at length and in detail the well-known facts of fetal development. If this suggestion of personhood is established, the appellant's case, of course, collapses, [410 U.S. 113, 157] for the fetus" right to life would then be guaranteed specifically by the Amendment. The appellant conceded as much on reargument.[51] On the other hand, the appellee conceded on reargument[52] that no case could be cited that holds that a fetus is a person within the meaning of the Fourteenth Amendment.

The Constitution does not define "person" in so many words. Section 1 of the Fourteenth Amendment contains three references to "person." The first, in defining "citizens," speaks of "persons born or naturalized in the United States." The word also appears both in the Due Process Clause and in the Equal Protection Clause. "Person" is used in other places in the Constitution: in the listing of qualifications for Representatives and Senators, Art. I, 2, cl. 2, and 3, cl. 3; in the Apportionment Clause, Art. I, 2, cl. 3;[53] in the Migration and Importation provision, Art. I, 9, cl. 1; in the Emolument Clause, Art. I, 9, cl. 8; in the Electors provisions, Art. II, 1, cl. 2, and the superseded cl. 3; in the provision outlining qualifications for the office of President, Art. II, 1, cl. 5; in the Extradition provisions, Art. IV, 2, cl. 2, and the superseded Fugitive Slave Clause 3; and in the Fifth, Twelfth, and Twenty-second Amendments, as well as in 2 and 3 of the Fourteenth Amendment. But in nearly all these instances, the use of the word is such that it has application only postnatally. None indicates, with any assurance, that it has any possible pre-natal application.[54] [410 U.S. 113, 158]

All this, together with our observation, supra, that throughout the major portion of the 19th century prevailing legal abortion practices were far freer than they are today, persuades us that the word "person," as used in the Fourteenth Amendment, does not include the unborn.[55] This is in accord with the results reached in those few cases where the issue has been squarely presented. McGarvey v. Magee-Womens Hospital, 340 F. Supp. 751 (WD Pa. 1972); Byrn v. New York City Health & Hospitals Corp., 31 N. Y. 2d 194, 286 N. E. 2d 887 (1972), appeal docketed, No. 72–434; Abele v. Markle, 351 F. Supp. 224 (Conn. 1972), appeal docketed, No. 72–730. Cf. Cheaney v. State, ____ Ind., at ____, 285 N. E. 2d, at 270; Montana v. Rogers, 278 F.2d 68, 72 (CA7 1960), aff'd sub nom. Montana v. Kennedy, 366 U.S. 308 (1961); Keeler v. Superior Court, 2 Cal. 3d 619, 470 P.2d 617 (1970); State v. Dickinson,

28 [410 U.S. 113, 159] Ohio St. 2d 65, 275 N. E. 2d 599 (1971). Indeed, our decision in United States v. Vuitch, 402 U.S. 62 (1971), inferentially is to the same effect, for we there would not have indulged in statutory interpretation favorable to abortion in specified circumstances if the necessary consequence was the termination of life entitled to Fourteenth Amendment protection.

This conclusion, however, does not of itself fully answer the contentions raised by Texas, and we pass on to other considerations.

B. The pregnant woman cannot be isolated in her privacy. She carries an embryo and, later, a fetus, if one accepts the medical definitions of the developing young in the human uterus. See Dorland's Illustrated Medical Dictionary 478–479, 547 (24th ed. 1965). The situation therefore is inherently different from marital intimacy, or bedroom possession of obscene material, or marriage, or procreation, or education, with which Eisenstadt and Griswold, Stanley, Loving, Skinner, and Pierce and Meyer were respectively concerned. As we have intimated above, it is reasonable and appropriate for a State to decide that at some point in time another interest, that of health of the mother or that of potential human life, becomes significantly involved. The woman's privacy is no longer sole and any right of privacy she possesses must be measured accordingly.

Texas urges that, apart from the Fourteenth Amendment, life begins at conception and is present throughout pregnancy, and that, therefore, the State has a compelling interest in protecting that life from and after conception. We need not resolve the difficult question of when life begins. When those trained in the respective disciplines of medicine, philosophy, and theology are unable to arrive at any consensus, the judiciary, at this point in the development of man's knowledge, is not in a position to speculate as to the answer. [410 U.S. 113, 160]

It should be sufficient to note briefly the wide divergence of thinking on this most sensitive and difficult question. There has always been strong support for the view that life does not begin until live birth. This was the belief of the Stoics.[56] It appears to be the predominant, though not the unanimous, attitude of the Jewish faith.[57] It may be taken to represent also the position of a large segment of the Protestant community, insofar as that can be ascertained; organized groups that have taken a formal position on the abortion issue have generally regarded abortion as a matter for the conscience of the individual and her family.[58] As we have noted, the common law found greater significance in quickening. Physicians and their scientific colleagues have regarded that event with less interest and have tended to focus either upon conception, upon live birth, or upon the interim point at which the fetus becomes "viable," that is, potentially able to live outside the mother's womb, albeit with artificial aid.[59] Viability is usually placed at about seven months (28

weeks) but may occur earlier, even at 24 weeks.[60] The Aristotelian theory of "mediate animation," that held sway throughout the Middle Ages
and the Renaissance in Europe, continued to be official Roman Catholic
dogma until the 19th century, despite opposition to this "ensoulment"
theory from those in the Church who would recognize the existence of
life from [410 U.S. 113, 161] the moment of conception.[61] The latter is
now, of course, the official belief of the Catholic Church. As one brief
amicus discloses, this is a view strongly held by many non–Catholics as
well, and by many physicians. Substantial problems for precise definition
of this view are posed, however, by new embryological data that purport
to indicate that conception is a "process" over time, rather than an event,
and by new medical techniques such as menstrual extraction, the "morning-after" pill, implantation of embryos, artificial insemination, and even
artificial wombs.[62]

In areas other than criminal abortion, the law has been reluctant to
endorse any theory that life, as we recognize it, begins before live birth
or to accord legal rights to the unborn except in narrowly defined situations and except when the rights are contingent upon live birth. For
example, the traditional rule of tort law denied recovery for prenatal
injuries even though the child was born alive.[63] That rule has been
changed in almost every jurisdiction. In most States, recovery is said to
be permitted only if the fetus was viable, or at least quick, when the
injuries were sustained, though few [410 U.S. 113, 162] courts have squarely
so held.[64] In a recent development, generally opposed by the commentators, some States permit the parents of a stillborn child to maintain an
action for wrongful death because of prenatal injuries.[65] Such an action,
however, would appear to be one to vindicate the parents" interest and
is thus consistent with the view that the fetus, at most, represents only the
potentiality of life. Similarly, unborn children have been recognized as
acquiring rights or interests by way of inheritance or other devolution of
property, and have been represented by guardians ad litem.[66] Perfection
of the interests involved, again, has generally been contingent upon live
birth. In short, the unborn have never been recognized in the law as persons in the whole sense.

X.

In view of all this, we do not agree that, by adopting one theory of life,
Texas may override the rights of the pregnant woman that are at stake.
We repeat, however, that the State does have an important and legitimate
interest in preserving and protecting the health of the pregnant woman,
whether she be a resident of the State or a nonresident who seeks med-

ical consultation and treatment there, and that it has still another important and legitimate interest in protecting the potentiality of human life. These interests are separate and distinct. Each grows in substantiality as the woman approaches [410 U.S. 113, 163] term and, at a point during pregnancy, each becomes "compelling."

With respect to the State's important and legitimate interest in the health of the mother, the "compelling" point, in the light of present medical knowledge, is at approximately the end of the first trimester. This is so because of the now-established medical fact, referred to above at 149, that until the end of the first trimester mortality in abortion may be less than mortality in normal childbirth. It follows that, from and after this point, a State may regulate the abortion procedure to the extent that the regulation reasonably relates to the preservation and protection of maternal health. Examples of permissible state regulation in this area are requirements as to the qualifications of the person who is to perform the abortion; as to the licensure of that person; as to the facility in which the procedure is to be performed, that is, whether it must be a hospital or may be a clinic or some other place of less-than-hospital status; as to the licensing of the facility; and the like.

This means, on the other hand, that, for the period of pregnancy prior to this "compelling" point, the attending physician, in consultation with his patient, is free to determine, without regulation by the State, that, in his medical judgment, the patient's pregnancy should be terminated. If that decision is reached, the judgment may be effectuated by an abortion free of interference by the State.

With respect to the State's important and legitimate interest in potential life, the "compelling" point is at viability. This is so because the fetus then presumably has the capability of meaningful life outside the mother's womb. State regulation protective of fetal life after viability thus has both logical and biological justifications. If the State is interested in protecting fetal life after viability, it may go so far as to proscribe abortion [410 U.S. 113, 164] during that period, except when it is necessary to preserve the life or health of the mother.

Measured against these standards, Art. 1196 of the Texas Penal Code, in restricting legal abortions to those "procured or attempted by medical advice for the purpose of saving the life of the mother," sweeps too broadly. The statute makes no distinction between abortions performed early in pregnancy and those performed later, and it limits to a single reason, "saving" the mother's life, the legal justification for the procedure. The statute, therefore, cannot survive the constitutional attack made upon it here.

This conclusion makes it unnecessary for us to consider the additional challenge to the Texas statute asserted on grounds of vagueness. See United States v. Vuitch, 402 U.S., at 67–72.

XI.

To summarize and to repeat:

1. A state criminal abortion statute of the current Texas type, that excepts from criminality only a life-saving procedure on behalf of the mother, without regard to pregnancy stage and without recognition of the other interests involved, is violative of the Due Process Clause of the Fourteenth Amendment.

(a) For the stage prior to approximately the end of the first trimester, the abortion decision and its effectuation must be left to the medical judgment of the pregnant woman's attending physician.

(b) For the stage subsequent to approximately the end of the first trimester, the State, in promoting its interest in the health of the mother, may, if it chooses, regulate the abortion procedure in ways that are reasonably related to maternal health.

(c) For the stage subsequent to viability, the State in promoting its interest in the potentiality of human life [410 U.S. 113, 165] may, if it chooses, regulate, and even proscribe, abortion except where it is necessary, in appropriate medical judgment, for the preservation of the life or health of the mother.

2. The State may define the term "physician," as it has been employed in the preceding paragraphs of this Part XI of this opinion, to mean only a physician currently licensed by the State, and may proscribe any abortion by a person who is not a physician as so defined.

In Doe v. Bolton, post, p. 179, procedural requirements contained in one of the modern abortion statutes are considered. That opinion and this one, of course, are to be read together.[67]

This holding, we feel, is consistent with the relative weights of the respective interests involved, with the lessons and examples of medical and legal history, with the lenity of the common law, and with the demands of the profound problems of the present day. The decision leaves the State free to place increasing restrictions on abortion as the period of pregnancy lengthens, so long as those restrictions are tailored to the recognized state interests. The decision vindicates the right of the physician to administer medical treatment according to his professional judgment up to the points where important [410 U.S. 113, 166] state interests provide compelling justifications for intervention. Up to those points, the abortion decision in all its aspects is inherently, and primarily, a medical decision, and basic responsibility for it must rest with the physician. If an individual practitioner abuses the privilege of exercising proper medical judgment, the usual remedies, judicial and intra-professional, are available.

XII.

Our conclusion that Art. 1196 is unconstitutional means, of course, that the Texas abortion statutes, as a unit, must fall. The exception of Art. 1196 cannot be struck down separately, for then the State would be left with a statute proscribing all abortion procedures no matter how medically urgent the case.

Although the District Court granted appellant Roe declaratory relief, it stopped short of issuing an injunction against enforcement of the Texas statutes. The Court has recognized that different considerations enter into a federal court's decision as to declaratory relief, on the one hand, and injunctive relief, on the other. Zwickler v. Koota, 389 U.S. 241, 252–255 (1967); Dombrowski v. Pfister, 380 U.S. 479 (1965). We are not dealing with a statute that, on its face, appears to abridge free expression, an area of particular concern under Dombrowski and refined in Younger v. Harris, 401 U.S., at 50.

We find it unnecessary to decide whether the District Court erred in withholding injunctive relief, for we assume the Texas prosecutorial authorities will give full credence to this decision that the present criminal abortion statutes of that State are unconstitutional.

The judgment of the District Court as to intervenor Hallford is reversed, and Dr. Hallford's complaint in intervention is dismissed. In all other respects, the judgment [410 U.S. 113, 167] of the District Court is affirmed. Costs are allowed to the appellee.

It is so ordered.

[For concurring opinion of MR. CHIEF JUSTICE BURGER, see post, p. 207.]

[For concurring opinion of MR. JUSTICE DOUGLAS, see post, p. 209.]

[For dissenting opinion of MR. JUSTICE WHITE, see post, p. 221.]

FOOTNOTES

[1] "Article 1191. Abortion
  "If any person shall designedly administer to a pregnant woman or knowingly procure to be administered with her consent any drug or medicine, or shall use towards her any violence or means whatever externally or internally applied, and thereby procure an abortion, he shall be confined in the penitentiary not less than two nor more than five years; if it be done without her consent, the punishment shall be doubled. By "abortion" is meant that the life of the fetus or embryo shall be destroyed in the woman's womb or that a premature birth thereof be caused.
  "Art. 1192. Furnishing the means
  "Whoever furnishes the means for procuring an abortion knowing the purpose intended is guilty as an accomplice.

"Art. 1193. Attempt at abortion

"If the means used shall fail to produce an abortion, the offender is nevertheless guilty of an attempt to produce abortion, provided [410 U.S. 113, 118] it be shown that such means were calculated to produce that result, and shall be fined not less than one hundred nor more than one thousand dollars.

"Art. 1194. Murder in producing abortion

"If the death of the mother is occasioned by an abortion so produced or by an attempt to effect the same it is murder.

"Art. 1196. By medical advice

"Nothing in this chapter applies to an abortion procured or attempted by medical advice for the purpose of saving the life of the mother."

The foregoing Articles, together with Art. 1195, compose Chapter 9 of Title 15 of the Penal Code. Article 1195, not attacked here, reads:

"Art. 1195. Destroying unborn child

"Whoever shall during parturition of the mother destroy the vitality or life in a child in a state of being born and before actual birth, which child would otherwise have been born alive, shall be confined in the penitentiary for life or for not less than five years."

[2] Ariz. Rev. Stat. Ann. 13–211 (1956); Conn. Pub. Act No. 1 (May 1972 special session) (in 4 Conn. Leg. Serv. 677 (1972)), and Conn. Gen. Stat. Rev. 53–29, 53–30 (1968) (or unborn child); Idaho Code 18–601 (1948); Ill. Rev. Stat., c. 38, 23–1 (1971); Ind. Code 35–1–58–1 (1971); Iowa Code 701.1 (1971); Ky. Rev. Stat. 436.020 (1962); La. Rev. Stat. 37:1285 (6) (1964) (loss of medical license) (but see 14:87 (Supp. 1972) containing no exception for the life of the mother under the criminal statute); Me. Rev. Stat. Ann., Tit. 17, 51 (1964); Mass. Gen. Laws Ann., c. 272, 19 (1970) (using the term "unlawfully," construed to exclude an abortion to save the mother's life, Kudish v. Bd. of Registration, 356 Mass. 98, 248 N. E. 2d 264 (1969)); Mich. Comp. Laws 750.14 (1948); Minn. Stat. 617.18 (1971); Mo. Rev. Stat. 559.100 (1969); Mont. Rev. Codes Ann. 94–401 (1969); Neb. Rev. Stat. 28–405 (1964); Nev. Rev. Stat. 200.220 (1967); N. H. Rev. Stat. Ann. 585:13 (1955); N. J. Stat. Ann. 2A:87–1 (1969) ("without lawful justification"); N. D. Cent. Code 12–25–01, 12–25–02 (1960); Ohio Rev. Code Ann. 2901.16 (1953); Okla. Stat. Ann., Tit. 21, 861 (1972–1973 Supp.); Pa. Stat. Ann., Tit. 18, [410 U.S. 113, 119] 4718, 4719 (1963) ("unlawful"); R. I. Gen. Laws Ann. 11–3–1 (1969); S. D. Comp. Laws Ann. 22–17–1 (1967); Tenn. Code Ann. 39–301, 39–302 (1956); Utah Code Ann. 76–2–1, 76–2–2 (1953); Vt. Stat. Ann., Tit. 13, 101 (1958); W. Va. Code Ann. 61–2–8 (1966); Wis. Stat. 940.04 (1969); Wyo. Stat. Ann. 6–77, 6–78 (1957).

[3] Long ago, a suggestion was made that the Texas statutes were unconstitutionally vague because of definitional deficiencies. The Texas Court of Criminal Appeals disposed of that suggestion peremptorily, saying only,

"It is also insisted in the motion in arrest of judgment that the statute is unconstitutional and void in that it does not sufficiently define or describe the offense of abortion. We do not concur in respect to this question." Jackson v. State, 55 Tex. Cr. R. 79, 89, 115 S. W. 262, 268 (1908).

The same court recently has held again that the State's abortion statutes are not unconstitutionally vague or overbroad. Thompson v. State (Ct. Crim. App. Tex. 1971), appeal docketed, No. 71–1200. The court held that "the State of Texas has a compelling interest to protect fetal life"; that Art. 1191 "is designed to protect fetal life"; that the Texas homicide statutes, particularly Art. 1205 of the Penal Code, are intended to protect a person "in existence by actual birth" and thereby implicitly recognize other human life that is not "in existence by actual birth"; that the definition of human life is for the legislature and not the courts; that Art. 1196 "is more definite than the District of Columbia statute upheld in [United States v.] Vuitch" (402 U.S. 62); and that the

Texas statute "is [410 U.S. 113, 120] not vague and indefinite or overbroad." A physician's abortion conviction was affirmed.

    In Thompson, n. 2, the court observed that any issue as to the burden of proof under the exemption of Art. 1196 "is not before us." But see Veevers v. State, 172 Tex. Cr. R. 162, 168–169, 354 S. W. 2d 161, 166–167 (1962). Cf. United States v. Vuitch, 402 U.S. 62, 69–71 (1971).

[4] The name is a pseudonym.

[5] These names are pseudonyms.

[6] The appellee twice states in his brief that the hearing before the District Court was held on July 22, 1970. Brief for Appellee 13. The docket entries, App. 2, and the transcript, App. 76, reveal this to be an error. The July date appears to be the time of the reporter's transcription. See App. 77.

[7] We need not consider what different result, if any, would follow if Dr. Hallford's intervention were on behalf of a class. His complaint in intervention does not purport to assert a class suit and makes no reference to any class apart from an allegation that he "and others similarly situated" must necessarily guess at the meaning of Art. 1196. His application for leave to intervene goes somewhat further, for it asserts that plaintiff Roe does not adequately protect the interest of the doctor "and the class of people who are physicians . . . [and] the class of people who are . . . patients . . . ." The leave application, however, is not the complaint. Despite the District Court's statement to the contrary, 314 F. Supp., at 1225, we fail to perceive the essentials of a class suit in the Hallford complaint.

[8] A. Castiglioni, A History of Medicine 84 (2d ed. 1947), E. Krumbhaar, translator and editor (hereinafter Castiglioni).

[9] J. Ricci, The Genealogy of Gynaecology 52, 84, 113, 149 (2d ed. 1950) (hereinafter Ricci); L. Lader, Abortion 75–77 (1966) (hereinafter Lader); K. Niswander, Medical Abortion Practices in the United States, in Abortion and the Law 37, 38–40 (D. Smith ed. 1967); G. Williams, The Sanctity of Life and the Criminal Law 148 (1957) (hereinafter Williams); J. Noonan, An Almost Absolute Value in History, in The Morality of Abortion 1, 3–7 (J. Noonan ed. 1970) (hereinafter Noonan); Quay, Justifiable Abortion—Medical and Legal Foundations (pt. 2), 49 Geo. L. J. 395, 406–422 (1961) (hereinafter Quay).

[10] L. Edelstein, The Hippocratic Oath 10 (1943) (hereinafter Edelstein). But see Castiglioni 227.

[11] Edelstein 12; Ricci 113–114, 118–119; Noonan 5.

[12] Edelstein 13–14.

[13] Castiglioni 148.

[14] Id., at 154.

[15] Edelstein 3.

[16] Id., at 12, 15–18.

[17] Id., at 18; Lader 76.

[18] Edelstein 63.

[19] Id., at 64.

[20] Dorland's Illustrated Medical Dictionary 1261 (24th ed. 1965).

[21] E. Coke, Institutes III *50; 1 W. Hawkins, Pleas of the Crown, c. 31, 16 (4th ed. 1762); 1 W. Blackstone, Commentaries *129–130; M. Hale, Pleas of the Crown 433 (1st Amer. ed. 1847). For discussions of the role of the quickening concept in English common law, see Lader 78; Noonan 223–226; Means, The Law of New [410 U.S. 113, 133] York Concerning Abortion and the Status of the Foetus, 1664–1968: A Case of Cessation of Constitutionality (pt. 1), 14 N. Y. L. F. 411, 418–428 (1968) (hereinafter Means I); Stern, Abortion: Reform and the Law, 59 J. Crim. L. C. & P. S. 84 (1968) (hereinafter Stern); Quay 430–432; Williams 152.

[22] Early philosophers believed that the embryo or fetus did not become formed and begin to live until at least 40 days after conception for a male, and 80 to 90 days for a female. See, for example, Aristotle, Hist. Anim. 7.3.583b; Gen. Anim. 2.3.736, 2.5.741; Hippocrates, Lib. de Nat. Puer., No. 10. Aristotle's thinking derived from his three-stage theory of life: vegetable, animal, rational. The vegetable stage was reached at conception, the animal at "animation," and the rational soon after live birth. This theory, together with the 40/80 day view, came to be accepted by early Christian thinkers.

The theological debate was reflected in the writings of St. Augustine, who made a distinction between embryo inanimatus, not yet endowed with a soul, and embryo animatus. He may have drawn upon Exodus 21:22. At one point, however, he expressed the view that human powers cannot determine the point during fetal development at which the critical change occurs. See Augustine, De Origine Animae 4.4 (Pub. Law 44.527). See also W. Reany, The Creation of the Human Soul, c. 2 and 83–86 (1932); Huser, The Crime of Abortion in Canon Law 15 (Catholic Univ. of America, Canon Law Studies No. 162, Washington, D.C., 1942).

Galen, in three treatises related to embryology, accepted the thinking of Aristotle and his followers. Quay 426–427. Later, Augustine on abortion was incorporated by Gratian into the Decretum, published about 1140. Decretum Magistri Gratiani 2.32.2.7 to 2.32.2.10, [410 U.S. 113, 134] in 1 Corpus Juris Canonici 1122, 1123 (A. Friedburg, 2d ed. 1879). This Decretal and the Decretals that followed were recognized as the definitive body of canon law until the new Code of 1917.

For discussions of the canon-law treatment, see Means I, pp. 411–412; Noonan 20–26; Quay 426–430; see also J. Noonan, Contraception: A History of Its Treatment by the Catholic Theologians and Canonists 18–29 (1965).

[23] Bracton took the position that abortion by blow or poison was homicide "if the foetus be already formed and animated, and particularly if it be animated." 2 H. Bracton, De Legibus et Consuetudinibus Angliae 279 (T. Twiss ed. 1879), or, as a later translation puts it, "if the foetus is already formed or quickened, especially if it is quickened," 2 H. Bracton, On the Laws and Customs of England 341 (S. Thorne ed. 1968). See Quay 431; see also 2 Fleta 60–61 (Book 1, c. 23) (Selden Society ed. 1955).

[24] E. Coke, Institutes III *50.

[25] 1 W. Blackstone, Commentaries *129–130.

[26] Means, The Phoenix of Abortional Freedom: Is a Penumbral or Ninth-Amendment Right About to Arise from the Nineteenth-Century Legislative Ashes of a Fourteenth-Century Common-Law Liberty?, 17 N. Y. L. F. 335 (1971) (hereinafter Means II). The author examines the two principal precedents cited marginally by Coke, both contrary to his dictum, and traces the treatment of these and other cases by earlier commentators. He concludes that Coke, who himself participated as an advocate in an abortion case in 1601, may have intentionally misstated the law. The author even suggests a reason: Coke's strong feelings against abortion, coupled with his determination to assert common-law (secular) jurisdiction to assess penalties for an offense that traditionally had been an exclusively ecclesiastical or canon-law crime. See also Lader 78–79, who notes that some scholars doubt that the common law ever was applied to abortion; that the English ecclesiastical courts seem to have lost interest in the problem after 1527; and that the preamble to the English legislation of 1803, 43 Geo. 3, c. 58, 1, referred to in the text, infra, at 136, states that "no adequate means have been hitherto provided for the prevention and punishment of such offenses."

[27] Commonwealth v. Bangs, 9 Mass. 387, 388 (1812); Commonwealth v. Parker, 50 Mass. (9 Metc.) 263, 265–266 (1845); State v. Cooper, 22 N. J. L. 52, 58 (1849); Abrams v. Foshee, 3 Iowa 274, 278–280 (1856); Smith v. Gaffard, 31 Ala. 45, 51 (1857); Mitchell v. Commonwealth, 78 Ky. 204, 210 (1879); Eggart v. State, 40 Fla. [410 U.S. 113, 136] 527, 532, 25 So. 144, 145 (1898); State v. Alcorn, 7 Idaho 599, 606, 64 P. 1014, 1016

(1901); Edwards v. State, 79 Neb. 251, 252, 112 N. W. 611, 612 (1907); Gray v. State, 77 Tex. Cr. R. 221, 224, 178 S. W. 337, 338 (1915); Miller v. Bennett, 190 Va. 162, 169, 56 S. E. 2d 217, 221 (1949). Contra, Mills v. Commonwealth, 13 Pa. 631, 633 (1850); State v. Slagle, 83 N.C. 630, 632 (1880).

[28] See Smith v. State, 33 Me. 48, 55 (1851); Evans v. People, 49 N. Y. 86, 88 (1872); Lamb v. State, 67 Md. 524, 533, 10 A. 208 (1887).

[29] Conn. Stat., Tit. 20, 14 (1821).

[30] Conn. Pub. Acts, c. 71, 1 (1860).

[31] N. Y. Rev. Stat., pt. 4, c. 1, Tit. 2, Art. 1, 9, p. 661, and Tit. 6, 21, p. 694 (1829).

[32] Act of Jan. 20, 1840, 1, set forth in 2 H. Gammel, Laws of Texas 177–178 (1898); see Grigsby v. Reib, 105 Tex. 597, 600, 153 S. W. 1124, 1125 (1913).

[33] The early statutes are discussed in Quay 435–438. See also Lader 85–88; Stern 85–86; and Means II 375–376.

[34] Criminal abortion statutes in effect in the States as of 1961, together with historical statutory development and important judicial interpretations of the state statutes, are cited and quoted in Quay 447–520. See Comment, A Survey of the Present Statutory and Case Law on Abortion: The Contradictions and the Problems, 1972 U. Ill. L. F. 177, 179, classifying the abortion statutes and listing 25 States as permitting abortion only if necessary to save or preserve the mother's life.

[35] Ala. Code, Tit. 14, 9 (1958); D.C. Code Ann. 22–201 (1967).

[36] Mass. Gen. Laws Ann., c. 272, 19 (1970); N. J. Stat. Ann. 2A:87–1 (1969); Pa. Stat. Ann., Tit. 18, 4718, 4719 (1963).

[37] Fourteen States have adopted some form of the ALI statute. See Ark. Stat. Ann. 41–303 to 41–310 (Supp. 1971); Calif. Health & Safety Code 25950–25955.5 (Supp. 1972); Colo. Rev. Stat. Ann. 40–2–50 to 40–2–53 (Cum. Supp. 1967); Del. Code Ann., Tit. 24, 1790–1793 (Supp. 1972); Florida Law of Apr. 13, 1972, c. 72–196, 1972 Fla. Sess. Law Serv., pp. 380–382; Ga. Code 26–1201 to 26–1203 (1972); Kan. Stat. Ann. 21–3407 (Supp. 1971); Md. Ann. Code, Art. 43, 137–139 (1971); Miss. Code Ann. 2223 (Supp. 1972); N. M. Stat. Ann. 40A-5–1 to 40A-5–3 (1972); N.C. Gen. Stat. 14–45.1 (Supp. 1971); Ore. Rev. Stat. 435.405 to 435.495 (1971); S. C. Code Ann. 16–82 to 16–89 (1962 and Supp. 1971); Va. Code Ann. 18.1–62 to 18.1–62.3 (Supp. 1972). Mr. Justice Clark described some of these States as having "led the way." Religion, Morality, and Abortion: A Constitutional Appraisal, 2 Loyola U. (L. A.) L. Rev. 1, 11 (1969).

By the end of 1970, four other States had repealed criminal penalties for abortions performed in early pregnancy by a licensed physician, subject to stated procedural and health requirements. Alaska Stat. 11.15.060 (1970); Haw. Rev. Stat. 453–16 (Supp. 1971); N. Y. Penal Code 125.05, subd. 3 (Supp. 1972–1973); Wash. Rev. Code 9.02.060 to 9.02.080 (Supp. 1972). The precise status of criminal abortion laws in some States is made unclear by recent decisions in state and federal courts striking down existing state laws, in whole or in part.

[38] "Whereas, Abortion, like any other medical procedure, should not be performed when contrary to the best interests of the patient [410 U.S. 113, 144] since good medical practice requires due consideration for the patient's welfare and not mere acquiescence to the patient's demand; and

"Whereas, The standards of sound clinical judgment, which, together with informed patient consent should be determinative according to the merits of each individual case; therefore be it

"RESOLVED, That abortion is a medical procedure and should be performed only by a duly licensed physician and surgeon in an accredited hospital acting only after consultation with two other physicians chosen because of their professional competency and in conformance with standards of good medical practice and the Medical Practice Act of his State; and be it further

"RESOLVED, That no physician or other professional personnel shall be compelled to perform any act which violates his good medical judgment. Neither physician, hospital, nor hospital personnel shall be required to perform any act violative of personally-held moral principles. In these circumstances good medical practice requires only that the physician or other professional personnel withdraw from the case so long as the withdrawal is consistent with good medical practice." Proceedings of the AMA House of Delegates 220 (June 1970).

[39] "The Principles of Medical Ethics of the AMA do not prohibit a physician from performing an abortion that is performed in accordance with good medical practice and under circumstances that do not violate the laws of the community in which he practices.

"In the matter of abortions, as of any other medical procedure, the Judicial Council becomes involved whenever there is alleged violation of the Principles of Medical Ethics as established by the House of Delegates."

[40] "UNIFORM ABORTION ACT

"SECTION 1. [Abortion Defined; When Authorized.]

"(a) "Abortion" means the termination of human pregnancy with an intention other than to produce a live birth or to remove a dead fetus.

"(b) An abortion may be performed in this state only if it is performed:

"(1) by a physician licensed to practice medicine [or osteopathy] in this state or by a physician practicing medicine [or osteopathy] in the employ of the government of the United States or of this state, [and the abortion is performed [in the physician's office or in a medical clinic, or] in a hospital approved by the [Department of Health] or operated by the United States, this state, or any department, agency, or political subdivision of either;] or by a female upon herself upon the advice of the physician; and

"(2) within 20 weeks after the commencement of the pregnancy [or after 20 weeks only if the physician has reasonable cause to believe (i) there is a substantial risk that continuance of the pregnancy would endanger the life of the mother or would gravely impair the physical or mental health of the mother, (ii) that the child would be born with grave physical or mental defect, or (iii) that [410 U.S. 113, 147] the pregnancy resulted from rape or incest, or illicit intercourse with a girl under the age of 16 years].

"SECTION 2. [Penalty.] Any person who performs or procures an abortion other than authorized by this Act is guilty of a [felony] and, upon conviction thereof, may be sentenced to pay a fine not exceeding [$1,000] or to imprisonment [in the state penitentiary] not exceeding [5 years], or both.

"SECTION 3. [Uniformity of Interpretation.] This Act shall be construed to effectuate its general purpose to make uniform the law with respect to the subject of this Act among those states which enact it.

"SECTION 4. [Short Title.] This Act may be cited as the Uniform Abortion Act.

"SECTION 5. [Severability.] If any provision of this Act or the application thereof to any person or circumstance is held invalid, the invalidity does not affect other provisions or applications of this Act which can be given effect without the invalid provision or application, and to this end the provisions of this Act are severable.

"SECTION 6. [Repeal.] The following acts and parts of acts are repealed: "(1) "(2) "(3)

"SECTION 7. [Time of Taking Effect.] This Act shall take effect
_____."

[41] "This Act is based largely upon the New York abortion act following a review of the more recent laws on abortion in several states and upon recognition of a more liberal trend in laws on this subject. Recognition was given also to the several decisions in state

and federal courts which show a further trend toward liberalization of abortion laws, especially during the first trimester of pregnancy.

"Recognizing that a number of problems appeared in New York, a shorter time period for "unlimited" abortions was advisable. The [410 U.S. 113, 148] time period was bracketed to permit the various states to insert a figure more in keeping with the different conditions that might exist among the states. Likewise, the language limiting the place or places in which abortions may be performed was also bracketed to account for different conditions among the states. In addition, limitations on abortions after the initial `unlimited" period were placed in brackets so that individual states may adopt all or any of these reasons, or place further restrictions upon abortions after the initial period.

"This Act does not contain any provision relating to medical review committees or prohibitions against sanctions imposed upon medical personnel refusing to participate in abortions because of religious or other similar reasons, or the like. Such provisions, while related, do not directly pertain to when, where, or by whom abortions may be performed; however, the Act is not drafted to exclude such a provision by a state wishing to enact the same."

[42] See, for example, YWCA v. Kugler, 342 F. Supp. 1048, 1074 (N. J. 1972); Abele v. Markle, 342 F. Supp. 800, 805–806 (Conn. 1972) (Newman, J., concurring in result), appeal docketed, No. 72–56; Walsingham v. State, 250 So.2d 857, 863 (Ervin, J., concurring) (Fla. 1971); State v. Gedicke, 43 N. J. L. 86, 90 (1881); Means II 381–382.

[43] See C. Haagensen & W. Lloyd, A Hundred Years of Medicine 19 (1943).

[44] Potts, Postconceptive Control of Fertility, 8 Int'l J. of G. & O. 957, 967 (1970) (England and Wales); Abortion Mortality, 20 Morbidity and Mortality 208, 209 (June 12, 1971) (U.S. Dept. of HEW, Public Health Service) (New York City); Tietze, United States: Therapeutic Abortions, 1963–1968, 59 Studies in Family Planning 5, 7 (1970); Tietze, Mortality with Contraception and Induced Abortion, 45 Studies in Family Planning 6 (1969) (Japan, Czechoslovakia, Hungary); Tietze & Lehfeldt, Legal Abortion in Eastern Europe, 175 J. A. M. A. 1149, 1152 (April 1961). Other sources are discussed in Lader 17–23.

[45] See Brief of Amicus National Right to Life Committee; R. Drinan, The Inviolability of the Right to be Born, in Abortion and the Law 107 (D. Smith ed. 1967); Louisell, Abortion, The Practice of Medicine and the Due Process of Law, 16 U. C. L. A. L. Rev. 233 (1969); Noonan 1.

[46] See, e. g., Abele v. Markle, 342 F. Supp. 800 (Conn. 1972), appeal docketed, No. 72–56.

[47] See discussions in Means I and Means II.

[48] See, e. g., State v. Murphy, 27 N. J. L. 112, 114 (1858).

[49] Watson v. State, 9 Tex. App. 237, 244–245 (1880); Moore v. State, 37 Tex. Cr. R. 552, 561, 40 S. W. 287, 290 (1897); Shaw v. State, 73 Tex. Cr. R. 337, 339, 165 S. W. 930, 931 (1914); Fondren v. State, 74 Tex. Cr. R. 552, 557, 169 S. W. 411, 414 (1914); Gray v. State, 77 Tex. Cr. R. 221, 229, 178 S. W. 337, 341 (1915). There is no immunity in Texas for the father who is not married to the mother. Hammett v. State, 84 Tex. Cr. R. 635, 209 S. W. 661 (1919); Thompson v. State (Ct. Crim. App. Tex. 1971), appeal docketed, No. 71–1200.

[50] See Smith v. State, 33 Me., at 55; In re Vince, 2 N. J. 443, 450, 67 A. 2d 141, 144 (1949). A short discussion of the modern law on this issue is contained in the Comment to the ALI's Model Penal Code 207.11, at 158 and nn. 35–37 (Tent. Draft No. 9, 1959).

[51] Tr. of Oral Rearg. 20–21.

[52] Tr. of Oral Rearg. 24.

[53] We are not aware that in the taking of any census under this clause, a fetus has ever been counted.

[54] When Texas urges that a fetus is entitled to Fourteenth Amendment protection as a

person, it faces a dilemma. Neither in Texas nor in any other State are all abortions prohibited. Despite broad proscription, an exception always exists. The exception contained [410 U.S. 113, 158] in Art. 1196, for an abortion procured or attempted by medical advice for the purpose of saving the life of the mother, is typical. But if the fetus is a person who is not to be deprived of life without due process of law, and if the mother's condition is the sole determinant, does not the Texas exception appear to be out of line with the Amendment's command?

There are other inconsistencies between Fourteenth Amendment status and the typical abortion statute. It has already been pointed out, n. 49, supra, that in Texas the woman is not a principal or an accomplice with respect to an abortion upon her. If the fetus is a person, why is the woman not a principal or an accomplice? Further, the penalty for criminal abortion specified by Art. 1195 is significantly less than the maximum penalty for murder prescribed by Art. 1257 of the Texas Penal Code. If the fetus is a person, may the penalties be different?

[55] Cf. the Wisconsin abortion statute, defining "unborn child" to mean "a human being from the time of conception until it is born alive," Wis. Stat. 940.04 (6) (1969), and the new Connecticut Statute, Pub. Act No. 1 (May 1972 special session), declaring it to be the public policy of the State and the legislative intent "to protect and preserve human life from the moment of conception."

[56] Edelstein 16.

[57] Lader 97–99; D. Feldman, Birth Control in Jewish Law 251–294 (1968). For a stricter view, see I. Jakobovits, Jewish Views on Abortion, in Abortion and the Law 124 (D. Smith ed. 1967).

[58] Amicus Brief for the American Ethical Union et al. For the position of the National Council of Churches and of other denominations, see Lader 99–101.

[59] L. Hellman & J. Pritchard, Williams Obstetrics 493 (14th ed. 1971); Dorland's Illustrated Medical Dictionary 1689 (24th ed. 1965).

[60] Hellman & Pritchard, supra, n. 59, at 493.

[61] For discussions of the development of the Roman Catholic position, see D. Callahan, Abortion: Law, Choice, and Morality 409–447 (1970); Noonan 1.

[62] See Brodie, The New Biology and the Prenatal Child, 9 J. Family L. 391, 397 (1970); Gorney, The New Biology and the Future of Man, 15 U. C. L. A. L. Rev. 273 (1968); Note, Criminal Law—Abortion—The "Morning-After Pill" and Other Pre-Implantation Birth-Control Methods and the Law, 46 Ore. L. Rev. 211 (1967); G. Taylor, The Biological Time Bomb 32 (1968); A. Rosenfeld, The Second Genesis 138–139 (1969); Smith, Through a Test Tube Darkly: Artificial Insemination and the Law, 67 Mich. L. Rev. 127 (1968): Note, Artificial Insemination and the Law, 1968 U. Ill. L. F. 203.

[63] W. Prosser, The Law of Torts 335–338 (4th ed. 1971); 2 F. Harper & F. James, The Law of Torts 1028–1031 (1956); Note, 63 Harv. L. Rev. 173 (1949).

[64] See cases cited in Prosser, supra, n. 63, at 336–338; Annotation, Action for Death of Unborn Child, 15 A. L. R. 3d 992 (1967).

[65] Prosser, supra, n. 63, at 338; Note, The Law and the Unborn Child: The Legal and Logical Inconsistencies, 46 Notre Dame Law. 349, 354–360 (1971).

[66] Louisell, Abortion, The Practice of Medicine and the Due Process of Law, 16 U. C. L. A. L. Rev. 233, 235–238 (1969); Note, 56 Iowa L. Rev. 994, 999–1000 (1971); Note, The Law and the Unborn Child, 46 Notre Dame Law. 349, 351–354 (1971).

[67] Neither in this opinion nor in Doe v. Bolton, post, p. 179, do we discuss the father's rights, if any exist in the constitutional context, in the abortion decision. No paternal right has been asserted in either of the cases, and the Texas and the Georgia statutes on their face

take no cognizance of the father. We are aware that some statutes recognize the father under certain circumstances. North Carolina, for example, N.C. Gen. Stat. 14–45.1 (Supp. 1971), requires written permission for the abortion from the husband when the woman is a married minor, that is, when she is less than 18 years of age, 41 N.C. A. G. 489 (1971); if the woman is an unmarried minor, written permission from the parents is required. We need not now decide whether provisions of this kind are constitutional.

MR. JUSTICE REHNQUIST, dissenting.

The Court's opinion brings to the decision of this troubling question both extensive historical fact and a wealth of legal scholarship. While the opinion thus commands my respect, I find myself nonetheless in fundamental disagreement with those parts of it that invalidate the Texas statute in question, and therefore dissent.

I.

The Court's opinion decides that a State may impose virtually no restriction on the performance of abortions during the first trimester of pregnancy. Our previous decisions indicate that a necessary predicate for such an opinion is a plaintiff who was in her first trimester of pregnancy at some time during the pendency of her law-suit. While a party may vindicate his own constitutional rights, he may not seek vindication for the rights of others. Moose Lodge v. Irvis, 407 U.S. 163 (1972); Sierra Club v. Morton, 405 U.S. 727 (1972). The Court's statement of facts in this case makes clear, however, that the record in no way indicates the presence of such a plaintiff. We know only that plaintiff Roe at the time of filing her complaint was a pregnant woman; for aught that appears in this record, she may have been in her last trimester of pregnancy as of the date the complaint was filed.

Nothing in the Court's opinion indicates that Texas might not constitutionally apply its proscription of abortion as written to a woman in that stage of pregnancy. Nonetheless, the Court uses her complaint against the Texas statute as a fulcrum for deciding that States may [410 U.S. 113, 172] impose virtually no restrictions on medical abortions performed during the first trimester of pregnancy. In deciding such a hypothetical lawsuit, the Court departs from the longstanding admonition that it should never "formulate a rule of constitutional law broader than is required by the precise facts to which it is to be applied." Liverpool, New York & Philadelphia S. S. Co. v. Commissioners of Emigration, 113 U.S. 33, 39 (1885). See also Ashwander v. TVA, 297 U.S. 288, 345 (1936) (Brandeis, J., concurring).

II.

Even if there were a plaintiff in this case capable of litigating the issue which the Court decides, I would reach a conclusion opposite to that reached by the Court. I have difficulty in concluding, as the Court does, that the right of "privacy" is involved in this case. Texas, by the statute here challenged, bars the performance of a medical abortion by a licensed physician on a plaintiff such as Roe. A transaction resulting in an operation such as this is not "private" in the ordinary usage of that word. Nor is the "privacy" that the Court finds here even a distant relative of the freedom from searches and seizures protected by the Fourth Amendment to the Constitution, which the Court has referred to as embodying a right to privacy. Katz v. United States, 389 U.S. 347 (1967).

If the Court means by the term "privacy" no more than that the claim of a person to be free from unwanted state regulation of consensual transactions may be a form of "liberty" protected by the Fourteenth Amendment, there is no doubt that similar claims have been upheld in our earlier decisions on the basis of that liberty. I agree with the statement of MR. JUSTICE STEWART in his concurring opinion that the "liberty," against deprivation of which without due process the Fourteenth [410 U.S. 113, 173] Amendment protects, embraces more than the rights found in the Bill of Rights. But that liberty is not guaranteed absolutely against deprivation, only against deprivation without due process of law. The test traditionally applied in the area of social and economic legislation is whether or not a law such as that challenged has a rational relation to a valid state objective. Williamson v. Lee Optical Co., 348 U.S. 483, 491 (1955). The Due Process Clause of the Fourteenth Amendment undoubtedly does place a limit, albeit a broad one, on legislative power to enact laws such as this. If the Texas statute were to prohibit an abortion even where the mother's life is in jeopardy, I have little doubt that such a statute would lack a rational relation to a valid state objective under the test stated in Williamson, supra. But the Court's sweeping invalidation of any restrictions on abortion during the first trimester is impossible to justify under that standard, and the conscious weighing of competing factors that the Court's opinion apparently substitutes for the established test is far more appropriate to a legislative judgment than to a judicial one.

The Court eschews the history of the Fourteenth Amendment in its reliance on the "compelling state interest" test. See Weber v. Aetna Casualty & Surety Co., 406 U.S. 164, 179 (1972) (dissenting opinion). But the Court adds a new wrinkle to this test by transposing it from the legal considerations associated with the Equal Protection Clause of the Fourteenth Amendment to this case arising under the Due Process

Clause of the Fourteenth Amendment. Unless I misapprehend the consequences of this transplanting of the "compelling state interest test," the Court's opinion will accomplish the seemingly impossible feat of leaving this area of the law more confused than it found it. [410 U.S. 113, 174]

While the Court's opinion quotes from the dissent of Mr. Justice Holmes in Lochner v. New York, 198 U.S. 45, 74 (1905), the result it reaches is more closely attuned to the majority opinion of Mr. Justice Peckham in that case. As in Lochner and similar cases applying substantive due process standards to economic and social welfare legislation, the adoption of the compelling state interest standard will inevitably require this Court to examine the legislative policies and pass on the wisdom of these policies in the very process of deciding whether a particular state interest put forward may or may not be "compelling." The decision here to break pregnancy into three distinct terms and to outline the permissible restrictions the State may impose in each one, for example, partakes more of judicial legislation than it does of a determination of the intent of the drafters of the Fourteenth Amendment.

The fact that a majority of the States reflecting, after all, the majority sentiment in those States, have had restrictions on abortions for at least a century is a strong indication, it seems to me, that the asserted right to an abortion is not "so rooted in the traditions and conscience of our people as to be ranked as fundamental," Snyder v. Massachusetts, 291 U.S. 97, 105 (1934). Even today, when society's views on abortion are changing, the very existence of the debate is evidence that the "right" to an abortion is not so universally accepted as the appellant would have us believe.

To reach its result, the Court necessarily has had to find within the scope of the Fourteenth Amendment a right that was apparently completely unknown to the drafters of the Amendment. As early as 1821, the first state law dealing directly with abortion was enacted by the Connecticut Legislature. Conn. Stat., Tit. 22, 14, 16. By the time of the adoption of the Fourteenth [410 U.S. 113, 175] Amendment in 1868, there were at least 36 laws enacted by state or territorial legislatures limiting abortion.[1] While many States have amended or updated [410 U.S. 113, 176] their laws, 21 of the laws on the books in 1868 remain in effect today.[2] Indeed, the Texas statute struck down today was, as the majority notes, first enacted in 1857 [410 U.S. 113, 177] and "has remained substantially unchanged to the present time." Ante, at 119.

There apparently was no question concerning the validity of this provision or of any of the other state statutes when the Fourteenth Amendment was adopted. The only conclusion possible from this history is that the drafters did not intend to have the Fourteenth Amendment withdraw from the States the power to legislate with respect to this matter.

III.

Even if one were to agree that the case that the Court decides were here, and that the enunciation of the substantive constitutional law in the Court's opinion were proper, the actual disposition of the case by the Court is still difficult to justify. The Texas statute is struck down in toto, even though the Court apparently concedes that at later periods of pregnancy Texas might impose these selfsame statutory limitations on abortion. My understanding of past practice is that a statute found [410 U.S. 113, 178] to be invalid as applied to a particular plaintiff, but not unconstitutional as a whole, is not simply "struck down" but is, instead, declared unconstitutional as applied to the fact situation before the Court. Yick Wo v. Hopkins, 118 U.S. 356 (1886); Street v. New York, 394 U.S. 576 (1969).

For all of the foregoing reasons, I respectfully dissent.

FOOTNOTES

[1] Jurisdictions having enacted abortion laws prior to the adoption of the Fourteenth Amendment in 1868:

1. Alabama—Ala. Acts, c. 6, 2 (1840).
2. Arizona—Howell Code, c. 10, 45 (1865).
3. Arkansas—Ark. Rev. Stat., c. 44, div. III, Art. II, 6 (1838).
4. California—Cal. Sess. Laws, c. 99, 45, p. 233 (1849–1850).
5. Colorado (Terr.)—Colo. Gen. Laws of Terr. of Colo., 1st Sess., 42, pp. 296–297 (1861).
6. Connecticut—Conn. Stat., Tit. 20, 14, 16 (1821). By 1868, this statute had been replaced by another abortion law. Conn. Pub. Acts, c. 71, 1, 2, p. 65 (1860).
7. Florida—Fla. Acts 1st Sess., c. 1637, subc. 3, 10, 11, subc. 8, 9, 10, 11 (1868), as amended, now Fla. Stat. Ann. 782.09, 782.10, 797.01, 797.02, 782.16 (1965).
8. Georgia—Ga. Pen. Code, 4th Div., 20 (1833).
9. Kingdom of Hawaii—Hawaii Pen. Code, c. 12, 1, 2, 3 (1850).
10. Idaho (Terr.)—Idaho (Terr.) Laws, Crimes and Punishments 33, 34, 42, pp. 441, 443 (1863).
11. Illinois—Ill. Rev. Criminal Code 40, 41, 46, pp. 130, 131 (1827). By 1868, this statute had been replaced by a subsequent enactment. Ill. Pub. Laws 1, 2, 3, p. 89 (1867).
12. Indiana—Ind. Rev. Stat. 1, 3, p. 224 (1838). By 1868 this statute had been superseded by a subsequent enactment. Ind. Laws, c. LXXXI, 2 (1859).
13. Iowa (Terr.)—Iowa (Terr.) Stat., 1st Legis., 1st Sess., 18, p. 145 (1838). By 1868, this statute had been superseded by a subsequent enactment. Iowa (Terr.) Rev. Stat., c. 49, 10, 13 (1843).
14. Kansas (Terr.)—Kan. (Terr.) Stat., c. 48, 9, 10, 39 (1855). By 1868 this statute had been superseded by a subsequent enactment. Kan. (Terr.) Laws, c. 28, 9, 10, 37 (1859).
15. Louisiana—La. Rev. Stat., Crimes and Offenses 24, p. 138 (1856).

16. Maine—Me. Rev. Stat., c. 160, 11, 12, 13, 14 (1840).

17. Maryland—Md. Laws, c. 179, 2, p. 315 (1868).

18. Massachusetts—Mass. Acts & Resolves, c. 27 (1845).

19. Michigan—Mich. Rev. Stat., c. 153, 32, 33, 34, p. 662 (1846). [410 U.S. 113, 176]

20. Minnesota (Terr.)—Minn. (Terr.) Rev. Stat., c. 100, 10, 11, p. 493 (1851).

21. Mississippi—Miss. Code, c. 64, 8, 9, p. 958 (1848).

22. Missouri—Mo. Rev. Stat., Art. II, 9, 10, 36, pp. 168, 172 (1835).

23. Montana (Terr.)—Mont. (Terr.) Laws, Criminal Practice Acts 41, p. 184 (1864).

24. Nevada (Terr.)—Nev. (Terr.) Laws, c. 28, 42, p. 63 (1861).

25. New Hampshire—N. H. Laws, c. 743, 1, p. 708 (1848).

26. New Jersey—N. J. Laws, p. 266 (1849).

27. New York—N. Y. Rev. Stat., pt. 4, c. 1, Tit. 2, 8, 9, pp. 12–13 (1828). By 1868, this statute had been superseded. N. Y. Laws, c. 260, 1–6, pp. 285–286 (1845); N. Y. Laws, c. 22, 1, p. 19 (1846).

28. Ohio—Ohio Gen. Stat. 111 (1), 112 (2), p. 252 (1841).

29. Oregon—Ore. Gen. Laws, Crim. Code, c. 43, 509, p. 528 (1845–1864).

30. Pennsylvania—Pa. Laws No. 374, 87, 88, 89 (1860).

31. Texas—Tex. Gen. Stat. Dig., c. VII, Arts. 531–536, p. 524 (Oldham & White 1859).

32. Vermont—Vt. Acts No. 33, 1 (1846). By 1868, this statute had been amended. Vt. Acts No. 57, 1, 3 (1867).

33. Virginia—Va. Acts, Tit. II, c. 3, 9, p. 96 (1848).

34. Washington (Terr.)—Wash. (Terr.) Stats., c. II, 37, 38, p. 81 (1854).

35. West Virginia—See Va. Acts., Tit. II, c. 3, 9, p. 96 (1848); W. Va. Const., Art. XI, par. 8 (1863).

36. Wisconsin—Wis. Rev. Stat., c. 133, 10, 11 (1849). By 1868, this statute had been superseded. Wis. Rev. Stat., c. 164, 10, 11; c. 169, 58, 59 (1858).

[2] Abortion laws in effect in 1868 and still applicable as of August 1970:

1. Arizona (1865). 2. Connecticut (1860). 3. Florida (1868). 4. Idaho (1863). 5. Indiana (1838). [410 U.S. 113, 177] 6. Iowa (1843). 7. Maine (1840). 8. Massachusetts (1845). 9. Michigan (1846). 10. Minnesota (1851). 11. Missouri (1835). 12. Montana (1864). 13. Nevada (1861). 14. New Hampshire (1848). 15. New Jersey (1849). 16. Ohio (1841). 17. Pennsylvania (1860). 18. Texas (1859). 19. Vermont (1867). 20. West Virginia (1863). 21. Wisconsin (1858). [410 U.S. 113, 179]

Bush v. Gore
2000

In the hotly contested Presidential election of 2000, George W. Bush won the popular vote for the State of Florida over Al Gore by a margin of less than 0.5%. As per Florida's election laws, a margin that small sets into motion an automatic machine recount of all votes, which, once completed, had Bush in the lead by an even smaller margin. Al Gore then requested a manual recount of the votes in four counties—Volusia, Palm Beach, Broward, and Miami-Dade—which, though granted, would not be completed by the deadline for submitting election results to the Florida Secretary of State. After the Florida Supreme Court ordered that the deadline be extended, Bush filed an application with the U.S. Supreme Court, requesting that the manual recount be stopped.

In a 5–4 decision, the U.S. Supreme Court ruled that the Florida recount was unconstitutional, citing a lack of uniformity in the ways the votes were being recounted as its primary basis. Though there was much dissent both in the court and throughout the country, the decision was upheld and George W. Bush was declared the winner of Florida's twenty-five electoral votes, and thus the Presidency.

U.S. SUPREME COURT

BUSH V. GORE. U.S. (2000)

V.S.

GEORGE W. BUSH, ET AL., PETITIONERS
v. ALBERT GORE, JR., ET AL.

ON WRIT OF CERTIORARI TO THE FLORIDA SUPREME COURT

December 12, 2000.

Per Curiam.

I.

ON December 8, 2000, the Supreme Court of Florida ordered that the Circuit Court of Leon County tabulate by hand 9,000 ballots in Miami-Dade County. It also ordered the inclusion in the certified vote totals of 215 votes identified in Palm Beach County and 168 votes identified in Miami-Dade County for Vice President Albert Gore, Jr., and Senator Joseph Lieberman, Democratic Candidates for President and Vice President. The Supreme Court noted that petitioner, Governor George W. Bush asserted that the net gain for Vice President Gore in Palm Beach County was 176 votes, and directed the Circuit Court to resolve that dispute on remand. ___ So. 2d, at ___ (slip op., at 4, n. 6). The court further held that relief would require manual recounts in all Florida counties where so-called "under-votes" had not been subject to manual tabulation. The court ordered all manual recounts to begin at once. Governor Bush and Richard Cheney, Republican Candidates for the Presidency and Vice Presidency, filed an emergency application for a stay of this mandate. On December 9, we granted the application, treated the application as a petition for a writ of certiorari, and granted certiorari. *Post,* p. ___.

The proceedings leading to the present controversy are discussed in some detail in our opinion in *Bush v. Palm Beach County Canvassing Bd.,* *ante,* p. ___ *(per curiam) (Bush I).* On November 8, 2000, the day following the Presidential election, the Florida Division of Elections reported that petitioner, Governor Bush, had received 2,909,135 votes, and respondent, Vice President Gore, had received 2,907,351 votes, a margin of 1,784 for Governor Bush. Because Governor Bush's margin of victory was less than "one-half of a percent . . . of the votes cast," an automatic machine recount was conducted under §102.141(4) of the election code, the results of which showed Governor Bush still winning the race but by a diminished margin. Vice President Gore then sought manual recounts in Volusia, Palm Beach, Broward, and Miami–Dade Counties, pursuant to Florida's election protest provisions. Fla. Stat. §102.166 (2000). A dispute arose concerning the deadline for local county canvassing boards to submit their returns to the Secretary of State (Secretary). The Secretary declined to waive the November 14 deadline imposed by statute. §§102.111, 102.112. The Florida Supreme Court, however, set the deadline at November 26. We granted certiorari and vacated the Florida Supreme Court's decision, finding considerable uncertainty as to the grounds on which it was based. *Bush I, ante,* at ___-___ (slip. op., at 6–7). On December 11, the Florida Supreme Court issued a decision on remand reinstating that date. ___ So. 2d ___, ___ (slip op. at 30–31).

On November 26, the Florida Elections Canvassing Commission certified the results of the election and declared Governor Bush the winner of Florida's 25 electoral votes. On November 27, Vice President Gore, pursuant to Florida's contest provisions, filed a complaint in Leon County Circuit Court contesting the certification. Fla. Stat. §102.168 (2000). He sought relief pursuant to §102.168(3)(c), which provides that "[r]eceipt of a number of illegal votes or rejection of a number of legal votes sufficient to change or place in doubt the result of the election" shall be grounds for a contest. The Circuit Court denied relief, stating that Vice President Gore failed to meet his burden of proof. He appealed to the First District Court of Appeal, which certified the matter to the Florida Supreme Court.

Accepting jurisdiction, the Florida Supreme Court affirmed in part and reversed in part. *Gore v. Harris,* ___ So. 2d. ___ (2000). The court held that the Circuit Court had been correct to reject Vice President Gore's challenge to the results certified in Nassau County and his challenge to the Palm Beach County Canvassing Board's determination that 3,300 ballots cast in that county were not, in the statutory phrase, "legal votes."

The Supreme Court held that Vice President Gore had satisfied his burden of proof under §102.168(3)(c) with respect to his challenge to Miami–Dade County's failure to tabulate, by manual count, 9,000 ballots on which the machines had failed to detect a vote for President ("undervotes"). ___ So. 2d., at ___ (slip. op., at 22–23). Noting the closeness of the election, the Court explained that "[o]n this record, there can be no question that there are legal votes within the 9,000 uncounted votes sufficient to place the results of this election in doubt." *Id.,* at ___ (slip. op., at 35). A "legal vote," as determined by the Supreme Court, is "one in which there is a "clear indication of the intent of the voter." *Id.,* at ___ (slip op., at 25). The court therefore ordered a hand recount of the 9,000 ballots in Miami-Dade County. Observing that the contest provisions vest broad discretion in the circuit judge to "provide any relief appropriate under such circumstances," Fla. Stat. §102.168(8) (2000), the Supreme Court further held that the Circuit Court could order "the Supervisor of Elections and the Canvassing Boards, as well as the necessary public officials, in all counties that have not conducted a manual recount or tabulation of the undervotes ... to do so forthwith, said tabulation to take place in the individual counties where the ballots are located." ___ So. 2d, at ___ (slip. op., at 38).

The Supreme Court also determined that both Palm Beach County and Miami-Dade County, in their earlier manual recounts, had identified a net gain of 215 and 168 legal votes for Vice President Gore. *Id.,* at ___ (slip. op., at 33–34). Rejecting the Circuit Court's conclusion that Palm Beach County lacked the authority to include the 215 net votes submitted past the November 26 deadline, the Supreme Court explained that the deadline was not intended to exclude votes identified after that date through ongoing manual recounts. As to Miami-Dade County, the Court concluded that although the 168 votes identified were the result of a partial recount, they were "legal votes [that] could change the outcome of the election." *Id.,* at (slip op., at 34). The Supreme Court therefore directed the Circuit Court to include those totals in the certified results, subject to resolution of the actual vote total from the Miami-Dade partial recount.

The petition presents the following questions: whether the Florida Supreme Court established new standards for resolving Presidential election contests, thereby violating Art. II, §1, cl. 2, of the United States Constitution and failing to comply with 3 U. S. C. §5, and whether the use of standardless manual recounts violates the Equal Protection and Due Process Clauses. With respect to the equal protection question, we find a violation of the Equal Protection Clause.

II.

A

The closeness of this election, and the multitude of legal challenges which have followed in its wake, have brought into sharp focus a common, if heretofore unnoticed, phenomenon. Nationwide statistics reveal that an estimated 2% of ballots cast do not register a vote for President for whatever reason, including deliberately choosing no candidate at all or some voter error, such as voting for two candidates or insufficiently marking a ballot. See Ho, More Than 2M Ballots Uncounted, AP Online (Nov. 28, 2000); Kelley, Balloting Problems Not Rare But Only In A Very Close Election Do Mistakes And Mismarking Make A Difference, Omaha World-Herald (Nov. 15, 2000). In certifying election results, the votes eligible for inclusion in the certification are the votes meeting the properly established legal requirements.

This case has shown that punch card balloting machines can produce an unfortunate number of ballots which are not punched in a clean, complete way by the voter. After the current counting, it is likely legislative bodies nationwide will examine ways to improve the mechanisms and machinery for voting.

B

The individual citizen has no federal constitutional right to vote for electors for the President of the United States unless and until the state legislature chooses a statewide election as the means to implement its power to appoint members of the Electoral College. U. S. Const., Art. II, §1. This is the source for the statement in *McPherson v. Blacker,* 146 U. S. 1, 35 (1892), that the State legislature's power to select the manner for appointing electors is plenary; it may, if it so chooses, select the electors itself, which indeed was the manner used by State legislatures in several States for many years after the Framing of our Constitution. *Id.,* at 28–33. History has now favored the voter, and in each of the several States the citizens themselves vote for Presidential electors. When the state legislature vests the right to vote for President in its people, the right to vote as the legislature has prescribed is fundamental; and one source of its fundamental nature lies in the equal weight accorded to each vote and the equal dignity owed to each voter. The State, of course, after granting the franchise in the special context of Article II, can take back the power to appoint electors. See *id.,* at 35 ("[T]here is no doubt of the right of the legislature to resume the power at any time, for it can neither be taken away nor abdicated") (quoting S. Rep. No. 395, 43d Cong., 1st Sess.).

The right to vote is protected in more than the initial allocation of the franchise. Equal protection applies as well to the manner of its exercise. Having once granted the right to vote on equal terms, the State may not, by later arbitrary and disparate treatment, value one person's vote over that of another. See, *e.g., Harper v. Virginia Bd. of Elections,* 383 U. S. 663, 665 (1966) ("[O]nce the franchise is granted to the electorate, lines may not be drawn which are inconsistent with the Equal Protection Clause of the Fourteenth Amendment"). It must be remembered that "the right of suffrage can be denied by a debasement or dilution of the weight of a citizen's vote just as effectively as by wholly prohibiting the free exercise of the franchise." *Reynolds v. Sims,* 377 U. S. 533, 555 (1964).

There is no difference between the two sides of the present controversy on these basic propositions. Respondents say that the very purpose of vindicating the right to vote justifies the recount procedures now at issue. The question before us, however, is whether the recount procedures the Florida Supreme Court has adopted are consistent with its obligation to avoid arbitrary and disparate treatment of the members of its electorate.

Much of the controversy seems to revolve around ballot cards designed to be perforated by a stylus but which, either through error or deliberate omission, have not been perforated with sufficient precision for a machine to count them. In some cases a piece of the card—a chad—is hanging, say by two corners. In other cases there is no separation at all, just an indentation.

The Florida Supreme Court has ordered that the intent of the voter be discerned from such ballots. For purposes of resolving the equal protection challenge, it is not necessary to decide whether the Florida Supreme Court had the authority under the legislative scheme for resolving election disputes to define what a legal vote is and to mandate a manual recount implementing that definition. The recount mechanisms implemented in response to the decisions of the Florida Supreme Court do not satisfy the minimum requirement for non-arbitrary treatment of voters necessary to secure the fundamental right. Florida's basic command for the count of legally cast votes is to consider the "intent of the voter." *Gore v. Harris,* ___ So. 2d, at ___ (slip op., at 39). This is unobjectionable as an abstract proposition and a starting principle. The problem inheres in the absence of specific standards to ensure its equal application. The formulation of uniform rules to determine intent based on these recurring circumstances is practicable and, we conclude, necessary.

The law does not refrain from searching for the intent of the actor in a multitude of circumstances; and in some cases the general command to ascertain intent is not susceptible to much further refinement. In this instance, however, the question is not whether to believe a witness but how to interpret the marks or holes or scratches on an inanimate object, a piece of cardboard or paper which, it is said, might not have registered as a vote during the machine count. The factfinder confronts a thing, not a person. The search for intent can be confined by specific rules designed to ensure uniform treatment.

The want of those rules here has led to unequal evaluation of ballots in various respects. See *Gore v. Harris,* ___ So. 2d, at ___ (slip op., at 51) (Wells, J., dissenting) ("Should a county canvassing board count or not count a "dimpled chad" where the voter is able to successfully dislodge the chad in every other contest on that ballot? Here, the county canvass-ing boards disagree"). As seems to have been acknowledged at oral argu-ment, the standards for accepting or rejecting contested ballots might vary not only from county to county but indeed within a single county from one recount team to another.

The record provides some examples. A monitor in Miami-Dade County testified at trial that he observed that three members of the county canvassing board applied different standards in defining a legal vote. 3 Tr. 497, 499 (Dec. 3, 2000). And testimony at trial also revealed that at least one county changed its evaluative standards during the counting process. Palm Beach County, for example, began the process with a 1990 guideline which precluded counting completely attached chads, switched to a rule that considered a vote to be legal if any light could be seen through a chad, changed back to the 1990 rule, and then abandoned any pretense of a *per se* rule, only to have a court order that the county consider dimpled chads legal. This is not a process with suf-ficient guarantees of equal treatment.

An early case in our one person, one vote jurisprudence arose when a State accorded arbitrary and disparate treatment to voters in its different counties. *Gray v. Sanders,* 372 U. S. 368 (1963). The Court found a con-stitutional violation. We relied on these principles in the context of the Presidential selection process in *Moore v. Ogilvie,* 394 U. S. 814 (1969), where we invalidated a county-based procedure that diluted the influ-ence of citizens in larger counties in the nominating process. There we observed that "[t]he idea that one group can be granted greater voting strength than another is hostile to the one man, one vote basis of our rep-resentative government." *Id.,* at 819.

The State Supreme Court ratified this uneven treatment. It mandated that the recount totals from two counties, Miami–Dade and Palm Beach, be included in the certified total. The court also appeared to hold *sub silentio* that the recount totals from Broward County, which were not completed until after the original November 14 certification by the Secretary of State, were to be considered part of the new certified vote totals even though the county certification was not contested by Vice President Gore. Yet each of the counties used varying standards to deter-mine what was a legal vote. Broward County used a more forgiving stan-dard than Palm Beach County, and uncovered almost three times as many new votes, a result markedly disproportionate to the difference in popu-lation between the counties.

In addition, the recounts in these three counties were not limited to so-called undervotes but extended to all of the ballots. The distinction has real consequences. A manual recount of all ballots identifies not only those ballots which show no vote but also those which contain more than one, the so-called overvotes. Neither category will be counted by the machine. This is not a trivial concern. At oral argument, respondents estimated there are as many as 110,000 overvotes statewide. As a result, the citizen whose ballot was not read by a machine because he failed to vote for a candidate in a way readable by a machine may still have his vote counted in a manual recount; on the other hand, the citizen who marks two candidates in a way discernable by the machine will not have the same opportunity to have his vote count, even if a manual examination of the ballot would reveal the requisite indicia of intent. Furthermore, the citizen who marks two candidates, only one of which is discernable by the machine, will have his vote counted even though it should have been read as an invalid ballot. The State Supreme Court's inclusion of vote counts based on these variant standards exemplifies concerns with the remedial processes that were under way.

That brings the analysis to yet a further equal protection problem. The votes certified by the court included a partial total from one county, Miami-Dade. The Florida Supreme Court's decision thus gives no assurance that the recounts included in a final certification must be complete. Indeed, it is respondent's submission that it would be consistent with the rules of the recount procedures to include whatever partial counts are done by the time of final certification, and we interpret the Florida Supreme Court's decision to permit this. See _____ So. 2d, at _____, n. 21 (slip op., at 37, n. 21) (noting "practical difficulties" may control outcome of election, but certifying partial Miami-Dade total nonetheless). This accommodation no doubt results from the truncated contest period established by the Florida Supreme Court in *Bush I,* at respondents' own urging. The press of time does not diminish the constitutional concern. A desire for speed is not a general excuse for ignoring equal protection guarantees.

In addition to these difficulties the actual process by which the votes were to be counted under the Florida Supreme Court's decision raises further concerns. That order did not specify who would recount the ballots. The county canvassing boards were forced to pull together ad hoc teams comprised of judges from various Circuits who had no previous training in handling and interpreting ballots. Furthermore, while others were permitted to observe, they were prohibited from objecting during the recount.

The recount process, in its features here described, is inconsistent with the minimum procedures necessary to protect the fundamental right of each voter in the special instance of a statewide recount under the authority of a single state judicial officer. Our consideration is limited to the present circumstances, for the problem of equal protection in election processes generally presents many complexities.

The question before the Court is not whether local entities, in the exercise of their expertise, may develop different systems for implementing elections. Instead, we are presented with a situation where a state court with the power to assure uniformity has ordered a statewide recount with minimal procedural safeguards. When a court orders a statewide remedy, there must be at least some assurance that the rudimentary requirements of equal treatment and fundamental fairness are satisfied.

Given the Court's assessment that the recount process underway was probably being conducted in an unconstitutional manner, the Court stayed the order directing the recount so it could hear this case and render an expedited decision. The contest provision, as it was mandated by the State Supreme Court, is not well calculated to sustain the confidence that all citizens must have in the outcome of elections. The State has not shown that its procedures include the necessary safeguards. The problem, for instance, of the estimated 110,000 overvotes has not been addressed, although Chief Justice Wells called attention to the concern in his dissenting opinion. See _____ So. 2d, at _____, n. 26 (slip op., at 45, n. 26).

Upon due consideration of the difficulties identified to this point, it is obvious that the recount cannot be conducted in compliance with the requirements of equal protection and due process without substantial additional work. It would require not only the adoption (after opportunity for argument) of adequate statewide standards for determining what is a legal vote, and practicable procedures to implement them, but also orderly judicial review of any disputed matters that might arise. In addition, the Secretary of State has advised that the recount of only a portion of the ballots requires that the vote tabulation equipment be used to screen out undervotes, a function for which the machines were not designed. If a recount of overvotes were also required, perhaps even a second screening would be necessary. Use of the equipment for this purpose, and any new software developed for it, would have to be evaluated for accuracy by the Secretary of State, as required by Fla. Stat. §101.015 (2000).

The Supreme Court of Florida has said that the legislature intended the State's electors to "participat[e] fully in the federal electoral process," as provided in 3 U. S. C. §5. _____ So. 2d, at _____ (slip op., at 27); see also *Palm Beach Canvassing Bd. v. Harris,* 2000 WL 1725434, *13 (Fla. 2000). That statute, in turn, requires that any controversy or contest that is designed to lead to a conclusive selection of electors be completed by December 12. That date is upon us, and there is no recount procedure in place under the State Supreme Court's order that comports with minimal constitutional standards. Because it is evident that any recount seeking to meet the December 12 date will be unconstitutional for the reasons we have discussed, we reverse the judgment of the Supreme Court of Florida ordering a recount to proceed.

Seven Justices of the Court agree that there are constitutional problems with the recount ordered by the Florida Supreme Court that demand a remedy. See *post*, at 6 (*Souter, J.,* dissenting); *post*, at 2, 15 (*Breyer, J.,* dissenting). The only disagreement is as to the remedy. Because the Florida Supreme Court has said that the Florida Legislature intended to obtain the safe-harbor benefits of 3 U. S. C. §5, *Justice Breyer's* proposed remedy—remanding to the Florida Supreme Court for its ordering of a constitutionally proper contest until December 18—contemplates action in violation of the Florida election code, and hence could not be part of an "appropriate" order authorized by Fla. Stat. §102.168(8) (2000).

* * *

None are more conscious of the vital limits on judicial authority than are the members of this Court, and none stand more in admiration of the Constitution's design to leave the selection of the President to the people, through their legislatures, and to the political sphere. When contending parties invoke the process of the courts, however, it becomes our unsought responsibility to resolve the federal and constitutional issues the judicial system has been forced to confront.

The judgment of the Supreme Court of Florida is reversed, and the case is remanded for further proceedings not inconsistent with this opinion.

Pursuant to this Court's Rule 45.2, the Clerk is directed to issue the mandate in this case forthwith.

It is so ordered.

GEORGE W. BUSH, ET AL., PETITIONERS
v. ALBERT GORE, *Jr.*, ET AL.
ON WRIT OF CERTIORARI TO THE FLORIDA SUPREME COURT
December 12, 2000.

Justice Stevens, with whom *Justice Ginsburg and Justice Breyer* join, dissenting.

The Constitution assigns to the States the primary responsibility for determining the manner of selecting the Presidential electors. See Art. II, §1, cl. 2. When questions arise about the meaning of state laws, including election laws, it is our settled practice to accept the opinions of the highest courts of the States as providing the final answers. On rare occasions, however, either federal statutes or the Federal Constitution may require federal judicial intervention in state elections. This is not such an occasion.

The federal questions that ultimately emerged in this case are not substantial. Article II provides that "[e]ach *State* shall appoint, in such Manner as the Legislature *thereof* may direct, a Number of Electors." *Ibid.* (emphasis added). It does not create state legislatures out of whole cloth, but rather takes them as they come—as creatures born of, and constrained by, their state constitutions. Lest there be any doubt, we stated over 100 years ago in *McPherson* v. *Blacker,* 146 U. S. 1, 25 (1892), that "[w]hat is forbidden or required to be done by a State" in the Article II context "is forbidden or required of the legislative power under state constitutions as they exist." In the same vein, we also observed that "[t]he [State's] legislative power is the supreme authority except as limited by the constitution of the State." *Ibid.*; cf. *Smiley* v. *Holm,* 285 U. S. 355, 367 (1932).[1] The legislative power in Florida is subject to judicial review pursuant to Article V of the Florida Constitution, and nothing in Article II of the Federal Constitution frees the state legislature from the constraints in the state constitution that created it. Moreover, the Florida Legislature's own decision to employ a unitary code for all elections indicates that it intended the Florida Supreme Court to play the same role in Presidential elections that it has historically played in resolving electoral disputes. The Florida Supreme Court's exercise of appellate jurisdiction therefore was wholly consistent with, and indeed contemplated by, the grant of authority in Article II.

It hardly needs stating that Congress, pursuant to 3 U. S. C. §5, did not impose any affirmative duties upon the States that their governmental branches could "violate." Rather, §5 provides a safe harbor for States to select electors in contested elections "by judicial or other methods" established by laws prior to the election day. Section 5, like Article II, assumes the involvement of the state judiciary in interpreting state election laws and resolving election disputes under those laws. Neither §5 nor Article II grants federal judges any special authority to substitute their views for those of the state judiciary on matters of state law.

Nor are petitioners correct in asserting that the failure of the Florida Supreme Court to specify in detail the precise manner in which the "intent of the voter," Fla. Stat. §101.5614(5) (Supp. 2001), is to be determined rises to the level of a constitutional violation.[2] We found such a violation when individual votes within the same State were weighted unequally, see, *e.g., Reynolds* v. *Sims,* 377 U. S. 533, 568 (1964), but we have never before called into question the substantive standard by which a State determines that a vote has been legally cast. And there is no reason to think that the guidance provided to the factfinders, specifically the various canvassing boards, by the "intent of the voter" standard is any less sufficient—or will lead to results any less uniform—than, for example, the "beyond a reasonable doubt" standard employed every day by ordinary citizens in courtrooms across this country.[3]

Admittedly, the use of differing substandards for determining voter intent in different counties employing similar voting systems may raise serious concerns. Those concerns are alleviated—if not eliminated—by the fact that a single impartial magistrate will ultimately adjudicate all objections arising from the recount process. Of course, as a general matter, "[t]he interpretation of constitutional principles must not be too literal. We must remember that the machinery of government would not work if it were not allowed a little play in its joints." *Bain Peanut Co. of Tex. v. Pinson,* 282 U. S. 499, 501 (1931) (Holmes, J.). If it were otherwise, Florida's decision to leave to each county the determination of what balloting system to employ—despite enormous differences in accuracy[4]—might run afoul of equal protection. So, too, might the similar decisions of the vast majority of state legislatures to delegate to local authorities certain decisions with respect to voting systems and ballot design.

Even assuming that aspects of the remedial scheme might ultimately be found to violate the Equal Protection Clause, I could not subscribe to the majority's disposition of the case. As the majority explicitly holds, once a state legislature determines to select electors through a popular vote, the right to have one's vote counted is of constitutional stature. As the majority further acknowledges, Florida law holds that all ballots that reveal the intent of the voter constitute valid votes. Recognizing these principles, the majority nonetheless orders the termination of the contest proceeding before all such votes have been tabulated. Under their own reasoning, the appropriate course of action would be to remand to allow more specific procedures for implementing the legislature's uniform general standard to be established.

In the interest of finality, however, the majority effectively orders the disenfranchisement of an unknown number of voters whose ballots reveal their intent—and are therefore legal votes under state law—but were for some reason rejected by ballot-counting machines. It does so on the basis of the deadlines set forth in Title 3 of the United States Code. *Ante,* at 11. But, as I have already noted, those provisions merely provide rules of decision for Congress to follow when selecting among conflicting slates of electors. *Supra,* at 2. They do not prohibit a State from counting what the majority concedes to be legal votes until a bona fide winner is determined. Indeed, in 1960, Hawaii appointed two slates of electors and Congress chose to count the one appointed on January 4, 1961, well after the Title 3 deadlines. See Josephson & Ross, Repairing the Electoral College, 22 J. Legis. 145, 166, n. 154 (1996).[5] Thus, nothing prevents the majority, even if it properly found an equal protection violation, from ordering relief appropriate to remedy that violation without depriving Florida voters of their right to have their votes counted. As the majority notes, "[a] desire for speed is not a general excuse for ignoring equal protection guarantees." *Ante,* at 10.

Finally, neither in this case, nor in its earlier opinion in *Palm Beach County Canvassing Bd. v. Harris,* 2000 WL 1725434 (Fla., Nov. 21, 2000), did the Florida Supreme Court make any substantive change in Florida electoral law.[6] Its decisions were rooted in long-established precedent and were consistent with the relevant statutory provisions, taken as a whole. It did what courts do[7]—it decided the case before it in light of the legislature's intent to leave no legally cast vote uncounted. In so doing, it relied on the sufficiency of the general "intent of the voter" standard articulated by the state legislature, coupled with a procedure for ultimate review by an impartial judge, to resolve the concern about disparate evaluations of contested ballots. If we assume—as I do—that the members of that court and the judges who would have carried out its mandate are impartial, its decision does not even raise a colorable federal question.

What must underlie petitioners" entire federal assault on the Florida election procedures is an unstated lack of confidence in the impartiality and capacity of the state judges who would make the critical decisions if the vote count were to proceed. Otherwise, their position is wholly without merit. The endorsement of that position by the majority of this Court can only lend credence to the most cynical appraisal of the work of judges throughout the land. It is confidence in the men and women who administer the judicial system that is the true backbone of the rule of law. Time will one day heal the wound to that confidence that will be inflicted by today's decision. One thing, however, is certain. Although we may never know with complete certainty the identity of the winner of this year's Presidential election, the identity of the loser is perfectly clear. It is the Nation's confidence in the judge as an impartial guardian of the rule of law.

I respectfully dissent.

GEORGE W. BUSH, ET AL., PETITIONERS
v. ALBERT GORE, JR., ET AL.
ON WRIT OF CERTIORARI TO THE FLORIDA SUPREME COURT
[December 12, 2000]

Justice Souter, with whom *Justice Breyer* joins and with whom *Justice Stevens* and *Justice Ginsburg* join with regard to all but Part C, dissenting.

The Court should not have reviewed either *Bush* v. *Palm Beach County Canvassing Bd., ante,* p. ___ (*per curiam*), or this case, and should not have stopped Florida's attempt to recount all undervote ballots, see *ante* at ___, by issuing a stay of the Florida Supreme Court's orders during the period of this review, see *Bush* v. *Gore, post* at ____ (slip op., at 1). If this Court had allowed the State to follow the course indicated by the opinions of its own Supreme Court, it is entirely possible that there would ultimately have been no issue requiring our review, and political tension could have worked itself out in the Congress following the procedure provided in 3 U. S. C. §15. The case being before us, however, its resolution by the majority is another erroneous decision.

As will be clear, I am in substantial agreement with the dissenting opinions of *Justice Stevens, Justice Ginsburg* and *Justice Breyer.* I write separately only to say how straightforward the issues before us really are.

There are three issues: whether the State Supreme Court's interpretation of the statute providing for a contest of the state election results somehow violates 3 U. S. C. §5; whether that court's construction of the state statutory provisions governing contests impermissibly changes a state law from what the State's legislature has provided, in violation of Article II, §1, cl. 2, of the national Constitution; and whether the manner of interpreting markings on disputed ballots failing to cause machines to register votes for President (the undervote ballots) violates the equal protection or due process guaranteed by the Fourteenth Amendment. None of these issues is difficult to describe or to resolve.

A

The 3 U. S. C. §5 issue is not serious. That provision sets certain conditions for treating a State's certification of Presidential electors as conclusive in the event that a dispute over recognizing those electors must be resolved in the Congress under 3 U. S. C. §15. Conclusiveness requires selection under a legal scheme in place before the election, with results determined at least six days before the date set for casting electoral votes. But no State is required to conform to §5 if it cannot do that (for whatever reason); the sanction for failing to satisfy the conditions of §5 is simply loss of what has been called its "safe harbor." And even that determination is to be made, if made anywhere, in the Congress.

B

The second matter here goes to the State Supreme Court's interpretation of certain terms in the state statute governing election "contests," Fla. Stat. §102.168 (2000); there is no question here about the state court's interpretation of the related provisions dealing with the antecedent process of "protesting" particular vote counts, §102.166, which was involved in the previous case, *Bush* v. *Palm Beach County Canvassing Board.* The issue is whether the judgment of the state supreme court has displaced the state legislature's provisions for election contests: is the law as declared by the court different from the provisions made by the legislature, to which the national Constitution commits responsibility for determining how each state's Presidential electors are chosen? See U. S. Const., Art. II, §1, cl. 2.

Bush does not, of course, claim that any judicial act interpreting a statute of uncertain meaning is enough to displace the legislative provision and violate Article II; statutes require interpretation, which does not without more affect the legislative character of a statute within the meaning of the Constitution. Brief for Petitioners 48, n. 22, in *Bush v. Palm Beach County Canvassing Bd., et al.,* 531 U. S. ___ (2000). What Bush does argue, as I understand the contention, is that the interpretation of §102.168 was so unreasonable as to transcend the accepted bounds of statutory interpretation, to the point of being a nonjudicial act and producing new law untethered to the legislative act in question.

The starting point for evaluating the claim that the Florida Supreme Court's interpretation effectively re-wrote §102.168 must be the language of the provision on which Gore relies to show his right to raise this contest: that the previously certified result in Bush's favor was produced by "rejection of a number of legal votes sufficient to change or place in doubt the result of the election." Fla. Stat. §102.168(3)(c) (2000). None of the state court's interpretations is unreasonable to the point of displacing the legislative enactment quoted. As I will note below, other interpretations were of course possible, and some might have been better than those adopted by the Florida court's majority; the two dissents from the majority opinion of that court and various briefs submitted to us set out alternatives. But the majority view is in each instance within the bounds of reasonable interpretation, and the law as declared is consistent with Article II.

1. The statute does not define a "legal vote," the rejection of which may affect the election. The State Supreme Court was therefore required to define it, and in doing that the court looked to another election statute, §101.5614(5), dealing with damaged or defective ballots, which contains a provision that no vote shall be disregarded "if there is a clear indication of the intent of the voter as determined by a canvassing board." The court read that objective of looking to the voter's intent as indicating that the legislature probably meant "legal vote" to mean a vote recorded on a ballot indicating what the voter intended. *Gore* v. *Harris,* __ So. 2d __ (slip op., at 23–25) (Dec. 8, 2000). It is perfectly true that the majority might have chosen a different reading. See, *e.g.,* Brief for Respondent Harris et al. 10 (defining "legal votes" as "votes properly executed in accordance with the instructions provided to all registered voters in advance of the election and in the polling places"). But even so, there is no constitutional violation in following the majority view; Article II is unconcerned with mere disagreements about interpretive merits.

2. The Florida court next interpreted "rejection" to determine what act in the counting process may be attacked in a contest. Again, the statute does not define the term. The court majority read the word to mean simply a failure to count. ____ So. 2d, at___ (slip op., at 26–27). That reading

is certainly within the bounds of common sense, given the objective to give effect to a voter's intent if that can be determined. A different reading, of course, is possible. The majority might have concluded that "rejection" should refer to machine malfunction, or that a ballot should not be treated as "reject[ed]" in the absence of wrongdoing by election officials, lest contests be so easy to claim that every election will end up in one. Cf. *id.,* at _____ (slip op., at 48) (Wells, C. J., dissenting). There is, however, nothing nonjudicial in the Florida majority's more hospitable reading.

3. The same is true about the court majority's understanding of the phrase "votes sufficient to change or place in doubt" the result of the election in Florida. The court held that if the uncounted ballots were so numerous that it was reasonably possible that they contained enough "legal" votes to swing the election, this contest would be authorized by the statute.[1] While the majority might have thought (as the trial judge did) that a probability, not a possibility, should be necessary to justify a contest, that reading is not required by the statute's text, which says nothing about probability. Whatever people of good will and good sense may argue about the merits of the Florida court's reading, there is no warrant for saying that it transcends the limits of reasonable statutory interpretation to the point of supplanting the statute enacted by the "legislature" within the meaning of Article II.

In sum, the interpretations by the Florida court raise no substantial question under Article II. That court engaged in permissible construction in determining that Gore had instituted a contest authorized by the state statute, and it proceeded to direct the trial judge to deal with that contest in the exercise of the discretionary powers generously conferred by Fla. Stat. §102.168(8) (2000), to "fashion such orders as he or she deems necessary to ensure that each allegation in the complaint is investigated, examined, or checked, to prevent or correct any alleged wrong, and to provide any relief appropriate under such circumstances." As *Justice Ginsburg* has persuasively explained in her own dissenting opinion, our customary respect for state interpretations of state law counsels against rejection of the Florida court's determinations in this case.

C

It is only on the third issue before us that there is a meritorious argument for relief, as this Court's *Per Curiam* opinion recognizes. It is an issue that might well have been dealt with adequately by the Florida courts if the state proceedings had not been interrupted, and if not disposed of at the state level it could have been considered by the Congress in any electoral vote dispute. But because the course of state proceedings has been interrupted, time is short, and the issue is before us, I think it sensible for the Court to address it.

Petitioners have raised an equal protection claim (or, alternatively, a due process claim, see generally *Logan* v. *Zimmerman Brush Co.,* 455 U. S. 422 (1982)), in the charge that unjustifiably disparate standards are applied in different electoral jurisdictions to otherwise identical facts. It is true that the Equal Protection Clause does not forbid the use of a variety of voting mechanisms within a jurisdiction, even though different mechanisms will have different levels of effectiveness in recording voters" intentions; local variety can be justified by concerns about cost, the potential value of innovation, and so on. But evidence in the record here suggests that a different order of disparity obtains under rules for determining a voter's intent that have been applied (and could continue to be applied) to identical types of ballots used in identical brands of machines and exhibiting identical physical characteristics (such as "hanging" or "dimpled" chads). See, *e.g.,* Tr., at 238–242 (Dec. 2–3, 2000) (testimony of Palm Beach County Canvassing Board Chairman Judge Charles Burton describing varying standards applied to imperfectly punched ballots in Palm Beach County during precertification manual recount); *id.,* at 497–500 (similarly describing varying standards applied in Miami-Dade County); Tr. of Hearing 8–10 (Dec. 8, 2000) (soliciting from county canvassing boards proposed protocols for determining voters" intent but declining to provide a precise, uniform standard). I can conceive of no legitimate state interest served by these differing treatments of the expressions of voters" fundamental rights. The differences appear wholly arbitrary.

In deciding what to do about this, we should take account of the fact that electoral votes are due to be cast in six days. I would therefore remand the case to the courts of Florida with instructions to establish uniform standards for evaluating the several types of ballots that have prompted differing treatments, to be applied within and among counties when passing on such identical ballots in any further recounting (or successive recounting) that the courts might order.

Unlike the majority, I see no warrant for this Court to assume that Florida could not possibly comply with this requirement before the date set for the meeting of electors, December 18. Although one of the dissenting justices of the State Supreme Court estimated that disparate standards potentially affected 170,000 votes, *Gore v. Harris, supra,* ____ So. 2d, at ____ (slip op., at 66), the number at issue is significantly smaller. The 170,000 figure apparently represents all uncounted votes, both undervotes (those for which no Presidential choice was recorded by a machine) and overvotes (those rejected because of votes for more than one candidate). Tr. of Oral Arg. 61–62. But as *Justice Breyer* has pointed out, no showing has been made of legal overvotes uncounted, and counsel for Gore made an uncontradicted representation to the Court that the statewide total of undervotes is about 60,000. *Id.,* at 62. To recount these manually would be a tall order, but before this Court stayed the effort to do that the courts of Florida were ready to do their best to get that job done. There is no justification for denying the State the opportunity to try to count all disputed ballots now.

I respectfully dissent.

GEORGE W. BUSH, ET AL., PETITIONERS
v. ALBERT GORE, *Jr.*, ET AL.
ON WRIT OF CERTIORARI TO THE
FLORIDA SUPREME COURT
December 12, 2000.

Justice Ginsburg, with whom *Justice Stevens* joins, and with whom *Justice Souter* and *Justice Breyer* join as to Part I, dissenting.

I.

The Chief Justice acknowledges that provisions of Florida's Election Code "may well admit of more than one interpretation." *Ante,* at 3. But instead of respecting the state high court's province to say what the State's Election Code means, *The Chief Justice* maintains that Florida's Supreme Court has veered so far from the ordinary practice of judicial review that what it did cannot properly be called judging. My colleagues have offered a reasonable construction of Florida's law. Their construction coincides with the view of one of Florida's seven Supreme Court justices. *Gore v. Harris,* __ So. 2d __, __ (Fla. 2000) (slip op., at 45–55) (Wells, C. J., dissenting); *Palm Beach County Canvassing Bd.* v. *Harris,* __ So. 2d __, __ (Fla. 2000) (slip op., at 34) (on remand) (confirming, 6–1, the construction of Florida law advanced in *Gore*). I might join *The Chief Justice* were it my commission to interpret Florida law. But disagreement with the Florida court's interpretation of its own State's law does not warrant the conclusion that the justices of that court have legislated. There is no cause here to believe that the members of Florida's high court have done less than "their mortal best to discharge their oath of office," *Sumner* v. *Mata,* 449 U. S. 539, 549 (1981), and no cause to upset their reasoned interpretation of Florida law.

This Court more than occasionally affirms statutory, and even constitutional, interpretations with which it disagrees. For example, when reviewing challenges to administrative agencies" interpretations of laws they implement, we defer to the agencies unless their interpretation violates "the unambiguously expressed intent of Congress." *Chevron U. S.A. Inc. v. Natural Resources Defense Council, Inc.,* 467 U. S. 837, 843 (1984). We do so in the face of the declaration in Article I of the United States Constitution that "All legislative Powers herein granted shall be vested in a Congress of the United States." Surely the Constitution does not call upon us to pay more respect to a federal administrative agency's construction of federal law than to a state high court's interpretation of its own state's law. And not uncommonly, we let stand state-court interpretations of *federal* law with which we might disagree. Notably, in the habeas context, the Court adheres to the view that "there is "no intrinsic reason why the fact that a man is a federal judge should make him more competent, or conscientious, or learned with respect to [federal law] than his neighbor in the state courthouse.'" *Stone* v. *Powell,* 428 U. S. 465, 494, n. 35 (1976) (quoting Bator, Finality in Criminal Law and Federal Habeas Corpus For State Prisoners, 76 Harv. L. Rev. 441, 509 (1963)); see *O'Dell* v. *Netherland,* 521 U. S. 151, 156 (1997) ("[T]he *Teague* doctrine validates reasonable, good-faith interpretations of existing precedents made by state courts even though they are shown to be contrary to later decisions.") (citing *Butler v. McKellar,* 494 U. S. 407, 414 (1990)); O'Connor, Trends in the Relationship Between the Federal and State Courts from the Perspective of a State Court Judge, 22 Wm. & Mary L. Rev. 801, 813 (1981) ("There is no reason to assume that state court judges cannot and will not provide a 'hospitable forum' in litigating federal constitutional questions.").

No doubt there are cases in which the proper application of federal law may hinge on interpretations of state law. Unavoidably, this Court must sometimes examine state law in order to protect federal rights. But we have dealt with such cases ever mindful of the full measure of respect we owe to interpretations of state law by a State's highest court. In the Contract Clause case, *General Motors Corp.* v. *Romein,* 503 U. S. 181 (1992), for example, we said that although "ultimately we are bound to decide for ourselves whether a contract was made," the Court "accord[s] respectful consideration and great weight to the views of the State's highest court." *Id.,* at 187 (citation omitted). And in *Central Union Telephone Co.* v. *Edwardsville,* 269 U. S. 190 (1925), we upheld the Illinois Supreme Court's interpretation of a state waiver rule, even though that interpretation resulted in the forfeiture of federal constitutional rights. Refusing to supplant Illinois law with a federal definition of waiver, we explained that the state court's declaration "should bind us unless so unfair or unreasonable in its application to those asserting a federal right as to obstruct it." *Id.,* at 195.[1]

In deferring to state courts on matters of state law, we appropriately recognize that this Court acts as an "'outside[r]" lacking the common exposure to local law which comes from sitting in the jurisdiction."

Lehman Brothers v. *Schein,* 416 U. S. 386, 391 (1974). That recognition has sometimes prompted us to resolve doubts about the meaning of state law by certifying issues to a State's highest court, even when federal rights are at stake. Cf. *Arizonans for Official English* v. *Arizona,* 520 U. S. 43, 79 (1997) ("Warnings against premature adjudication of constitutional questions bear heightened attention when a federal court is asked to invalidate a State's law, for the federal tribunal risks friction-generating error when it endeavors to construe a novel state Act not yet reviewed by the State's highest court."). Notwithstanding our authority to decide issues of state law underlying federal claims, we have used the certification devise to afford state high courts an opportunity to inform us on matters of their own State's law because such restraint "helps build a cooperative judicial federalism." *Lehman Brothers,* 416 U. S., at 391.

Just last Term, in *Fiore v. White,* 528 U. S. 23 (1999), we took advantage of Pennsylvania's certification procedure. In that case, a state prisoner brought a federal habeas action claiming that the State had failed to prove an essential element of his charged offense in violation of the Due Process Clause. *Id.,* at 25–26. Instead of resolving the state-law question on which the federal claim depended, we certified the question to the Pennsylvania Supreme Court for that court to "help determine the proper state-law predicate for our determination of the federal constitutional questions raised." *Id.,* at 29; *id.,* at 28 (asking the Pennsylvania Supreme Court whether its recent interpretation of the statute under which Fiore was convicted "was always the statute's meaning, even at the time of Fiore's trial"). *The Chief Justice's* willingness to *reverse* the Florida Supreme Court's interpretation of Florida law in this case is at least in tension with our reluctance in *Fiore* even to interpret Pennsylvania law before seeking instruction from the Pennsylvania Supreme Court. I would have thought the "cautious approach" we counsel when federal courts address matters of state law, *Arizonans,* 520 U. S., at 77, and our commitment to "build[ing] cooperative judicial federalism," *Lehman Brothers,* 416 U. S., at 391, demanded greater restraint.

Rarely has this Court rejected outright an interpretation of state law by a state high court. *Fairfax's Devisee v. Hunter's Lessee,* 7 Cranch 603 (1813), *NAACP* v. *Alabama ex rel. Patterson,* 357 U. S. 449 (1958), and Bouie v. City of Columbia, 378 U. S. 347 (1964), cited by *The Chief Justice,* are three such rare instances. See *ante,* at 4, 5, and n. 2. But those cases are embedded in historical contexts hardly comparable to the situation here. *Fairfax's Devisee,* which held that the Virginia Court of Appeals had misconstrued its own forfeiture laws to deprive a British subject of lands secured to him by federal treaties, occurred amidst vociferous States" rights attacks on the Marshall Court. G. Gunther & K. Sullivan, Constitutional Law 61–62 (13th ed. 1997). The Virginia court refused to obey this Court's *Fairfax's Devisee* mandate to enter judgment for the British subject's successor in interest. That refusal led to the Court's path-marking decision in *Martin* v. *Hunter's Lessee*,[1] Wheat. 304 (1816). *Patterson,* a case decided three months after *Cooper* v. *Aaron,* 358 U. S. 1 (1958), in the face of Southern resistance to the civil rights movement, held that the Alabama Supreme Court had irregularly applied its own procedural rules to deny review of a contempt order against the NAACP arising from its refusal to disclose membership lists. We said that "our jurisdiction is not defeated if the nonfederal ground relied on by the state court is without any fair or substantial support." 357 U. S., at 455. *Bouie,* stemming from a lunch counter "sit-in" at the height of the civil rights movement, held that the South Carolina Supreme Court's construction of its trespass laws—criminalizing conduct not covered by the text of an otherwise clear statute—was "unforeseeable" and thus violated due process when applied retroactively to the petitioners. 378 U. S., at 350, 354.

The *Chief Justice's* casual citation of these cases might lead one to believe they are part of a larger collection of cases in which we said that the Constitution impelled us to train a skeptical eye on a state court's portrayal of state law. But one would be hard pressed, I think, to find additional cases that fit the mold. As *Justice Breyer* convincingly explains, see *post,* at 5–9 (dissenting opinion), this case involves nothing close to the kind of recalcitrance by a state high court that warrants extraordinary action by this Court. The Florida Supreme Court concluded that counting every legal vote was the overriding concern of the Florida Legislature when it enacted the State's Election Code. The court surely should not be bracketed with state high courts of the Jim Crow South.

The *Chief Justice* says that Article II, by providing that state legislatures shall direct the manner of appointing electors, authorizes federal superintendence over the relationship between state courts and state legislatures, and licenses a departure from the usual deference we give to state court interpretations of state law. *Ante,* at 5 ("To attach definitive weight to the pronouncement of a state court, when the very question at issue is whether the court has actually departed from the statutory meaning, would be to abdicate our responsibility to enforce the explicit requirements of Article II."). The Framers of our Constitution, however, understood that in a republican government, the judiciary would construe the legislature's enactments. See U. S. Const., Art. III; The Federalist No. 78 (A. Hamilton). In light of the constitutional guarantee to States of a "Republican Form of Government," U. S. Const., Art. IV, §4, Article II can hardly be read to invite this Court to disrupt a State's republican regime. Yet The *Chief Justice* today would reach out to do just that. By holding that Article II requires our revision of a state court's construction of state laws in order to protect one organ of the State from another, *The*

Chief Justice contradicts the basic principle that a State may organize itself as it sees fit. See, *e.g., Gregory* v. *Ashcroft,* 501 U. S. 452, 460 (1991) ("Through the structure of its government, and the character of those who exercise government authority, a State defines itself as a sovereign."); *Highland Farms Dairy, Inc.* v. *Agnew,* 300 U. S. 608, 612 (1937) ("How power shall be distributed by a state among its governmental organs is commonly, if not always, a question for the state itself.").[2] Article II does not call for the scrutiny undertaken by this Court.

The extraordinary setting of this case has obscured the ordinary principle that dictates its proper resolution: Federal courts defer to state high courts" interpretations of their state's own law. This principle reflects the core of federalism, on which all agree. "The Framers split the atom of sovereignty. It was the genius of their idea that our citizens would have two political capacities, one state and one federal, each protected from incursion by the other." *Saenz* v. *Roe,* 526 U. S. 489, 504, n. 17 (1999) (citing *U. S. Term Limits, Inc.* v. *Thornton,* 514 U. S. 779, 838 (1995) (*Kennedy,* J., concurring)). *The Chief Justice's* solicitude for the Florida Legislature comes at the expense of the more fundamental solicitude we owe to the legislature's sovereign. U. S. Const., Art. II, §1, cl. 2 ("Each *State* shall appoint, in such Manner as the Legislature *thereof* may direct," the electors for President and Vice President) (emphasis added); *ante,* at 1–2 (*Stevens,* J., dissenting).[3] Were the other members of this Court as mindful as they generally are of our system of dual sovereignty, they would affirm the judgment of the Florida Supreme Court.

II.

I agree with *Justice Stevens* that petitioners have not presented a substantial equal protection claim. Ideally, perfection would be the appropriate standard for judging the recount. But we live in an imperfect world, one in which thousands of votes have not been counted. I cannot agree that the recount adopted by the Florida court, flawed as it may be, would yield a result any less fair or precise than the certification that preceded that recount. See, *e.g., McDonald* v. *Board of Election Comm'rs of Chicago,* 394 U.S. 802, 807 (1969) (even in the context of the right to vote, the state is permitted to reform "'one step at a time'") (quoting *Williamson* v. *Lee Optical of Oklahoma, Inc.,* 348 U.S. 483, 489 (1955)).

Even if there were an equal protection violation, I would agree with *Justice Stevens, Justice Souter,* and *Justice Breyer* that the Court's concern about "the December 12 deadline," *ante,* at 12, is misplaced. Time is short in part because of the Court's entry of a stay on December 9, several hours after an able circuit judge in Leon County had begun to superintend the recount process. More fundamentally, the Court's reluctance to let the recount go forward—despite its suggestion that "[t]he search for intent can be confined by specific rules designed to ensure uniform treatment," *ante,* at 8—ultimately turns on its own judgment about the practical realities of implementing a recount, not the judgment of those much closer to the process.

Equally important, as *Justice Breyer* explains, *post,* at 12 (dissenting opinion), the December 12 "deadline" for bringing Florida's electoral votes into 3 U. S. C. §5's safe harbor lacks the significance the Court assigns it. Were that date to pass, Florida would still be entitled to deliver electoral votes Congress *must* count unless both Houses find that the votes "ha[d] not been . . . regularly given." 3 U. S. C. §15. The statute identifies other significant dates. See, *e.g.,* §7 (specifying December 18 as the date electors "shall meet and give their votes"); §12 (specifying "the fourth Wednesday in December"—this year, December 27—as the date on which Congress, if it has not received a State's electoral votes, shall request the state secretary of state to send a certified return immediately). But none of these dates has ultimate significance in light of Congress" detailed provisions for determining, on "the sixth day of January," the validity of electoral votes. §15.

The Court assumes that time will not permit "orderly judicial review of any disputed matters that might arise." *Ante,* at 12. But no one has doubted the good faith and diligence with which Florida election officials, attorneys for all sides of this controversy, and the courts of law have performed their duties. Notably, the Florida Supreme Court has produced two substantial opinions within 29 hours of oral argument. In sum, the Court's conclusion that a constitutionally adequate recount is impractical is a prophecy the Court's own judgment will not allow to be tested. Such an untested prophecy should not decide the Presidency of the United States.

I dissent.

GEORGE W. BUSH, ET AL., PETITIONERS
v. ALBERT GORE, Jr., ET AL.

ON WRIT OF CERTIORARI TO THE
FLORIDA SUPREME COURT

December 12, 2000.

Justice Breyer, with whom *Justice Stevens* and *Justice Ginsburg* join except as to Part I-A-1, and with whom *Justice Souter* joins as to Part I, dissenting.

The Court was wrong to take this case. It was wrong to grant a stay. It should now vacate that stay and permit the Florida Supreme Court to decide whether the recount should resume.

I.

The political implications of this case for the country are momentous. But the federal legal questions presented, with one exception, are insubstantial.

A

1

The majority raises three Equal Protection problems with the Florida Supreme Court's recount order: first, the failure to include overvotes in the manual recount; second, the fact that *all* ballots, rather than simply the undervotes, were recounted in some, but not all, counties; and third, the absence of a uniform, specific standard to guide the recounts. As far as the first issue is concerned, petitioners presented no evidence, to this Court or to any Florida court, that a manual recount of overvotes would identify additional legal votes. The same is true of the second, and, in addition, the majority's reasoning would seem to invalidate any state provision for a manual recount of individual counties in a statewide election.

The majority's third concern does implicate principles of fundamental fairness. The majority concludes that the Equal Protection Clause requires that a manual recount be governed not only by the uniform general standard of the "clear intent of the voter," but also by uniform subsidiary standards (for example, a uniform determination whether indented, but not perforated, "undervotes" should count). The opinion points out that the Florida Supreme Court ordered the inclusion of Broward County's undercounted "legal votes" even though those votes included ballots that were not perforated but simply "dimpled," while newly recounted ballots from other counties will likely include only votes determined to be "legal" on the basis of a stricter standard. In light of our previous remand, the Florida Supreme Court may have been reluctant to adopt a more specific standard than that provided for by the legislature for fear of exceeding its authority under Article II. However, since the use of different standards could favor one or the other of the candidates, since time was, and is, too short to permit the lower courts to iron out significant differences through ordinary judicial review, and since the relevant distinction was embodied in the order of the State's highest court, I agree that, in these very special circumstances, basic principles of fairness may well have counseled the adoption of a uniform standard to address the problem. In light of the majority's disposition, I need not decide whether, or the extent to which, as a remedial matter, the Constitution would place limits upon the content of the uniform standard.

2

Nonetheless, there is no justification for the majority's remedy, which is simply to reverse the lower court and halt the recount entirely. An appropriate remedy would be, instead, to remand this case with instructions that, even at this late date, would permit the Florida Supreme Court to require recounting *all* undercounted votes in Florida, including those from Broward, Volusia, Palm Beach, and Miami-Dade Counties, whether or not previously recounted prior to the end of the protest period, and to do so in accordance with a single-uniform substandard.

The majority justifies stopping the recount entirely on the ground that there is no more time. In particular, the majority relies on the lack of time for the Secretary to review and approve equipment needed to separate undervotes. But the majority reaches this conclusion in the absence of *any* record evidence that the recount could not have been completed in the time allowed by the Florida Supreme Court. The majority finds facts outside of the record on matters that state courts are in a far better position to address. Of course, it is too late for any such recount to take place by December 12, the date by which election disputes must be decided if a State is to take advantage of the safe harbor provisions of 3 U. S. C. §5. Whether there is time to conduct a recount prior to December 18, when the electors are scheduled to meet, is a matter for the state courts to determine. And whether, under Florida law, Florida could or could not take further action is obviously a matter for Florida courts, not this Court, to decide. See *ante,* at 13 *(per curiam).*

By halting the manual recount, and thus ensuring that the uncounted legal votes will not be counted under any standard, this Court crafts a remedy out of proportion to the asserted harm. And that remedy harms the very fairness interests the Court is attempting to protect. The manual recount would itself redress a problem of unequal treatment of ballots. As *Justice Stevens* points out, see *ante,* at 4 and n. 4 (*Stevens, J.,* dissenting opinion), the ballots of voters in counties that use punch-card systems are more likely to be disqualified than those in counties using optical-scanning systems. According to recent news reports, variations in the undervote rate are even more pronounced. See Fessenden, No-Vote Rates Higher in Punch Card Count, N. Y. Times, Dec. 1, 2000, p. A29 (reporting that 0.3% of ballots cast in 30 Florida counties using optical-scanning systems registered no Presidential vote, in comparison to 1.53% in the 15 counties using Votomatic punch card ballots). Thus, in a system that allows counties to use different types of voting systems, voters already arrive at the polls with an unequal chance that their votes will be counted. I do not see how the fact that this results from counties" selection of different voting machines rather than a court order makes the outcome any more fair. Nor do I understand why the Florida Supreme Court's recount order, which helps to redress this inequity, must be entirely prohibited based on a deficiency that could easily be remedied.

B

The remainder of petitioners' claims, which are the focus of the *Chief Justice's* concurrence, raise no significant federal questions. I cannot agree that the *Chief Justice's* unusual review of state law in this case, see *ante,* at 5–8 (*Ginsburg, J.,* dissenting opinion), is justified by reference either to Art. II, §1, or to 3 U. S. C. §5. Moreover, even were such review proper, the conclusion that the Florida Supreme Court's decision contravenes federal law is untenable.

While conceding that, in most cases, "comity and respect for federalism compel us to defer to the decisions of state courts on issues of state law," the concurrence relies on some combination of Art. II, §1, and 3 U. S. C. §5 to justify the majority's conclusion that this case is one of the few in which we may lay that fundamental principle aside. *Ante,* at 2 (Opinion of *Rehnquist,* C. J. The concurrence's primary foundation for this conclusion rests on an appeal to plain text: Art. II, §1's grant of the power to appoint Presidential electors to the State "Legislature." *Ibid.* But neither the text of Article II itself nor the only case the concurrence cites that interprets Article II, *McPherson* v. *Blacker,* 146 U. S. 1 (1892), leads to the conclusion that Article II grants unlimited power to the legislature, devoid of any state constitutional limitations, to select the manner of appointing electors. See *id.,* at 41 (specifically referring to state constitutional provision in upholding state law regarding selection of electors). Nor, as *Justice Stevens* points out, have we interpreted the Federal constitutional provision most analogous to Art. II, §1—Art. I, §4—in the strained manner put forth in the concurrence. *Ante,* at 1–2 and n. 1 (dissenting opinion).

The concurrence's treatment of §5 as "inform[ing]" its interpretation of Article II, §1, cl. 2, *ante,* at 3 (*Rehnquist,* C. J., concurring), is no more convincing. The *Chief Justice* contends that our opinion in *Bush* v. *Palm Beach County Canvassing Bd., ante,* p. ____, *(per curiam) (Bush I),* in which we stated that "a legislative wish to take advantage of [§5] would counsel against" a construction of Florida law that Congress might deem to be a change in law, *id.,* (slip op. at 6), now means that *this Court* "must ensure that post-election state court actions do not frustrate the legislative desire to attain the "safe harbor" provided by §5." *Ante,* at 3. However, §5 is part of the rules that govern Congress" recognition of slates of electors. Nowhere in *Bush I* did we establish that *this Court* had the authority to enforce §5. Nor did we suggest that the permissive "counsel against" could be transformed into the mandatory "must ensure." And nowhere did we intimate, as the concurrence does here, that a state court decision that threatens the safe harbor provision of §5 does so in violation of Article II. The concurrence's logic turns the presumption that legislatures would wish to take advantage of § 5's "safe harbor" provision into a mandate that trumps other statutory provisions and overrides the intent that the legislature *did* express.

But, in any event, the concurrence, having conducted its review, now reaches the wrong conclusion. It says that "the Florida Supreme Court's interpretation of the Florida election laws impermissibly distorted them beyond what a fair reading required, in violation of Article II." *Ante,* at 4–5 (*Rehnquist,* C. J, concurring). But what precisely is the distortion? Apparently, it has three elements. First, the Florida court, in its earlier opinion, changed the election certification date from November 14 to November 26. Second, the Florida court ordered a manual recount of "undercounted" ballots that could not have been fully completed by the December 12 "safe harbor" deadline. Third, the Florida court, in the opinion now under review, failed to give adequate deference to the determinations of canvassing boards and the Secretary.

To characterize the first element as a "distortion," however, requires the concurrence to second-guess the way in which the state court resolved a plain conflict in the language of different statutes. Compare Fla. Stat. §102.166 (2001) (foreseeing manual recounts during the protest period) with §102.111 (setting what is arguably too short a deadline for manual recounts to be conducted); compare §102.112(1) (stating that the Secretary "may" ignore late returns) with §102.111(1) (stating that the Secretary "shall" ignore late returns). In any event, that issue no longer has any practical importance and cannot justify the reversal of the different Florida court decision before us now.

To characterize the second element as a "distortion" requires the concurrence to overlook the fact that the inability of the Florida courts to conduct the recount on time is, in significant part, a problem of the Court's own making. The Florida Supreme Court thought that the recount could be completed on time, and, within hours, the Florida Circuit Court was moving in an orderly fashion to meet the deadline. This Court improvidently entered a stay. As a result, we will never know whether the recount could have been completed.

Nor can one characterize the third element as "impermissibl[e] distort[ing]" once one understands that there are two sides to the opinion's argument that the Florida Supreme Court "virtually eliminated the Secretary's discretion." *Ante,* at 9 (*Rehnquist,* C. J. concurring). The Florida statute in question was amended in 1999 to provide that the "grounds for contesting an election" include the "rejection of a number of legal votes sufficient to . . . place in doubt the result of the election." Fla. Stat. §§102.168(3), (3)(c) (2000). And the parties have argued about the proper meaning of the statute's term "legal vote." The Secretary has claimed that a "legal vote" is a vote "properly executed in accordance with the instructions provided to all registered voters." Brief for Respondent Harris et al. 10. On that interpretation, punchcard ballots for which the machines cannot register a vote are not "legal" votes. *Id.*, at 14. The Florida Supreme Court did not accept her definition. But it had a reason. Its reason was that a different provision of Florida election laws (a provision that addresses damaged or defective ballots) says that no vote shall be disregarded "if there is a clear indication of the intent of the voter as determined by the canvassing board" (adding that ballots should not be counted "if it is impossible to determine the elector's choice"). Fla. Stat. §101.5614(5) (2000). Given this statutory language, certain roughly analogous judicial precedent, *e.g., Darby* v. *State ex rel. McCollough,* 75 So. 411 (Fla. 1917) *(per curiam),* and somewhat similar determinations by courts throughout the Nation, see cases cited *infra,* at 9, the Florida Supreme Court concluded that the term "legal vote" means a vote recorded on a ballot that clearly reflects what the voter intended. *Gore* v. *Harris,* ___ So. 2d ___, ___ (2000) (slip op., at 19). That conclusion differs from the conclusion of the Secretary. But nothing in Florida law requires the Florida Supreme Court to accept as determinative the Secretary's view on such a matter. Nor can one say that the Court's ultimate determination is so unreasonable as to amount to a constitutionally "impermissible distort[ion]" of Florida law.

The Florida Supreme Court, applying this definition, decided, on the basis of the record, that respondents had shown that the ballots undercounted by the voting machines contained enough "legal votes" to place "the results" of the election "in doubt." Since only a few hundred votes separated the candidates, and since the "undercounted" ballots numbered tens of thousands, it is difficult to see how anyone could find this conclusion unreasonable—however strict the standard used to measure the voter's "clear intent." Nor did this conclusion "strip" canvassing boards of their discretion. The boards retain their traditional discretionary authority during the protest period. And during the contest period, as the court stated, "the Canvassing Board's actions [during the protest period] may constitute evidence that a ballot does or does not qualify as a legal vote." *Id.*, at ★13. Whether a local county canvassing board's discretionary judgment during the protest period not to conduct a manual recount will be set aside during a contest period depends upon whether a candidate provides additional evidence that the rejected votes contain enough "legal votes" to place the outcome of the race in doubt. To limit the local canvassing board's discretion in this way is not to eliminate that discretion. At the least, one could reasonably so believe.

The statute goes on to provide the Florida circuit judge with authority to "fashion such orders as he or she deems necessary to ensure that each allegation . . . is *investigated, examined, or checked,* . . . and to provide any relief appropriate." Fla. Stat. §102.168(8) (2000) (emphasis added). The Florida Supreme Court did just that. One might reasonably disagree with the Florida Supreme Court's interpretation of these, or other, words in the statute. But I do not see how one could call its plain language interpretation of a 1999 statutory change so misguided as no longer to qualify as judicial interpretation or as a usurpation of the authority of the State legislature. Indeed, other state courts have interpreted roughly similar state statutes in similar ways. See, e.g., *In re Election of U. S. Representative for Second Congressional Dist.,* 231 Conn. 602, 621, 653 A. 2d 79, 90–91 (1994) ("Whatever the process used to vote and to count votes, differences in technology should not furnish a basis for disregarding the bedrock principle that the purpose of the voting process is to ascertain the intent of the voters"); *Brown* v. *Carr,* 130 W. Va. 401, 460, 43 S. E.2d 401, 404–405 (1947) ("[W]hether a ballot shall be counted . . . depends on the intent of the voter . . . . Courts decry any resort to technical rules in reaching a conclusion as to the intent of the voter").

I repeat, where is the "impermissible" distortion?

II.

Despite the reminder that this case involves "an election for the President of the United States," *ante,* at 1 (*Rehnquist,* C. J., concurring), no preeminent legal concern, or practical concern related to legal questions, required this Court to hear this case, let alone to issue a stay that stopped Florida's recount process in its tracks. With one exception, petitioners" claims do not ask us to vindicate a constitutional provision designed to protect a basic human right. See, e.g., *Brown* v. *Board of Education,* 347 U. S. 483 (1954). Petitioners invoke fundamental fairness, namely, the need for procedural fairness, including finality. But with the one "equal protection" exception, they rely upon law that focuses, not upon that basic need, but upon the constitutional allocation of power. Respondents invoke a competing fundamental consideration—the need to determine the voter's true intent. But they look to state law, not to federal constitutional law, to protect that interest. Neither side claims electoral fraud, dishonesty, or the like. And the more fundamental equal protection claim might have been left to the state court to resolve if and when it was discovered to have mattered. It could still be resolved through a remand conditioned upon issuance of a uniform standard; it does not require reversing the Florida Supreme Court.

Of course, the selection of the President is of fundamental national importance. But that importance is political, not legal. And this Court should resist the temptation unnecessarily to resolve tangential legal disputes, where doing so threatens to determine the outcome of the election.

The Constitution and federal statutes themselves make clear that restraint is appropriate. They set forth a road map of how to resolve disputes about electors, even after an election as close as this one. That road map foresees resolution of electoral disputes by *state* courts. See 3 U. S. C. §5 (providing that, where a "State shall have provided, by laws enacted prior to [election day], for its final determination of any controversy or contest concerning the appointment of . . . electors . . . by *judicial* or other methods," the subsequently chosen electors enter a safe harbor free from congressional challenge). But it nowhere provides for involvement by the United States Supreme Court.

To the contrary, the Twelfth Amendment commits to Congress the authority and responsibility to count electoral votes. A federal statute, the Electoral Count Act, enacted after the close 1876 Hayes-Tilden Presidential election, specifies that, after States have tried to resolve disputes (through "judicial" or other means), Congress is the body primarily authorized to resolve remaining disputes. See Electoral Count Act of 1887, 24 Stat. 373, 3 U. S. C. §§5, 6, and 15.

The legislative history of the Act makes clear its intent to commit the power to resolve such disputes to Congress, rather than the courts:

"The two Houses are, by the Constitution, authorized to make the count of electoral votes. They can only count legal votes, and in doing so must determine, from the best evidence to be had, what are legal votes . . . . The power to determine rests with the two Houses, and there is no other constitutional tribunal." H. Rep. No. 1638, 49th Cong., 1st Sess., 2 (1886) (report submitted by Rep. Caldwell, Select Committee on the Election of President and Vice-President).

The Member of Congress who introduced the Act added:

> "The power to judge of the legality of the votes is a necessary consequent of the power to count. The existence of this power is of absolute necessity to the preservation of the Government. The interests of all the States in their relations to each other in the Federal Union demand that the ultimate tribunal to decide upon the election of President should be a constituent body, in which the States in their federal relationships and the people in their sovereign capacity should be represented." 18 Cong. Rec. 30 (1886).

"Under the Constitution who else could decide? Who is nearer to the State in determining a question of vital importance to the whole union of States than the constituent body upon whom the Constitution has devolved the duty to count the vote?" *Id.,* at 31.

The Act goes on to set out rules for the congressional determination of disputes about those votes. If, for example, a state submits a single slate of electors, Congress must count those votes unless both Houses agree that the votes "have not been . . . regularly given." 3 U. S. C. § 15. If, as occurred in 1876, one or more states submits two sets of electors, then Congress must determine whether a slate has entered the safe harbor of §5, in which case its votes will have "conclusive" effect. *Ibid.* If, as also occurred in 1876, there is controversy about "which of two or more of such State authorities . . . is the lawful tribunal" authorized to appoint electors, then each House shall determine separately which votes are "supported by the decision of such State so authorized by its law." *Ibid.* If the two Houses of Congress agree, the votes they have approved will be counted. If they disagree, then "the votes of the electors whose appointment shall have been certified by the executive of the State, under the seal thereof, shall be counted." *Ibid.*

Given this detailed, comprehensive scheme for counting electoral votes, there is no reason to believe that federal law either foresees or requires resolution of such a political issue by this Court. Nor, for that matter, is there any reason to think that the Constitution's Framers would have reached a different conclusion. Madison, at least, believed that allowing the judiciary to choose the presidential electors "was out of the question." Madison, July 25, 1787 (reprinted in 5 Elliot's Debates on the Federal Constitution 363 (2d ed. 1876)).

The decision by both the Constitution's Framers and the 1886 Congress to minimize this Court's role in resolving close federal presidential elections is as wise as it is clear. However awkward or difficult it may be for Congress to resolve difficult electoral disputes, Congress, being a political body, expresses the people's will far more accurately than does an unelected Court. And the people's will is what elections are about.

Moreover, Congress was fully aware of the danger that would arise should it ask judges, unarmed with appropriate legal standards, to resolve a hotly contested Presidential election contest. Just after the 1876 Presidential election, Florida, South Carolina, and Louisiana each sent two slates of electors to Washington. Without these States, Tilden, the Democrat, had 184 electoral votes, one short of the number required to win the Presidency. With those States, Hayes, his Republican opponent, would have had 185. In order to choose between the two slates of electors, Congress decided to appoint an electoral commission composed of five Senators, five Representatives, and five Supreme Court Justices. Initially the Commission was to be evenly divided between Republicans and Democrats, with Justice David Davis, an Independent, to possess the decisive vote. However, when at the last minute the Illinois Legislature elected Justice Davis to the United States Senate, the final position on the Commission was filled by Supreme Court Justice Joseph P. Bradley.

The Commission divided along partisan lines, and the responsibility to cast the deciding vote fell to Justice Bradley. He decided to accept the votes by the Republican electors, and thereby awarded the Presidency to Hayes.

Justice Bradley immediately became the subject of vociferous attacks. Bradley was accused of accepting bribes, of being captured by railroad interests, and of an eleventh-hour change in position after a night in which his house "was surrounded by the carriages" of Republican partisans and railroad officials. C. Woodward, Reunion and Reaction 159–160 (1966). Many years later, Professor Bickel concluded that Bradley was honest and impartial. He thought that "'the great question" for Bradley was, in fact, whether Congress was entitled to go behind election returns or had to accept them as certified by state authorities," an "issue of principle." The Least Dangerous Branch 185 (1962). Nonetheless, Bickel points out, the legal question upon which Justice Bradley's decision turned was not very important in the contemporaneous political context. He says that "in the circumstances the issue of principle was trivial, it was overwhelmed by all that hung in the balance, and it should not have been decisive." *Ibid.*

For present purposes, the relevance of this history lies in the fact that the participation in the work of the electoral commission by five Justices, including Justice Bradley, did not lend that process legitimacy. Nor did it assure the public that the process had worked fairly, guided by the law. Rather, it simply embroiled Members of the Court in partisan conflict, thereby undermining respect for the judicial process. And the Congress that later enacted the Electoral Count Act knew it.

This history may help to explain why I think it not only legally wrong, but also most unfortunate, for the Court simply to have terminated the Florida recount. Those who caution judicial restraint in resolving political disputes have described the quintessential case for that restraint as a case marked, among other things, by the "strangeness of the issue," its "intractability to principled resolution," its "sheer momentousness, . . . which tends to unbalance judicial judgment," and "the inner vulnerability, the self-doubt of an institution which is electorally irresponsible and has no earth to draw strength from." Bickel, *supra,* at 184. Those characteristics mark this case.

At the same time, as I have said, the Court is not acting to vindicate a fundamental constitutional principle, such as the need to protect a basic human liberty. No other strong reason to act is present. Congressional statutes tend to obviate the need. And, above all, in this highly politicized matter, the appearance of a split decision runs the risk of undermining the public's confidence in the Court itself. That confidence is a public treasure. It has been built slowly over many years, some of which were marked by a Civil War and the tragedy of segregation. It is a vitally necessary ingredient of any successful effort to protect basic liberty and, indeed, the rule of law itself. We run no risk of returning to the days when a President (responding to this Court's efforts to protect the Cherokee Indians) might have said, "John Marshall has made his decision; now let him enforce it!" Loth, *Chief Justice John Marshall and The Growth of the American Republic* 365 (1948). But we do risk a self-inflicted wound—a wound that may harm not just the Court, but the Nation.

I fear that in order to bring this agonizingly long election process to a definitive conclusion, we have not adequately attended to that necessary "check upon our own exercise of power," "our own sense of self-restraint." *United States* v. *Butler,* 297 U. S. 1, 79 (1936) (Stone, J., dissenting). Justice Brandeis once said of the Court, "The most important thing we do is not doing." Bickel, *supra,* at 71. What it does today, the Court should have left undone. I would repair the damage done as best we now can, by permitting the Florida recount to continue under uniform standards.

I respectfully dissent.

FOOTNOTES

[1] Similarly, our jurisprudence requires us to analyze the "background principles" of state property law to determine whether there has been a taking of property in violation of the Takings Clause. That constitutional guarantee would, of course, afford no protection against state power if our inquiry could be concluded by a state supreme court holding that state property law accorded the plaintiff no rights. See *Lucas* v. *South Carolina Coastal Council,* 505 U. S. 1003 (1992). In one of our oldest cases, we similarly made an independent evaluation of state law in order to protect federal treaty guarantees. In *Fairfax's Devisee* v. *Hunter's Lessee,* 7 Cranch 603 (1813), we disagreed with the Supreme Court of Appeals of Virginia that a 1782 state law had extinguished the property interests of one Denny Fairfax, so that a 1789 ejectment order against Fairfax supported by a 1785 state law did not constitute a future confiscation under the 1783 peace treaty with Great Britain. See *id.,* at 623; *Hunter* v. *Fairfax's Devisee,* 1 Munf. 218 (Va. 1809).

[2] We vacated that decision and remanded that case; the Florida Supreme Court reissued the same judgment with a new opinion on December 11, 2000, ___ So. 2d, ___.

[3] Specifically, the Florida Supreme Court ordered the Circuit Court to include in the certified vote totals those votes identified for Vice President Gore in Palm Beach County and Miami-Dade County.

[4] It is inconceivable that what constitutes a vote that must be counted under the "error in the vote tabulation" language of the protest phase is different from what constitutes a vote that must be counted under the "legal votes" language of the contest phase.

FOOTNOTES

[1] "Wherever the term "legislature" is used in the Constitution it is necessary to consider the nature of the particular action in view." 285 U. S., at 367. It is perfectly clear that the meaning of the words "Manner" and "Legislature" as used in Article II, §1, parallels the usage in Article I, §4, rather than the language in Article V. *U. S. Term Limits, Inc.* v. *Thornton,* 514 U. S. 779, 805 (1995). Article I, §4, and Article II, §1, both call upon legislatures to act in a lawmaking capacity whereas Article V simply calls on the legislative body to deliberate upon a binary decision. As a result, petitioners" reliance on *Leser* v. *Garnett,* 258 U. S. 130 (1922), and *Hawke* v. *Smith (No. 1),* 253 U. S. 221 (1920), is misplaced.

[2] The Florida statutory standard is consistent with the practice of the majority of States, which apply either an "intent of the voter" standard or an "impossible to determine the elector's choice" standard in ballot recounts. The following States use an "intent of the voter" standard: Ariz. Rev. Stat. Ann. §16–645(A) (Supp. 2000) (standard for canvassing write–in votes); Conn. Gen. Stat. §9–150a(j) (1999) (standard for absentee ballots, including three conclusive presumptions); Ind. Code §3–12–1–1 (1992); Me. Rev. Stat. Ann., Tit. 21-A, §1(13) (1993); Md. Ann. Code, Art. 33, §11–302(d) (2000 Supp.) (standard for absentee ballots); Mass. Gen. Laws §70E (1991) (applying standard to Presidential primaries); Mich. Comp. Laws §168.799a(3) (Supp. 2000); Mo. Rev. Stat. §115.453(3) (Cum. Supp. 1998) (looking to voter's intent where there is substantial compliance with statutory requirements); Tex. Elec. Code Ann. §65.009(c) (1986); Utah Code Ann. §20A–4–104(5)(b) (Supp. 2000) (standard for write–in votes), §20A–4–105(6)(a) (standard for mechanical ballots); Vt. Stat. Ann., Tit. 17, §2587(a) (1982); Va. Code Ann. §24.2–644(A) (2000); Wash. Rev. Code §29.62.180(1) (Supp. 2001) (standard for write–in votes); Wyo. Stat. Ann. §22–14–104 (1999). The following States employ a standard in which a vote is counted unless it is "impossible to determine the elector's [or voter's] choice": Ala. Code §11–46–44(c) (1992), Ala. Code §17–13–2 (1995); Ariz. Rev. Stat. Ann. §16–610 (1996) (standard for rejecting ballot); Cal. Elec. Code Ann. §15154(c) (West Supp. 2000); Colo. Rev. Stat. §1–7–309(1) (1999) (standard for paper ballots), §1–7–508(2) (standard for electronic ballots); Del. Code Ann., Tit. 15, §4972(4) (1999); Idaho Code §34–1203 (1981); Ill. Comp. Stat., ch. 10, §5/7–51 (1993) (standard for primaries), id., ch. 10, §5/17–16 (1993) (standard for general elections); Iowa Code §49.98 (1999); Me. Rev. Stat. Ann., Tit. 21-A §§696(2)(B), (4) (Supp. 2000); Minn. Stat. §204C.22(1) (1992); Mont. Code Ann. §13–15–202 (1997) (not counting votes if "elec-

tor's choice cannot be determined"); Nev. Rev. Stat. §293.367(d) (1995); N. Y. Elec. Law §9–112(6) (McKinney 1998); N. C. Gen. Stat. §§163–169(b), 163–170 (1999); N. D. Cent. Code §16.1–15–01(1) (Supp. 1999); Ohio Rev. Code Ann. §3505.28 (1994); 26 Okla. Stat., Tit. 26, §7–127(6) (1997); Ore. Rev. Stat. §254.505(1) (1991); S. C. Code Ann. §7–13–1120 (1977); S. D. Codified Laws §12–20–7 (1995); Tenn. Code Ann. §2–7–133(b) (1994); W. Va. Code §3–6–5(g) (1999).

[3] Cf. *Victor* v. *Nebraska,* 511 U. S. 1, 5 (1994) ("The beyond a reasonable doubt standard is a requirement of due process, but the Constitution neither prohibits trial courts from defining reasonable doubt nor requires them to do so").

[4] The percentage of nonvotes in this election in counties using a punch-card system was 3.92%; in contrast, the rate of error under the more modern optical-scan systems was only 1.43%. *Siegel* v. *LePore,* No. 00–15981, 2000 WL 1781946, ★31, ★32, ★43 (charts C and F) (CA11, Dec. 6, 2000). Put in other terms, for every 10,000 votes cast, punch–card systems result in 250 more nonvotes than optical–scan systems. A total of 3,718,305 votes were cast under punch–card systems, and 2,353,811 votes were cast under optical–scan systems. *Ibid.*

[5] Republican electors were certified by the Acting Governor on November 28, 1960. A recount was ordered to begin on December 13, 1960. Both Democratic and Republican electors met on the appointed day to cast their votes. On January 4, 1961, the newly elected Governor certified the Democratic electors. The certification was received by Congress on January 6, the day the electoral votes were counted. Josephson & Ross, 22 J. Legis., at 166, n. 154.

[6] When, for example, it resolved the previously unanswered question whether the word "shall" in Fla. Stat. §102.111 or the word "may" in §102.112 governs the scope of the Secretary of State's authority to ignore untimely election returns, it did not "change the law." Like any other judicial interpretation of a statute, its opinion was an authoritative interpretation of what the statute's relevant provisions have meant since they were enacted. *Rivers v. Roadway Express, Inc.,* 511 U. S. 298, 312–313 (1994).

[7] "It is emphatically the province and duty of the judicial department to say what the law is." *Marbury v. Madison.,* 1 Cranch 137, 177 (1803).

FOOTNOTES

[1] When the Florida court ruled, the totals for Bush and Gore were then less than 1,000 votes apart. One dissent pegged the number of uncounted votes in question at 170,000. *Gore v. Harris, supra,* __ So. 2d __ , (slip op., at 66) (opinion of Harding, J.). Gore's counsel represented to us that the relevant figure is approximately 60,000, Tr. of Oral Arg. 62, the number of ballots in which no vote for President was recorded by the machines.

FOOTNOTES

[1] See also *Lucas v. South Carolina Coastal Council,* 505 U. S. 1003, 1032, n. 18 (1992) (South Carolina could defend a regulatory taking "if an objectively reasonable application of relevant precedents [by its courts] would exclude . . . beneficial uses in the circumstances in which the land is presently found"); *Bishop v. Wood,* 426 U. S. 341, 344–345 (1976) (deciding whether North Carolina had created a property interest cognizable under the Due Process Clause by reference to state law as interpreted by the North Carolina Supreme Court). Similarly, in *Gurley v. Rhoden,* 421 U. S. 200 (1975), a gasoline retailer claimed that due process entitled him to deduct a state gasoline excise tax in computing the amount of his sales subject to a state sales tax, on the grounds that the legal incidence of the excise tax fell on his customers and that he acted merely as a collector of the tax. The Mississippi Supreme Court held that the legal incidence of the excise tax fell on petitioner. Observing that "a State's highest court is the final judicial arbiter of the meaning of state statutes," we said that "[w]hen a state court has made its own definitive determination as to the operating incidence, . . . [w]e give this finding great weight in determining the natural effect of a statute, and if it is consistent with the statute's reasonable interpretation it will be deemed conclusive." *Id.,* at 208.

[2] Even in the rare case in which a State's "manner" of making and construing laws might implicate a structural constraint, Congress, not this Court, is likely the proper governmental entity to enforce that constraint. See U. S. *Const.,* amend. XII; 3 U. S. C. §§1–15; cf. *Ohio ex rel. Davis v. Hildebrant,* 241 U. S. 565, 569 (1916) (treating as a nonjusticiable political question whether use of a referendum to override a congressional districting

plan enacted by the state legislature violates Art. I, §4); *Luther* v. *Borden,* 7 How. 1, 42 (1849).

[3] "[B]ecause the Framers recognized that state power and identity were essential parts of the federal balance, see The Federalist No. 39, the Constitution is solicitous of the prerogatives of the States, even in an otherwise sovereign federal province. The Constitution . . . grants States certain powers over the times, places, and manner of federal elections (subject to congressional revision), Art. I, §4, cl. 1 . . . , and allows States to appoint electors for the President, Art. II, §1, cl. 2." *U. S. Term Limits, Inc.* v. *Thornton,* 514 U. S. 779, 841–842 (1995) (*Kennedy,* J., concurring).

Gratz v. Bollinger
2003

In 1995 and 1997, respectively, white Michigan residents Jennifer Gratz and Patrick Hamacher were denied admission to the University of Michigan's College of Literature, Science, and the Arts. At the time, it was the policy of the University of Michigan to judge applicants based on a 150-point system that granted admission to those with the highest scores. Under this system, certain minority groups were awarded an automatic 20 points, while whites were not. In the fall of 1997, both Gratz and Hamacher filed suit against the University of Michigan, claiming that they were unfairly denied admission based on race, in violation of their Fourteenth Amendment rights. After the District Court for the Eastern District of Michigan found for the respondents only for admissions years 1998–2000, Gratz and Hamacher appealed to the U. S. Supreme Court for review in 2003.

The Supreme Court found that the University of Michigan's 20-point policy was not "narrowly tailored" enough to achieve a valid diversity interest for the university, and thus unconstitutional. As a result of this decision, all universities would have to do away with point systems for judging race as a factor for admission, using only individual review in making such decisions.

U.S. SUPREME COURT

GRATZ V. BOLLINGER, U.S. (2003)

VS.

GRATZ ET AL. v. BOLLINGER ET AL.

CERTIORARI TO THE UNITED STATES COURT
OF APPEALS FOR THE SIXTH CIRCUIT

No. 02–516. Argued April 1, 2003—Decided June 23, 2003.

PETITIONERS Gratz and Hamacher, both of whom are Michigan residents and Caucasian, applied for admission to the University of Michigan's (University) College of Literature, Science, and the Arts (LSA) in 1995 and 1997, respectively. Although the LSA considered Gratz to be well qualified and Hamacher to be within the qualified range, both were denied early admission and were ultimately denied admission. In order to promote consistency in the review of the many applications received, the University's Office of Undergraduate Admissions (OUA) uses written guidelines for each academic year. The guidelines have changed a number of times during the period relevant to this litigation. The OUA considers a number of factors in making admissions decisions, including high school grades, standardized test scores, high school quality, curriculum strength, geography, alumni relationships, leadership, and race. During all relevant periods, the University has considered African-Americans, Hispanics, and Native Americans to be "underrepresented minorities," and it is undisputed that the University admits virtually every qualified applicant from these groups. The current guidelines use a selection method under which every applicant from an underrepresented racial or ethnic minority group is automatically awarded 20 points of the 100 needed to guarantee admission.

Petitioners filed this class action alleging that the University's use of racial preferences in undergraduate admissions violated the Equal Protection Clause of the Fourteenth Amendment, Title VI of the Civil

Rights Act of 1964, and 42 U. S. C. §1981. They sought compensatory and punitive damages for past violations, declaratory relief finding that respondents violated their rights to nondiscriminatory treatment, an injunction prohibiting respondents from continuing to discriminate on the basis of race, and an order requiring the LSA to offer Hamacher admission as a transfer student. The District Court granted petitioners" motion to certify a class consisting of individuals who applied for and were denied admission to the LSA for academic year 1995 and forward and who are members of racial or ethnic groups that respondents treated less favorably on the basis of race. Hamacher, whose claim was found to challenge racial discrimination on a classwide basis, was designated as the class representative. On cross-motions for summary judgment, respondents relied on Justice Powell's principal opinion in *Regents of Univ. of Cal.* v. *Bakke,* 438 U. S. 265, 317, which expressed the view that the consideration of race as a factor in admissions might in some cases serve a compelling government interest. Respondents contended that the LSA has just such an interest in the educational benefits that result from having a racially and ethnically diverse student body and that its program is narrowly tailored to serve that interest. The court agreed with respondents as to the LSA's current admissions guidelines and granted them summary judgment in that respect. However, the court also found that the LSA's admissions guidelines for 1995 through 1998 operated as the functional equivalent of a quota running afoul of Justice Powell's *Bakke* opinion, and thus granted petitioners summary judgment with respect to respondents" admissions programs for those years. While interlocutory appeals were pending in the Sixth Circuit, that court issued an opinion in *Grutter* v. *Bollinger, post,* p. ___, upholding the admissions program used by the University's Law School. This Court granted certiorari in both cases, even though the Sixth Circuit had not yet rendered judgment in this one.

Held:
    1. Petitioners have standing to seek declaratory and injunctive relief. The Court rejects *Justice Stevens"* contention that, because Hamacher did not actually apply for admission as a transfer student, his future injury claim is at best conjectural or hypothetical rather than real and immediate. The "injury in fact" necessary to establish standing in this type of case is the denial of equal treatment resulting from the imposition of the barrier, not the ultimate inability to obtain the benefit. *Northeastern Fla. Chapter, Associated Gen. Contractors of America* v. *Jacksonville,* 508 U. S. 656, 666. In the face of such a barrier, to establish standing, a party need only demonstrate that it is able and ready to perform and that a discriminatory policy prevents it from doing so on an equal basis. *Ibid.* In bringing

his equal protection challenge against the University's use of race in undergraduate admissions, Hamacher alleged that the University had denied him the opportunity to compete for admission on an equal basis. Hamacher was denied admission to the University as a freshman applicant even though an underrepresented minority applicant with his qualifications would have been admitted. After being denied admission, Hamacher demonstrated that he was "able and ready" to apply as a transfer student should the University cease to use race in undergraduate admissions. He therefore has standing to seek prospective relief with respect to the University's continued use of race. Also rejected is *Justice Stevens"* contention that such use in undergraduate transfer admissions differs from the University's use of race in undergraduate freshman admissions, so that Hamacher lacks standing to represent absent class members challenging the latter. Each year the OUA produces a document setting forth guidelines for those seeking admission to the LSA, including freshman and transfer applicants. The transfer applicant guidelines specifically cross-reference factors and qualifications considered in assessing freshman applicants. In fact, the criteria used to determine whether a transfer applicant will contribute to diversity are *identical* to those used to evaluate freshman applicants. The *only* difference is that all underrepresented minority freshman applicants receive 20 points and "virtually" all who are minimally qualified are admitted, while "generally" all minimally qualified minority transfer applicants are admitted outright. While this difference might be relevant to a narrow tailoring analysis, it clearly has no effect on petitioners" standing to challenge the University's use of race in undergraduate admissions and its assertion that diversity is a compelling state interest justifying its consideration of the race of its undergraduate applicants. See *General Telephone Co. of Southwest* v. *Falcon,* 457 U. S. 147, 159; *Blum* v. *Yaretsky,* 457 U. S. 991, distinguished. The District Court's carefully considered decision to certify this class action is correct. Cf. *Coopers & Lybrand* v. *Livesay,* 437 U. S. 463, 469. Hamacher's personal stake, in view of both his past injury and the potential injury he faced at the time of certification, demonstrates that he may maintain the action. Pp. 11–20.

2. Because the University's use of race in its current freshman admissions policy is not narrowly tailored to achieve respondents" asserted interest in diversity, the policy violates the Equal Protection Clause. For the reasons set forth in *Grutter* v. *Bollinger, post,* at 15–21, the Court has today rejected petitioners" argument that diversity cannot constitute a compelling state interest. However, the Court finds that the University's current policy, which automatically distributes 20 points, or one-fifth of the points needed to guarantee admission, to every single "underrepresented minority" applicant solely because of race, is not narrowly tailored

to achieve educational diversity. In *Bakke,* Justice Powell explained his view that it would be permissible for a university to employ an admissions program in which "race or ethnic background may be deemed a "plus" in a particular applicant's file." 438 U. S., at 317. He emphasized, however, the importance of considering each particular applicant as an individual, assessing all of the qualities that individual possesses, and in turn, evaluating that individual's ability to contribute to the unique setting of higher education. The admissions program Justice Powell described did not contemplate that any single characteristic automatically ensured a specific and identifiable contribution to a university's diversity. See *id.,* at 315. The current LSA policy does not provide the individualized consideration Justice Powell contemplated. The only consideration that accompanies the 20-point automatic distribution to all applicants from underrepresented minorities is a factual review to determine whether an individual is a member of one of these minority groups. Moreover, unlike Justice Powell's example, where the race of a "particular black applicant" could be considered without being decisive, see *id.,* at 317, the LSA's 20-point distribution has the effect of making "the factor of race . . . decisive" for virtually every minimally qualified underrepresented minority applicant, *ibid.* The fact that the LSA has created the possibility of an applicant's file being flagged for individualized consideration only emphasizes the flaws of the University's system as a whole when compared to that described by Justice Powell. The record does not reveal precisely how many applications are flagged, but it is undisputed that such consideration is the exception and not the rule in the LSA's program. Also, this individualized review is only provided *after* admissions counselors automatically distribute the University's version of a "plus" that makes race a decisive factor for virtually every minimally qualified underrepresented minority applicant. The Court rejects respondents" contention that the volume of applications and the presentation of applicant information make it impractical for the LSA to use the admissions system upheld today in *Grutter.* The fact that the implementation of a program capable of providing individualized consideration might present administrative challenges does not render constitutional an otherwise problematic system. See, *e.g., Richmond* v. *J. A. Croson Co.,* 488 U. S. 469, 508. Nothing in Justice Powell's *Bakke* opinion signaled that a university may employ whatever means it desires to achieve diversity without regard to the limits imposed by strict scrutiny. Pp. 20–27.

3. Because the University's use of race in its current freshman admissions policy violates the Equal Protection Clause, it also violates Title VI and §1981. See, *e.g., Alexander* v. *Sandoval,* 532 U. S. 275, 281; *General Building Contractors Assn.* v. *Pennsylvania,* 458 U. S. 375, 389–390. Accordingly, the Court reverses that portion of the District Court's deci-

sion granting respondents summary judgment with respect to liability. Pp. 27–28.

Reversed in part and remanded.

Rehnquist, C. J. delivered the opinion of the Court, in which *O'Connor, Scalia, Kennedy,* and *Thomas, JJ.,* joined. *O'Connor, J.,* filed a concurring opinion, in which *Breyer, J.,* joined in part. *Thomas, J.,* filed a concurring opinion. *Breyer, J.,* filed an opinion concurring in the judgment. *Stevens, J.,* filed a dissenting opinion, in which *Souter, J.,* joined. *Souter, J.,* filed a dissenting opinion, in which *Ginsburg, J.,* joined as to Part II. *Ginsburg, J.,* filed a dissenting opinion, in which *Souter, J.,* joined, and in which *Breyer, J.,* joined as to Part I.

JENNIFER GRATZ AND PATRICK HAMACHER, PETITIONERS v. LEE BOLLINGER ET AL.

ON WRIT OF CERTIORARI TO THE UNITED STATES COURT OF APPEALS FOR THE SIXTH CIRCUIT

June 23, 2003.

Chief Justice Rehnquist delivered the opinion of the Court.

We granted certiorari in this case to decide whether "the University of Michigan's use of racial preferences in undergraduate admissions violate[s] the Equal Protection Clause of the Fourteenth Amendment, Title VI of the Civil Rights Act of 1964 (42 U. S. C. §2000d), or 42 U. S. C. §1981." Brief for Petitioners i. Because we find that the manner in which the University considers the race of applicants in its undergraduate admissions guidelines violates these constitutional and statutory provisions, we reverse that portion of the District Court's decision upholding the guidelines.

I.

A

Petitioners Jennifer Gratz and Patrick Hamacher both applied for admission to the University of Michigan's (University) College of Literature, Science, and the Arts (LSA) as residents of the State of Michigan. Both petitioners are Caucasian. Gratz, who applied for admission for the fall of 1995, was notified in January of that year that a final decision regarding her admission had been delayed until April. This delay was based upon the University's determination that, although Gratz was "'well qualified,'" she was "'less competitive than the students who ha[d] been admitted on first review.'" App. to Pet. for Cert. 109a. Gratz was notified in April that the LSA was unable to offer her admission. She enrolled in the University of Michigan at Dearborn, from which she graduated in the spring of 1999.

Hamacher applied for admission to the LSA for the fall of 1997. A final decision as to his application was also postponed because, though his "'academic credentials [were] in the qualified range, they [were] not at the level needed for first review admission.'" *Ibid.* Hamacher's application was subsequently denied in April 1997, and he enrolled at Michigan State University.[1]

In October 1997, Gratz and Hamacher filed a lawsuit in the United States District Court for the Eastern District of Michigan against the University of Michigan, the LSA,[2] James Duderstadt, and Lee Bollinger.[3] Petitioners" complaint was a class-action suit alleging "violations and threatened violations of the rights of the plaintiffs and the class they represent to equal protection of the laws under the Fourteenth Amendment . . . , and for racial discrimination in violation of 42 U. S. C. §§1981, 1983, and 2000d *et seq.*" App. 33. Petitioners sought, *inter alia,* compensatory and punitive damages for past violations, declaratory relief finding that respondents violated petitioners" "rights to nondiscriminatory treatment," an injunction prohibiting respondents from "continuing to discriminate on the basis of race in violation of the Fourteenth Amendment," and an order requiring the LSA to offer Hamacher admission as a transfer student.[4] *Id.,* at 40.

The District Court granted petitioners" motion for class certification after determining that a class action was appropriate pursuant to Federal Rule of Civil Procedure 23(b)(2). The certified class consisted of "those individuals who applied for and were not granted admission to the College of Literature, Science and the Arts of the University of Michigan for all academic years from 1995 forward and who are members of those racial or ethnic groups, including Caucasian, that defendants treated less favorably on the basis of race in considering their application for admission." App. 70–71. And Hamacher, whose claim the District Court found to challenge a "'practice of racial discrimination pervasively applied on a classwide basis,'" was designated as the class representative. *Id.,* at 67, 70. The court also granted petitioners" motion to bifurcate the proceedings into a liability and damages phase. *Id.,* at 71. The liability phase was to determine "whether [respondents'] use of race as a factor in admissions decisions violates the Equal Protection Clause of the Fourteenth Amendment to the Constitution." *Id.,* at 70.[5]

B

The University has changed its admissions guidelines a number of times during the period relevant to this litigation, and we summarize the most significant of these changes briefly. The University's Office of Undergraduate Admissions (OUA) oversees the LSA admissions process.[6] In order to promote consistency in the review of the large number of applications received, the OUA uses written guidelines for each academic year. Admissions counselors make admissions decisions in accordance with these guidelines.

OUA considers a number of factors in making admissions decisions, including high school grades, standardized test scores, high school quality, curriculum strength, geography, alumni relationships, and leadership. OUA also considers race. During all periods relevant to this litigation, the University has considered African-Americans, Hispanics, and Native Americans to be "underrepresented minorities," and it is undisputed that the University admits "virtually every qualified . . . applicant" from these groups. App. to Pet. for Cert. 111a.

During 1995 and 1996, OUA counselors evaluated applications according to grade point average combined with what were referred to as the "SCUGA" factors. These factors included the quality of an applicant's high school (S), the strength of an applicant's high school curriculum (C), an applicant's unusual circumstances (U), an applicant's geographical residence (G), and an applicant's alumni relationships (A). After these scores were combined to produce an applicant's "GPA 2" score, the reviewing admissions counselors referenced a set of "Guidelines" tables, which listed GPA 2 ranges on the vertical axis, and American College Test/Scholastic Aptitude Test (ACT/SAT) scores on the horizontal axis. Each table was divided into cells that included one or more courses of action to be taken, including admit, reject, delay for additional information, or postpone for reconsideration.

In both years, applicants with the same GPA 2 score and ACT/SAT score were subject to different admissions outcomes based upon their racial or ethnic status.[7] For example, as a Caucasian in-state applicant, Gratz's GPA 2 score and ACT score placed her within a cell calling for a postponed decision on her application. An in-state or out-of-state minority applicant with Gratz's scores would have fallen within a cell calling for admission.

In 1997, the University modified its admissions procedure. Specifically, the formula for calculating an applicant's GPA 2 score was restructured to include additional point values under the "U" category in the SCUGA factors. Under this new system, applicants could receive points for underrepresented minority status, socioeconomic disadvantage, or attendance at a high school with a predominantly underrepresented minority population, or underrepresentation in the unit to which the student was applying (for example, men who sought to pursue a career in nursing). Under the 1997 procedures, Hamacher's GPA 2 score and ACT score placed him in a cell on the in-state applicant table calling for postponement of a final admissions decision. An underrepresented minority applicant placed in the same cell would generally have been admitted.

Beginning with the 1998 academic year, the OUA dispensed with the Guidelines tables and the SCUGA point system in favor of a "selection index," on which an applicant could score a maximum of 150 points. This index was divided linearly into ranges generally calling for admissions dispositions as follows: 100–150 (admit); 95–99 (admit or postpone); 90–94 (postpone or admit); 75–89 (delay or postpone); 74 and below (delay or reject).

Each application received points based on high school grade point average, standardized test scores, academic quality of an applicant's high school, strength or weakness of high school curriculum, in-state residency, alumni relationship, personal essay, and personal achievement or leadership. Of particular significance here, under a "miscellaneous" category, an applicant was entitled to 20 points based upon his or her membership in an underrepresented racial or ethnic minority group. The University explained that the " "development of the selection index for admissions in 1998 changed only the mechanics, not the substance of how race and ethnicity were considered in admissions.'" App. to Pet. for Cert. 116a.

In all application years from 1995 to 1998, the guidelines provided that qualified applicants from underrepresented minority groups be admitted as soon as possible in light of the University's belief that such applicants were more likely to enroll if promptly notified of their admission. Also from 1995 through 1998, the University carefully managed its rolling admissions system to permit consideration of certain applications submitted later in the academic year through the use of "protected seats." Specific groups—including athletes, foreign students, ROTC candidates, and underrepresented minorities—were "protected categories" eligible for these seats. A committee called the Enrollment Working Group (EWG) projected how many applicants from each of these protected categories the University was likely to receive after a given date and then paced admissions decisions to permit full consideration of expected applications from these groups. If this space was not filled by qualified candidates from the designated groups toward the end of the admissions season, it was then used to admit qualified candidates remaining in the applicant pool, including those on the waiting list.

During 1999 and 2000, the OUA used the selection index, under which every applicant from an underrepresented racial or ethnic minority group was awarded 20 points. Starting in 1999, however, the University established an Admissions Review Committee (ARC), to provide an additional level of consideration for some applications. Under the new system, counselors may, in their discretion, "flag" an application for the ARC to review after determining that the applicant (1) is academically prepared to succeed at the University,[8] (2) has achieved a minimum selection index score, and (3) possesses a quality or characteristic important to the University's composition of its freshman class, such as high class rank, unique life experiences, challenges, circumstances, interests or talents, socioeconomic disadvantage, and underrepresented race, ethnicity, or geography. After reviewing "flagged" applications, the ARC determines whether to admit, defer, or deny each applicant.

C

The parties filed cross-motions for summary judgment with respect to liability. Petitioners asserted that the LSA's use of race as a factor in admissions violates Title VI of the Civil Rights Act of 1964, 78 Stat. 252, 42 U. S. C. §2000d, and the Equal Protection Clause of the Fourteenth Amendment. Respondents relied on Justice Powell's opinion in *Regents of Univ. of Cal. v. Bakke,* 438 U. S. 265 (1978), to respond to petitioners" arguments. As discussed in greater detail in the Court's opinion in *Grutter v. Bollinger, post,* at 10–13, Justice Powell, in *Bakke,* expressed the view that the consideration of race as a factor in admissions might in some cases serve a compelling government interest. See 438 U. S., at 317. Respondents contended that the LSA has just such an interest in the educational benefits that result from having a racially and ethnically diverse student body and that its program is narrowly tailored to serve that interest. Respondent-intervenors asserted that the LSA had a compelling interest in remedying the University's past and current discrimination against minorities.[9]

The District Court began its analysis by reviewing this Court's decision in *Bakke.* See 122 F. Supp. 2d 811, 817 (ED Mich. 2001). Although the court acknowledged that no decision from this Court since *Bakke* has explicitly accepted the diversity rationale discussed by Justice Powell, see 122 F. Supp. 2d, at 820–821, it also concluded that this Court had not, in the years since *Bakke,* ruled out such a justification for the use of race. 122 F. Supp. 2d, at 820–821. The District Court concluded that respondents and their *amici curiae* had presented "solid evidence" that a racially and ethnically diverse student body produces significant educational benefits such that achieving such a student body constitutes a compelling governmental interest. See *id.,* at 822–824.

The court next considered whether the LSA's admissions guidelines were narrowly tailored to achieve that interest. See *id.,* at 824. Again relying on Justice Powell's opinion in *Bakke,* the District Court determined that the admissions program the LSA began using in 1999 is a narrowly tailored means of achieving the University's interest in the educational benefits that flow from a racially and ethnically diverse student body. See 122 F. Supp. 2d, at 827. The court emphasized that the LSA's current program does not utilize rigid quotas or seek to admit a predetermined number of minority students. See *ibid.* The award of 20 points for membership in an underrepresented minority group, in the District Court's view, was not the functional equivalent of a quota because minority candidates were not insulated from review by virtue of those points. See *id.,* at 828. Likewise, the court rejected the assertion that the LSA's program operates like the two-track system Justice Powell found objectionable in *Bakke* on the grounds that LSA applicants are not competing for different groups of seats. See 122 F. Supp. 2d, at 828–829. The court also dismissed petitioners" assertion that the LSA's current system is nothing more than a means by which to achieve racial balancing. See *id.,* at 831. The court explained that the LSA does not seek to achieve a certain proportion of minority students, let alone a proportion that represents the community. See *ibid.*

The District Court found the admissions guidelines the LSA used from 1995 through 1998 to be more problematic. In the court's view, the University's prior practice of "protecting" or "reserving" seats for underrepresented minority applicants effectively kept nonprotected applicants from competing for those slots. See *id.,* at 832. This system, the court concluded, operated as the functional equivalent of a quota and ran afoul of Justice Powell's opinion in *Bakke.*[10] See 122 F. Supp. 2d, at 832.

Based on these findings, the court granted petitioners" motion for summary judgment with respect to the LSA's admissions programs in existence from 1995 through 1998, and respondents" motion with respect to the LSA's admissions programs for 1999 and 2000. See *id.,* at 833. Accordingly, the District Court denied petitioners" request for injunctive relief. See *id.,* at 814.

The District Court issued an order consistent with its rulings and certified two questions for interlocutory appeal to the Sixth Circuit pursuant to 28 U. S. C. §1292(b). Both parties appealed aspects of the District Court's rulings, and the Court of Appeals heard the case en banc on the same day as *Grutter* v. *Bollinger.* The Sixth Circuit later issued an opinion in *Grutter,* upholding the admissions program used by the University of Michigan Law School, and the petitioner in that case sought a writ of certiorari from this Court. Petitioners asked this Court to grant certiorari in this case as well, despite the fact that the Court of Appeals had not yet rendered a judgment, so that this Court could address the constitutionality of the consideration of race in university admissions in a wider range of circumstances. We did so. See 537 U. S. 1044 (2002).

II.

As they have throughout the course of this litigation, petitioners contend that the University's consideration of race in its undergraduate admissions decisions violates §1 of the Equal Protection Clause of the Fourteenth Amendment,[11] Title VI,[12] and 42 U. S. C. §1981.[13] We consider first whether petitioners have standing to seek declaratory and injunctive relief, and, finding that they do, we next consider the merits of their claims.

A

Although no party has raised the issue, *Justice Stevens* argues that petitioners lack Article III standing to seek injunctive relief with respect to the University's use of race in undergraduate admissions. He first contends that because Hamacher did not "actually appl[y] for admission as a transfer student[,] [h]is claim of future injury is at best "conjectural or hypothetical" rather than "real and immediate.'" *Post,* at 5 (dissenting opinion). But whether Hamacher "actually applied" for admission as a transfer student is not determinative of his ability to seek injunctive relief in this case. If Hamacher had submitted a transfer application and been rejected, he would still need to allege an intent to apply again in order to seek prospective relief. If *Justice Stevens* means that because Hamacher did not apply to transfer, he must never *really* have intended to do so, that conclusion directly conflicts with the finding of fact entered by the District Court that Hamacher "intends to transfer to the University of Michigan when defendants cease the use of race as an admission preference." App. 67.[14]

It is well established that intent may be relevant to standing in an Equal Protection challenge. In *Clements* v. *Fashing,* 457 U. S. 957 (1982), for example, we considered a challenge to a provision of the Texas Constitution requiring the immediate resignation of certain state officeholders upon their announcement of candidacy for another office. We concluded that the plaintiff officeholders had Article III standing because they had alleged that they *would have announced their candidacy* for other offices were it not for the "automatic resignation" provision they were challenging. *Id.,* at 962; accord, *Turner* v. *Fouche,* 396 U. S. 346, 361–362, n. 23 (1970) (plaintiff who did not own property had standing to challenge property ownership requirement for membership on school board even though there was no evidence that plaintiff had applied and been rejected); *Quinn* v. *Millsap*, 491 U. S. 95, 103, n. 8 (1989) (plaintiffs who did not own property had standing to challenge property ownership requirement for membership on government board even though they lacked standing to challenge the requirement "as applied"). Likewise, in *Northeastern Fla. Chapter, Associated Gen. Contractors of America* v. *Jacksonville,* 508 U. S. 656 (1993), we considered whether an association challenging an ordinance that gave preferential treatment to certain minority-owned businesses in the award of city contracts needed to show that one of its members would have received a contract absent the ordinance in order to establish standing. In finding that no such showing was necessary, we explained that "[t]he "injury in fact" in an equal protection case of this variety is the denial of equal treatment resulting from the imposition of the barrier, not the ultimate inability to obtain the benefit. . . . And in the context of a challenge to a set-aside program, the "injury in fact" is the inability to compete on an equal footing in the bidding process, not the loss of contract." *Id.,* at 666. We concluded that in the face of such a barrier, "[t]o establish standing, a party challenging a set-aside program like Jacksonville's need only demonstrate that it is able and ready to bid on contracts and that a discriminatory policy prevents it from doing so on an equal basis." *Ibid.*

In bringing his equal protection challenge against the University's use of race in undergraduate admissions, Hamacher alleged that the University had denied him the opportunity to compete for admission on an equal basis. When Hamacher applied to the University as a freshman applicant, he was denied admission even though an underrepresented minority applicant with his qualifications would have been admitted. See App. to Pet. for Cert. 115a. After being denied admission, Hamacher demonstrated that he was "able and ready" to apply as a transfer student should the University cease to use race in undergraduate admissions. He therefore has standing to seek prospective relief with respect to the University's continued use of race in undergraduate admissions.

Justice Stevens raises a second argument as to standing. He contends that the University's use of race in undergraduate transfer admissions differs from its use of race in undergraduate freshman admissions, and that therefore Hamacher lacks standing to represent absent class members challenging the latter. *Post,* at 5 (dissenting opinion). As an initial matter, there is a question whether the relevance of this variation, if any, is a matter of Article III standing at all or whether it goes to the propriety of class certification pursuant to Federal Rule of Civil Procedure 23(a). The parties have not briefed the question of standing versus adequacy, however, and we need not resolve the question today: Regardless of whether the requirement is deemed one of adequacy or standing, it is clearly satisfied in this case.[15]

From the time petitioners filed their original complaint through their brief on the merits in this Court, they have consistently challenged the University's use of race in undergraduate admissions and its asserted justification of promoting "diversity." See, *e.g.,* App. 38; Brief for Petitioners 13. Consistent with this challenge, petitioners requested injunctive relief prohibiting respondent "from continuing to discriminate on the basis of race." App. 40. They sought to certify a class consisting of all individuals who were not members of an underrepresented minority group who either had applied for admission to the LSA and been rejected or who intended to apply for admission to the LSA, for all academic years from 1995 forward. *Id.,* at 35–36. The District Court determined that the proposed class satisfied the requirements of the Federal Rules of Civil Procedure, including the requirements of numerosity, commonality, and typicality. See Fed. Rule Civ. Proc. 23(a); App. 70. The court further concluded that Hamacher was an adequate representative for the class in the pursuit of compensatory and injunctive relief for purposes of Rule 23(a)(4), see App. 61–69, and found "the record utterly devoid of the presence of . . . antagonism between the interests of . . . Hamacher, and the members of the class which [he] seek[s] to represent," *id.,* at 61. Finally, the District Court concluded that petitioners" claim was appropriate for class treatment because the University's "'practice of racial discrimination pervasively applied on a classwide basis.'" *Id.,* at 67. The court certified the class pursuant to Federal Rule of Civil Procedure 23(b)(2), and designated Hamacher as the class representative. App. 70.

Justice Stevens cites *Blum* v. *Yaretsky,* 457 U. S. 991 (1982), in arguing that the District Court erred. *Post,* at 8. In *Blum,* we considered a class action suit brought by Medicaid beneficiaries. The named representatives in *Blum* challenged decisions by the State's Medicaid Utilization Review Committee (URC) to transfer them to lower levels of care without, in their view, sufficient procedural safeguards. After a class was certified, the plaintiffs obtained an order expanding class certification to include challenges to URC decisions to transfer patients to *higher* levels of care as well. The defendants argued that the named representatives could not represent absent class members challenging transfers to higher levels of care because they had not been threatened with such transfers. We agreed. We noted that "[n]othing in the record . . . suggests that any of the individual respondents have been either transferred to more intensive care or threatened with such transfers." 457 U. S., at 1001. And we found that transfers to lower levels of care involved a number of fundamentally different concerns than did transfers to higher ones. *Id.,* at 1001–1002 (noting, for example, that transfers to lower levels of care implicated beneficiaries' property interests given the concomitant decrease in Medicaid benefits, while transfers to higher levels of care did not).

In the present case, the University's use of race in undergraduate transfer admissions does not implicate a significantly different set of concerns than does its use of race in undergraduate freshman admissions. Respondents challenged Hamacher's standing at the certification stage, but *never* did so on the grounds that the University's use of race in undergraduate transfer admissions involves a different set of concerns than does its use of race in freshman admissions. Respondents" failure to allege any such difference is simply consistent with the fact that no such difference exists. Each year the OUA produces a document entitled "COLLEGE OF LITERATURE SCIENCE AND THE ARTS GUIDELINES FOR ALL TERMS," which sets forth guidelines for all individuals seeking admission to the LSA, including freshman applicants, transfer applicants, international student applicants, and the like. See, *e.g.,* 2 App. in No. 01–1333 etc. (CA6), pp. 507–542. The guidelines used to evaluate transfer applicants specifically cross-reference factors and qualifications considered in assessing freshman applicants. In fact, the criteria used to determine whether a transfer applicant will contribute to the University's stated goal of diversity are *identical* to that used to evaluate freshman applicants. For example, in 1997, when the class was certified and the District Court found that Hamacher had standing to represent the class, the transfer guidelines contained a separate section entitled "CONTRIBUTION TO A DIVERSE STUDENT BODY." 2 *id.,* at 531. This section explained that any transfer applicant who could *"contribut[e] to a diverse student body"* should "generally be admitted" even with substantially lower qualifications than those required of other transfer applicants. *Ibid.* (emphasis added). To determine whether a transfer applicant was capable of "contribut[ing] to a diverse student body," admissions counselors were instructed to determine whether that transfer applicant met the "criteria as defined in Section IV of the "U" category of [the] SCUGA" factors used to assess freshman applicants. *Ibid.* Section IV of the "U" category, entitled "Contribution to a Diverse Class," explained that "[t]he University is committed to a rich educational experience for its students. A diverse, as opposed to a homogenous, student population enhances the educational experience for all students. To insure a diverse class, significant weight will be given in the admissions process to indicators of student's contribution to a diverse class." 1 *id.,* at 432. These indicators, used in evaluating freshman and transfer applicants alike, list being a member of an underrepresented minority group as establishing an applicant's contribution to diversity. See 3 *id.,* at 1133–1134, 1153–1154. Indeed, the *only* difference between the University's use of race in considering freshman and transfer applicants is that all underrepresented minority freshman applicants receive 20 points and "virtually" all who are minimally qualified are admitted, while "generally" all minimally qualified minority transfer applicants are admitted outright. While this difference might be relevant to a narrow tailoring analysis, it clearly has no effect on petitioners" standing to challenge the University's use of race in undergraduate admissions and its assertion that diversity is a compelling state interest that justifies its consideration of the race of its undergraduate applicants.[16]

Particularly instructive here is our statement in *General Telephone Co. of Southwest v. Falcon,* 457 U. S. 147 (1982), that "[i]f [defendant-employer] used a biased testing procedure to evaluate both applicants for employment and incumbent employees, a class action on behalf of every applicant or employee who might have been prejudiced by the test *clearly* would satisfy the . . . requirements of Rule 23(a)." *Id.,* at 159, n. 15 (emphasis added). Here, the District Court found that the sole rationale the University had provided for any of its race-based preferences in undergraduate admissions was the interest in "the educational benefits that result from having a diverse student body." App. to Pet. for Cert. 8a. And petitioners argue that an interest in "diversity" is not a compelling state interest that is *ever* capable of justifying the use of race in undergraduate admissions. See, *e.g.,* Brief for Petitioners 11–13. In sum, the same set of concerns is implicated by the University's use of race in evaluating all undergraduate admissions applications under the guidelines.[17] We therefore agree with the District Court's carefully considered decision to certify this class-action challenge to the University's consideration of race in undergraduate admissions. See App. 67 ("'It is a singular policy . . . applied on a classwide basis'"); cf. *Coopers & Lybrand v. Livesay,* 437 U. S. 463, 469 (1978) ("[T]he class determination generally involves considerations that are enmeshed in the factual and legal issues comprising the plaintiff's cause of action" (internal quotation marks omitted)). Indeed, class action treatment was particularly important in this case because "the claims of the individual students run the risk of becoming moot" and "[t]he class action vehicle . . . provides a mechanism for ensuring that a justiciable claim is before the Court." App. 69. Thus, we think it clear that Hamacher's personal stake, in view of both his past injury and the potential injury he faced at the time of certification, demonstrates that he may maintain this class-action challenge to the University's use of race in undergraduate admissions.

B

Petitioners argue, first and foremost, that the University's use of race in undergraduate admissions violates the Fourteenth Amendment. Specifically, they contend that this Court has only sanctioned the use of racial classifications to remedy identified discrimination, a justification on which respondents have never relied. Brief for Petitioners 15–16. Petitioners further argue that "diversity as a basis for employing racial preferences is simply too open–ended, ill–defined, and indefinite to constitute a compelling interest capable of supporting narrowly-tailored means." *Id.,* at 17–18, 40–41. But for the reasons set forth today in *Grutter* v. *Bollinger, post,* at 15–21, the Court has rejected these arguments of petitioners.

Petitioners alternatively argue that even if the University's interest in diversity can constitute a compelling state interest, the District Court erroneously concluded that the University's use of race in its current freshman admissions policy is narrowly tailored to achieve such an interest. Petitioners argue that the guidelines the University began using in 1999 do not "remotely resemble the kind of consideration of race and ethnicity that Justice Powell endorsed in *Bakke*." Brief for Petitioners 18. Respondents reply that the University's current admissions program *is* narrowly tailored and avoids the problems of the Medical School of the University of California at Davis program (U. C. Davis) rejected by Justice Powell.[18] They claim that their program "hews closely" to both the admissions program described by Justice Powell as well as the Harvard College admissions program that he endorsed. Brief for Respondents 32. Specifically, respondents contend that the LSA's policy provides the individualized consideration that "Justice Powell considered a hallmark of a constitutionally appropriate admissions program." *Id.,* at 35. For the reasons set out below, we do not agree.

It is by now well established that "all racial classifications reviewable under the Equal Protection Clause must be strictly scrutinized." *Adarand Constructors, Inc.* v. *Peña,* 515 U. S. 200, 224 (1995). This "'standard of review . . . is not dependent on the race of those burdened or benefited by a particular classification.'" *Ibid.* (quoting *Richmond* v. *J. A. Croson Co.,* 488 U. S. 469, 494 (1989) (plurality opinion)). Thus, "any person, of whatever race, has the right to demand that any governmental actor subject to the Constitution justify any racial classification subjecting that person to unequal treatment under the strictest of judicial scrutiny." *Adarand,* 515 U. S., at 224.

To withstand our strict scrutiny analysis, respondents must demonstrate that the University's use of race in its current admission program employs "narrowly tailored measures that further compelling governmental interests." *Id.,* at 227. Because "[r]acial classifications are simply too pernicious to permit any but the most exact connection between justification and classification," *Fullilove* v. *Klutznick,* 448 U. S. 448, 537 (1980) (*Stevens,* J., dissenting), our review of whether such requirements have been met must entail "'a most searching examination.'" *Adarand, supra,* at 223 (quoting *Wygant* v. *Jackson Bd. of Ed.,* 476 U. S. 267, 273 (1986) (plurality opinion of Powell, J.)). We find that the University's policy, which automatically distributes 20 points, or one-fifth of the points needed to guarantee admission, to every single "underrepresented minority" applicant solely because of race, is not narrowly tailored to achieve the interest in educational diversity that respondents claim justifies their program.

In *Bakke,* Justice Powell reiterated that "[p]referring members of any one group for no reason other than race or ethnic origin is discrimination for its own sake." 438 U. S., at 307. He then explained, however, that in his view it would be permissible for a university to employ an admissions program in which "race or ethnic background may be deemed a "plus" in a particular applicant's file." *Id.,* at 317. He explained that such a program might allow for "[t]he file of a particular black applicant [to] be examined for his potential contribution to diversity without the factor of race being decisive when compared, for example, with that of an applicant identified as an Italian-American if the latter is thought to exhibit qualities more likely to promote beneficial educational pluralism." *Ibid.* Such a system, in Justice Powell's view, would be "flexible enough to consider all pertinent elements of diversity in light of the particular qualifications of each applicant." *Ibid.*

Justice Powell's opinion in *Bakke* emphasized the importance of considering each particular applicant as an individual, assessing all of the qualities that individual possesses, and in turn, evaluating that individual's ability to contribute to the unique setting of higher education. The admissions program Justice Powell described, however, did not contemplate that any single characteristic automatically ensured a specific and identifiable contribution to a university's diversity. See *id.,* at 315. See also *Metro Broadcasting, Inc.* v. *FCC,* 497 U. S. 547, 618 (1990) (*O'Connor, J.,* dissenting) (concluding that the FCC's policy, which "embodie[d] the related notions that a particular applicant, by virtue of race or ethnicity alone, is more valued than other applicants because [the applicant is] "likely to provide [a] distinct perspective," "impermissibly value[d] individuals" based on a presumption that "persons think in a manner associated with their race"). Instead, under the approach Justice Powell described, each characteristic of a particular applicant was to be considered in assessing the applicant's entire application.

The current LSA policy does not provide such individualized consideration. The LSA's policy automatically distributes 20 points to every single applicant from an "underrepresented minority" group, as defined by the University. The only consideration that accompanies this distribution of points is a factual review of an application to determine whether an individual is a member of one of these minority groups. Moreover, unlike Justice Powell's example, where the race of a "particular black applicant" could be considered without being decisive, see *Bakke,* 438 U. S., at 317, the LSA's automatic distribution of 20 points has the effect of making "the factor of race . . . decisive" for virtually every minimally qualified underrepresented minority applicant. *Ibid.*[19]

Also instructive in our consideration of the LSA's system is the example provided in the description of the Harvard College Admissions Program, which Justice Powell both discussed in, and attached to, his opinion in *Bakke.* The example was included to "illustrate the kind of significance attached to race" under the Harvard College program. *Id.,* at 324. It provided as follows:

> "The Admissions Committee, with only a few places left to fill, might find itself forced to choose between A, the child of a successful black physician in an academic community with promise of superior academic performance, and B, a black who grew up in an inner-city ghetto of semi-literate parents whose academic achievement was lower but who had demonstrated energy and leadership as well as an apparently abiding interest in black power. If a good number of black students much like A but few like B had already been admitted, the Committee might prefer B; and vice versa. If C, a white student with extraordinary artistic talent, were also seeking one of the remaining places, his unique quality might give him an edge over both A and B. Thus, the critical criteria are often individual qualities or experience *not dependent upon race but sometimes associated with it.*" *Ibid.* (emphasis added).

This example further demonstrates the problematic nature of the LSA's admissions system. Even if student C's "extraordinary artistic talent" rivaled that of Monet or Picasso, the applicant would receive, at most, five points under the LSA's system. See App. 234–235. At the same time, every single underrepresented minority applicant, including students A and B, would automatically receive 20 points for submitting an application. Clearly, the LSA's system does not offer applicants the individualized selection process described in Harvard's example. Instead of considering how the differing backgrounds, experiences, and characteristics of students A, B, and C might benefit the University, admissions counselors reviewing LSA applications would simply award both A and B 20 points because their applications indicate that they are African-American, and student C would receive up to 5 points for his "extraordinary talent."[20]

Respondents emphasize the fact that the LSA has created the possibility of an applicant's file being flagged for individualized consideration by the ARC. We think that the flagging program only emphasizes the flaws of the University's system as a whole when compared to that described by Justice Powell. Again, students A, B, and C illustrate the point. First, student A would never be flagged. This is because, as the University has conceded, the effect of automatically awarding 20 points is that virtually every qualified underrepresented minority applicant is admitted. Student A, an applicant "with promise of superior academic performance," would certainly fit this description. Thus, the result of the automatic distribution of 20 points is that the University would never consider student A's individual background, experiences, and characteristics to assess his individual "potential contribution to diversity," *Bakke, supra,* at 317. Instead, every applicant like student A would simply be admitted.

It is possible that students B and C would be flagged and considered as individuals. This assumes that student B was not already admitted because of the automatic 20-point distribution, and that student C could muster at least 70 additional points. But the fact that the "review committee can look at the applications individually and ignore the points," once an application is flagged, Tr. of Oral Arg. 42, is of little comfort under our strict scrutiny analysis. The record does not reveal precisely how many applications are flagged for this individualized consideration, but it is undisputed that such consideration is the exception and not the rule in the operation of the LSA's admissions program. See App. to Pet. for Cert. 117a ("The ARC reviews only a portion of all of the applications. The bulk of admissions decisions are executed based on selection index score parameters set by the EWG").[21] Additionally, this individualized review is only provided *after* admissions counselors automatically distribute the University's version of a "plus" that makes race a decisive factor for virtually every minimally qualified underrepresented minority applicant.

Respondents contend that "[t]he volume of applications and the presentation of applicant information make it impractical for [LSA] to use the . . . admissions system" upheld by the Court today in *Grutter.* Brief for Respondents 6, n. 8. But the fact that the implementation of a program capable of providing individualized consideration might present administrative challenges does not render constitutional an otherwise problematic system. See *J. A. Croson Co.,* 488 U. S., at 508 (citing *Frontiero v. Richardson,* 411 U. S. 677, 690 (1973) (plurality opinion of Brennan, J.) (rejecting "'administrative convenience'" as a determinant of constitutionality in the face of a suspect classification)). Nothing in Justice Powell's opinion in *Bakke* signaled that a university may employ whatever means it desires to achieve the stated goal of diversity without regard to the limits imposed by our strict scrutiny analysis.

We conclude, therefore, that because the University's use of race in its current freshman admissions policy is not narrowly tailored to achieve respondents" asserted compelling interest in diversity, the admissions policy violates the Equal Protection Clause of the Fourteenth Amendment.[22] We further find that the admissions policy also violates Title VI and 42 U. S. C. § 1981.[23] Accordingly, we reverse that portion of the District Court's decision granting respondents summary judgment with respect to liability and remand the case for proceedings consistent with this opinion.

It is so ordered.

JENNIFER GRATZ AND PATRICK HAMACHER, PETITIONERS v. LEE BOLLINGER ET AL.

ON WRIT OF CERTIORARI TO THE UNITED STATES COURT OF APPEALS FOR THE SIXTH CIRCUIT

June 23, 2003.

Justice Stevens, with whom *Justice Souter* joins, dissenting.

Petitioners seek forward-looking relief enjoining the University of Michigan from continuing to use its current race-conscious freshman admissions policy. Yet unlike the plaintiff in *Grutter* v. *Bollinger, post,* p. 1,[1] the petitioners in this case had already enrolled at other schools before they filed their class–action complaint in this case. Neither petitioner was in the process of reapplying to Michigan through the freshman admissions process at the time this suit was filed, and neither has done so since. There is a total absence of evidence that either petitioner would receive any benefit from the prospective relief sought by their lawyer. While some unidentified members of the class may very well have standing to seek prospective relief, it is clear that neither petitioner does. Our precedents therefore require dismissal of the action.

I.

Petitioner Jennifer Gratz applied in 1994 for admission to the University of Michigan's (University) College of Literature, Science, and the Arts (LSA) as an undergraduate for the 1995–1996 freshman class. After the University delayed action on her application and then placed her name on an extended waiting list, Gratz decided to attend the University of Michigan at Dearborn instead; she graduated in 1999. Petitioner Patrick Hamacher applied for admission to LSA as an undergraduate for the 1997–1998 freshman class. After the University post-poned decision on his application and then placed his name on an extended waiting list, he attended Michigan State University, graduating in 2001. In the complaint that petitioners filed on October 14, 1997, Hamacher alleged that "[h]e intends to apply to transfer [to the University of Michigan] if the discriminatory admissions system described herein is eliminated." App. 34.

At the class certification stage, petitioners sought to have Hamacher represent a class pursuant to Federal Rule Civil Procedure 23(b)(2).[2] See App. 71, n. 3. In response, Michigan contended that "Hamacher lacks standing to represent a class seeking declaratory and injunctive relief." Id., at 63. Michigan submitted that Hamacher suffered "'no threat of imminent future injury'" given that he had already enrolled at another undergraduate institution.[3] Id., at 64. The District Court rejected Michigan's contention, concluding that Hamacher had standing to seek injunctive relief because the complaint alleged that he intended to apply to Michigan as a transfer student. See id., at 67 ("To the extent that plain-tiff Hamacher reapplies to the University of Michigan, he will again face the same "harm" in that race will continue to be a factor in admissions"). The District Court, accordingly, certified Hamacher as the sole class representative and limited the claims of the class to injunctive and declaratory relief. See id., at 70–71.

In subsequent proceedings, the District Court held that the 1995–1998 admissions system, which was in effect when both petition-ers" applications were denied, was unlawful but that Michigan's new 1999–2000 admissions system was lawful. When petitioners sought cer-tiorari from this Court, Michigan did not cross-petition for review of the District Court's judgment concerning the admissions policies that Michigan had in place when Gratz and Hamacher applied for admission in 1994 and 1996 respectively. See Brief for Respondents 5, n. 7. Accordingly, we have before us only that portion of the District Court's judgment that upheld Michigan's new freshman admissions policy.

II.

Both Hamacher and Gratz, of course, have standing to seek damages as compensation for the alleged wrongful denial of their respective appli-cations under Michigan's old freshman admissions system. However, like the plaintiff in Los Angeles v. Lyons, 461 U. S. 95 (1983), who had stand-ing to recover damages caused by "chokeholds" administered by the police in the past but had no standing to seek injunctive relief prevent-ing future chokeholds, petitioners" past injuries do not give them standing to obtain injunctive relief to protect third parties from similar harms. See *id.,* at 102 ("[P]ast exposure to illegal conduct does not in itself show a present case or controversy regarding injunctive relief . . . if unaccompanied by any continuing, present adverse effects" (quoting *O'Shea* v. *Littleton,* 414 U. S. 488, 495–496 (1974))). To seek forward-looking, injunctive relief, petitioners must show that they face an imminent threat of future injury. See *Adarand Constructors, Inc.* v. *Peña,* 515 U. S. 200, 210–211 (1995). This they cannot do given that when this suit was filed, neither faced an impending threat of future injury based on Michigan's new freshman admissions policy.[4]

Even though there is not a scintilla of evidence that the freshman admissions program now being administered by respondents will ever have any impact on either Hamacher or Gratz, petitioners nonetheless argue that Hamacher has a personal stake in this suit because at the time the complaint was filed, Hamacher intended to apply to transfer to Michigan once certain admission policy changes occurred.[5] See App. 34; see also Tr. of Oral Arg. 4–5. Petitioners" attempt to base Hamacher's standing in this suit on a hypothetical transfer application fails for several reasons. First, there is no evidence that Hamacher ever actually applied for admission as a transfer student at Michigan. His claim of future injury is at best "conjectural or hypothetical" rather than "real and immediate." *O'Shea* v. *Littleton,* 414 U. S., at 494 (internal quotation marks omitted); see also *Lujan* v. *Defenders of Wildlife,* 504 U. S. 555, 560 (1992).

Second, as petitioners" counsel conceded at oral argument, the transfer policy is not before this Court and was not addressed by the District Court. See Tr. of Oral Arg. 4–5 (admitting that "[t]he transfer admissions policy itself is not before you—the Court"). Unlike the University's freshman policy, which is detailed at great length in the Joint Appendix filed with this Court, the specifics of the transfer policy are conspicuously missing from the Joint Appendix filed with this Court. Furthermore, the transfer policy is not discussed anywhere in the parties' briefs. Nor is it ever even referenced in the District Court's Dec. 13, 2000, opinion that upheld Michigan's new freshman admissions policy and struck down Michigan's old policy. Nonetheless, evidence filed with the District Court by Michigan demonstrates that the criteria used to evaluate transfer applications at Michigan differ significantly from the criteria used to evaluate freshman undergraduate applications. Of special significance, Michigan's 2000 freshman admissions policy, for example, provides for 20 points to be added to the selection index scores of minority applicants. See *ante,* at 23. In contrast, Michigan does not use points in its transfer policy; some applicants, including minority and socioeconomically disadvantaged applicants, "will generally be admitted" if they possess certain qualifications, including a 2.5 undergraduate grade point average (GPA), sophomore standing, and a 3.0 high school GPA. 10 Record 16 (Exh. C). Because of these differences, Hamacher cannot base his right to complain about the *freshman* admissions policy on his hypothetical injury under a wholly separate *transfer* policy. For "[i]f the right to complain of *one* administrative deficiency automatically conferred the right to complain of *all* administrative deficiencies, any citizen aggrieved in one respect could bring the whole structure of state administration before the courts for review." *Lewis* v. *Casey,* 518 U. S. 343, 358–359, n. 6 (1996) (emphasis in original); see also *Blum* v. *Yaretsky,* 457 U. S. 991, 999 (1982) ("[A] plaintiff who has been subject to injurious conduct of one kind [does not] possess by virtue of that injury the necessary stake in litigating conduct of another kind, although similar").[6]

Third, the differences between the freshman and the transfer admissions policies make it extremely unlikely, at best, that an injunction requiring respondents to modify the freshman admissions program would have any impact on Michigan's transfer policy. See *Allen* v. *Wright,* 468 U. S. 737, 751 (1984) ("[R]elief from the injury must be "likely" to follow from a favorable decision"); *Schlesinger* v. *Reservists Comm. to Stop the War,* 418 U. S. 208, 222 (1974) ("[T]he discrete factual context within which the concrete injury occurred or is threatened insures the framing of relief no broader than required by the precise facts to which the court's ruling would be applied"). This is especially true in light of petitioners" unequivocal disavowal of any request for equitable relief that would totally preclude the use of race in the processing of all admissions applications. See Tr. of Oral Arg. 14–15.

The majority asserts that petitioners "have challenged *any* use of race by the University in undergraduate admissions"—freshman and transfer alike. *Ante,* at 18, n. 16 (emphasis in original). Yet when questioned at oral argument about whether petitioners" challenge would impact both private and public universities, petitioners" counsel stated: "Your Honor, I want to be clear about what it is that we're arguing for here today. *We are not suggesting an absolute rule forbidding any use of race under any circumstances.* What we are arguing is that the interest asserted here by the University, this amorphous, ill-defined, unlimited interest in diversity is not a compelling interest." Tr. of Oral Arg. 14 (emphasis added). In addition, when asked whether petitioners took the position that the only permissible use of race is as a remedy for past discrimination, petitioners' lawyer stated: "I would not go that far. . . . [T]here may be other reasons. I think they would have to be extraordinary and rare. . . ." *Id.,* at 15. Consistent with these statements, petitioners' briefs filed with this Court attack the University's asserted interest in "diversity" but acknowledge that race could be considered for remedial reasons. See, *e.g.,* Brief for Petitioners 16–17.

Because Michigan's transfer policy was not challenged by petitioners and is not before this Court, see *supra,* at 5, we do not know whether Michigan would defend its transfer policy on diversity grounds, or whether it might try to justify its transfer policy on other grounds, such as a remedial interest. Petitioners' counsel was therefore incorrect in asserting at oral argument that if the University's asserted interest in "diversity" were to be "struck down as a rationale, then the law would be [the] same with respect to the transfer policy as with respect to the original [freshman admissions] policy." Tr. of Oral Arg. 7–8. And the majority is likewise mistaken in assuming that "the University's use of race in undergraduate transfer admissions does not implicate a significantly different set of concerns than does its use of race in undergraduate freshman admissions." *Ante,* at 16. Because the transfer policy has never been the subject of this suit, we simply do not know (1) whether Michigan would defend its transfer policy on "diversity" grounds or some other grounds, or (2) how the absence of a point system in the transfer policy might impact a narrow tailoring analysis of that policy.

At bottom, petitioners' interest in obtaining an injunction for the benefit of younger third parties is comparable to that of the unemancipated minor who had no standing to litigate on behalf of older women in *H. L. v. Matheson,* 450 U. S. 398, 406–407 (1981), or that of the Medicaid patients transferred to less intensive care who had no standing to litigate on behalf of patients objecting to transfers to more intensive care facilities in *Blum* v. *Yaretsky,* 457 U. S., at 1001. To have standing, it is elementary that the petitioners" own interests must be implicated. Because neither petitioner has a personal stake in this suit for prospective relief, neither has standing.

III.

It is true that the petitioners' complaint was filed as a class action and that Hamacher has been certified as the representative of a class, some of whose members may well have standing to challenge the LSA freshman admissions program that is presently in effect. But the fact that "a suit may be a class action . . . adds nothing to the question of standing, for even named plaintiffs who represent a class 'must allege and show that they personally have been injured, not that injury has been suffered by other, unidentified members of the class to which they belong and which they purport to represent.'" *Simon* v. *Eastern Ky. Welfare Rights Organization,*

426 U. S. 26, 40, n. 20 (1976) (quoting *Warth* v. *Seldin,* 422 U. S. 490, 502 (1975)); see also 1 A. Conte & H. Newberg, Class Actions §2:5 (4th ed. 2002) ("[O]ne cannot acquire individual standing by virtue of bringing a class action").[7] Thus, in *Blum,* we squarely held that the interests of members of the class could not satisfy the requirement that the class representatives have a personal interest in obtaining the particular equitable relief being sought. The class in *Blum* included patients who wanted a hearing before being transferred to facilities where they would receive more intensive care. The class representatives, however, were in the category of patients threatened with a transfer to less intensive care facilities. In explaining why the named class representatives could not base their standing to sue on the injury suffered by other members of the class, we stated:

> "Respondents suggest that members of the class they represent have been transferred to higher levels of care as a result of [utilization review committee] decisions. Respondents, however, "must allege and show that they personally have been injured, not that injury has been suffered by other, unidentified members of the class to which they belong and which they purport to represent." *Warth* v. *Seldin,* 422 U. S. 490, 502 (1975). Unless these individuals "can thus demonstrate the requisite case or controversy between themselves personally and [petitioners], "none may seek relief on behalf of himself or any other member of the class." *O'Shea* v. *Littleton,* 414 U. S. 488, 494 (1974)." *Ibid."* 457 U. S., at 1001, n. 13.

Much like the class representatives in *Blum,* Hamacher—the sole class representative in this case—cannot meet Article III's threshold personal-stake requirement. While unidentified members of the class he represents may well have standing to challenge Michigan's current freshman admissions policy, Hamacher cannot base his standing to sue on injuries suffered by other members of the class.

IV.

As this case comes to us, our precedents leave us no alternative but to dismiss the writ for lack of jurisdiction. Neither petitioner has a personal stake in the outcome of the case, and neither has standing to seek prospective relief on behalf of unidentified class members who may or may not have standing to litigate on behalf of themselves. Accordingly, I respectfully dissent.

JENNIFER GRATZ AND PATRICK HAMACHER, PETITIONERS v. LEE BOLLINGER ET AL.

ON WRIT OF CERTIORARI TO THE UNITED STATES COURT OF APPEALS FOR THE SIXTH CIRCUIT

June 23, 2003.

Justice Souter, with whom *Justice Ginsburg* joins as to Part II, dissenting.

I agree with *Justice Stevens* that Patrick Hamacher has no standing to seek declaratory or injunctive relief against a freshman admissions policy that will never cause him any harm. I write separately to note that even the Court's new gloss on the law of standing should not permit it to reach the issue it decides today. And because a majority of the Court has chosen to address the merits, I also add a word to say that even if the merits were reachable, I would dissent from the Court's judgment.

I.

The Court's finding of Article III standing rests on two propositions: first, that both the University of Michigan's undergraduate college's transfer policy and its freshman admissions policy seek to achieve student body diversity through the "use of race," *ante,* at 12–20, and second, that Hamacher has standing to challenge the transfer policy on the grounds that diversity can never be a "compelling state interest" justifying the use of race in any admissions decision, freshman or transfer, *ante,* at 18. The Court concludes that, because Hamacher's argument, if successful, would seal the fate of both policies, his standing to challenge the transfer policy also allows him to attack the freshman admissions policy. *Ante,* at 18, n. 16 ("[P]etitioners challenged any use of race by the University to promote diversity, including through the transfer policy"); *ibid.* ("'[T]he University considers race for a purpose to achieve a diversity that we believe is not compelling, and if that is struck down as a rationale, then the [result] would be [the] same with respect to the transfer policy as with respect to the [freshman] admissions policy, Your Honor'" (quoting Tr. of Oral Arg. 7–8)). I agree with *Justice Stevens's* critique that the Court thus ignores the basic principle of Article III standing that a plaintiff cannot challenge a government program that does not apply to him. See *ante,* at 6, and n. 6 (dissenting opinion).[1]

But even on the Court's indulgent standing theory, the decision should not go beyond a recognition that diversity can serve as a compelling state interest justifying race-conscious decisions in education. *Ante,* at 20 (citing *Grutter* v. *Bollinger,* at 15–21). Since, as the Court says, "petitioners did not raise a narrow tailoring challenge to the transfer policy," *ante,* at 18, n. 16, our decision in *Grutter* is fatal to Hamacher's sole attack upon the transfer policy, which is the only policy before this Court that he claims aggrieved him. Hamacher's challenge to that policy having failed, his standing is presumably spent. The further question whether the freshman admissions plan is narrowly tailored to achieving student body diversity remains legally irrelevant to Hamacher and should await a plaintiff who is actually hurt by it.[2]

II.

The cases now contain two pointers toward the line between the valid and the unconstitutional in race-conscious admissions schemes. *Grutter* reaffirms the permissibility of individualized consideration of race to achieve a diversity of students, at least where race is not assigned a preordained value in all cases. On the other hand, Justice Powell's opinion in *Regents of Univ. of Cal.* v. *Bakke,* 438 U. S. 265 (1978), rules out a racial quota or set-aside, in which race is the sole fact of eligibility for certain places in a class. Although the freshman admissions system here is subject to argument on the merits, I think it is closer to what *Grutter* approves than to what *Bakke* condemns, and should not be held unconstitutional on the current record.

The record does not describe a system with a quota like the one struck down in *Bakke,* which "insulate[d]" all nonminority candidates from competition from certain seats. *Bakke, supra*, at 317 (opinion of Powell, J.); see also *Richmond* v. *J. A. Croson Co.,* 488 U. S. 469, 496 (1989) (plurality opinion) (stating that *Bakke* invalidated "a plan that completely eliminated nonminorities from consideration for a specified percentage of opportunities"). The *Bakke* plan "focused *solely* on ethnic diversity" and effectively told nonminority applicants that "[n]o matter how strong their qualifications, quantitative and extracurricular, including their own potential for contribution to educational diversity, they are never afforded the chance to compete with applicants from the preferred groups for the [set-aside] special admissions seats." *Bakke, supra*, at 315, 319 (opinion of Powell, J.) (emphasis in original).

The plan here, in contrast, lets all applicants compete for all places and values an applicant's offering for any place not only on grounds of race, but on grades, test scores, strength of high school, quality of course of study, residence, alumni relationships, leadership, personal character, socioeconomic disadvantage, athletic ability, and quality of a personal essay. *Ante,* at 6. A nonminority applicant who scores highly in these other categories can readily garner a selection index exceeding that of a minority applicant who gets the 20-point bonus. Cf. *Johnson* v. *Transportation Agency, Santa Clara Cty.,* 480 U. S. 616, 638 (1987) (upholding a program in which gender "was but one of numerous factors [taken] into account in arriving at [a] decision" because "[n]o persons are automatically excluded from consideration; all are able to have their qualifications weighed against those of other applicants" (emphasis deleted)).

Subject to one qualification to be taken up below, this scheme of considering, through the selection index system, all of the characteristics that the college thinks relevant to student diversity for every one of the student places to be filled fits Justice Powell's description of a constitutionally acceptable program: one that considers "all pertinent elements of diversity in light of the particular qualifications of each applicant" and places each element "on the same footing for consideration, although not necessarily according them the same weight." *Bakke, supra,* at 317. In the Court's own words, "each characteristic of a particular applicant [is] considered in assessing the applicant's entire application." *Ante,* at 23. An unsuccessful nonminority applicant cannot complain that he was rejected "simply because he was not the right color"; an applicant who is rejected because "his combined qualifications . . . did not outweigh those of the other applicant" has been given an opportunity to compete with all other applicants. *Bakke, supra,* at 318 (opinion of Powell, J.).

The one qualification to this description of the admissions process is that membership in an underrepresented minority is given a weight of 20 points on the 150-point scale. On the face of things, however, this assignment of specific points does not set race apart from all other weighted considerations. Nonminority students may receive 20 points for athletic ability, socioeconomic disadvantage, attendance at a socioeconomically disadvantaged or predominantly minority high school, or at the Provost's discretion; they may also receive 10 points for being residents of Michigan, 6 for residence in an underrepresented Michigan county, 5 for leadership and service, and so on.

The Court nonetheless finds fault with a scheme that "automatically" distributes 20 points to minority applicants because "[t]he only consideration that accompanies this distribution of points is a factual review of an application to determine whether an individual is a member of one of these minority groups." *Ante,* at 23. The objection goes to the use of points to quantify and compare characteristics, or to the number of points awarded due to race, but on either reading the objection is mistaken.

The very nature of a college's permissible practice of awarding value to racial diversity means that race must be considered in a way that increases some applicants' chances for admission. Since college admission is not left entirely to inarticulate intuition, it is hard to see what is inappropriate in assigning some stated value to a relevant characteristic, whether it be reasoning ability, writing style, running speed, or minority race. Justice Powell's plus factors necessarily are assigned some values. The college simply does by a numbered scale what the law school accomplishes in its "holistic review," *Grutter, post,* at 25; the distinction does not imply that applicants to the undergraduate college are denied individualized consideration or a fair chance to compete on the basis of all the various merits their applications may disclose.

Nor is it possible to say that the 20 points convert race into a decisive factor comparable to reserving minority places as in *Bakke.* Of course we can conceive of a point system in which the "plus" factor given to minority applicants would be so extreme as to guarantee every minority applicant a higher rank than every nonminority applicant in the university's admissions system, see 438 U. S., at 319, n. 53 (opinion of Powell, J.). But petitioners do not have a convincing argument that the freshman admissions system operates this way. The present record obviously shows that nonminority applicants may achieve higher selection point totals than minority applicants owing to characteristics other than race, and the fact that the university admits "virtually every qualified under-represented minority applicant," App. to Pet. for Cert. 111a, may reflect nothing more than the likelihood that very few qualified minority applicants apply, Brief for Respondents Bollinger et al. 39, as well as the possibility that self-selection results in a strong minority applicant pool. It suffices for me, as it did for the District Court, that there are no *Bakke*-like set-asides and that consideration of an applicant's whole spectrum of ability is no more ruled out by giving 20 points for race than by giving the same points for athletic ability or socioeconomic disadvantage.

Any argument that the "tailoring" amounts to a set-aside, then, boils down to the claim that a plus factor of 20 points makes some observers suspicious, where a factor of 10 points might not. But suspicion does not carry petitioners' ultimate burden of persuasion in this constitutional challenge, *Wygant* v. *Jackson Bd. of Ed.,* 476 U. S. 267, 287–288 (1986) (plurality opinion of Powell, J.), and it surely does not warrant condemning the college's admissions scheme on this record. Because the District Court (correctly, in my view) did not believe that the specific point assignment was constitutionally troubling, it made only limited and general findings on other characteristics of the university's admissions practice, such as the conduct of individualized review by the Admissions Review Committee. 122 F. Supp. 2d 811, 829–830 (ED Mich. 2000). As the Court indicates, we know very little about the actual role of the review committee. *Ante,* at 26 ("The record does not reveal precisely how many applications are flagged for this individualized consideration [by the committee]"); see also *ante,* at 4 (*O'Connor,* J., concurring) ("The evidence in the record . . . reveals very little about how the review committee actually functions"). The point system cannot operate as a *de facto* set-aside if the greater admissions process, including review by the committee, results in individualized review sufficient to meet the Court's standards. Since the record is quiet, if not silent, on the case-by-case work of the committee, the Court would be on more defensible ground by vacating and remanding for evidence about the committee's specific determinations.[3]

Without knowing more about how the Admissions Review Committee actually functions, it seems especially unfair to treat the candor of the admissions plan as an Achilles" heel. In contrast to the college's forthrightness in saying just what plus factor it gives for membership in an underrepresented minority, it is worth considering the character of one alternative thrown up as preferable, because supposedly not based on race. Drawing on admissions systems used at public universities in California, Florida, and Texas, the United States contends that Michigan could get student diversity in satisfaction of its compelling interest by guaranteeing admission to a fixed percentage of the top students from each high school in Michigan. Brief for United States as *Amicus Curiae* 18; Brief for United States as *Amicus Curiae* in *Grutter* v. *Bollinger,* O. T. 2002, No. 02–241, pp. 13–17.

While there is nothing unconstitutional about such a practice, it nonetheless suffers from a serious disadvantage.[4] It is the disadvantage of deliberate obfuscation. The "percentage plans" are just as race-conscious as the point scheme (and fairly so), but they get their racially diverse results without saying directly what they are doing or why they are doing it. In contrast, Michigan states its purpose directly and, if this were a doubtful case for me, I would be tempted to give Michigan an extra point of its own for its frankness. Equal protection cannot become an exercise in which the winners are the ones who hide the ball.

III.

If this plan were challenged by a plaintiff with proper standing under Article III, I would affirm the judgment of the District Court granting summary judgment to the college. As it is, I would vacate the judgment for lack of jurisdiction, and I respectfully dissent.

JENNIFER GRATZ AND PATRICK HAMACHER, PETITIONERS v. LEE BOLLINGER ET AL.

ON WRIT OF CERTIORARI TO THE UNITED STATES COURT OF APPEALS FOR THE SIXTH CIRCUIT

June 23, 2003.

Justice Ginsburg, with whom *Justice Souter* joins, dissenting.

I.

Educational institutions, the Court acknowledges, are not barred from any and all consideration of race when making admissions decisions. *Ante,* at 20; see *Grutter* v. *Bollinger, post,* at 13–21. But the Court once again maintains that the same standard of review controls judicial inspection of all official race classifications. *Ante,* at 21 (quoting *Adarand Constructors, Inc.* v. *Peña,* 515 U. S. 200, 224 (1995); *Richmond* v. *J.A. Croson Co.,* 488 U. S. 469, 494 (1989) (plurality opinion)). This insistence on "consistency," *Adarand,* 515 U. S., at 224, would be fitting were our Nation free of the vestiges of rank discrimination long reinforced by law, see *id.,* at 274–276, and n. 8 (*Ginsburg, J.,* dissenting). But we are not far distant from an overtly discriminatory past, and the effects of centuries of law-sanctioned inequality remain painfully evident in our communities and schools.

In the wake "of a system of racial caste only recently ended," *id.,* at 273 (*Ginsburg, J.,* dissenting), large disparities endure. Unemployment,[1] poverty,[2] and access to health care[3] vary disproportionately by race. Neighborhoods and schools remain racially divided.[4] African-American and Hispanic children are all too often educated in poverty-stricken and underperforming institutions.[5] Adult African-Americans and Hispanics generally earn less than whites with equivalent levels of education.[6] Equally credentialed job applicants receive different receptions depending on their race.[7] Irrational prejudice is still encountered in real estate markets[8] and consumer transactions.[9] "Bias both conscious and unconscious, reflecting traditional and unexamined habits of thought, keeps up barriers that must come down if equal opportunity and nondiscrimination are ever genuinely to become this country's law and practice." *Id.,* at 274 (*Ginsburg, J.,* dissenting); see generally Krieger, Civil Rights Perestroika: Intergroup Relations After Affirmative Action, 86 Calif. L. Rev. 1251, 1276–1291 (1998).

The Constitution instructs all who act for the government that they may not "deny to any person . . . the equal protection of the laws." Amdt. 14, §1. In implementing this equality instruction, as I see it, government decisionmakers may properly distinguish between policies of exclusion and inclusion. See *Wygant* v. *Jackson Bd. of Ed.,* 476 U. S. 267, 316 (1986) (*Stevens, J.,* dissenting). Actions designed to burden groups long denied full citizenship stature are not sensibly ranked with measures taken to hasten the day when entrenched discrimination and its after effects have been extirpated. See Carter, When Victims Happen To Be Black, 97 Yale L. J. 420, 433–434 (1988) ("[T]o say that two centuries of struggle for the most basic of civil rights have been mostly about freedom from racial categorization rather than freedom from racial oppressio[n] is to trivialize the lives and deaths of those who have suffered under racism. To pretend . . . that the issue presented in [*Regents of Univ. of Cal.* v. *Bakke,* 438 U. S. 265 (1978)] was the same as the issue in [*Brown* v. *Board of Education,* 347 U. S. 483 (1954)] is to pretend that history never happened and that the present doesn't exist.").

Our jurisprudence ranks race a "suspect" category, "not because [race] is inevitably an impermissible classification, but because it is one which usually, to our national shame, has been drawn for the purpose of maintaining racial inequality." *Norwalk Core* v. *Norwalk Redevelopment Agency,* 395 F. 2d 920, 931–932 (CA2 1968) (footnote omitted). But where race is considered "for the purpose of achieving equality," *id.,* at 932, no automatic proscription is in order. For, as insightfully explained, "[t]he Constitution is both color blind and color conscious. To avoid conflict with the equal protection clause, a classification that denies a benefit, causes harm, or imposes a burden must not be based on race. In that sense, the Constitution is color blind. But the Constitution is color conscious to prevent discrimination being perpetuated and to undo the effects of past discrimination." *United States* v. *Jefferson County Bd. of Ed.,* 372 F. 2d 836, 876 (CA5 1966) (Wisdom, J.); see Wechsler, The Nationalization Of Civil Liberties And Civil Rights, Supp. to 12 Tex. Q. 10, 23 (1968) (*Brown* may be seen as disallowing racial classifications that "impl[y] an invidious assessment" while allowing such classifications when "not invidious in implication" but advanced to "correct inequalities"). Contemporary human rights documents draw just this line; they distinguish between policies of oppression and measures designed to accelerate *de facto* equality. See *Grutter, post* at 1 (*Ginsburg, J.,* concurring) (citing the United Nations-initiated Conventions on the Elimination of All Forms of Racial Discrimination and on the Elimination of All Forms of Discrimination against Women).

The mere assertion of a laudable governmental purpose, of course, should not immunize a race-conscious measure from careful judicial inspection. See *Jefferson County*, 372 F. 2d, at 876 ("The criterion is the relevancy of color to a legitimate governmental purpose."). Close review is needed "to ferret out classifications in reality malign, but masquerading as benign," *Adarand*, 515 U. S., at 275 (*Ginsburg, J.,* dissenting), and to "ensure that preferences are not so large as to trammel unduly upon the opportunities of others or interfere too harshly with legitimate expectations of persons in once-preferred groups," *id.*, at 276.

II.

Examining in this light the admissions policy employed by the University of Michigan's College of Literature, Science, and the Arts (College), and for the reasons well stated by *Justice Souter,* I see no constitutional infirmity. See *ante,* at 3–8 (dissenting opinion). Like other top-ranking institutions, the College has many more applicants for admission than it can accommodate in an entering class. App. to Pet. for Cert. 108a. Every applicant admitted under the current plan, petitioners do not here dispute, is qualified to attend the College. *Id.*, at 111a. The racial and ethnic groups to which the College accords special consideration (African-Americans, Hispanics, and Native-Americans) historically have been relegated to inferior status by law and social practice; their members continue to experience class-based discrimination to this day, see *supra*, at 1–4. There is no suggestion that the College adopted its current policy in order to limit or decrease enrollment by any particular racial or ethnic group, and no seats are reserved on the basis of race. See Brief for Respondents 10; Tr. of Oral Arg. 41–42 (in the range between 75 and 100 points, the review committee may look at applications individually and ignore the points). Nor has there been any demonstration that the College's program unduly constricts admissions opportunities for students who do not receive special consideration based on race. Cf. Liu, The Causation Fallacy: *Bakke* and the Basic Arithmetic of Selective Admissions, 100 Mich. L. Rev. 1045, 1049 (2002) ("In any admissions process where applicants greatly outnumber admittees, and where white applicants greatly outnumber minority applicants, substantial preferences for minority applicants will not significantly diminish the odds of admission facing white applicants.").[10]

The stain of generations of racial oppression is still visible in our society, see Krieger, 86 Calif. L. Rev., at 1253, and the determination to hasten its removal remains vital. One can reasonably anticipate, therefore, that colleges and universities will seek to maintain their minority enrollment—and the networks and opportunities thereby opened to minority graduates—whether or not they can do so in full candor through adoption of affirmative action plans of the kind here at issue. Without recourse to such plans, institutions of higher education may resort to camouflage. For example, schools may encourage applicants to write of their cultural traditions in the essays they submit, or to indicate whether English is their second language. Seeking to improve their chances for admission, applicants may highlight the minority group associations to which they belong, or the Hispanic surnames of their mothers or grandparents. In turn, teachers" recommendations may emphasize who a student is as much as what he or she has accomplished. See, *e.g.,* Steinberg, Using Synonyms for Race, College Strives for Diversity, N. Y. Times, Dec. 8, 2002, section 1, p. 1, col. 3 (describing admissions process at Rice University); cf. Brief for United States as *Amicus Curiae* 14–15 (suggesting institutions could consider, *inter alia,* "a history of overcoming disadvantage," "reputation and location of high school," and "individual outlook as reflected by essays"). If honesty is the best policy, surely Michigan's accurately described, fully disclosed College affirmative action program is preferable to achieving similar numbers through winks, nods, and disguises.[11]

* * *

For the reasons stated, I would affirm the judgment of the District Court.

FOOTNOTES

[1] Although Hamacher indicated that he "intend[ed] to apply to transfer if the [LSA's] discriminatory admissions system [is] eliminated," he has since graduated from Michigan State University. App. 34.

[2] The University of Michigan Board of Regents was subsequently named as the proper defendant in place of the University and the LSA. See *id.,* at 17.

[3] Duderstadt was the president of the University during the time that Gratz's application was under consideration. He has been sued in his individual capacity. Bollinger was the president of the University when Hamacher applied for admission. He was originally sued in both his individual and official capacities, but he is no longer the president of the University. *Id.,* at 35.

[4] A group of African-American and Latino students who applied for, or intended to apply for, admission to the University, as well as the Citizens for Affirmative Action's Preservation, a nonprofit organization in Michigan, sought to intervene pursuant to Federal Rule of Civil Procedure 24. See App. 13–14. The District Court originally denied this request, see *id.,* at 14–15, but the Sixth Circuit reversed that decision. See *Gratz* v. *Bollinger,* 188 F. 3d 394 (1999).

[5] The District Court decided also to consider petitioners' request for injunctive and declaratory relief during the liability phase of the proceedings. App. 71.

[6] Our description is taken, in large part, from the "Joint Proposed Summary of Undisputed Facts Regarding Admissions Process" filed by the parties in the District Court. App. to Pet. for Cert. 108a–117a.

[7] In 1995, counselors used four such tables for different groups of applicants: (1) in-state, nonminority applicants; (2) out-of-state, non-minority applicants; (3) in-state, minority

applicants; and (4) out-of-state, minority applicants. In 1996, only two tables were used, one for in-state applicants and one for out-of-state applicants. But each cell on these two tables contained separate courses of action for minority applicants and nonminority applicants whose GPA 2 scores and ACT/SAT scores placed them in that cell.

[8] LSA applicants who are Michigan residents must accumulate 80 points from the selection index criteria to be flagged, while out-of-state applicants need to accumulate 75 points to be eligible for such consideration. See App. 257.

[9] The District Court considered and rejected respondent-intervenors' arguments in a supplemental opinion and order. See 135 F. Supp. 2d 790 (ED Mich. 2001). The court explained that respondent-intervenors "failed to present any evidence that the discrimination alleged by them, or the continuing effects of such discrimination, was the real justification for the LSA's race-conscious admissions programs." *Id.*, at 795. We agree, and to the extent respondent-intervenors reassert this justification, a justification the University has *never* asserted throughout the course of this litigation, we affirm the District Court's disposition of the issue.

[10] The District Court determined that respondents Bollinger and Duderstadt, who were sued in their individual capacities under Rev. Stat. §1979, 42 U. S. C. §1983, were entitled to summary judgment based on the doctrine of qualified immunity. See 122 F. Supp. 2d, at 833–834. Petitioners have not asked this Court to review this aspect of the District Court's decision. The District Court denied the Board of Regents' motion for summary judgment with respect to petitioners' Title VI claim on Eleventh Amendment immunity grounds. See *id.*, at 834–836. Respondents have not asked this Court to review this aspect of the District Court's decision.

[11] The Equal Protection Clause of the Fourteenth Amendment explains that "[n]o State shall . . . deny to any person within its jurisdiction the equal protection of the laws."

[12] Title VI provides that "[n]o person in the United States shall, on the ground of race, color, or national origin, be excluded from participation in, be denied the benefits of, or be subjected to discrimination under any program or activity receiving Federal financial assistance." 42 U. S. C. §2000d.

[13] Section 1981(a) provides that:

"All persons within the jurisdiction of the United States shall have the same right in every State and Territory to make and enforce contracts, . . . and to the full and equal benefit of all laws and proceedings for the security of persons and property as is enjoyed by white citizens."

[14] This finding is further corroborated by Hamacher's request that the District Court "[r]equir[e] the LSA College to offer [him] admission as a transfer student." App. 40.

[15] Although we do not resolve here whether such an inquiry in this case is appropriately addressed under the rubric of standing or adequacy, we note that there is tension in our prior cases in this regard. See, *e.g.,* Burns, Standing and Mootness in Class Actions: A Search for Consistency, 22 U. C. D. L. Rev. 1239, 1240–1241 (1989); *General Telephone Co. of Southwest* v. *Falcon,* 457 U. S. 147, 149 (1982) (Mexican-American plaintiff alleging that he was passed over for a promotion because of race was not an adequate representative to "maintain a class action on behalf of Mexican-American applicants" who were not hired by the same employer); *Blum* v. *Yaretsky,* 457 U. S. 991 (1982) (class representatives who had been transferred to lower levels of medical care lacked standing to challenge transfers to higher levels of care).

[16] Because the University's guidelines concededly use race in evaluating both freshman and transfer applications, and because petitioners have challenged *any* use of race by the University in undergraduate admissions, the transfer admissions policy is very much before this Court. Although petitioners did not raise a narrow tailoring challenge to the transfer policy, as counsel for petitioners repeatedly explained, the transfer policy is before this Court in that petitioners challenged any use of race by the University to pro-

omote diversity, including through the transfer policy. See Tr. of Oral Arg. 4 ("[T]he [transfer] policy is essentially the same with respect to the consideration of race"); *id.,* at 5 ("The transfer policy considers race"); *id.,* at 6 (same); *id.,* at 7 ("[T]he transfer policy and the [freshman] admissions policy are fundamentally the same in the respect that they both consider race in the admissions process in a way that is discriminatory"); *id.,* at 7–8 ("[T]he University considers race for a purpose to achieve a diversity that we believe is not compelling, and if that is struck down as a rationale, then the [result] would be [the] same with respect to the transfer policy as with respect to the [freshman] admissions policy, Your Honor").

[17] Indeed, as the litigation history of this case demonstrates, "the class-action device save[d] the resources of both the courts and the parties by permitting an issue potentially affecting every [class member] to be litigated in an economical fashion." *Califano* v. *Yamasaki,* 442 U. S. 682, 701 (1979). This case was therefore quite unlike *General Telephone Co. of Southwest* v. *Falcon,* 457 U. S. 147 (1982), in which we found that the named representative, who had been passed over for a promotion, was not an adequate representative for absent class members who were never hired in the first instance. As we explained, the plaintiff's "evidentiary approaches to the individual and class claims were entirely different. He attempted to sustain his individual claim by proving intentional discrimination. He tried to prove the class claims through statistical evidence of disparate impact. . . . It is clear that the maintenance of respondent's action as a class action did not advance "the efficiency and economy of litigation which is a principal purpose of the procedure.'" *Id.,* at 159 (quoting *American Pipe & Constr. Co.* v. *Utah,* 414 U. S. 538, 553 (1974)).

[18] U. C. Davis set aside 16 of the 100 seats available in its first year medical school program for "economically and/or educationally disadvantaged" applicants who were also members of designated "minority groups" as defined by the university. "To the extent that there existed a pool of at least minimally qualified minority applicants to fill the 16 special admissions seats, white applicants could compete only for 84 seats in the entering class, rather than the 100 open to minority applicants." *Regents of Univ. of Cal.* v. *Bakke,* 438 U. S. 265, 274, 289 (1978) (principal opinion). Justice Powell found that the program employed an impermissible two-track system that "disregard[ed] . . . individual rights as guaranteed by the Fourteenth Amendment." *Id.,* at 315. He reached this conclusion even though the university argued that "the reservation of a specified number of seats in each class for individuals from the preferred ethnic groups" was "the only effective means of serving the interest of diversity." *Ibid.* Justice Powell concluded that such arguments misunderstood the very nature of the diversity he found to be compelling. See *ibid.*

[19] *Justice Souter* recognizes that the LSA's use of race is decisive in practice, but he attempts to avoid that fact through unsupported speculation about the self-selection of minorities in the applicant pool. See *Post,* at 6 (dissenting opinion).

[20] *Justice Souter* is therefore wrong when he contends that "applicants to the undergraduate college are [not] denied individualized consideration." *Post,* at 6. As *Justice O'Connor* explains in her concurrence, the LSA's program "ensures that the diversity contributions of applicants cannot be individually assessed." *Post,* at 4.

[21] *Justice Souter* is mistaken in his assertion that the Court "take[s] it upon itself to apply a newly formulated legal standard to an undeveloped record." *Post,* at 7, n. 3. He ignores the fact that the respondents have told us all that is necessary to decide this case. As explained above, respondents concede that only a portion of the applications are reviewed by the ARC and that the "bulk of admissions decisions" are based on the point system. It should be readily apparent that the availability of this review, which comes *after* the automatic distribution of points, is far more limited than the individualized review given to the "large middle group of applicants" discussed by Justice Powell

and described by the Harvard plan in *Bakke.* 438 U. S., at 316 (internal quotation marks omitted).

[22] *Justice Ginsburg* in her dissent observes that "[o]ne can reasonably anticipate . . . that colleges and universities will seek to maintain their minority enrollment . . . whether or not they can do so in full candor through adoption of affirmative action plans of the kind here at issue." *Post,* at 7–8. She goes on to say that "[i]f honesty is the best policy, surely Michigan's accurately described, fully disclosed College affirmative action program is preferable to achieving similar numbers through winks, nods, and disguises." *Post,* at 8. These observations are remarkable for two reasons. First, they suggest that universities—to whose academic judgment we are told in *Grutter* v. *Bollinger, post,* at 16, we should defer—will pursue their affirmative-action programs whether or not they violate the United States Constitution. Second, they recommend that these violations should be dealt with, not by requiring the universities to obey the Constitution, but by changing the Constitution so that it conforms to the conduct of the universities.

[23] We have explained that discrimination that violates the Equal Protection Clause of the Fourteenth Amendment committed by an institution that accepts federal funds also constitutes a violation of Title VI. See *Alexander* v. *Sandoval,* 532 U. S. 275, 281 (2001); *United States* v. *Fordice,* 505 U. S. 717, 732, n. 7 (1992); *Alexander* v. *Choate,* 469 U. S. 287, 293 (1985). Likewise, with respect to §1981, we have explained that the provision was "meant, by its broad terms, to proscribe discrimination in the making or enforcement of contracts against, or in favor of, any race." *McDonald* v. *Santa Fe Trail Transp. Co.,* 427 U. S. 273, 295–296 (1976). Furthermore, we have explained that a contract for educational services is a "contract" for purposes of §1981. See *Runyon* v. *McCrary,* 427 U. S. 160, 172 (1976). Finally, purposeful discrimination that violates the Equal Protection Clause of the Fourteenth Amendment will also violate §1981. See *General Building Contractors Assn., Inc.* v. *Pennsylvania,* 458 U. S. 375, 389–390 (1982).

FOOTNOTES

[*] *Justice Breyer* joins this opinion, except for the last sentence.
[1] In challenging the use of race in admissions at Michigan's law school, Barbara Grutter alleged in her complaint that she "has not attended any other law school" and that she "still desires to attend the Law School and become a lawyer." App. in No. 02–241, p. 30.
[2] Petitioners did not seek to have Gratz represent the class pursuant to Federal Rule Civil Procedure 23(b)(2). See App. 71, n. 3.
[3] In arguing that Hamacher lacked standing, Michigan also asserted that Hamacher "would need to achieve a 3.0 grade point average to attempt to transfer to the University of Michigan." *Id.,* at 64, n. 2. The District Court rejected this argument, concluding that "Hamacher's present grades are not a factor to be considered at this time." *Id.,* at 67.
[4] In responding to questions about petitioners" standing at oral argument, petitioners' counsel alluded to the fact that Michigan might continually change the details of its admissions policy. See Tr. of Oral Arg. 9. The change in Michigan's freshman admissions policy, however, is not the reason why petitioners cannot establish standing to seek prospective relief. Rather, the reason they lack standing to seek forward-looking relief is that when this suit was filed, neither faced a "real and immediate threat" of future injury under Michigan's freshman admissions policy given that they had both already enrolled at other institutions. *Adarand Constructors, Inc.* v. *Peña,* 515 U. S. 200, 210 (1995) (quoting *Los Angeles* v. *Lyons,* 461 U. S. 95, 105 (1983)). Their decision to obtain a college education elsewhere distinguishes this case from Allan Bakke's single-minded pursuit of a medical education from the University of California at Davis. See *Regents of Univ. of*

   Cal. v. *Bakke,* 438 U. S. 265 (1978); cf. *DeFunis* v. *Odegaard,* 416 U. S. 312 (1974) *(per curiam).*

[5] Hamacher clearly can no longer claim an intent to transfer into Michigan's undergraduate program given that he graduated from college in 2001. However, this fact alone is not necessarily fatal to the instant class action because we have recognized that, if a named class representative has standing at the time a suit is initiated, class actions may proceed in some instances following mootness of the named class representative's claim. See, *e.g., Sosna* v. *Iowa,* 419 U. S. 393, 402 (1975) (holding that the requisite Article III "case or controversy" may exist "between a named defendant and a member of the class represented by the named plaintiff, even though the claim of the named plaintiff has become moot"); *Franks* v. *Bowman Transp. Co.,* 424 U. S. 747 (1976). The problem in this case is that neither Gratz nor Hamacher had standing to assert a forward-looking, injunctive claim in federal court at the time this suit was initiated.

[6] Under the majority's view of standing, there would be no end to Hamacher's ability to challenge any use of race by the University in a variety of programs. For if Hamacher's right to complain about the *transfer* policy gives him standing to challenge the *freshman* policy, presumably his ability to complain about the *transfer* policy likewise would enable him to challenge Michigan's *law school* admissions policy, as well as any other race-based admissions policy used by Michigan.

[7] Of course, the injury to Hamacher would give him standing to claim damages for past harm on behalf of class members, but he was certified as the class representative for the limited purpose of seeking injunctive and declaratory relief.

FOOTNOTES

[1] The Court's holding arguably exposes a weakness in the rule of *Blum* v. *Yaretsky,* 457 U. S. 991 (1982), that Article III standing may not be satisfied by the unnamed members of a duly certified class. But no party has invited us to reconsider *Blum,* and I follow *Justice Stevens* in approaching the case on the assumption that *Blum* is settled law.

[2] For that matter, as the Court suggests, narrow tailoring challenges against the two policies could well have different outcomes. *Ante,* at 18. The record on the decisionmaking process for transfer applicants is understandably thin, given that petitioners never raised a narrow tailoring challenge against it. Most importantly, however, the transfer policy does not use a points-based "selection index" to evaluate transfer applicants, but rather considers race as one of many factors in making the general determination whether the applicant would make a "'contribution to a diverse student body.'" *Ante,* at 17 (quoting 2 App. in No. 01–1333 etc. (CA6), p. 531 (capitalization omitted)). This limited glimpse into the transfer policy at least permits the inference that the University engages in a "holistic review" of transfer applications consistent with the program upheld today in *Grutter* v. *Bollinger, post,* at 25.

[3] The Court surmises that the committee does not contribute meaningfully to the University's individualized review of applications. *Ante,* at 25–26. The Court should not take it upon itself to apply a newly-formulated legal standard to an undeveloped record. Given the District Court's statement that the committee may examine "any number of applicants, including applicants other than under-represented minority applicants," 122 F. Supp. 2d 811, 830 (ED Mich. 2000), it is quite possible that further factual development would reveal the committee to be a "source of individualized consideration" sufficient to satisfy the Court's rule, *ante,* at 4 (*O'Connor,* J., concurring). Determination of that issue in the first instance is a job for the District Court, not for this Court on a record that is admittedly lacking.

[4] Of course it might be pointless in the State of Michigan, where minorities are a much smaller fraction of the population than in California, Florida, or Texas. Brief for Respondents Bollinger et al. 48–49.

FOOTNOTES

Justice Breyer joins Part I of this opinion.

[1] See, *e.g.,* U. S. Dept. of Commerce, Bureau of Census, Statistical Abstract of the United States: 2002, p. 368 (2002) (Table 562) (hereinafter Statistical Abstract) (unemployment rate among whites was 3.7% in 1999, 3.5% in 2000, and 4.2% in 2001; during those years, the unemployment rate among African-Americans was 8.0%, 7.6%, and 8.7%, respectively; among Hispanics, 6.4%, 5.7%, and 6.6%).

[2] See, *e.g.,* U. S. Dept of Commerce, Bureau of Census, Poverty in the United States: 2000, p. 291 (2001) (Table A) (In 2000, 7.5% of non-Hispanic whites, 22.1% of African-Americans, 10.8% of Asian-Americans, and 21.2% of Hispanics were living in poverty); S. Staveteig & A. Wigton, Racial and Ethnic Disparities: Key Findings from the National Survey of America's Families 1 (Urban Institute Report B-5, 2000) ("Blacks, Hispanics, and Native Americans . . . each have poverty rates almost twice as high as Asians and almost three times as high as whites.").

[3] See, *e.g.,* U. S. Dept. of Commerce, Bureau of Census, Health Insurance Coverage: 2000, p. 391 (2001) (Table A) (In 2000, 9.7% of non-Hispanic whites were without health insurance, as compared to 18.5% of African-Americans, 18.0% of Asian-Americans, and 32.0% of Hispanics.); Waidmann & Rajan, Race and Ethnic Disparities in Health Care Access and Utilization: An Examination of State Variation, 57 Med. Care Res. and Rev. 55, 56 (2000) ("On average, Latinos and African-Americans have both worse health and worse access to effective health care than do non-Hispanic whites . . . .").

[4] See, *e.g.,* U. S. Dept. of Commerce, Bureau of Census, Racial and Ethnic Residential Segregation in the United States: 1980–2000 (2002) (documenting residential segregation); E. Frankenberg, C. Lee, & G. Orfield, A Multiracial Society with Segregated Schools: Are We Losing the Dream? 4 (Jan. 2003), http://www.civilrightsproject.-harvard.edu/research/reseg03/AreWeLosingtheDream.pdf (all Internet materials as visited June 2, 2003, and available in Clerk of Court's case file), ("[W]hites are the most segregated group in the nation's public schools; they attend schools, on average, where eighty percent of the student body is white."); *id.,* at 28 ("[A]lmost three-fourths of black and Latino students attend schools that are predominantly minority . . . . More than one in six black children attend a school that is 99–100% minority . . . . One in nine Latino students attend virtually all minority schools.").

[5] See, *e.g.,* Ryan, Schools, Race, and Money, 109 Yale L. J. 249, 273–274 (1999) ("Urban public schools are attended primarily by African-American and Hispanic students"; students who attend such schools are disproportionately poor, score poorly on standardized tests, and are far more likely to drop out than students who attend nonurban schools.).

[6] See, *e.g.,* Statistical Abstract 140 (Table 211).

[7] See, *e.g.,* Holzer, Career Advancement Prospects and Strategies for Low-Wage Minority Workers, in Low-Wage Workers in the New Economy 228 (R. Kazis & M. Miller eds. 2001) ("[I]n studies that have sent matched pairs of minority and white applicants with apparently equal credentials to apply for jobs, whites routinely get more interviews and job offers than either black or Hispanic applicants."); M. Bertrand & S. Mullainathan, Are Emily and Brendan More Employable than Lakisha and Jamal?: A Field Experiment on Labor Market Discrimination (Nov. 18, 2002), http://gsb.uchicago.edu/pdf/bertrand.pdf; Mincy, The Urban Institute Audit Studies: Their Research and Policy

Context, in Clear and Convincing Evidence: Measurement of Discrimination in America 165–186 (M. Fix & R. Struyk eds. 1993).

[8] See, *e.g.,* M. Turner et al., Discrimination in Metropolitan Housing Markets: National Results from Phase I HDS 2000, pp. i, iii (Nov. 2002), http://www.huduser.org/Publications/pdf/Phase1_Report.pdf (paired testing in which "two individuals—one minority and the other white—pose as otherwise identical homeseekers, and visit real estate or rental agents to inquire about the availability of advertised housing units" revealed that "discrimination still persists in both rental and sales markets of large metropolitan areas nationwide"); M. Turner & F. Skidmore, Mortgage Lending Discrimination: A Review of Existing Evidence 2 (1999) (existing research evidence shows that minority homebuyers in the United States "face discrimination from mortgage lending institutions.").

[9] See, *e.g.,* Ayres, Further Evidence of Discrimination in New Car Negotiations and Estimates of its Cause, 94 Mich. L. Rev. 109, 109–110 (1995) (study in which 38 testers negotiated the purchase of more than 400 automobiles confirmed earlier finding "that dealers systematically offer lower prices to white males than to other tester types").

[10] The United States points to the "percentage plans" used in California, Florida, and Texas as one example of a "race-neutral alternativ[e]" that would permit the College to enroll meaningful numbers of minority students. Brief for United States as *Amicus Curiae* 14; see Commission on Civil Rights, Beyond Percentage Plans: The Challenge of Equal Opportunity in Higher Education 1 (Nov. 2002), http://www.usccr.gov/pubs/percent2/percent2.pdf (percentage plans guarantee admission to state universities for a fixed percentage of the top students from high schools in the State). Calling such 10 or 20% plans "race-neutral" seems to me disingenuous, for they "unquestionably were adopted with the specific purpose of increasing representation of African-Americans and Hispanics in the public higher education system." Brief for Respondents 44; see C. Horn & S. Flores, Percent Plans in College Admissions: A Comparative Analysis of Three States" Experiences 14–19 (2003), http://www.civilrightsproject.harvard.edu/research/affirmativeaction/tristate.pdf. Percentage plans depend for their effectiveness on continued racial segregation at the secondary school level: They can ensure significant minority enrollment in universities only if the majority-minority high school population is large enough to guarantee that, in many schools, most of the students in the top 10 or 20% are minorities. Moreover, because such plans link college admission to a single criterion—high school class rank—they create perverse incentives. They encourage parents to keep their children in low-performing segregated schools, and discourage students from taking challenging classes that might lower their grade point averages. See Selingo, What States Aren't Saying About the "X-Percent Solution," Chronicle of Higher Education, June 2, 2000, p. A31. And even if percentage plans could boost the sheer numbers of minority enrollees at the undergraduate level, they do not touch enrollment in graduate and professional schools.

[11] Contrary to the Court's contention, I do not suggest "changing the Constitution so that it conforms to the conduct of the universities." *Ante,* at 27, n. 22. In my view, the Constitution, properly interpreted, permits government officials to respond openly to the continuing importance of race. See *supra,* at 4–5. Among constitutionally permissible options, those that candidly disclose their consideration of race seem to me preferable to those that conceal it.